TUTORIAL TUTORIAL TUTORIAL TUTORIAL TUTORIAL

REDUCED INSTRUCTION SET COMPUTERS

William Stallings

IEEE Computer Society Order Number 713
Library of Congress Number 86-45871
IEEE Catalog Number EH0251-9
ISBN 0-8186-0713-0

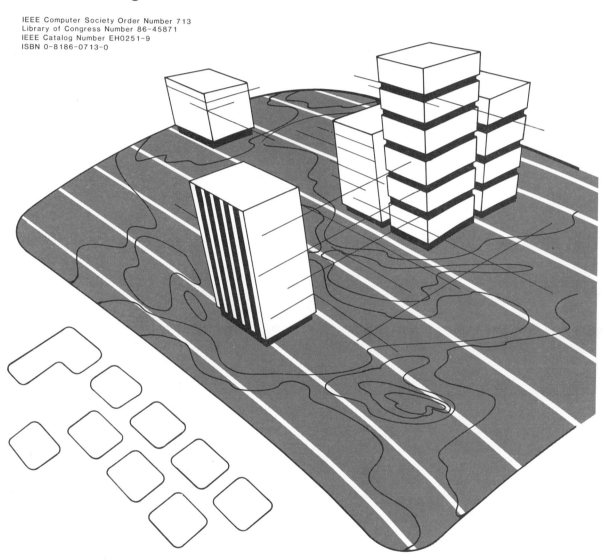

 **THE COMPUTER SOCIETY**
OF THE IEEE

  IEEE THE INSTITUTE OF ELECTRICAL AND ELECTRONICS ENGINEERS, INC.

 IEEE
**COMPUTER
SOCIETY
PRESS**

Published by IEEE Computer Society Press
1730 Massachusetts Avenue, N.W.
Washington, D.C. 20036-1903

COVER DESIGNED BY JACK I. BALLESTERO

Copyright and Reprint Permissions: Abstracting is permitted with credit to the source. Libraries are permitted to photocopy beyond the limits of U.S. copyright law for private use of patrons those articles in this volume that carry a code at the bottom of the first page, provided the per-copy fee indicated in the code is paid through the Copyright Clearance Center, 29 Congress Street, Salem, MA 01970. Instructors are permitted to photocopy isolated articles for noncommercial classroom use without fee. For other copying, reprint or republication permission, write to Director, Publishing services, IEEE, 345 E. 47 St., New York, NY 10017. All rights reserved. Copyright © 1986 by The Institute of Electrical and Electronics Engineers, Inc.

IEEE Computer Society Order Number 713
Library of Congress Number 86-45871
IEEE Catalog Number EH0251-9
ISBN 0-8186-0713-0 (Paper)
ISBN 0-8186-4713-2 (Microfiche)

Order from: IEEE Computer Society   IEEE Service Center
            Post Office Box 80452   445 Hoes Lane
            Worldway Postal Center   Piscataway, NJ 08854
            Los Angeles, CA 90080

 THE INSTITUTE OF ELECTRICAL AND ELECTRONICS ENGINEERS, INC.

Preface

Since the development of the stored-program computer around 1950, there have been remarkably few true innovations in the areas of computer organization and architecture. One of the most interesting and, potentially, one of the most important innovations is the reduced instruction set computer (RISC). The RISC architecture is a dramatic departure from the historical trend in CPU architecture and challenges the conventional wisdom expressed in words and deeds by most computer architects. An analysis of the RISC architecture brings into focus many of the important issues in computer organization and architecture. Although most of the work has been on experimental systems, commercial RISC systems have begun to appear.

P.1 Objectives

The objectives of this tutorial text are to (1) provide a comprehensive introduction to RISC and (2) give the reader an understanding of RISC design issues and the ability to assess their importance relative to other approaches. The articles have been selected based on topic and style to support these aims.

P.2 Intended Audience

The tutorial is intended for a broad range of readers who will benefit from an understanding of RISC concepts. These include students and professionals in the fields of computer science and computer engineering, designers and implementers, and data processing managers who now find RISC machines among their available processor choices. A basic, general background in computer architecture is recommended. However, some tutorial material is provided for the reader with little or no background in this area.

P.3 Organization

This tutorial text is a combination of original material and reprinted articles and is organized as follows:

1. *Instruction Execution Characteristics:* This section presents results on studies of the execution characteristics of compiled high-level language instructions. These results form the base on which the RISC approach has evolved.

2. *RISC Overview:* This section introduces the concept of RISC and provides an overview of its key characteristics.

3. *Optimized Register Usage:* One of the major design goals for RISC is to maximize the use of registers and minimize memory reads and writes. Several approaches to optimization have been explored by RISC designers.

4. *RISC Compilers:* A vital element in achieving high performance on a RISC system is an optimizing compiler. This section presents reports on three RISC compilers.

5. *Example Systems:* This section surveys systems that have been implemented using the RISC approach.

6. *An Assessment of RISC:* This section explores the relative merits of the RISC approach compared to the more conventional approaches to computer architecture.

7. *Glossary:* This includes definitions for most of the key terms appearing in the text.

8. *List of Acronyms:* Includes most of the acronyms appearing in the text.

9. *Annotated Bibliography:* Provides a guide to further reading.

Table of Contents

Section 1: Instruction Execution Characteristics

1.1 Background

One of the most visible forms of evolution associated with computers is that of programming languages. As the cost of hardware has dropped, the relative cost of software has risen. Along with that, a chronic shortage of programmers has driven up software costs in absolute terms. Thus the major cost in the life cycle of a system is software, not hardware. Adding to the cost, and to the inconvenience, is the element of unreliability: It is common for programs, both system and application, to continue to exhibit new bugs after years of operation.

The response from researchers and industry has been to develop ever more powerful and complex high-level programming languages (compare FORTRAN to Ada). These high-level languages (HLL) allow the programmer to express algorithms more concisely, take care of much of the detail, and often support naturally the use of structured programming.

Alas, this solution gave rise to another problem, known as the *semantic gap*, the difference between the operations provided in HLLs and those provided in computer architecture. Symptoms of this gap are alleged to include execution inefficiency, excessive program size, and compiler complexity. Designers responded with architectures intended to close this gap. Key features include large instruction sets, dozens of addressing modes, and various HLL statements implemented in hardware. An example of the latter is the CASE machine instruction on the VAX-11. Such complex instruction sets are intended to

- Ease the task of the compiler writer;
- Improve execution efficiency, since complex sequences of operations can be implemented in microcode;
- Provide support for even more complex and sophisticated HLLs.

Meanwhile, a number of studies have been done over the years to determine the characteristics and patterns of execution of machine instructions generated from HLL programs. The results of these studies inspired some researchers to look for an altogether different approach, namely, to make the architecture that supports the HLL simpler, rather than more, complex.

The articles in this section present results on studies of the execution characteristics of compiled HLL instructions. These results form the base on which the RISC approach has

evolved. For the reader unfamiliar with some of the issues in instruction set design, the following subsections provide some background.

1.2 The Machine Instruction Set

The operation of a computer's central processing unit (CPU) is determined by the instructions it executes. These instructions are referred to as *machine instructions* or *computer instructions*. The CPU may perform a variety of functions, and these are reflected in the variety of instructions defined for the CPU. The collection of different instructions that the CPU can execute is referred to as the CPU's *instruction set*.

Most of the details of a computer's organization and implementation are hidden from the user. One boundary where the computer designer and the computer programmer can view the same machine is the machine instruction set. From the designer's point of view, the machine instruction set provides the functional requirements for the CPU: Implementing the CPU is a task that in large part involves implementing the machine instruction set. From the user's side, the user that chooses to program in machine language or assembly language becomes aware of the register and memory structure, the types of data directly supported by the machine, and the functioning of the arithmetic and logic unit (ALU). Today, few programmers employ machine or assembly language. However, the machine instruction set remains of concern to the compiler writer.

1.3 Elements of a Machine Instruction

The basic function performed by a computer is program execution. The central processing unit (CPU) does the actual work by performing the instructions specified by the program. A program consisting of a set of instructions is stored in memory. The CPU typically reads (*fetches*) instructions from memory one at a time, executes each instruction, and then fetches the next instruction. This process is repeated indefinitely. The processing required for a single instruction is called an *instruction cycle* and is depicted in simplified form in Figure 1-1. The figure is in the form of a state diagram. For any given instruction cycle, some states may be null and others may be visited more than once. The states can be described as follows

- *instruction.address.calculation (iac):* Determine the address of the next instruction to be executed. Usually,

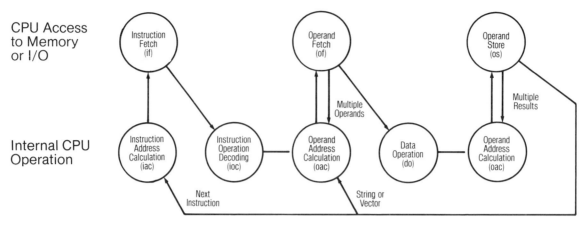

CPU Access to Memory or I/O

Internal CPU Operation

Note: Any state may be null

Figure 1.1: Instruction Cycle State Diagram

this involves adding 1 to the address of the previous instruction.

- *instruction.fetch (if):* Read instruction from its memory location into the CPU.

- *instruction.operation.decoding (iod):* Analyze instruction to determine the type of operation to be performed and operands to be used.

- *operand.address.calculation (oac):* If the operation involves reference to an operand in memory or available via I/O, then determine the address of the operand.

- *operand.fetch (of):* Fetch the operand from memory or read it in from I/O.

- *data.operation (do):* Perform the operation indicated.

- *operand.store (os):* Write the result into memory or out to I/O.

States in the upper part of the diagram involve an exchange between the CPU and either memory or an I/O module. States in the lower part of the diagram involve only internal CPU operations. The oac state appears twice, since an instruction may involve a read, a write, or both. However, the action performed during that state is fundamentally the same in both cases, so only a single state identifier is needed.

Also note that the diagram allows for multiple operands and multiple results, since some instructions on some machines require this. For example, the PDP-11 instruction ADD A,B results in the following sequence of states: iac, if, iod, oac, of, oac, of, do, oac, os.

Finally, on some machines, a single instruction can specify an operation to be performed on a vector (one-dimensional array) of numbers or a string (one-dimensional array) of characters, and this is also reflected in the state diagram.

From Figure 1-1, we can deduce the essential elements of a machine instruction. These elements are

- *Operation code:* Specifies the operation to be performed (e.g., ADD, I/O). The operation is specified by a binary code, known as the operation code, or *opcode*.

- *Source Operand Reference:* The operation may involve one or more source operands, that is, operands that are inputs for the operation.

- *Result Operand Reference:* The operation may produce a result.

- *Next Instruction Reference:* This tells the CPU where to fetch the next instruction after the execution of this instruction is complete.

The next instruction to be fetched is located in main memory or, in the case of a virtual memory system, in either main memory or secondary memory (disk). In most cases, the next instruction to be fetched immediately follows the current instruction, and there is no explicit reference to the next instruction. When an explicit reference is needed, then the main memory or virtual memory address must be supplied. The form in which that address is supplied is discussed below.

Source and result operands can be in one of three areas

- *Main or Virtual Memory:* As with next instruction references, the main or virtual memory address must be supplied.

- *CPU Register:* With rare exceptions, a CPU contains one or more registers that may be referenced by machine instructions. If only one register exists, reference to it may be implicit. If more than one register exists, then each register is assigned a unique number, and the instruction must contain the number of the desired register.

- *I/O Device:* The instruction must specify the I/O module and device for the operation. If memory-mapped I/O is used, this is just another main or virtual memory address.

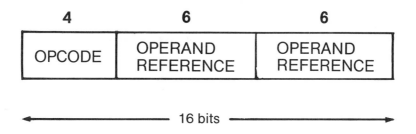

Figure 1.2: A simple Instruction Format

1.4 Instruction Representation

Within the computer, each instruction is represented by a sequence of bits. The instruction is divided into fields, corresponding to the constituent elements of the instruction. This layout of the instruction is known as the *instruction format*. A simple example is shown in Figure 1-2. With most instruction sets, more than one format is used. During instruction execution, an instruction is read into an instruction register (IR) in the CPU. The CPU must be able to extract the data from the various instruction fields to perform the required operation.

It is difficult both for the programmer and for the reader of textbooks to deal with binary representations of machine instructions. Thus it has become common practice to use a *symbolic representation* of machine instructions.

Opcodes are represented by abbreviations, called mnemonics, that indicate the operation. Common examples are

ADD	Add
SUB	Subtract
MPY	Multiply
DIV	Divide
LOAD	Load data from memory
STOR	Store data to memory

Operands are also represented symbolically. For example, the instruction

ADD R, Y

may mean add the value contained in data location Y to the contents of register R. In this example, Y refers to the address of a location in memory, and R refers to a particular register.

1.5 Instruction Types

Consider a high-level language instruction that could be expressed in a language such as BASIC or FORTRAN. For example

X = X + Y

This statement instructs the computer to add the value stored in Y to the value stored in X and put the result in X. How might this be accomplished with machine instructions? Let us assume that the variables X and Y correspond to locations 513 and 514. If we assume a simple set of machine instruc-

tions, this operation could be accomplished with three instructions

1. Load a register with the contents of memory location 513.
2. Add the contents of memory location 514 to the register.
3. Store the contents of the register in memory location 513.

As can be seen, the single BASIC instruction may require three machine instructions. This is typical of the relationship between a high-level language and a machine language. A high-level language expresses operations in a concise algebraic form, using variables. A machine language expresses operations in a basic form involving the movement of data to or from registers.

With this simple example to guide us, consider the type of instructions that must be included in a practical computer. A computer should have a set of instructions that allows the user to formulate any data processing task. Another way to view it is to consider the capabilities of a high-level programming language. Any program written in a high-level language must be translated into machine language in order to be executed. Thus the set of machine instructions must be sufficient to express any of the instructions from a high-level language. With this in mind we can list some of the most important types of instructions

- *Data Transfer:* This is the most fundamental type of machine instruction and results in the movement of data from one location to another. The data transfer instruction must specify the location of the source and destination operands and the length of data to be transferred.

- *Arithmetic:* These provide computational capabilities for processing numeric data (e.g., add, subtract, multiply, divide).

- *Logic:* These operate on individual bits of data and include boolean functions (e.g., AND, OR, NOT) and shifting functions.

- *Input/Output:* I/O instructions are used to transfer programs and data into main memory and results back out to the user or the secondary memory.

- *Transfer of Control:* These instructions are used to

cause the CPU to continue execution from a different point in the program rather than the next instruction in sequence.

1.6 Number of Addresses

One of the traditional ways of describing processor architecture is in terms of the number of addresses contained in each instruction. This dimension has become less significant with the increasing complexity of instruction set design. Nevertheless, it is useful at this point to draw and analyze this distinction.

What is the maximum number of addresses one might need in an instruction? Evidently, arithmetic and logic instructions will require the most operands. Virtually all arithmetic and logic operations are either unary (one operand) or binary (two operands). Thus we would need a maximum of two addresses to reference source operands. The result of an operation must be stored, suggesting a third address. Finally, after completion of an instruction, the next instruction must be fetched, and its address is needed.

The above line of reasoning suggests that an instruction could plausibly be required to contain four address references: two source operands, one result, and the address of the next instruction. In practice, four-address instructions are extremely rare. Most CPU's are of the one-, two-, or three-address variety, with the address of the next instruction being implicit (the next instruction in sequence).

Figure 1-3 compares typical one-, two-, and three-address instructions that could be used to compute $Y = (A - B) \div (C + D * E)$. With three addresses, each instruction specifies two operand locations and a result location. Because we would like to not alter the value of any of the operand locations, a temporary location, T, is used to store some intermediate results. Note that there are four instructions and that the original expression had four operands.

Three-address instruction formats are not common because they require a relatively long instruction format to hold the three address references. With two-address instructions, and for binary operations, one address must do double duty as both an operand and a result. Thus the instruction SUB Y, B carries out the calculation Y - B and stores the result in Y. The two-address format reduces the space requirement, but also introduces some awkwardness. To avoid altering the value of an operand, a MOVE instruction is used to move one of the values to a result or temporary location before performing the operation. Our sample program expands to six instructions.

Simpler yet is the one-address instruction. For this to work, a second address must be implicit. This was common in earlier machines, with the implied address being a CPU register known as the accumulator, or AC. The accumulator contains one of the operands and is used to store the result. In our example, eight instructions are needed to accomplish the task.

Instruction		Comment
SUB	Y,A,B	$Y \leftarrow A - B$
MPY	T,D,E	$T \leftarrow D \times E$
ADD	T,T,C	$T \leftarrow T + C$
DIV	Y,Y,T	$Y \leftarrow Y \div T$

(a) Three-Address Instructions

Instruction		Comment
MOVE	Y,A	$Y \leftarrow A$
SUB	Y,B	$Y \leftarrow Y - B$
MOVE	T,D	$T \leftarrow D$
MPY	T,E	$T \leftarrow T \times E$
ADD	T,C	$T \leftarrow T + C$
DIV	Y,T	$Y \leftarrow Y \div T$

(b) Two-Address Instructions

Instruction		Comment
LOAD	D	$AC \leftarrow D$
MPY	E	$AC \leftarrow AC \times E$
ADD	C	$AC \leftarrow AC + C$
STOR	Y	$Y \leftarrow AC$
LOAD	A	$AC \leftarrow A$
SUB	B	$AC \leftarrow AC - B$
DIV	Y	$AC \leftarrow AC \div Y$
STOR	Y	$Y \leftarrow AC$

(c) One-Address Instructions

Figure 1.3: Programs to Execute
$Y = (A - B) \div (C + D \times E)$

It is, in fact, possible to make do with zero addresses for some instructions. Zero-address instructions are applicable to a special memory organization, called a stack. A stack is a last-in first-out set of locations. The stack is in a known location and, often, at least the top two elements are in CPU registers. Thus zero-address instructions would reference the top two stack elements.

The number of addresses per instruction is a basic design decision. Fewer addresses per instruction results in more primitive instructions, which requires a less complex CPU. It also results in instructions of shorter length. On the other hand, with fewer addresses per instruction, programs contain more total instructions, which in general results in longer execution times and longer and more complex programs. Also, there is an important threshold between one-

Table 1.1: Basic Addressing Modes

Mode	Algorithm	Principal Advantage	Principal Disadvantage
Immediate	Operand = A	No Memory Reference	Limited Operand Magnitude
Direct	EA = A	Simple	Limited Address Space
Indirect	EA = (A)	Large Address Space	Multiple Memory References
Register	EA = R	No Memory Reference	Limited Address Space
Register Indirect	EA = (R)	Large Address Space	Extra Memory Reference
Displacement	EA = A + (R)	Flexibility	Complexity
Stack	EA = Top of Stack	No Memory Reference	Limited Applicability

address and multiple-address instructions. With one-address instructions, the programmer generally has available only one general-purpose register, the accumulator. With multiple-address instructions, it is common to have multiple general-purpose registers. This allows some operations to be performed solely on registers. Since register references are faster than memory references, this speeds up execution. For reasons of flexibility and ability to use multiple registers, most contemporary machines employ a mixture of two- and three-address instructions.

The design tradeoffs involved in choosing the number of addresses per instruction are complicated by other factors. There is the issue of whether an address references a memory location or a register. Since there are fewer registers, fewer bits are needed for a register reference. Also, as we shall see below, a machine may offer a variety of addressing modes, and the specification of mode takes one or more bits. The result is that most CPU designs involve a variety of instruction formats.

1.7 Addressing Modes

The address field or fields in a typical instruction format is quite limited. We would like to be able to reference a large range of locations in main memory or, for some systems, virtual memory. To achieve this objective, a variety of addressing techniques have been employed. They all involve some tradeoff between address range and/or addressing flexibility on the one hand and the number of memory references and/or the complexity of address calculation on the other.

Table 1.1 summarizes the most common addressing modes in use in various instruction sets. The table uses the following notation

A = contents of the (an) address field in the instruction

EA = actual (effective) address of the location containing the referenced operand

(X) = contents of location X

Briefly, the modes are

- *Immediate:* The operand is actually present in the instruction. This mode can be used to define and use constants or set initial values of variables.

- *Direct:* The address field in the instruction contains the effective address of the operand. This is a very simple form of addressing. Its limitation is that the size of memory (range of addresses) is limited by the length of the address field in the instruction.

- *Indirect:* Indirect addressing expands the range of addresses by having the address field refer to the address of a word in memory which in turn contains a full-length address of the operand. The disadvantage of this approach is that two memory accesses are required to access the operand.

- *Register:* The address field refers to a register. This saves time, since register access is faster than memory access, and also saves bits in the instruction format, since there are fewer registers than memory locations. However, because there are few registers, this technique has limited applicability.

5

- *Register Indirect:* The address field refers to a register that contains a full-length memory address of the operand. As with indirect, this mode provides for a large address range, yet it only requires one memory access.
- *Displacement:* In this mode, the effective address consists of the sum of the contents of a register plus a displacement value. The displacement value may be in another instruction address field or in another register. This powerful mode of addressing is used for a variety of functions, including segmentation of memory and indexing.
- *Stack:* The address is implicit and refers to the top of a stack. This is a useful but specialized mode.

To complete this discussion, two comments need to be made. First, virtually all instruction sets provide more than one of the addressing modes listed above. The question arises as to how the CPU can determine which address mode is being used in a particular instruction. Several approaches are taken. Often, different opcodes will use different addressing modes. Alternatively, one or more bits in the instruction format can be used as a *mode field*. The value of the mode field determines which addressing mode is to be used.

The second comment concerns the interpretation of the effective address (EA). In a system without virtual memory, the *effective address* will either be a main memory address or a register. In a virtual memory system, the effective address is a virtual address or a register. The actual mapping of a virtual address to a physical address is a function of the paging mechanism and is invisible to the programmer.

1.8 Instruction Formats

An instruction format defines the layout of the bits of an instruction, in terms of its constituent parts. An instruction format must include an opcode and, implicitly or explicitly, one or more operands. Each explicit operand is referenced by using one of the addressing modes described above. The format must, implicitly or explicitly, indicate the addressing mode for each operand. For most instruction sets, more than one instruction format is used.

The design of an instruction format is a complex art, and an amazing variety of designs have been implemented. In this section, we look at some of the key design issues.

1.8.1 Instruction Length

The most basic design issue to be faced is the instruction format length. This decision affects, and is affected by, memory size, memory organization, bus structure, CPU complexity, and CPU speed. This decision determines the richness and flexibility of the machine as seen by the assembly-language programmer.

The most obvious tradeoff here is between the desire for a powerful instruction repertoire versus a need to save space. Programmers want more opcodes, more operands, more

addressing modes, and greater address range. More opcodes and more operands make life easier for the programmer, since shorter programs can be written to accomplish given tasks. Similarly, more addressing modes give the programmer greater flexibility in implementing certain functions, such as table manipulations and multiple-way branching. And, of course, with the increase in main memory size and the increasing use of virtual memory, programmers want to be able to address larger memory ranges. All of these things (opcodes, operands, addressing modes, address range) require bits and push in the direction of longer instruction lengths. But longer instruction length may be wasteful. A 32-bit instruction occupies twice the space of a 16-bit instruction, but is probably much less than twice as useful.

Beyond this basic tradeoff, there are other considerations. The instruction length should either be equal to the memory-transfer length (in a bus system, data-bus length) or one should be a multiple of the other. Otherwise, we will not get an integral number of instructions during the fetch cycle. A related consideration is the memory transfer rate. This rate has not kept up with increases in processor speed. Accordingly, memory can become a bottleneck if the processor can execute instructions faster than it can fetch them. One solution to this problem is the use of cache memory; another is to use shorter instructions. Again, 16-bit instructions can be fetched at twice the rate of 32-bit instructions, but probably can be executed less than twice as fast.

1.8.2 Allocation of Bits

We have looked at some of the factors that go into deciding the length of the instruction format. An equally difficult issue is how to allocate the bits in that format. The tradeoffs here are complex.

For a given instruction length, there is clearly a tradeoff between the number of opcodes and the power of the addressing capability. More opcodes obviously means more bits in the opcode field. For an instruction format of a given length, this reduces the number of bits available for addressing. There is one interesting refinement to this tradeoff, and that is the use of variable-length opcodes. In this approach, there is a minimum opcode length but, for some opcodes, additional operations may be specified by using additional bits in the instruction. For a fixed-length instruction, this leaves fewer bits for addressing. Thus this feature is used for those instructions that require fewer operands and/or less powerful addressing.

The following interrelated factors go into determining the allocation of bits for addressing

- *Number of addressing modes:* Sometimes, an address mode can be indicated implicitly. For example, certain opcodes might always call for indexing. In other cases, the address modes must be explicit, and one or more mode bits will be needed.
- *Number of operands:* Typical instructions on today's machines provide for two operands. Each operand ad-

dress in the instruction might require its own mode indicator, or the use of a mode indicator could be limited to just one of the address fields.

- *Register versus Memory:* A machine must have registers so that data can be brought into the CPU for processing. With a single user-visible register (usually called the accumulator), one operand address is implicit and consumes no instruction bits. However, single-register programming is awkward and requires many instructions. Even with multiple registers, only a few bits are needed to specify the register. The more that registers can be used for operand references, the fewer bits are needed. A number of studies indicate that a total of 8 to 32 user-visible registers is desirable [e.g., article by Lunde in this section].

- *Number of register sets:* A number of machines have one set of general-purpose registers, with typically 8 or 16 registers in the set. These registers can be used to store data and can be used to store addresses for displacement addressing. The trend recently has been away from one bank of general-purpose registers and toward a collection of two or more specialized sets (such as data and displacement). This trend shows up everywhere from single-chip microprocessors to supercomputers. One advantage of this approach is that, for a fixed number of registers, a functional split requires fewer bits to be used in the instruction. For example, with two sets of eight registers, a functional split requires fewer bits to be used in the instruction. For example, with two sets of eight registers, only three bits are required to identify a register; the opcode implicitly will determine which set of registers is being referenced. There seems to be little disadvantage to this approach [LUND77]. In systems such as the S/370, which has one set of general-purpose registers, programmers usually establish conventions that assign about half the registers to data and half to displacement and maintain a fixed assignment.

- *Address range:* For addresses that reference memory, the range of addresses that can be referenced is related to the number of address bits. Because this imposes a severe limitation, direct addressing is rarely used. With displacement addressing, the range if opened up to the length of the address register. Even so, it is still convenient to allow rather large displacements from the register address, which requires a relatively large number of address bits in the instruction.

- *Address granularity:* For addresses that reference memory rather than registers, another factor is the granularity of addressing. In a system with 16- or 32-bit words, the designer can choose that addresses reference a word or a byte. Byte addressing is convenient for character manipulation but requires, for a fixed-size memory, more address bits.

Thus the designer is faced with a host of factors to consider and balance.

1.9 Instruction Set Design

One of the most intersting, and most analyzed, aspects of computer design is instruction set design. The design of an instruction set is very complex, since it affects so many aspects of the computer system. The instruction set defines many of the functions performed by the CPU, and thus has a significant effect on the implementation of the CPU. The instruction set is the programmer's means of controlling the CPU. Thus, programmer requirements must be considered in designing the instruction set.

Some of the most fundamental issues relating to the design of instruction sets remain in dispute. Indeed, in recent years the level of disagreement concerning these fundamentals has actually grown. This dispute is at the core of the research and development effort on RISC design and the controversy that that effort has generated. In this section, we have examined a number of these design issues. To summarize, the most important of these fundamental design issues include

- *Operation repertoire:* How many and which operations to provide, and how complex operations should be.
- *Data types:* The various types of data upon which operations are performed.
- *Instruction format:* Instruction length (in bits), number of addresses, size of various fields, etc.
- *Registers:* Number of CPU registers that can be referenced by instructions, and their use.
- *Addressing:* The mode or modes by which the address of an operand is specified.

These issues are highly interrelated and must be considered together in designing an instruction set. In this tutorial, we will be examining the design choices made by those involved in the design of RISC machines.

1.10 Article Summary

The first article, "Understanding Execution Behavior of Software Systems," presents the case for an analysis of instruction execution characteristics as a guide to the design of new architectures.

Next, "The Nature of General-Purpose Computations" surveys virtually all of the studies on instruction execution characteristics that are relevant to processor design. The author summarizes the key results that lead to a RISC approach.

The final two articles are perhaps the two most important papers on the subject. They have been referenced widely not only in the RISC literature, but in works on computer architecture in general. Lunde examines a set of numeric-computation programs written in five different high-level languages (2 FORTRAN versions, BASIC, Algol, BLISS). Tanenbaum presents measurements, from over 300 procedures used in operating-system programs and written in a language (SAL) that supports structured programming.

Without an understanding of micro- and macro-execution behavior, potential benefits from enhancements of computer architectures will be lost. Models of execution behavior are needed to connect measurement to theory.

Understanding Execution Behavior of Software Systems

James C. Browne, University of Texas at Austin

Modern computer architectures are primarily designed on a basis of compatibility with past architectures, engineering convenience, and limited context analysis of the execution behavior of current architectures. Only the latter has much value for improving the effectiveness of new architectures. Microelectronics technology permits cost-effective implementation and thus permits designers to utilize data or products developed during recent research on the execution behavior of current architectures. Consequently, hardware designers can, with relative ease, implement tremendously complex architectures or simple architectures with greatly increased computational speeds. However, the designer needs sufficient knowledge of or data on the execution behavior of a new architecture to predict the effectiveness of innovations in instruction set design or data access mechanisms. For example, (1) proposed architectures on which operations on complex data objects can be performed are likely to be inefficient unless the architectures are well matched to the workload, and (2) proposed architectures using simple instruction sets will not succeed unless the operations being performed can span the requirements of higher level language systems and efficiently map complex data structures to the architecture.

Our hopes for more effective computer architectures motivate us to establish the foundation for their development. Our goals include

- more economical use of the components of the hardware system; that is, more deliverable computations per dollar invested in hardware;
- simplification of development and maintenance of compilers and other basic software elements; and
- high-level language programs that obtain a greater fraction of the potential execution power of a given architecture for a given problem.

Two major barriers limit the development of innovative and cost-effective architectures. First, architecture designers lack knowledge of the execution structure of programs on existing architectures. (The execution structure of a program is determined by the way the logical operations and data structures of the program are bound to the instruction set and by the type of data storage facilities implemented in the architecture.) Second, any new architecture will be commercially important only when a useful body of software for it is available. The cost and time required for the development of such software will surely greatly exceed the cost for the development of the architecture itself; in fact, longer than typical lags in software availability may result because of the possible need for establishing techniques for utilizing innovative developments in software. Therefore, we should expect only limited enthusiasm for any truly innovative architectures.

Improvements in software development technology are, however, lessening the time and effort for development of software for new architectures. Parser and compiler generator systems and the trend towards writing basic software in higher level languages have aided in reducing the problems just cited. The porting of Unix to many different architectures is a good example of improved portability—from a clean system structure implemented in a higher level language. There are, however, avenues for more direct, short time-delay applications of significant new concepts in architectures or instruction sets. For instance, many major architectures are at least partially founded on microcoding; therefore, new capabilities can be added through microcoding while retaining compatibility with all current capabilities. Also, special-purpose or dedicated function units can be added to bus-based architectures to quickly implement useful new functions in an existing architecture.

In this article, no single form of instruction set is promoted; nor is one side or the other supported in the controversy involving proponents of the reduced instruction

Reprinted from *Computer*, July 1984, pages 83-87. Copyright © 1984 by The Institute of Electrical and Electronics Engineers, Inc.

EH0251-9/86/0000/0008$01.00 © 1984 IEEE

set[1] versus the complex instruction sets[2] controversy (see Jensen's article[3]). Rather, it is essential to recognize that proposals for new architectures should be based on an in-depth knowledge of the execution patterns of a spectrum of significant computation structures. This article investigates models of computation that can guide both the experimental analysis of execution behavior and the design of new generations of architectures.

Models of computation, architectures, and execution behavior

An algorithm or a computation can be described in terms of the model of computation required for execution, while a computer architecture can be described by the model of computation it implements. The cost-effectiveness of an architecture for execution of an algorithm is heavily influenced by the mapping between the models of computation of the algorithm and the architecture. A model of computation is defined by specification of at least the following properties:

- The primitive units of computation;
- The rules for turning the primitive units of computation into computation structures;
- The rules for constructing address spaces in which the complex computation structures execute;
- The modes of synchronization of parallel executions; and
- The modes of communication between computation structures and their address spaces.

The primitive units of computation for an architecture are defined by the instruction set of the processor. An instruction expresses an operation on some data structure or tuples of data structures and the operators of most architectures—arithmetic and logic—are applied to tuples of scalars or vectors of operands.

The common rule for turning primitive operations (instructions) into logical computation structures is to apply a stream of instructions—in some sequence which will usually be data dependent—to some set of basic storage units such as words or bytes. Parallel architectures may simultaneously process parallel streams of data and/or instructions.

An address space is the set of information (program and data) reachable by a composed unit of computation. It is determined in most computations by the specification of the set of memory cells that the currently executing instruction stream can address.

Synchronization is a concept brought into models of computation by the use of parallel instruction streams to execute a single logical computation. These instruction streams must often be executed in a specific sequence in order to implement the computation.

Communication mechanisms move information between the address spaces associated with distinct instruction streams: either the serially occurring instruction streams of sequential computation or the concurrently executing instruction streams of parallel computation structures.

Fundamental questions regarding the features of any architecture are "Which operators and operands should be selected and what are their capabilities for accessing memory in logical patterns?" To answer these questions requires that we first notice the relationship between operations, memory, and data structures; their interrelationship is determined by the time and mode of binding a computation structure to a sequence of elementary operations and a set of memory cells. Current conventional architectures bind structure to operators, at both compile time and execution time, by inserting data movement instructions between primitive instructions to do such things as map implicitly stored structures to registers. An object-based architecture such as a vector processor binds structures to operands in memory when the object is loaded in memory. This early binding is necessary to obtain the predictable behavior on which successful vector streaming operations depend.

Current architectures and research issues

Most current architectures execute their operations based on operands held in registers. Operand registers—in essence, caches for functional units—are introduced into the architectures because logic is faster than memory. The registers tend to limit the range of data structures to which operations can be applied, however, because they typically have simple structures. This limitation may be overcome by microelectronics, particularly by incorporating very large register sets into processor architectures. Programmers (and compilers) can then explicitly compose complex computations based on data held in fast registers.

Registers have a major impact on the instruction set of a processor. Instruction counts are strongly influenced by the movement of data structures between registers and memory. Instruction counts for register-oriented architectures are also skewed by sequence control and counter management instructions, which result from the mapping of complex data structures to operations on scalar registers. The logical structure of the computations executed on register-oriented machines may be obscured by the volume of register operations in instruction traces, unless the effects of the register operations are carefully characterized.

Composition sequencing rules determine how code for operations on complex structures will be produced from the code for the same operation on simple or scalar systems architectures. The composition rules and resulting execution structures could be simplified if instructions and high-level languages could be introduced into architectures to allow execution against objects closer to the object types of algorithms. There are several avenues of approach. One is to extend the application of operators to complex, conformable structures. Another is to introduce data structures into the architecture, then implement appropriate, preferably simple operations for execution against these data structures. In short, since faster execution will be attained only if the mapping between the operations of the algorithm and architectures are effective, analysis of algorithms and architectures on the same basis is very important. The direct-execution Lisp machines[4] testify to the results of an effective match of architecture to computations.

Synchronization among instruction streams depends on the characteristics of the units of computation and the data structures against which they are defined. However, though operating system[5] and database researchers have developed a large number of constructs for synchronization, there has been little systematic study of the effectiveness of mechanisms for coordination of computation structures with a variety of characteristics.

Communication among units of computation is commonly recognized as a concern only for parallel models of execution. Even in serial computation structures, however, the results from one operation on a tuple of operands must be made available (and sometimes reformatted) for the next sequenced or composed operation, a procedure that may involve movements among registers or storing in data structures held in memory. Communication between logical units of computation which execute in different address contexts also engenders execution costs. Reliable software isolates the address spaces of logical units of computation, so execution sequences at this level require either multiple bindings of addresses to names or the movement of values between address spaces. The communication costs of procedure calls can be a substantial fraction of the execution cost for highly modular programs.

An instruction set should provide clean and simple links between its instructions and the stream of control. A requirement for register shuffling or excessive storing and fetching from memory between computational or logical instructions can run up instruction counts to complete a logical unit of computation. Most data movement in sequential computation is caused by the need to compose operations on logical operands from operations on scalars.

A programming language also implements some spectrum of models of computation. Perhaps even more important than the links between the models of computation of algorithms and architectures are those between the models of computations of algorithms and programming languages, and those between programming languages and architectures. Since direct mapping from algorithms to architectures (assembly language programming) is rare, the representations of the models of computations of algorithms are realized in a programming language representation, which is actually executed on an architecture. This situation is sketched in Figure 1.

Analysis of previous research

The approach common in previous research is to analyze the execution of actual programs on existing architectures, then extrapolate from this information. Industry uses this approach to improve the effectiveness of instruction sets across generations of similar processors. Analysis involves counts of instruction frequency both by static occurrence in codes and dynamic occurrence in code execution sequences, as well as architecture dependent searches for patterns such as increment index and store. There are numerous papers and technical reports reporting

the results of such analyses. They often provide insights into execution patterns at a micro-level for a specific architecture, but they seldom relate the observations to the characteristics of the algorithms being executed, or apply the measurements to more abstract models of computation, or assess execution behavior on alternate architectures. The enhancement of operating system performance in the IBM 370 architecture is an obvious success of this approach.

Numerous recent projects in universities have also provided architectures with careful micro-level design, for instance, the MIPS project at Stanford.[6] Major industrial projects have also generated architectures based on detailed micro-level analyses. These include the 801 project at IBM[7] and the Bellmac project at Bell Laboratories.[8]

It is also appropriate to mention the research focused on major issues in models of computation: the Intel-432[9] and the Bellmac, which integrates data structures and instructions for implementation of processes. In addition, Lampson provides an example of a macro-level problem followed by modeling analysis and implementation design.[10]

An important omission in most of these studies has been analysis of patterns of access to memory. This omission has delayed extending analyses to more abstract models of computation. For example, it is difficult to define effective, complex memory structures without knowledge of the access of patterns of reference to data. It has been impossible to predict the behavior on significantly different architectures. There are exceptions, of course, in the work of Davidson and his students,[11,12] Batson and his students,[13] J. E. Smith,[14] and Cook and Donde.[15] The analysis of reference string behavior for support of virtualization of paged memory architectures is, of course, a notable body of experimental literature which is too large to detail here. The work on locality patterns and cache design is another significant body of work.[16]

Goals and directions for future research

Research in architecture should be structured by the scientific approach of constructing models, designing ex-

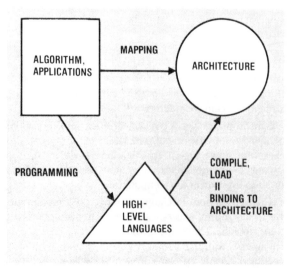

Figure 1. The interrelationships of models of computation.

periments, and measuring in well - understood environments with feedback into new models and experiments. Measurements have frequently been made without the beneficial structuring of models, and they are rarely compared to similar measurements on other architectures. More insight will result from analysis of models of execution behavior at a more macro-level than the instruction level of current-day architecture. There also remains a need for more consideration of the elements that comprise models of computation. Studies of execution of compiler-generated code seldom include implementation of protection structures and vice versa.

It is worthwhile to consider more sophisticated analyses of instruction-level data. A substantial set of analytical tools for determining the properties of graphs, and subgraphs constructed according to various algorithms, and direct construction of graph partitions of specified properties serve as a point of departure. A graph where the nodes represent application of primitive instructions to elementary data structures and the arcs are flow of control may represent a logical unit of computation. Analysis of commonly occurring or logically coherent sequences should reveal the logical elements of the computation. Then conversion of instruction streams to graph models, each representing a computation in terms of primitive computations and data movement in a given architecture, may suggest new instructions or define new data or memory structures.

Complementary research on real architectures could involve execution of abstract algorithms or representations of computations on paper architectures implementing interesting occurrences of significant models of computation. Since the computer industry encourages researchers to establish valid gate-level and micro-level architectures, why not support a similar thrust in the design of macro architectures?

Another major focus might be the organizational structures of modern software development and the increasing need for reliable, robust systems. Defining and maintaining separate address spaces for logical units of computation is a major problem which is neither well characterized nor well explored. For example, architectural suport for an access-list-based protection scheme has not been seriously discussed in the literature, although capability-based architectures have been extensively explored. [17]

Likewise the interaction among architectures, high-level languages, and their compilers is an interesting problem that has already received a great deal of attention. Wulf lists a set of principles for efficiently supporting higher level languages. [18] Still remaining to resolve are the differences between execution patterns for identical computations when the programs are prepared and compiled in different high-level language systems. A comparison might be made of the instruction sequences arising from execution of the same algorithm programmed in one language system using static memory allocation and the other using dynamic memory allocation. Interesting results should also come from a comparison between languages with rich data structuring and with limited data declarational power for their efficiency to execution of operations on complex data structures. The results might

resemble the RISC/CISC analyses, but at a slightly higher level of abstraction.

Other areas of controversy are the interactions between translation techniques for higher level languages and the conceptual gaps between the models of computation specified in high-level languages on the one hand, and those realized in architectures, on the other. The RISC approach argues for increasing the conceptual distance while simplifying the interface. The CISC approach argues for decreasing the conceptual gap while making the interface more complicated. Experiments on translation to the two targets are needed.

I/O architecture is likewise an area hardly touched in previous measurements. What, for example, is the pattern of use of data transferred to executable memories in fixed size pages?

The increasing representational power of microelectronic devices opens opportunities for innovations in architecture, which can lead to much more cost-effective, reliable, and easy-to-use computer systems. Progress must, however, be founded on an in-depth knowledge of the logical execution patterns of a spectrum of significant algorithms on realized and realizable computation architectures. Ultimately it can be the basis for design of more effective computer architectures. ∗

Acknowledgments

This research was sponsored in part by the Department of Energy (under grant DE-AS05-81-ER10987) and by the National Science Foundation (under grant MCS-8116099).

References

1. D. A. Patterson and C. H. Seguin, "RISC-I: A Reduced Instruction SET VLSI Computer," *Proc. Eighth Annual Symp. on Computer Architectures,* May 1981, pp. 443-458.

2. D. W. Clark and W. D. Strecker, "Comments on the Case for the Reduced Instruction Set Computer," *Computer Architecture News,* Aug. 1980, pp. 34-38.

3. E. D. Jensen, R. P. Colwell, and C. Y. Hitchcock, "Peering Through the RISC/CISC Fog," *Computer Architecture News,* Nov. 1982.

4. D. Weinreb and D. Moon, *LISP Machine Manual,* Symbolics Inc., Cambridge, Mass., 1981.

5. J. Bloom, "Evaluating Synchronization Primitives," *Proc. Seventh Symp. Operating Systems Princicples,* 1979, pp. 24-32.

6. J. Hennessy et. al, "Hardware/Software Tradeoffs for Increased Performance," *Proc. Symp. on Architectural Support for Programming Languages and Operating Systems,* Mar. 1982, pp. 2-11.

7. G. Radin, "The 801 Minicomputer," *Proc. Symp. Architectural Support for Programming Languages and Operating Systems,* Mar. 1982, pp. 39-47.

8. A. Berenbaum, M. Condry, and P. Lu, "The Operating System and Language Support Features of the BELL-MAC-32," *Proc. Symp. Architectural Support for Programming Languages and Operating Systems,* Mar. 1982, pp. 30-38.

9. J. Rattner and G. Cox, "Object-Based Computer Architectures," *Computer Architecture News,* Aug. 1980, pp. 4-11.

10. B. W. Lampson, "Fast Procedure Calls," *Proc. Symp. Architectural Support for Programming Languages and Operating Systems,* Mar. 1982, pp. 66-76.

11. D. W. Hammerstrom and E. S. Davidson, "Information Content of CPU Memory Referencing Behavior," *Fourth Annual Symp. Computer Architectures,* Mar. 1977, pp. 184-192.

12. A. R. Pleszkun and E. S. Davidson, "Structured Memory Access Architecture," *Proc. Int'l Conf. Parallel Processing,* Aug. 1983, pp. 461-471.

13. A. W. Madison and A. P. Batson, "Characteristics of Program Localities," *Comm. ACM,* Vol. 18, 1975, pp. 285-294.

14. "Decoupled Access/Execute Computer Architectures," *Proc. Ninth Annual Symp. on Computer Architecture,* 1982, pp. 112-119.

15. R. P. Cook and N. Donde, "An Experiment to Improve Operand Addressing," *Proc. Symp. on Architectural Support for Programming Languages and Operating Systems,* Mar. 1982, pp. 87-95.

16. A. J. Smith, "Cache Memories," *Computing Surveys 14,* 1982, pp. 473-530.

17. M. V. Wilkes, "Hardware Support for Memory Protection," *Proc. Symp. on Architectural Support for Programming Languages and Operating Systems,* Mar. 1982, pp. 107-116.

18. W. A. Wulf, "Compilers and Computer Architecture," *Computer,* Vol. 14, No. 7, July 1981, pp. 41-47.

James C. Browne received a BA degree from Hendrix College, Conway, Arkansas, in 1956 and a PhD in physical chemistry from the University of Texas at Austin in 1960. From 1960 to 1964, he was an assistant professor of physics, University of Texas at Austin, carrying out quantum mechanical calculations of small molecules, and research and development work on operating systems. From 1964 to 1965, he was an NSF postdoctoral fellow at Queen's University of Belfast, Northern Ireland, and from 1965 to 1968, professor of computer science and director of the computation laboratory at Queen's University. In 1968, he returned to the University of Texas at Austin as professor of computer science and physics, and served as chairman of the Dept. of Computer Sciences. His research interests include operating systems, systems modeling and design, performance evaluation of computer systems, and parallel computing. He is a fellow of the American Physical Society and the British Computer Society, and a member of the Association of Computing Machinery. He can be contacted at the Dept. of Computer Sciences, University of Texas, Austin, TX 78712.

The Nature
of General-Purpose Computations

In the design of a computer system, two issues must be studied carefully:

(1) FUNCTION: What is the purpose of the computer system? What is the nature of the computations it will perform? What are the necessary features that will enable it to perform those computations with high efficiency?

(2) COST: Can the desirable architectural features be implemented at a reasonable cost and with a reasonable performance, in a particular technology? What are the trade-offs imposed by the constraints of a given implementation technology?

This chapter focuses on the first question of what it is that computer systems usually do, leaving the bulk of the discussion on implementation issues for the next chapters. We are interested in "general-purpose computer systems". Although it is difficult to define this term, we use it to refer to systems not biased towards the execution of a particular algorithm, and, specifically, systems that execute a mix of word processing, data base applications, mail and communications, compilations, CAD, control, and numerical applications. The chapter will assemble a picture of the nature of such "general-purpose" computations, by collecting program measurements from the literature, and by studying the critical loops of some representative programs. The resulting picture will be used in the next chapters.

2.1   Goal and Methods of Program Measurement

The main vehicle for a qualitative and quantitative understanding of the nature of computations is the measurement of the important properties on some real programs. It is very difficult for such a study to be made *abstractly* -- not in connection with a particular model of computers and computations, because real programs and programming languages *are* written and defined with a particular model in mind, and because the properties to be measured depend on this model.

Throughout this dissertation, a *von Neumann model* of computers and computations is assumed. Programs written in corresponding languages are considered in this chapter. C and FORTRAN program fragments are studied, and measurements from the literature are reported, which were collected by looking at programs written in FORTRAN, XPL, PL/I, Algol, Pascal, C, BLISS, Basic, and SAL. This section identifies the main properties of computations which are important in the design of von Neumann architectures, and lists tools and methods for their measurement.

2.1.1 Architecturally Important Properties of Computations

In the von Neumann model, computations are performed by sequentially executing operations on operands which are kept in a storage device. The sequence of

Reprinted with permission from *Reduced Instruction Set Computer Architectures for VLSI*, edited by M. Katevenis, 1985, pages 9-41. Copyright © 1985 by MIT Press.

operations is dynamically controlled by operand values. Thus, the properties of computations that will interest us are:

- **Operands used.** Their type, size, structure, and the nature of their usage determines the storage organization for keeping them and the addressing modes for accessing them. In particular:

  - Constant or variable operands.
  - Types of operands: integers, floating-point, characters, pointers.
  - Structure of operands: scalars, arrays, strings, structures of records.
  - Declaration of operands: globals, procedure arguments, procedure locals.
  - Number of operands, sizes, and frequency of accesses for the above categories.
  - Amount and nature of locality-of-reference, possibly determined individually for each one of the above categories, for example, for scalars, arrays, (dynamic) structures, globals, and procedure activation records.

- **Operations performed.** These will determine the required operational units, and their connection to the storage units. The relative frequency of operations such as the ones listed below is important, and the variation of those frequencies with the operands' categories is also of interest.

  - Test, compare, add, subtract, multiply, divide, and so on.
  - Operation type, such as integer, floating-point, or string.
  - Higher level operations, such as I/O, buffer, list, and so forth.

- **Execution sequencing.** This will determine the control and pipeline organization:

  - Control transfers: conditional/unconditional jumps, calls, returns. What is their frequency, distance, conditions, predictability, and earliness of condition resolution.
  - Amount and nature of extractable parallelism. This is a very general and important question; for von Neumann architectures, we are interested in low-level parallelism.

While quantitative measurements are essential, the large number of properties to be measured -- especially if correlation among them is also studied -- makes a qualitative understanding of the global picture equally important. Methods for both kinds of analysis are presented below.

2.1.2 Static and Dynamic Measurements

Program measurements are usually collected by running the program under study through a suitable filter, or by executing it in a suitable environment. In both cases the result of this processing is a count of the numbers of times that some feature has appeared or that some particular property has held true in the text of the program or in its execution.

Measurements referring to the text of a program are called static. They give no useful information on performance, because they are not weighted relative to the number of times each statement was executed. They can show the size of storage required for the machine code and for the statically allocated objects, and they can show what the compiler has to deal with. Under crude assumptions, the static characteristics of programs can also give some indication on their dynamic behaviour.

Measurements referring to the execution of a program are called dynamic. Execution of the program requires previous compilation into object code for some machine, except if expensive interpretation is used. Thus, dynamic measurements usually refer to machine rather than source code, introducing another - often unwanted - parameter into the study. Machine code can be correlated back to source code, so that dynamic measurements at the source level can be inferred. However, this correlation is not always easy or precise.

Static and dynamic program measurements have frequently appeared in the literature, and have also been collected early in the RISC project (spring 1980). Section 2.2 reviews some of them.

2.1.3 Source-Code Profiling and Studying

Because the list of important properties of computations is very long, and because several of them are difficult to quantify or to measure, the static and dynamic program measurements have some limitations. There is another method of looking at the nature of computations which is less quantitative but more qualitative, and which can complement these measurements or give a better idea of what specific other measurements should be taken. That method is to carefully study the source code of a program and, if possible, the underlying algorithms, concentrating on those portions of it which account for most of the execution time.

It has been observed, time and again, that programs spend most of their execution time in small portions of their code, the so-called "critical loops". This makes it feasible and worthwhile to study those portions in detail, to understand the nature and properties of the computation that is carried out. The critical loops can be identified by profiling the program during execution. Profiling is the dynamic measurement of how much of the execution "cost" is spent at each place in the program's code. The "cost" may be:

- time spent,
- number of source-code lines executed,
- number of memory accesses, and so forth.

In section 2.3 we will study some critical loops that have been identified by other researchers. Section 2.4 studies some more critical loops, which were identified by this author using two profiling systems. The first was the standard profiling facility of UNIX: compilation using the *-p* or *-pg* switch, execution, and then interpretation of the results by the *prof* or *gprof* program. This method arranges that the program-counter of an executing process be sampled at "random" intervals (on clock interrupts, every 1/60th of a second). The sampled value is used to determine which procedure was executing at that time. If a program runs for a long time, the above samples can be used to construct estimates of how much time was spent in each of the program's procedures. There is no straightforward way to find out the time spent in executing any smaller program portions.

The second profiling system that was used, for programs written in C, belongs to Bell Laboratories (Murray Hill), and was used under special authorization [Wein]. It counts the number of times that each source-code line is executed (but gives no indication as to how long its execution takes). A special version of the C compiler is used, which inserts code at appropriate locations to increment appropriate counters. At the end of execution the counts are saved in a file. Another program is then invoked to correlate those counts with the original source code, and to generate an annotated program listing †.

2.2 Review of some Program Measurements from the Literature

In this section interesting program measurements from the literature are reviewed. Measurements on all properties mentioned in section 2.1.1 are not present here, because some of them either have not received enough attention in the literature, or were difficult to measure. The measurements were selected from:

[AlWo75]: Alexander and Wortman collected static and dynamic measurements from 19 programs (mostly compilers), written in XPL and executed on the IBM/360 architecture.

[Elsh76]: Elshoff presented static measurements of 120 commercial, production PL/I programs for business data processing.

[HaKe80],

[TaSe83]: Halbert and Kessler, in their study of multiple overlapping windows early during the RISC project, collected dynamic measurements on the number of arguments and local scalars per procedure, and on the locality property of procedure-nesting-depth. They measured the C compiler, the Pascal interpreter, the troff typesetter, and 6 other smaller non-numeric programs (all written in C). Tamir and Séquin collected some more dynamic data on the locality of nesting depth, measuring the RISC C compiler, the towers-of-Hanoi program, and the Puzzle program (all written in C).

[Lund77]: Lunde used the concept of "register-lives" in his measurements. He analyzed half a dozen numeric-computation programs written in 5 different HLL's (2 FORTRAN versions, Basic, Algol, BLISS), plus some compilers, all running on a DECsystem10 architecture.

[Shus78]: Shustek studied the usage made of the PDP-11 addressing modes, by statically measuring 10,000 lines of code of an operating system.

[PaSe82]: Patterson and Séquin presented the most important measurements collected during the early stages of the RISC project, in spring 1980,

---

† the count is not always what one would expect for lines like: " } else { ". The listings in section 2.4 have been corrected by hand in those situations.

in collaboration with E. Cohen and N. Soiffer. Measurements are dynamic, and were collected from compilers, typesetters, and programs for CAD, sorting, and file comparison. Four of those were written in C, and the other four in Pascal.

[Tane78]: Tanenbaum published static and dynamic measurements of HLL constructs, collected from more than 300 procedures used in operating-system programs and written in a language that supports structured programming (SAL).

2.2.1 Measurements on Operations

The operations performed by programs are the most frequent object of measurement, in the form of statement types (source level) or opcodes (machine level). The following tables summarize such measurements.

Property:	Measurement:	Reference:
Dynamically executed instructions:		
moves between registers and memory	40 %	[Lund77,p.149]
branching instructions	30 %	(numeric &
fixed-point add/sub's	12 %	compilers)
load, load address (more than normal, due to 360 archit.)	33 %	[AlWo75] (mostly compil.
store	10 %	in XPL
branch	14 %	on IBM/360)
compare	6 %	
Statically counted HLL statements:		
assignments	42 %	[AlWo75]
if	13 %	(mostly compil.
call	13 %	in XPL)
Dynamically executed HLL statements:		
assignments	42 ± 12 %	[PaSe82]
if	36 ± 15 %	(non-numeric,
call/return	14 ± 4 %	in C & Pascal)
loops	4 ± 3 %	
....weighted with the number of machine instructions executed for each:		
loops	37 ± 5 %	[PaSe82]
call/return	32 ± 12 %	(non-numeric,
if	16 ± 7 %	in C & Pascal)
assign	13 ± 4 %	
....weighted with the number of memory accesses necessary for each:		
call/return	45 ± 16 %	[PaSe82]
loops	30 ± 4 %	(non-numeric,
assign	15 ± 5 %	in C & Pascal)
if	10 ± 4 %	

More on procedure calls:

procedure calls as percentage of dynamically executed HLL statm.	12 %	[Tane78] (O.S., structured pr.)
procedure call administration as percentage of execution time	25 %	[Lund77,p.151] (BLISS compiler)

an amazing exception case:
   procedures def. within 100 K statm.
   perc. of calls relative to all statem.
	
	83 (only!)
	2 % (!)
		[Elsh76] (PL/I business prog., static)

Other frequent high-level operations:

• vector operations (inner product, move, sum, search,...)	[Lund77]
• character-string ops (table-controlled substitute, delete, branch)	
• loop control (incr. a reg., compare it to another reg., and branch)	

Jump distance, measured dynamically:

< 128 bytes	55 %	[AlWo75]
< 16 Kbytes	93 %	

Jump conditions, measured dynamically:

unconditional jumps as % of all jumps	55 %	[AlWo75]
..."the comparison of two non-zero values is about twice as common as compr. with zero".		[Lund77]

Expressions, register lives:

one-term expressions in assignments†	66 %	[Tane78]
two-term expressions in assignments†	20 %	(dynamic)
operators per expression (average)	0.76	[AlWo75](st)
relative to all register lives:		
lives w. no arithm. performed on them	50% (20-90%)	[Lund77]
lives w. max†† integer add/sub on them	25% (1-70%)	(dynamic,
lives w. max†† integer mult/div on them	5% (2-20%)	numeric &
lives used in floating-point operations	15% (0-40%)	compilers)
lives used for indexing	40% (20-70%)	[Lund77]

† on the right-hand-side of assignments.

†† "maximum-complexity" operation performed on the register, where int-add/sub < int-mult/div < floating-point-op.

These measurements are not very helpful in understanding the high-level nature of computations, but they do show:

- The importance of the procedure call mechanism, since so much time is spent in it.
- The importance of the sequencing control mechanism (compare and branch), since loops and if's are so frequent.
- The importance of simple arithmetic and of addressing, accessing, and moving operands around, since expressions are usually very short, and since half of the operands appearing in registers ("register lives" in [Lund77]) have no arithmetic performed on them.

2.2.2 Measurements on Operands

Measurements on the operands in programs have not been so frequent in the literature, even though this subject is very important. Lunde [Lund77] measured on a DECsystem10 that each instruction on the average references 0.5 operands in memory and 1.4 in registers dynamically. These figures depend highly on the architecture and on the compiler, but they do illustrate, nevertheless, the importance of fast operand accessing, since that occurs so frequently.

Property:	Measurement:	Reference:
Dynamic percentage of operands (HLL):		
integer constants	20 ± 7 %	[PaSe82]
scalars	55 ± 11 %	(non-numeric,
array/structure	25 ± 14 %	in C & Pascal)
local-scalar references as percentage of all scalar references	> 80 %	[PaSe82]
global-array/structure references as percentage of all arr/str. references	> 90 %	[PaSe82]

Use of PDP-11 addressing modes:		
"The 4 most common modes are perhaps the 4 simplest":		[Shus78]
register	32 %	(static,
indexed (e.g. for fields of structures)	17 %	O.S.)
immediate (constants)	15 %	
PC-relative (direct addressing)	11 %	
all others	25 %	
"The 4 least-used modes are precisely the 4 memory indirect ones (1%)".		
"Half of the move instr. had a register as their dest."		[Shus78]
"Half of the compare/add/subtract instructions had one of their operands be an immediate"		

A property that had attracted very little attention in the past is the high locality of references to local scalar variables. The figures from [PaSe82] given above show that over half of the accesses to non-constant values are made to local scalars. On top of that, references to arrays/structures require a previous reference to their index or pointer, which is again a - usually local - scalar. Most of the time, the number of local scalars per procedure is small.

Tanenbaum [Tane78] found that 98 % of the dynamically called procedures had less than 6 arguments, and that 92 % of them had less than 6 local scalar variables. Similar numbers were found by Halbert and Kessler:

Procedure Activation Records: [HaKe80] Percentage of executed procedure calls with:		
	compiler, interpr. and typesetter	other smaller programs (non-numer.)
> 3 arguments	0 to 7 %	0 to 5 %
> 5 arguments	0 to 3 %	0 %
> 8 words of arg's & locals	1 to 20 %	0 to 6 %
> 12 words of arg's & locals	1 to 6 %	0 to 3 %

Thus, the number of words per procedure activation is not large. The following measurements show that the number of procedure activations touched during a reasonable time span is not large either. This establishes the locality-of-reference property for local scalars.

Locality of Procedure Nesting Depth: [HaKe80] [TaSe83] Percentage of executed procedure calls which overflow from last span of nesting depths:		
(assuming that the span of nesting depths has constant size, and that its position moves by one on every over/under-flow; this corresponds to a RISC register file with as many windows as the span size, and with no window reserved for interrupts. See section 3.2).		
	2 compilers, interpr. typesetter, Hanoi	6+1 other smaller programs (non-numeric)
span sz = 4 (4 wind.)	8 to 15 %	0 to 2.5 %
span sz = 8 (8 wind.)	1 to 3 %	0 to 0.2 %

2.3 Study of some Critical FORTRAN Loops (collected mostly by Knuth)

Knuth, in [Knut71], presents a study of where FORTRAN programs spend most of their time. The programs he measured varied from text-editing to scientific number-crunching programs. Dynamic measurements of the HLL statements executed showed that:

- 67% were assignments,
- one third of those assignments were of the type A=B,
- 11% were IF, 9% were GOTO, 3% were DO,
- 3% were CALL, and 3% were RETURN,
- More than 25% of the execution time was spent in I/O formatting.

However, what is most interesting for our study is that he gives the actual code fragments where 17 of those programs (chosen at random) spent most of their time. He used those fragments (''examples'') to test the effectiveness of various techniques for optimization of compiled code. We will briefly study those same examples from our point of interest: understanding the nature of computations, and in particular answering the questions of section 2.1.1. The 17 examples have been classified in three categories of array-numeric, array-searching, and miscellaneous style examples. Their code (or a summary of it) is given below in a modernized-FORTRAN format. An eighteenth example of a critical loop, collected by the author of this dissertation, was added to the first category. It is the main loop of a procedure that inverts a positive-definite symmetric matrix. It was included in the study after two researchers in structural mechanics and in fluid dynamics independently told this author that they felt matrix inversion was the most time-consuming computation done by people in their area.

2.3.1 "Array-Numeric" Style Examples

Example 3:
```
double A, B, D
do 1 k=1,N
1    A = T[I-k, 1+k] ;  B = T[I-k, J+k] ;  D = D - A*B
```

Example 7:
```
do 1 i=1,N
    A = X**2 + Y**2 - 2.*X*Y*C[i]
1    B = SQRT(A) ;  K = 100.*B+1.5 ;  D[i] = S[i]*T[K]
    Q = D[1] - D[N]
    do 2 i=2,M,2
2    Q = Q + 4.*D[i]  + 2.*D[i+1]
```

Example 9:
```
do 2 k=1,M
do 2 j=1,M
initialize...
do 1 i=1,M
    N = j + j + (i-1)*M2 ;  B = A[k,i]
1    X = X + B*Z[N] ;  Y = Y + B*Z[N-1]
2    more computations...
```

Example 11:   a Fast Fourier Transform. It computes sums and products of floating-point elements of two linear arrays. One array is those same examples from our point of interest: understanding the nature of computations, and in particular answering the questions of section 2.1.1. The 17 examples have been classified in three categories of array-numeric, array-searching, and miscellaneous style examples. Their code (or a summary of it) is given below in a modernized-FORTRAN format. An eighteenth example of a critical loop, collected by the author of this dissertation, was added to the first category. It is the main loop of a procedure that inverts a positive-definite symmetric matrix. It was included in the study after two researchers in structural mechanics and in fluid dynamics independently told this author that they felt matrix inversion was the most time-consuming computation done by people in their area.

2.3.1 "Array-Numeric" Style Examples

Example 3:
```
double A, B, D
do 1 k=1,N
1    A = T[I-k, 1+k] ;  B = T[I-k, J+k] ;  D = D - A*B
```

Example 7:
```
do 1 i=1,N
    A = X**2 + Y**2 - 2.*X*Y*C[i]
1    B = SQRT(A) ;  K = 100.*B+1.5 ;  D[i] = S[i]*T[K]
    Q = D[1] - D[N]
    do 2 i=2,M,2
2    Q = Q + 4.*D[i]  + 2.*D[i+1]
```

Example 9:
```
do 2 k=1,M
do 2 j=1,M
initialize...
do 1 i=1,M
    N = j + j + (i-1)*M2 ;  B = A[k,i]
1   X = X + B*Z[N] ;  Y = Y + B*Z[N-1]
2 more computations...
```

Example 11:   a Fast Fourier Transform. It computes sums and products of floating-point elements of two linear arrays. One array is accessed sequentially, and the other one with a step of N.

Example 12:   a very long inner loop, with counter arithmetic, array accesses (many 3-dimensional arrays, some 2- and 1- dimensional), and floating-point multiplications and additions. There is one expression with 32 operators! In spite of its heavy computation character, this program has no more floating-point operations than it has simple counter and index operations.

Example 15:
```
do 1 j=i,N
    H[i,j] = H[i,j] + S[i]*S[j]/D1 - S[k+i]*S[k+j]/D2
1   H[j,i] = H[i,j]
```

Example 17:
```
do 1 i=1,N
1   A = A + B[i] + C[k+i]
```

Example - Matrix Inversion:
Figure 2.3.1 shows the aforementioned critical loop of positive-definite symmetric matrix inversion, in an abstract flow-chart form.

All these critical loops are of the same style: They perform floating-point operations on elements of arrays. Two almost independent "processes" exist. First, array elements are accessed in a *regular* fashion, i.e. in an arithmetic progression of memory addresses; the loop control is related to the array indexes, and does not depend on the array data. The second "process" is that of doing the actual numerical data computations.

2.3.2 "Array-Searching" Style Examples

Example 1:   a search for the maximum of the absolute values:
```
do 2 j=1,N
    t = ABS( A[i,j] ) ;  if (t>s) then s=t ;
2   continue
```

Example 2:   a search for a match:
```
do 1 j=38,53
    if (K[i]==L[j]) then goto 2
1   continue
```

Example 10:
```
do 1 i=L,M
1   if ( X[i-1,j] < Q and  X[i,j] ≥ Q ) then rare
```

22

Example 13:   a binary search:
```
1    j = (i+k)/2
     if (j==i) then  goto 2
     if ( X[j] == XKEY ) then  goto 3
     if ( X[j] < XKEY ) then  i=j else  k=j
     goto 1
```

These examples are non-numeric. Most of them access the array(s) in a regular manner, like the examples in 2.3.1. However, the control of their sequencing is *dynamic* in nature: it depends on the actual data being visited, rather than on regularly incremented counters.

2.3.3 "Miscellaneous" Style Examples

Example 4:   first a poor quality random-number generator is defined:
```
     subroutine RAND(R)
     j = i * 65539
     if (j<0) then  j = j + 2147483647 + 1
     R = j ;  R = R * 0.4656613e-9
     i = j ;  k = k+1 ;  return
then it is called:
     do 1 k=M,20
        call RAND(R)
1       if ( R > 0.81 ) then  N[k] = 1
```
Knuth comments: "...the most interesting thing here, however, is the effect of subroutine linkage, since the long prologue and epilogue significantly increase the time of the inner loop".

Example 5:   this is a long inner loop that does lots of floating-point computations. It contains some simple arithmetic and compare & branch operations on integer counters, sequential addressing of two linear arrays, and several floating-point exponentiations, multiplications, and additions. The loop is badly written, with many large common subexpressions. There is lots of low-level parallelism present, mainly among the floating-point computations, but also between them and the integer ones.

Example 6:   a subroutine S is defined:
```
     subroutine  S(A,B,X)
     dimension A[2], B[2]
     X=0 ;  Y = (B[2]-A[2])*12 + B[1] - A[1]
     if (Y<0) then goto 1
     X=Y
1    return
then W is defined, which is called multiple times, and which
calls S:
     subroutine  W(A,B,C,D,X)
     dimension A[2], B[2], C[2], D[2], U[2], V[2]
     X=0 ;  call S(A,D,X) ;  if (X==0) then goto 3
     call S(C,B,X) ;  if (X==0) then goto 3
     rarely executed code
3    return
```

Example 8:	subroutine COMPUTE ; common ....

```
Example 8:        subroutine COMPUTE ;  common ....
                  complex Y[10], Z[10]
                  R=real(Y[n]) ;  P=sin(R) ;  Q=cos(R)
                  S = C * 6.0 * (P/3.0 - Q*Q*P)
                  T = 1.414214 * P * P * Q * C * 6.0
                  U=T/2.
                  V = -2.0 * C * 6.0 * (P/3.0 - Q*Q*P/2.0)
                  Z[1] = (0.0,-1.0)   *  ( S*Y[1] + T*Y[2] )
                  Z[2] = (0.0,-1.0)   *  ( U*Y[1] + V*Y[2] )
                  return

Example 14:       do 1 i=1,N
               1   C = C/D*R ;  D = D-1 ;  R = R+1


Example 16:       real function F(X)
                  Y = X * 0.7071068
                  if ( Y < 0.0 ) then goto 1
                  rarely executed code
               1   F = 1.0 - 0.5 * (1.0 + ERF(-Y)) ;  return
```

These examples help us remember that real programs are not always as simple and straightforward as those seen in sections 2.3.1 and 2.3.2. Relative to those simpler ones, these "miscellaneous" programs are characterized by more numeric computations, the same number or fewer array accesses, less index/counter arithmetic, less or unusual-style comparisons and branches, and -- in some cases -- more procedure calls.

2.3.4 The Nature of Numeric Computations

The above examples give a picture of typical numeric computations, which can be summarized as follows:

1. The absolutely predominant data structure is the **array.** Most of the arrays are 1- or 2- dimensional. (Of course, the predominance of arrays over other data-structures can not be deduced by studying FORTRAN programs, since arrays are the only data-structure allowed in that language. However, it is known that the vast majority of numerical computations is performed to solve engineering or other similar problems, where the array arises as the natural data-structure.)

2. In the vast majority of the cases, the array elements are **accessed in regular sequence(s).** There are a few "working locations" in the array(s), and their addresses change as arithmetic progressions. The step is quite often equal to one element size, or, at other times, it is the column size or some other constant.

3. A few integer scalar variables are used as **loop-counters and array-indexes.** The arithmetic performed on them is simple and corresponds to the above "regular sequence" of array accesses: increment by a constant, compare & branch. **Address computations** for multi-dimensional arrays require integer multiplication. Most of the times, it is feasible and advantageous for the optimizing compiler (or the very sophisticated programmer) to replace those integer counters/indexes by actual memory pointers; the address computations

are avoided in this way (see [AhUl77], p.466: Induction Variable Elimination).

4. The numeric computations are usually **floating-point operations** (multiplications and additions/subtractions being the most frequent). Several such operations are performed, but usually not many more in number than the integer operations on counters.

5. **Low-level parallelism** is present in many cases, and has two forms: (1) among various floating-point operations, usually when long expressions are computed, and when a series of assignment statements is executed with no control-transfers in between; and (2) between counter/address calculations and floating-point operations, especially when program sequencing (if's, loop's) depend on the former only. This quite common "static nature" of program sequencing is an important characteristic of programs which perform a certain computation on all elements of a vector or of an array.

6. The last property also gives to these programs significant amounts of **higher-level parallelism**. Subsequent loop iterations are independent and could proceed in parallel. Some times, they are completely independent (Example 15 of section 2.3.1), so that a highly pipelined von Neumann processor could take advantage of them. Other times, they are less independent (Example 17 in section 2.3.1 would require a tree-organized addition); von Neumann architectures and languages typically cannot exploit that parallelism.

2.4 A Study of four C Programs for Text Processing and CAD of IC's

In this section we study the critical loops of four non-numeric programs, written in C and taken out of the Berkeley UNIX† and CAD environment:

fgrep   the UNIX program which searches a file for occurrences of fixed strings,

sed   the UNIX stream (batch) text editor,

sort   the UNIX program to sort the lines in a file, and

mextra   a circuit extractor [FitzMe] which, given a description of the IC's geometry, generates a list of the transistors and their interconnections present in an integrated circuit. It works by first reading-in the description of the geometry and building a corresponding dynamic data structure, and then "scanning" the IC following horizontal scan-lines of gradually increasing y-coordinate. It may be considered an example of a program that *manipulates a non-trivial dynamic data structure*.

As an argument in support of the representativeness of the above sample of programs, let us look at a typical compiler. Kessler's Pascal compiler spends

---

†UNIX is a trademark of Bell Laboratories.

most of its time [Kess82] scanning the input (i.e. reading and recognizing characters), generating assembly code (i:e. character I/O), and walking through tree structures and interrogating them. These functions are similar to what *fgrep, sed,* and *mextra* do.

The tools described in section 2.1.3 were used for locating the critical loops. Below, wherever code is shown, the number on the left of each line is the count of how many times the line was executed during the test run.

2.4.1 FGREP: a String Search Program

In the test run, *fgrep* was used to search for occurrences of the string "kateveni" in a file of size ≈ 230 KBytes (there were a few hundred such occurrences). The run took about 6 seconds CPU time, allocated as follows:

- ≈ 87% in the procedure *execute()*,
- ≈ 11% in _*read* (i.e. in the operating system),
- ≈ 2% in everything else.

The procedure *execute()* follows:

---

fgrep: execute() [87%]:

```
        | # define ccomp(a,b) (yflag ? lca(a)==lca(b) : a==b)
        | # define lca(x) (isupper(x) ? tolower(x) : x)
        |
        | struct words {
        |      char  inp, out;
        |      struct words *nst,  *link,  *fail;
        | } w[MAXSIZ];
        | int    yflag;
        |
        | ....
        |
      1 | execute(file)   char *file;
        | { register struct words  *c;
        |   register int  ccount;
        |   register char  ch, *p;
        |   char  buf[2*BUFSIZ];
        |   int  f, failed;  char *nlp;
        |
      1 |       ....  Initial Set-Up Work  ....
 229253 |       for (;;)
 229253 |          {  if (--ccount <= 0)
    226 |               { read-in a new 1Kbyte block or exit loop }
        |             nstate:
 229252 |             if (ccomp(c->inp, *p))    /* in-line expansion */
    923 |                 {  c = c->nst; }
 228329 |             else if (c->link != 0)
      0 |                 {  c = c->link; goto nstate; }
        |             else
```

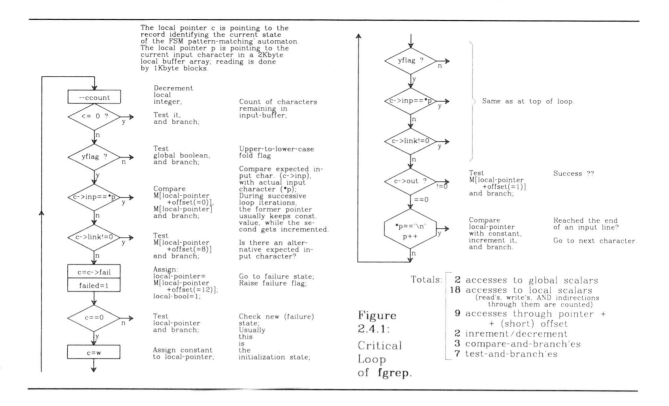

Figure 2.4.1: Critical Loop of fgrep.

Totals:
- 2 accesses to global scalars
- 18 accesses to local scalars (read's, write's, AND indirections through them are counted)
- 9 accesses through pointer + + (short) offset
- 2 inrement/decrement
- 3 compare-and-branch'es
- 7 test-and-branch'es

```
228329 |              { c = c->fail;
228329 |                failed = 1;
228329 |                if (c==0)
228329 |                   { c = w;
       |               istate:
228329 |                   if (ccomp(c->inp,*p)) /*in-line exp*/
     0 |                      { c = c->nst; }
228329 |                   else if (c->link != 0)
     0 |                      { c=c->link; goto istate; }
       |                   }
     0 |                else goto nstate;
       |                }
229252 |             if (c->out)
    48 |                { Code for Success }
229204 |             if (*p++ == '\n')
  4237 |                { Code for End-of-Line }
       |             }
     1 |          .... Final Wrap-Up Work ....
       | }
```

Figure 2.4.1 contains a flow-chart of the critical loop of this run of *fgrep*. The vast majority of the operations performed are simply:

• accesses to scalars (mostly locals) and indirections through them to access fields of structures to which they are pointing, and

• comparisons (mostly to zero) & subsequent branches. The high frequency of compare-&-branches is in part a result of the nature of the program (pattern matching), but is also a general characteristic of the non-numeric programs, as the next examples will show.

2.4.2 SED: a Batch Text Editor

In our test run, *sed* copies a 2.2 Mbyte file to output, searching for occurrences of three short fixed patterns. It replaces two of them with 2 others (one shorter, one longer), and upon encountering the third one, it appends a specified new line after the current one. The run took about 160 sec CPU time, allocated as follows:

- ≈ 23% in the procedure *execute()*,
- ≈ 23% in the procedure *match()*,
- ≈ 16% in the procedure *gline()*, and
- all other procedures accounted for < 8% each.

---

sed: execute() [23%]:

```
        1 | execute(file)      char *file;
          | { register char *p1, *p2;
          |   register union reptr  *ipc;
          |   int c;   char *execp;
          |
        1 | ....  Initial Set-Up Work...
    52820 |   for(;;)
    52820 |     { if((execp = gline(linebuf)) == badp) { rare }
    52819 |       spend = execp;
   158457 |       for(ipc = ptrspace; ipc->command; )
   158457 |           { p1 = ipc->ad1;
   158457 |             p2 = ipc->ad2;
   158457 |             if(p1)
    52819 |                 { if(ipc->inar) { never }
    52819 |                   else if(*p1 == CEND) { never }
    52819 |                   else if(*p1 == CLNUM) { never }
    52819 |                   else if(match(p1, 0)) {22,000 if's exct'd}
    30899 |                   else {62,000 stmnts exect'd; continue;}
          |                 }
   127558 |             if(ipc->negfl) { never }
   127558 |             command(ipc);
   127558 |             if(delflag) { never }
   127558 |             if(jflag) { never }
   127558 |             else  ipc++;
          |           }
    52819 |       if(!nflag && !delflag)
  2143025 |           { for(p1 = linebuf; p1 < spend; p1++)
          |                       /*"spend" is a global pointer*/
  2143025 |                 putc(*p1, stdout);
```
/*Note: in-line expanded to: */
/* (--_iob[1]._cnt>=0 ? *(_iob[1]._ptr)++ = *p1 : {rare}) */
/* _iob[1]._cnt, _iob[1]._ptr are global scalars (compiler knows their addr.)*/
```
    52819 |                 putc('\n', stdout);
          |           }
```

```
52819 |        if(aptr > abuf) { 22,000 calls: arout(); }
52819 |        delflag = 0;
      |      }
      |  }
```

Here, we have:

- 0.26 M procedure calls,
- 2.35 M compare-&-branch,
- 3.10 M test-&-branch,
- 4.40 M incrementations, and
- 0.50 M assignments with no operation (move-type).

The vast majority of operands are accessed indirectly, through local pointers with a zero or small offset. Other accesses are to local and global scalars. Certainly, a lot of this procedure's time is spent in the tight **for** loop that copies characters to standard output.

---

sed: match() [23%]:

```
161106 | match(expbuf, gf)   char *expbuf;
       | { register char       *p1, *p2, c;
       |
161106 |      if(gf) { Execute ≈ 150,000 statements }
158457 |      else { p1 = linebuf; locs = 0; }
161106 |      p2 = expbuf;
161106 |      if(*p2++) { never }
       |      /* fast check for first character: */
161106 |      if(*p2 == CCHR)
161106 |         {  c = p2[1];
5242476 |            do  {  if(*p1 != c) continue;
269623 |                    if(advance(p1, p2)) { infrequent }
5189445 |                 } while(*p1++);
108075 |            return(0);
       |         }
     0 |      ...Various  others, never executed...
       | }
```

---

sed: gline() [16%]:

```
 52820 | char *gline(addr)   char *addr;
       | { register char *p1, *p2;   register c;
       |      ...Initial Set-Up Work (100,000 statements total)...
2174691 |      for (;;)
2174691 |         {  if (p2 >= ebp) { rare }
2174690 |            if ((c = *p2++) == '\n') { infrequent }
2121871 |            if(c) if(p1 < lbend)
2121871 |                   *p1++ = c;
```

```
|         }
|     ...Final Wrap-Up Work (200,000 statements total)...
| }
```

These two procedures spend most of their time scanning characters. *Match()* scans characters searching for some particular one. *Gline()* scans characters copying and checking them.

2.4.3 SORT: an Extreme, but Real Case

The particular sorting program that was studied, namely the one installed on our UNIX machines, spent one third of the test run time in its calls to a trivial procedure *blank()* used to scan over blanks. Obviously, it is preferable that *blank()* were defined as a macro, so that it be expanded in-line. The test run consisted of sorting a 2.2 Mbyte file, relative to the second-in-line field and with elimination of duplicates. It took half-an-hour of CPU time.

sort: blank() [31%]:

```
26087970 | blank(c)
26087970 | { if(c==' ' || c=='\t')
 6279488 |              return(1);
19808482 |       else  return(0);
         | }
```

In general, text-processing programs spend a lot of their time in inner loops where they sequentially "walk" through the characters in buffers, copying, comparing, or testing various things.

It is important to notice that programs dealing with text waste a lot of memory bandwidth in the usual architectures, where a full memory word is accessed each time a byte transaction takes place.

Exploitation of parallelism is difficult in these programs, because of the high frequency of conditional branches. The amount of work done between two consecutive branches is usually quite small, with limited parallelism. Parallelism is often available between operations in two different blocks B1 and B2 separated by a conditional branch, where the branch *usually* follows the path that makes B2 execute after B1. Programs are usually written in such a way that execution of B2 cannot start before it is certain that it should start. The programmer could rearrange the code and introduce temporary variables to hold tentative results, but doing so would lead to complicated and hard to maintain programs.

2.4.4 MEXTRA: a Circuit Extraction Program

Mextra's test run consisted of extracting the circuitry in the control section of the RISC II chip. It took 330 sec CPU time, allocated as follows:

- $\approx 14\%$ in the procedure *ScanSubSwath()*,
- $\approx 11\%$ in the procedure *Propagate()*,
- $\approx 10\%$ in the procedure *alloc()*,
- $\approx 8\%$ in the procedure *EndTrap()*,
- $\approx 5\%$ in the procedure *Free()*, and
- the remaining procedures took $< 4\%$ of the total time each.

mextra: ScanSubSwath() [14%]:

```
   771 | ScanSubSwath(bin)    int bin;
        | {   int i, newCount, n;
        |     register edge *new,*old,*last,  *oldList,*newList;
        |
        |        ...Initial  Set-Up Work (30,000 statements)...
353237  |        while(new != NIL && old != NIL)    /* NIL is 0 */
352466  |            {  if(new->bb.l < old->bb.l) { infrequent }
        |               else
302554  |                  {  if(n < old->bb.t)
254342  |                        {  if(last == NIL) { rare }
253628  |                           else {last->next=old; last=old;}
254342  |                           old = oldList;
254342  |                           if (old!=NIL) oldList=old->next;
        |                        }
 48212  |                     else { infrequent }
        |                  }
304254  |               if(depth[last->layer] == 0)
140442  |                     StartTrap(last->layer,last);
304254  |               if((depth[last->layer] += last->dir) == 0)
139794  |                     EndTrap(last->layer,last);
304254  |               nextEnd =
        |                  (nextEnd<last->bb.t ? nextEnd : last->bb.t);
        |            }
        |        ...Final  Wrap-Up Work (250,000 statements)...
        |    }
```

This procedure performs extensive list operations, using local pointers. The total operations performed in its critical loop are:

- 0.6 M procedure calls;
- 0.3 M additions (not counting address computations).
- 1.8 M test-&-branches;
- 1.0 M compare-&-branches;
- ≈ 0.6 M accesses to a global scalar (nextEnd);
- 6.5 M accesses to locals (96% of them to pointers)
     (these include accesses for indirecting through them);
- 3.1 M accesses to fields of structures via a local pointer, and
- 1.0 M (random) accesses to a small array *depth[10]*.

The basic pattern of memory accesses is the list traversal, which places a corresponding limit on locality-of-reference. However, during each loop iteration there are 11 accesses to fields of the structures pointed to by ''old->'' and by ''last->''. Accesses to various fields of the same structure are obviously accesses to neighboring memory locations, since the structure nodes here have a size of 8 words. Moreover, there are repeated accesses to the same field of the same structure, for example ≈ 4 accesses per iteration to ''last->layer''.

The available parallelism, is again limited by the high frequency of conditional branches. Some parallelism can be seen between accessing a memory location and computing the effective address for a subsequent memory access. For example:

```
if ( new->bb.l < old->bb.l )
if ( (depth[last->layer] += last->dir) == 0)
```

---

mextra: Propagate() [11%]:

```
   773 | Propagate(y,yNext)    int y, yNext;
       | { int   layer, height, tempx,tempy;
       |   register segment *above, *below, *next, *poly, *diff;
       |
       |        ...Initial Set-Up Work (8,000 statements)...
       |        for( above=Above[layer]; above!=NIL;
       |                   above=above->next )
141443 |           {
       |              for(    ; below!=NIL &&
       |                          below->right < above->left;
       |                       below=below->next)
138000 |                   if(below->area != 0) { rare }
       |               for( next=below;
       |                  next!=NIL && next->left <= above->right;
       |                  next=below->next)
136083 |                { below = next;
136083 |                    if(above->node == 0)
       |                         {
135024 | above->node = below->node;
135024 | above->area = below->area +
       |                height*(above->right - above->left - 1)/100;
135024 | above->perim = below->perim +
       |                2 * (height + above->right - above->left -
       |                    MIN(above->right,below->right) +
       |                    MAX(above->left,below->left) ) / 10;
       |                /* Note: In-line expansions:  */
       |                /*    MIN(x,y) into: (x<y ? x : y) */
       |                /*    MAX(x,y) into: (x<y ? y : x) */
135024 | below->perim = below->area = 0;
       |                         }
       |                    else { rare }
136083 |                    if(below->area != 0) { never }
       |                }
141443 |             if(above->node == 0) { rare }
       |           }
       |        ...Final Wrap-Up Work (500,000 statements)...
       | }
```

Here again, extensive list operations are performed. The list-nodes have a size of 8 words, and are accessed via local pointers. During each loop iteration, 16 accesses are made to fields of a certain list-node, and 15 to fields of another. Each individual field is accessed an average of 3 times. This procedure has more numeric computations than the other procedures in this section, but these are still not the dominant factor.

---

mextra: alloc() [10%]:

```
283165 | alloc(n)
       | { register int tmp; register struct cell *ptr;
       |
283165 |     if(n<CELLSIZE-4) { rare }
283165 |     n = (n+WORDSIZE-1)/WORDSIZE;
       |                 /* WORDSIZE is 2 in this example */
283165 |     if(TBLSIZE<=n) { rare }
283138 |     else if(FreeTbl[n]!=0)
258662 |         { ptr = FreeTbl[n];
258662 |             FreeTbl[n] = ptr->next;
258662 |             --FreeCnt[n];
258662 |             if(ptr->status!=FREE || ptr->count!=n) {never}
258662 |             if(FreeCnt[n]!=0)
241417 |                 {  if(FreeTbl[n]->status!=FREE) {never}
241417 |                     if(FreeTbl[n]->count!=n) {never}
       |                 }
       |             else { rare }
       |         }
       |     else { infrequent }
283165 |     ptr->status = ALLOC;
283165 |     ptr->count = n;
283165 |     tmp = (int) ptr;
283165 |     if (n<TBLSIZE) AllocCnt[n]++;
283165 |     return(tmp+4);
       | }
```

This last procedure has no loop; it is entered many times, and does a little work each time. Besides accessing fields of structures via pointers, it also makes many references to the n-th elements of several arrays. These latter are *not* sequential array-element accesses. However, if the information were kept in a single array of structures, instead of in multiple simple arrays, then the above accesses would all be to neighboring memory locations. Slightly more parallelism can be found here, for example:

{ptr->status=ALLOC; ptr->count=n; tmp=(int)ptr; if(n<TBLSIZE)}

Also, notice that the *if's* that lead to *then-clauses* which never get executed are consistency checks, and they could all be done in parallel if the language allowed some way of expressing that.

The overall picture from this CAD program is one of many conditional branches and of many accesses to fields of structures using local pointers pointing to them. Although the application has some arithmetic that needs to be done, it does not play a dominant role. There are very few increment operations, contrary to the previous programs studied in earlier sections, because this program deals with dynamic data structures. The locality-of-references to the elements of the data structures stems from the computation pattern of performing several accesses to various fields of a few structure instances, before interest shifts to some new such instances.

2.5   Summary of Findings

In this chapter, we first reviewed static and dynamic program statistics collected by other researchers. Their results indicate that the simplest operations are also the ones that are executed most of the time.

Then, we looked at several FORTRAN programs, most of them doing numerical computations. We observed that they perform primarily floating-point arithmetic operations on operands which frequently are elements of arrays. The inner loops usually traverse the arrays in a "regular" fashion, using indexes that are incremented by a constant amount and compared to a limit. The use of pointers rather than indexes, by the programmer or by the optimizing compiler, would be advantageous.

Then, we studied some text-processing programs written in C, and saw that they spend a large fraction of their time running sequentially through character buffers. These are array elements, again, but here programmers usually access them indirectly through local pointers. The dominant operations are not arithmetic any more -- they are tests or comparisons for branching and mere copying.

Finally, we analyzed a program for CAD of IC's, which manipulates a nontrivial dynamic data structure. The fields of a few nodes (structures) are accessed several times indirectly through local pointers, before the program shifts its attention to some other nodes linked to the previous ones. Again, we found high frequencies of test/compare-&-branch and of copying.

In all cases, we saw that programs are organized in procedures and that procedure calls are frequent and costly in terms of execution time. Procedures usually have a few arguments and local variables, most of which are scalars, and are heavily used. The nesting depth fluctuates within narrow ranges for long periods of time.

We found low-level parallelism although usually in small amounts, mainly between address and data computations. The frequent occurrence of conditional-branch instructions greatly limits its exploitation.

General-purpose computations, as usually expressed in von Neumann languages, are carried out by walking through static or dynamic data structures in some - usually regular - path. Operand addressing, copying, and comparing for decision making, are factors of prime importance. Procedures are heavily used for hierarchical organizations. Numeric computations are frequent and expensive in some applications.

In the next chapters, possible architectural features for exploiting these program characteristics will be presented.

Computer
Systems   G. Bell, D. Siewiorek,
and S.H. Fuller, Editors

Empirical Evaluation of Some Features of Instruction Set Processor Architectures

Åmund Lunde
Carnegie-Mellon University

This paper presents methods for empirical evaluation
of features of Instruction Set Processors (ISPs). ISP
features are evaluated in terms of the time used or
saved by having or not having the feature. The methods
are based on analysis of traces of program executions.
The concept of a register life is introduced, and used to
answer questions like: How many registers are used
simultaneously? How many would be sufficient all of
the time? Most of the time? What would the overhead
be if the number of registers were reduced? What are
registers used for during their lives? The paper also
discusses the problem of detecting desirable but nonexisting instructions. Other problems are briefly discussed. Experimental results are presented, obtained by
analyzing 41 programs running on the DECsystem10
ISP.

Key Words and Phrases: computer architecture,
program behavior, instruction sets, opcode utilization,
register structures, register utilization, simultaneous
register lives, instruction tracing, execution time
CR Categories: 6.20, 6.21, 6.33

Copyright © 1977, Association for Computing Machinery, Inc.
General permission to republish, but not for profit, all or part
of this material is granted provided that ACM's copyright notice
is given and that reference is made to the publication, to its date
of issue, and to the fact that reprinting privileges were granted
by permission of the Association for Computing Machinery.
This work was supported in part by the Advanced Research
Projects Agency of the office of the Secretary of Defense (F44620-
73-C-0074) monitored by the Air Force Office of Scientific Research, in part by The Norwegian Research Council for Science
and the Humanities (Norges Almenvitenskapelige Forskningsråd).
Author's present address: EDB-sentret, Universitetet i Oslo;
P.O. Box 1059, Blindern, Oslo 3, Norway.
* Notes for this article appear on p. 152.

1. Introduction

A quick survey of current computers reveals a great
variation in the structure of Instruction Set Processors.[1]*
This observation is true even for computers intended
for the same general market. Current ISPs designed
with the scientific market in mind, for example, have
word lengths ranging from 24 to 64 bits; the number of
different instructions varies from about 70 to over 400;
register structures span the area from one accumulator
plus a few index registers, through designs with 8 to
24 general or specialized registers, to designs with up
to 64 registers, again relatively general. A natural conclusion from such a survey is that very little is known
about the optimal structure of ISPs. Further study reveals that very little has been published about measuring techniques or other methods designed to obtain
such knowledge.

This paper presents a step towards the development
of such measuring techniques. It describes methods
designed to study the detailed behavior of programs as
they are executing on some ISP. Experimental results
are presented which reflect the behavior of one particular set of programs on one particular ISP.

The need for such measures and their utility is
vindicated by the results found by the designers of the
Burroughs B1700 central processor [14, 15]. These
results clearly show the dependence of program efficiency on a good ISP.

Previous authors have measured the frequency of
execution of the individual instructions or groups of
instructions [7 (The Gibson mix), 8, 4, 12, and 9].
Only a few more comprehensive studies are known to
this author: Foster et al. [5, 6] have developed measures
of opcode utilization and studied alternative encodings
of the opcodes into fewer bits than those required by a
conventional encoding. Similar results are presented
by Wilner [15]. Winder [16, 17] has gathered miscellaneous statistics on ISP usage. Alexander [1] has
made extensive study of how one particular programming language uses ISP features.

None of the above studies report on ISP behavior
reflecting more than two or three consecutive instructions. Also, register use is barely touched upon. The
methods described in this paper improve this situation. They are only to a small extent, or not at all,
restricted to the study of a small fixed length sequence
of instructions. On the contrary, we may follow a
phenomenon for as many instructions as seems rele-

"Empirical Evaluation of Some Features of Instruction Set Processor Archi-
tectures" by A. Lunde from *Communications of the ACM*, Volume 20,
Number 3, March 1977, pages 143-153. Copyright 1977, Association for
Computing Machinery, Inc., reprinted by permission.

vant, while at the same time retaining full knowledge about every instruction executed.

2. Basic Methodology

The basic idea of the methods is to analyze traces of a representative set of programs, the *subject set*, written as these are executed by an interpreter for the ISP being studied. Information is recorded for every instruction executed by the *subject program*. The major advantages of this approach are:

—ISP behavior may be studied in great detail.

—The methods are not restricted to special languages or compilers.

—Analysis programs are easily written, and programs for new analysis methods may be developed after the data have been collected.

—All analyses of the same program (trace) see exactly the same instruction stream; hence the results are not perturbed by random influences caused by external devices or by multiprogramming of jobs.

Each individual analysis, therefore, studies the behavior of a user program running on the user ISP and the suitability of this ISP to that particular program, as opposed to studying the suitability of the full ISP to a collection of multiprogrammed programs. For the latter purpose a device is needed to trace executive mode programs, probably at full speed. Statistical validity comes from studying many programs individually.

The methods are easily modifiable to apply to all register structured ISPs, and to some extent even to stack ISPs or other ISPs. The specific results obtained are, however, strongly dependent on the structure of the ISP analyzed. The extent to which they can be applied to similar ISPs depends on the degree of similarity and on the result in question. On the other hand, the results are relatively independent of technology; hence they may be used by ISP architects to compare the cost/utility ratios of different structures across different technologies.

Our methods evaluate ISP features in terms of their associated time cost, i.e. the change in execution time or instruction count caused by including or removing the feature. Of these, the instruction count is most independent of technology, but it hides the fact that certain operations take a longer time than others, regardless of technology. Hence execution time is also computed in some cases by summing the individual instruction execution times.

Other relevant costs are the space occupied in primary memory by program and data, and the cost of designing, coding, and debugging programs. Both of these are highly dependent on the ISP, and are as important to a good design as the time cost. They are not, however, measured by our methods, but should be otherwise measured or estimated by the ISP architect before he makes his decisions.

3. Experimental Environment

3.1 ISP Studied

The emphasis of our experimental work was on studying the methods, and estimating the dependence of the results on the major parameters of the subject set. In order to reduce the work, experiments were performed on one ISP only: the DECsystem10 (KA-10). The structure of this ISP is unusually general; some of its properties are:

(1) It has a large instruction repertoire of about 420 user instructions including:

—A rich set of instructions for arithmetic and bitwise comparison. These compare memory, register, immediate or implicit (0) operands, and all 6 arithmetic conditions are available.

—Programmer defined stacks.

—Three different mechanisms for subroutine calls.

—All 16 Boolean functions of two variables.

—Immediate operands and several result destinations (register, memory or both) for arithmetic and logic instructions.

—31 Monitor calls and 32 user-definable trap instructions (UUOs).

(2) The register structure is equally general. The 16 registers are part of the memory address space. All of them may be used for all standard purposes with only insignificant exceptions.

(3) Indirection may be carried to any depth, with indexing at each level.

Hence this ISP is a good starting point for detection of unnecessary generality or superfluous features. This is vindicated by our results reported here and in [10]. We did, however, also discover features which we would like to see incorporated into this ISP. Some of these have, in fact, been included in later processors of the DECsystem10 family.

3.2 Subject Set

Another restriction on our experiments was that we analyzed programs only from a scientific environment. On the other hand, we tried to choose a subject set which would show the influence of the choice of algorithm, programming language, and compiler.

Hence one part of our subject set consisted of six algorithms from *Collected Algorithms of the ACM* (CALGO). These were selected to contain as many as possible of the commonly used program structures, and to give a reasonable covering of the modified SHARE classification for algorithms. Each of these algorithms was coded in four languages: ALGOL, BASIC, BLISS, and FORTRAN. Two different FORTRAN systems were used. BLISS [18] is a high-

Table I. Distribution of Lives by Lifelength, Unweighted Sum of All Programs—Logarithmic Table Division.

Length	No. of lives	Fraction	Cum. fraction
1 - 1	174927	0.09	0.09
2 - 3	728346	0.38	0.48
4 - 7	547072	0.29	0.77
8 - 15	252508	0.13	0.90
16 - 31	116404	0.06	0.96
32 - 63	41673	0.02	0.98
64 - 127	17790	0.01	0.99
128 - up	15603	0.01	1.00
Total number of lives	1894323		

level language for systems programming. The other languages should be well known. The six algorithms were:

No. 30: Polynomial roots by Bairstow's method (Bairstow)

No. 43: Linear equations by Crout's method (Crout)

No. 113: Treesort

No. 119: PERT

No. 257: Numerical integration by Håvies method (Håvie)

No. 355: Generation of Ising configurations (Ising).

The latter could not easily be coded in BASIC, hence that version was omitted.

To investigate the influence of coding style, we included an algorithm for polynomial interpolation (Aitken) as coded in BLISS by four different programmers, plus a carefully tuned version of this algorithm. These are denoted E (efficient), B, A, L, and G. A medium-sized numeric FORTRAN program, SEC, was also analyzed. Again both FORTRAN systems were used. Finally we analyzed the five compilers used for the CALGO set: these are denoted ALGOL, BASIC, BLISS, FORFOR, and FORTEN. ALGOL, BASIC, and FORFOR are written in MACRO (the assembly language), BLISS and FORTEN are written in BLISS.

Thus our final subject set consisted of 41 programs, comprising about 5.3 million instructions or 16.8 seconds of CPU time. 38 of these were written in high-level languages. One would a priori expect that such programs do not make as good use of the ISP as do assembly language programs. On the other hand, we are already restricted to the user ISP, and certainly the majority of user programs are written in high-level languages.

4. Register Structure

Methods were developed for two problems connected with register structure:

—How many registers are used efficiently?

—What is the need for generality of registers?

Both are attacked through the concept of a *register life*. A register life consists of all activity associated with a given register during a period of time starting with a load into that register, and terminating with the last use of the register before the next load into it. A register is *loaded* when a new value is brought into it which is unrelated to its old value. Use of the old value during address calculation is not considered a relation in this context.

The start of a register life is analogous to the "open effects" situation described by Tjaden and Flynn [13]. The terms *live* and *dead* now have obvious meanings. A register is *dormant* when it is live but not used. The resolution of our time measure is one instruction. Hence two successive lives of the same register may overlap if the old value is used to load the new one. Usually there will be a dead period between two consecutive lives of a register. Finally we note that for a machine with several registers, any number of them may be live at any given time.

It seems unreasonable to use these concepts unmodified for registers which have long dormant periods. Hence the results below were obtained under the assumption that a register was dead when it had been dormant for 200 or more instructions. This is discussed further below.

4.1 Analysis Program

The analysis program detects register lives, classifies them according to the operations they contain, and finds the number of live registers at each point in time during program execution.

As the trace is read, one can not in general tell whether a register is dead or live until the next LOAD into it is encountered. This may be any length of time after the register actually died. Hence the analysis of register usage is a two-phase process. In the first phase register lives are detected and classified. Phase I also writes a file of descriptions of each life which is used by phase II. Phase II then finds how many registers were live at each point in time, and computes various results based on this.

In the analysis a relatively fine classification was used for the lives. For purposes of presentation the following seven classes were considered:

—All lives (the total class—TOT).

—Lives used for indexing (INX).

—Lives used for temporary storage only (TMP).

—The four classes defined by the "strongest" arithmetic used:

    No arithmetic (NOA).

    Fixed-point additions and subtractions (FAS).

    Fixed-point multiplications and divisions (FMD).

    Floating-point operations (FLO).

The latter four classes are disjoint and their union is the class TOT.

4.1.1 Phase I. As the trace is read, phase I keeps track of the times of the most recent load and the most recent use of each register. Hence each time a register

Table II. Average Lifelength in Instructions.

Language:		ALGOL	BASIC	BLISS	FORFOR	FORTEN	Mean
Bairstow		12.3	12.3	11.2	12.9	12.9	12.3
Crout		13.6	11.3	18.2	15.1	15.9	14.8
Treesort		6.1	11.9	9.0	4.2	5.8	7.4
PERT		10.9	11.4	8.4	5.0	7.9	8.7
Havie		16.6	11.2	13.5	14.3	20.0	15.1
Ising		16.5	–	9.7	5.5	9.2	10.2
Secant		–	–	–	8.1	9.6	8.9
Programmer:		E	B	A	G	L	Mean
Aitken		14.3	14.7	13.0	8.9	11.9	12.6
Compiler:		ALGOL	BASIC	BLISS	FORFOR	FORTEN	Mean
		17.4	23.8	9.7	14.9	11.4	15.4
Language:	MACRO	ALGOL	BASIC	BLISS	FORFOR	FORTEN	Mean
Mean	18.7	12.7	11.6	11.8	9.3	11.6	11.9

Table V. Memory References per Instruction Excluding Instruction Fetches.

Language:		ALGOL	BASIC	BLISS	FORFOR	FORTEN	Mean
Bairstow		.61	.52	.50	.62	.60	.57
Crout		.44	.59	.50	.55	.64	.54
Treesort		.65	.50	.51	.57	.63	.57
PERT		.51	.47	.53	.69	.63	.57
Havie		.30	.45	.31	.44	.35	.37
Ising		.40	–	.60	.67	.60	.57
Secant		–	–	–	.60	.53	.57
Programmer:		E	B	A	G	L	Mean
Aitken		.45	.48	.52	.50	.53	.50
Compiler:		ALGOL	BASIC	BLISS	FORFOR	FORTEN	Mean
		.40	.32	.45	.42	.40	.40
Language:	MACRO	ALGOL	BASIC	BLISS	FORFOR	FORTEN	Mean
Mean	.38	.49	.51	.48	.59	.57	.51

Table III. Usages per Register Life.

Language:		ALGOL	BASIC	BLISS	FORFOR	FORTEN	Mean
Bairstow		4.6	3.6	4.6	4.6	4.4	4.4
Crout		3.8	3.7	6.6	3.7	3.9	4.3
Treesort		3.9	3.5	4.8	2.9	2.9	3.6
PERT		4.1	3.4	3.8	3.1	3.2	3.5
Havie		4.4	3.7	5.8	5.4	5.2	4.9
Ising		4.0	–	4.5	3.1	3.3	3.7
Secant		–	–	–	3.8	3.8	3.8
Programmer:		E	B	A	G	L	Mean
Aitken		5.4	5.5	5.2	3.9	5.2	5.0
Compiler:		ALGOL	BASIC	BLISS	FORFOR	FORTEN	Mean
		3.7	6.0	3.5	4.1	3.2	4.1
Language:	MACRO	ALGOL	BASIC	BLISS	FORFOR	FORTEN	Mean
Mean	4.6	4.1	3.6	4.8	3.8	3.8	4.2

Table VI. Register References per Instruction.

Language:		ALGOL	BASIC	BLISS	FORFOR	FORTEN	Mean
Bairstow		1.66	1.05	1.58	1.35	1.37	1.40
Crout		1.67	1.21	1.67	1.56	1.46	1.51
Treesort		1.62	1.04	1.65	1.28	1.32	1.38
PERT		1.58	1.05	1.61	1.25	1.22	1.34
Havie		1.57	1.14	1.61	1.36	1.16	1.37
Ising		1.58	–	1.66	1.11	1.13	1.37
Secant		–	–	–	1.39	1.33	1.36
Programmer:		E	B	A	G	L	Mean
Aitken		1.66	1.67	1.69	1.69	1.64	1.67
Compiler:		ALGOL	BASIC	BLISS	FORFOR	FORTEN	Mean
		1.09	1.13	1.32	1.39	1.17	1.22
Language:	MACRO	ALGOL	BASIC	BLISS	FORFOR	FORTEN	Mean
Mean	1.20	1.61	1.10	1.59	1.33	1.28	1.40

Table IV. Average Number of Live Registers, Computed as ⟨Sum of Lifelengths⟩/⟨Program Length⟩.

Language:		ALGOL	BASIC	BLISS	FORFOR	FORTEN	Mean
Bairstow		4.4	3.6	3.8	3.8	4.0	3.9
Crout		6.0	3.7	4.7	6.4	6.0	5.4
Treesort		2.5	3.5	3.1	1.8	2.7	2.7
PERT		4.2	3.6	3.6	2.0	3.0	3.3
Havie		6.0	3.5	3.7	3.6	4.5	4.3
Ising		6.5	–	3.6	1.9	3.2	3.8
Secant		–	–	–	3.0	3.4	3.2
Programmer:		E	B	A	G	L	Mean
Aitken		4.4	4.5	4.2	3.9	3.7	4.1
Compiler:		ALGOL	BASIC	BLISS	FORFOR	FORTEN	Mean
		5.1	4.5	3.6	5.1	4.2	4.5
Language:	MACRO	ALGOL	BASIC	BLISS	FORFOR	FORTEN	Mean
Mean	4.9	4.9	3.6	3.9	3.2	3.8	3.9

Table VII. Fraction of Lives with No Arithmetic.

Language:		ALGOL	BASIC	BLISS	FORFOR	FORTEN	Mean
Bairstow		.213	.637	.574	.494	.470	.478
Crout		.528	.716	.214	.349	.440	.449
Treesort		.315	.686	.257	.784	.565	.521
PERT		.597	.735	.547	.457	.416	.550
Havie		.628	.680	.482	.496	.412	.540
Ising		.695	–	.620	.744	.622	.670
Secant		–	–	–	.263	.266	.265
Programmer:		E	B	A	G	L	Mean
Aitken		.317	.390	.402	.475	.391	.395
Compiler:		ALGOL	BASIC	BLISS	FORFOR	FORTEN	Mean
		.844	.744	.921	.802	.886	.839
Language:	MACRO	ALGOL	BASIC	BLISS	FORFOR	FORTEN	Mean
Mean	.797	.496	.691	.498	.512	.456	.538

is loaded, the endpoints of its previous life are immediately available. For each register life, phase I determines its class, and also the number of references to it. Finally phase I computes the total number of register references and memory references. The data items written on the file for phase II contain most of this information, together with the register name.

Some results from phase I are given in Tables I through XII. Results are given for each individual program, as well as the averages for each algorithm, for all the compilers, and for all programs written in each language. All the programs are equally weighted in these averages.

We note that most lives (68% of the total) are between 2 and 7 instructions long. Only 4% are 32 instructions or longer. For each individual program over half the lives are less than 8 instructions long. Only 3 programs have more than 10% of their lives 32 instructions or longer. The average lifelength is 11.9 instructions, but ranges from 4 to 24 instructions for the individual programs. The average number of references to a life is 4.2, it ranges between 3 and 7 for the individual programs. The average number of simultaneously live registers ranges between 2 and 6. Operands, including indices and nominators (indirect addresses), are found in registers 2 to 4 times as often as in primary memory.

The classes FLO and FMD are significant only for those algorithms that use floating-point arithmetic, or where FMD arithmetic is used to access data. This is as one would expect. Even for highly numeric programs at most 50% of the lives are in class FLO, less than

Table VIII. Fraction of Lives with Fixed Point Add/Subtract.

Language:	ALGOL	BASIC	BLISS	FORFOR	FORTEN	Mean
Bairstow	.504	.106	.054	.118	.141	.185
Crout	.304	.009	.096	.186	.122	.143
Treesort	.355	.103	.710	.208	.056	.286
PERT	.380	.122	.397	.516	.552	.393
Hävie	.278	.085	.149	.123	.156	.158
Ising	.300	–	.373	.250	.370	.323
Secant	–	–	–	.359	.303	.331
Programmer:	E	B	A	G	L	Mean
Aitken	.210	.202	.302	.423	.389	.305
Compiler:	ALGOL	BASIC	BLISS	FORFOR	FORTEN	Mean
	.130	.234	.074	.190	.108	.147

Language:	MACRO	ALGOL	BASIC	BLISS	FORFOR	FORTEN	Mean
Mean	.185	.354	.085	.268	.251	.243	.245

Table IX. Fraction of Lives with Fixed Point Multiply/Divide.

Language:	ALGOL	BASIC	BLISS	FORFOR	FORTEN	Mean
Bairstow	.009	.001	.018	.042	.019	.018
Crout	.006	.064	.433	.156	.142	.160
Treesort	.317	.000	.011	.000	.370	.140
PERT	.002	.000	.004	.006	.006	.004
Hävie	.002	.001	.031	.018	.015	.013
Ising	.006	–	.007	.006	.008	.007
Secant	–	–	–	.175	.199	.187
Programmer:	E	B	A	G	L	Mean
Aitken	.000	.000	.000	.000	.085	.017
Compiler:	ALGOL	BASIC	BLISS	FORFOR	FORTEN	Mean
	.026	.019	.005	.009	.008	.013

Language:	MACRO	ALGOL	BASIC	BLISS	FORFOR	FORTEN	Mean
Mean	.018	.057	.013	.046	.058	.108	.054

Table X. Fraction of Lives with Floating Point Arithmetic.

Language:	ALGOL	BASIC	BLISS	FORFOR	FORTEN	Mean
Bairstow	.274	.256	.354	.347	.369	.320
Crout	.163	.211	.257	.306	.296	.247
Treesort	.014	.211	.022	.008	.009	.053
PERT	.021	.143	.053	.021	.026	.053
Hävie	.092	.233	.339	.363	.418	.289
Ising	.000	–	.000	.000	.000	.000
Secant	–	–	–	.203	.232	.218
Programmer:	E	B	A	G	L	Mean
Aitken	.473	.408	.296	.102	.136	.238
Compiler:	ALGOL	BASIC	BLISS	FORFOR	FORTEN	Mean
	.000	.003	.000	.000	.000	.001

Language:	MACRO	ALGOL	BASIC	BLISS	FORFOR	FORTEN	Mean
Mean	.001	.094	.211	.188	.178	.193	.162

40% in all but two programs. In spite of the fact that all variables in BASIC are floating point, the percentage of FLO lives in the BASIC programs is never above 25.

For the classes FAS and NOA, the dependence on language is larger than the dependence on algorithm. This is in particular true for ALGOL and BASIC, which enforce a stronger regimen on programs than do the other languages.

Between 18% and 68% of the lives, 39% on the average, are used for indexing.

4.1.2 Phase II. Phase II reads the file written by phase I in reverse order, and simulates a backwards execution of the subject program. Initially the descriptions of the last lives of each register are read. For each

register the program keeps the description of one life, viz. that which is now valid, or will next be valid, during the backwards simulation. The loading and final uses of each register are entered in a list sorted by decreasing time. This list is processed in order, and a counter of live registers is suitably updated.

Each time a loading use of a register is processed, all information about that life may be discarded. The program is then ready to receive the description of the previous (at execution) life for that register. This description was written by phase I as it processed the same load instruction which is now being processed by phase II. Hence the desired data item is in the correct position to be read off the file.

We now know exactly how many registers were live at each point in time, and the fraction of the total time when exactly N registers were live can easily be computed for each N. Since the usage class was written on the intermediate file, this analysis may be done simultaneously for any suitably defined classes of lives. The results for the 7 classes previously defined are given in Tables XIII through XV.

As is seen, no program uses more than 15 registers simultaneously. 17 of the 41 programs would get by with 10 or fewer registers. This maximum is only used for short periods of time. Thus 10 registers would suffice 90% of the time for all 41 programs, 98% of the time for 36 of the 41 programs. The results for the compilers and for the BLISS programs (BLISS has a highly optimizing compiler) show that neither the size and complexity of the programs nor their efficiency imply the use of many registers. On the contrary, the BLISS results seem to indicate the opposite conclusion. Hence we would attribute the relatively high number of live registers for the other compilers to the fact that these are written in assembly language. If specialized registers were to be used, it would seem appropriate to have 2 floating point accumulators, 2 fixed-point accumulators, and 8 index registers with simple fixed-point operations.

4.2 Reducing the Register Block

The results just presented suggest that programs might run almost equally time-efficiently on an ISP with fewer registers than the one analyzed, but otherwise having the same structure. Increased execution time would ensue from having to store and reload registers whenever the number of lives in the original version was too high. We use two methods, called *interleaving* and *bedding*, to compute an upper bound on this increase in execution time.

4.2.1 Interleaving. Interleaving is applied in phase II. Assume that our reduced ISP has M registers. For each period when the program requires N registers, $N > M$, we select the $N - M$ least useful lives as described below, and assume the associated values to be stored in memory. Each time one of these values is

Table XI. Fraction of Lives Used as Temporaries Only.

Language:		ALGOL	BASIC	BLISS	FORFOR	FORTEN	Mean
Bairstow		.028	.067	.179	.101	.121	099
Crout		.018	.101	.049	.137	.142	.098
Treesort		.001	.107	.000	.000	.001	.022
PERT		.016	.128	.188	.069	.104	.101
Hàvie		.072	.279	.062	.250	.019	.136
Ising		.059	–	.086	.147	.067	.090
Secant		–	–	–	.041	.030	.036
Programmer:		E	B	A	G	L	Mean
Aitken		.062	.078	.092	.112	.015	.072
Compiler:		ALGOL	BASIC	BLISS	FORFOR	FORTEN	Mean
		.096	.089	.180	151	153	134
Language:	MACRO	ALGOL	BASIC	BLISS	FORFOR	FORTEN	Mean
Mean	.112	.032	.136	.097	.106	.069	.090

Table XII. Fraction of Lives Used for Indexing.

Language:		ALGOL	BASIC	BLISS	FORFOR	FORTEN	Mean
Bairstow		.513	.407	.226	.341	.251	.347
Crout		.519	.374	.520	.195	.244	.370
Treesort		.482	.412	.683	.431	.476	.497
PERT		.592	.421	.556	.445	.497	.502
Hàvie		.524	.365	.387	.278	.203	.351
Ising		.571	–	.484	.267	.249	.393
Secant		–	–	–	.376	.406	.392
Programmer:		E	B	A	G	L	Mean
Aitken		.185	.196	.232	.318	.474	.281
Compiler:		ALGOL	BASIC	BLISS	FORFOR	FORTEN	Mean
		.401	.364	.341	.509	.313	.386
Language:	MACRO	ALGOL	BASIC	BLISS	FORFOR	FORTEN	Mean
Mean	.425	.534	.396	.378	.333	.332	.391

needed, some register has to be temporarily stored, and the required value loaded into it. Hence each reference to one of the selected lives costs at most two STORE LOAD pairs.

The following four criteria were used for usefulness of lives:
— The number of references to the life was high.
— The density of references to the life was high.
— The life was long.
— The life was short.

The fourth criterion never gave the lowest cost. The third one rarely gave a low cost, the first two gave the lowest cost almost equally often. Furthermore the criterion that gave the lowest cost often changed with M within the same analysis. The interleaving cost is computed only when needed, i.e. when $N > M$. On the other hand, neither the selection of useless lives nor the cost computation takes local properties of the lives into account; both are based on their global characteristics.

4.2.2 Bedding. The bedding method, on the other hand, is based on the local properties of lives. The idea is to store ("bed") registers in memory when they have long dormant periods. In each such period the number of live registers is reduced by one, at the cost of one STORE LOAD pair. Such periods are known during phase I, but the information is not easily carried into phase II. In phase I, however, we do not know when registers are scarce ($N > M$). Hence bedding must be applied each time a life has been dormant longer than some time K, regardless of the need for registers during that time.

Our results were obtained using a hybrid method. Registers were bedded by phase I whenever they were dormant more than 200 instructions, and interleaving was used in phase II. The results, given as relative increase in instruction count, are displayed in Table XVI. As is seen, the increase caused by a reduction to 8 registers is less than 1% for 21 of the 41 programs, less than 5% for 30 of them, but runs as high as 50% or more in a few cases. The average increase is 7.9%.

We investigated the bad cases further by using lower values for K, i.e. lives were bedded when they had been dormant for as little as 22 instructions (in one case). Interleaving was applied in phase II as before. As K is reduced the interleaving cost decreases, since there are fewer periods when $N > M$. On the other hand, the bedding cost increases since there are more dormant periods. We have at present no way of telling which K will give the best result. In fact, in a similar analysis of two programs where the cost for $K = 200$ was already low, we found that the cost was lower for $K = 200$ in one case, $K = 100$ in the other. To produce the results given in Table XVII, different values of K were tried until a minimum seemed close. As is seen, the cost has been dramatically reduced for all of the programs, although it still is high for some. These results would reduce the mean of Table XVI from 7.9% to 2.7%.

The values obtained by bedding and interleaving are upper bounds, in the sense that any satisfactory compiler or programmer, knowing the local properties of the program, will select better "useless" lives, and only store them when N is high. He will also avoid unnecessary STOREs. On the other hand, the results were obtained using complete knowledge of the path taken through the program. When the code is written, all possible paths have to be provided for. This implies a less than optimal use of registers in each particular execution. In view of the fact that most lives are short, it is reasonable to assume that the gain by the former factor far outweighs the loss by the latter.

5. Operator Utility

We also used traces to study the utility of data types, data operators, and control operators. For existing operators and types, frequency counts were used. Some desirable but nonexisting operators were detected by observing frequencies of dynamic sequences of instructions.

Frequency studies for individual instructions or groups of instructions have been reported by various authors [1, 2, 4, 8, 9, 12, 16, 17]. Our results agree well with those of Gibson [7] (the Gibson mix), which

Table XIII. Number of Registers Sufficient 100%, 98%, and 90% of the Time (K = 200).

Language:		ALGOL	BASIC	BLISS	FORFOR	FORTEN	Mean
Bairstow	100%	13	10	9	13	12	11.4
	98%	11	7	6	10	9	8.6
	90%	8	6	5	9	7	7.0
Crout	100%	13	7	7	13	12	10.4
	98%	11	7	7	12	8	9.0
	90%	10	6	6	10	7	7.8
Treesort	100%	14	7	6	4	12	8.6
	98%	4	7	5	4	5	5.0
	90%	3	6	5	3	4	4.2
PERT	100%	14	10	7	11	12	10.8
	98%	10	7	6	8	8	7.8
	90%	8	6	5	3	5	5.4
Hàvie	100%	14	10	9	10	13	11.2
	98%	11	6	6	6	9	7.6
	90%	9	5	5	5	5	5.8
Ising	100%	14	–	7	11	12	11.0
	98%	11	–	5	7	9	8.0
	90%	10	–	5	3	6	6.0
Secant	100%	–	–	–	13	12	12.5
	98%	–	–	–	6	6	6.0
	90%	–	–	–	5	5	5.0
Programmer:		E	B	A	G	L	Mean
Aitken	100%	7	7	8	7	8	7.4
	98%	7	7	7	7	7	7.0
	90%	7	6	6	6	7	6.4
Compiler:		ALGOL	BASIC	BLISS	FORFOR	FORTEN	Mean
	100%	15	11	13	13	11	12.6
	98%	10	9	6	8	8	8.2
	90%	8	7	5	7	6	6.6
Language:	MACRO	ALGOL	BASIC	BLISS	FORFOR	FORTEN	Mean
Mean 100%	13.0	13.7	8.8	8.2	10.7	12.1	10.4
98%	9.0	9.7	6.8	6.5	7.6	7.7	7.6
90%	7.3	8.0	5.8	5.7	5.4	5.6	6.1

Table XIV. Number of Registers Sufficient 90% of the Time for the Arithmetic Classes FLO, FMD, and FAS (FLO = Floating, FMD = Fixed Mul/Div, FAS = Fixed Add/Sub).

Language:		ALGOL	BASIC	BLISS	FORFOR	FORTEN	Mean
Bairstow	FLO	2	1	2	2	2	1.8
	FMD	1	0	0	1	0	0.4
	FAS	4	2	2	1	2	2.2
Crout	FLO	1	1	1	3	2	1.6
	FMD	0	1	2	4	2	1.8
	FAS	5	1	3	3	3	3.0
Treesort	FLO	0	1	0	0	0	.2
	FMD	1	0	0	0	1	.4
	FAS	1	2	3	1	2	1.8
PERT	FLO	0	1	1	0	0	.4
	FMD	0	0	0	0	0	.0
	FAS	4	2	3	2	3	2.8
Hàvie	FLO	1	2	2	2	2	1.8
	FMD	0	0	1	0	0	.2
	FAS	5	2	2	2	3	2.8
Ising	FLO	0	–	0	0	0	.0
	FMD	0	–	0	0	0	.0
	FAS	5	–	4	1	3	3.3
Secant	FLO	–	–	–	2	1	1.5
	FMD	–	–	–	1	1	1.0
	FAS	–	–	–	2	4	3.0
Programmer:		E	B	A	G	L	Mean
Aitken	FLO	2	2	2	2	2	2.0
	FMD	0	0	0	0	1	.2
	FAS	3	2	3	4	3	3.0
Compiler:		ALGOL	BASIC	BLISS	FORFOR	FORTEN	Mean
	FLO	0	0	0	0	0	.0
	FMD	0	1	0	0	0	.2
	FAS	3	2	2	2	2	3.2
Language:	MACRO	ALGOL	BASIC	BLISS	FORFOR	FORTEN	Mean
Mean FLO	.0	.7	1.2	1.2	1.3	1.0	1.0
FMD	.3	.3	.2	.3	.9	.6	.4
FAS	2.3	4.0	1.8	2.8	1.7	2.9	2.4

should be well known. We refer the reader to [10] and [11].

274 of the over 400 instructions were used by our subject set. 75% of the instructions executed were accounted for by the 29 most executed instructions. 133 instructions accounted for 99% of the executed instructions. Over 40% of the executed instructions were moves between registers and primary memory, almost 30% were branching instructions, 12% were fixed-point adds or subtracts. The other categories of [7] each accounted for less than 5%.

We would also point out one particular result, relating to the addressing problem for tests, where the rich set of test instructions on the DECsystem10 permitted some possibly new observations. The test instructions were divided into groups according to the form of their operands, as seen in Table XVIII. Similarly, the programs were divided into three obvious groups. The programs were weighted in inverse proportion to their instruction count, and the distribution of the different groups of test instructions was observed.

Table XVIII clearly shows that comparison of two nonzero values is twice as common as comparison with zero. This is particularly true for recently computed values (contained in registers), in which case the factor is 3. Hence one is led to doubt the utility of condition codes as compared with the more general test instructions. Also noteworthy is the fact that compilers frequently test against small values known when the compiler was written (immediate operands).

5.1 Instruction Sequences

We now describe our attempt to detect data types and operators that could be included in the ISP at a benefit. Such operators manifest themselves as sequences of instructions, viz. those sequences used to interpret the desirable instructions in terms of the existing instruction set. Since such sequences may be of considerable length, a major difficulty is to limit the space and time used by the analysis program. Thus, for one of our subject programs, the number of different pairs of instructions was as high as 2000. If all these were to be extended to triples, quadruples or longer sequences, both space and time required for the analysis would be prohibitive.

We avoided this problem by using a multipass algorithm. Each pass scanned the whole trace; the first pass built the pairs, successive passes extended the existing sequences by one. After each pass the data structure was pruned; only those sequences thought to be significant were retained. The program ran until no sequences were retained, or until an arbitrary preset length of 20 was reached (after 19 passes). Before the results were printed, the counts for all those sequences which had been extended were reduced by the counts of the extensions. Hence only the unextendable fraction of each sequence was included in the final counts.

Five heuristics were used to detect candidates for deletion:

—All sequences whose counts were low compared to the most frequent sequence of the same length were deleted.

—All sequences that were not a significant extension of their leading and trailing longest subsequences were deleted. The intent was to isolate the common part of overlapping sequences as the interesting part.

—By the algorithm used, loops of length L may be represented at L different places in the data structure. When sequences of length $L + 2$ had been generated, all those for which the two last and two first instructions were the same, and which contained a jump instruction, were assumed to be loops of length L. One representation of such loops was retained, the others deleted.

—An attempt was made to detect all but one of several overlapping sequences representing the same longer sequence. Assume that the sequence A B C D E F G occurs frequently in the trace. At the end of pass 4 the sequences A B C D E, B C D E F, and C D E F G are observed to have approximately the same count. The latter two may be deleted, since the former will be extended in later passes.

—An attempt was made to detect all but the most frequent of long sequences with a large degree of overlap.

Using these pruning heuristics, about half the analyses produced one or more sequences of length 20. All analyses produced sequences of length 10 or more.

The heuristics above, as used in our experiments, were not as good as one might desire. In particular, in most analyses several of the sequences obviously overlapped. This caused the reduced counts for the overlapping parts to be much too low. Other sequences were extended too much, or they included only part of what was known from other considerations to be "the right" sequence. Hence a manual, and therefore subjective, analysis was necessary to extract significant results. This was also needed to relate the results back to program fragments with more or less intuitive meaning. During this analysis, the final results were compared with the unreduced counts printed after each pass. This manual analysis could be reduced by improving the existing heuristics and devising new ones. More accurate counts could be obtained by running a second analysis, observing only predetermined sequences or classes of sequences. This was, however, not done.

5.2 Sequence Results

Specific results are presented in [10]. Below we give a survey of those that seemed most important, and a few specific examples.

5.2.1 Subroutine calling sequences. Calling sequences for subroutines should be better supported by suitable

Table XV. Number of Registers Sufficient 90% of the Time for the Classes NOA, INX, and TOT (NOA = No Arithmetic, INX = Indexing, TOT = Total Class).

Language:		ALGOL	BASIC	BLISS	FORFOR	FORTEN	Mean
Bairstow	NOA	4	4	3	7	5	4.6
	INX	6	3	2	5	5	4.2
	TOT	8	6	5	9	7	7.0
Crout	NOA	6	4	2	3	5	4.0
	INX	9	3	3	2	3	4.0
	TOT	10	6	6	10	7	7.8
	NOA	2	4	2	2	2	2.4
	INX	2	3	3	2	2	2.4
	TOT	3	6	5	3	4	4.2
PERT	NOA	4	4	2	2	3	3.0
	INX	7	3	3	2	2	3.4
	TOT	8	6	5	3	5	5.4
Håvie	NOA	5	3	2	2	2	2.8
	INX	8	3	2	2	2	3.4
	TOT	9	5	5	5	5	5.8
Ising	NOA	6	–	2	2	4	3.5
	INX	9	–	2	2	4	4.3
	TOT	10	–	5	3	6	6.0
Secant	NOA	–	–	–	2	2	2.0
	INX	–	–	–	2	2	2.0
	TOT	–	–	–	5	5	5.0
Programmer:		E	B	A	G	L	Mean
Aitken	NOA	4	4	4	3	2	3.4
	INX	4	3	3	2	5	3.4
	TOT	7	6	6	6	7	6.4
Compiler:		ALGOL	BASIC	BLISS	FORFOR	FORTEN	Mean
	NOA	6	5	4	6	4	5.0
	INX	4	4	2	4	2	3.2
	TOT	8	7	5	7	6	6.6

Language:		MACRO	ALGOL	BASIC	BLISS	FORFOR	FORTEN	Mean
Mean	NOA	5.7	4.5	3.8	2.9	2.9	3.3	3.5
	INX	4.0	6.8	3.0	2.9	2.4	2.9	3.5
	TOT	7.3	8.0	5.8	5.7	5.4	5.6	6.1

Table XVI. Sum Interleaving and Bedding Costs for $K = 200$ When the Number of Registers is Reduced to 10, 8, or 7, Given as Relative Increase in Instruction Count.

Language:		ALGOL	BASIC	BLISS	FORFOR	FORTEN	Mean
Bairstow	10 rg	.057	.000	.005	.017	.009	.018
	8 rg	.231	.001	.005	.136	.095	.094
	7 rg	.371	.002	.009	.254	.184	.164
Crout	10 rg	.077	.000	.004	.440	.016	.107
	8 rg	.385	.000	.004	.757	.022	.234
	7 rg	.773	.000	.004	1.046	.097	.384
Treesort	10 rg	.002	.000	.011	.000	.015	.006
	8 rg	.005	.000	.011	.000	.016	.006
	7 rg	.007	.000	.011	.000	.016	.007
PERT	10 rg	.017	.000	.000	.004	.004	.005
	8 rg	.133	.000	.000	.036	.038	.041
	7 rg	.213	.001	.000	.053	.067	.070
Håvie	10 rg	.060	.000	.002	.001	.006	.014
	8 rg	.575	.001	.003	.005	.045	.126
	7 rg	.734	.003	.008	.018	.072	.167
Ising	10 rg	.068	–	.005	.002	.005	.020
	8 rg	.438	–	.005	.010	.052	.127
	7 rg	.998	–	.005	.031	.106	.285
Secant	10 rg	–	–	–	.004	.005	.005
	8 rg	–	–	–	.012	.017	.015
	7 rg	–	–	–	.018	.023	.021
Programmer:		E	B	A	G	L	Mean
Aitken	10 rg	.003	.003	.002	.001	.002	.002
	8 rg	.003	.003	.002	.001	.002	.002
	7 rg	.003	.003	.013	.001	.005	.005
Compiler:		ALGOL	BASIC	BLISS	FORFOR	FORTEN	Mean
	10 rg	.031	.004	.000	.013	.008	.011
	8 rg	.081	.040	.002	.072	.016	.042
	7 rg	.134	.085	.010	.225	.030	.097

Language:		MACRO	ALGOL	BASIC	BLISS	FORFOR	FORTEN	Mean
Mean	10 rg	.016	.047	.000	.004	.067	.009	.035
	8 rg	.064	.295	.000	.004	.136	.041	.079
	7 rg	.148	.516	.001	.007	.202	.081	.137

instructions to handle parameter transmission, return addresses, and to save and restore registers and other parts of the runtime representation.

The cost of call administration is easily detected for BLISS programs, since stack instructions are used only in this context. There is, however, no reason to believe that this cost is less for other languages usually considered to be "efficient."

The BLISS compiler, which is written in BLISS, and which contains many small subroutines for trivial bookkeeping tasks, spent approximately 25% of its time (to compile the BLISS version of Treesort) in call administration. For one of the FORTRAN compilers, which is also written in BLISS, the same number was approximately 15%.[2]

About $\frac{1}{8}$ of the instructions executed by the BLISS compiler could be saved if the subroutine call and exit instructions (PUSHJ and POPJ) were extended to manipulate the run-time registers, and to remove parameters from the stack on exit.

This would reduce 6 or 8 instructions to 2, and 10 or 12 memory cycles to 5, for each subroutine call. This improvement would fit well into the existing instruction format. In the case of FORTRAN programs it would be useful if parameter descriptors were recognized by the hardware, so that local copies of the actuals could be made by the calling instructions.

The suggested improvements would force representations on the language implementors, and hence reduce flexibility. However, such representations are rarely changed once they are decided, so this would not be a serious objection, particularly not if the instruction set were microprogrammed.

Another observation is interesting in this context: From observing the use of the stack instructions, we know that the BLISS compiler saves and restores about 16,000 registers per second (about 1.15 per routine call). This is the same number as would be saved and restored by 1,000 complete process swaps per second. We believe this to be a high frequency of process swaps for the KA-10 processor. Hence it seems that the cost of register saving caused by routine calls may be considerably larger than the corresponding cost caused by interrupts.

One remark is in order: the BLISS compiler has very many small and frequently called subroutines, and is not typical of common or garden programs. We do not, however, consider this a deficiency. Subroutines are an important ingredient in structuring programs, and should be cheap to use. The experimental results support our plea for more efficient hardware to handle registers and state information in calling mechanisms.

5.2.2 Vector descriptors and operands. A vector type should be introduced. This is motivated not only by the importance of vectors as a mathematical structure, but also by the vector structure of central memory and the effect this has on program structure in general. A vector descriptor should be provided. This should

Table XVII. Best Upper Bound for Relative Increase in Instruction Count, Selected Subject Programs, Best K Tried.

Language:	ALGOL	FORFOR	ALGOL	FORFOR
Algorithm	Bairstow	Bairstow	Crout	Crout
Bedding cost	.049	.017	.078	.114·
Interleaving cost	.007	.011	.001	.015
Total cost	.056	.028	.079	.129
K where obtained	25	40	27	22
Same cost for K = 200	.231	.136	.385	.757

Language:	ALGOL	ALGOL	ALGOL
Algorithm	PERT	Håvie	Ising
Bedding cost	.043	.065	.102
Interleaving cost	.001	.005	.008
Total cost	.044	.070	.110
K where obtained	25	30	27
Same cost for K = 200	.133	.575	.438

Table XVIII. Use of Test Instructions, Percentages of Total Instruction Count.

Program type	Compilers	Non-numeric programs	Highly numeric programs	Total subject set
Instruction form				
Register vs. memory	3.0	4.9	4.5	4.5
Register vs. immediate	7.7	1.7	1.0	2.1
Memory vs. 0	2.3	1.7	.9	1.3
Register vs. 0	2.5	1.8	2.1	2.0

make no distinction between vectors allocated by the compilers, and those allocated at run time. Furthermore, it should permit easy description of both row and column vectors of matrices. Operations should include common mathematical operators such as inner product, and also moves, summation, searches in ordered vectors etc. By permitting vectors of different lengths, and in particular length 1, interesting specializations may be obtained, such as initialization by a constant value.

Vector types would, in the extreme, change the ISP radically, as is exemplified by the CDC STAR. We do think, however, that some vector operations would be useful even in more conventional ISPs. Examples are frequent in our programs, although none are as dramatic as the others cited in this section.

5.2.3 String handling. Introduction of a "character string" type would speed up the compilers by a significant amount. Instructions operating on this type should be controlled by a table, indexed by the set of possible characters. The options for each character should include substitution, removal, branching to a special action routine, and termination of the instruction. It should be easy to use these instructions to change encodings, move strings, remove multiple blanks, remove extraneous characters etc. Analysis of routines for I/O formatting, and of COBOL programs, would suggest further options. Typical examples which illustrate the need for such instructions come from the compilers, particularly from BASIC.[3]

5.2.4 Run-time support for languages. The routines for run-time space management, parameter transmis-

43

sion and similar functions in ALGOL and similar languages are exceedingly expensive. They may consume as much as 50% of the execution time of some ALGOL programs.[4]

5.2.5 Miscellaneous data operators. Other data operators which could be included are: memory to memory moves (unless subsumed under the vector type), type conversions, and packing and unpacking of partwords. Some of these are already in the DECsystem10 ISP, but are not accessible to high-level language programmers. Hence this is a language problem as much as an ISP problem.[5]

5.2.6 Loop control. There should be an instruction for loop control which increments a fullword counter in one register and tests it against a fullword upper bound in another register. This instruction is also easily accommodated within the DECsystem10 ISP structure. It would save up to 5% of the execution time of some programs, reduce program size, and increase readability.[6]

6. Conclusions

In spite of the restricted set of experiments performed, we believe some of the results produced to be valid, not only for the DECsystem10, but for all register structured ISPs. This is in particular true for the results on simultaneous use of registers, and on the cost of subroutine calls.

It seems, for instance, that eight registers would be sufficient for a general register ISP similar to the DECsystem10. The result is no longer valid when the registers are used for other tasks than in this ISP, such as base register addressing, program counter, hardware defined stacks, etc.

Similarly the results on overhead in subroutine calling are both important and portable. Results from other ISPs would often exhibit an even worse situation, since the handling of return linkages for recursive or reentrant subprograms is more cumbersome. On the other hand, the situation can easily be improved by introducing instructions tailored to the needs of the commonly used languages. An ideal solution would be to permit a restricted form of writable microprogram, defining special instructions for each language. This would also be helpful with respect to run-time support for ALGOL and other languages.

Some of the results presented here and in [10], particularly those stemming from unnecessary generality, might seem like a severe criticism of the DECsystem10. This is a consequence of the deplorable fact that our methods only measure the time cost of ISP features. The richness and generality of the DECsystem10 ISP make it a good ISP to program for, and contribute to a low programming cost and a low memory space for programs. For our other points of

criticism we note that although the DECsystem10 leaves room for improvement, the problems we point out are not solved in a better way in other common ISPs.

Our work has barely scratched the surface of a large area of investigation. In particular, it would be interesting to study information used for address calculation and information used for control purposes. We would like to know more about how such information is computed, and how the two kinds interact. We hope to make this the subject of further research. The various solutions to the addressing problem for test instructions should also be investigated.

Acknowledgment. W.A. Wulf provided initial impetus to and considerable support and ideas throughout the project that led to this paper.

Received April 1975, revised January 1976

Notes

1. By an Instruction Set Processor, or ISP [3], we mean the logical processor which processes the instruction set, as divorced from its physical realization. Example: The IBM 360/370 is one ISP which has several physical realizations.

2. This is illustrated by the following sequences from the BLISS compiler:

PUSH PUSHJ JSP PUSH HRRZ	(14.3% of the execution time)
JRST POP POPJ SUB	(7.2% of the execution time)
JRST POP POP POPJ SUB	(3.5% of the execution time)

Only 3 of these 14 instructions are used in connection with parameter transmission; the rest are used for state saving, environment definition, and linkage handling.

3. The sequence:

SKIPE ILDB JRST CAIE CAIN CAIN CAIE CAIN CAIE CAIN CAIG CAIA CAIGE IDPB SKIPE SOSLE AOJA

consumed 20.7% of the compilation time. Its purpose is to move a line while removing extraneous characters like TABs, LINEFEEDS, etc. Similarly the sequence

ILDB CAIN IDPB JRST

moves a line stopping at a RETURN. It consumed 8% of the compilation time.

4. The following example is from the Ising program:

AOBJP MOVE MOVE ADDI HLLZ SETZB ROTC EXCH ROTC ROT ANDI HLRZ HRRZ ANDI LSH ANDI LSH

It consumed 19% of the time. From PERT we have:

XCT PUSHJ PUSHJ MOVE PUSH MOVEI MOVE PUSH HLRZ PUSHJ MOVE ADD MOVE POPJ POP POP TLNE POPJ MOVE POPJ

This is a complete call of a formal parameter by name (thunk), starting at the call within the procedure body (XCT) and ending at the POPJ back into it. The actual parameter is a vector element. Time consumed by this sequence was about 20% of the total.

5. An example is the sequence MOVE IDIV, used to unpack left halfwords, which consumes 45% of the time for the FORTEN version of Treesort. The HLRZ instruction used for the same purpose in the BLISS version consumes only 7.5% of the time of that version. The rest of these routines are about equally efficient.

6. The function shows up as:

ADDI AOJL or GAMGE AOJA MOVEM in FORTRAN
JRST AOS CAMLE in ALGOL,
MOVE FADR JRST CAMLE MOVEM in BASIC, and
AOJA CAMLE in BLISS.

References

1. Alexander, W.G. How a programming language is used. Rep. CSRG-10, Comptr. Res. Group, U. of Toronto, Toronto, Canada, Feb. 1972.

2. Arbuckle, R.A. Computer analysis and thruput evaluation. *Computers and Automation* (Jan. 1966), 12–15 and 19.

3. Bell, C.G., and Newell, A. *Computer Structures, Readings and Examples.* McGraw-Hill, New York, 1971.

4. Connors, W.D., Mercer, V.S., and Sorlini, T.A. S/360 instruction usage distribution. Rep. TR 00.2025, IBM Systems Development Div., Poughkeepsie, N.Y., May 8, 1970.

5. Foster, C.C., Gonter, R.H., and Riseman, E.M. Measures of opcode utilization. *IEEE Trans. Computers C-20*, 5 (May 1971), 582–584.

6. Foster, C.C., and Gonter, R.M. Conditional interpretation of operation codes. *IEEE Trans. Computers C-20*, 1 (Jan. 1971), 108–111.

7. Gibson, J.C. The Gibson mix. Rep. TR 00.2043, IBM Systems Development Div., Poughkeepsie, N. Y., 1970.

8. Gonter, R.H. Comparison of the Gibson mix with the UMASS mix. Pub. No. TN/RCC/004, Res. Comptg. Center, U. of Massachusetts, Amherst, Mass.

9. Herbst, E.H., Metropolis, N., and Wells, M.B. Analysis of problem codes on the MANIAC. *Math. Tables and Other Aids to Comput. 9* (Jan. 1955), 14–20.

10. Lunde, Å. Evaluation of instruction set processor architecture by program tracing. Ph.D. Th., Dep. Comptr. Sci., Carnegie-Mellon U., Pittsburgh, Pa., July 1974 (available as AD A004824 from Nat. Tech. Inform. Service, Springfield, Va).

11. Lunde, Å. More data on the O/W ratios. A note on a paper by Flynn. *Computer Architecture News 4*, 1 (March 1975), 9–13.

12. Raichelson, E., and Collins, G. A method for comparing the internal operating speeds of computers. *Comm. ACM 7*, 5 (May 1966), 309–310.

13. Tjaden, G.S., and Flynn, M.J. Detection and parallel execution of independent instructions. *IEEE Trans. Computers C-19*, 10 (Oct. 1970), 889–895.

14. Wilner, W.T. Design of the Burroughs B1700. Proc. AFIPS 1972 FJCC, Vol. 41, AFIPS Press, Montvale, N.J., pp. 489–497.

15. Wilner, W.T. Burroughs B1700 memory utilization. Proc. AFIPS 1972 FJCC, Vol. 41, AFIPS Press, Montvale, N.J., pp. 579–586.

16. Winder, R.O. Data base for computer performance evaluation. RCA-reprint PE-517, RCA David Sarnoff Res. Ctr., Princeton, N.J., 1971.

17. Winder, R.O. A data base for computer evaluation. *Computer 6*, 3 (March 1973), 25–29.

18. Wulf, W.A., Russell, D.B., and Habermann, A.N. BLISS: A language for systems programming. *Comm. ACM 14*, 12 (Dec. 1971), 780–790.

"Implications of Structured Programming for Machine Architecture" by A.S. Tanenbaum from *Communications of the ACM*, Volume 21, Number 3, March 1978, pages 237-246. Copyright 1978, Association for Computing Machinery, Inc., reprinted by permission.

Computer Systems   G. Bell, S. H. Fuller, and D. Siewiorek, Editors

Implications of Structured Programming for Machine Architecture

Andrew S. Tanenbaum
Vrije Universiteit, The Netherlands

Based on an empirical study of more than 10,000 lines of program text written in a GOTO-less language, a machine architecture specifically designed for structured programs is proposed. Since assignment, CALL, RETURN, and IF statements together account for 93 percent of all executable statements, special care is given to ensure that these statements can be implemented efficiently. A highly compact instruction encoding scheme is presented, which can reduce program size by a factor of 3. Unlike a Huffman code, which utilizes variable length fields, this method uses only fixed length (1-byte) opcode and address fields. The most frequent instructions consist of a single 1-byte field. As a consequence, instruction decoding time is minimized, and the machine is efficient with respect to both space and time.

Key Words and Phrases: machine architecture, computer architecture, computer organization, instruction set design, program characteristics
CR Categories: 4.12, 4.22, 4.9, 6.21

General permission to make fair use in teaching or research of all or part of this material is granted to individual readers and to nonprofit libraries acting for them provided that ACM's copyright notice is given and that reference is made to the publication, to its date of issue, and to the fact that reprinting privileges were granted by permission of the Association for Computing Machinery. To otherwise reprint a figure, table, other substantial excerpt, or the entire work requires specific permission as does republication, or systematic or multiple reproduction.
Author's address: Computer Science Group, Vrije Universteit, Amsterdam, The Netherlands.
© 1978 ACM 0001-0782/78/0300-0237 $00.75

1. Introduction

Information about the way computers are actually used is of great importance to computer architects, programming language designers, and compiler writers. Whether or not a certain semantic primitive should be included in a machine's instruction set, made a language construct, or carefully optimized depends primarily upon its projected frequency of usage. This information can only be obtained empirically, since there is no way to predict a priori, whether, for example, REPEAT . . . UNTIL statements are more useful than CASE statements.

The ways in which certain programming languages are used has already been studied: Knuth [6] has examined Fortran; Salvadori, Gordon, and Capstick [9] have examined Cobol; Alexander and Wortman [1] have examined XPL; Wortman [15] has examined student PL.

In recent years unstructured programs have fallen into disrepute. A growing number of people have come to recognize the importance of structuring programs so that they can be easily understood. Although there is no generally accepted definition of structured programming yet (see [2] for discussion), most programmers intuitively realize that breaking programs up into small, easily understood procedures, and drastically reducing or even eliminating GOTO statements greatly improves readability. We are even beginning to see the development of new programming languages which have been intentionally designed without a GOTO statement [16].

In order to determine what characteristics structured programs have, it is necessary to collect and dissect a number of them. These data can then be used as a basis for designing computer architectures that can execute structured programs efficiently. The next section of this article describes a GOTO-less language we have developed to encourage good programming style. The third and fourth section contain an analysis of a collection of procedures written in this language. The fifth and sixth sections propose and discuss a machine architecture based upon our findings.

2. The Experiment

We have developed a typeless GOTO-less language (SAL) specifically intended for system programming [10]. It has been implemented [11] on a PDP-11/45, and used, among other things, to construct a general purpose time sharing system for that computer. The language resembles BCPL [8]; its control structures are similar to those of Pascal [5]. A summary of the executable statements follows.

Assignment
CALL
IF . . . THEN . . . ELSE . . . FI
RETURN

```
FOR ... FROM ... TO ... BY ... DO ... OD
WHILE ... DO ... OD
REPEAT ... UNTIL ... LITNU
DO FOREVER ... OD
EXITLOOP
CASE ... IN ..., ..., ..., OUT ... ESAC
PRINT
```

Expressions are evaluated strictly left to right, with no precedence or parentheses. ELSE parts in IF statements are optional. RETURN statements exit the current procedure, and optionally return a value, so that a procedure may be used as a function. Procedures not returning an explicit value may terminate by "falling through", i.e. the END statement implies RETURN.

The WHILE statement tests at the top of the loop, whereas the REPEAT statement tests at the end of the loop. DO FOREVER statements are the same as WHILE TRUE DO; they are useful in operating system modules that endlessly get and carry out service requests, the "get" primitive blocking the process in the absence of a message. EXITLOOP is a forward jump out of one level of enclosing loop of any kind (FOR, WHILE, REPEAT, or DO FOREVER). Our experience indicates that this, plus RETURN, is sufficient most of the time. The CASE statement contains an integer expression that selects one of the clauses to be executed, or the OUT clause if the integer is out of range (as in Algol 68 [12]). There is no GOTO statement.

In addition to the above statements, there are a variety of declarations, debugging facilities and compiler directives.

The basic data types are machine words (including the general registers and the i/o device registers, accessible as the top 4K memory words), one-dimensional arrays of words and characters, bit fields, and programmer defined data structures consisting of a collection of named fields, each field being a word, character, bit field, or array. There are two scope levels, local (stack storage, reserved upon procedure entry, and released upon procedure exit), and global (static storage). A program consists of one or more procedures, and zero or more modules that declare and initialize external variables.

The programs examined for this research were all written by the faculty and graduate students of the Computer Science Group at the Vrije Universiteit. All the programmers involved made a very deliberate effort to produce "clean," well structured programs, knowing full well that succeeding generations of students would pore over their code line by line. This is clearly a different situation than one finds in the average, garden variety, computer center.

The amount of memory available on our PDP-11/45 was so small that the initial compiler could not handle procedures much larger than two pages of source code. This defect was remedied by declaring it to be a virtue, and by continually exhorting the programmers to produce short, well structured procedures. (The mean number of executable statements per procedure turned out to be 18.2). The combination of the GOTO-less language, the quality of the programmers, an environment with a long Algol tradition and no Fortran tradition, and our deliberate efforts to produce intelligible programs has resulted in what we believe to be state-of-the-art structured programs.

3. Characteristics of the Programs

For this study we have used a specially instrumented compiler to collect information on more than 300 procedures used in various system programs. Most of these were related to the time sharing system project. The results presented should be interpreted keeping in mind that operating system modules may systematically differ from say, applications programs, in certain ways, e.g. they have little i/o.

Where relevant, both static and dynamic measurements are given. Static measurements were obtained by having the compiler count the number of occurrences of the item in the source text. Dynamic measurements were obtained by having the compiler insert code into the object program to increment counters during program execution. The results are given in Tables I–VIII.

4. Discussion of the Results

According to our data, a typical procedure consists of 8 or 9 assignment statements, 4 calls to other procedures, 3 IF statements, 1 loop, and 1 escape (RETURN or EXITLOOP). Two of the assignment statements simply assign a constant to a scalar variable, one assigns one scalar variable to another, and 3 or 4 more involve only one operand on the right hand size. The entire procedure probably contains only 2 arithmetic operators. Two of the three conditions in the IF statements involve only a single relational operator, probably = or ≠.

The general conclusion that can be drawn from this data is the same as Knuth drew from his Fortran study: programs tend to be very simple. Combining this conclusion with the Bauer principle (If you do not use a feature, you should not have to pay for it), we suggest that most present day machine architectures could be considerably improved by catering more to the commonly occurring special cases. This will be discussed in detail in the next section. First we have a few more comments about the measurements.

In some cases there are significant differences between the static and dynamic measurements. Some of these differences are genuine, e.g. the operating system is constantly looking for internal inconsistencies in its tables. If an error is detected, an error handling

Table I. Percent Distribution of Executable Statements.

Statement Type	Static	Dynamic
Assignment	46.5	41.9
CALL	24.6	12.4
IF	17.2	36.0
RETURN	4.2	2.6
FOR	3.4	2.1
EXITLOOP	1.4	1.6
WHILE	1.1	1.5
REPEAT	0.5	0.1
DO FOREVER	0.5	0.8
CASE	0.3	1.2
PRINT	0.3	<0.05

Table II. Percent Distribution of Assignment Statement Types.

Type	Static	Dynamic
variable=constant	21.7	19.2
variable=variable	9.5	9.1
variable=function call	4.4	1.9
variable=array element	4.3	3.3
array element=constant	4.1	2.8
array element=variable	4.1	2.9
array element=array element	0.9	1.8
array element=function call	0.5	0.1
other forms with 1 rhs term	30.5	25.2
forms with 2 rhs terms	15.2	20.4
forms with 3 rhs terms	3.0	6.9
forms with 4 rhs terms	1.5	5.9
forms with ≥5 rhs terms	0.3	0.3

Table III. Percent Distribution of Operand Types

Type	Static	Dynamic
constant	40.0	32.8
simple variable	35.6	41.9
array element	9.3	9.2
field of structure	7.1	11.1
function call	4.8	1.6
bit field	3.2	3.3

Table IV. Percent Distribution of Arithmetic Operators.

Operator	Static	Dynamic
+	50.0	57.4
−	28.3	25.5
×	14.6	13.2
/	7.0	3.8

Table V. Percent Distribution of Relational Operators.

Operator	Static	Dynamic
=	48.3	50.6
≠	22.1	18.6
>	11.8	10.2
<	9.5	9.0
≥	4.5	8.4
≤	3.8	3.3

Table VI. Percent of all Procedures with N Formal Parameters.

N	Static	Dynamic
0	41.0	21.2
1	19.0	27.6
2	15.0	23.3
3	9.3	10.8
4	7.3	8.8
5	5.3	6.6
6	2.3	0.6
7	0.3	0.2
8	0.3	<0.05
≥9	<0.05	1.0

Table VII. Percent of all Procedures with N Local Scalar Variables.

N	Static	Dynamic
0	21.5	30.7
1	17.2	26.5
2	19.8	15.4
3	13.5	4.2
4	8.3	4.9
5	5.3	10.0
6	4.6	1.6
7	3.6	1.0
8	1.3	1.6
9	1.0	0.8
10	0.7	<0.05
≥11	3.3	3.0

Table VIII. Percent Distribution of Number of Statements in "THEN" Part of IF Statements.

Statements	Static
1	47.4
2	20.5
3	9.9
4	5.8
5	2.3
6	3.4
7	1.2
8	1.1
9	2.0
≥10	6.1

procedure is called. During normal operation there are no inconsistencies, so these error handlers are not called. These CALL statements increase the static number of CALL's but not the dynamic number.

Furthermore, an IF statement containing a single CALL statement in its THEN part and a single CALL statement in its ELSE part will be counted as one IF and two CALL's in the static statistics, but one IF and one CALL in the dynamic statistics, since only one branch is actually taken per execution. This effect increases the proportion of IF statements relative to other statements in the dynamic statistics.

On the other hand, a single loop executed 10,000 times gives grossly disproportionate weight to the statements in the loop in (only) the dynamic statistics. Thus the dynamic statistics may in fact be based on a very much smaller sample than the more than 10,000 lines of source text used to derive the static statistics. For this reason the static statistics are probably more meaningful. In the remainder of this paper we will use the static statistics.

From the fact that 5.5 percent of the statements are loops, and 1.4 percent are EXITLOOP's, we estimate that at least 25 percent of the loops are "abnormally" terminated. (In addition, an unknown number of loops are terminated by RETURN). The

Table IX. Comparison of Static Executable Statement Distribution (percent).

Statement type	SAL	XPL	Fortran
Assignment	47	55	51
CALL	25	17	5
IF	17	17	10
Loops	6	5	9
RETURN	4	4	4
GOTO	0	1	9

Table X. Summary of EM-1 Instructions and Number of Opcodes Allocated to Each.

Instruction description	Format 1	2	3A
push constant onto stack	3	2	
push local onto stack	12	1	
push external onto stack	8	1	
pop local from stack	12	1	
pop external from stack	8	1	
zero address ADD, SUB, MUL, DIV	4		
increment local	12	1	
zero local	12	1	
increment top word on stack	1		
push array element onto stack		2	
pop array element from stack		2	
call		1	
load address		1	
load indirect		1	
mark	3	1	
advance stack pointer		1	
return	1		
for instruction			2
branch forward unconditionally	34	1	
branch backward unconditionally		1	
branch if operand 1=operand 2	12	1	
branch if operand 1≠operand 2	20	1	
branch if operand 1≤operand 2	8	1	
branch if operand 1≥operand 2	8	1	
branch if operand 1<operand 2	4	1	
branch if operand 1>operand 2	4	1	
branch if operand=0	12	1	
branch if operand≠0	20	1	
branch if operand≤0	8	1	
branch if operand≥0	8	1	
branch if operand<0	4	1	
branch if operand>0	4	1	
opcode 255 (i.e. use formats 3B, 4)	1		

discussion currently raging in the literature [7] about how premature loop termination should be incorporated into language syntax is not irrelevant.

Since measurements of the type presented in this paper are obviously very sensitive to idiosyncracies of one's programming style, it is interesting to compare our results to previously published work. Table IX compares executable statement distribution for 3 studies cited in Section 1. One difference between Fortran and the other languages stands out immediately: Fortran programs have relatively few procedure calls. This suggests that they are not well modularized. From Knuth's data (his Table I) we compute that the average Fortran subroutine has 86.3 executable statements, vs. 28.6 for XPL and 18.2 for SAL, which agrees with this hypothesis.

Our data gives an average of 0.45 arithmetic operators per expression, which agrees well with Alexander's and Wortman's figure of 0.41. Likewise, our measurement of 1.22 operators per conditional expression agrees with their value of 1.19 logical plus relational operators. Such good agreement enhances one's confidence in the universality of the results.

5. A Proposal for a Machine Architecture

Most present day computers have an architecture designed in the early 1960's. They have remained substantially unchanged for a decade in the name of compatibility in spite of their obstacles to generating efficient code from high level languages. A machine architecture based on the characteristics of the programs described in the previous sections is sketched below. The architecture is specifically intended for block structured languages that permit recursion, i.e. Algol-like languages.

Our architecture has two explicit goals: 1. minimizing program size, and 2. providing a target language to which compilation is straightforward. We choose to minimize program size rather than maximize execution speed for several reasons. First, execution speed depends not only on the raw clock rate, but also on the characteristics of the underlying microinstruction set. Given a high level language benchmark program and two proposed instruction sets, it is possible to determine unambiguously which object program is smaller, but not which is faster. (By hypothesizing a faster clock or better microarchitecture either machine can be speeded up). In other words, minimizing size is a more clearly defined goal than maximizing speed.

Second, size and speed are highly intertwined. All other factors being equal, a shorter program will execute faster than a longer one since fewer bits need be processed. If the memory bandwidth is N bits/sec and the mean instruction size is L bits, the maximum instruction execution rate will be N/L instructions/sec. The smaller L is, the faster the machine can be. Furthermore, on a machine with virtual memory, reducing program size reduces the number of page faults, which, in turn, reduces the time required to process the page faults, thereby speeding up execution.

Third, on large computers with sophisticated multiprogramming systems, a decrease in program size means an increase in the degree of multiprogramming, hence a higher CPU utilization, as well as less swapping.

Fourth, the small amount of memory available on minicomputers is often a serious limitation. Making the program fit into the memory may take precedence over all other considerations.

Fifth, on mini and micro computer systems, the cost of memory frequently is much larger than the CPU cost. Reducing memory requirements has a much greater effect on total system cost than reducing execution time.

The fact that few compilers for third generation computers can produce code that even comes close to what a skilled assembly language programmer can generate argues strongly for redesigning machine architectures so that compilers can do their job better. (See [11] for some statistics). It is for this reason that we consider a stack machine, since generating efficient reverse Polish is simpler than generating efficient code for a register oriented machine. We assume the presence of a cache to eliminate the need for memory cycles when referencing the stack.

The design described below is intended for implementing modern programming languages such as Algol 60, Algol 68, Pascal, XPL, BCPL, SAL, and others of this genre, since they tend to facilitate rather than hinder the writing of well structured programs.

The proposed machine, which we shall call EM-1 (Experimental Machine-1) has a paged, segmented virtual memory. The program and data reside in different address spaces (like the PDP-11/45), so that instruction space segment 0 is distinct from data segment 0. An instruction space segment is a sequence of 8-bit bytes, each with a unique address. A data space segment is a sequence of words of N bits each (N is left unspecified here). The word length for data space segments may be different from that of instruction space segments. (See Table X.)

One data space segment is special: the stack. The stack has associated with it a stack pointer register (SP) that points to the top word on it. Whenever a procedure is entered, a new frame is allocated on the stack for the administration, actual parameters, and locals. The frame is released upon procedure exit. Figure 1 depicts the stack for the following Algol 60 program.

```
begin integer e1, e2, e3; integer array e4[1:3];
  proc p1;
  begin integer k1, k2; p2(k1, k2)
  end;
  proc p2(formal1, formal2);
  begin integer k1, k2; p2(k1, k2)
    integer array n5[1:4], n6[0:1];
    comment snapshot of Figure 1 taken here;
  end;
  p1
end
```

When $p2$ returns, SP will be reset to point to $k2$, thus removing that part of the stack marked "current stack frame" in Figure 1.

The stack frame for a procedure consists of 4 areas: (1) the administration information; (2) the actual parameters; (3) the local scalar variables and array descriptors; and (4) the elements of local arrays. The sizes of areas (1–3) are always known at compile time; the size of area (4) may not be known until run time.

A special hardware register, LB (Local Base) points

Fig. 1.

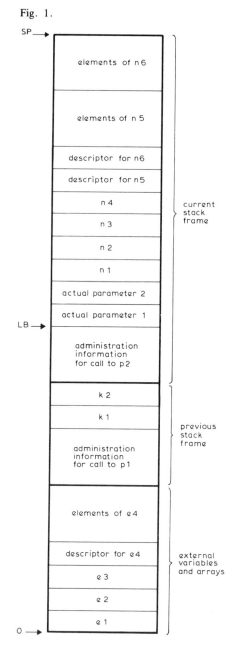

to the beginning of the local variables. Local variables are specified by giving their positions relative to LB.

The administration area contains the calling procedure's return address, the previous value of LB, and other (language dependent) information. It is assumed that the microprogram knows the size and organization of the administration area; a special instruction could be executed at the beginning of each program to tell it. Actual parameters can be addressed by giving their distance from LB, just as locals. Note that the administration area is not counted in order to reduce the size of the constants needed.

A procedure call takes place in the following steps:

1. A MARK instruction is executed to deposit the static and dynamic links on the stack. The MARK instruction has one operand which tells how much the static depth of nesting is increased or decreased.

This is needed to update the static chain. The MARK instruction also reserves space for the return address to be deposited subsequently.

2. The calling procedure pushes the actual parameters onto the stack.

3. A call instruction is executed, transferring control to the called procedure. The call instruction has as operand the index of a procedure descriptor, discussed later. This instruction must deposit the return address in the place reserved for it by the MARK instruction, update LB and transfer control.

4. The called procedure executes a single instruction that increments SP to reserve as much local storage as is initially needed; this instruction could also initialize the local variables to 0 or a special "undefined" value such as 1000 . . . 000 (two's complement -0). If more local storage is needed during execution of the procedure, e.g. for an Algol 68 local generator, SP can simply be advanced again.

We propose an addressing mechanism with distinct instructions for the 2 most important cases: local and external variables. Each instruction must provide an integer offset telling which variable is intended. Locals are offset above LB, and externals are offset from address 0 of the stack segment. For the purposes of addressing, procedure parameters are the same as locals.

Two other addressing forms are needed but are much less important. One is for full virtual addresses consisting of a segment and word within the segment. The other is for accessing intermediate lexicographical levels in block structured languages by means of a (relative lexicographical level, offset) pair. Rather than using a display, which must be frequently updated at considerable cost, we propose that at some position within the administration area known to the microprogram is the LB value of the most recent incarnation of the procedure in which the current procedure is nested (i.e. the static link). Given a (relative lexicographical level, offset) pair, the microprogram can follow the chain and locate variables at any outer static level. Note that the penalty for accessing intermediate levels is only a few microinstructions and one memory reference for each level of nesting followed. The combination of infrequent usage and a small penalty per use makes this method attractive since it reduces procedure call overhead, which is far more crucial.

The stack is also used for all arithmetic and logical operations, shifting, etc. An assignment is performed by first pushing the value to be assigned onto the stack (or perhaps its descriptor, if provision is made for assigning entire arrays in one instruction), and then popping it to its destination, a total of 2 instructions. The statement $A = B \times C$ is handled by 4 instructions: PUSH B; PUSH C; MULTIPLY; POP A.

The advantage of a stack type architecture for arithmetic is clear: compilers can translate expressions to reverse Polish very simply, with no complicated

register optimization needed. High execution speed can be attained by a hardware cache memory that retains the most recently referenced words (i.e. the top of the stack) in high speed storage, or by having the microprogram keep them in its scratchpad memory. If the arithmetic expressions evaluated are simple, little cache or scratchpad storage will be needed. Our data indicate that 80 percent of all expressions consist of a single term, 95 percent consists of 1 or 2 terms and 99.7 percent consists of 4 or fewer terms, meaning that rarely will more than 4 operands be on the stack simultaneously.

Most of the instructions require an opcode and a small constant, which we call the "offset." The offset is generally used to select one of the local variables, one of the external variables, the number of bytes to skip (branch instructions), etc. The following five instruction formats are used by EM-1.

Format	Bytes	Description
1	1	byte 1 = opcode + offset (arithmetic sum)
2	2	byte 1 = opcode, byte 2 = offset
3A	3	byte 1 = opcode, bytes 2,3 = offset
3B	3	byte 1 = 255, byte 2 = opcode, byte 3 = offset
4	4	byte 1 = 255, byte 2 = opcode, bytes 3,4 = offset

The choice of machine instructions, and their assignment to formats, should be carefully arranged to minimize program size (based on the data of Section 3). In particular, an effort should be made to insure that the most common statements can be translated into 1 byte instructions most of the time. The scheme described below is constrained by the fact that the total number of format 1 instructions plus format 2 instructions plus format 3A instructions must not exceed 255. Some instructions, may occur several times in the order code, e.g. push constant onto the stack occurs in formats 1, 2, and 4, with a different range of constants provided in each form.

The idea of using shorter bit patterns for common instructions and longer bit patterns for infrequent instructions is not new. Huffman [4] gives a method for encoding items whose probabilities of occurrence are known, in the minimum number of bits. An approximation of this technique has been used in the design of the Burroughs B1700 S-machines (Wilner, [13, 14]). In the SDL S-machine, opcodes can be 4, 6, or 10 bits, and addresses 8, 11, 13, or 16 bits. A single address instruction can have a length of 12, 14, 15, 17, 18, 19, 20, 21, 22, 23, or 26 bits. Since the B1700 microarchitecture is extremely flexible (among other things being able to read an arbitrary length bit string — up to 24 bits — out of memory beginning at an arbitrary bit, in a single microinstruction) the use of peculiar length instructions does not slow down interpretation.

However, nearly all other computers are based upon a memory organization using fixed length words. For a microprogram with internal registers, bus widths etc. of 8, 16, or 32 bits interpreting a "machine" language whose instructions came in units of 12, 14, 15, 17, 18, 19, 20, 21, 22, 23, or 26 bits would be unbearably slow, since nearly every instruction would straddle word or byte boundaries, necessitating time consuming shifting and masking operations to extract the opcode and address fields. The scheme described by Wilner is only feasible if every single bit in memory has a unique address, a situation which is rarely the case.

The instruction set of EM-1, in contrast, also provides a very efficient method for encoding instructions, but is based on a memory in which every 8-bit byte has a unique address, rather than every bit having a unique address. This makes the principles of the EM-1 design applicable to a much larger number of computers than one utilizing arbitrary length bit fields.

From Table I we see that the assignment, IF, CALL, RETURN and FOR statements together account for 96 percent of the source statements. Therefore we will design an instruction set to handle the object code from these statements efficiently. To push local variables (including parameters) onto the stack, we propose 12 distinct 1-byte (format 1) opcodes, one each for offsets 0–11. Twelve instructions allow access to all the locals (and parameters) in 94.6 percent of the procedures, and to more than 50 percent of the locals in the remaining procedures. For example, opcodes 114–125 might be used for PUSH LOCAL 0, PUSH LOCAL 1, . . . , PUSH LOCAL 11. There is no need to have distinct "opcode" and "address" bits.

Eight opcodes will be allocated to stacking the 8 external variables at the base of the stack segment. Since 81.4 percent of the constants in our data were either 0, 1, or 2, we allocate 3 opcodes for pushing these constants onto the stack.

At this point 23 of the 255 available 1 byte instructions have been used. Another 20 are needed for popping values from the stack. To handle programs with up to 256 locals, or externals, 4 format 2 instructions are needed: 2 push and 2 pop. Two more opcodes (format 2) are needed to push positive and negative constants up to 256 onto the stack. Format 4 (16 bit offset) can contain instructions with larger offsets for truly pathological programs. By including zero address (stack) instructions for add, subtract, multiply, and divide, we have sufficient instructions to evaluate most scalar expressions, using 53 of the opcodes.

Setting local variables to zero, and incrementing them by 1, are so common that we allocate 24 format 1 and two format 2 opcodes for this purpose. Incrementing the top of the stack is also worth an opcode.

Array accesses are accomplished using descriptors on the stack. Each descriptor (which may be 1 or more words, depending on N, the word length) contains the bounds and strides, S_i, for the array. For example, the address of $A[i, j, k]$ can be found from

address $= S_0 + S_1 \times i + S_2 \times j + S_3 \times k$

where the strides can be computed once and for all as soon as the bounds are known, at compile time in many cases, and at run time in the others. The descriptor must also contain the number of dimensions and the element size (and the segment number, for nonlocal arrays).

Array elements are accessed as follows. First the subscripts are stacked, requiring at least one instruction per subscript. Then a PUSH ELEMENT instruction is executed, specifying the offset of the descriptor from LB. This instruction removes all the subscripts from the stack, and replaces them with the selected element. The instruction also performs all bounds checking (unless disabled) and traps upon detecting a subscript error. A second opcode is needed for a POP ELEMENT instruction that first pops the subscripts and then the value. With these two instructions, the statement $A[I] := B[J]$ can usually be compiled into only 6 bytes of object code, including all bounds checking (PUSH J; PUSH ELEM; PUSH I; POP ELEM). This is a substantial improvement over most conventional designs. Four format 2 instructions are needed for pushing and popping local and external array elements.

Note that this addressing scheme is not affected by the size of the arrays. Assuming that a descriptor can fit in a single machine word, a procedure with ≤ 256 large arrays could nevertheless perform all array accesses using exclusively format 2 instructions.

For calling procedures, we envision one format 2 instruction whose offset is an index into a table held in a special data segment. Each table entry could contain the segment and address of the object code, possibly a "not yet linked" bit, to implement dynamic linking as in MULTICS, and possibly some protection machinery to keep less privileged procedures from calling more privileged ones. The symbolic name might also be present for debugging purposes and a counter to be incremented by the microprogram upon each call might be provided for performance monitoring.

To allow the instruction to locate the administration area in order to deposit the return address there, and to update LB, the number of words of parameters is also needed. For programs with up to 256 procedures, the call instruction will be 2 bytes, although a method to reduce this to 1 byte in most cases will be described below.

No additional instructions are needed for call-by-value. For call-by-reference an additional format 2 instruction to push an address onto the stack would be useful, along with one to fetch a parameter passed by reference (i.e. load indirect). The three most common types of procedure calls are to increase the depth of static nesting by 1, leave it unchanged, and decrease it by 1. Three opcodes are devoted to the three corresponding MARK instructions.

After a MARK instruction the distribution of the next few instructions is radically more different than the normal one. This fact can be exploited to reduce the procedure call instruction to 1 byte in many cases, using a generalization of the idea of Foster and Gonter [3]. The only instructions than can follow a MARK instruction are those needed to pass the parameters, if any, and the CALL itself. Most parameters are constants, variables, or simple expressions, which can usually be passed using only a limited number of different instructions, mostly load type instructions. About 200 opcodes could be reserved for CALL's, each corresponding to a specific procedure descriptor. These CALL instructions would each require only 1 byte.

The simplest way to implement this would be to have the microprogram maintain the microaddress of the start of the instruction fetch loop in one of its registers. At the end of the execution phase of each interpreted instruction the microprogram would jump indirectly to this register. The MARK instruction would reload this register with the address of an alternative fetch loop, which would merely use a different branch table, in effect temporarily remapping the opcodes. The CALL instruction could restore the normal opcodes by resetting just one internal register. The use of opcode remapping can also be used in any other context with explicit first and last instructions.

An instruction with a 1-byte offset is needed by the called program to advance SP. The return instruction, which needs no offset, restores the stacked program counter and previous LB value (which are at known positions below the current LB) and resets SP.

Our proposed FOR statement instructions are based upon our measurement that 95 percent of the loops have a BY part of +1 or −1. Before the loop, the controlled variable is initialized, and the TO part is evaluated and pushed onto the stack. The EM-1 FOR instruction reads the TO part and the controlled variable. If the termination condition is met, a forward branch out of the loop occurs. Otherwise the controlled variable is updated and the next instruction is executed. The TO part is only removed from the stack when the loop is terminated. To allow both tests for both upward and downward counting, two opcodes are needed. (For languages in which the TO and BY parts may change during execution of the loop, variants of these instructions will be needed). Both instructions use format 3A. The offset of the controlled variable is in the second byte of the instruction, and the forward branch distance is specified in the third byte. The body of the loop is terminated by an unconditional branch backward to the FOR instruction.

At this point we must devise instructions to handle IF statements. A number of third generation machines perform conditional branching by first setting condition code bits, and then testing them in a subsequent instruction. EM-1, in contrast, combines these functions, and eliminates the need for condition codes.

There are three types of branch instructions, distinguished by the number of operands they remove from the stack. The unconditional branch forward and backward instructions do not remove any operands from the stack. The second group removes one operand and compares it to zero, branching forward if the condition specified by the opcode ($=, \neq, <, >, \leq,$ or $\geq$) is met. This group is useful for statements such as IF N = 0 THEN . . . If Boolean variables represent FALSE by 0 and TRUE by 1, this group can also be used for statements such as IF FLAG THEN. . . .

The third group of branch instructions removes two operands from the stack, compares them, and branches forward if the specified condition is met. Backward conditional branches are not needed for translating IF statements (or WHILE statements either).

Each branch instruction specifies an offset which is the branch distance in bytes relative to the instruction itself. (Offset = k means skip $k + 1$ bytes.) Intersegment branches are prohibited, so that the procedure call mechanism can be used to limit access to privileged procedures. The size of the offsets required can be estimated from the data of Table VIII. Based upon the design proposed above, we estimate that the average source statement will require not more than 4 bytes of object code. This means that an offset with a range of 0–3 (i.e. 4 instructions) is sufficient for nearly half the IF statements, and a range of 0–15 (i.e. 16 instructions) is sufficient for more than 4/5 of the cases. We need 14 opcodes to provide format 2 instructions for the unconditional branch, 1 operand conditional branch, and 2 operand conditional branch instructions.

This leaves 141 opcodes over for the format 1 opcodes. A possible allocation covering most of the frequently occurring cases is given in the summary of opcode usage below. If the average statement needs 4 bytes of object code, the division proposed below will handle 77 percent of the IF tests in a single byte. Note that "IF $A = B$" compiles into a branch NOT equal instruction to skip over the THEN part.

We will not discuss the instruction set further here. Suffice to say that all the instructions that could not be included in format 1 or format 2 for lack of encoding room, are included in format 3B. Also versions of all the above instructions should be provided as format 4 instructions (16-bit offset). Instructions needed, but not discussed above, e.g. accessing intermediate lexicographical levels of block structured languages should also be provided as format 3B and 4 instructions. There should also be instructions for multiple precision arithmetic, floating point, shifting, rotating, Boolean operations, etc.

It should be obvious that our design is not optimal in the information theory sense. More data and detailed simulation are needed to fine tune the choice of format 1 opcodes. On a user microprogrammable computer, one can envision tuning the format 1 instruction set to match the measured characteristics of important production programs, and loading a special highly optimized microprogram before beginning program execution. Alternately, a whole collection of single chip microprocessors could be kept in house, each with a read only microprogram tuned to a different application.

6. Discussion of the Machine Architecture

Our major point in this whole discussion is to illustrate that 1 byte instructions in this design can often do the work of 4 byte or longer instructions in conventional machines. To illustrate the savings of EM-1, Table XI gives some examples of the size of the EM-1 code compared to DEC PDP-11 code and CDC Cyber code, as examples of mini and mainframe computers. The PDP-11 and Cyber code sequences used for comparison are those a good compiler might reasonably expect to generate in order to minimize object program size. It is assumed that these are fragments from a block structured language that permits recursion and requires subscript checking. All local variables are assumed to be on the stack, not in registers (except loop indices) and EM-1 is assumed to be able to use the shortest instruction format. Both the PDP-11 and Cyber make use of calls to run-time subroutines whose size is not counted here.

As a second test, 4 programs were carefully coded in assembly language for EM-1, the PDP-11 and the Cyber. In contrast to the above examples, these were complete programs, and the ground rules permitted the use of registers. There was no run time system (i.e. everything was coded in-line) and subscripts were not checked. The results are given in Table XII. It should be noted that the PDP-11 and Cyber test programs were carefully hand coded by an experienced assembly language programmer. Few compilers could ever generate object code this compact, whereas it would be easy to have a compiler generate the EM-1 code used in the examples due to the close match between the EM-1 instruction set and reverse Polish. This means that EM-1 is actually much better than the above data might at first indicate.

It is important to realize that in an environment consisting of many short procedures, the register sets provided by a third generation machine are of little value. They can be used for temporary results during expression evaluation, but from our data, that of Alexander and Wortman, and also Knuth's, one register is usually enough. The registers cannot be used effectively to hold local variables, because they must be constantly saved and restored upon procedure calls. This save-restore overhead will be very severe if, as our data shows, one out of every four statements is a procedure call.

Although we have not emphasized execution speed, a microprogrammed EM-1 machine is potentially very

Table XI. A Comparison of EM-1, PDP-11, and Cyber Object Code Size (in Bits).

| | | | | Ratios | |
| | | | | PDP-11/ | Cyber/ |
Statements	EM-1	PDP-11	Cyber	EM-1	EM-1
I := 0	8	32	45	4.0	5.6
I := 3	16	48	60	3.0	3.8
I := J	16	48	75	3.0	4.7
I := I + 1	8	16	60	2.0	7.5
I := I + J	32	48	90	1.5	2.8
I := J + K	32	96	105	3.0	3.3
I := J + 1	24	80	75	3.3	3.1
I := A[J]	32	128	120	4.0	3.8
A[I] := 0	32	112	105	3.5	3.3
A[I] := B[J]	48	192	180	4.0	3.8
A[I] := B[J] + C[K]	80	304	285	3.8	3.6
A[I, J, K] := 0	48	176	165	3.7	3.4
IF I = J THEN . . .	24	64	105	2.7	4.4
IF I = 0 THEN . . .	16	48	60	3.0	3.8
IF I = J + K THEN . . .	40	112	150	2.8	3.8
IF FLAG THEN . . .	16	48	60	3.0	3.8
CALL P	16	64	60	4.0	3.8
CALL P1(I) (by value)	24	96	90	4.0	3.8
CALL P2(I, J) (by value)	32	128	120	4.0	3.8
CALL P3(I) (by reference)	32	112	90	3.5	2.8
FOR I FROM 1 TO N DO A [I] := 0 OD	88	176	225	2.0	2.6

fast. The microprogram would fetch the opcode and then execute a 256-way branch. Since each of the format 1 instructions is relatively simple, each instruction could be handled by a small number of microinstructions. In contrast microprograms for machines like the PDP-11 and IBM 370 must do considerable extraction and manipulation of short fields within the target instruction. This is avoided in EM-1. By having a distinct microroutine for each of the twelve instructions that push a local variable onto the stack, none of these microroutines would have to do any decoding or bit extraction, providing for very fast execution. The other format 1 instructions would also be fast for the same reason. Alternately, to reduce the size of the microprogram at the expense of execution speed, all the target instructions of a given type could share one microroutine.

At first it may appear that producing code for EM-1 would give compiler writers nightmares, due to the multiple instruction formats. This problem can be easily solved by first writing an optimizing assembler that has a single mnemonic for "load local variable onto the stack" (e.g. LODLOC SYM), etc. The assembler, and not the compilers, chooses the shortest feasible instruction format. The assembler should also recognize sequences such as PUSH 0; POP X and PUSH X; PUSH 1; ADD; POP X and replace them by ZERO X and INCR X respectively. Compilers might also leave the task of sorting the local variables on number of occurrences, and assigning the most heavily used ones lower offsets to the assembler. Once such an assembler was written, it could be used as the last

Table XII. A Comparison of EM-1, PDP-11 and Cyber Object Code Size (in Bits)

Program	EM/1	PDP-11	Cyber	PDP-11/ EM-1	Cyber/ EM-1
				Ratios	
Towers of Hanoi	352	992	2205	2.8	6.3
sort integer array	562	1248	1260	2.2	2.2
dot product	552	832	1140	1.5	2.0
find primes	306	704	1020	2.3	3.3

pass of all compilers, allowing them to produce straightforward reverse Polish, and still get locally optimal code.

7. Summary

There is a certain analogy between a Huffman code used to encode text in a minimal number of bits, and our proposal for a machine language with a compact instruction set. In both cases it is necessary to determine the frequencies of occurrence of the data to be encoded (letters and instructions, respectively) by empirical measurements. We have done this and reported the results in Section 3. Then an encoding scheme must be devised in which the most commonly occurring cases are assigned the shortest bit patterns, and the least commonly occurring cases are assigned the longest bit patterns. This is in contrast to a scheme in which all cases are assigned the same length bit pattern. In EM-1 the most frequently occurring instructions are encoded in a single byte, which is both efficient in storage and avoids the problems associated with variable length bit strings produced by true Huffman coding. This leads to object programs that require little memory and are capable of being executed very easily (i.e. fast).

Received February 1976; revised January 1977

References
1. Alexander, W.G., and Wortman, D.B. Static and dynamic characteristics of XPL programs. *Computer 8* (1975), 41–46.
2. Denning, P.J. Is it not time to define 'structured programming'? *Operating Syst. Rev. 8* (Jan. 1974), 6–7.
3. Foster, C.C., and Gonter, R.H. Conditional interpretation of operation codes. *IEEE Trans. Comptrs. C-20*, 1 (1971), 108–111.
4. Huffman, D. A method for the construction of minimum redundancy codes. *Proc. IRE 40* (1952), 1098–1101.
5. Jensen, K., and Wirth, N. *PASCAL User Manual and Report.* Springer-Verlag, New York, 1974.
6. Knuth, D.E. An empirical study of FORTRAN programs. *Software – Practice and Experience 1* (1971), 105–133.
7. Knuth, D.E. Structured programming with go to statements, *Computing Surveys 6* (1974), 261–301.
8. Richards, M. BCPL: A tool for compiler writing and system programming. Proc. AFIPS SJCC, Vol. 34, AFIPS Press, Montvale, N.J., 1969, pp. 557–566.
9. Salvadori, A., Gordon, J., and Capstick, C. Static profile of COBOL programs. Sigplan Notices (ACM) 10 (1975), 20–33.
10. Tanenbaum, A.S. A programming language for writing operating systems. Rep. IR-3, Wiskundig Seminarium, Vrije U., Amsterdam, 1974.
11. Tanenbaum, A.S. A general purpose macro processor as a poor man's compiler. *IEEE Trans. Software Eng. SE-2* (1976), 121–125.
12. van Wijngaarden, A., Mailloux, B., Peck, J.E.L., and Koster, C.H.A. Report on the algorithmic language ALGOL 68, Num. Math. *14* (1969), 79–218.
13. Wilner, W.T. Design of the Burroughs B1700. Proc. AFIPS FJCC, Vol. 41, 497, AFIPS Press, Montvale, N.J., 1972, pp. 489–497.
14. Wilner, W.T. Burroughs B1700 Memory Utilization. Proc. AFIPS FJCC, Vol. 41, AFIPS Press, Montvale, N.J., 1972, 579–586.
15. Wortman, D.B. A study of language directed computer design. CSRG-20, U. of Toronto, Toronto, Ont. (1972).
16. Wulf, W.A., Russell, D.B., and Habermann, A.N. BLISS: A language for systems programming. *Comm. ACM 14* (1971), 780–790.

Section 2: RISC Overview

2.1 Background

While RISC systems have been defined and designed in a variety of ways by different groups, the key elements shared by most (not all) designs are these

- A limited and simple instruction set;
- A large number of general-purpose registers;
- An emphasis on optimizing the instruction pipeline.

The proponents of the RISC architecture cite two main advantages to this approach: improved performance and optimized use of VLSI. With respect to performance

- A simplified instruction set reduces or eliminates the need for microcode, which is slower than a hardwired implementation.
- A simplified instruction set makes it possible to exploit more effectively instruction pipelining.
- The use of a large number of registers makes it possible to reduce the rate of memory access, thus increasing speed.

The second area of benefit relates to the use of VLSI to implement an entire processor on a single chip. A RISC architecture is simpler and therefore easier to design and implement. Furthermore, the scarce resource of chip surface area can be optimized, since the RISC design does not require a complex control unit and lots of ROM to store the microcode.

Although the RISC approach is relatively new, extensive research has been carried out and reported, and commercial products have begun to appear.

2.2 Article Summary

The first article provides a comprehensive overview of the subject and is intended to provide a context for the remainder of the text.

The second article, by Patterson, is a survey article that focuses on two topics. First, the historical background and motivation that led to the research in RISC architecture is examined. Second, the various RISC approaches are analyzed and compared.

The next article, "VLSI Processor Architecture," is an exhaustive look at the relevant design issues for both RISC and complex-instruction-set computer (CISC) designs, from the perspective of a RISC designer.

The final article, "RISC: Back to the Future?," is by the chief architect of one of the most complex of CISCs, the VAX. Bell places RISC technology in the historical context of computer development since 1948, and shows that the roots of RISC can be traced to the CDC 6600.

Reduced Instruction Set Computers

Since the development of the stored-program computer around 1950, there have been remarkably few true innovations in the areas of computer organization and architecture. The following, though not constituting a complete list, are some of the major advances since the birth of the computer.

- *The Family Concept:* Introduced by IBM with its System/360 in 1964, followed shortly thereafter by DEC, with its PDP- 8. The family concept decouples the architecture of a machine from its implementation. A set of computers are offered, with different price/performance characteristics, that present the same architecture to the user. The differences in price and performance are due to different implementations of the same architecture.
- *Microprogrammed Control Unit:* Suggested by Wilkes in 1951, and introduced by IBM on the S/360 line in 1964. Microprogramming eases the task of designing and implementing the control unit and provides support for the family concept.
- *Cache Memory:* First introduced commercially on IBM S/360 Model 85 in 1968. The insertion of this element into the memory hierarchy dramatically improves performance.
- *Pipelining:* A means of introducing parallelism into the essentially sequential nature of a machine-instruction program. Examples are instruction pipelining and vector processing.

Reprinted with permission of Macmillan Publishing Company from *Computer Organization and Architecture* by William Stallings. Copyright © 1986 by Macmillan Publishing Company.

TABLE 14-1   Characteristics of some CISCs AND RISCs

Characteristic	Complex Instruction Set Computers (CISCs)			Reduced Instruction Set Computers (RISCs)	
	IBM 370/168	VAX-11/780	Intel 8086	Berkeley RISC I	IBM 801
Year developed	1973	1978	1978	1981	1980
Number of instructions	208	303	133	31	120
Instruction size (bits)	16-48	16-456	8-32	32	32
Addressing modes	4	22	6	3	5
Number of general purpose registers	16	16	4	138	32
Control memory size	420 Kb	480 Kb		0	0
Cache size	64 Kb	64 Kb		0	

- *Multiple Processors:* This category covers a number of different organizations and objectives.

To this list must now be added one of the most interesting and, potentially, one of the most important innovations: reduced instruction set computer (RISC) architecture. The RISC architecture is a dramatic departure from the historical trend in CPU architecture and challenges the conventional wisdom expressed in words and deeds by most computer architects. An analysis of the RISC architecture brings into focus many of the important issues in computer organization and architecture, and thus is a fitting close to this text.

Most of the work has been on experimental systems, but commercial RISC systems have begun to appear ([OHR85], [MILL85], [GANN85]). Recently, both IBM (with its RT PC) and Hewlett-Packard (with its 900 series) have introduced machines that have both RISC and conventional characteristics [MOKH86]. Although RISC systems have been defined and designed in a variety of ways by different groups, the key elements shared by most (not all) designs are these:

- A limited and simple instruction set.
- A large number of general-purpose registers.
- An emphasis on optimizing the instruction pipeline.

Table 14-1 compares several RISC and non-RISC systems.

We begin this chapter with a brief survey of some results on instruction sets, then examine each of the three topics just listed. This is followed by a description of one of the best-documented RISC designs.

14-1

INSTRUCTION EXECUTION CHARACTERISTICS

One of the most visible forms of evolution associated with computers is that of programming languages. As the cost of hardware has dropped, the relative cost of software has risen. Along with that, a chronic shortage of programmers has driven up software costs in absolute terms. Thus the major cost in the life cycle of a system is software, not hardware. Adding to the cost, and to the inconvenience, is the element of unreliability: it is common for programs, both system and application, to continue to exhibit new bugs after years of operation.

The response from researchers and industry has been to develop ever more powerful and complex high-level programming languages (compare FORTRAN to Ada). These high-level languages (HLL) allow the programmer to express algorithms more concisely, take care of much of the detail, and often support naturally the use of structured programming.

Alas, this solution gave rise to another problem, known as the *semantic gap*, the difference between the operations provided in HLLs and those provided in computer architecture. Symptoms of this gap are alleged to include execution inefficiency, excessive machine program size, and compiler complexity. Designers responded with architectures intended to close this gap. Key features include large instruction sets, dozens of addressing modes, and various HLL statements implemented in hardware. An example of the latter is the CASE machine instruction on the VAX-11. Such complex instruction sets are intended to

- Ease the task of the compiler writer.
- Improve execution efficiency, since complex sequences of operations can be implemented in microcode.
- Provide support for even more complex and sophisticated HLLs.

Meanwhile, a number of studies have been done over the years to determine the characteristics and patterns of execution of machine instructions generated from HLL programs. The results of these studies inspired some researchers to look for an altogether different approach: namely, to make the architecture that supports the HLL simpler, rather than more complex.

So, to understand the line of reasoning of the RISC advocates, we begin with a brief review of instruction execution characteristics. The aspects of computation of interest are

- *Operations Performed:* These determine the functions to be performed by the CPU and its interaction with memory.
- *Operands Used:* The types of operands and the frequency of their use determine the memory organization for storing them and the addressing modes for accessing them.
- *Execution Sequencing:* This determines the control and pipeline organization.

In the remainder of this section, we summarize the results of a number of studies of high-level-language programs. All of the results are based on dynamic measurements. That is, measurements are collected by executing the program and counting the number of times some feature has appeared or a particular property has held true. In contrast, static measurements merely perform these counts on the source text of a program. They give no useful information on performance, because they are not weighted relative to the number of times each statement is executed.

Operations

A variety of studies have been made to analyze the behavior of HLL programs. Table 14-2 includes key results from the following studies. The earliest study of

**TABLE 14-2   Relative Dynamic Frequency
of High-Level Language Operations**

Study	[HUCK83]	[KNUT71]	[PATT82a]		[TANE78]
Language	Pascal	FORTRAN	Pascal	C	SAL
Workload	Scientific	Student	System	System	System
Assign	74	67	45	38	42
Loop	4	3	5	3	4
Call	1	3	15	12	12
IF	20	11	29	43	36
GOTO	2	9	—	3	—
Other		7	6	1	6

programming language, performed by Knuth [KNUT71], examined a collection of FORTRAN programs used as student exercises. Dynamic measurements showed that two-thirds of all statements were assignment and, of these, one-third were of the type A = B. The remainder seldom had more than one operator. Tanenbaum [TANE78] published measurements of HLL constructs, collected from over 300 procedures used in operating-system programs and written in a language that supports structured programming (SAL). Patterson and Sequin [PATT82a], two of the key figures in the Berkeley RISC project, analyzed a set of measurements taken in the early stages of the RISC effort. Measurements were collected from compilers and from programs for typesetting, CAD, sorting, and file comparison. The programming languages C and Pascal were studied. Huck [HUCK83] analyzed four programs intended to represent a mix of general-purpose scientific computing, including fast Fourier transform and integration of systems of differential equations.

There is quite good agreement in the results of this mixture of languages and applications. Assignment statements predominate, suggesting that the simple movement of data is of high importance. There is also a preponderance of conditional statements (IF, LOOP). These statements are implemented in machine language with some sort of compare and branch instruction. This suggests that the sequence control mechanism of the instruction set is important.

These results are instructive to the machine instruction set designer, indicating which types of statements occur most often and therefore should be supported in an "optimal" fashion. However, these results do not reveal which statements use the most time in the execution of a typical program. That is, given a compiled machine language program, which statements in the source language cause the execution of the most machine-language instructions?

To get at this underlying phenomenon, the Patterson programs [PATT82a] were compiled on the VAX, PDP-11, and Motorola 68000 to determine the average number of machine instructions and memory references per statement type. By multiplying the frequency of occurrence of each statement type by these averages, Table 14-3 is obtained. Columns 2 and 3 provide surrogate measures of the actual time spent executing the various statement types. The results suggest that the procedure call/return is the most time-consuming operation in typical HLL programs.

The reader should be clear on the significance of Table 14-3. This table indicates the relative significance of various statement types in an HLL, when that HLL is compiled for a typical contemporary instruction set architecture. Some other architecture could conceivably produce different results. However, this study pro-

TABLE 14-3 Weighted Relative Dynamic Frequency of HLL Operations

	Dynamic Occurence		Machine-Instruction Weighted		Memory-Reference Weighted	
	Pascal	C	Pascal	C	Pascal	C
ASSIGN	45	38	13	13	14	15
LOOP	5	3	42	32	33	26
CALL	15	12	31	33	44	45
IF	29	43	11	21	7	13
GOTO	—	3	—	—	—	—
OTHER	6	1	3	1	2	1

Source: [PATT82a]

duces results that are representative for contemporary complex instruction set computer (CISC) architectures. Thus, they can provide guidance to those looking for more efficient ways to support HLLs.

Operands

Much less work has been done on the occurrence of types of operands, despite the importance of this topic. There are several aspects that are significant.

The Patterson study already referenced [PATT82a] also looked at the dynamic frequency of occurrence of classes of variables (Table 14-4). The results, consistent between Pascal and C programs, show that the majority of references are to simple scalar variables. Further, over 80% of the scalars were local (to the procedure) variables. In addition, references to arrays/structures require a previous reference to their index or pointer, which again is usually a local scalar. Thus, there is a preponderance of references to scalars, and these are highly localized.

The Patterson study examined the dynamic behavior of HLL programs, independent of the underlying architecture. As discussed before, it is necessary to deal with actual architectures to examine program behavior more deeply. One study, [LUND77], examined DEC-10 instructions dynamically and found that each instruction on the average references 0.5 operands in memory and 1.4 registers. Similar results are reported in [HUCK83] for C, Pascal, and FORTRAN programs on S/370, PDP-11, and VAX-11. Of course, these figures depend highly on both the architecture and the compiler, but they do illustrate the frequency of operand accessing.

These latter studies suggest the importance of an architecture that lends itself to fast operand accessing, since this operation is performed so frequently. The Pat-

TABLE 14-4 Dynamic Percentage of Operands

	Pascal	C	Average
Integer Constant	16	23	20
Scalar Variable	58	53	55
Array/Structure	26	24	25

TABLE 14-5   Procedure Arguments and Local Scalar Variables

Percentage of Executed Procedure Calls With	Compiler, Interpreter and Typesetter	Small Nonnumeric Programs
> 3 arguments	0-7%	0-5%
> 5 arguments	0-3%	0%
> 8 words of arguments and local scalars	1-20%	0-6%
> 12 words of arguments and local scalars	1-6%	0-3%

terson study suggests that a prime candidate for optimization is the mechanism for storing and accessing local scalar variables.

Procedure Calls

We have seen that procedure calls and returns are an important aspect of HLL programs. The evidence (Table 14-3) suggests that these are the most time-consuming operations in compiled HLL programs. Thus, it will be profitable to consider ways of implementing these operations efficiently. Two aspects are significant: the number of parameters and variables that a procedure deals with, and the depth of nesting.

In Tanenbaum's study [TANE78], he found that 98% of dynamically called procedures were passed fewer than six arguments, and that 92% of them used fewer than six local scalar variables. Similar results were reported by the Berkeley RISC team [KATE83], as shown in Table 14-5. These results show that the number of words required per procedure activation is not large. The studies reported earlier indicated that a high proportion of operand references are to local scalar variables. These studies show that those references are in fact confined to relatively few variables.

The same Berkeley group also looked at the pattern of procedure calls and returns in HLL programs. They found that it is rare to have a long uninterrupted sequence of procedure calls followed by the corresponding sequence of returns. Rather, they found that a program remains confined to a rather narrow window of procedure-invocation depth. This is illustrated in Figure 14-1. The graph illustrates call-return behavior. Each call is represented by the line moving down and to the right, and each return by the line moving up and to the right. In the figure, a *window* with depth equal to 5 is defined. Only a sequence of calls and returns with a net movement of 6 in either direction causes the window to move. As can be seen, the executing program can remain within this window for quite long periods of time. The Berkeley results (for C and Pascal) showed that a window of depth 8 will need to shift only on less than 1% of the calls or returns [TAMI83]. These results reinforce the conclusion that operand references are highly localized.

Implications

A number of groups have looked at results such as those just reported and have concluded that the attempt to make the instruction set architecture close to HLLs

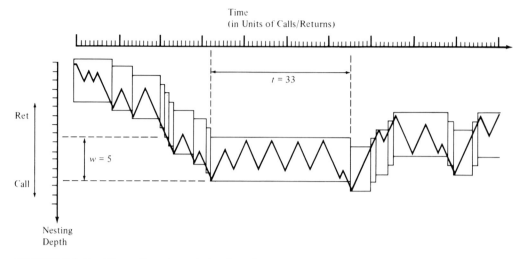

FIGURE 14-1.   The call—return behavior of programs.

is not the most effective design strategy. Rather, the HLLs can best be supported by optimizing performance of the most time-consuming features of typical HLL programs.

Generalizing from the work of a number of researchers, three elements emerge that, by and large, characterize RISC architectures. First, use a large number of registers. This is intended to optimize operand referencing. The studies just discussed show that there are several references per HLL instruction, and that there is a high proportion of move (assignment) statements. This, coupled with the locality and predominance of scalar references, suggests that performance can be improved by reducing memory references at the expense of more register references. Because of the locality of these references, an expanded register set seems practical.

Second, careful attention needs to be paid to the design of instruction pipelines. Because of the high proportion of conditional branch and procedure call instructions, a straightforward instruction pipeline will be inefficient. This manifests itself as a high proportion of instructions that are pre-fetched but never executed.

Finally, a simplified (reduced) instruction set is indicated. This point is not as obvious as the others, but should become clearer in the ensuing discussion. In addition, we will see that the desire to implement an entire CPU on a single chip suggests a reduced instruction set solution.

14-2

THE USE OF A LARGE REGISTER FILE

The results summarized in Section 14-1 point out the desirability of quick access to operands. We have seen that there is a large proportion of assignment statements in HLL programs, and many of these are of the simple form A = B. Also, there are a significant number of operand accesses per HLL statement. If we couple these results with the fact that most accesses are to local scalars, heavy reliance on register storage is suggested.

The reason that register storage is indicated is that it is the fastest available storage device, faster than both main memory and cache. The register file is physically small, generally on the same chip as the ALU and control unit, and employs much shorter addresses than addresses for cache and memory. Thus a strategy is needed that will allow the most frequently accessed operands to be kept in registers and to minimize register-memory operations.

Two basic approaches are possible, one based on software and the other on hardware. The software approach is to rely on the compiler to maximize register usage. The compiler will attempt to allocate registers to those variables that will be used the most in a given time period. This approach requires the use of sophisticated program-analysis algorithms. The hardware approach is simply to use more registers so that more variables can be held in registers for longer periods of time.

In this section, we will discuss the hardware approach. This approach has been pioneered by the Berkeley RISC group [PATT82a] and is used in the first commercial RISC product, the Pyramid [RAGA83].

Register Windows

On the face of it, the use of a large set of registers should decrease the need to access memory. The design task is to organize the registers in such a fashion that this goal is realized.

Since most operand references are to local scalars, the obvious approach is to store these in registers, with perhaps a few registers reserved for global variables. The problem is that the definition of *local* changes with each procedure call and return, operations that occur frequently. On every call, local variables must be saved from the registers into memory, so that the registers can be reused by the called program. Furthermore, parameters must be passed. On return, the variables of the parent program must be restored (loaded back into registers) and results must be passed back to the parent program.

The solution is based on two other results reported in Section 14-1. First, a typical procedure employs only a few passed parameters and local variables. Second, the depth of procedure activation fluctuates within a relatively narrow range (Figure 14-1). To exploit these properties, multiple small sets of registers are used, each assigned to a different procedure. A procedure call automatically switches the CPU to use a different fixed-size window of registers, rather than saving registers in memory. Windows for adjacent procedures are overlapped to allow parameter passing.

The concept is illustrated in Figure 14-2. At any time, only one window of registers is visible and is addressable as if it were the only set of registers (e.g., address 0 through N − 1). The window is divided into three fixed-size areas. Parameter registers hold parameters passed down from the procedure that called the current procedure and results to be passed back up. Local registers are used for local variables, as assigned by the compiler. Temporary registers are used to exchange parameters and results with the next lower level (procedure called by current procedure). The temporary registers at one level are physically the same as the parameter registers at the next lower level. This overlap permits parameters to be passed without the actual movement of data.

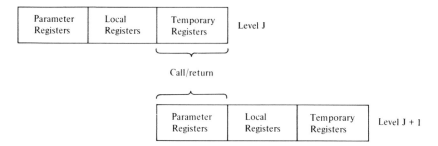

FIGURE 14-2. Overlapping register windows.

To handle any possible pattern of calls and returns, the number of register windows would have to be unbounded. Instead, the register windows can be used to hold the few most recent procedure activations. Older activations must be saved in memory and later restored when the nesting depth decreases. Thus, the actual organization of the register file is as a circular buffer of overlapping windows.

This organization is shown in Figure 14-3, which depicts a circular buffer of six windows. The buffer is filled to a depth of 4 (A called B; B called C; C called D) with procedure D active. The current-window pointer (CWP) points to the window

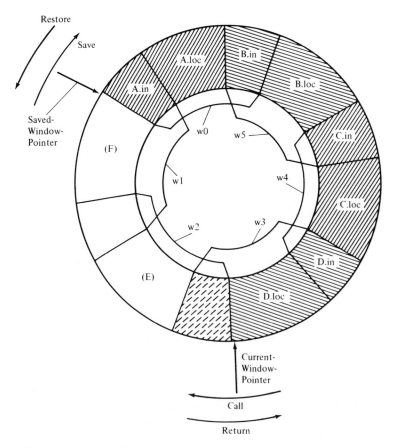

FIGURE 14-3. Circular-buffer organization of overlapped windows.

of the currently active procedure. Register references by a machine instruction are offset by this pointer to determine the actual physical register. The saved-window pointer identifies the window most recently saved in memory. If procedure D now calls procedure E, arguments for E are placed in D's temporary registers (the overlap between w3 and w2) and the CWP is advanced by one window.

If procedure E then makes a call to procedure F, the call cannot be made with the current status of the buffer. This is because F's window overlaps A's window. If F begins to load its temporary registers, preparatory to a call, it will overwrite the parameter registers of A (A.In). Thus when CWP is incremented (modulo 6) so that it becomes equal to SWP, an interrupt occurs and A's window is saved. Only the first two portions (A.In and A.loc) need be saved. Then the SWP is incremented and the call to F proceeds. A similar interrupt can occur on returns. For example, subsequent to the activation of F, when B returns to A, CWP is decremented and becomes equal to SWP. This causes an interrupt that results in the restoral of A's window.

From the preceding, it can be seen that an N-window register file can hold only $N - 1$ procedure activations. The value of N need not be large. As was mentioned earlier, one study [TAMI83] found that, with eight windows, a save or restore is needed on only 1% of the calls or returns. The Berkeley RISC computers use 8 windows of 16 registers each. The Pyramid computer employs 16 windows of 32 registers each.

Global Variables

The window scheme just described provides an efficient organization for storing local scalar variables in registers. However, this scheme does not address the need to store global variables, those accessed by more than one procedure (e.g., COMMON variables in FORTRAN). Two options suggest themselves. First, variables declared as global in an HLL can be assigned memory locations by the compiler, and all machine instructions that reference these variables will use memory-reference operands. This is straightforward, from both the hardware and software (compiler) points of view. However, for frequently-accessed global variables, this scheme is inefficient.

An alternative is to incorporate a set of global registers in the CPU. These registers would be fixed in number and available to all procedures. A unified numbering scheme can be used to simplify the instruction format. For example, references to registers 0 through 7 could refer to unique global registers, and references to registers 8 through 31 could be offset to refer to physical registers in the current window. Thus, there is an increased hardware burden to accommodate the split in register addressing. In addition, the compiler must decide which global variables should be assigned to registers.

Large Register File Versus Cache

The register file, organized into windows, acts as a small, fast buffer for holding a subset of all variables that are likely to be used the most heavily. From this point of view, the register file acts much like a cache memory. The question therefore arises as to whether it would be simpler and better to use a cache and a small traditional register file.

TABLE 14-6 Characteristics of Large-Register-File and Cache Organizations

Large Register File	Cache
All local scalars	Recently-used local scalars
Individual variables	Blocks of memory
Compiler-assigned global variables	Recently-used global variables
Save/Restore based on procedure nesting depth	Save/Restore based on cache replacement algorithm
Register addressing	Memory addressing

Table 14-6 compares characteristics of the two approaches. The window-based register file holds all of the local scalar variables (except in the rare case of window overflow) of the most recent $N - 1$ procedure activations. The cache holds a selection of recently used scalar variables. The register file should save time, since all local scalar variables are retained. On the other hand, the cache may make more efficient use of space, since it is reacting to the situation dynamically. Furthermore, caches generally treat all memory references alike, including instructions and other types of data. Thus, savings in these other areas are possible with a cache and not a register file.

A register file may make inefficient use of space, since not all procedures will need the full window space allotted to them. On the other hand, the cache suffers from another sort of inefficiency: Data are read in in blocks. Whereas the register file contains only those variables in use, the cache reads in a block of data, some or much of which will not be used.

The cache is capable of handling global as well as local variables. There are usually many global scalars, but only a few of them are heavily used [KATE83]. A cache will dynamically discover these variables and hold them. If the window-based register file is supplemented with global registers, it too can hold some global scalars. However, it is difficult for a compiler to determine which globals will be heavily used.

With the register file, the movement of data between registers and memory is determined by the procedure nesting depth. Since this depth usually fluctuates within a narrow range, the use of memory is relatively infrequent. Most cache memories are set-associative with a small set size. Thus, there is the danger that other data or instructions will overwrite frequently used variables.

Based on the discussion so far, the choice between a large window-based register file and a cache is not clear cut. There is one characteristic, however, in which the register approach is clearly superior and which suggests that a cache-based system will be noticeably slower. This distinction shows up in the amount of addressing overhead experienced by the two approaches.

Figure 14-4 illustrates the difference. To reference a local scalar in a window-based register file, a "virtual" register number and a window number are used. These can pass through a relatively simple decoder to select one of the physical registers. To reference a memory location in cache, a full-width memory address must be generated. The complexity of this operation depends on the addressing mode. In a set-associative cache, a portion of the address is used to read a number of words and tags equal to the set size. Another portion of the address is compared to the tags, and one of the words that were read is selected. It should be clear that

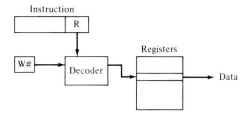

(a) Window-Based Register File

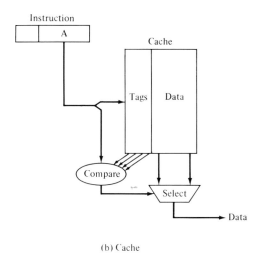

(b) Cache

FIGURE 14-4. Referencing a local scalar.

even if the cache is as fast as the register file, the access time will be considerably longer. Thus, from the point of view of performance, the window-based register file is superior for local scalars. Further performance improvement could be achieved by the addition of a cache for instructions only.

REDUCED INSTRUCTION SET ARCHITECTURE

In this section, we look at some of the general characteristics of and the motivation for a reduced instruction set architecture. Specific examples will be seen later in this chapter. We begin with a discussion of motivations for contemporary complex instruction set architectures.

Why CISC

We hve noted the trend to richer instruction sets, which include a larger number of instructions and more-complex instructions. Two principal reasons have motivated this trend: a desire to simplify compilers and a desire to improve performance. Underlying both of these reasons was the shift to high-level languages (HLL) on the part of programmers; architects attempted to design machines that provided better support for HLLs.

It is not the intent of this chapter to say that the CISC designers took the wrong direction. RISC technology is very new and so the CISC versus RISC debate cannot now be settled. Indeed, because technology continues to evolve and because architectures exist along a spectrum rather than in two neat categories, a black-and-white assessment is unlikely ever to emerge. Thus, the comments that follow are simply meant to point out some of the potential pitfalls in the CISC approach and to provide some understanding of the motivation of the RISC adherents.

The first of the reasons cited, compiler simplification, seems obvious. The task of the compiler writer is to generate a sequence of machine instructions for each HLL statement. If there are machine instructions that resemble HLL statements, this task is simplified. This reasoning has been disputed by the RISC researchers ([HENN82], [RADI82], [PATT82b]). They have found that complex machine instructions are often hard to exploit since the compiler must find those cases that exactly fit the construct. The task of optimizing the generated code to minimize code size, reduce instruction execution count, and enhance pipelining is much more difficult with a complex instruction set. As evidence of this, studies cited earlier in this chapter indicate that most of the instructions in a compiled program are the relatively simple ones.

The other major reason cited is the expectation that a CISC will yield smaller, faster programs. Let us examine both aspects of this assertion: that programs will be smaller and that they will execute faster.

There are two advantages to smaller programs. First, because the program takes up less memory, there is a savings in that resource. With memory today being so inexpensive, this potential advantage is no longer compelling. More importantly, smaller programs should improve performance, and this will happen in two ways. First, fewer instructions means fewer instruction bytes to be fetched. And second, in a paging environment, smaller programs occupy fewer pages, reducing page faults.

The problem with this line of reasoning is that it is far from certain that a CISC program will be smaller than a corresponding RISC program. In many cases, the CISC program, expressed in symbolic machine language, may be *shorter* (i.e., fewer instructions), but the number of bits of memory occupied may not be noticeably *smaller*. Table 14-7 shows results from three studies that compared the size of compiled C programs on a variety of machines, including RISC I, which has a reduced instruction set architecture. Note that there is little or no savings using a CISC over a RISC. It is also interesting to note that the VAX-11, which has a much more complex instruction set than the PDP-11, achieves very little

TABLE 14-7 Code Size Relative to RISC I

	[PATT82a] 11 C Programs	[KATE83] 12 C Programs	[HEAT84] 5 C Programs
RISC I	1.0	1.0	1.0
VAX-11/780	0.8	0.67	
M68000	0.9		0.9
Z8002	1.2		1.12
PDP-11/70	0.9	0.71	

savings over the latter. These results were confirmed by IBM researchers [RADI82], who found that the IBM 801 (a RISC) produced code that was 0.9 times the size of code on an IBM S/370. The study used a set of PL/I programs.

There are several reasons for these rather surprising results. We have already noted that compilers on CISCs tend to favor simpler instructions, so that the conciseness of the complex instructions seldom comes into play. Also, since there are more instructions on a CISC, longer op codes are required, producing longer instructions. Finally, RISCs tend to emphasize register rather than memory references, and the former require fewer bits. An example of this last effect is discussed presently (see Figure 14-5).

So, the expectation that a CISC will produce smaller programs, with the attendant advantages, may not be realized. The second motivating factor for increasingly complex instruction sets was that instruction execution would be faster. It seems to make sense that a complex HLL operation will execute more quickly as a single machine instruction rather than as a series of more-primitive instructions. However, because of the bias towards the use of those simpler instructions, this may not be so. The entire control unit must be made more complex, and/or the microprogram control store must be made larger, to accommodate a richer instruction set. Either factor increases the execution time of the simple instructions.

In fact, some researchers have found that the speed up in the execution of complex functions is due not so much to the power of the complex machine instructions as to their residence in high-speed control store [RADI82]. In effect, the control store acts as an instruction cache. Thus, the hardware architect is in the position of trying to determine which subroutines or functions will be used most frequently and assigning those to the control store by implementing them in microcode. The results have been less than encouraging. Thus on S/370 systems, instructions such as Translate and Extended-Precision-Floating-Point-Divide reside

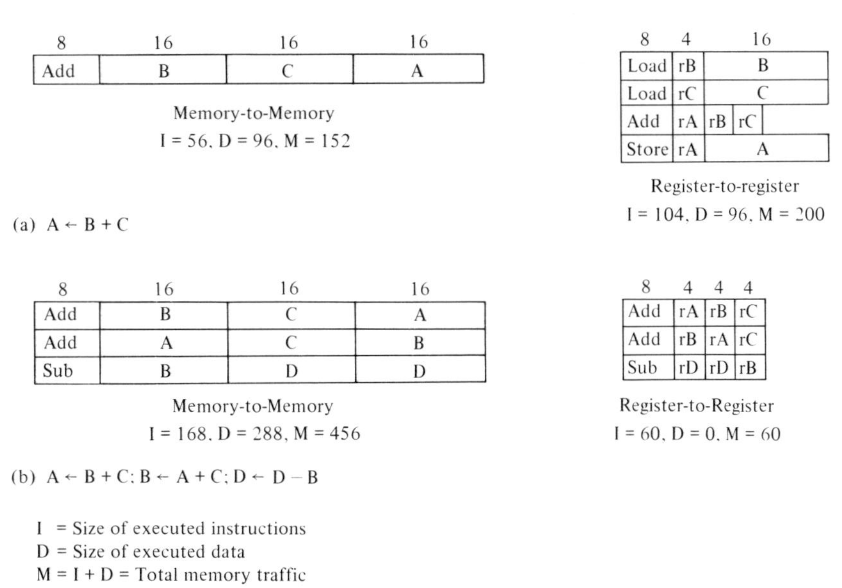

FIGURE 14-5. Two comparisons of register-to-register and memory-to-memory approaches.

in high-speed storage, while the sequence involved in setting up procedure calls or initiating an interrupt handler are in slower main memory.

Thus, it is far from clear that the trend to increasingly complex instruction sets is appropriate. This has led a number of groups to pursue the opposite path.

Characteristics of Reduced Instruction Set Architectures

Although a variety of different approaches to reduced instruction set architecture have been taken, certain characteristics are common to all of them. These characteristics are listed in Table 14-8 and described here. Specific examples are explored later in this chapter.

The first characteristic listed in Table 14-8 is that there is one machine instruction per machine cycle. A *machine cycle* is defined to be the time it takes to fetch two operands from registers, perform an ALU operation, and store the result in a register. Thus, RISC machine instructions should be no more complicated, than, and execute about as fast as, microinstructions on CISC machines. With simple, one-cycle instructions, there is little or no need for microcode; the machine instructions can be hardwired. Such instructions should execute faster than comparable machine instructions on other machines, since it is not necessary to access a microprogram control store during instruction execution.

A second characteristic is that most operations should be register-to-register, with only simple LOAD and STORE operations accessing memory. This design feature simplifies the instruction set and therefore the control unit. For example, a RISC instruction set may include only one or two ADD instructions (e.g., integer add, add with carry); the VAX-11 has 25 different ADD instructions. Another benefit is that such an architecture encourages the optimization of register use, so that frequently accessed operands remain in high-speed storage.

This emphasis on register-to-register operations is unique to RISC designs. Other contemporary machines provide such instructions but also include memory-to-memory and mixed register/memory operations. Attempts to compare these approaches were made in the 1970s, before the appearance of RISCs. Figure 14-5a illustrates the approach taken. Hypothetical architectures were evaluated on program size and the number of bits of memory traffic. Results such as this one led one researcher to suggest that future architectures should contain no registers at all [MYER78]. One wonders what he would have thought, at the time, of the RISC machine marketed by Pyramid, which contains no less than 528 registers!

What was missing from those studies was a recognition of the frequent access to a small number of local scalars and that, with a large bank of registers or an optimizing compiler, most operands could be kept in registers for long periods of time. Thus Figure 14-5b may be a fairer comparison.

Returning to Table 14-8, a third characteristic is the use of simple addressing modes. Almost all instructions use simple register addressing. Several additional modes, such as displacement and PC-relative, may be included. Other, more-complex modes can be synthesized in software from the simple ones. Again, this design feature simplifies the instruction set and the control unit.

A final common characteristic is the use of simple instruction formats. Generally, only one or a few formats are used. Instruction length is fixed and aligned on word

TABLE 14-8 Characteristics of Reduced Instruction Set Architectures

One Instruction Per Cycle
Register-to-Register Operations
Simple Address Modes
Simple Instruction Formats

boundaries. Field locations, especially the op code, are fixed. This design feature has a number of benefits. With fixed fields, op code decoding and register operand accessing can occur simultaneously. Simplified formats simplify the control unit. Instruction fetching is optimized since word-length units are fetched. This also means that a single instruction does not cross page boundaries.

Taken together, these characteristics can be assessed to determine the potential benefits of the RISC approach. These benefits fall into two main categories: those related to performance and those related to VLSI implementation.

With respect to performance, a certain amount of "circumstantial evidence" can be presented. First, more-effective optimizing compilers can be developed. With more-primitive instructions, there are more opportunities for moving functions out of loops, reorganizing code for efficiency, maximizing register utilization, and so forth. It is even possible to compute parts of complex instructions at compile time. For example, the S/370 Move Characters (MVC) instruction moves a string of characters from one location to another. Each time it is executed, the move will depend on the length of the string, whether and in which direction the locations overlap, and what the alignment characteristics are. In most cases, these will all be known at compile time. Thus the compiler could produce an optimized sequence of primitive instructions for this function.

A second point, already noted, is that most instructions generated by a compiler are relatively simple anyway. It would seem reasonable that a control unit built specifically for those instructions and using little or no microcode could execute them faster than a comparable CISC.

A third point relates to the use of instruction pipelining. RISC researchers feel that the instruction pipelining technique can be applied much more effectively with a reduced instruction set. We examine this point in some detail presently.

A final, and somewhat less significant point, is that RISC programs should be more responsive to interrupts since interrupts are checked between rather elementary operations. Architectures with complex instructions either restrict interrupts to instruction boundaries or must define specific interruptible points and implement mechanisms for restarting an instruction.

The case for improved performance for a reduced instruction set architecture is far from proven. A number of studies have been done but not on machines of comparable technology and power. Further, most studies have not attempted to separate the effects of a reduced instruction set and the effects of a large register file. The "circumstantial evidence," however, is suggestive.

The second area of potential benefit, which is more clear-cut, relates to VLSI implementation. When VLSI is used, the design and implementation of the CPU are fundamentally changed. Traditional CPUs, such as the IBM S/370 and the VAX-11, consist of one or more printed circuit boards containing standardized SSI and MSI packages. With the advent of LSI and VLSI, it is possible to put an entire

TABLE 14-9 Design and Layout Effort For Some Microprocessors

CPU	Transistors (thousands)	Design (Person-Months)	Layout (Person-Months)
RISC I	44	15	12
RISC II	41	18	12
M68000	68	100	70
Z8000	18	60	70
Intel iAPx-432	110	170	90

CPU on a single chip. For a single-chip CPU, there are two motivations for following a RISC strategy. First, there is the issue of performance. On-chip delays are of much shorter duration than inter-chip delays. Thus it makes sense to devote scarce chip real estate to those activities that occur frequently. We have seen that simple instructions and access to local scalars are, in fact, the most frequent activities. The Berkeley RISC chips were designed with this consideration in mind. Whereas a typical single-chip microprocessor dedicates about half of its area to the microcode control store, the RISC I chip devotes only about 6% of its area to the control unit [SHER84].

A second VLSI-related issue is design-and-implementation time. A VLSI processor is difficult to develop. Instead of relying on available SSI/MSI parts, the designer must perform circuit design, layout, and modeling at the device level. With a reduced instruction set architecture, this process is far easier, as evidenced by Table 14-9 [FITZ81]. If, in addition, the performance of the RISC chip is equivalent to comparable CISC microprocessors, then the advantages of the RISC approach become evident.

14-4

RISC PIPELINING

Pipelining with Regular Instructions

As we discussed in Section 10-4, instruction pipelining is often used to enhance performance. Let us reconsider this in the context of a RISC architecture. Most instructions are register-to-register, and an instruction cycle has the following two phases:

- I: Instruction fetch.
- E: Execute. Performs an ALU operation with register input and output.

For load and store operations, three phases are required:

- I: Instruction fetch.
- E: Execute. Calculates memory address
- D: Memory. Register-to-memory or memory-to-register operation.

Figure 14-6 depicts the timing of a sequence of instructions using no pipelining. Clearly, this is a wasteful process. Even very simple pipelining can substantially improve performance. Figure 14-7 shows a two-way pipelining scheme, in which the I and E phases of two different instructions are performed simultaneously. This

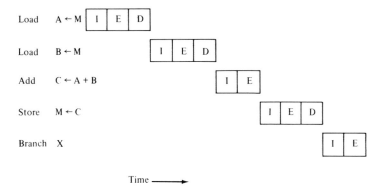

FIGURE 14-6. Timing of sequential execution.

scheme can yield up to twice the execution rate of a serial scheme. Two problems prevent the maximum speed-up from being achieved. First, we assume that a single-port memory is used and that only one memory access is possible per phase. This requires the insertion of a wait state in some instructions. Second, a branch instruction interrupts the sequential flow of execution. To accommodate this with minimum circuitry, a NOOP instruction can be inserted into the instruction stream by the compiler or assembler.

Pipelining can be improved further by permitting two memory accesses per phase. This yields the sequence shown in Figure 14-8. Now, up to three instructions can be overlapped, and the improvement is as much as a factor of three. Again, branch instructions cause the speed-up to fall short of the maximum possible. Also, note that data dependencies have an effect. If an instruction needs an operand that is altered by the preceding instruction, a delay is required. Again, this can be accomplished by a NOOP.

The pipelining discussed so far works best if the three phases are of approximately equal duration. Because the E phase usually involves an ALU operation, it may be longer. In this case, we can divide into two subphases:

- E_1: Register file read
- E_2: ALU operation and register write.

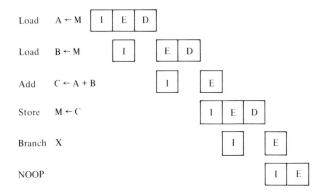

FIGURE 14-7. Two-way pipelined timing.

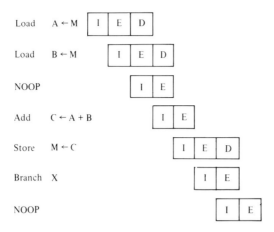

FIGURE 14-8. Three-way pipelined timing.

Because of the simplicity and regularity of the instruction set, the design of the phasing into three or four phases is easily accomplished. Figure 14-9 shows the result with a four-way pipeline. Up to four instructions at a time can be under way, and the maximum potential speed-up is a factor of four. Note again the use of NOOPs to account for data and branch delays.

Optimization of Pipelining

Because of the simple and regular nature of RISC instructions, pipelining schemes can be efficiently employed. There are few variations in instruction execution duration, and the pipeline can be tailored to reflect this. However, we have seen that data and branch dependencies reduce the overall execution rate.

To compensate for these dependencies, code reorganization techniques have been developed. First, let us consider branching instructions. *Delayed branch*, a way of

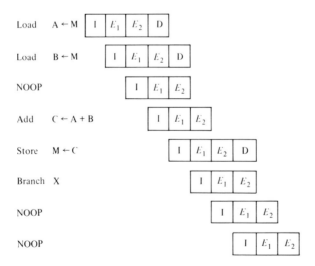

FIGURE 14-9. Four-way pipelined timing.

TABLE 14-10   Normal And Delayed Branch

Address	Normal Branch		Delayed Branch		Optimized Delayed Branch	
100	LOAD	X,A	LOAD	X,A	LOAD	X,A
101	ADD	1,A	ADD	1,A	JUMP	105
102	JUMP	105	JUMP	106	ADD	1,A
103	ADD	A,B	NOOP		ADD	A,B
104	SUB	C,B	ADD	A,B	SUB	C,B
105	STORE	A,Z	SUB	C,B	STORE	A,Z
106			STORE	A,Z		

increasing the efficiency of the pipeline, makes use of a branch that does not take effect until after the following instruction. This strange procedure is illustrated in Table 14-10. In the first column, we see a normal symbolic instruction machine-language program. After 102 is executed, the next instruction to be executed is 105. In order to regularize the pipeline, a NOOP is inserted after this branch. However, increased performance is achieved if the instructions at 101 and 102 are interchanged. Figure 14-10 shows the result. The JUMP instruction is fetched before the ADD instruction. Note, however, that the ADD instruction is fetched before the execution of the JUMP instruction has a chance to alter the program counter. Thus, the original semantics of the program are retained.

This interchange of instructions will work successfully for unconditional branches, calls, and returns. For conditional branches, this procedure cannot be blindly applied. If the condition that is tested for the branch can be altered by the immediately preceding instruction, then the compiler must refrain from doing the interchange

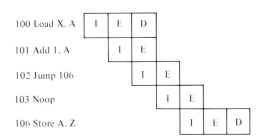

(a) Inserted NOOP

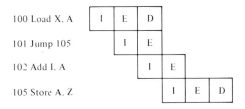

(b) Reversed Instructions

FIGURE 14-10.   Use of the delayed branch.

and instead insert a NOOP. The experience with both the Berkeley RISC and IBM 801 systems is that the majority of conditional branch instructions can be optimized in this fashion ([PATT82a], [RADI82]).

A similar sort of tactic, called the delayed load, can be used on LOAD instructions. On LOAD instructions, the register that is to be the target of the load is locked by the CPU. The CPU then continues execution of the instruction stream until it reaches an instruction requiring that register, at which point it idles until the load is complete. If the compiler can rearrange instructions so that useful work can be done while the load is in the pipeline, efficiency is increased.

14-5

BERKELEY RISC

The best-documented RISC project is that conducted at the University of California at Berkeley. Two similar machines, RISC I and RISC II, were produced. The Berkeley RISC architecture was the inspiration for a commercially available product, the Pyramid [RAGA83].

Instruction Set

Table 14-11 lists the instructions for the Berkeley RISC computers.

As can be seen, most of the instructions reference only register operands. Register-to-register instructions have three operands and can be expressed in the form

$$Rd \leftarrow R_{S1} \; op \; S2$$

Rd and R_{S1} are register references. S2 can refer either to a register or to a 13-bit immediate operand. Register zero (R_0) is hardwired with the value 0. This form is well suited to typical programs, which have a high proportion of local scalars and constants.

The available ALU operations can be grouped as follows:

- Integer addition (with or without carry)
- Integer subtraction (with or without carry)
- Bitwise Boolean AND, OR, XOR
- Shift left logical, right logical, or right arithmetic

All of these instructions can optionally set the four condition codes (ZERO, NEGATIVE, OVERFLOW, CARRY). Integers are represented in 32-bit 2's-complement form.

Only simple load and store instructions reference memory. There are separate load and store instructions for word (32 bits), halfword, and byte. For the latter two cases, there are instructions for loading these quantities as signed or unsigned numbers. Signed numbers are sign-extended to fill out the 32-bit destination register. Unsigned numbers are padded with 0s.

On the RISC I, the only available addressing mode, other than register, is a displacement mode. That is, the effective address of an operand consists of a displacement from an address contained in a register:

$$EA = (R_{S1}) + S2$$
$$\text{or } EA = (R_{S1}) + (R_{S2})$$

TABLE 14-11 RISC Instruction Set

Instruction	Operands	Comments	
ADD	Rs,S2,Rd	Rd←Rs + S2	integer add
ADDC	Rs,S2,Rd	Rd←Rs + S2 + carry	add with carry
SUB	Rs,S2,Rd	Rd←Rs − S2	integer subtract
SUBC	Rs,S2,Rd	Rd←Rs − S2 − carry	subtract with carry
SUBR	Rs,S2,Rd	Rd←S2 − Rs	integer subtract
SUBCR	Rs,S2,Rd	Rd←S2 − Rs − carry	subtract with carry
AND	Rs,S2,Rd	Rd←Rs | S2	logical and
OR	Rs,S2,Rd	Rd←Rs | S2	logical or
XOR	Rs,S2,Rd	Rd←Rs xor S2	logical exclusive or
SLL	Rs,S2,Rd	Rd←Rs shifted by S2	shift left
SRL	Rs,S2,Rd	Rd←Rs shifted by S2	shift right logical
SRA	Rs,S2,Rd	Rd←Rs shifted by S2	shift right arithmetic
LDXW	(Rx)S2,Rd	Rd←M[Rx + S2]	load word
LDXHU	(Rx)S2,Rd	Rd←M[Rx + S2]	load halfword unsigned
LDXHS	(Rx)S2,Rd	Rd←M[Rx + S2]	load halfword signed
LDXBU	(Rx)S2,Rd	Rd←M[Rx + S2]	load byte unsigned
LDXBS	(Rx)S2,Rd	Rd←M[Rx + S2]	load byte signed
STXW	Rm,(Rx)S2	M[Rx + S2]←Rm	store word
STXH	Rm,(Rx)S2	M[Rx + S2]←Rm	store halfword
STXB	Rm,(Rx)S2	M[Rx + S2]←Rm	store byte
LDRW	S2,Rd	Rd←M[PC + S2]	load word relative
LDRHU	S2,Rd	Rd←M[PC + S2]	load halfword unsigned relative
LDRHS	S2,Rd	Rd←M[PC + S2]	load halfword signed relative
LDRBU	S2,Rd	Rd←M[PC + S2]	load byte unsigned relative
LDRBS	S2,Rd	Rd←M[PC + S2]	load byte signed relative
STRW	Rm,S2	M[PC + S2]←Rm	store word
STRH	Rm,S2	M[PC + S2]←Rm	store halfword
STRB	Rm,S2	M[PC + S2]←Rm	store byte
JMP	COND,S2(Rx)	pc←Rx + S2	conditional jump
JMPR	COND,Y	pc←pc + Y	conditional relative
CALL	Rd,S2(Rx)	Rd←pc, next	call
		pc←Rx + S2, CWP←CWP − 1	and change window
CALLR	Rd,Y	Rd←pc, next	call relative
		pc←pc + Y, CWP←CWP − 1	and change window
RET	Rm,S2	pc←Rm + S2, CWP←CWP + 1	return and change window
CALLINT	Rd	Rd←last pc; next CWP←CWP − 1	disable interrupts
RETINT	Rm,S2	pc←Rm + S2; next CWP←CWP + 1	enable interrupts
LDHI	Rd,Y	Rd<31:13>←Y; Rd<12:0>←0	load immediate high
GTLPC	Rd	Rd←last pc	to restart delayed jump
GETPSW	Rd	Rd←PSW	load status word
PUTPSW	Rm	PSW←Rm	set status word

according as the second operand is immediate or a register reference. To perform a load or store, an extra phase is added to the instruction cycle. During the second phase, the address is calculated using the ALU; the load or store occurs in a third phase. This single addressing mode is quite versatile and can be used to synthesize other addressing modes, as indicated in Table 14-12.

The RISC II includes an additional version of each load and store instruction

TABLE 14-12 Synthesizing Other Addressing Modes With RISC Addressing Modes

Mode	Algorithm	RISC Equivalent	Instruction Type
Immediate	operand = A	S2	Register–Register
Direct	EA = A	$R_0 + S_2$	Load, Store
Register	EA = R	Rs_1, Rs_2	Register–Register
Register Indirect	EA = (R)	$Rs_1 + 0$	Load, Store
Displacement	EA = (R) + A	$Rs_1 + S_2$	Load, Store

using relative addressing:

$$EA = (PC) + S2$$

The remaining instructions include control-transfer instructions and some miscellaneous instruction. The control-transfer instructions include conditional jump, call, and conditional return instructions. Both forms of RISC II addressing can be used.

Instruction Format

One of the major factors in the complexity of instruction processing is instruction decoding, especially the task of extracting the various instruction fields. To minimize this chore, the ideal instruction set would use a single fixed-length format with fixed field positions. The RISC instruction set comes close to this goal.

All RISC instructions are a single word (32 bits) in length (Figure 14-11). The first 7 bits are the op code, allowing up to 128 different op codes. RISC I and RISC II use only 31 and 39 codes, respectively. The SCC bit indicates whether to set the condition codes. The DEST field usually contains a 5-bit destination register reference. For conditional branch instructions, 4 bits of the field designate which condition or conditions are to be tested.

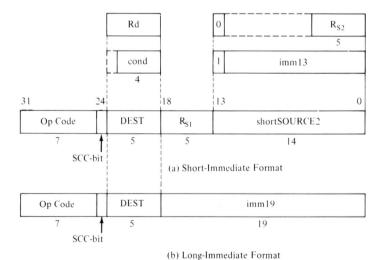

(a) Short-Immediate Format

(b) Long-Immediate Format

FIGURE 14-11. RISC instruction formats.

The remaining 19 bits designate one or two operands, depending on op code. A single 19-bit 2's-complement immediate operand is used for all PC-relative instructions. Otherwise the first of the two operands is a register reference. The second operand is either a register reference or a 13-bit 2's-complement immediate operand.

Register File

The RISC register file contains 138 registers. Physical registers 0 through 9 are global registers shared by all procedures. The remaining registers are grouped into eight windows. Each process sees logical registers 0 through 31 (Figure 14-12). Logical registers 26 through 31 are shared with the calling (parent) procedure, and logical registers 10 through 15 are shared with any called (child) procedure. These two portions overlap with other windows.

Pipelining

The RISC I processor uses a two-stage pipeline, dividing each instruction into fetch and execute states. RISC II uses three stages. The second stage performs ALU operations. The third stage stores a result in Rd or accesses memory with an effective address computed in the second stage.

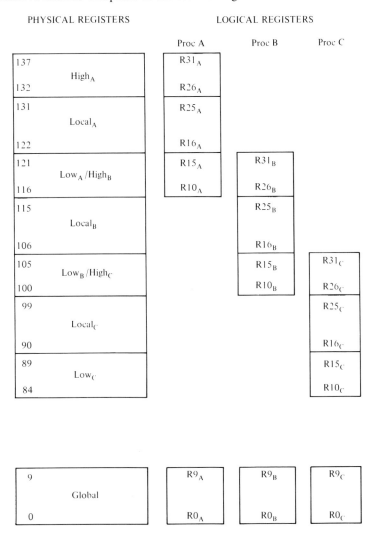

FIGURE 14-12. Berkeley RISC register windows.

"Reduced Instruction Set Computers" by D.A. Patterson from *Communications of the ACM*, Volume 28, Number 1, January 1985, pages 8-21. Copyright 1985, Association for Computing Machinery, Inc., reprinted by permission.

REDUCED INSTRUCTION SET COMPUTERS

Reduced instruction set computers aim for both simplicity in hardware and synergy between architectures and compilers. Optimizing compilers are used to compile programming languages down to instructions that are as unencumbered as microinstructions in a large virtual address space, and to make the instruction cycle time as fast as possible.

DAVID A. PATTERSON

As circuit technologies reduce the relative cost of processing and memory, instruction sets that are too complex become a distinct liability to performance. The designers of reduced instruction set computers (RISCs) strive for both simplicity in hardware and synergy between architecture and compilers, in order to streamline processing as much as possible. Early experience indicates that RISCs can in fact run much faster than more conventionally designed machines.

BACKGROUND

The IBM System/360, first introduced in 1964, was the real beginning of modern computer architecture. Although computers in the System/360 "family" provided a different level of performance for a different price, all ran identical software. The System/360 originated the distinction between *computer architecture*—the abstract structure of a computer that a machine-language programmer needs to know to write programs—and the *hardware implementation* of that structure. Before the System/360, architectural trade-offs were determined by the effect on price and performance of a single implementation; henceforth, architectural trade-offs became more esoteric. The consequences of single implementations would no longer be sufficient to settle an argument about instruction set design.

Microprogramming was the primary technological innovation behind this marketing concept. Microprogramming relied on a small control memory and was an elegant way of building the processor control unit for a large instruction set. Each word of control memory is

© 1985 ACM 0001-0782/85/0100-0008 75¢

called a *microinstruction*, and the contents are essentially an interpreter, programmed in microinstructions. The main memories of these computers were magnetic core memories, the small control memories of which were usually 10 times faster than core.

Minicomputer manufacturers tend to follow the lead of mainframe manufacturers, especially when the mainframe manufacturer is IBM, and so microprogramming caught on quickly. The rapid growth of semiconductor memories also speeded this trend. In the early 1970s, for example, 8192 bits of read-only memory (ROM) took up no more space than 8 bits of register. Eventually, minicomputers using core main memory and semiconductor control memory became standard in the minicomputer industry.

With the continuing growth of semiconductor memory, a much richer and more complicated instruction set could be implemented. The architecture research community argued for richer instruction sets. Let us review some of the arguments they advanced at that time:

1. *Richer instruction sets would simplify compilers.* As the story was told, compilers were very hard to build, and compilers for machines with registers were the hardest of all. Compilers for architectures with execution models based either on stacks or memory-to-memory operations were much simpler and more reliable.

2. *Richer instruction sets would alleviate the software crisis.* At a time when software costs were rising as fast as hardware costs were dropping, it seemed

appropriate to move as much function to the hardware as possible. The idea was to create machine instructions that resembled programming language statements, so as to close the "semantic gap" between programming languages and machine languages.

3. *Richer instruction sets would improve architecture quality.* After IBM differentiated architecture from implementation, the research community looked for ways to measure the quality of an architecture, as opposed to the speed at which implementations could run programs. The only architectural metrics then widely recognized were program size, the number of bits of instructions, and bits of data fetched from memory during program execution (see Figure 1).

Memory efficiency was such a dominating concern in these metrics because main memory—magnetic core memory—was so slow and expensive. These metrics are partially responsible for the prevailing belief in the 1970s that execution speed was proportional to program size. It even became fashionable to examine long lists of instruction execution to see if a pair or triple of old instructions could be replaced by a single, more powerful instruction. The belief that larger programs were invariably slower programs inspired the invention of

many exotic instruction formats that reduced program size.

The rapid rise of the integrated circuit, along with arguments from the architecture research community in the 1970s led to certain design principles that guided computer architecture:

1. *The memory technology used for microprograms was growing rapidly, so large microprograms would add little or nothing to the cost of the machine.*

2. *Since microinstructions were much faster than normal machine instructions, moving software functions to microcode made for faster computers and more reliable functions.*

3. *Since execution speed was proportional to program size, architectural techniques that led to smaller programs also led to faster computers.*

4. *Registers were old fashioned and made it hard to build compilers; stacks or memory-to-memory architectures were superior execution models. As one architecture researcher put it in 1978, "One's eyebrows should rise whenever a future architecture is developed with a register-oriented instruction set."*[1]

Computers that exemplify these design principles are the IBM 370/168, the DEC VAX-11/780, the Xerox

---
[1] Myers, G.J. The case against stack-oriented instruction sets. *Comput. Archit. News 6*, 3 (Aug. 1977), 7–10.

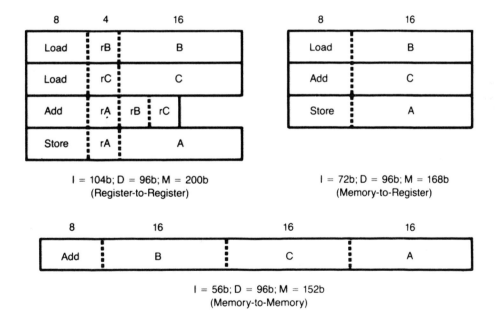

I = 104b; D = 96b; M = 200b
(Register-to-Register)

I = 72b; D = 96b; M = 168b
(Memory-to-Register)

I = 56b; D = 96b; M = 152b
(Memory-to-Memory)

In this example, the three data words are 32 bits each and the address field is 16 bits. Metrics were selected by research architects for deciding which architecture is best; they selected the total size of executed instructions (I), the total size of executed data (D), and the total memory traffic—that is, the sum of I and D, which is (M).

These metrics suggest that a memory-to-memory architecture is the "best" architecture, and a register-to-register architecture the "worst." This study led one research architect in 1978 to suggest that future architectures should not include registers.

FIGURE 1. The Statement A ← B + C Translated into Assembly Language for Three Execution Models: Register-to-Register, Memory-to-Register, and Memory-to-Memory

TABLE I. Four Implementations of Modern Architectures

	IBM 370/168	VAX-11/780	Dorado	iAPX-432
Year	1973	1978	1978	1982
Number of instructions	208	303	270	222
Control memory size	420 Kb	480 Kb	136 Kb	64 Kb
Instruction sizes (bits)	16–48	16–456	8–24	6–321
Technology	ECL MSI	TTL MSI	ECL MSI	NMOS VLSI
Execution model	reg-mem	reg-mem	stack	stack
	mem-mem	mem-mem		mem-mem
	reg-reg	reg-reg		
Cache size	64 Kb	64 Kb	64 Kb	0

These four implementations, designed in the 1970s, all used microprogramming. The emphasis on memory efficiency at that time led to the varying-sized instruction formats of the VAX and the 432. Note how much larger the control memories were than the cache memories.

Dorado, and the Intel iAPX-432. Table I shows some of the characteristics of these machines.

Although computer architects were reaching a consensus on design principles, the implementation world was changing around them:

- Semiconductor memory was replacing core, which meant that main memories would no longer be 10 times slower than control memories.
- Since it was virtually impossible to remove all mistakes for 400,000 bits of microcode, control store ROMs were becoming control store RAMs.
- Caches had been invented—studies showed that the locality of programs meant that small, fast buffers could make substantial improvement in the implementation speed of an architecture. As Table I shows, caches were included in nearly every machine, though control memories were much larger than cache memories.
- Compilers were subsetting architectures—simple compilers found it difficult to generate the complex new functions that were included to help close the "semantic gap." Optimizing compilers subsetted architectures because they removed so many of the unknowns at compiler time that they rarely needed the powerful instructions at run time.

WRITABLE CONTROL STORE

One symptom of the general dissatisfaction with architectural design principles at this time was the flurry of work in writable control memory, or writable control store (WCS). Researchers observed that microcoded machines could not run faster than 1 microcycle per instruction, typically averaging 3 or 4 microcycles per instruction; yet the simple operations in many programs could be found directly in microinstructions. As long as machines were too complicated to be implemented by ROMs, why not take advantage of RAMs by loading different microprograms for different applications?

One of the first problems was to provide a programming environment that could simplify the task of writing microprograms, since microprogramming was the most tedious form of machine-language programming. Many researchers, including myself, built compilers and debuggers for microprogramming. This was a formidable assignment, for virtually no inefficiencies could be tolerated in microcode. These demands led to the invention of new programming languages for microprogramming and new compiler techniques.

Unfortunately for me and several other researchers, there were three more impediments that kept WCSs from being very popular. (Although a few machines offer WCS as an option today, it is unlikely that more than one in a thousand programmers take this option.) These impediments were

1. *Virtual memory complications.* Once computers made the transition from physical memory to virtual memory, microprogrammers incurred the added difficulty of making sure that any routine could start over if any memory operand caused a virtual memory fault.
2. *Limited address space.* The most difficult programming situation occurs when a program must be forced to fit in too small a memory. With control memories of 4096 words or less, some unfortunate WCS developers spent more time squeezing space from the old microcode than they did writing the new microcode.
3. *Swapping in a multiprocess environment.* When each program has its own microcode, a multiprocess operating system has to reload the WCS on each process switch. Reloading time can range from 1,000 to 25,000 memory accesses, depending on the machine. This added overhead decreased the performance benefits gained by going to a WCS in the first place.

These last two difficulties led some researchers to conclude that future computers would have to have virtual control memory, which meant that page faults could occur during microcode execution. The distinction between programming and microprogramming was becoming less and less clear.

THE ORIGINS OF RISCS

About this point, several people, including those who had been working on microprogramming tools, began to rethink the architectural design principles of the 1970s. In trying to close the "semantic gap," these principles had actually introduced a "performance gap." The attempt to bridge this gap with WCSs was unsuccessful, although the motivation for WCS—that instructions should be no faster than microinstructions and that programmers should write simple operations that map directly onto microinstructions—was still valid. Furthermore, since caches had allowed "main" memory accesses at the same speed as control memory accesses, microprogramming no longer enjoyed a ten-to-one speed advantage.

A new computer design philosophy evolved: Optimizing compilers could be used to compile "normal" programming languages down to instructions that were as unencumbered as microinstructions in a large virtual address space, and to make the instruction cycle time as fast as the technology would allow. These machines would have fewer instructions—a *reduced set*—and the remaining instructions would be simple and would generally execute in one cycle—*reduced instructions*—hence the name *reduced instruction set computers* (RISCs). RISCs inaugurated a new set of architectural design principles:

1. *Functions should be kept simple unless there is a very good reason to do otherwise.* A new operation that increases cycle time by 10 percent must reduce the number of cycles by at least 10 percent to be worth considering. An even greater reduction might be necessary, in fact, if the extra development effort and hardware resources of the new function, as they impact the rest of the design, are taken into account.

2. *Microinstructions should not be faster than simple instructions.* Since cache is built from the same technology as writable control store, a simple instruction should be executed at the same speed as a microinstruction.

3. *Microcode is not magic.* Moving software into microcode does not make it better, it just makes it harder to change. To paraphrase the Turing Machine argument, *anything that can be done in a microcoded machine can be done in assembly language in a simple machine.* The same hardware primitives assumed by the microinstructions must be available in assembly language. The run-time library of a RISC has all the characteristics of a function in microcode, except that it is easier to change.

4. *Simple decoding and pipelined execution are more important than program size.* Imagine a model in which the total work per instruction is broken into pieces, and different pieces for each instruction execute in parallel. At the peak rate a new instruction is started every cycle (Figure 2). This assembly-line approach performs at the rate determined by the length of individual pieces rather than by the total length of all pieces. This kind of model gave rise to instruction formats that are simple to decode and to pipeline.

5. *Compiler technology should be used to simplify instructions rather than to generate complex instructions.* RISC compilers try to remove as much work as possible at compile time so that simple instructions can be used. For example, RISC compilers try to keep operands in registers so that simple register-to-register instructions can be used. Traditional compilers, on the other hand, try to discover the ideal addressing mode and the shortest instruction format to add the operands in memory. In general, the designers of RISC compilers prefer a register-to-register model of execution so that compilers can keep operands that will be reused in registers, rather than repeating a memory access or a calculation. They therefore use LOADs and STOREs to access memory so that operands are not implicitly discarded after being fetched, as in the memory-to-memory architecture (see Figure 3).

COMMON RISC TRAITS

We can see these principles in action when we look at some actual RISC machines: the 801 from IBM Research, the RISC I and the RISC II from the University of California at Berkeley, and the MIPS from Stanford University.

All three RISC machines have actually been built and are working (see Figure 4). The original IBM 801 was built using off-the-shelf MSI ECL, whereas the Berkeley RISCs and the Stanford MIPS were built with custom NMOS VLSI. Table II shows the primary characteristics of these three machines.

Although each project had different constraints and goals, the machines they eventually created have a great deal in common:

1. *Operations are register-to-register, with only LOAD and STORE accessing memory.* Allowing compilers to reuse operands requires registers. When only LOAD and STORE instructions access memory, the instruction set, the processor, and the handling of page faults in a virtual memory environment are greatly simplified. Cycle time is shortened as well.

2. *The operations and addressing modes are reduced.* Operations between registers complete in one cycle, permitting a simpler, hardwired control for each RISC, instead of microcode. Multiple-cycle instructions such as floating-point arithmetic are either executed in software or in a special-purpose coprocessor. (Without a coprocessor, RISCs have mediocre floating-point performance.) Only two simple addressing modes, indexed and PC-relative, are provided. More complicated addressing modes can be synthesized from the simple ones.

3. *Instruction formats are simple and do not cross word boundaries.* This restriction allows RISCs to re-

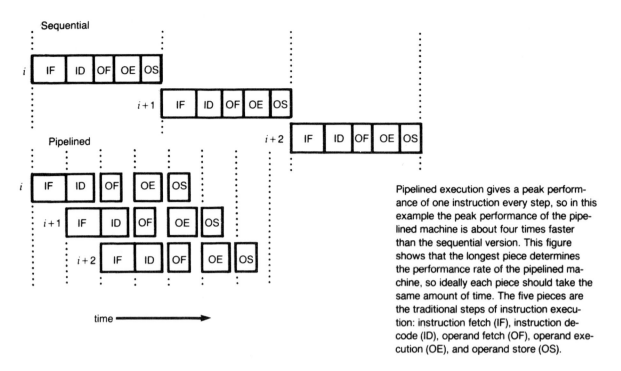

Pipelined execution gives a peak performance of one instruction every step, so in this example the peak performance of the pipelined machine is about four times faster than the sequential version. This figure shows that the longest piece determines the performance rate of the pipelined machine, so ideally each piece should take the same amount of time. The five pieces are the traditional steps of instruction execution: instruction fetch (IF), instruction decode (ID), operand fetch (OF), operand execution (OE), and operand store (OS).

FIGURE 2a.   Execution of Three Instructions for Sequential and Pipelined Execution

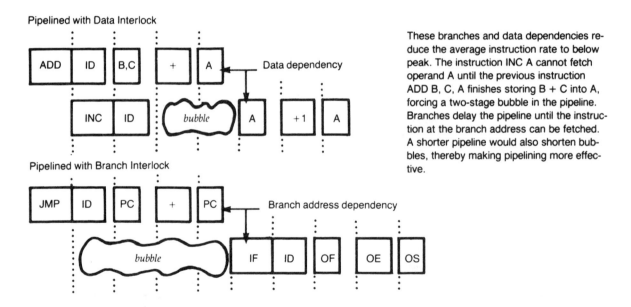

These branches and data dependencies reduce the average instruction rate to below peak. The instruction INC A cannot fetch operand A until the previous instruction ADD B, C, A finishes storing B + C into A, forcing a two-stage bubble in the pipeline. Branches delay the pipeline until the instruction at the branch address can be fetched. A shorter pipeline would also shorten bubbles, thereby making pipelining more effective.

FIGURE 2b.   Branches and Data Dependencies between Instructions Force Delays, or "Bubbles," into Pipelines

move instruction decoding time from the critical execution path. As Figure 5 shows, the Berkeley RISC register operands are always in the same place in the 32-bit word, so register access can take place simultaneously with opcode decoding. This removes the instruction decoding stage from the pipelined execution, making it more effective by shortening the pipeline (Figure 2b). Single-sized in-

structions also simplify virtual memory, since they cannot be broken into parts that might wind up on different pages.

4. *RISC branches avoid pipeline penalties.*   A branch instruction in a pipelined computer will normally delay the pipeline until the instruction at the branch address is fetched (Figure 2b). Several pipelined machines have elaborate techniques for fetching

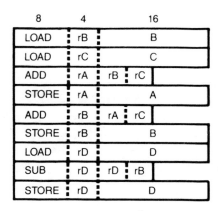

8	4	16
LOAD	rB	B
LOAD	rC	C

A ← B + C
B ← A + C
D ← D − B

Reuse of Operands
I = 228b; D = 192b; M = 420b
(Register-to-Register)

8	4	4	4
ADD	rA	rB	rC
ADD	rB	rA	rC
SUB	rD	rD	rB

Compiler allocates Operands in Registers
I = 60b; D = 0b; M = 60b
(Register-to-Register)

8	16	16	16
ADD	B	C	A
ADD	A	C	B
SUB	B	D	D

I = 168b; D = 288b; M = 456b
(Memory-to-Memory)

This new version assumes optimizing compiler technology for the sequence A ← B + C; B ← A + C; D ← D − B. Note that the memory-to-memory architecture has no temporary storage, which means that it must reload operands. The register-to-register architecture now appears to be the "best."

FIGURE 3. A New Version of the Architectural Metrics Presented in Figure 1

the appropriate instruction after the branch, but these techniques are too complicated for RISCs. The generic RISC solution, commonly used in microinstruction sets, is to redefine jumps so that they do not take effect until after the *following* instruction; this is called the *delayed branch*. The delayed branch allows RISCs to always fetch the next instruction during the execution of the current instruction. The machine-language code is suitably arranged so that the desired results are obtained. Because RISCs are designed to be programmed in high-level languages, the programmer is not required to consider this issue; the "burden" is carried by the programmers of the compiler, the optimizer, and the debugger. The delayed branch also removes the branch bubbles normally associated with pipelined execution (see Figure 2b). Table III illustrates the delayed branch.

RISC optimizing compilers are able to successfully rearrange instructions to use the cycle after the delayed branch more than 90 percent of the time. Hennessy has found that more than 20 percent of all instructions are executed in the delay after the branch.

Hennessy also pointed out how the delayed branch

illustrates once again the folly of architectural metrics. Virtually all machines with variable-length instructions use a buffer to supply instructions to the CPU. These units blindly fill the prefetch buffer no matter what instruction is fetched and thus load the buffer with instructions after a branch, despite the fact that these instructions will eventually be discarded. Since studies show that one in four VAX instructions changes the program counter, such variable-length instruction machines really fetch about 20 percent more instruction words from memory than the architecture metrics would suggest. RISCs, on the other hand, nearly always execute something useful because the instruction is fetched after the branch.

RISC VARIATIONS
Each RISC machine provides its own particular variations on the common theme. This makes for some interesting differences.

Compiler Technology versus Register Windows
Both IBM and Stanford pushed the state of the art in compiler technology to maximize the use of registers. Figure 6 shows the graph-coloring algorithm that is the cornerstone of this technology.

The IBM 801, above, was completed in 1979 and had a cycle time of 66 ns. It was built from off-the-shelf ECL. The RISC II, on the right, designed by Manolis Katevenis and Robert Sherburne, was designed in a four-micron single-level metal custom NMOS VLSI. This 41,000-transistor chip worked the first time at 500 ns per 32-bit instruction. The small control area accounts for only 10 percent of the chip and is found in the upper right-hand corner. The RISC II was rescaled and fabricated in three-micron NMOS. The resulting chip is 25 percent smaller than a 68000 and ran on first silicon at 330 ns per instruction. The Stanford MIPS, shown on page 16, chip was fabricated using the same conservative NMOS architecture and runs at 500 ns per instruction. This 25,000-transistor chip has about the same chip area as the RISC II. On-chip memory management support plus the two-instruction-per-word format increase the control area of the MIPS.

FIGURE 4. Photographs of the Hardware for Three RISC Machines

The Berkeley team did not include compiler experts, so a hardware solution was implemented to keep operands in registers. The first step was to have enough registers to keep all the local scalar variables and all the parameters of the current procedure in registers. Attention was directed to these variables because of two very opportune properties: Most procedures only have a few variables (approximately a half-dozen), and these are heavily used (responsible for one-half to two-thirds of all dynamically executed references to operands). Normally, it slows procedure calls when there are a great many registers. The solution was to have many sets, or windows, of registers, so that registers would not have to be saved on every procedure call and restored on every return. A procedure call automatically switches the processor to use a fresh set of registers. Such buffering can only work if programs naturally behave in a way that matches the buffer. Caches work because programs do not normally wander randomly about the address space. Similarly, through experimentation, a locality of procedure nesting was found; programs rarely execute a long uninterrupted sequence of calls followed by a long uninterrupted sequence of returns. Figure 7 illustrates this nesting behavior. To further improve performance, the Berkeley RISC machines have a unique way of speeding up procedure calls. Rather than copy the parameters from one window to another on each call, windows are overlapped so that some registers are simultaneously part of two windows. By putting parameters into the overlapping registers, operands are passed automatically.

What is the "best" way to keep operands in registers? The disadvantages of register windows are that they use more chip area and slow the basic clock cycle. This is due to the capacitive loading of the longer bus, and although context switches rarely occur—about 100 to 1000 procedure calls for every switch—they require that two to three times as many registers be saved, on average. The only drawbacks of the optimizing compiler are that it is about half the speed of a simple compiler and ignores the register-saving penalty of procedure calls. Both the 801 and the MIPS mitigate this call cost by expanding some procedures in-line, although this means these machines cannot provide separate compilation of those procedures. If compiler technology can reduce the number of LOADs and STOREs to the extent that register windows can, the optimizing compiler will stand in clear superiority. About 30 percent of the 801 instructions are LOAD or STORE when large programs are run; the MIPS has 16 registers compared to 32 for the 801, about 35 percent of them being LOAD or STORE instructions. For the Berkeley RISC machines, this percentage drops to about 15 percent, including the LOADs and STOREs used to save and restore registers when the register-window buffer overflows.

Delayed Loads and Multiple Memory and Register Ports
Since it takes one cycle to calculate the address and one cycle to access memory, the straightforward way to implement LOADs and STOREs is to take two cycles. This is what we did in the Berkeley RISC architecture. To reduce the costs of memory accesses, both the 801 and the MIPS provide "one-cycle" LOADs by following the style of the delayed branch. The first step is to have two ports to memory, one for instructions and one for data, plus a second write port to the registers. Since the address must still be calculated in the first cycle and the operand must still be fetched during the second cycle, the data are not available until the third cycle.

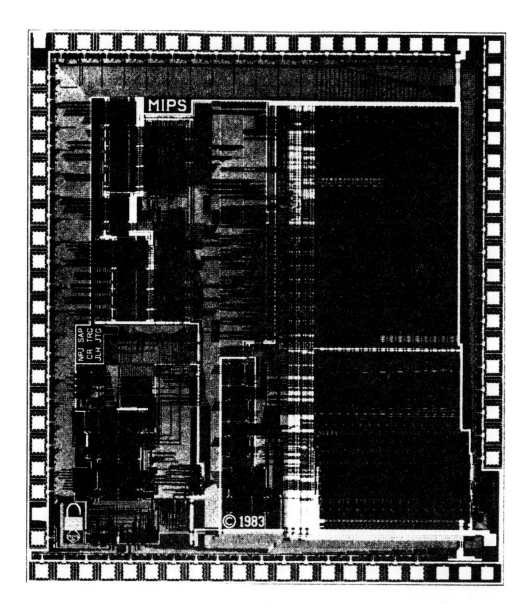

Therefore, the instruction executed following the one-cycle LOAD must not rely on the operand coming from memory. The 801 and the MIPS solve this problem with a *delayed load*, which is analogous to the delayed branch described above. The two compilers are able to put an independent instruction in the extra slot about 90 percent of the time. Since the Berkeley RISC executes many fewer LOADs, we decided to bypass the extra expense of an extra memory port and an extra register write port. Once again, depending on goals and implementation technology, either approach can be justified.

Pipelines

All RISCs use pipelined execution, but the length of the pipeline and the approach to removing pipeline bubbles vary. Since the peak pipelined execution rate is determined by the longest piece of the pipeline, the trick is to find a balance between the four parts of a RISC

TABLE II. Primary Characteristics of Three Operational RISC Machines

	IBM 801	RISC I	MIPS
Year	1980	1982	1983
Number of instructions	120	39	55
Control memory size	0	0	0
Instruction sizes (bits)	32	32	32
Technology	ECL MSI	NMOS VLSI	NMOS VLSI
Execution model	reg-reg	reg-reg	reg-reg

None of these machines use microprogramming; all three use 32-bit instructions and follow the register-to-register execution model. Note that the number of instructions in each of these machines is significantly lower than for those in Table I.

90

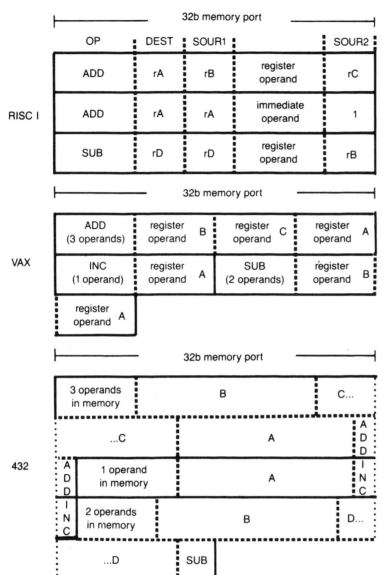

RISC I

OP	DEST	SOUR1		SOUR2
ADD	rA	rB	register operand	rC
ADD	rA	rA	immediate operand	1
SUB	rD	rD	register operand	rB

32b memory port

VAX

ADD (3 operands)	register operand B	register operand C	register operand A
INC (1 operand)	register operand A	SUB (2 operands)	register operand B
register operand A			

32b memory port

432

3 operands in memory	B	C...
...C	A	A D D
A D D	1 operand in memory	A	I N C
I N C	2 operands in memory	B	D...
...D	SUB	

FIGURE 5. Three Machines Are Compared for the Instruction Sequence A ← B + C; A ← A + 1; D ← D − B

Although variable-sized instructions improve the architectural metrics in Figure 1, they also make instruction decoding more expensive and thus may not be good predictors of performance. Three machines—the RISC I, the VAX, and the 432—are compared for the instruction sequence A ← B + C; A ← A + 1; D ← D − B. VAX instructions are byte variable from 16 to 456 bits, with an average size of 30 bits. Operand locations are not part of the main opcode but are spread throughout the instruction. The 432 has bit-variable instructions that range from 6 to 321 bits. The 432 also has multipart opcodes: The first part gives the number of operands and their location, and the second part gives the operation. The 432 has no registers, so all operands must be kept in memory. The specifier of the operand can appear anywhere in a 32-bit instruction word in the VAX or the 432. The RISC I instructions are always 32 bits long, they always have three operands, and these operands are always specified in the same place in the instruction. This allows overlap of instruction decoding with fetching the operand. This technique has the added benefit of removing a stage from the execution pipeline.

instruction execution:

1. instruction fetch,
2. register read,
3. arithmetic/logic operation, and
4. register write.

The 801 assumes that each part takes the same amount of time, and thus uses a four-stage pipeline. We at Berkeley assumed that instruction fetch was equal to the sum of register read and the arithmetic/logic operation, and thus selected the three-stage pipeline shown in Figure 8.

The biggest difference is in handling instruction sequences that cause bubbles in a pipeline. For example, the first instruction in Figure 2b stores a result in A,

which the following instruction needs to read. In most machines this forces the second instruction to delay execution until the first one completes storing its result. The 801 and the RISC II avoid inserting a bubble by means of an internal forwarding technique that checks operands and automatically passes the result of one instruction to the next.

The MIPS, in contrast, uses software to prevent interlocks from occurring; this, in fact, is what prompted the machine's name: *Microprocessor without Interlocked Pipelined Stages.* A routine passes over the output of the assembler to ensure that there cannot be conflicts. NO-OPs are inserted when necessary, and the optimizing compiler tries to shuffle instructions to avoid executing them. Traditional pipelined machines can spend

TABLE III. A Comparison of the Traditional Branch Instruction with the Delayed Branch Found in RISC Machines

Address	Normal branch		Delayed branch		Optimized delayed branch	
100	LOAD	X,A	LOAD	X,A	LOAD	X,A
101	ADD	1,A	ADD	1,A	**JUMP**	**105**
102	**JUMP**	**105**	**JUMP**	**106**	**ADD**	**1,A**
103	ADD	A,B	**NO-OP**		ADD	A,B
104	SUB	C,B	ADD	A,B	SUB	C,B
105	**STORE**	**A,Z**	SUB	C,B	**STORE**	**A,Z**
106			**STORE**	**A,Z**		

The delayed branch is used to avoid a branch dependency bubble in the pipeline (Figure 2b). Machines with normal branches would execute the sequence 100, 101, 102, 105,.... To get that same effect with a RISC computer, it would be necessary to insert a NO-OP in the Delayed branch column. The sequence of instructions for RISCs would then be 100, 101, 102, *103*, 106,.... In the worst case, every branch would take two instructions. The RISC compilers, however, include optimizers that try to rearrange the se-

quence of instructions to do the equivalent operations while making use of the instruction slot where the NO-OP appears. The Optimized delayed branch column shows that the optimized RISC sequence is 100, 101, *102*, 105,.... Because the instruction following a branch is always executed and the branch at 101 is not dependent on the add at 102 (in this example), this sequence is equivalent to the original program segment in the Normal branch column.

a fair amount of their clock cycle detecting and blocking interlocks, but the simple pipeline and register model of RISCs also simplifies interlocking. Hennessy believes the MIPS cycle would be lengthened by 10 percent if hardware interlocking were added. The designers of the RISC II measured the internal forwarding logic and found that careful hardware design prevented

forwarding from lengthening the RISC II clock cycle.

Multiple Instructions per Word
The designers of the MIPS tried an interesting variation on standard RISC philosophy by packing two instructions into every 32-bit word whenever possible. This improvement could potentially double performance if

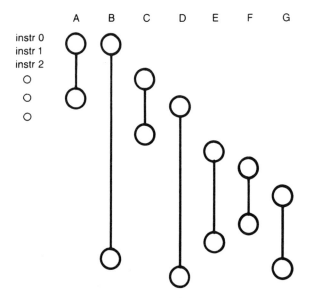

IBM's solution was to deal with register allocation according to the rules prescribed for painting a directed graph with a fixed number of colors. Each color represents one of the machine registers. The simultaneous lifetimes of A through G are shown, from first use to last. Here we assume only four registers, so the problem is to map the seven variables into the four registers. This is equivalent to painting the graph with only four colors.

FIGURE 6a. IBM's Solution to the Register Allocation Problem

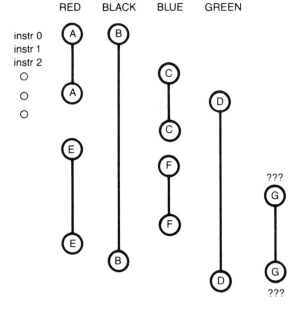

We start by mapping the first four variables onto the four colors. Variable E does not conflict with variable A, so they can share the same color, in this case RED. Similarly, F can share BLUE with C. With G all four colors are used, so the compiler must use LOADs and STOREs to free a register to make space for G.

FIGURE 6b. A Partial Solution to Register Allocation

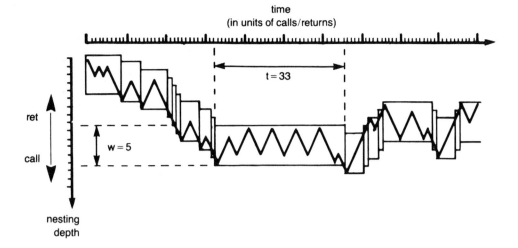

This graph shows the call–return behavior of programs that inspired the register window scheme used by the Berkeley RISC machines. Each call causes the line to move down and to the right, and each return causes the line to move up and to the right. The rectangles show how long the machine stays within the buffer. The longest case is 33 calls and returns ($t = 33$) inside the buffer. In this figure we assume that there are five windows ($w = 5$). We have found that about eight windows hits the knee of the curve and that locality of nesting is found in programs written in C, Pascal, and Smalltalk.

FIGURE 7.   The Call–Return Behavior of Programs

twice as many operations were executed for every 32-bit instruction fetch. Since memory-access instructions and jump instructions generally need the full 32-bit word, and since data dependencies prevented some combinations, most programs were sped up by 10 to 15 percent. Arithmetic routines written in assembly language had much higher savings. Hennessy believes the two-instruction-per-word format adds 10 percent to the MIPS cycle time because of the more complicated de-coding. He does not plan to use the two-instruction-per-word technique in his future designs.

HIDDEN RISCS

If building a new computer around a reduced instruction set results in a machine with a better price/performance ratio, what would happen if the same techniques were used on the RISC subset of a traditional machine? This interesting question has been explored

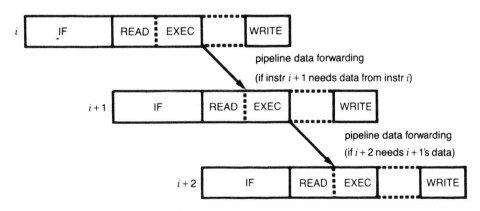

The memory is kept busy 100 percent of the time, the register file is reading or writing 100 percent of the time, and the execution unit (ALU) is busy 50 percent of the time. The short pipeline and pipeline data forwarding allow the RISC II to avoid pipeline bubbles when data dependencies like those shown in Figure 2b are present.

FIGURE 8.   The Three-Stage Pipeline of the RISC II

by RISC advocates and, perhaps unintentionally, by the designers of more traditional machines.

DEC reported a subsetting experiment on two implementations of the VAX architecture in VLSI. The VLSI VAX has nine custom VLSI chips and implements the complete VAX-11 instruction set. DEC found that 20.0 percent of the instructions are responsible for 60.0 percent of the microcode and yet are only 0.2 percent of all instructions executed. By trapping to software to execute these instructions, the MicroVAX 32 was able to fit the subset architecture into only one chip, with an optional floating-point coprocessor in another chip. As shown in Table IV, the VLSI VAX, a VLSI implementation of the full VAX architecture, uses five to ten times the resources of the MicroVAX 32 to implement the full instruction set, yet is only 20 percent faster.

Michael L. Powell of DEC obtained improved performance by subsetting the VAX architecture from the software side. His experimental DEC Modula-2 compiler generates code that is comparable in speed to the best compilers for the VAX, using only a subset of the addressing modes and instructions. This gain is in part due to the fact that optimization reduces the use of complicated modes. Often only a subset of the functions performed by a single complicated instruction is needed. The VAX has an elaborate CALL instruction, generated by most VAX compilers, that saves registers on procedure entry. By replacing the CALL instruction with a sequence of simple instructions that do only what is necessary, Powell was able to improve performance by 20 percent.

The IBM S/360 and S/370 were also targets of RISC studies. The 360 model 44 can be considered an ancestor of the MicroVAX 32, since it implements only a subset of the 360 architecture in hardware. The rest of the instructions are implemented by software. The 360/44 had a significantly better cost/performance ratio than its nearest neighbors. IBM researchers performed a software experiment by retargetting their highly optimizing PL/8 compiler away from the 801 to the System/370. The optimizer treated the 370 as a register-to-register machine to increase the effectiveness of register allocation. This subset of the 370 ran programs 50 percent faster than the previous best opti-

mizing compiler that used the full 370 instruction set.

Software and hardware experiments on subsets of the VAX and IBM 360/370, then, seem to support the RISC arguments.

ARCHITECTURAL HERITAGE

All RISC machines borrowed good ideas from old machines, and we hereby pay our respects to a long line of architectural ancestors. In 1946, before the first digital computer was operational, von Neumann wrote

> The really decisive considerations from the present point of view, in selecting a code [instruction set], are more of a practical nature: the simplicity of the equipment demanded by the code, and the clarity of its application to the actually important problems together with the speed of its handling of those problems.[2]

For the last 25 years Seymour Cray has been quietly designing register-based computers that rely on LOADs and STOREs while using pipelined execution. James Thornton, one of his colleagues on the CDC-6600, wrote in 1963

> The simplicity of *all* instructions allows quick and simple evaluation of status to begin execution. . . . Adding complication to a special operation, therefore, degrades all the others.

and also

> In my mind, the greatest potential for improvement is with the internal methods. . .at the risk of loss of fringe operations. The work to be done is really engineering work, pure and simple. As a matter of fact, that's what the results should be—pure and simple.[3]

John Cocke developed the idea of pushing compiler technology with fast, simple instructions for text and integer applications. The IBM 801 project, led by George Radin, began experimenting with these ideas in 1975 and produced an operational ECL machine in 1979. The results of this project could not be published, however, until 1982.

In 1980 we started the RISC project at Berkeley. We were inspired by an aversion to the complexity of the VAX and Intel 432, the lack of experimental evidence in architecture research, rumors of the 801, and the desire to build a VLSI machine that minimized design effort while maximizing the cost/performance factor. We combined our research with course work to build the RISC I and RISC II machines.

In 1981 John Hennessy started the MIPS project, which tried to extend the state of the art in compiler optimization techniques, explored pipelined techniques, and used VLSI to build a fast microcomputer.

Both university projects built working chips using much less manpower and time than traditional microprocessors.

TABLE IV. Two VLSI Implementations of the VAX

	VLSI VAX	MicroVAX 32	
VLSI Chips (including floating point)	9	2	(22%)
Microcode	480K	64K	(13%)
Transistors	1250K	101K	(8%)

These two implementations, although not yet in products, illustrate the difficulty of building the complete VAX architecture in VLSI. The VLSI VAX is 20 percent faster than the MicroVAX 32 but uses five to ten times the resources for the processor. Both are implemented from the same three-micron double-level metal NMOS technology. (The VLSI VAX also has external data and address caches not counted in this table.)

---

[2] Burks, A.W., Goldstine, H.H., and von Neumann, J. Preliminary discussion of the logical design of an electronic computing instrument. Rep. to U.S. Army Ordinance Dept., 1946.
[3] Thornton, J.E. *Considerations in Computer Design—Leading Up to the Control Data 6600.* Control Data Chippewa Laboratory, 1963.

CONCLUSIONS

In my view, the remaining technical difficulty is how to get good floating-point performance from RISCs. The RISCs mentioned here have mediocre floating-point performance without special hardware assists. Another issue is whether RISCs will provide the same advantages in the cost/performance factor for exploratory programming environments such as Lisp and Smalltalk. Initial experiments are promising.

I believe the split between architecture and implementation has caused architects to ignore the implementation consequences of architecture decisions, which has led to "good" architectures with disappointing implementations. Complex architecture requires lengthy development cycles, and long development cycles using implementation technologies that routinely double in speed and capacity can potentially mean producing a computer in an antiquated technology. RISCs reduce this danger.

Simple machines can also dramatically simplify design verification. As things stand now, it can take a year or two to discover all the important design flaws in a mainframe. VLSI technology will soon allow a single-chip computer to be built that is as complicated as a mainframe. Unfortunately, VLSI manufacturing will also produce hundreds of thousands of computers in the time it takes to debug a mainframe in the field. RISC machines offer the best chance of heading off "computer recall" as a new step in the development cycle.

A final observation: Technology runs in cycles, so trade-offs in instruction set design will change over time, if there is change in the balance of speeds in memory and logic. Designers who reconcile architecture with implementation will reduce their RISCs.

Acknowledgments. I thank the many Berkeley students who worked hard to create RISCs, and my colleagues at IBM and Stanford for pursuing RISCs. I must also acknowledge the excellent papers by Hennessy and Hopkins for providing me with insights to help explain the RISC phenomenon.

Thanks also go to Gordon Bell, Peter Denning, Susan Eggers, Robert Garner, Garth Gibson, Paul Hansen, John Hennessy, Paul Hilfiger, Mark Hill, Normam Jouppi, Manolis Katevenis, Randy Katz, John Ousterhout, Joan Pendleton, Michael Powell, George Taylor, Tom West, and David Ungar for their useful suggestions in improving this paper.

The Berkeley RISC project was sponsored by DARPA, order number 3803, monitored by NAVALEX under contract number N00034-K-025.

Further Reading. Items [1, 4, 9] should provide a good introduction to RISCs for the general reader. The remaining references may help to explain some of the ideas presented in this paper in greater depth. The IBM 801 is described in [12], while the two papers by Martin Hopkins of IBM [5, 6] provide historical and philosophical perspective on RISC machines. The IBM graph-coloring algorithm is found in [2], and the subsetted use of one instruction set in [8]. The primary reference for the Berkeley RISC machines is [11], although [10] contains the latest information on performance of the RISC II and [7] a thorough explanation of the motivation for RISCs in general and the RISC II in particular. An attempt to use RISCs in an exploratory programming environment, in this case the object-oriented Smalltalk system, is described in [13]. Joseph Fisher, a Writable Control Store refugee like myself, is now working on compiling "normal" programming languages into very wide instructions (or horizontal microinstructions, depending on your perspective) for a high-performance multiple arithmetic unit computer [3].

REFERENCES
1. Bernhard, R. More hardware means less software. *IEEE Spectrum 18*, 12 (Dec. 1981), 30–37.
2. Chaitin, G.J. Register allocation and spilling via graph coloring. In Proceedings of the SIGPLAN 82 Symposium on Compiler Construction. *SIGPLAN Not. 17*, 6 (June 1982), 98–105.
3. Fisher, J.A. Very long instruction word architectures and the ELI-512. In *The 10th Annual International Symposium on Computer Architecture* (Stockholm, Sweden, June 13–17). ACM, New York, 1983, pp. 140–150.
4. Hennessy, J.L. VLSI processor architecture. *IEEE Trans. Comput.* To be published.
5. Hopkins, M. A perspective on microcode. In *Proceedings of the 21st Annual IEEE Computer Conference (Spring COMPCON 83)* (San Francisco, Calif., Feb.). IEEE, New York, 1983, pp. 108–110.
6. Hopkins, M. Definition of RISC. In *Proceedings of the Conference on High Level Language Computer Architecture* (Los Angeles, Calif., May). 1984.
7. Katevenis, M.G.H. Reduced instruction set computer architectures for VLSI. Ph.D. dissertation, Computer Science Dept., Univ. of California, Berkeley, Oct. 1983.
8. Lunde, A. Empirical evaluation of some features of instruction set processor architecture. *Commun. ACM 20*, 3 (Mar. 1977), 143–153.
9. Patterson, D.A. Microprogramming. *Sci. Am. 248*, 3 (Mar. 1983), 36–43.
10. Patterson, D.A. RISC watch. *Comput. Archit. News 12*, 1 (Mar. 1984), 11–19.
11. Patterson, D.A., and Séquin, C. A VLSI RISC. *Computer 15*, 9 (Sept. 1982), 8–21.
12. Radin, G. The 801 minicomputer. *IBM J. Res. Dev. 27*, 3 (May 1983), 237–246.
13. Ungar, D., Blau, R., Foley, P., Samples, D., and Patterson, D. Architecture of SOAR: Smalltalk on a RISC. In *Proceedings of the 11th Symposium on Computer Architecture* (Ann Arbor, Mich., June 5–7). ACM, New York, 1984, pp. 188–197.

CR Categories and Subject Descriptors: B.1.1 [**Control Structures and Microprogramming**]: Control Design Styles: B.2.1 [**Arithmetic and Logic Structures**]: Design Styles: B.7.1 [**Integrated Circuits**]: Types and Design Styles: C.1.0 [**Processor Architectures**]: General
  General Terms: Design, Performance
  Additional Key Words and Phrases: RISC, VLSI, microprocessors. CPU

Author's Present Address: David A. Patterson, Dept. of Electrical Engineering and Computer Sciences, Computer Science Division, University of California, Berkeley, CA 94720.

Permission to copy without fee all or part of this material is granted provided that the copies are not made or distributed for direct commercial advantage, the ACM copyright notice and the title of the publication and its date appear, and notice is given that copying is by permission of the Association for Computing Machinery. To copy otherwise, or to republish, requires a fee and/or specific permission.

VLSI Processor Architecture

JOHN L. HENNESSY

Abstract — A processor architecture attempts to compromise between the needs of programs hosted on the architecture and the performance attainable in implementing the architecture. The needs of programs are most accurately reflected by the dynamic use of the instruction set as the target for a high level language compiler. In VLSI, the issue of implementation of an instruction set architecture is significant in determining the features of the architecture. Recent processor architectures have focused on two major trends: large microcoded instruction sets and simplified, or reduced, instruction sets. The attractiveness of these two approaches is affected by the choice of a single-chip implementation. The two different styles require different tradeoffs to attain an implementation in silicon with a reasonable area. The two styles consume the chip area for different purposes, thus achieving performance by different strategies. In a VLSI implementation of an architecture, many problems can arise from the base technology and its limitations. Although circuit design techniques can help alleviate many of these problems, the architects must be aware of these limitations and understand their implications at the instruction set level.

Index Terms — Computer organization, instruction issue, instruction set design, memory mapping, microprocessors, pipelining, processor architecture, processor implementation, VLSI.

I. INTRODUCTION

ADVANCES in semiconductor fabrication capabilities have made it possible to design and fabricate chips with tens of thousands to hundreds of thousands of transistors, operating at clock speeds as fast as 16 MHz. Single-chip processors that have transistor complexity and performance comparable to CPU's found in medium- to large-scale mainframes can be designed. Indeed, both commercial and experimental nMOS processors have been built that match the performance of large minicomputers, such as DEC's VAX 11/780.

In the context of this paper, a processor architecture is defined by the view of the programmer; this view includes user visible registers, data types and their formats, and the instruction set. The memory system and I/O system architectures may be defined either on or off the chip. Because we are concerned with chip-level processors we must also include the definition of the interface between the chip and its environment. The chip interface defines the use of individual pins, the bus protocols, and the memory architecture and I/O architecture to the extent that these architectures are controlled by the processor's external interface.

Manuscript received April 30, 1984; revised July 31, 1984. This work was supported by the Defense Advanced Research Projects Agency under Grants MDA903-79-C-680 and MDA903-83-C-0335.

The author is with the Computer Systems Laboratory, Stanford University, Stanford, CA 94305.

In many ways, the architecture and organization of these VLSI processors is similar to the designs used in the CPU's of modern machines implemented using standard parts and bipolar technology. However, the tremendous potential of MOS technology has not only made VLSI an attractive implementation medium, but it has also encouraged the use of the technology for new experimental architectures. These new architectures display some interesting concepts both in how they utilize the technology and in how they overcome performance limitations that arise both from the technology and from the standard barriers to high performance encountered in any CPU.

This paper investigates the architectural design of VLSI uniprocessors. We divide the discussion into six major segments. First, we examine the goals of a processor architecture; these goals establish a framework for examining various architectural approaches. In the second section, we explore the two major styles: reduced instruction set architectures and high level microcoded instruction set architectures. Some specific techniques for supporting both high level languages and operating systems functions are discussed in the third and fourth sections, respectively. The fifth section of the paper surveys several major processor architectures and their implementations; we concentrate on showing the salient features that make the processors unique. In the sixth section we investigate an all-important issue — implementation. In VLSI, the organization and implementation of a CPU significantly affect the architecture. Using some examples, we show how these features interact with each other, and we indicate some of the principles involved.

II. ARCHITECTURAL GOALS

A computer architecture is measured by its effectiveness as a host for applications and by the performance levels obtainable by implementations of the architecture. The applications are written in high level languages, translated to the processor's instruction set by a compiler, and executed on the processor using support functions provided by the operating system. Thus, the suitability of an architecture as a host is determined by two factors: its effectiveness in supporting high level languages, and the base it provides for system level functions. The efficiency of an architecture from an implementation viewpoint must be evaluated both on the cost and on the performance of implementations of that architecture. Since a computer's role as program host is so important, the

Reprinted from *IEEE Transactions on Computers*, Volume C-33, Number 12, December 1984, pages 1221-1246. Copyright © 1984 by The Institute of Electrical and Electronics Engineers, Inc.

EH0251-9/86/0000/0096$01.00 © 1984 IEEE

instruction set designer must carefully consider both the usefulness of the instruction set for encoding programs and the performance of implementations of that instruction set.

Although the instruction set design may have several goals, the most obvious and usually most important goal is *performance*. Performance can be measured in many ways; typical measurements include instructions per second, total required memory bandwidth, and instructions needed both statically and dynamically for an application. Although all these measurements have their place, they can also be misleading. They either measure an irrelevant point, or they assume that the implementation and the architecture are independent.

The key to performance is the ability of the architecture to execute high level language programs. Measures based on assembly language performance are much less useful because such measurements may not reflect the same patterns of instruction set usage as compiled code. Of course, compiler interaction clouds the issue of high level language performance; that is to be expected. The architecture also influences the ease and difficulty of building compilers.

Implementation related effects can cause serious problems if the abstract measurements are used as a gauge of the real hardware performance. The architecture profoundly influences the complexity, cost, and potential performance of the implementation. On the basis of abstract architecturally oriented benchmarks, the most complex, highest level instruction sets seem to make the most sense; these include machines like the VAX [1], the Intel-432 [2], the DEL approaches [3], and the Xerox Mesa architectures [4]. However, the cost of implementing such architectures is higher, and their performance is not necessarily as good as architectural measures, such as instructions executed per high level statement, might indicate. Many VAX benchmarks show impressive architectural measurements, especially for instruction bytes fetched. However, data from implementations of the architecture show that the same performance is not attained. VAX instructions are short; the instruction fetch unit must constantly prefetch instructions to keep the rest of the machine busy. This includes fetching one or more instructions that sequentially follow a branch. Since branches are frequent and they are taken with higher than 50 percent probability, the instructions fetched following a branch are most often not executed. This leads to a significantly higher instruction bandwidth than the architectural measurements indicate.

Since most programs are written in high level languages, the role of the architecture as a host for programs depends on its ability to serve as a target for the code generated by compilers for high level languages of interest. The effectiveness is a function of the architecture, the compiler technology, and, to a lesser extent, the programming language. Much commonality exists among languages in their need for hardware support; furthermore, compilers tend to translate common features to similar types of code sequences. Some special language features may be significant enough to influence the architecture. Examples of such of features are support for tags, support for floating point arithmetic, and support for parallel constructs.

Program optimization is becoming a standard part of many compilers. Thus, the architecture should be designed to support the code produced by an optimizing compiler. An implication of this observation is that the architecture should expose the details of the hardware to allow the compiler to maximize the efficiency of its use of that hardware. The compiler should also be able to compare alternative instruction sequences and choose the more time or space efficient sequence. Unless the execution implications of each machine instruction are visible, the compiler cannot make a reasonable choice between two alternatives. Likewise, hidden computations cannot be optimized away. This view of the optimizing compiler argues for a simplified instruction set that maximizes the visibility of all operations needed to execute the program.

Large instruction set architectures are usually implemented with microcode. In VLSI, silicon area limitations often force the use of microcode for all but the smallest and simplest instruction sets: all of the commercial 16 and 32 bit processors make extensive use of microcode in their implementations. In a processor that is microcoded, an additional level of translation, from the machine code to microinstructions, is done by the hardware. By allowing the compiler to implement this level of translation, the cost of the translation is taken once at compile-time rather than repetitively every time a machine instruction is executed. The view of an optimizing compiler as generating microcode for a simplified instruction set is explained in depth in a paper by Hopkins [5]. In addition to eliminating a level of translation, the compiler "customizes" the generated code to fit the application [6]. This customizing by the compiler can be thought of as a realizable approach to dynamically microcoding the architecture. Both the IBM 801 and MIPS exploit this approach by "compiling down" to a low level instruction set.

The architecture and its strength as a compiler target determine much of the performance at the architectural level. However, to make the hardware usable an operating system must be created on the hardware. The operating system requires certain architectural capabilities to achieve full functional performance with reasonable efficiency. If the necessary features are missing, the operating system will be forced to forego some of its user-level functions, or accept significant performance penalities. Among the features considered necessary in the construction of modern operating systems are

• privileged and user modes, with protection of specialized machine instructions and of system resources in user mode;

• support for external interrupts and internal traps;

• memory mapping support, including support for demand paging, and provision for memory protection; and

• support for synchronization primitives, in multiprocessor configurations, if conventional instructions cannot be used for that purpose.

Some architectures provide additional instructions for supporting the operating system. These instructions are included for two primary reasons. First, they establish a standard interface for hardware dependent functions. Second, they may enhance the performance of the operating system by supporting some special operation in the architecture.

Standardizing an interface by including it in the architecture has been cited as a goal both for conventional high level instructions, e.g., on the VAX [7], and for operating system interfaces [2]. Standardizing an interface in the architectural specification can be more definitive, but it can carry performance penalties when compared to a standard at the assembly language level. This standard can be implemented by macros, or by standard libraries. Putting the interface into the architecture commits the hardware designers to supporting it, but it does not inherently enforce or solidify the interface.

Enhancing operating system performance via the architecture can be beneficial. However, such enhancements must be compared to alternative improvements that will increase general performance. Even when significant time is spent in the operating system, the bulk of the time is spent executing general code rather than special functions, which might be supported in the architecture. The architect must carefully weigh the proposed feature to determine how it affects other components of the instruction set (overhead costs, etc.), as well as the opportunity cost related to the components of the instruction set that could have been included instead. Many times the performance gained by such high level features is small because the feature is not heavily used or because it yields only a minor improvement over the same function implemented with a sequence of other instructions. Often the combination of a feature's cost and performance merit forms a strong argument against its presence in the architecture.

Hardware organization can dramatically affect performance. This is especially true when the implementation is in VLSI where the interaction of the architecture and its implementation is more pronounced. Some of the more important architectural implications are as follows.

• The limited speed of the technology encourages the use of parallel implementations. That is, many slower components are used rather than a smaller number of fast components. This basic method has been used by many designers on projects as varied as systolic arrays [8] to the MicroVAX I datapath chip [9].

• The cost of complexity in the architecture. This is true in any implementation medium, but is exacerbated in VLSI, where complexity becomes more difficult to accommodate. A corollary of this rule is that no architectural feature is free.

• Communication is more expensive than computation. Architectures that require significant amounts of global interaction will suffer in implementation.

• The chip boundaries have two major effects. First, they impose hard limits on data bandwidth on and off the chip. Second, they create a substantial disparity between on-chip and off-chip communication delays.

The architecture affects the performance of the hardware primarily at the organizational level where it imposes certain requirements. Smaller effects occur at the implementation level where the technology and its properties become relevant. The technology acts strongly as a weighting factor favoring some organizational approaches and penalizing others. For example, VLSI technology typically makes the use of memory on the chip attractive: relatively high densities can be obtained and chip crossings can be eliminated.

A goal in implementation is to provide the fastest hardware possible; this translates into two rules.

1) Minimize the clock cycle of the system. This implies both reducing the overhead on instructions as well as organizing the hardware to minimize the delays in each clock cycle.

2) Minimize the number of cycles to perform each instruction. This minimization must be based on the expected dynamic frequency of instruction use. Of course, different programming languages may differ in their frequency of instruction usage.

This second rule may dictate sacrificing performance in some components of the architecture in return for increased performance of the more heavily used parts.

The observation that these types of tradeoffs are needed, together with the fact that larger architectures generate additional overhead, have led to the reduced (or simplified) instruction set approach [10], [11]. Such architectures are streamlined to eliminate instructions that occur with low frequency in favor of building such complex instructions out of sequences of simpler instructions. The overhead per instruction can be significantly reduced and the implementor does not have to discriminate among the instructions in the architecture. In fact, most simplified instruction set machines use single cycle execution of every instruction; this eliminates complex tradeoffs both by the hardware implementor and the compiler writer. The simple instruction set permits a high clock speed for the instruction execution, and the one-cycle nature of the instructions simplifies the control of the machine. The simplification of control allows the implementation to more easily take advantage of parallelism through pipelining. The pipeline allows simultaneous execution of several instructions, similar to the parallel activity that would occur in executing microinstructions for the interpretation of a more complex instruction set.

III. Basic Architectural Trends

The major trend that has emerged among computer architectures in the recent past has been the emphasis on targeting to and support for high level languages. This trend is especially noticeable within the microprocessor area where it represents an abrupt change from the assembly-language-oriented architectures of the 1970's. The most recent generation of commercially available processors, the Motorola 68000, the Intel 80X86, Intel iAPX-432, the Zilog 8000, and the National 16032, clearly show the shift from the 8-bit assembly language oriented machines to the 16-bit compiled language orientation. The extent of this change is influenced by the degree of compatibility with previous processor design. The machines that are more compatible (the Intel 80X86 and the Zilog processors) show their heritage and the compatibility has an effect on the entire instruction set. The Motorola and National products show much less compatibility and more of a compiled language direction.

This trend is more obvious among designs done in universities. The Mead and Conway [12] structured design approach has made it possible to design VLSI processors within the university environment. These projects have been language-directed. The RISC project at Berkeley and the MIPS project at Stanford both aim to support high level languages with simplified instruction sets. The MIT Scheme project [13] supports LISP via a built-in interpreter for the language.

A. RISC-Style Machines

A RISC, reduced instruction set computer, is a machine with simplified instruction set. The architectures that are generally considered to be RISC's are the Berkeley RISC I and II processors, the Stanford MIPS processor, and the IBM 801 processor (which is *not* a microprocessor). These machines certainly have instruction sets that are simpler than most other machines; however, they may still have many instructions: the 801 has over 100 instructions, MIPS has over 60. They may also have conceptually complex details: the 801 has instructions for programmer cache management, while MIPS requires that pipeline dependence hazards be removed in software. All three architectures avoid features that require complex control structures, though they may use a complex implementation structure where the complexity is merited by the performance gained.

The adjective *streamlined* is probably a better description of the key characteristics of such architectures. The most important features are

1) regularity and simplicity in the instruction set allows the use of the same, simple hardware units in a common fashion to execute almost all instructions;

2) single cycle execution — most instructions execute in one machine (or pipeline) cycle. These architectures are register-oriented: all operations on data objects are done in the registers. Only load and store instructions access memory; and

3) fixed length instructions with a small variety of formats.

The advantages of streamlined instruction set architectures come from a close interaction between architecture and implementation. The simplicity of the architecture lends a simplicity to the implementation. The advantages gained from this include the following.

1) The simplified instruction formats allow very fast instruction decoding. This can be used to reduce the pipeline length (without reducing throughput), and/or shorten the instruction execution time.

2) Most instructions can be made to execute in a single cycle; the register-oriented (or load/store) nature of the architecture provides this capability.

3) The simplicity of the architecture means that the organization can be streamlined; the overhead on each instruction can be reduced, allowing the clock cycle to be shortened.

4) The simpler design allows silicon resources and human resources to be concentrated on features that enhance performance. These may be features that provide additional high level language performance, or resources may be concentrated on enhancing the throughput of the implementation.

5) The low level instruction set provides the best target for state-of-the-art optimizing compiler technology. Nearly every transformation done by the optimizer on the intermediate form will result in an improved running time because the transformation will eliminate one or more instructions. The benefits of register allocation are also enhanced by eliminating entire instructions needed to access memory.

6) The simplified instruction set provides an opportunity to eliminate a level of translation at runtime, in favor of translating at compile-time. The microcode of a complex instruction set is replaced by the compiler's code generation function.

The potential disadvantages of the streamlined architecture come from two areas: memory bandwidth and additional software requirements. Because a simplified instruction set will require more instructions to perform the same function, instruction memory bandwidth requirements are potentially higher than for a machine with more powerful and more tightly encoded instructions. Some of this disadvantage is mitigated by the fact that instruction fetching will be more complicated when the architecture allows multiple sizes of instructions, especially if the instructions require multiple fetches due to lack of alignment or instruction length.

Register-oriented architectures have *significantly* lower data memory bandwidth [10], [14]. Lower data memory bandwidth is highly desirable since data access is less predictable than instruction access and can cause more performance problems. The existing streamlined instruction set implementations achieve this reduction in data bandwidth from either special support for on-chip data accessing, as in the RISC register windows (see Section IV-A), or the compiler doing register allocation. The load/store nature of these architectures is very suitable for effective register allocation by the compiler; furthermore, each eliminated memory reference results in saving an entire instruction. In a memory-oriented instruction set only a portion of an instruction is saved.

If implementations of the architecture are expected to have a cache, trading increased instruction bandwidth for decreased data bandwidth can be advantageous. Instruction caches typically achieve higher hit rates than data caches for the same number of lines because of greater locality in code. Instruction caches are also simpler since they can be read-only. Thus, a small on-chip instruction cache might be used to lower the required off-chip instruction bandwidth.

The question of instruction bandwidth is a tricky one. Statically, programs for machines with simplier, less densely encoded instruction sets, will obviously be larger. This static size has some secondary effect on performance due to increased working set sizes both for the instruction cache and the virtual memory. However, the potentially higher bandwidth requirements are much more important. Here we see a more unclear picture.

While the streamlined machines will definitely need more instruction bytes fetched at the architectural level, they have some benefits at the implementation level. The MIPS and RISC architectures use *delayed branches* [15] to reduce the fetching of instructions that will not be executed. A delayed branch means that instructions following a branch will be executed until the branch destination can be gotten into the pipeline. Data taken on MIPS had shown that 21 percent of the instructions that are executed occur during a branch delay cycle; in the case of an architecture without the delayed branch, that 21 percent of the cycles would be wasted. In many machine implementations the instructions are independently fetched by an instruction prefetch unit so that when the branch is taken the instruction prefetch is wasted. Another data point that points to the same conclusion is from the VAX; Clark found that 25 percent of the VAX instructions executed are *taken* branches. This means that 25 percent of the time, the fetched instruction (i.e., the one following the branch) is not executed. Thus the bandwidth is only 80 percent of its effective bandwidth.

There are some important differences in peak bandwidth and average bandwidth for instruction memory. To be competitive in performance the complex instruction set machines must come close to achieving single cycle execution for the simple instructions, e.g., register–register instructions. To achieve this goal, the peak bandwidth must at least come close to the same bandwidth that a reduced instruction set machine will require. This peak bandwidth determines the real complexity of the memory system needed to support the processor.

Code generation for both streamlined machines and simplified machines is believed to be equally difficult. In the case of the streamlined machine, optimization is more important, but code generation is simpler since the alternative implementations of code sequences do not exist [16]. The use of code optimization, which is usually done on an intermediate form whose level is below the level of the machine instruction set, means that code generation must coalesce sequences of low level intermediate form instructions into larger more powerful machine instructions. This process is complicated by the detail in the machine instruction set and by complex tradeoffs the compiler faces in choosing what sequence of instructions to synthesize. Experience at Stanford with our retargetable compiler system [17] has shown that the streamlined instruction sets have an easier code generation problem than the more complex instruction machines. We have also found that the simplicity of the instruction set makes it easier to determine whether an optimizing transformation is effective. In retargetting the compiler system to multiple architectures, we have found better optimization results for simpler machines [18]. In an experiment at Berkeley, a program for the Berkeley RISC processor showed little improvement in running time between a compiled and carefully hand-coded version, while substantial improvement was possible on the VAX [19]. Since the same compiler was used in both instances, a reasonable conclusion is that less work is needed to achieve good code for the RISC processor when compared to the VAX and that a simpler compiler suffices for the RISC processor.

B. Microcoded Instruction Sets

The alternative to a streamlined machine is a higher level instruction set. For the purposes of this paper, we will use the term *high level instruction set* to mean an architecture with more powerful instructions; one of the key arguments of the RISC approach is that the high level nature of the instruction set is not necessarily a better fit for high level languages. The reader should take care to keep these two different interpretations of "high level" architecture distinct. The complications of such an instruction set will usually require that the implementation be done through microcode. A large instruction set with support for multiple data types and addressing modes must use a denser instruction encoding. In addition to more opcode space, the large number of combinations of opcode, data type, and addressing mode must be encoded efficiently to prevent an explosion in code size.

A high level instruction set has one major technological advantage and several strategic advantages. The denser encoding of the instruction set lowers the static size of the program; the dynamic instruction bandwidth depends on the static size of the most active portions of the program. The major strategic advantage for a high level microcoded instruction set comes from the ability to span a wide range of application environments. Although compilers will tend to use the simpler and straightforward instructions more often, different applications will emphasize different parts of the instruction set [7], [20]. A large instruction set can attempt to accommodate a wide range of application with high level instructions suited to the needs of these applications. This allows the standardization of the instruction set and the ability to interchange object code across a wide range of implementations of the architecture.

In addition to not sharing some of the implementation advantages of a simplified instruction set, a more complex architecture suffers from its own complexity. Instruction set complexity makes it more difficult to ensure correctness and achieve high performance in the implementation. The latter occurs because the size of the instruction set makes it more difficult to tune the sections that are critical to high performance. In fact, one of the advantages claimed for large instruction set machines is that they do not *a priori* discriminate against languages or applications by prejudicing the instruction set. However, similarities in the translation of high level languages could easily allow prejudices that benefited the most common languages and which penalized other languages. There is also a question of design and implementation efficiency with this type of instruction set: some portions of it may see little use in many environments. However, the overhead of that portion of the instruction set is paid by all instructions to the extent that the critical path for the instructions runs through the control unit.

IV. Architectural Support for High Level Languages

Several computers have included special language support in the architecture. This support most often focuses on a small set of primitives for performing frequent language-oriented actions. The most often attacked area is support for procedure calls. This may include anything from a call instruction with simple program counter (PC) saving and branching, to very elaborate instructions that save the PC and some set of registers, set up the parameter list and create the new activation record. A wide range of machines, from the Intel-432, to the VAX, to the Berkeley RISC microprocessor all have special reasonably powerful instructions for supporting procedure calls.

Extensive measurements of procedure call activity have been made. Source language measurements for C and Pascal have been done on the VAX by the RISC group at Berkeley [21]. Clark [7] has measured the VAX instruction set (including call) using a hardware monitor. These measurements confirm two facts. First, procedure calls are infrequent (about

10 percent of the high level statements) compared to the most common simpler instructions (data moves, adds, etc). Second, the procedure call is one of the most costly instructions in terms of execution time; the data from Berkeley indicates that it is the most costly source language statement (i.e., more machine instructions are needed to execute this source statement than most others). This high cost is sufficient to make call one of the most expensive statements, both at the machine instruction set level and at the source language level.

There are a few important caveats to examine when considering these data. The most important observation is that register allocation bloats the cost of procedure call. A simple procedure call in compiled code without register allocation is not very expensive: save the program counter, the old activation record pointer, and create a new activation record. This can be easily done in a few simple instructions, particularly if activation record maintenance is minimized. However, when an additional half-dozen register-allocated variables need to be saved the cost is in the neighborhood of 10–15 instructions. This additional cost is not inherent in the procedure call itself but is an artifact of the register allocator. Such costs should be accounted for by the register allocation algorithm [18], but are often ignored. Despite this, there is merit in lumping these saves and restores as part of the call, if this means that they can be reduced by an efficient method of executing procedure calls.

Before we look at such a method in detail, consider one other possible attack on the problem: reducing call frequency. Modern programming practice encourages the use of many small procedures; often procedures are called exactly once. While this may be good programming practice, an intelligent optimizer can expand inline any procedure that is called exactly once, and perhaps a large number of procedures that are small. For a small procedure, the call overhead may easily be comparable to the procedure size. In such cases, inline expansion of the procedure will increase the execution speed with little or no size penalty. The IBM PL.8 compiler [22] does inline expansion of all leaf-level procedures (i.e., ones that do not call another procedure), while the Stanford U-Code optimizer includes a cost-driven inline expansion phase [18].

A. Support for Procedure Call: The Register Stack

VLSI implementation greatly favors on-chip communication versus off-chip communication. This fact has led many designers to keep small caches (usually for instructions only) or instruction prefetch buffers on the chip as in the VAX microprocessors [23], [24] and the Motorola 68020. However, current limitations prevent the integration of a full size cache (e.g., 2K words) onto the same chip as the processor. An alternative approach is to use a large on-chip register set. This approach sacrifices the dynamic tracking ability of a cache, but it is possible to put a reasonably large register set on the chip because the area per stored bit can be smaller than in a cache. By allowing the compiler to allocate scalar locals and globals to the register set, the amount of main memory data traffic can be lowered substantially. Additionally, the

use of register references versus memory references lowers the amount of addressing overhead. For example, in the Berkeley RISC register–register instructions execute twice as fast as memory accesses. The compiler can be selective about its allocation effectively increasing the "hit rate" of the register file. However, only scalar variables may be allocated to the registers. Thus, some programs may benefit little from this technique, although data [21] has shown that the bulk of the accessed variables are local and global scalars.

Any large register set can achieve the elimination of off-chip references and reduction of addressing overhead. However, to make use of such a large register set without burdening the cost of procedure call by an enormous amount, the register file can be organized as a stack of register sets, allocated dynamically on a per procedure basis. This concept was originally proposed for use in VLSI by Sites [25], expanded by Baskett [26], and has been studied by a wide range of people including Ditzel for a C machine [27], the BBN C machine [28], Lampson [29], and Wakefield for a direct execution style architecture [30]. A full exploration of the concept was done by the Berkeley RISC design group and implemented with some important extensions in their RISC-I microprocessor [21]. The Pyramid supermini computer [31] has a register stack as its main innovative architectural feature. We will explain the register stack concept in detail using the RISC design.

Numerous on-chip registers are arranged in a stack. On each call instruction a new frame, or window, of registers is allocated on the stack and the old set is pushed; on a return instruction the stack is popped. Of course, the push and pop actions are done by manipulation of pointers that indicate the current register frame. Each procedure addresses the registers as $0 \cdots n$ and gets a set of n registers. The compiler attempts to allocate variables to the register frame, eliminating memory accesses. Scalar global variables can be allocated to a base level frame that is accessible to all procedures and does not change during the running of the program. The effectiveness of this scheme for allocating global scalars is limited for languages that may use large numbers of base-level variables; many modern languages with module support, e.g., Ada and Modula, have this property. In addition, any variables that are visible to multiple, separately compiled routines cannot be allocated to registers. There are similar problems in allocating local variables to registers, when those variables may be referenced by inward-nested procedures; we will discuss this problem in detail shortly.

Although this concept is straightforward, there are a number of complications to consider. First, should these frames be fixed in size or variable, and if fixed how large? The advantage of using a fixed frame size is that an appropriately chosen frame size can avoid an addition cycle which is otherwise needed to choose the correct register from the register file. It also has some small simplifications in the call instruction. However, a fixed size frame will provide insufficient registers for some procedures and waste registers for others. Studies by various groups have shown that a small number of registers (around eight) works for most procedures and that an even smaller number can obtain over 80 percent of the benefits. Most implementations of register files use a fixed size frame with from 8 to 16 registers per frame. The stack cache design of Ditzel demonstrates an elegant variable size approach.

In today's technology a processor can contain only a small number of such register frames; e.g., the RISC-II processor has 8 such frames of 16 registers each. Increasing integrated circuit densities may allow more frames but the diminishing returns and implementation disadvantages, which we will discuss shortly, indicate that the number of frames should be kept low. Because it is impossible either to bound at compile-time, or to restrict the calling depth *a priori,* the processor must deal with register stack overflow.

When the register stack overflows, which only happens on a call instruction as a new frame is allocated, the oldest frame must be migrated off the chip to main memory. This function can be done with hardware assist, in microcode as on the Pyramid, or in macrocode as on RISC. In a more complex processor, the oldest stack frames might be migrated off-chip in background using the available data memory cycles. When the processor returns from the call that caused the overflow, the register stack will have an empty frame and the frame saved on the overflow can be reloaded from memory. Alternatively, the reloading can be postponed until execution returns to the procedure whose frame was migrated.

One of the interesting results obtained by the studies done for the RISC register file concerns measurements done of call patterns and the implications for register migration strategies [32]. If we assume that calls are quite random in their behavior, the benefits of the register stack can be quite small. In particular, if the call depth varies widely, then a large number of saves and restores of the register stack frames will be needed. In such a case, the register stack with a fixed size frame can even be slower than a processor without such a stack because all registers are saved and restored whether or not they are being used. However, if the call pattern tends to be something like "call to depth k, make a significant number of calls from level k and higher but mostly within a few levels of k, before backing out," then register stack scheme can perform quite well. It will need to save and restore frames getting to and returning from level k, but once at level k the number of migrations could be very small.

Data collected by the Berkeley RISC designers indicate the latter behavior dominates. This also leads to another important insight: it may be more efficient to migrate frames in batches, thus cutting down on the number of overflows and underflows encountered. However, a recent paper [32] shows that the optimal number of frames to move varies between programs. Furthermore, that study shows that past behavior is not necessarily a good guide when choosing the number of frames to migrate. Simple strategies of moving a single frame or two frames are a good static approximation and should be used.

Because the language C does not have nested scopes of reference, a register file scheme for C need provide addressability only to the local frame and the global frame. This can be easily done by splitting the register set seen by the procedure so tnat registers $0 \cdots m$ address $m + 1$ global registers

and registers $m \cdots n$ reference the $n - m + 1$ local registers. Furthermore, since these global registers are the only globally accessible registers they are never swapped out.

Languages like Ada, Modula, and Pascal have nested scopes and allow up-level referencing from any nested scope to a surrounding scope. This means that the processor must allow addressing to all the register frames that are global to the currently active procedure. Because up-level referencing to intermediate scopes (i.e., to a scope that is not the most global scope) is rare, such addressing can be penalized without significant overall performance loss. In the simple case, the addressing is straightforward: the instruction can give a relative register-set number and a register number (offset in the register-set) and the processor can do the addressing. Even if this instruction is very slow, the performance penalty will be negligible. The complicated case arises when a register stack overflow has occurred and the addressed register frame has been swapped out. In this case, the register reference must become a memory reference.

A similar problem exists with reference (or pass by address) parameters. Variables that are passed as reference parameters may be allocated in a register and may not even have a memory address that can be passed. The language C allows the address of a variable to be obtained by an operator; this causes problems since register-allocated variables will not have addresses.

Fortunately, there are two solutions [29] to these problems. The first is to rely on a two-pass compilation scheme to detect all up-level references or address references and to prevent the associated variable from being allocated in the register stack. This requires a slightly more complex compiler and has some small performance impact. An alternative solution uses some additional hardware capability and will handle both types of nonlocal references. Let us assume that each register frame (and hence each register) has a main memory address, where it resides if it is swapped out. A nonlocal reference (up-level in the scope of the reference) can be translated by computing the address of the desired frame, which is a function of

• the address in memory for the current frame (which is based only on the absolute frame number), and

• the number of frames offset from the current frame, which is based on the differences in lexical levels between the current procedure and the scope of the referenced variable.

With these two pieces of information we can calculate the memory address of the desired frame. Likewise, for a reference parameter that is in a register we can calculate and pass the memory address assigned to the register location in the frame.

Now, this leaves only one problem: some memory addresses can refer to registers that may or may not currently be in the processor. If the referenced register window has overflowed into memory, then we can treat the reference as a conventional memory reference. If the register is currently on-chip, then we need to find the register set and access the on-chip version. Since this access need not be fast, it is easy to check the current register file and get the contents, or to allow the memory references to complete [33].

A register stack allows the use of a fairly simple register allocator, as well as mitigating the cost of register save/restore at call statements. Compilers often attempt to speed up procedure linkage by communicating parameters and return values in the registers. If the compiler is not doing global register allocation, this task is easy; otherwise, the compiler must integrate the register allocation in existence at the call site with the register usage needed for parameter passing. This communication of parameters in registers can improve performance by about 10 percent. However, using this improvement with a straightforward register stack is impossible since neither procedure can address the registers of the other in a fast and efficient manner.

The RISC processor extended the idea of the register stack to solve this problem [14]. On RISC the frames of a caller and callee overlap by a small number of registers. That is, the j high order registers of the caller correspond to the j low order registers of the callee. The caller uses these registers to pass the actual parameters, and the callee can use them to return the procedure result. The number of overlapping registers is based on the number of expected parameters and on hardware design considerations.

The disadvantages of the register set idea come from three areas. First, improved compiler technology, mostly in the form of good models for register allocation [34]–[36], makes it possible for compilers to achieve very high register "hit" rates and to more efficiently handle saving and restoring at procedure call boundaries. Good allocation of a single register set with a cache for unassigned references could be extremely effective. Since the registers are multiport, the size of the individual register cells and their decode logic means the silicon area per word of storage may approach the area occupied per word in a set associative cache. Another disadvantage with respect to a cache is that the register stack is inefficient: only a small fraction (i.e., one frame) is actively being used at any time. In a cache a larger portion of the storage could be used. Of course, the effectiveness of the register stack is increased when procedure calls are frequent and the portion of the register stack being used changes quickly.

A second disadvantage is that the use of a register set clearly increases the process switching time, by dramatically increasing the processor state. Although process switches happen much less frequently than procedure calls, the true cost of this impact is not known. Studies [37]–[39] have shown that the effect of process switches on TLB and cache hit ratios can be significant.

Third, the register set concept presents a challenging implementation problem, particularly in VLSI. The number of frames is ideally as large as possible; however, if the register file is to be fast it must be on-chip and close to the central data path. The size and tight coupling to the data path will result in slowing down the data path at a rate dependent on the size of the register file; this cost at some point exceeds the merit of a larger register file. The best size for the register stack and its impact on the cycle time is difficult to determine since it depends a great deal on both the implementation and the benchmarks chosen to measure performance. We will discuss the issue of implementation impact later in the paper. The final worth of the register stack ideas remains to be seen; they

have been incorporated in a commercial machine [31] and used in the RISC chip. However, when measured against improved compiler technology and the cost in the cycle time, the real benefits remain unknown.

V. Systems Support

A processor executes compiled programs; however, without an operating system the processor is essentially useless. The operating system requires certain architectural capabilities to achieve functional performance with reasonable efficiency. Perhaps the most important area for operating systems support is in memory management.

Support for memory management has become a feature of almost all computer architectures. The initial microprocessors did not provide such support and even in machines as late as the M68000 no support for demand paging is provided, although support is provided in the M68010. Current microprocessors must compromise between providing all necessary memory management features on-chip and the real limitations of silicon area and interchip delays. Thus, some design compromises are usually made to achieve an acceptable memory mapping mechanism. After looking at the requirements, we will examine the memory mapping support in three processors: the 8-chip VLSI VAX, the Intel iAPX432, and the Stanford MIPS processor. Each of these processors makes a different set of design compromises.

Modern memory systems provide virtual memory support for programs. In addition, the system must also implement memory protection and help to minimize the cost of using virtual memory as well as improve memory utilization. Program relocation is a function of the memory mapping system; segmentation provides a level of relocation that may be used instead of or in addition to paging. Implementing a paged virtual memory requires translation of virtual addresses into real addresses via some type of memory map. Support for demand paging will require the ability to stop and restart instructions when page faults occur. Protection can be provided by the hardware on a segment and/or page basis.

A. VAX and VLSI VAX Memory Management

The memory management scheme used in the VAX architecture is a fairly conventional paging strategy. Some of the more interesting aspects of the memory architecture arise when the implementation techniques used in the VLSI VAX's are examined.

The 2^{32} byte virtual address space is broken into several segments. The main division into two halves provides for a system space (a system wide common address space) and a user process address space. The process address space is further subdivided into a P0 region, used for programs, and a P1 region, used for stack-allocated data. The heap, from which dynamically managed nonstack data are allocated, is placed above the code in the P0 region. Fig. 1 shows this breakdown. The P0 and P1 regions grow towards each other, while the system region grows towards its upper half, which is currently reserved. The decomposition into system and process space has two main effects: it guarantees in the architecture a shared region for processes as well as for the operating system, and it allows the processor implementation to

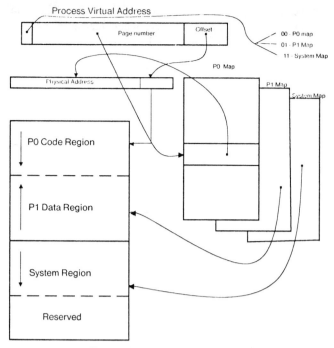

Fig. 1. VAX address space mapping.

distinguish between memory references that belong to a single process and those that are owned by the operating system or shared among processes. Both the operating system and the memory mapping hardware can take advantage of this knowledge. The operating system can use the page address to determine if a page is shared; this may affect the way in which it is handled by the page replacement routines. The use of the P0 and P1 spaces results in increased efficiency in page table utilization, as we will see shortly.

The two high order bits of a virtual address serve to classify the reference into the P0, P1, or system region. Each region uses its own page table. The next twenty high order bits are used to index the page table, while the low order nine bits are used as the page offset. A set of registers tracks the location of the page table for each region. These registers also keep the current length of the page table, so that the entire table need not be allocated in memory, if it is not used. The relatively small page size (512 bytes) is probably not optimal for most VAX machines that are used with real memory of 1–8 MB.

From an architectural viewpoint the major distinguishing factor of the VAX memory management scheme is the decomposition of the address space into four regions with separate page tables. An advantage of this scheme is that it helps prevent contention in caches and translation lookaside buffers (TLB's) by separating those portions of the address space. Another advantage is that the size of the page tables needed can be reduced since each area can have its own table with its own limit register. A single page table with a limit register cannot be used for this purpose because high level language programs typically include two areas whose memory allocations must grow: the heap (for dynamically allocated objects) and the stack. Furthermore, in growing the stack, the compiler assumes that stack frames will be contiguous in virtual address space. Thus, if a single page table is to be used it will require a pair of limit registers. This need is obviated

by splitting user space into the P0 and P1 region, each with a single register. This solution is an interesting contrast to the MIPS approach, which we will discuss shortly.

On the VAX 11/780, the translation lookaside buffer uses some portion of the high order part of the virtual address as the index. This splits the buffer into two partitions: the first to hold references to pages in system space and the second to hold references to pages in the active process' space. The benefit of this approach is that only the second partition of the TLB need be cleared on a process switch; the first partition is process independent. However, studies by Clark [40] have shown that this split is not necessarily beneficial. For example, substantially higher TLB miss rates for system space references, indicate that the partition in the TLB sizes is suboptimal.

There are two VAX implementations that are in VLSI; we discuss these in further detail in the survey section. We will look at the memory management implementation on the 8-chip VLSI VAX. In the 8-chip set, memory management is handled at two levels.

1) The main processor chip, responsible for instruction fetch and execution, has a mini-TLB with 5 entries.

2) The Memory/Peripheral Subsystem chip contains the tag array for a 512-entry TLB as well as the tag array for a 2K cache.

The mini-TLB allows very fast (50 ns) address translation on-chip. The small size allows the buffer to be fully associative; however, the TLB is partitioned into a one-entry instruction-stream buffer (always used for the currently executing instruction) and a four-entry data-stream buffer. This prevents the ambitious instruction prefetch unit from interfering with the execution of the current instruction, which may require up to five operands to be mapped. When a hit is obtained on the internal TLB, a physical address is driven out to the memory subsystem chip, which acts as the cache. This whole process occurs in a 200 ns cycle. If the internal TLB misses, but the external TLB hits, a single cycle penalty is taken and the data are moved into the internal TLB.

This design is an interesting compromise between the limitations of silicon area that prohibited a large on-chip TLB and the need to have efficient memory address translation. The relatively small penalty incurred when the mini-TLB misses but the main TLB hits, allows operation as if the TLB were quite large. A substantial penalty is only incurred if the main TLB misses, and microcode intervention is required to compute the physical address. The larger 512 entry TLB will yield a higher hit ratio than the 128 entry TLB used in the VAX 11/780. In fact the judicious choice of a small on-chip TLB coupled with a larger off-chip TLB with a minimal penalty, can probably achieve performance comparable to the one-level TLB used in the 11/780.

B. Intel iAPX432 Memory Management

The 432 supports a capability-based addressing scheme. Every memory address consists of a segment and an offset; there may be up to 2^{24} segments and each segment has at most 2^{16} bytes. Although few individual objects will require more than one segment, many programs will use a total stack or heap size that requires multiple segments. Because such allocation requirements are nearly impossible to predict at compile-time, the compiler must assume that references to other parts of the stack and references to the heap will require a segment change. This will result in a performance loss if the number of segments that are simultaneously active becomes large.

The 432 uses a more powerful scheme than segment plus offset: the segment designator is an access descriptor that contains the access rights for the segment, as well as information for addressing the segment. These access descriptors are similar to the concept of capabilities [41]. The access descriptors are collected into an access segment, which is indexed by a segment selector. The address portion of the access descriptor contains a pointer to a segment table, which specifies the entry providing the base address of the segment. The offset to the segment is part of the original operand address, whose format is described in a following section. This two-level mapping process is illustrated in Fig. 2. The 432's data processor chip contains a 22 element cache on the access segment and the segment table; 14 of the 20 entries are preassigned for each procedure, two are reserved for object table entries, and six entries are available for generic use. This cache reduces the frequency with which the hardware must examine the two-level map in memory.

The 432 architecture uses the access segment to define a domain for a program. A program's domain of access consists of an access segment that provides addressing to multiple data and program segments. For program segments, the access descriptor indicates that the object is a program and checks that the execution of instructions occurs only from an instruction segment. Similarly, all branches are checked to be sure that they will transfer to an instruction segment. In addition to the instruction segments, the 432 defines both data and stack segments, as well as constant segments.

The 432 addressing scheme achieves two primary objectives: support for capabilities, and support for fine-grained protection. The major objection raised to the addressing scheme is that it is more complicated and powerful than is necessary. The use of capabilities has been explored in several systems [42], [43] with limited success at least partially due to a lack of hardware support. Most of these systems found that capability based addressing was expensive and this may have prevented its use. An interesting discussion of the issues is contained in a paper by Wilkes [44]. The other major advantage claimed for the 432 is that it provides fine grained protection to allow users to protect against array bounds violations and references out of a module, by limiting the size of the segment. However, a careful examination of the requirements imposed by Ada, the host language for the 432, shows that the segment based approach is only usable when each object that can be indexed or addressed dynamically is in a single segment. When this is not the case, runtime checks are required by the compiler and these checks guarantee that the reference is legal, making the hardware segment checking superfluous. There are several reasons why allocating each such data object to a unique segment is an unsuitable approach. The most important reason is that it will cause a large increase in the number of segments (one per data object to be protected), which will decrease the locality of segment references and hamper the effectiveness of the address cache. Address cache

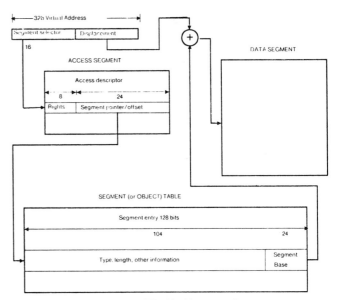

Fig. 2.   iAPX-432 address mapping.

misses must be translated at a much slower rate (approximately 5 μs per translation) causing a substantial degradation in performance.

Despite these objections, the 432 addressing mechanism does provide the most cost effective implementation of capabilities in hardware to date. Future evolution of software systems, such as Smalltalk, may make object-based environments more important. When such environments are very dynamic and a high level of protection is desired, the 432 capability-based mechanism offers an attractive vehicle for implementation. The challenge to such architectures will be to make the performance penalties for a capability-based system insignificant when compared to their functional benefits.

C. MIPS Memory Management

In addition to the standard requirements for virtual memory mapping, the Stanford MIPS processor attempts to support a large uniform address space for each process, and fast context switching. One mechanism for facilitating context switching is the incorporation of a process identification number into the virtual memory address. The use of the process id number helps achieve fast context switches by allowing the cache and memory address translation units to avoid the cold start penalties. These penalties appear in systems that require caches and translation buffers to be flushed because processes share the same virtual address space. The process id approach also allows the use of a large linear address space, avoiding the difficulties that arise when segment boundaries are introduced. The realities of the MIPS implementation technology (a 4 μm channel length nMOS) meant that it was not feasible to include all of the virtual to physical translation on the same chip as the processor.

Consequently, a novel memory segmentation scheme was added to the architecture; it is designed to work with a conventional page mapping scheme implemented with the use of an off-chip TLB. Each process has a process address space of 2^{32} words. The first step of the translation is to remove the top n bits of the address and replace them by an n-bit *process identifier* (PID). Fig. 3 shows the generation of this virtual

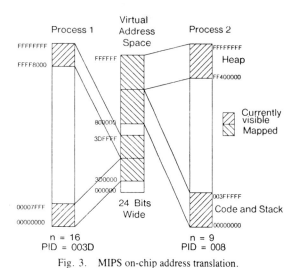

Fig. 3. MIPS on-chip address translation.

TABLE I
SUMMARY OF TRANSLATION BUFFER FEATURES ON VAX IMPLEMENTATIONS

Machine	Entries	Features
11/780	128	Direct mapped; 1/2 system, 1/2 user
VLSI VAX	5 on processor chip	Fully associative; limit one instruction entry
	512 on companion-chip	Set associative; not reserved
MicroVAX-32	8	Fully associative

address. By restricting the process address under the mask to be all ones or all zeros, the accessible portion of the process address space becomes the low 2^{32-n-1} and the high 2^{32-n-1} words; this allows two large-address segments to grow towards one another but not overlap. An attempt to access any of the nonvisible words (by generating an address that fails to have all ones or all zeros under the mask) will cause an exception. The operating system can then remap the process identifier in such a way as to give the faulting process a smaller PID number and thus a larger visible portion of its process address space. This will only happen if the program used more heap or stack space then it was initially allocated. This is similar to the procedure of expanding the VAX page tables by increasing the page table limit register for one of the address spaces.

An additional level of translation maps the processor's virtual address to a physical address. This level of mapping could be implemented with a wide variety of hardware ranging from a direct map to a TLB.

The constraining factor on MIPS is that the total size of all the visible process address spaces must be less than the size of the implementation's virtual address space. This restricts the number of processes that can actively use the memory map; should this number of processes become very large, the operating system will need to periodically reuse a PID. Whenever a process with a shared PID is made active, a process and cache sweep will be needed. This should not happen frequently, since the number of small processes that can be created is very large.

D. Summary

Modern memory management techniques seem to have become an issue of major concern for VLSI processor architectures. The approaches described in this section have interesting differences.

The VAX architecture defines a partitioning of its address space and a two-level memory mapping scheme. This scheme permits the use of a small number of page limit registers to control the mapping of several potentially growing user storage areas. Table I makes the comparison among translation buffers (which are required to achieve acceptable memory mapping performance on the VAX) used on the

VAX 11/780 mainframe, the 9-chip VLSI VAX, and the single-chip MicroVAX-32.

The Intel 432 offers one of the most sophisticated memory mapping and protection schemes. It provides access to a large segmented address space (with small segments, unfortunately). Segments are protected by capabilities that provide extremely flexible control over access to the segment. An address cache (or translation buffer) reduces the need for a costly two-level translation of addresses.

MIPS uses the simplest memory mapping scheme of these three architectures. Its important features are a large, (optionally) unpartitioned address space that allows any of a variety of page mapping schemes implemented off-chip. The architecture has the novel feature of a variable-sized process id that is included as part of the virtual address; this helps decrease the loss of performance when a context switch occurs as well as communicating the process id to allow for protection checks by off-chip hardware.

VI. SOME INTERESTING VLSI ARCHITECTURES

In this section we discuss some of the interesting points of several commercial and experimental microprocessor architectures. The purpose of this examination is not a definitive comparison of the architectures. Our goal is to discuss some of the architectural features, examine tradeoffs in the architecture, and analyze the methods used to achieve performance as well as the limitations on performance. The architectures chosen represent only a portion of the available VLSI processors. We have chosen these processors because they provide interesting and contrasting viewpoints. The implementations of these processors vary: some are commercial, and some are university-based experiments. Thus, implementation specific data should be used for interpreting the general behavior of an architecture; differences in the levels of implementation and the size of the implementation efforts make direct performance comparisons unreasonable.

A. The Berkeley RISC Microprocessor

The Berkeley RISC I and II processors [21] were the first microprocessors to explore the concept of a simplified, or reduced, instruction set. The architecture has a total of 31 instructions and is a load/store machine. The 32-bit integer ALU operations (which include add, subtract, logical, and shift operations, but not multiply or divide) all have a 3-operand format, where the operands are registers, or one of the source operands may be a 13-bit immediate constant. The Berkeley RISC provides memory addressing support for bytes, half-words (16 bits), and words (32 bits). The single addressing mode is: register contents plus offset; it can be used to synthesize absolute addressing (by ignoring the register) and register indirect (by making the offset zero).

In addition to the ALU, load, and store instructions, RISC has a set of delayed branch instructions, call and return instructions, and processor status instructions. By simplifying the instruction set, instruction fetch and decode was straightforward, and the amount of control logic needed on the processor was substantially reduced. However, this very loose encoding of instructions means that instruction density is much lower than for other architectures, in the range of 40–70 percent lower. The RISC processor is able to achieve a one machine cycle execution of register–register instructions and a two machine cycle memory access instruction. Its instruction set is summarized in Table II.

The major innovation of the RISC processor has been the addition of a large register stack with overlapping register windows. This idea was explained in detail in the section on register stacks. The register window concept is responsible for much of the performance benefits that RISC demonstrates. The simplicity of the other parts of the instruction set allow reduction in the silicon area needed to implement the processor's control portion, thus freeing up space for the large register file.

There have been two implementations of RISC. The first, RISC-I, did not obtain the desired speed but was nearly perfect functionally. Its 1.5 MHz clock cycle with three clock cycles per instruction, yields an execution rate of one-half million register–register instructions per second. The RISC-II implementation is a completely new, and more sophisticated design; it is functionally correct and runs with an 8 MHz clock cycle at room temperature using a 4 μm single-metal, nMOS process. With four clock cycles per machine cycle, the 4 μm part has a register–register instruction execution rate of 2 MIPS. A 3 μm version has also been fabricated; it achieves a 3 MIPS execution rate for register–register instructions by using a 12 MHz clock. All the Berkeley RISC processors execute load or store instructions at one-half the rate of register–register instructions. The RISC architecture and the microengine are discussed in detail in Katevenis' thesis [33].

B. The Stanford MIPS Processor

The MIPS processor [45]–[47] probably represents the most streamlined processor design to date. A key point in the MIPS philosophy is to expose, in the instruction set, all the processor activity that could affect performance. This philosophy coupled with the concept of a streamlined instruction set allows a shift of functions from hardware to software. This shift in responsibility simplifies the requirements placed on the hardware allowing the machine to have a higher clock speed (4 MHz) than it would otherwise and a fast pipeline (one instruction initiated every two clock cycles).

The best example of this shift of responsibility is that the compiler assumes responsibility for simple register access conflicts in the pipeline. The pipeline hardware has no register interlocks; instead, the compiler is forced to compile code that accounts for the pipeline structure and the register usage patterns. Since storage access may take an undetermined amount of time (due to cache misses, memory delays, etc.),

TABLE II
SUMMARY OF RISC INSTRUCTION SET

Instruction	Operands		Comments
add	Rd,Rs,S2	Rd := Rs + S2	integer add
addc	Rd,Rs,S2	Rd := Rs + S2 + carry	add with carry
sub	Rd,Rs,S2	Rd := Rs - S2	integer subtract
subc	Rd,Rs,S2	Rd := Rs - S2 - borrow	subtract with borrow
subi	Rd,Rs,S2	Rd := S2 - Rs	integer subtract reverse
subci	Rd,Rs,S2	Rd := S2 - Rs - borrow	reverse subtract with borrow
and	Rd,Rs,S2	Rd := Rs & S2	bitwise AND
or	Rd,Rs,S2	Rd := Rs | S2	bitwise OR
xor	Rd,Rs,S2	Rd := Rs xor S2	bitwise EXCLUSIVE OR
sll	Rd,Rs,S2	Rd := Rs shifted by S2	shift left
srl	Rd,Rs,S2	Rd := Rs shifted by S2	shift right logical
sra	Rd,Rs,S2	Rd := Rs shifted by S2	shift right arithmetic
ldw	Rd,(Rx)S2	Rd:=M[Rx+S2]	load word
ldhu	Rd,(Rx)S2	Rd:=M[Rx+S2] (align, zero-fill)	load half unsigned
ldhs	Rd,(Rx)S2	Rd:=M[Rx+S2] (align, sign-ext)	load half signed
ldbu	Rd,(Rx)S2	Rd:=M[Rx+S2] (align, zero-fill)	load byte unsigned
ldbs	Rd,(Rx)S2	Rd:=M[Rx+S2] (align, sign-ext)	load byte signed
stw	Rm,(Rx)S2	M[Rx+S2]:=Rm	store word
sth	Rm,(Rx)S2	M[Rx+S2]:=Rm (align)	store half
stb	Rm,(Rx)S2	M[Rx+S2]:=Rm (align)	store byte
jmpx	COND,(Rx)S2	if COND then PC:=Rx+S2	cond. jump, indexed
jmpr	COND,Y	if COND then PC:=PC+Y	cond. jump, PC-rel.
callx	Rd,(Rx)S2	Rd:=PC; PC:=Rx+S2; CWP--	call indexed
callr	Rd,Y	Rd:=PC; PC:=PC+Y; CWP--	call PC-rel.
ret	(Rx)S2	PC:=Rx+S2; CWP++	return
ldhi	Rd,Y	Rd<31:13>:=Y; Rd<12:0>:=0	load immediate high
gtlpc	Rd	Rd:=lastPC	save value for restarting pipeline
getpsw	Rd	Pd:=PSW	read status word
putpsw	Rm	PSW:=Rm	set status word
reti	(Rx)S2	PC:=Rx+S2; CWP++;	return from interrupt
calli			call an interrupt

Rd, Rs, Rx, Rm: a register (one of 32, where R0=0)
S2: either a register or a 13-bit immediate constant;
COND: 4-bit condition;
Y: 19-bit immediate constant;
PC: Program Counter;
CWP: Current Window-Pointer;
All instructions can optionally set the Condition-Codes.

the pipeline control must delay instructions in the pipeline; however, the compiler is still responsible for scheduling the minimum appropriate delay (i.e., the cache access time). This process amounts to scheduling the code on the processor and has two benefits: it speeds up the code by eliminating pipeline delays due to register utilization, and it makes the pipeline hardware simpler and more regular. This simplicity and regularity allows for a faster clock cycle for the pipeline. This pipeline scheduling as well as other features in the MIPS architecture are oriented towards the use of optimizing compiler technology.

Like most streamlined machines MIPS is a load/store architecture. However, unlike most other new processor architectures, it provides only word-addressing. This choice was made because word addressing dominates in frequency and is also simpler and faster. Byte addressing is supported using a set of instructions for manipulating byte pointers, which are single-word addresses whose two low order are bits used to specify a byte within a word. The MIPS' byte pointer facilities are similar to those supported in the DEC-10 architecture, but are slightly easier to deal with in a compiler and handle primarily 8-bit bytes.

MIPS has 16 orthogonal general purpose registers. All ALU instructions are register–register and are available in two and three operand formats. One of the source registers may be replaced by a small constant. Support for integer multiplication and division consists of special multiply and divide instructions that provide two bits of a Booth multiply sequence and one bit of a divide sequence. The assembly language includes multiply and divide instructions that are expanded into sequences of multiply or divide steps. No hardware is provided for floating point arithmetic.

The architecture has no condition codes. Instead, there is a compare-and-branch operation. Abandoning condition codes in favor of a compare-and-branch instruction has bene-

TABLE III
MIPS ASSEMBLY INSTRUCTIONS

Operation	Operands	Comments	
Arithmetic and logical operations			
Add	src1, src2, dst	dst: = src2 + src1	Integer addition
And	src1, src2, dst	dst: = src2 & src1	Logical and
Ic	src1, src2, dst	dst: = byte src1 of dst is replaced by src2	Insert byte
Or	src1, src2, dst	dst: = src2 | src1	Logical or
Rlc	src1, src2, src3, dst	dst: = src2||src3 rotated by src1 positions	Rotate combined
Rol	src1, src2, dst	dst: = src2 rotated by src1 positions	Rotate
Sll	src1, src2, dst	dst: = src2 shifted left by src1 positions	Shift left logical
Sra	src1, src2, dst	dst: = src2 shifted right by src1 positions	Shift right arithmetic
Srl	src1, src2, dst	dst: = src2 shifted right by src1 positions	Shift right logical
Sub	src1, src2, dst	dst: = src2 - src1	Integer subtraction
Subr	src1, src2, dst	dst: = src1 - src2	Reverse integer subtraction
Xc	src1, src2, dst	dst: = byte src1 of src2	Extract byte
Xor	src1, src2, dst	dst: = src2 ⊕ src1	Logical xor
Transport operations			
Ld	A[src], dst	dst: = M[A + src]	Load based
Ld	[src1 + src2], dst	dst: = M[src1 + src2]	Load based-indexed
Ld	[src1>>src2], dst	dst: = M[src1 shifted by src2]	Load based-shifted
Ld	A, dst	dst: = M[A]	Load direct
Ld	I, dst	dst: = I	Load immediate
Mov	src, dst	dst: = src	Move (byte or register)
St	src1, A[src]	M[A + src]: = src1	Store based
St	src1, [src2 + src3]	M[src2 + src3]: = src1	Store based-indexed
St	src1, [src2>>src3]	M[src2 shifted by src3]: = src1	Store based-shifted
St	src, A	M[A]: = src	Store direct
Control transfer operations			
Bra	dst	PC: = dst + PC	Unconditional relative jump
Bra	Cond, src1, src2, dst	PC: = dst + PC if Cond(src1,src2)	Conditional jump
Jmp	dst	PC: = dst	Unconditional jump direct
Jmp	A[src]	PC: = A + src	Unconditional jump based
Jmp	@A[src]	PC: = M[A + src]	Unconditional jump indirect
Trap	Cond, src1, src2	PC: = 0 if Cond(src1, src2)	Trap instruction
Other operations			
SavePC	A	M[A]: = PC_{-3}	Save multi-stage PC after trap or interrupt
Set	Cond, src, dst	dst: = -1 if Cond(src,dst) dst: = 0 if not Cond(src,dst)	Set conditional

fits for both the compiler and the processor implementation [48]. It simplifies pipelining and branch handling in the implementation and eliminates the need to attempt optimization of the condition code setting.

The compiler and operating system would prefer to see a simple well-structured instruction set. However, this conflicts with the goal of exposing all operations, and allowing the internal processor organization to closely match the architecture. To overcome these two conflicting requirements, the MIPS instruction set architecture is defined at two levels. The first level is visible to the compiler or assembly language programmer. It presents the MIPS machine as a simple streamlined processor. Table III summarizes the MIPS definition at this level.

Each MIPS assembly-level instruction is translated to machine level instructions; this translation process includes a number of machine-dependent optimizations: organizing the instructions to avoid pipeline interlocks and branch delays, expanding instructions that are macros, and packing multiple assembly language instructions into one machine instruction.

The machine-level instruction set of MIPS is closely tied to the pipeline structure. The pipeline structure can be explained by examining the memory and ALU utilization. Each instruction goes through the five stages of the pipeline, with an instruction started on every other stage. During a single instruction, two pipestages are allocated for instruction fetch and decode, two for ALU usage, and one for a data memory

access cycle. The use of two ALU cycles makes it possible to accommodate compare and branch in a single instruction, although the data memory cycle is unused in such an instruction.

The execution of a load instruction requires the use of the ALU only once to compute the effective address of the item that is to be retrieved from memory. This arrangement leaves the ALU idle for one machine cycle during the execution of a simple load instruction. Since the ALU is not busy and most load instructions do not require a full 32-bit instruction word, an additional register–register operation can be done in the same instruction. The companion ALU instruction is an independent two operand register–register instruction. Some forms of the load (e.g., long immediate) sacrifice the ALU instruction encoding space for another use. Since an ALU instruction only uses the ALU once and is a small instruction, the instruction set allows a three operand ALU operation and a two operand ALU operation to be combined in every instruction word. This combination is particularly effective for executing arithmetic code that tends to be operation intensive. Store instructions, and to a lesser extent branch instructions that involve a reference to memory, are treated correspondingly.

These two component instructions consist of two separate and independent halves. The same is true of most other instructions. For example, a compare-and-branch instruction involves a condition test and a PC-relative address calculation. This separation of the instruction into two distinct parts allows the instruction to be viewed as a series of distinct single operators to be executed in the pipeline. This approach simplifies the pipeline control and allows the pipeline to run faster.

Translation between Assembly language (the architectural level) and the hardware instructions (organizational level) is done by the reorganizer [49]. The reorganizer reorders the instructions for each basic block to satisfy the constraints imposed by the pipeline organization; this reorganization establishes at compile time the schedule of instruction execution. Scheduling instructions in software has two benefits: it enhances performance by eliminating instances of pipeline interlocking, and it simplifies the pipeline control hardware allowing a shorter time per pipestage. The disadvantage in the MIPS case is that the absence of a legal instruction to schedule will force the insertion of a no-op instruction; this results in a slight code size increase (less than 5 percent in typical applications [49], [50]) but has no impact on execution speed. MIPS also includes a delayed branch, which is the natural extension of the absence of interlocks to the program counter.

Studies on the MIPS instruction set show that the combination of a simplified pipeline structure and the optimizations performed by the code reorganizer are responsible for a factor of two in performance improvement.

C. The Intel iAPX-432 Processor

The Intel iAPX-432 [2] represents the most complete approach to integrating the needs of an entire software environment onto silicon. Among the characteristics of the iAPX-432 architecture are the following:
• a dense encoding of instructions with variable instruction lengths in bits. Instructions may also start and stop on arbitrary bit boundaries;
• an object-oriented support mechanism, allowing for creation and protection of an object;
 • a packet-switched bus protocol;
 • support for many standard operating system functions;
 • provision for transparent multiprocessing; and
 • support for fault-tolerant operation.

The iAPX-432 also represents an architecture that meets many of the goals and specific design principles of Flynn's ideal machine [51]. The similarities between the iAPX-432 and the high level DEL machines proposed by Hoevel (for Fortran [52]) and Wakefield (for Pascal [30]) are considerable. The major difference is the absence of a register set or stack cache in the iAPX-432. However, the use of memory and stack operands, bit encoded instructions, data typing, and symmetric addressing are all key principles in the DEL designs.

The iAPX-432 implementation consists of three major chips: two of these comprise the general data processor (GDP) and the other is the interface processor (IDP). The two-chip GDP consists of an instruction decode unit, which also contains most of the microcode, and the microexecution unit. In addition to executing microinstructions, the microexecution unit performs the memory mapping and protection functions within the iAPX-432 architecture. In this section we will concentrate on the components of the instruction set

not related to memory mapping; we will briefly mention the other operating system support features.

Among the most significant features in the iAPX-432 architecture is its support for a wide variety of data types, including
• 8-bit characters,
• 16-bit signed and unsigned integers,
• 32-bit signed and unsigned integers,
• a variable length bit field: 1–31, or 1–16 bits in length, and
• 32-bit, 64-bit, and 80-bit reals.

Complete sets of arithmetic and (where appropriate) logical operators are defined for each data type. The iAPX-432 is the first microprocessor to define and implement floating point support in the architecture. Conditional branch instructions are defined as taking Boolean operands. The remainder of the instruction set is largely devoted to operators for: object manipulation, protection, context management (which we discuss in Section V), and process communication.

Data operands reside either in data memory or on an operand stack implemented in memory with caching of the top element of the stack. Although the stack is efficient when measured by the number of bits needed to represent a computation, it is not believed to be a good representation for compilers and code optimization [53]. Memory–memory operations are efficient when measured by the number of operations needed for a program. However, since there are no on-chip registers, it is not possible to optimize references to commonly used variables.

The iAPX-432 instructions have one, two, or three operands and complete symmetry with respect to addressing modes. Since the instruction formats allow arbitrary bit lengths, memory operands can be mixed with stack operands with no loss of encoding efficiency. Of course, the task of instruction fetching and decoding is substantially more complex; we will discuss this topic further in a latter section.

The iAPX-432 uses a two-part memory address consisting of a segment and a displacement. Segment-based addressing has been discussed in the earlier section on memory management and is summarized by Fig. 2. The segments may be up to 2^{16} bytes long; although fixed limited size segments help provide memory protection, they pose a major problem for segments that need to grow larger than this size. Managing the activation record stack and heap as growing objects requires using a multisegment approach from the start. It also implies that most programs will need to include segment numbers in addresses.

The displacement portion of an address is the displacement within a segment and may be specified using one of four addressing modes. Each addressing mode is composed of a base address and an index; either component may be indirect, i.e., the address contains the value of the base or index. Indirect index values are scaled according to the byte size of the object being accessed.

The iAPX-432 is unique among architectures in its support for multiprocessing. Multiprocessing is supported by defining a number of instructions for both processor and process intercommunication and by the interconnect bus. The interconnect bus is a packet bus that allows multiple processors to be connected. The bus offers up to a 16 Mbyte bandwidth when the packets are the maximum size. Data from memory can be 1–10 bytes in length per access.

The process communication instructions include operations to send and receive messages, as well as conditional send and receive. Operations that send to processors as well as broadcasting to all processors are supported. Since these operations are supported by the architecture and the bus provides communication of these messages, multiprocessing can be performed independently of the process count, processor count, or distribution of processes on processors. However, the single bus provides a limit on the ability to do multiprocessing; the current bus design for the iAPX-432 can handle approximately three processors without undue bus contention. Peripheral chips have been developed to allow multiple buses to be incorporated into a design.

D. The Motorola 68000

The 68000 [54], [55] represents the first microprocessor to support a large, uniform (i.e., unsegmented), virtual addressing space ($>2^{16}$ bytes) and complete support for a 32-bit data type. The MC68000 architecture has many things in common with the PDP-11 architecture. It offers a number of addressing modes and features orthogonality between instructions and addressing modes for many but not nearly all instructions (as compared to a VAX). The MC68000 is a 16-bit implementation, but almost all the instructions support 32-bit data.

Some interesting compromises were made in the MC68000 architecture. Possibly the most obvious is the partitioning of the 16 general purpose registers into two sets: address and data registers. For the compiler this partitioning is troublesome since most addressing modes require the use of an address register and most arithmetic instructions use data registers. Because of this dichotomy, excess register copies are required and the number of data registers is too small to allow register allocation to be easily done. Because the split lowers the number of bits needed for a register designator from four to three bits, this choice is motivated by the instruction coding.

For the most part the addressing modes of the MC68000 follow those of the PDP-11: the major change is the elimination of the infrequently used indirect modes and their replacement with an indexed mode that computes the effective address as the sum of the contents of two registers plus an offset. The MC68000 is a one and a half address machine: instructions have a source and a source/destination specifier and only one of these may be a memory operand. The major exception is the move instruction that can move between two arbitrary operands.

One interesting new instruction in the MC68000 is "check register against bounds." This instruction checks a register contents against an arbitrary upper bound and causes a trap if the contents exceeds the upper bound. If the register contents is a zero-based array index, then this instruction can be used to do the upper array bound check and trap if the bound is exceeded. The MC68000 also obtains reasonably high code density due to its useful addressing modes, a good match between instructions and compiled code, and its support for a wide variety of immediate data. Besides having immediate addressing formats for byte, word, and long word data types, many of the arithmetic and logical instructions allow a short immediate constant ($1 \cdots 8$) as an operand. This combination of immediate data types and the short immediate (quick) format helps increase code density substantially.

The MC68000 made two instruction set additions that help support high level languages. Support for procedure linkage was built in with several instructions; the most important addition was the link instruction, which can be used to set up and maintain activation records. The multiple register move instruction helps shorten the save/restore sequence during a call or return.

Since the original MC68000 has been announced two important new versions of the architecture have been produced. The MC68010 provides support for demand paging by providing instruction restartability in the event of a page fault. The three year delay between the original MC68000 and the MC68010 is a good indication of the complexity of this capability. The recently announced MC68020 provides some extensions to the instruction set, but more importantly represents a 32-bit implementation both internally in the chip and externally on the pins. This provides important performance improvements in instruction access and 32-bit data memory access.

E. The DEC VLSI-Based VAX Processors

There are now three VLSI-based implementations of the VAX architecture. They differ in chip count, amount of custom silicon, and performance. All three implementations are interesting because they reflect different design compromises needed to put the large instruction set into a chip-based implementation. The first implementation, the MicroVAX-I, uses a custom data path chip [9] and keeps the microcode and microsequencer off chip. The second implementation is the VLSI VAX [23], a nine-chip set that implements the full VAX instruction set. The third VLSI-based VAX, the MicroVAX-32 [24], is a single chip that implements a subset of the VAX architecture in hardware.

Several key features characterize the VAX instruction set and help provide organization for the 304 instructions and tens of thousands of combinations of instructions and addressing modes:

• a large number of instructions with nearly complete orthogonality among opcode, addressing mode, and data type;

• support for bytes, words (16 bits), and long words (32 bits) as data types. Special instructions for bit data types;

• many high level instructions including procedure call and return, string instructions, and instructions for floating point and decimal arithmetic; and

• a large number of addressing modes, summarized in Table IV.

The table gives the frequency as percent of all operand memory addressing; the notation (R) indicates the contents of register R. These memory addressing modes represent just less than one-half of the operands. The other operands are register and literal operands. The VAX supports a short literal mode (5 bits) and an immediate mode (defined as PC-relative followed by an autoincrement of the PC). Several common operand addressing formats are obtained using PC-relative addressing since the PC is in the register set. Hence PC-

TABLE IV
SUMMARY OF VAX ADDRESSING MODES

Addressing Mode	Form	Effective Address	Frequency
Register Deferred	(Rn)	(Rn)	7.7%
Autodecrement	-(Rn)	(Rn) - size of operand	0.7%
Autoincrement	(Rn)+	(Rn) Rn := (Rn) + size of operand	6.1%
Autoincrement Deferred	@(Rn)+	((Rn)) Rn := (Rn) + size of operand	0.2%
Byte,Word,Long Displacement	D(Rn)	D+(Rn) D is byte, word, longword	23.8%
Byte,Word,Long Displacement, Deferred	@D(Rn)	(D+(Rn)) D is byte, word, longword	1.2%
Index	base[Rn]	base is addr. mode the address is base + Rn*size of operand	5.3
Total			45%

relative and absolute addressing, as well as immediate addressing, are all done with standard addressing modes using the PC as the register operand.

The MicroVAX-I is not a self-contained VLSI processor since only the data path is integrated. The rest of the processor (including the microcode sequencing, the microcode, and instruction fetch unit) are implemented with standard MSI and LSI parts. The data path was designed to support the VAX architecture and improves upon the structure used in the VAX 11/730 implementation. The advantages of the custom data path are that it consumes far less space and power than a discrete implementation, and it yields higher performance. This performance advantage comes from the tailoring of the data path to the needs of the VAX architecture, as opposed to using off-the-shelf components, which results in a less than optimal implementation of the data path. This tailoring consists primarily of several improvements to the match between the data path and the architecture; these include

1) the ability to handle registers as byte, word, and long word quantities;

2) the ability to read two 32-bit registers in parallel and send them either to the ALU or the barrel shifter in a single cycle;

3) automatic back-up of registers that might be affected by autoincrement and autodecrement addressing modes; and

4) better support for multiply operations.

By limiting the use of custom silicon to the portion of the processor where it most effective and to a point where the design complexity could be handled, the MicroVAX-I achieved its design goals. Performance exceeds that of a VAX 11/730 and the design and implementation time was kept under one year [9].

Two new implementations of the VAX architecture use primarily custom VLSI chips. The first of these, the VLSI VAX, uses a nine-chip set to implement a version of the architecture comparable in performance to a VAX 11/780 CPU. These nine chips include most of the CPU functions, including memory mapping and cache control. The nine-chip set contains about 1.25 million transistors and consists of five different cutsom chips.

1) The instruction fetch/execution chip that performs instruction fetch and decode, ALU operations, and address translation using a small on-chip translation lookaside buffer (TLB).

2) The memory subsystem chip holds a larger TLB, the tag array and control for a 2 KW cache, and performs additional peripheral control functions.

3) A floating point accelerator chip uses an 81b-wide data path and a 100 ns cycle time to provide floating point speeds comparable to those on a 780.

4) The 480K bits of microprogram are stored in five patchable control store chips. Each chip contains nine bits of each 40 byte control word. The amount of microcode is comparable to the MSI based 11/780, 11/750, and 11/730 implementations.

5) The CPU uses a custom bus interface chip [56] to couple to a high speed external system bus.

The single chip implementation of the VAX-11 architecture [24], the MicroVAX-32, uses a single chip to implement a subset of the VAX instruction set including support for memory mapping. When operated with a 20 MHz clock, it is about 20 percent slower than the VLSI VAX in performance. The chip supports 6 of the 12 VAX data types and all 21 addressing modes. Only a subset of instructions are supported on the chip; the breakdown is as follows:

• 175 instructions are supported in the processor's hardware;

• the 70 floating point instructions are supported only with the addition of the floating point chip; and

• 59 instructions (including, e.g., instructions for the less heavily used data formats) are trapped by the processor and interpreted in macrocode.

Interestingly, the 58 percent of the instructions implemented in the processor require only 15 percent of the microcode of a full VAX implementation and constitute 98 percent of the most frequently executed instructions for typical benchmarks (ignoring floating point). A few instructions in the VAX have low utilization (1–2 percent) but long execution times [7] that inflate the effect of the instruction in determining program execution time. By including these instructions in the hardware implementation, the execution time effects of only implementing 58 percent of the instruction set are negligible.

Both VLSI-based VAX processors are implemented on a two-level metal, 3 μm drawn, nMOS process with four implants. First silicon for both processors was completed in February 1984. The design tradeoffs made in the MicroVAX-32 are in strong contrast to the ambitious design of the 9-chip VLSI VAX. Table V clearly shows the dramatic reductions in size and complexity of the implementation accomplished by the subsetting of the architecture that was used in the MicroVAX-32. The less than 20 percent performance impact makes it an effective technique and calls into doubt the need for the software-based part of the instruction set to be defined in the architecture.

VII. ORGANIZATION AND IMPLEMENTATION ISSUES

The interaction between a processor architecture and its organization has always had a profound influence on the cost-performance ratios attainable for the architecture. In VLSI this effect is extended through to low levels of the implementation. To explain some of these interactions and

TABLE V
SUMMARY COMPARISON OF THE VAX MICROPROCESSORS

	VLSI VAX	MicroVAX-32
Chip count (incl. floating pt.)	9	2
Microcode (bits)	460K	64K
Transistors	1250K	101K
TLB	5 entry mini-TLB 512 entries off chip	8 entry fully assoc.
Cache	Yes	No. instruction prefetch buffer

tradeoffs, we have used examples from the MIPS processor. Although the examples are specific to that processor, the issues that they illustrate are common to most VLSI processor designs.

A. Organizational Techniques

Many of the techniques used to obtain high performance in conventional processor designs are applicable to VLSI processors. Some changes in these approaches have been made due to the implementation technology; some of these changes have been adapted into designs for non-VLSI processors. We will look at the motivating influences at the organizational level and then look at pipelining and instruction unit design.

MOS offers the designer a technology that sacrifices speed to obtain very high densities. Although switching time is somewhat slower than in bipolar technologies, communication speed has more effect on the organization and implementation. The organization of an architecture in MOS must attempt to exploit the density of the technology by favoring local computation to global communication.

1) Pipelining: A classical technique for enhancing the performance of a processor is pipelining. Pipelining increases performance by a factor determined by the depth of the pipeline: if the maximum rate at which operators can be executed is r, then pipelining to a depth of d provides an *idealized* execution rate of $r \times d$. Since the speed with which individual operations can be executed is limited, this approach is an excellent technique to enhance performance in MOS.

The depth of the pipeline is an idealized performance multiplier. Several factors prevent achievement of this increase. First, delays are introduced whenever data needed to execute an instruction is still in the pipeline. Second, pipeline breaks occur because of branches. A branch requires that the processor calculate the effective destination of the branch and fetch that instruction; for conditional branches, it is impossible to do this without delaying the pipe for at least one stage (unless both successors of the branch instruction are fetched, or the branch outcome is correctly predicted). Conditional branches may cause further delays because they require the calculation of the condition, as well as the target address. For most programs and implementations, pipeline breaks due to branches are the most serious cause of degraded pipeline performance. Third, the complexity of managing the pipeline and handling breaks adds additional overhead to the basic logic, causing a degradation in the rate at which pipestages can be executed.

The designer, in an attempt to maximize performance, might increase the number of pipestages per instruction; this meets with two problems. First, not all instructions will contain the same number of pipestages. Many instructions, in particular the simpler ones, fit best in pipelines of length two, three, or four, at most. On average, longer pipelines will waste a number of cycles equal to the difference between the number of stages in the pipeline and the average number of stages per instruction. This might lead one to conclude that more complex instructions that could use more pipestages would be more effective. However, this potential advantage is negated by the two other problems: branch frequency and operand hazards.

The frequency of branches in compiled code limits the length of the pipeline since it determines the average number of instructions that occurs before the pipeline must be flushed. This number of course depends on the instruction set. Measurements of the VAX taken by Clark [7] have shown an average of three instructions are executed between every *taken* branch. For simplicity, we call any instruction that changes the program counter (not including incrementing it to obtain the next sequential instruction) a taken branch. Measurements on the Pascal DEL architecture Adept have turned up even shorter runs between branches. Branches that are not taken may also cause a delay in the pipeline since the instructions following the branch may not change the machine state before the branch condition has been determined, unless such changes can be undone if the branch is taken.

Similar measurements for more streamlined architectures such as MIPS and the 801 have shown that branches (both taken and untaken) occupy 15–20 percent of the dynamic instruction mix. When the levels of the instruction set are accounted for and some special anomalies that increase the VAX branch frequency are eliminated, the VAX and streamlined machine numbers are equivalent. This should be the case: if no architectural anomalies that introduce branches exist, the branch frequency will reflect that in the source language programs. The number of operations (not instructions) between branches is independent of the instruction set. This number, often called the run length, and the ability to pipeline individual instructions should determine the optimal choice for the depth of the pipeline. Since more complex instruction sets have shorter run lengths, pipelining across instruction boundaries is less productive.

The streamlined VLSI processor designs have taken novel approaches to the control of the pipeline and attempted to improve the utilization of the pipeline by lowering the frequency of pipeline breaks. The RISC and MIPS processor have only delayed branches; thus, a pipeline break on a branch only occurs when the compiler can not find useful instructions to execute during the stages that are needed to determine the branch address, test the branch condition, and prefetch the destination if the branch is taken. Measurements have found that these branch delays can be effectively used in 80–90 percent of the cases [15]. In fact, measurements of MIPS' benchmarks have shown that almost 20 percent of the instructions executed by the processor occur during a branch delay slot! The 801 offers both delayed and nondelayed branches; the latter allow the processor to avoid inserting a no-op when a useful instruction cannot be found. This delayed branch approach is an interesting contrast to the branch prediction and multiple target fetch techniques used on high-end machines. The delayed branch approach offers performance that is nearly as good as the more sophisticated approaches and does not consume any silicon area.

A stall in the pipeline caused by an instruction with an operand that is not yet available is called a data or operand hazard. MIPS, the 801 and some larger machines, such as the Cray-1, include pipeline scheduling as a process done by the compiler. This scheduling can be completely done for operations with deterministic execution times (such as most register–register operations) and be optimistically scheduled for operations whose execution time is indeterminate (such as memory references in a system with a cache). This optimization typically provides improvements in the 5–10 percent range. In MIPS, this improvement is compounded by the increase in execution rate achieved by simplifying the pipeline hardware when the interlocks are eliminated for register–register operations. Dealing with indeterminate occurrences, such as cache misses, requires stopping the pipeline. The algorithms used for scheduling the MIPS pipeline are discussed in [49]; Sites describes the scheduling process for the Cray-I in [57].

Because the code sequences between branches are often short, it is often impossible for either the compiler or the hardware to reduce the effects of data dependencies between instructions in the sequence. There are simply not enough unrelated instructions in many segments to keep the pipeline busy executing interleaved and unrelated sequences of instructions. In such cases, neither a pipeline scheduling technique nor a sophisticated pipeline that allows instructions to execute out-of-order can find useful instructions to execute.

Operand hazards cause more difficulty for architectures with powerful instructions and shorter run lengths. When no pipeline scheduling is being done, the dependence between adjacent instructions is high. When scheduling is used it may be ineffective since the small number of instructions between basic blocks makes it difficult to find useful instructions to place between two interdependent instructions.

Another approach to migrating the effect of operand hazards and increasing pipeline performance is to allow *out-of-order instruction execution*. In the most straightforward scenario, the processor keeps a buffer of sequential instructions (up to and including a branch) and examines each of the instructions in parallel to decide if it is ready to execute. An instruction is executed as soon as its operands are available. In most implementations, instructions also complete out-of-order. The alternative is to buffer the results of an instruction, until all the previous instructions have completed; this becomes complex, especially if an instruction can have results longer than a word (since as a block move instruction). Out-of-order completion leads to a fundamental problem: imprecise interrupts. An *imprecise interrupt* occurs when a program is interrupted at an instruction that does not serve as a clean boundary between completed and uncompleted instructions; that is, some of the instructions before the interrupted instruction may not have completed and some of the instructions after the interrupted instruction may have been completed. Continuing execution of a program after an imprecise interrupt is nearly impossible; at best, to continue requires extensive analysis of the executing code segment and simulation of the uncompleted instructions to create a precise interrupt location. Imprecise interrupts can be largely avoided by choosing the instruction to interrupt as the successor of the last (in the sequence) that has completed; this will guarantee that no completed instructions follow the interrupted instruction. This approach has some performance penalty on interrupt speed and prohibits interrupts that can not be scheduled, such as page faults. Because the occurrence of a page fault is not known until the instruction execution is attempted, imprecise interrupts cannot be tolerated on a processor that allows demand paging. This fundamental incompatibility has limited the use of out-of-order instruction issue and completion to high performance machines.

2) Instruction Fetch and Decode: One goal of pipelining is to approach as closely as possible the target of one instruction execution every clock cycle. For most instructions, this can be achieved in the execution unit of the machine. Long running instructions like floating point will take more time, but they can often be effectively pipelined within the execution box. More serious bottlenecks exist in the instruction unit.

As we discussed in an earlier segment, densely encoded instruction sets with multiple instruction lengths lower memory bandwidth but suffer a performance penalty during fetch and decode of the instructions. This penalty comes from the inability to decode the entire instruction in parallel due to the large number of possible interpretations of instruction fields and interdependencies among the fields. This penalty is serious for two reasons. First, it cannot be pipelined away. High level instruction sets have very short sequences between branches (due to the high level nature of the instruction set). Thus, the processor must keep the number of pipestages devoted to instruction fetch and decode to as near to one as possible. If more stages are devoted to this function, the processor will often have idle pipestages. This lack of ability to pipeline high level instruction sets has been observed for the DEL architecture Adept [30]. Note that the penalty will be seen both at instruction prefetch and instruction decode; both phases are made more complex by multiple instruction lengths.

The second reason is that most instructions that are executed are still simple instructions. The most common instructions for VAX, PDP-11, and S/370 style architectures are MOV and simple ALU instructions, combined with "register" and "register with byte displacement" addressing for the operands. Thus, the cost of the fetch and decode can often be as high or even higher than the execution cost. The complexities of instruction decoding can also cause the simple, short instructions to suffer a penalty. For example, on the VAX 11/780 register–register operands take two cycles to complete, although only one cycle is required for the data path to execute the operation. Half the cycle time is spent in fetch and decode; similar results can be found for DEL machines. In contrast, MIPS takes one third of the total cycle time of each instruction for fetch and decode. A processor can achieve single-cycle execution for the simple instructions in a complex architecture, but to do so requires very careful design and an instruction encoding that simplifies fetch and decode for such instructions.

B. Control Unit Design

The structure of the control unit on a VLSI processor most clearly reflects the make-up of the instruction set. For example, streamlined architectures usually employ a single cycle decode because the simplicity of the instruction set allows the instruction contents to be decoded in parallel. Even in such a machine, a multistate microengine is needed to run the pipeline and control the processor during unpredictable events that cause significant change in the processor states, such as interrupts and page faults. However, the microengine does not participate in either instruction decoding or execution except to dictate the sequencing of pipestages. In a more complex architecture, the microcode must deal both with instruction sequencing and the handling of exceptional events. The cascading of logic needed to decode a complex instruction slows down the decode time, which impacts performance when the control unit is in the critical path. Since decoding is usually done with PLA's, ROM's, or similar programmable structures, substantial delays can be incurred communicating between these structures and in the logic delays within the structures, which themselves are usually clocked.

In addition to the instruction fetch and decode unit, the instruction set and system architecture has a profound effect on the design of the master control unit. This unit is responsible for managing the major cycles of the processor, including initiating normal processor instruction cycles under usual conditions and handling exceptional conditions (page faults, interrupts, cache misses, internal faults, etc.) when they arise. The difficult component of this task is in handling exceptional conditions that require the intervention of the operating system; the process typically involves shutting down the execution of the normal instruction stream, saving the state of execution, and transferring to supervisor level code to save user state and begin handling the condition. Simpler conditions, such as a cache miss or DMA cycle, require only that the processor delay its normal cycle.

Exceptional conditions that require the interruption of execution during an instruction have a significant effect on the implementation. Two distinct types of problems arise: state saving and partially completed instructions. To allow processing of the interrupt, execution of the current instruction stream must be stopped and the machine state must be saved. In a machine with multicycle instructions, some of the internal instruction state may not be visible to user-level instructions. Forcing such state to be visible is often unworkable since the exact amount of state depends on the implementation. Defining such state in the instruction set locks in a particular implementation of the instruction. Thus, the processor must include microcode to save and restore the state of the partially executed instruction. To avoid this problem, some architectures force instructions that execute for a comparatively long time and generate results throughout the instruction, to employ user visible registers for their operation; most architectures that support long string instructions

use just this approach. For example, on the S/370 long string instructions use the general purpose registers to hold the state of the instruction during execution; shorter instructions, such as Move Character (MVC), inhibit interrupts during execution. Because the MVC instruction can still access multiple memory words, the processor must first check to ensure that no page faults will occur before beginning instruction execution.

Instructions that do not have very long running times can be dealt with by a two-part strategy. The architecture may prohibit most interrupts during the execution of the instruction. For those interrupts that cannot be prohibited, e.g., a page fault in the executing instruction, the architecture can stop the execution of instruction, process the interrupt, and restart the instruction. This process is reasonably straightforward, except when the instruction is permitted to alter the state of the processor before completion of the instruction without interrupt can be guaranteed. If such changes are allowed, then the implementation must either continue the instruction in the middle, or restore the state of the processor before restarting the instruction. Neither of these approaches is particularly attractive since they require either special hardware support, or extensive examination of the executing instruction. If the processor can decode the instruction and knows how much of the instruction was completed, the microcontrol could simulate the completion of the instruction, or (under most cases) undo the effect of the completed portions. However, both of these approaches incur substantial overhead for determining the exact state of the partially executed instruction, and taking the remedial action. Additionally, some classes of instructions may not be undone; for example, an instruction component that clears a register cannot be reversed, without saving the contents of the register. Since this overhead must be taken on common types of interrupts, such as page faults, this solution is not attractive.

To circumvent these problems, the architecture must either prohibit such instructions, as streamlined architectures do, or provide hardware assist. To keep the amount of special hardware assistance needed within bounds, only limited types of changes in the states are allowed before guaranteed completion. The most common example of such a limited feature is autoincrement/autodecrement addressing modes. Like most instructions that change state midway through the instruction, only the general purpose registers can be changed. This offers an opportunity to try to restore the machine state to its state prior to instruction execution.

Let us consider the possibilities that occur on the VAX. The most obvious scheme would be to decode the faulting instruction and unwind its effect by inverting the increment or decrement (which can only change the register contents by a fixed constant). However, on the VAX, with up to five operands per instruction, decoding the·faulting instruction and determining which registers have been changed is a major undertaking. Because the instruction cannot be restarted until all values that have been altered are restored, the cost would be prohibitive. The solution used for the MVC instruction on the S/370—make sure you can complete the instruction before you start it—can be adapted. Because of the possibility of page faults, this approach requires that the instruction be simulated to determine that all the pages accessed by the instruction's operands are in memory. This could be quite expensive, especially if the addressing mode is used often. Because only limited modifications to the processor state are allowed before instruction completion, there are several hardware-based solutions that have smaller impacts on performance.

1) Save the register contents before they are changed, along with the register designator. Restore all the saved registers using their designator when an interrupt occurs.

2) Save the register designator and the amount of the increment or decrement (in the range of 1–4 on the VAX). If an interrupt occurs, compute the original value of the registers corresponding to the saved designators and constants.

3) Compute the altered register value, but do not store it into the register until the end of the instruction execution. The above list gives the rough order of the hardware complexity of these solutions. The last solution is complicated because a list of changed registers and the register numbers must be kept until the instruction ends. It is also the least efficient solution; since most instructions do not fault, the cost of the update must be added to the execution time. The second solution is simpler and requires the least storage, but it still requires some decoding overhead. The first solution is the simplest; it can be implemented by saving the registers as they are read for incrementing/decrementing.

C. Data Path Design

The data paths of most VLSI processors share many common features since most instruction sets require a small number of basic micro-operations. Special features may be included to support structures such as the queue that saves altered registers during instruction execution.

The main data path of the processor is usually distinguished by the presence of two or more buses, serving as a common communication link among the components of the bus. Many common components may be associated with smaller, auxiliary data paths because they do not need frequent or time-critical access to the resources provided by the main data path or for performance reasons, which we will discuss shortly.

The data path commonly includes the following components.

• A register file for the processor's general purpose registers and any other registers included in the main data path for performance. In a microprogrammed machine, temporary registers used by the microcode may reside here. The function of the register file depends on the instruction set. In some cases, it is removed from the data path for reasons we will discuss shortly.

• An ALU providing both addition/subtraction and some collection of logical operations, and perhaps providing support for multiplication and division. We will discuss the design of the ALU in some more detail shortly.

• A shifter used to implement shifts and rotates and to implement bit string instructions or assist instruction decoding. Some processors include a barrel shifter (rather than a single-bit shifter) because although they consume a fair amount of area, they dramatically increase the speed of multiple-bit shifts.

• The program counter. Positioning the program counter in the main data path simplifies calculation of PC-based displacements. In a high performance or pipelined processor, the program counter will usually have its own incrementer. This allows both faster calculation of the next sequential instruction address and overlap of PC increment with ALU operation. A pipelined processor will often have multiple PC registers to simplify state saving and returning from interrupts.

These are the primary components of the data path; micro-architectures may have special features designed to improve the performance of some particular part of the instruction set. Fig. 4 shows the data path from the MIPS processor. It is typical of the data path designs found on many VLSI processors. Some data paths are simpler (e.g., the RISC data path, ignoring the register stack) and some are more complicated (e.g., the VAX data path). Although the basic components are common, the communication paths are often customized to the needs of the instruction set and varying speed, space, and power tradeoffs may made in designing the data path components (e.g., a ripple carry adder versus a carry lookahead adder).

1) Data Bus Design: The minimum machine cycle time is limited by the time needed to move data from one resource to another in the data path. This delay consists of the propagation time on the control wires and the propagation time on the data buses, which are usually longer than the control lines. In a process with only one level of low resistance interconnect (metal) the data bus would be run in metal, while the control lines would run in polysilicon. The delay on the control lines can be reduced by minimizing the pitch in the data path. Partly because of these delays, almost all data paths in VLSI processors use a two bus design. The extra delays due to the wide data path pitch in a three bus design may not be compensated for by the extra throughput available on the third bus.

Power constraints and the need to communicate signals as quickly as possible across the data path lead to heavy use of bootstrapped control drivers. Large numbers of bootstrap drivers put a considerable load on clock signals, and the designer must be careful to avoid skew problems by routing clocks in metal and using low resistance crossovers. Bootstrap drivers require a setup period and cannot be used when a control signal is active on both clock phases. Static super-buffers can be used in such cases, but they have a much higher static power usage. The tight pitch and use of bootstrap drivers helps minimize the control delay time. In MIPS the tight pitch (33 λ) and the extensive use of dynamic bootstrap drivers holds the control delay to 10 ns.

Although reducing the control communication delays is important, the main bus delays normally constitute a much larger portion of the processor cycle time. The main reason for this is that the bus delay is proportional to the product of the bus capacitance and the voltage swing divided by the driver size. When the number of drivers on the bus gets large (25–50, or more), the bus capacitance is dominated by the drivers themselves, i.e., it is proportional to driver size times the driver count. Thus, the bus delay becomes proportional to the product of the driver count and the voltage swing!

This delay can be reduced by either lowering the number of drivers or by reducing the voltage swing. For many data

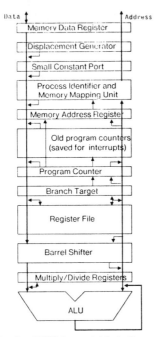

Fig. 4.   MIPS data path block diagram.

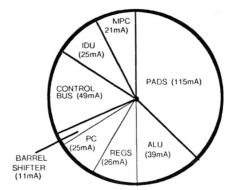

Fig. 5.   MIPS current distribution.

paths the register file is the major source of bus drivers. Those bus drivers are directly responsible for a slower clock cycle. This penalty on processor cycle time is a major drawback for a large register file implemented in MOS technology. To partially overcome this problem, many processor designs implement the register file as a small RAM off of the data bus. Although this eliminates a large fraction of the load from drivers, it may introduce several other problems. The register file is usually a multiported device for at least reads and sometimes for writes. The smallest RAM cell designs may not provide this capability. Thus, maintaining the same level of performance requires operating the RAM at a higher speed or duplicating the RAM to increase bandwidth (a typical technique for high performance ECL machines). Isolating the RAM or register file from the bus may also incur extra delays due to communication time or the presence of latches between the registers and the bus.

Another approach is to try to reduce the switching time of the bus by circuit design techniques. There are three major styles of bus design that can be used:

• a nonprecharged rail-to-rail bus which has the above stated problem;

• a precharged bus which reduces the problem by replacing the slower pull-up time but having the same the pull-down time. Precharging requires a separate idle bus cycle to charge the bus to the high state; and

• a limited voltage-swing bus that still allows a bus active on every clock cycle.

The use of precharged buses is discussed in many introductory texts on VLSI design [12]. Precharging is most useful in a design when the bus is idle every other cycle due to the organization of the processor. For example, if the ALU cycle time is comparatively long and the processor is otherwise idle during that time, the ALU can be isolated from the bus, and the precharge can occur during that cycle. When such idle cycles are not present in the global timing strategy, the attrac-

tion of precharging vanishes. The limited swing bus uses an approach similar to the techniques used in dynamic RAM design [58]. The bus is clamped to reduce its voltage swing and sense-amplifier-like circuits are used to detect the change in voltage. A version of MIPS was fabricated using a clamped bus structure to reduce the effective voltage swing by about a factor of 4. This approach was the most attractive, since MIPS uses the bus on every clock phase. The use of a restricted voltage swing does require careful circuit design since important margins, such as noise immunity, may be reduced.

2) The Data Path ALU: Arithmetic operations are often in a processor's critical timing paths and thus require careful logic and circuit design. Although some designs use straightforward Manchester-carry adders and universal logic blocks (see, e.g., the description of the OM2 [12]), more powerful techniques are needed to achieve high performance. Since the addition circuitry is usually the critical path, it can be separated from the logic operation unit to achieve minimal loading on the adder. A fast adder will need to use carry lookahead, carry bypass, or carry select. For example, MIPS uses a full carry-lookahead tree, with propagate signals and generate signals produced for each pair of bits, which results in a total ALU delay of less than 80-ns with a one-level metal 3 μm process. To obtain high speed addition, the ALU may also consume a substantial portion of the processor's power budget.

Supporting integer multiply and divide (and the floating point versions) with reasonable performance can provide a real challenge to the designer. One approach is to code these operations out of simpler instructions, using Booth's algorithm. This will result in multiply or divide performance at the rate of approximately one bit per every three or four instructions. The RISC processor uses this approach. Most microprocessors implement multiply/divide via microcode using either individual shift and add operations or relying on special support for executing Booth's algorithm. The 68000 uses this approach. MIPS implements special instructions for doing steps of a multiply or divide operation; these instructions are used to expand the macros for a 32-bit multiply or divide, into a sequence of 8 or 16 instructions, respectively. This type of support, similar to that used in the 68000 microengine, requires the ability to do an add (depending on the low-order bits of the register) and a shift in the same instruction step. Limited silicon area and power budgets often make it impractical to include hardware for more parallel multiplication on the CPU chip.

Fast arithmetic operations can be supported in a coprocessor that does both integer and floating point operations as in the VLSI VAX. The design of a floating point coprocessor that achieves high performance for floating point operations can be extremely difficult. The coprocessor design must be taken into account in the design of the main CPU as well as in the software for the floating point routines. An inefficient or ineffective coprocessor interface will mean that the coprocessor does not perform as well as an integral floating point unit. Many current microprocessors exhibit this property: they execute integer operations at a rate close to that of a minicomputer, but are substantially slower on floating point instructions. Furthermore, the floating point instruction time is often dominated by communication and coordination with the coprocessor, not by the time for the arithmetic operation. A well-designed floating point coprocessor, such as the floating point processor for the VLSI VAX, can achieve performance equal to the performance obtained in an integral floating point unit.

3) The Package Constraint: Packaging introduces pin limitations and power constraints. Limited pins force the designer to choose his functional boundaries to minimize interconnection. Pin multiplexing can partially relieve the pin constraints, but it costs time, especially when the pins are frequently active.

Two types of power constraints exist: total static power and package inductance. The packaging technology defines the maximum static power the chip may consume. Because power can eliminate delays in the critical path, the power budget must be used carefully. Typical packages for processors with more than 64 pins can dissipate 2–3 W.

The problem of package inductance [59] is more subtle and can be difficult to overcome. Suppose the processor drives a large number of pins simultaneously, e.g., 32 data and 32 address pins, then the current required to drive the pins can be temporarily quite large. In such cases the package inductance (due largely to the power leads between the die and the package) can lead to a transient in the on-chip power supply voltage. This problem can be mitigated by using multiple power and ground wires or by more sophisticated die bonding and packaging technology.

The power distribution plot for MIPS (see Fig. 5) shows how this power budget might be consumed. Power is used for three principle goals in nMOS: to overcome delays due to serial combinations of gates, to reduce communication delays between functional blocks, and to reduce off-chip communication delays. The MIPS power distribution plot shows the major power consumers are

• the ALU with its extensive multilevel logic,
• the pins with the drive logic, and
• the control bus, which provides most of the time-critical interchip communication.

D. Summary

VLSI technology has a fundamental effect on the design decisions made in the architecture and organization of processors. Since pipelining is a basic technique by which VLSI

processors achieve performance, the architect and designer must consider a series of issues that affect performance improvements achievable by pipelining. These issues include the suitability of the instruction set for pipelining, the frequency of branches, the ease of decomposing instructions, and the interaction between instructions.

Pipelining adds a major complication to the task of controlling the execution of instructions. The parallel and simultaneous interpretation of multiple instructions dramatically complicates the control unit since it must consider all the ways in which all the instructions under execution can require special control. Complications in the instruction set can make this task overwhelming. In addition to controlling instruction sequencing, the control unit (or its neighbor) often contains the instruction decoding logic. The complexity and size of the decoding logic is influenced by the size and complexity of the instruction set and how the instruction set is encoded. The observation that most microprocessors use 50 percent or more of their limited silicon area for control functions was a consideration when RISC architectures were proposed [60].

Although the high level design of the data path is largely functionally independent of the architecture, the detailed requirements of data path components are affected by the architecture. For example, an architecture with instructions for bytes, half-words, and words requires special support in the register file (to read and write fragments) and in the ALU to detect overflow on small fragments (or to shift smaller data items into the high order bits of the ALU). Although the functionality of most data path components is independent of the processor architecture, the architecture and organization affect the data path design in two important ways. First, different processors will have different critical timing paths, and data path components in the critical path will need to be designed for maximum performance. Second, specific features of the architecture will cause specialization of the data path; examples of this specialization include support for bytes and half words in a register file and the register stack used to handle autoincrement/autodecrement in VAX microprocessors. The role of good implementation is magnified in VLSI where what is obtainable is much broader in range and much more significantly affected by the technology.

VIII. FUTURE TRENDS

VLSI processor technology combines several different areas: architecture, organization, and implementation technology. Until recently, technology has been the driving force: rapid improvements in density and chip size have made it possible to double the on-chip device count every few years. These improvements have led to both architectural changes (from 8- to 16- to 32-bit data paths, and to larger instruction sets) and organizational changes (incorporation of pipelining and caches). As the technology to implement a full 32-bit processor has become available, architectural issues, rather than implementation concerns, have assumed a larger role in determining what is designed.

A. Architectural Trends

In the past few years many designers have been occupied with exploring the tradeoffs between streamlined and more complex architectures. Future architectures will probably embrace some combination of both these ideas. Three major areas, parallel processing, support for nonprocedural languages, and more attention to systems-level issues, stand out as foci of future architectures.

Parallel processing is an ideal vehicle for increasing performance using VLSI-based processors. The low-cost of replicating these processors makes a parallel processor attractive as a method for attaining higher performance. However, many unsolved problems still exist in this arena. Another paper in this issue address the development of concurrent processor architectures for VLSI in more detail [61].

Another architectural area that is currently being explored is the architecture of processors for nonprocedural languages, such as Lisp, Smalltalk, and Prolog. There are several important reasons for interest in this area. First, such languages perform less well than procedural languages (Pascal, Fortran, C, etc.) on most architectures. Thus, one goal of the architectural investigations is to determine whether there are significant ways to achieve improved performance for such languages through architectural support. A second important issue is the role of such languages in exploiting parallelism. Many advocates of this class of languages contend that they offer a better route to obtaining parallelism in programs. If efforts to develop parallel processors are successful, then this advantage can be best exploited by supporting the execution of programs in an efficient manner, both for sequential and parallel activities.

Several important VLSI processors have been designed to support this class of languages. The SCHEME chips [13], [62] (called SCHEME-79 and SCHEME-81) are processors designed at MIT to directly execute SCHEME, a statically-scoped variant of Lisp. In addition to direct support for interpreting SCHEME, the SCHEME chips include hardware support for garbage collection (a microcoded garbage collector) and dynamic type checking.

SCHEME-81 includes tag bits to type each data item. The tag specifies whether a word is a datum (e.g., list, integer, etc.), or an instruction. Special support is provided for accessing tags and using them either as opcodes, to be interpreted by the microcode, or as data type specifications, to be checked dynamically when the datum is used. A wide microcode word is used to control multiple sets of register-operator units that function in parallel within the data path. The SCHEME-81 design supports multiple SCHEME processors. The primary mechanism to support multiprocessing is the SBUS. The novel feature of the SBUS is that it provides a protocol to manipulate Lisp structures over the bus.

The SOAR (Smalltalk on a RISC) processor [63] is a chip designed at U.C. Berkeley to support Smalltalk. SOAR provides efficient execution of Smalltalk by concentrating on three key areas. First, SOAR supports the dynamic type checking of tagged objects required by Smalltalk. SOAR handles tagged data by executing instructions and checking the tag in parallel; if both operands are not simple integers, the processor does a trap to a routine for the data type specified by the tag. This makes the frequent case where both tags are integers extremely fast. Second, SOAR provides fast procedure call with a variation of the RISC register windowing scheme and with hardware support to simplify software

caching of methods. In Smalltalk, the destination of a procedure call may depend on the argument passed. Caching the method in the instruction stream requires special support for nonreentrant code. Third, SOAR has hardware support for an efficient storage reclamation algorithm, called generation scavenging [64]. To support this technique requires the ability to trap on a small percentage of the store operations (about 0.2 percent). Checking for this infrequent trap condition is done by the SOAR hardware.

The SOAR architecture and implementation shows how the RISC philosophy of building support for the most frequent cases can be extended to a dynamic object-oriented environment. Smalltalk is supported by providing fast and simple ways to handle the most common situations (e.g., integer add) and using traps to routines that handle the exceptional cases. This approach is very different from the Xerox Smalltalk implementations [65], [66] that use a custom instruction set which is heavily encoded and implemented with extensive microcode.

Another major problem facing VLSI processor architects arises as the performance of these architectures approaches mainframe performance. Prior to the most recent processor designs, architects did not have to devote as much attention to systems issues: memory speeds were adequate to keep the processor busy, off-chip memory maps sufficed, and simple bus designs were fast enough for the needs of the processor. As these processors have become faster and have been adopted into complete computers (with large mapped memories and multiple I/O devices), these issues assume increasing importance. VLSI processors will need to be more concerned with the memory system: how it is mapped, what memory hierarchy is available, and the design of special processor-memory paths that can keep the processor's bandwidth requirements satisfied. Likewise, interrupt structure and support for a wide variety of high speed I/O devices will become more important.

B. Organizational Trends

Increasing processor speeds will bring increased need for memory bandwidth. Packaging constraints will make it increasing disadvantageous to obtain that bandwidth from off-chip. Thus, caches will migrate onto the processor chip. Similarly, memory address translation support will also move onto the processor chip. Two important instances of this move can be seen: the Intel iAPX432 includes an address cache, while the Motorola 68020 includes a small (256 byte) instruction cache. Cache memory is an attractive use of silicon because it can directly improve performance and its regularity limits the design effort per unit of silicon area.

Although today's microprocessors are used as CPU's in many computers, much of the functionality required in the CPU is handled off-chip. Many of the required functions not supported on the processor require powerful coprocessors. Among the functions performed by coprocessors, floating point and I/O interfacing are the most common. In the case of floating point, limited on-chip silicon area prevents the integration of a high performance floating point unit unto the chip. For the near future, designers will be faced with the difficult task of choosing what to incorporate on the processor chip. Without the cache both the fixed point and floating point performance of the processor may suffer. Thus, using a separate coprocessor is a concession to the lack of silicon area. The challenge is to design a coprocessor interface that avoids performance loss due to communication and coordination required between the processor and the coprocessor.

I/O coprocessors allow another processor to be devoted to the detailed control of an I/O device. A separate I/O processor not only eliminates the need for such functionality on the processor chip, it also supports overlapped processing by removing the I/O interface from the set of active tasks to be executed by the processor. As I/O processors become more powerful, they migrate from a coprocessor model to a separate I/O processor that uses DMA and the bus to interface to the memory and main processor.

C. Technology Trends

One of the most fundamental changes in technology is the shift to CMOS as the fabrication technology for VLSI processors [67]. The major advantage of CMOS is the low power consumption: CMOS designs use essentially no static power. This advantage simplifies circuit design and allows designers to use their power budget more effectively to reduce critical paths. Another advantage of CMOS is the absence of ratios in the design of logic structures; this simplifies the design process compared to nMOS design.

The major drawbacks of CMOS are in layout density. These disadvantages come from two factors: logic design and design rule requirements. Static logic designs in CMOS will often require more transistors and hence more connections than the nMOS counterpart. Many designs will also require both a signal and its complement; this increases the wiring space needed for the logic. CMOS designs can also take more space because of well separation rules. The p and n transistor types must be placed into different wells; since the well spacing rules are comparatively large, the separation between transistors of different types must be large. This can lead to cell designs whose density and area are dominated by the well spacing rules.

One important development that will help MOS technologies (but is particularly important for CMOS) is the availability of multiple levels of low resistance interconnect. The larger number of connections in CMOS makes this almost mandatory to avoid dominating layout density by interconnection constraints. A two-level metal process provides another level of interconnect and is the best solution. A silicide process allows the designer access to a low resistance polysilicon layer; this allows polysilicon to be used for longer routes but does not provide an additional layer of interconnect.

The design of faster and larger VLSI processors will require improvements in packaging both to lower delays and to increase the package connectivity. The development of pin grid packages has helped solve both of these problems to a significant extent. Packaging technologies that use wafers with multiple levels of interconnect as a substrate are being developed. These wafer-based packaging technologies provide high density and a large number of connections; they offer an alternative to the multilayer ceramic package.

Two of the biggest areas of unknown opportunity are gallium arsenide (GaAs) and wafer-scale integration. A GaAs medium for integrated circuits offers the advantage of significantly higher switching speeds versus silicon-based integrated circuits [68]. The primary advantage of GaAs comes from increased mobility of electrons, which leads to improvements in transistor switching speed over silicon by about an order of magnitude; furthermore, its power dissipation per gate is similar to nMOS (but still considerably higher than CMOS). Several fundamental problems must be overcome before GaAs becomes a viable technology for a processor. The most mature GaAs processes are for depletion mode MESFETS; logic design with such devices is more complex and consumes more transistors than MOS design. Currently, many problems prevent the fabrication of large (>10 000 transistors) GaAs integrated circuits with acceptable yields. Until these problems are overcome, the advantages of silicon technologies will make them the choice for VLSI processors.

Wafer scale integration allows effective use of silicon and high bandwidth interconnect between blocks on the same wafer. If the blocks represent components similar to individual IC's, their integration on a single wafer yields increased packing density and communication bandwidth because of shorter wires and more connections. Lower total packaging costs are also possible. There are several major hurtles that must be surpassed to make wafer-scale technology suitable for high performance custom VLSI processors. A major problem is to create a design methodology that generates individual testable blocks that will have high yields and that can be selectively interconnected to other working blocks. The need for multiple connection paths among the blocks and the high bandwidth of these connections makes this problem very difficult.

D. Summary

New and future architectural concepts are serving as driving forces for the design of new VLSI processors. Interest in nonprocedural languages leads to the creation of processors such as SCHEME and SOAR that are specifically designed to support such languages. The potential of a parallel processor constructed using VLSI microprocessors is an exciting possibility. The Intel iAPX432 specifically provides for multiprocessing. The importance of this type of system architecture will influence other processors to provide support for multiprocessing.

The increasing performance of VLSI processors will force designers to consider system performance, memory hierarchies, and floating point performance. Systems level products constructed using these processors will require support for memory mapping, interrupts, and high speed I/O. To attain the desired performance goals both on and off chip caches will be needed to reduce the bandwidth demands on main memory. The next generation of VLSI processors will be easily competitive with minicomputers and superminicomputers in integer performance; however, without floating point support they will be much slower than the larger machines with integrated floating point support. High performance floating point is a function both of the available coprocessor hardware for floating point and a low overhead coprocessor interface.

Despite the increased input from the architectural and software directions to the design of VLSI processors, technology remains a powerful driving force. CMOS will bring relief from the power problems associated with large nMOS integrated circuits; the problems presented by CMOS technology are minor compared to its benefits. Steady improvements in packaging technology can be predicted; more radical packaging technologies offer substantial increases in packaging density and interconnection bandwidth.

Wafer-scale integration and GaAs FET's stand as two new technologies that may substantially alter VLSI processor design. Wafer-scale integration offers several benefits but its success will depend on a balanced design methodology that can overcome fabrication defects without substantially impacting performance. GaAs offers very high speed devices; to be useful for large IC's, such as a VLSI CPU, will require major improvements in yield.

IX. Conclusions

A processor architecture supplies the definition of a host environment for applications. The use of high level languages requires that we evaluate the environment defined by the instruction set in terms of its suitability as a target for compilers of these languages. New instruction set designs *must* use measurements based on compiled code to ascertain the effectiveness of certain features.

The architect must trade off the suitability of the feature (as measured by its use in compiled code), against its cost, which is measured by the execution speed in an implementation, the area and power (which help calibrate the opportunity cost), and the overhead imposed on other instructions by the presence of this instruction set feature or collection of features. This approach can be used to measure the effectiveness of support features for the operating system; the designer must consider the frequency of use of such a feature, the performance improvement gained, and the cost of the feature. All three of these measurements must be considered before deciding to include the feature.

The investigation of these tradeoffs has led to two significantly different styles of instruction sets: simplified instruction sets and microcoded instruction sets. These styles of instruction sets have devoted silicon resources to different uses, resulting in different performance tradeoffs. The simplified instruction set architectures use silicon area to implement more on-chip data storage. Processors with more powerful instructions and denser instruction encodings require more control logic to interpret the instructions. This use of available silicon leads to a tradeoff between data and instruction bandwidth: the simplified architectures have lower data bandwidth and higher instruction bandwidth than the microcode-based architectures.

VLSI appears to be the first choice implementation media for many processor architectures. Increased densities and decreased switching times make the technology continuously more competitive. These advantages have motivated designers to use VLSI as the medium to explore new architectures. By combining improvements in technology, better processor organizations, and architectures that are good hosts for high level language programs, a VLSI processor can reach performance levels formerly attainable only by large-scale mainframes.

Acknowledgment

The material in this paper concerning MIPS and several of the figures are due to the collective efforts of the MIPS team: T. Gross, N. Jouppi, S. Przybylski, and C. Rowen; T. Gross and N. Jouppi also made suggestions on an early draft of the paper. M. Katevenis (who supplied the table of instructions for the Berkeley RISC processor) and J. Moussouris also made numerous valuable suggestions from a non-MIPS perspective.

References

[1] *DEC VAX11 Architecture Handbook*, Digital Equipment Corp., Maynard, MA, 1979.
[2] J. Rattner, "Hardware/Software Cooperation in the iAPX 432," in *Proc. Symp. Architectural Support for Programming Languages and Operating Systems*, Ass. Comput. Mach., Palo Alto, CA, Mar. 1982, p. 1.
[3] M. Flynn, "Directions and issues in architecture and language: Language → Architecture → Machine →," *Computer*, vol. 13, no. 10, pp. 5–22, Oct. 1980.
[4] R. Johnnson and D. Wick, "An overview of the Mesa processor architecture," in *Proc. Symp. Architectural Support for Programming Languages and Operating Systems*, Ass. Comput. Mach., Palo Alto, CA, Mar. 1982, pp. 20–29.
[5] M. Hopkins, "A perspective on microcode," in *Proc. COMPCON Spring '83*, IEEE, San Francisco, CA, Mar. 1983, pp. 108–110.
[6] ——, "Compiling high level functions on low-level machines," in *Proc. Int. Conf. Computer Design*, IEEE, Port Chester, NY, Oct. 1983.
[7] D. Clark and H. Levy, "Measurement and analysis of instruction use in the VAX 11/780," in *Proc. 9th Annu. Symp. Computer Architecture*, ACM/IEEE, Austin, TX, Apr. 1982.
[8] H. T. Kung and C. E. Leiserson, "Algorithms for VLSI processor arrays," in *Introduction to VLSI Systems*, C. A. Mead and L. Conway, Eds. Reading, MA: Addison-Wesley, 1978.
[9] G. Louie, T. Ho, and E. Cheng, "The MicroVAX I data-path chip," *VLSI Design*, vol. 4, no. 8, pp. 14–21, Dec. 1983.
[10] G. Radin, "The 801 minicomputer," in *Proc. SIGARCH/SIGPLAN Symp. Architectural Support for Programming Languages and Operating Systems*, Ass. Comput. Mach., Palo Alto, CA, Mar. 1982, pp. 39–47.
[11] D. A. Patterson and D. R. Ditzel, "The case for the reduced instruction set computer," *Comput. Architecture News*, vol. 8, no. 6, pp. 25–33, Oct. 1980.
[12] C. Mead and L. Conway, *Introduction to VLSI Systems*. Menlo Park, CA: Addison-Wesley, 1980.
[13] J. Holloway, G. Steele, G. Sussman, and A. Bell, "SCHEME-79 — LISP on a chip," *Computer*, vol. 14, no. 7, pp. 10–21, July 1981.
[14] R. Sherburne, M. Katevenis, D. Patterson, and C. Sequin, "Local memory in RISCs," in *Proc. Int. Conf. Computer Design*, IEEE, Rye, NY, Oct. 1983, pp. 149–152.
[15] T. R. Gross and J. L. Hennessy, "Optimizing delayed branches," in *Proc. Micro-15*, IEEE, Oct. 1982, pp. 114–120.
[16] W. A. Wulf, "Compilers and computer architecture," *Computer*, vol. 14, no. 7, pp. 41–48, July 1981.
[17] J. Hennessy, "Overview of the Stanford UCode compiler system," Stanford Univ., Stanford, CA.
[18] F. Chow, "A portable, machine-independent global optimizer — design and measurments," Ph.D. dissertation, Stanford Univ., Stanford, CA, 1984.
[19] J. R. Larus, "A comparison of microcode, assembly code, and high level languages on the VAX-11 and RISC-I," *Comput. Architecture News*, vol. 10, no. 5, pp. 10–15, Sept. 1982.
[20] L. J. Shustek, "Analysis and performance of computer instruction sets," Ph.D. dissertation, Stanford University, Stanford, CA, May 1977; also published as SLAC Rep. 205.
[21] D. A. Patterson and C. H. Sequin, "A VLSI RISC," *Computer*, vol. 15, no. 9, pp. 8–22, Sept. 1982.
[22] M. Auslander and M. Hopkins, "An overview of the PL.8 compiler," in *Proc. SIGPLAN Symp. Compiler Construction*, Ass. Comput. Mach., Boston, MA, June 1982, pp. 22–31.

[23] W. Johnson, "A VLSI superminicomputer CPU," in *Dig. 1984 Int. Solid-State Circuits Conf.*, IEEE, San Francisco, CA, Feb. 1984, pp. 174–175.

[24] J. Beck, D. Dobberpuhl, M. Doherty, E. Dornekamp, R. Grondalski, D. Grondalski, K. Henry, M. Miller, R. Supnik, S. Thierauf, and R. Witek, "A 32b microprocessor with on-chip virtual memory management," in *Dig. 1984 Int. Solid-State Circuits Conf.*, IEEE, San Francisco, CA, Feb. 1984, pp. 178–179.

[25] R. Sites, "How to use 1000 registers," in *Proc. 1st Caltech Conf. VLSI*, California Inst. Technol., Pasadena, CA, Jan. 1979.

[26] F. Baskett, "A VLSI Pascal machine," Univ. California, Berkeley, lecture.

[27] D. Ditzel and R. McLellan, "Register allocation for free: The C machine stack cache," in *Proc. Symp. Architectural Support for Programming Languages and Operating Systems*, Ass. Comput. Mach., Palo Alto, CA, Mar. 1982, pp. 48–56.

[28] *The C/70 Macroprogrammer's Handbook*, Bolt, Beranek, and Newman, Inc., Cambridge, MA, 1980.

[29] B. Lampson, "Fast procedure calls," in *Proc. SIGARCH/SIGPLAN Symp. Architectural Support for Programming Languages and Operating Systems*, Ass. Comput. Mach., Mar. 1982, pp. 66–76.

[30] S. Wakefield, "Studies in execution architectures," Ph.D. dissertation, Stanford Univ., Stanford, CA, Jan. 1983.

[31] R. Ragan-Kelly, "Performance of the pyramid computer," in *Proc. COMPCON*, Feb. 1983.

[32] Y. Tamir and C. Sequin, "Strategies for managing the register file in RISC," *IEEE Trans. Comput.*, vol. C-32, no. 11, pp. 977–988, Nov. 1983.

[33] M. Katevenis, "Reduced instruction set computer architectures for VLSI," Ph.D. dissertation, Univ. California, Berkeley, Oct. 1983.

[34] G. J. Chaitin, M. A. Auslander, A. K. Chandra, J. Cocke, M. E. Hopkins, and P. W. Markstein, "Register allocation by coloring," IBM Watson Research Center, Res. Rep. 8395, 1981.

[35] B. Leverett, "Register allocation in optimizing compilers," Ph.D. dissertation, Carnegie-Mellon Univ., Pittsburgh, PA, Feb. 1981.

[36] F. C. Chow and J. L. Hennessy, "Register allocation by priority-based coloring," in *Proc. 1984 Compiler Construction Conf.*, Ass. Comput. Mach., Montreal, P.Q., Canada, June 1984.

[37] A. J. Smith, "Cache memories," *Ass. Comput. Mach. Comput. Surveys*, vol. 14, no. 3, pp. 473–530, Sept. 1982.

[38] D. Clark, "Cache Performance in the VAX 11/780," *ACM Trans. Comput. Syst.*, vol. 1, no. 1, pp. 24–37, Feb. 1983.

[39] M. Easton and R. Fagin, "Cold start vs. warm start miss ratios," *Commun. Ass. Comput. Mach.*, vol. 21, no. 10, pp. 866–872, Oct. 1978.

[40] D. Clark and J. Emer, "Performance of the VAX-11/780 translation buffer," to be published.

[41] R. Fabry, "Capability based addressing," *Commun. Ass. Comput. Mach.*, vol. 17, no. 7, pp. 403–412, July 1974.

[42] W. Wulf, R. Levin, and S. Harbinson, *Hydra:C.mmp: An Experimental Computer System*. New York: McGraw-Hill, 1981.

[43] M. Wilkes and R. Needham, *The Cambridge CAP Computer and Its Operating System*. New York: North Holland, 1979.

[44] M. Wilkes, "Hardware support for memory management functions," in *Proc. SIGARCH/SIGPLAN Symp. Architectural Support for Programming Languages and Operating Systems*, Ass. Comput. Mach., Mar. 1982, pp. 107–116.

[45] J. Hennessy, N. Jouppi, S. Przybylski, and T. Gross, "Design of a high performance VLSI processor," in *Proc. 3rd Caltech Conf. VLSI*, California Inst. Technol., Pasadena, CA, Mar. 1983, pp. 33–54.

[46] S. Przybylski, T. Gross, J. Hennessy, N. Jouppi, and C. Rowen, "Organization and VLSI implementation of MIPS," *J. VLSI Comput. Syst.*, vol. 1, no. 3, Spring 1984; see also Tech. Rep. 83-259.

[47] J. Hennessy, N. Jouppi, F. Baskett, and J. Gill, "MIPS: A VLSI processor architecture," in *Proc. CMU Conf. VLSI Systems and Computations*, Rockville, MD: Computer Science Press, Oct. 1981, pp. 337–346; see also Tech. Rep. 82-223.

[48] J. L. Hennessy, N. Jouppi, F. Baskett, T. R. Gross, and J. Gill, "Hardware/software tradeoffs for increased performance," in *Proc. SIGARCH/SIGPLAN Symp. Architectural Support for Programming Languages and Operating Systems*, Ass. Comput. Mach., Palo Alto, CA, Mar. 1982, pp. 2–11.

[49] J. L. Hennessy and T. R. Gross, "Postpass code optimization of pipeline constraints," *ACM Trans. on Programming Lang. Syst.*, vol. 5, no. 3, July 1983.

[50] T. R. Gross, "Code optimization of pipeline constraints," Ph.D. dissertation, Stanford Univ., Stanford, CA, Aug. 1983.

[51] M. Flynn, *The Interpretive Interface: Resources and Program Representation in Computer Organization*. New York: Academic, 1977, ch. I-3, pp. 41–70; see also *Proc. Symp. High Speed Computer and Algorithm Organization*.

[52] M. Flynn and L. Hoevel, "Execution architecture: The DELtran experiment," *IEEE Trans. Comput.*, vol. C-32, no. 2, pp. 156–174, Feb. 1983.

[53] G. Meyer, "The case against stack-oriented instruction sets," *Comput. Architecture News*, vol. 6, no. 3, Aug. 1977.

[54] *MC68000 Users Manual*, 2nd ed., Motorola Inc., Austin, TX, 1980.

[55] E. Stritter and T. Gunther, "A microprocessor architecture for a changing world: The Motorola 68000," *Computer*, vol. 12, no. 2, pp. 43–52, Feb. 1979.

[56] R. Schumann and W. Parker, "A 32b bus interface chip," in *Dig. 1984 Int. Solid-State Circuits Conf.*, IEEE, San Francisco, CA, Feb. 1984, pp. 176–177.

[57] R. Sites, "Instruction ordering for the Cray-1 computer," University of California, San Diego, Tech. Rep. 78-CS-023, July 1978.

[58] J. Mavor, M. Jack, and P. Denyer, *Introduction to MOS LSI Design*. London, England: Addison-Wesley, 1983.

[59] A. Rainal, "Computing inductive noise of chip packages," *Bell Lab. Tech. J.*, vol. 63, no. 1, pp. 177–195, Jan. 1984.

[60] D. A. Patterson and C. H. Sequin, "RISC-I: A reduced instruction set VLSI computer," in *Proc. 8th Annu. Symp. Computer Architecture*, Minneapolis, MN, May 1981, pp. 443–457.

[61] C. Seitz, "Concurrent VLSI architectures," *IEEE Trans. Comput.*, this issue, pp. 1247–1265.

[62] J. Batali, E. Goodhue, C. Hanson, H. Shrobe, R. Stallman, and G. Sussman, "The SCHEME-81 architecture—system and chip," in *Proc. Conf. Advanced Research in VLSI*, Paul Penfield, Jr., Ed, Cambridge, MA: MIT Press, Jan. 1982, pp. 69–77.

[63] D. Ungar, R. Blau, P. Foley, D. Simples, and D. Patterson, "Architecture of SOAR: Smalltalk on a RISC," in *Proc. 11th Symp. Computer Architecture*, ACM/IEEE, Ann Arbor, MI, June 1984, pp. 188–197.

[64] D. Ungar, "Generation scavenging: A nondisruptive high performance storage reclaimation algorithm," in *Proc. Software Eng. Symp. Practical Software Development Environments*, ACM, Pittsburgh, PA, Apr. 1984, pp. 157–167.

[65] A. Goldberg and D. Robson, *Smalltalk-80: The Language and Its Implementation*. Reading, MA: Addison-Wesley, 1983.

[66] L. Deutsch, "The Dorado Smalltalk-80 implementation: Hardware architecture's impact on software architecture," in *Smalltalk-80: Bits of History, Words of Advice*, Glenn Krasner, Ed. Reading, MA: Addison-Wesley, 1983, pp. 113–126.

[67] R. Davies, "The case for CMOS," *IEEE Spectrum*, vol. 20, no. 10, pp. 26–32, Oct. 1983.

[68] R. Eden, A. Livingston, and B. Welch, "Integrated circuits: The case for gallium arsenide," *IEEE Spectrum*, vol. 20, no. 12, pp. 30–37, Dec. 1983.

John L. Hennessy received the B.E. degree in electrical engineering from Villanova University, Villanova, PA, in 1973 and is the recipient of the 1983 John J. Gallen Memorial Award. He received the Masters and Ph.D. degrees in computer science from the State University of New York, Stony Brook, in 1975 and 1977, respectively.

Since September 1977 he has been with the Computer Systems Laboratory at Stanford University where he is currently an Associate Professor of Electrical Engineering and Director of the Computer Systems Laboratory. He has done research on several issues in compiler design and optimization. Much of his current work is in VLSI. He is the designer of the SLIM system, which constructs VLSI control implementations from high level language specifications. He is also the leader of the MIPS project. MIPS is a high performance VLSI microprocessor designed to execute code for high level languages.

An old idea may influence new computer designs.

RISC: BACK TO THE FUTURE?

by C. Gordon Bell

Several recent announcements indicate that computers will be changing over the next decade. The new high-speed architectures announced by Hewlett-Packard, IBM, and a startup in Sunnyvale, Calif., called MIPS Computer Systems Inc., challenge today's reliance on microprogrammed processors—a legacy of the original IBM 360.

The primary development involves the application of the so-called reduced instruction set computer (RISC) concept. RISC

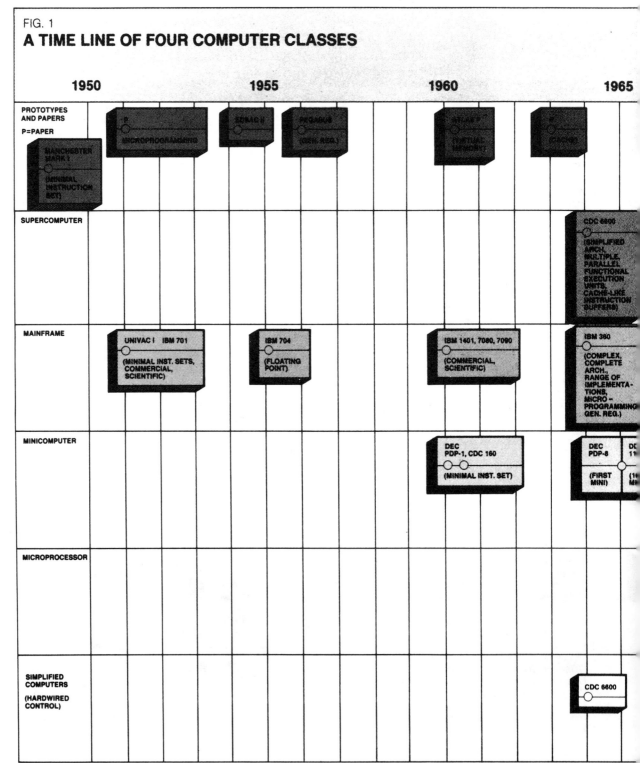

FIG. 1
A TIME LINE OF FOUR COMPUTER CLASSES

Reprinted with permission of DATAMATION® magazine, © Copyright Technical Publishing Company, A Dun & Bradstreet Company, 1986—rights reserved.

designs contrast with those of complex (or complete) instruction set computers (CISC), which are meant to contain a repertoire of machine instructions to handle all the data types and operations of today's high-level languages. (The CISC approach reduces the size of object programs by attempting to provide each high-level source code statement with a single machine instruction.)

The concept of RISC involves an attempt to reduce execution time by simplifying the central processor's tasks. Conventional microprogrammed architectures are predicated on relatively slow access to primary memory and read-only memories for microprograms that are five to 10 times faster. In CISC machines, which do more processing per instruction than in RISC, the processor requires five to 10 clock ticks to carry out a typical instruction.

But with continuing hardware refinements, especially in chip technology over the last decade, logic and memory speeds are now nearly identical. RISC machines exploit this development by transferring certain logical steps that are required to interpret instructions out of processor microcode and into memory as a run-time library program (see Figs. 2c and 2d). In a RISC design, all high-level language functions are constructed from simple software primitives in a fashion resembling microprogramming, except that they are stored outside the processor as regular programs.

Reducing the instruction set further reduces the work a RISC processor has to do. Since RISC has fewer types of instructions than CISC, a RISC instruction requires less processing logic to interpret than a

CHART BY CYNTHIA STODDARD

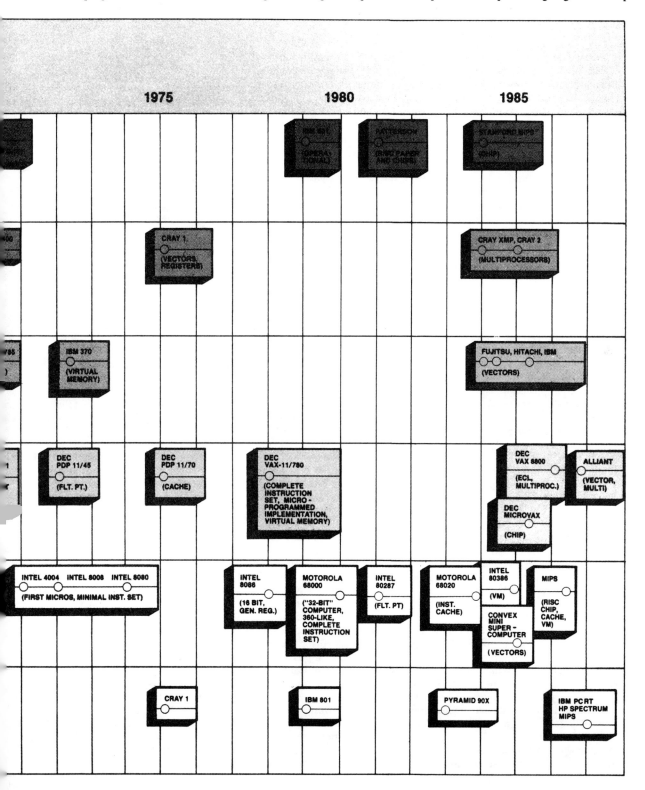

Nearly all the RISC machines resemble the simple, Cray-style architectures pioneered in the CDC 6600.

CISC instruction. The effect of such simplification is to speed up the execution rate for RISC instructions. In a RISC implementation it is theoretically possible to execute an instruction each time the computer's logic clock ticks. In practice the clock rate of a RISC processor is usually three times that of the instruction rate.

Of course, a typical instruction in a RISC machine is much less powerful than a typical CISC instruction—making comparisons of MIPS rates virtually meaningless. Benchmark tests in high-level languages are the only way to compare computers.

RISC's gains in processing time involve a cost in memory space. But since virtually all programs are implemented in high-level languages, machine-level trade-offs are scarcely noticeable to end users. If the notion of a RISC proves sound, users will see a gradual increase in performance as manufacturers go back to hard-wired control implementations and abandon the more complex microprogrammed approach used over the last two decades.

The second major development in recent architectures is the use of vector data types to speed up scientific computation. Cray Research pioneered this in 1975 with its Cray-1, and it has now been introduced in the IBM-compatible mainframes and a plethora of new minisupercomputers from Alliant Computer Systems Corp. of Acton, Mass., Convex of Dallas, and Scientific Computing Systems of Portland, Ore.

Finally, the multiprocessor approach to computing is being introduced in all computer families, from supercomputers to workstations, in order to provide the seemingly unbounded increases in performance available through parallel processing. The multiprocessor approach is independent of the architecture of the processors (i.e., whether a processor is "reduced" or "complex").

HOW RISC BEGAN

The groundwork for RISC was laid in the mid-1970s. In 1975, a team at the IBM Research Center in Yorktown Heights, N.Y., formed what was called the 801 project around a design approach credited to IBM fellow John Cocke. The goal of the project was to "achieve significantly better cost/performance for high-level language programs than that attainable by existing systems." The 801 group, which was led by George Radin, one of the primary authors of the PL/1 language, produced an operational minicomputer in 1979 (see "IBM Mini a Radical Departure," October 1979, p. 53). The IBM group acknowledged being influenced by the design simplifications—such

as hard-wired control—pioneered by Seymour Cray in his design of the first supercomputer, the CDC 6600 (c. 1964).

Professor David Patterson of the University of California at Berkeley has been the main proponent of reexamining architectures along RISC lines. His first paper on RISC, published in *Computer Architecture News* in October 1980, made the case for a simplified instruction set.

The phrase "reduced instruction set computer" was coined to describe the subsequent Berkeley effort. Berkeley researchers and engineers went on to implement operational prototypes, RISC I and RISC II, in the early '80s; a third Berkeley RISC design is oriented to multiprocessing and symbolic programming.

Pyramid Technology Corp., Mountain View, Calif., was among the first companies to build computers based on the new RISC ideas. Pyramid's 90X supermini was released in 1983.

IBM's newly introduced PC RT for scientific and engineering applications evolved from the basic 801 effort, although the machine is hardly noteworthy in terms of the initial performance or functionality. The RT chip was implemented with older generation MOS technology using a relatively slow clock of 6MHz. Performance does not appear to measure up to comparable microprocessors based on, for example, Intel's 80386 design. By using modern CMOS technology, a speedup of at least a factor of 3 is easily attainable, which would demonstrate the validity of the design approach.

The HP Spectrum series announced in February may also be related to the 801 effort. The manager of the section sponsoring the work at IBM, Joel Birnbaum, went to HP to head its research lab. As with the PC RT, Spectrum performance is uninspiring, but the series is not an adequate test of RISC since the technology used is hardly state of the art.

The chip built by MIPS Co. presents a more compelling case for RISC. MIPS Co. was formed in 1984 to build a high-performance chip based on the design ideas developed by Prof. John Hennessy and his associates at Stanford University. Initial benchmarks of the MIPS chip indicate it is five to 10 times faster than a DEC VAX-11/780 or the Motorola 68020 for the same clock speed. The MIPS Co. chip is simpler, considerably smaller, and significantly faster than any of today's microprocessors. The Defense Department's R&D arm, which sponsored the MIPS work, has adopted the architecture as a standard for high-performance implementations.

Fairchild Semiconductor Corp., Mountain View, Calif., has given further

support to the RISC approach with its recently announced microprocessor called Clipper. The leader of the Clipper development group, Howard Sachs, came from Cray Research. Clipper, implemented as three CMOS chips, is reported to be about the speed of a VAX 8600.

RISC MACHINES CRAY-LIKE

Nearly all the RISC machines unveiled so far resemble the simple, Cray-style architectures pioneered in the CDC 6600 and oriented to scientific processing (which stresses binary data types). How well a RISC design can handle the variable-length decimal and string data inherent in many commercial applications still remains to be seen. Provided the proper focus on the data types is maintained, there's no reason to believe the RISC approach will be unsuccessful.

The first operational stored program computer, the Manchester Mark I (c. 1948) was a minimal instruction set computer (MISC). The Mark I, which had a memory of 32 words (expandable to 8K words), each 32 bits long, had only six instructions: jump, load accumulator negative, subtract, store accumulator, test for zero, and stop.

Beginning with the Univac I (c. 1951), the computers that followed the Mark I in the '50s and '60s likewise had simple instruction sets, appropriately embellished with index registers to assist in the access of arrays. The design objectives of the earliest machines were that they have a minimum of registers, efficient encoding of programs (often oriented to assembly language programming), small primary memories, and processors matched to the memory's performance. The instruction sets were small and the instructions were simple and operated only on integers. Floating point hardware was introduced in the IBM 704 in 1955.

By the mid-1960s, computers had evolved to having a single set of general purpose registers combining accumulators, index and base registers, and subroutine linkage registers. The control unit for simple processors was straightforward. Each machine had a few allowable data types and instructions. Memories were slow, relative to the rate at which information could be transferred among the internal registers of the machine. By 1960, core memories had a 2μsec cycle time, with a 1μsec access time. Since internal logic operated at a 5MHz to 10MHz clock rate, five to 10 hardware operations could thus be carried out after one memory access and before the next. This ratio would change as chip technology progressed.

A simple computer of the early '60s operated at about 250,000 instructions per second since typically two memory references were required per instruction (e.g., load accumulator, add memory to accumulator, store accumulator). Performance was increased by providing overlapped memory so that a processor could access memory at a faster rate. The objective of computer design was to match the instruction processing rate of the processor to the memory. Fig. 2a shows the configuration of a hardwired processor, matched to a memory.

The second computer generation began in 1960 with many important, transistorized, core memory machines brought out by the early leaders in the minicomputer, mainframe, and supercomputer classes: DEC (PDP-1), IBM (1401 for operating on strings, 7070 for operating on decimal numbers, and 7090 for operating on scientific numbers), and Control Data (160, 1604). (Seymour Cray developed the architecture for Control Data's first supercomputer in the 1960s. He later left CDC and, in 1972, founded Cray Research, the leader in the supercomputer class.)

By the mid-1960s, a second round of significant computers from these vendors established their three respective classes: DEC PDP-5 (1964), the forerunner of the PDP-8, the first minicomputer; IBM 360 (April 1964), the mainframe; and Cray's CDC 6600 (1964), the first supercomputer. Fig. 1 depicts the evolution of the "mainline" computer classes—micros, as we shall see, came with the 1970s—demonstrating how prototype ideas that first appeared on high-priced machines later spread to wide-scale use.

The IBM 360, introduced in 1964, was one of the earliest computer families to span a range of price and performance. Along with the 360, IBM introduced the word architecture to refer to the various processing characteristics of a machine as seen by the programmer and his programs. In the initial 360 product family, the model 91 exceeded the model 20 in performance by a factor of 300, in memory size by a factor of 512, and in price by a factor of 100.

360 LINE SET NEW STANDARD

The enormously successful 360 product line set an important new standard for CISC design. By virtually all measures, the instruction set was more complete and complex than any previous design, and included instructions to handle data in both the commercial and scientific environments: integers, floating point, decimal, and character strings.

The primary goal for the product line was to merge IBM's scientific and com-

FIG. 2
FOUR MAINLINE COMPUTER ARCHITECTURES

2a. Early, hardwired simple computers (c. 1950 - 60) and conventional microprocessors (c. 1971 -)

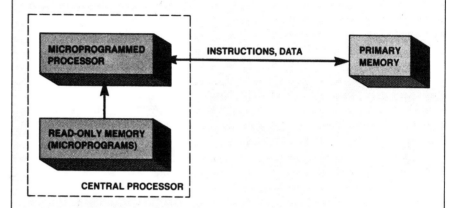

2b. Microprogrammed processor to interpret instruction set (c. 1964)

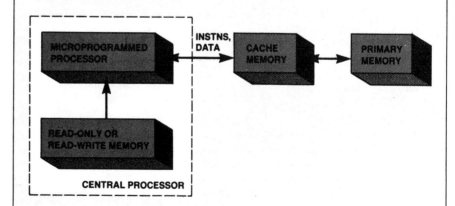

2c. Microprogrammed processor with cache (c. 1968)

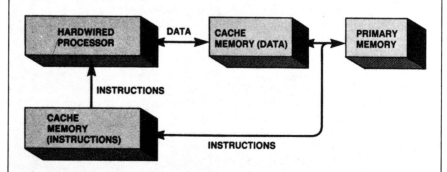

2d. Hardwired, pipelined processor with separate caches for instructions and data (c. 1985)

The goal of these early architectures was to provide processors that operated at the memory rate.

mercial computer families into a single product line in order to have a single architecture and to maximize the compatibility of the peripherals and operating systems. Since the memory sizes were small, a complex architecture was adopted in order to most efficiently encode programs of the various languages. The benefits to users were configuration flexibility and compatibility across the range.

Microprogramming, first described in a 1951 paper by the English computer pioneer Maurice Wilkes, was the technique used to implement most of the 360 line. A microprogrammed processor carries out its functions with a program, stored in a read-only memory, that interprets the larger instruction set. In effect, it is a computer within the central processor (see Fig. 2b). The microprogrammed processor is also useful for implementing the complex I/O processors that were part of the 360 architecture.

Since the 360 included a range of computers, the specific models were separate and distinct. A few of the early 360s were developed using hard-wired (non-microprogram) implementations. These were the highest-priced, high-performance models. The model 44, introduced in the late '60s, used hard-wired control, and provided an exceptionally high price/performance ratio.

CDC 6600 WAS MODEL FOR RISC

The goal behind the CDC 6600 was simply to build the largest, fastest scientific computer of the day. Hard-wired control, radical packaging (heat exchangers, for example), and an emphasis on parallelism were among the innovations of the first supercomputer.

The 6600 architecture was radically simplified compared with contemporary architectures of 1964, especially the 360's. The 6600 is now recognized as something of a RISC prototype because it used a relatively small set of general registers; only register-load and register-store instructions were used to access memory, and a minimum number of instructions were defined to operate on integer, boolean vector, and floating point data. More complex operations such as character string operations were coded from the basic operations.

The processor was completely hard-wired, with a great amount of control capabilities, so that several different instructions could be executed in parallel, through pipelining. In the 6600, a large instruction buffer, which is almost identical to today's instruction caches, was used to hold instructions without having to access the slower core memory.

By 1975, Cray had extended the 6600 architectural concept in the Cray 1 to include a small register array as a set of "vector" registers in order to maximize the performance of the computer for inherently pipelined operations.

With vector operations, a single instruction may specify a list of numbers, such as a column of a matrix, to be operated on at a given time. With the extension of vectors, it is very hard to characterize such an architecture as either simple or RISC-based. A vector processor, however, maintains the goal of delivering a result every clock tick, using a complex data type, namely a vector.

Roughly 10 years later, IBM and the Japanese 360/370-compatible vendors used the same concepts for extending the 360 architecture for high-performance scientific computation. By 1985, IBM had also introduced the vector processor in the 3090, model 200/VF.

MINIS APE LARGER COMPUTERS

Minicomputers followed the same evolutionary path taken by computers in the mainframe and supercomputer classes. Developers of the PDP-8, the first minicomputer, sought to build the smallest computer possible that would still be both widely useful and widely affordable ($18,000 in 1966).

The design of the PDP-8 followed that of its predecessor, the PDP-5, which had been implemented as the smallest (MISC) computer the design team could think of. As in the original Manchester Mark I, only two registers were included in the PDP-5 (and the original PDP-8) architecture: the accumulator and the program counter—which meant that subroutines were required for multiply/divide and floating point operations.

Registers were so expensive when the PDP-5 was built that the program counter was stored in memory location 0. The original architecture had only eight basic instructions. Subsequent additions to the architecture provided arithmetic, including floating point. The PDP-8 continued this pattern of adding complexity within the processor design.

By the early '70s, the 360 had evolved to include virtual memory, a concept first realized a decade earlier in Manchester's Atlas. The 360/85 (c. 1968) was the first computer to use the cache memory, described by computer pioneer Wilkes in 1965 as a small storage area used to hold recent fetches from primary memory (see Fig. 2c). The 370 (c. 1972) represented a high-end introduction of integrated circuits, which were used for, among other

things, both primary and cache memories. The gap between memory and logic speed had begun to close.

The advent of low-cost logic using integrated circuits led to the explosive growth of the the minicomputer industry in the 1970s. The evolution of minis followed "mainline" development, including a family of compatible computers, floating point arithmetic, virtual memory, cache memory, multiprocessors, and a complex instruction set (commercial and scientific) as pioneered by the 360.

The introduction of DEC's VAX-11/780 in 1978, which evolved from the PDP-11, marked the emergence of a high-performance or superminicomputer class that combined the design concepts of mainframes with relatively lower-cost technology.

By all accounts, VAX has about the most complete architecture, with separate sets of basic operations for each of the scientific and commercial data types and primitives to assist the operating system, including the management of virtual memory. The architecture also includes single instructions for procedure calls, DO loop control, and case statements. The initial microprogram size, in words or bits, was roughly double that of the first 360s.

MICRO ALSO APES LARGE COMPUTERS

The development of the micro has followed the evolution pattern of the mainframe and minicomputer. The first micro, the Intel 4004, was a minimal instruction set computer. Intel's subsequent microprocessors evolved from an 8-bit data orientation and small (16-bit) address to include floating point arithmetic, provide for memory management, and eventually support a large virtual address space (the 80386). The technology for implementing micros favors the microprogrammed approach in order to simplify the design whereby read-only memory arrays occupy a large area of the chip.

Motorola followed a similarly evolutionary path based on a near-360 architecture. After about 10 years of evolution, the 68020 chip set provides for floating point, a large virtual memory, and an on-chip instruction cache. National Semiconductor adopted a near look-alike to the VAX architecture.

Unlike either mainframes or minis, microprocessors are not fixed architectures. Rather, microprocessors approach a complete architecture as each new model extends the architecture of its predecessor. The chip technology determines the architecture of each implementation, which embellishes the architecture of its predecessor by adding capabilities. All the "standard" chips by Intel, Motorola, and National have followed the traditional path of evolutionary complexity: all of the chips are substantially larger and more complex (by a factor of 2 to 4) than their RISC counterparts. They require a relatively long design time and operate at a comparatively slower processing rate.

The academic and commercial interest in RISC, implemented with a simple hard-wired control unit, is motivated by trends in memory and logic technology. When memory rates were considerably slower than logic rates, microprogramming improved performance by reducing the time spent outside the processor in memory fetches. Although the microprogrammed idea originated in 1951, IBM pioneered this style of design with the 360 family.

By the early '70s, the cache memory was introduced (in the 360/85), providing in effect a substantially faster memory. New semiconductor memories also offered reduced access and cycle times. Further, the speed of small read-write memories used for registers and caches began to approach that of logic. The result was that cache-based computers underscored CISC performance limitations because no faster memory could be used for the microprogram. It was after the introduction of cache memory that the IBM research project leading to the 801 was established.

Today's large IBM mainframes require about three clock ticks per instruction, which makes the question of whether CISC is a performance limitation almost academic.

RISC GOAL IS MORE FUNCTIONS

The goal of a reduced instruction set is to make a simple hard-wired processor and to carry out as many functions as possible with software. (Fig. 2d shows the essential RISC scheme derived from the 801. Fig. 3 summarizes the two approaches.)

RISC focuses on reducing the number of instructions that operate on a conventional register array, and separating them into two classes: simple load/store of the registers, including use of the registers as base and/or index registers; and operations among the registers utilizing a three-register address format. In effect, this separation into instruction types means that a statement is compiled into the parts that access the data, and the part that performs the arithmetic of the statement.

In contrast, CISC schemes have a range of instruction formats that effectively combine memory access with the operations. The essential goal of the VAX, for example, is to provide a separate microcoded machine instruction for every statement that could be written in a high-level language, e.g., a single VAX instruction is C[i] = A[j] + B[k] and would correspond to at least four RISC instructions:

1. load accumulator 1 with A[j];
2. load accumulator 2 with B[k];
3. add accumulator 1 to accumulator 2;
4. store contents of accumulator 2 in C[i].

Because they are simple, one or more RISC instructions are usually held in a word (typically 32 bits), as in the early, word-oriented RISC machines.

The second way that a RISC scheme simplifies processing (besides having only load/stores and arithmetic operations) is by eliminating the complex data types such as floating point, decimal, and byte strings. In RISC, the necessary "primitive" operations (e.g., decimal add) are best considered part of the architecture. In the case of floating point, separate execution units are used for a completely hard-wired and parallel implementation.

The processor is controlled by a hard-wired logic unit, not a microprogrammed processor. The goal of an implementation is to be able to carry out one operation every clock tick or every memory cycle, using a pipeline of, say, four stages, just as in early processors that matched the memory bandwidth. The single best test for a RISC architecture is to observe whether the instruction rate is within a factor of 2 of the clock rate of the processor.

Here is the basic equation governing the execution rate of a simple, scalar computer:

$\#P \times$ (clock rate) $\times$ (1/ticks/instruction) $\times$ (operations + operands)/instruction $\times$ (statements/ (operations + operands)) $\times$ (compiler efficiency)

(The number of central processors is represented by P.) This general structure using multiprocessors is likely to be the basis of mainline computing in the next decade because of the negligible cost of incremental microprocessors based on CMOS technology. For scientific processors, a vector pro-

---

FIG. 3

TWO APPROACHES TO COMPUTER DESIGN

	COMPLEX	REDUCED
Registers	8-16 gen. reg. floating pt.	16-32 gen. reg., + opt. floating pt.
Data types	bytes...double precision fl. pt. decimal, byte strings, page tables, queues, etc.	bytes...integers, fl. pt. (opt.), ? decimal, ? byte strings (software processing of O/S data)
Instructions	correspond to data types, instructions assist O/S and run-time utilities	load/store general registers, operations on data types in registers
Inst. formats	variable length, many types: load/store, R := R op R, R := Mem. op R, M: = M, M := Mem op Mem	fixed length, two main types: load/store, R := R op R
Encoding	1 instruction = 1 statement	1 inst. = 1 operand or 1 operation
Design objective	min. program length, max. work per. instruction	trade-off program length, minimize time to execute instruction
Implementation	microprogrammed processor; slow, primary memory and fast clock; instructions take var. time; pipeline is complex; larger implementation may result in longer design time	hard-wired processor and software; fast processor and fast cache for instructions; instructions take one clocktime; simple pipeline
Caching	useful	essential for instructions
Compiler Design	should stress finding right instructions	should stress best ordering
Philosophy	move any useful software function into hardware, incl. diagnostics, hardware changes	move all functions to software

The efficiency of the compiler is a major factor that may favor the RISC approach.

cessing unit operating in parallel with the conventional processor is the surest way to increase performance by a factor of 3 to 20, depending on the problem.

PROCESSOR NUMBER IS CRUCIAL The number of processors potentially has the greatest effect, because it can quite possibly be increased indefinitely, with relatively little extra cost, depending on the amount of parallelism inherent in the problem. Companies such as Alliant, Encore, and Sequent are using multiple microprocessors (i.e., a multi) to increase performance in a radical fashion and provide substantially greater performance in the superminicomputer market. Cray is using the multiprocessor to increase performance in exactly the same fashion.

The efficiency of the compiler is a major factor that may favor the RISC approach, since there is usually only one way to carry out a given function. In the case of a complex architecture, the difficulty is finding the best way to carry out a statement, including the use of temporary general registers. There is little understanding or data that indicate that the compiler is substantially different in either case. We simply must wait for some competitive studies.

This review of the evolution of computer architecture has demonstrated the ultimate appeal of simple designs. For example, the advantages of complex microprogramming diminish directly as access time to memory is reduced. Given a relatively constant or smaller amount of a given technology, it now appears that a pipelined RISC computer could outperform a microprogrammed machine by a factor of 2 or 3. Based on the rate at which such slowly evolving technologies as TTL or ECL have been registering performance gains (i.e., 15% yearly), RISC would thus represent an immediate five- to seven-year advance over CISC. For rapidly advancing technology like CMOS, the performance of which has been improving at up to 40% per year, the switch to RISC is equivalent to a two- to three-year advance in the state of the art.

Many factors determine a computer's performance. The number of processors will have the greatest long-term effect, regardless of the number or type of instructions they execute. For the scientific market, the introduction of vectors is essential, which hardly makes the architecture very simple. For a simple instruction set, including vector operations and now multiprocessors, the best advice for today's architect is simply, "Follow Cray." If the computer is to process decimal and string data for the commercial environment, care must be taken to provide the primitive operations for the languages in the architecture. ◉

C. Gordon Bell is the assistant director of the newly formed computer and information science and engineering directorate of the National Science Foundation. He is also the chief scientist for the DANA Group, Sunnyvale, Calif., which is designing a personal supercomputer using a RISC chip. He was a vice president for engineering at DEC from 1960 to 1983, and the chief architect for the PDP-8, the System/20, the PDP-11, and the VAX-11/780. He has taught at Carnegie-Mellon University and is an IEEE fellow.

Section 3: Optimized Register Usage

3.1 Background

The results summarized in section 1 point out the desirability of quick access to operands. There is a large proportion of assignment statements in HLL programs, and many of these are of the simple form A = B. Also, there are a significant number of operand accesses per HLL statement. Finally, most accesses are to local scalars. On the basis of these results, heavy reliance on register storage is suggested. Register storage is the fastest available storage, faster than both main memory and cache. The register file is physically small, generally on the same chip as the ALU and control unit, and employs much shorter addresses than for cache and memory. Thus a strategy is needed that will allow the most frequently accessed operands to be kept in registers and to minimize register-memory operations.

Two basic approaches are possible, one based on software and the other on hardware. The software approach is to rely on the compiler to maximize register usage. The compiler will attempt to allocate registers to those variables that will be used the most in a given time period. This approach requires the use of sophisticated program-analysis algorithms. The hardware approach is simply to use more registers so that more variables can be held in registers for longer periods of time. This section presents both approaches.

To provide some context for this section, the following subsections discuss design issues related to CPU registers.

3.2 Registers

To understand the role of registers in the CPU, let us consider the requirements placed on the CPU, the things that it must do

- *Fetch instructions:* The CPU must read instructions from memory.

- *Interpret instructions:* The instruction must be decoded to determine what action is required.

- *Fetch data:* The execution of an instruction may require reading data from memory or an I/O module.

- *Process data:* The execution of an instruction may require performing some arithmetic or logical operation on data.

- *Write data:* The results of an execution may require writing data to memory or an I/O module.

To be able to do these things, it should be clear that the CPU needs to temporarily store some data. The CPU must remember the location of the last instruction so that it can know where to get the next instruction. It needs to store instructions and data temporarily while an instruction is being executed. In other words, the CPU needs a small internal memory. This memory consists of a set of high-speed registers. The registers in the CPU serve two functions

- *User-visible registers:* These enable the machine- or assembly-language programmer to minimize main-memory references by optimizing use of registers.

- *Control and status registers:* These are used by the control unit to control the operation of the CPU and by privileged, operating system programs to control the execution of programs.

There is not a clean separation of registers into these two categories. For example, on some machines the program counter is user visible (e.g., VAX), but on many it is not. For purposes of the following discussion, however, we will use these categories.

3.3 User-Visible Registers

A user-visible register is one which may be referenced by means of the machine language that the CPU executes. Virtually all contemporary CPU designs provide for a number of user-visible registers, as opposed to a single accumulator. We can characterize these in the following categories

- General purpose
- Data
- Address
- Condition codes

General-purpose registers can be assigned to a variety of functions by the programmer. Sometimes, their use within the instruction set is orthogonal to the operation; that is, any general-purpose register can contain the operand for any opcode. This provides true general-purpose register use. Often, however, there are restrictions. For example, there may be dedicated registers for floating-point operations.

In some cases, general-purpose registers can be used for addressing functions (e.g., register indirect, displacement). In other cases, there is a partial or clean separation between data registers and address registers. *Data registers* may only be used to hold data and cannot be employed in the calculation of an operand address. *Address registers* may themselves be somewhat general purpose, or they may be devoted to a particular addressing mode. Examples are

- *Segment pointers:* In a machine with segmented addressing, a segment register holds the address of the base of the segment. There may be multiple registers, for example, one for the operating system and one for the current process.
- *Index registers:* These are used for indexed addressing, and may be autoindexed.
- *Stack pointer:* If there is user-visible stack addressing, then typically the stack is in memory and there is a dedicated register that points to the top of the stack. This allows implicit addressing; that is, push, pop, and other stack instructions need not contain an explicit stack operand.

There are several design issues to be addressed here. An important one is whether to use completely general-purpose registers or to specialize their use. We have already touched on this issue in section 1, since it affects instruction set design. With the use of specialized registers, it can generally be implicit in the opcode which type of register a certain operand specifier refers to. The operand specifier must only identify one of a set of specialized registers rather than one out of all the registers, thus saving bits. On the other hand, this specialization limits the programmer's flexibility. There is no final and best solution to this design issue, but, as was mentioned, the trend seems to be toward the use of specialized registers.

Another design issue is the number of registers, either general-purpose or data plus address, to be provided. Again, this affects instruction set design since more registers require more operand specifier bits. As we previously discussed, somewhere between 8 and 32 registers appears optimum. Fewer registers result in more memory references; more registers do not noticeably reduce memory references. However, a new approach, which finds advantage in the use of hundreds of registers, is exhibited in some RISC systems.

Finally, there is the issue of register length. Registers that must hold addresses obviously must be at least long enough to hold the largest address. Data registers should be able to hold values of most data types. Some machines allow two contiguous registers to be used as one for holding double-length values.

A final category of registers, which is at least partially visible to the user, holds *condition codes* (also referred to as flags). Condition codes are bits set by the CPU hardware as the result of operations. For example, an arithmetic operation may produce a positive, negative, zero, or overflow result. In addition to the result itself being stored in a register or memory, a condition code is also set. The code may subsequently be tested as part of a conditional branch operation.

Condition code bits are collected into one or more registers. Usually, they form part of a control register. Generally, machine instructions allow these bits to be read by implicit reference, but they can not be altered by the programmer.

In some machines a subroutine call will result in the automatic saving of all user-visible registers, which are to be restored on return. The saving and restoring is performed by the CPU as part of the execution of call and return instructions. This allows each subroutine to use the user-visible registers independently. On other machines, it is the responsibility of the programmer to save the contents of the relevant user-visible registers prior to a subroutine call by including instructions for this purpose in the program.

3.4 Control and Status Registers

There are a variety of CPU registers employed to control the operation of the CPU. Most of these, on most machines, are not visible to the user. Some of them may be visible to machine instructions executed in a control or operating-system mode.

Of course, different machines will have different register organizations and use different terminology. We list here a reasonably complete list of register types, with a brief description.

Four registers are essential to instruction execution

- *Program counter (PC):* contains the address of an instruction to be fetched.
- *Instruction register (IR):* contains the instruction most recently fetched.
- *Memory address register (MAR):* contains the address of a location in memory.
- *Memory buffer register (MBR):* contains a word of data to be written to memory or the word most recently read.

The program counter contains an instruction address. Typically, the program counter is updated by the CPU after each instruction fetch so that it always points to the next instruction to be executed. A branch or skip instruction will also modify the contents of the PC. The fetched instruction is loaded into an instruction register, where the opcode and operand specifiers are analyzed. Data are exchanged with memory by using the MAR and MBR. In a bus organized system, the MAR connects directly to the address bus, and the MBR connects directly to the data bus. User-visible registers, in turn, exchange data with the MBR.

The four registers just mentioned are used for the movement of data between the CPU and memory. Within the CPU, data must be presented to the ALU for processing. The ALU may have direct access to the MBR and user-visible registers. Alternatively, there may be additional buffering registers at the boundary to the ALU; these registers serve as input and output registers for the ALU and exchange data with the MBR and user-visible registers.

All CPU designs include a register or set of registers containing status information, often known as the *program status word* (PSW). The PSW typically contains condition codes plus other status information. Common fields or flags include the following

- *Sign:* Contains the sign bit of the result of the last arithmetic operation.
- *Zero:* Set when the result is zero.
- *Carry:* Set if an operation resulted in a carry (addition) or borrow (subtraction) out of a high-order bit. Used for multiword arithmetic operations.
- *Equal:* Set if a logical compare result is equality.
- *Overflow:* Used to indicate arithmetic overflow.
- *Interrupt Enable/Disable:* Used to enable or disable interrupts.
- *Supervisor:* Indicates whether CPU is executing in supervisor or user mode. Certain privileged instructions can only be executed in supervisor mode, and certain areas of memory can only be accessed in supervisor mode.

There are a number of other registers related to status and control that might be found in a particular CPU design. In addition to the PSW, there may be a pointer to a block of memory containing additional status information (e.g., process control blocks). In machines using vectored interrupts, an interrupt vector register may be provided. If a stack is used to implement certain functions (e.g., subroutine call), then a system stack pointer is needed. A page table pointer is used with a virtual memory system. Finally, registers may be used in the control of I/O operations.

A number of factors go in to the design of the control and status register organization. One key issue is operating system support. Certain types of control information are of specific utility to the operating system. If the CPU designer were to have a functional understanding of the operating system to be used, then the register organization could to some extent be tailored to the operating system.

Another key design decision is the allocation of control information between registers and memory. It is common to dedicate the first (lowest) few hundred or thousand words of memory for control purposes. The designer must decide how much control information should be in registers and how much in memory. The usual tradeoff of cost versus speed arises.

3.5 Example Microprocessor Register Organizations

It is instructive to examine and compare the register organization of comparable systems. In this section, we look at three 16-bit microprocessors that were designed at about the same time: the Zilog Z8000, the Intel 8086, and the Motorola MC68000. Figure 3-1 depicts the register organization of each; purely internal registers, such as a

memory address register, are not shown.

The Z8000 makes use of sixteen 16-bit general-purpose registers, which can be used for data, addresses, and indexing. The designers felt that it was more important to provide a regularized, general set of registers than to save instruction bits by using special-purpose registers. Further, they preferred to leave it to the programmer to assign functions to registers, assuming that there might be a different functional breakdown for different applications. The registers can also be used for 8-bit and 32-bit operations. A segmented address space is used (7-bit segment number, 16-bit offset), and two registers are needed to hold a single address. Two of the registers are also used as implied stack pointers for system mode and normal mode.

The Z8000 also includes five registers related to program status. Two registers hold the program counter and two hold the address of a Program Status Area in memory. A 16-bit flag register holds various status and control bits.

The Intel 8086 takes a different approach to register organization. Every register is special-purpose, although some registers are also usable as general-purpose. The 8086 contains four 16-bit data registers addressable on a byte or 16-bit basis, and four 16-bit pointer and index registers. The data registers can be used as general-purpose in some instructions. In others, the registers are used implicitly. For example, a multiply instruction always uses the accumulator. The four pointer registers are also used implicitly in a number of operations; each contains a segment offset. There are also four 16-bit segment registers. Three of the four segment registers are used in a dedicated, implicit fashion to point to the segment of the current instruction (useful for branch instructions), a segment containing data, and a segment containing a stack, respectively. These dedicated and implicit uses provide for compact encoding at the cost of reduced flexibility. The 8086 also includes an instruction pointer and a set of 1-bit status and control flags.

The Motorola MC68000 falls somewhere between the design philosophies of the Zilog and Intel microprocessors. Although the MC68000 is considered a 16-bit processor because of its use of 16-bit internal and external data paths and a 16-bit ALU, it provides 32-bit registers. The MC68000 partitions its 32-bit registers into eight data registers and nine address registers. The eight data registers are used primarily for data manipulation, and are used in addressing only as index registers. The width of the registers allow 8-, 16-, and 32-bit data operations, determined by opcode. The address registers contain 32-bit (no segmentation) addresses; two of these registers are also used as stack pointers, one for users and one for the operating system, depending on the current execution mode. Both registers are numbered 7, since only one can be used at a time.

Like the Zilog designers, the Motorola team wanted a very regular instruction set, with no special-purpose registers. A concern for code efficiency led them to divide the

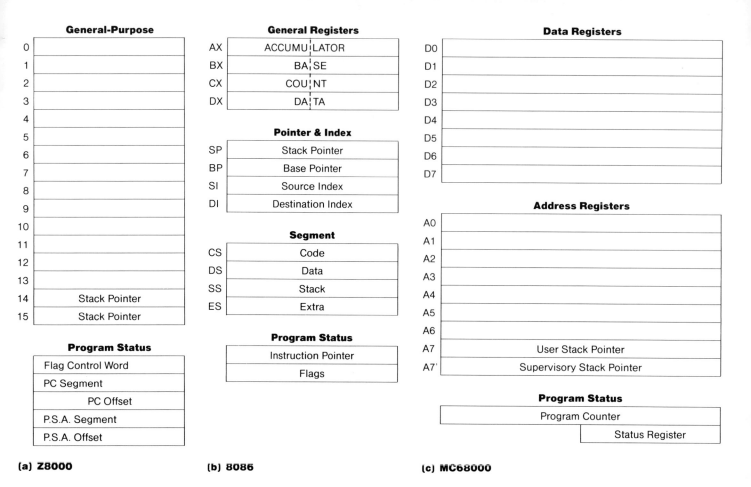

Figure 3.1: Microprocessor Register Organizations

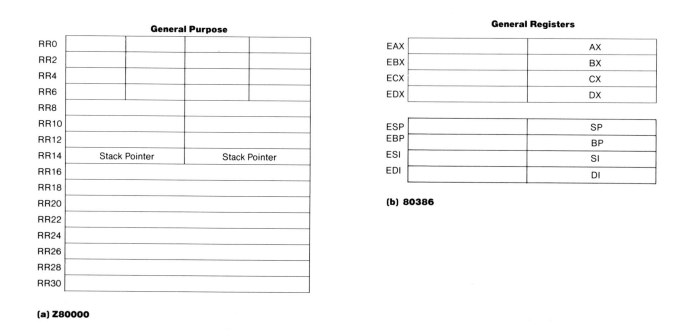

Figure 3.2: Register Organization Extensions for 32-Bit Microprocessors.

registers into two functional components, saving one bit on each register specifier. This seems a reasonable compromise between complete generality and code compaction. The point of this comparison should be clear. There is, as yet, no universally accepted philosophy concerning the best way to organize CPU registers. As with overall instruction set design and so many other CPU design issues, it is still a matter of judgment and taste.

A second instructive point concerning register organization design is illustrated in Figure 3-2. This figure shows the user-visible register organization for the Zilog Z80000 and Intel 80386, which are 32-bit microprocessors designed as extensions of the Z8000 and 8086, respectively. (Since the MC68000 already uses 32-bit registers, the MC68020, which is a full 32-bit extension, uses the same register organization.) Both of these new processors use 32-bit registers. However, to provide upward compatibility for programs written on the earlier machines, both of the new processors retain the original register organization embedded in the new organization. Given this design constraint, the architects of the new 32-bit processors had limited flexibility in designing the register organization. Virtually all of the RISC designs are free of this constraint, since they are not extensions of previous systems.

3.6 Article Summary

In "Register Allocation via Graph Coloring," it is observed that the register-allocation problem is equivalent to the graphcoloring problem in topology. From this observation, a technique is developed that was used on the IBM 801 RISC machine and is used on the IBM PC RT. A similar approach, used in the machine from MIPS Computer Systems, is described in the next paper, by Chow and Hennessy.

Next, "Strategies for Managing the Register File in RISC" explains the multiple-window approach used on the Berkeley RISC machine and analyzes alternative techniques for optimizing register use.

Finally, "Analyzing Multiple Register Sets" reports results that attempt to separate the effects of a large register file from a reduced instruction set in RISC systems.

REGISTER ALLOCATION VIA COLORING

Computer Languages 6 (1981), pp. 47-57.

Gregory J. Chaitin, Marc A. Auslander, Ashok K. Chandra, John Cocke,
Martin E. Hopkins and Peter W. Markstein

IBM T. J. Watson Research Center, Yorktown Heights, NY 10598, U.S.A.

(Received 9 October 1980)

Abstract

Register allocation may be viewed as a graph coloring problem. Each node in the graph stands for a computed quantity that resides in a machine register, and two nodes are connected by an edge if the quantities interfere with each other, that is, if they are simultaneously live at some point in the object program. This approach, though mentioned in the literature, was never implemented before. Preliminary results of an experimental implementation in a PL/I optimizing compiler suggest that global register allocation approaching that of hand-coded assembly language may be attainable.

Key Words and Phrases

register allocation, optimizing compilers, graph coloring

1. Overview of Register Allocation

In this paper we describe the Register Allocation Phase of an experimental PL/I compiler for the IBM System/370. (For an overview of the entire compiler see Cocke and Markstein [1], for background information on optimization, see Refs. [1] and [2].) It is the responsibility of this phase to map the unlimited number of symbolic registers assumed in the intermediate language into the 17 real machine registers, namely the 16 general-purpose registers ($R0$-$R15$), and the condition-code (CC).

The essence of our approach is that it is uniform and systematic. Compiler back-ends must deal with the idiosyncrasies of the machine instructions; for example, register pairs, the fact that register $R0$ is an invalid base register, and that the contents of some machine registers are destroyed as a side-effect of particular instructions. In our approach all these idiosyncrasies are entered in a uniform manner in our data structure, the interference graph. Afterwards this data structure is manipulated in a very systematic way.

Also, our approach has a rather different personality than traditional ones because we do *global* register allocation across entire procedures. Furthermore, except for the register which always contains the address of the DSA ("dynamic storage area," i.e. current stack frame) and is the anchor for all addressability, all other registers are considered to be part of a uniform pool and all computations compete on an equal basis for these registers. Most compilers reserve subsets of the registers for specific purposes; we do the exact opposite.

In our compiler a deliberate effort is made to make things as hard as possible for register allocation, i.e. to keep as many computations as possible in registers rather than in storage. For example, automatic scalars are usually kept in registers rather than in the DSA, and subroutine linkage also attempts to pass as much information as possible through registers. It is the responsibility of code generation and optimization to take advantage of the unlimited number of registers allowed in the intermediate language in order to minimize the number of loads and stores in the program, since these are much more expensive than register to register instructions. Then hopefully register allocation will map all these registers into the 17 that are actually available in the hardware. If not, it is register allocation's

Reprinted with permission from *Computer Languages*, Volume 6, Number 1, 1981, pages 47-57. Copyright © 1981 by Pergamon Press.

responsibility to put back into the object program the minimum amount of spill code, i.e. of stores and reloads of registers, that is needed.

As long as no spill code need be introduced, we feel that our approach to register allocation does a better job than can be done by hand-coders. For example, if there is a slight change in a program, when it is recompiled the Register Allocation Phase may produce a completely different allocation to accommodate the change. A hand-coder would be irresponsible to proceed in such a fashion. We also feel that our compiler succeeds in keeping things in registers rather than in storage better than other compilers, and that this is one of the salient features of the personality of the object code we produce. Moreover the mathematical elegance of the graph coloring approach described below, its systematic and uniform way of dealing with hardware idiosyncrasies, and the fact that its algorithms are computationally highly efficient, are convincing arguments in its favor.

2. Register Allocation as a Graph Coloring Problem

Our approach to register allocation is via graph coloring. This has been suggested by Cocke [1], Yershov [3], Schwartz [4], and others, but has never been worked-out in detail nor implemented before. Recall that a coloring of a graph is an assignment of a color to each of its nodes in such a manner that if two nodes are adjacent, i.e. connected by an edge of the graph, then they have different colors. A coloring of a graph is said to be an n-coloring if it does not use more than n different colors. And the chromatic number of a graph is defined to be the minimal number of colors in any of its colorings, i.e. the least n for which there is an n-coloring of it.

It is well-known [5] that given a graph G and a natural number $n > 2$, the problem of determining whether G is n-colorable, i.e. whether or not there is an n-coloring of G, is NP-complete. This suggests that in some cases an altogether impractical amount of computation is needed to decide this, i.e. that in some cases the amount of computation must be an exponential function of the size of G.

In fact experimental evidence indicates that the NP-completeness of graph coloring is not a significant obstacle to a register allocation scheme based on graph coloring. However it should be pointed out that given an arbitrary graph it is possible to construct a program whose register allocation is formulated in terms of coloring this graph (see Appendix 2). Thus some programs must give rise to serious coloring problems.

Our approach to register allocation is to build a *register interference graph* for each procedure in the source program, and to obtain 17-colorings of these interference graphs. Roughly speaking, two computations which reside in machine registers are said to interfere with each other if they are live simultaneously at any point in the program.

For each procedure P in the source program an interference graph is constructed whose nodes stand for the 17 machine registers and for all computations in the procedure P which reside in machine registers, and whose edges stand for register interferences. If the chromatic number of this graph is 17, then a register allocation has been achieved, and the register assigned to a computation is that one of the 17 machine registers which has the same color that it does. Thus computations which interfere cannot be assigned to the same machine register. On the other hand, if the chromatic number is greater than 17, then spill code must be introduced to store and reload registers in order to obtain a program whose chromatic number is 17.

3. The Concept of Interference

If a program has two loops of the form $DO\ J = 1\ TO\ 100$, J could be kept in a different register in each of the loops. In order to make this possible, each symbolic register is split into the connected components of its def-use (definition-use) chains, and it is these components, called names, which are the nodes of our interference graph. This is especially important because we always do global register allocation for entire procedures. Much additional freedom in coloring is obtained by uncoupling distant regions of the procedure by using names instead of symbolic registers as the nodes of the interference graph. However, as we explain below, some of these names are later coalesced, at which point the mapping from symbolic registers to names becomes many-many rather than one-many.

Our notion of liveness is not quite the same as that used in optimization. We consider a name X to be live at a point L in a program P if there is a control flow path from the entry point of P to a definition of X and then through L to a use of X at point U, which has the property that there is no redefinition of X on the path between L and the use of X at U. I.e. a computation is live if it has been computed and will be used before being recomputed.

Above it was stated that two names interfere if they are ever live simultaneously. Thus if at a point in the program there are k live names N_i, it is necessary to add $k(k-1)/2$ edges to the interference graph. However, we do not actually do this. If k names N_i are live at the definition point of another name N', we add the k interferences (N', N_i) to the graph. In other words, the notion of interference that we actually use is that two names interfere if one of them is live at a definition point of the other. This interference concept is better than the previous one for two reasons: it is less work to build the interference graph (k edges added vs $k(k+1)/2$), and there are programs for which the resulting interference graph has a smaller chromatic number. Here is an example of such a program:

```
P: PROC(MODE);

    DCL
       MODE            BIT(1),
       (A1,A2,A3,A4,A5,A6,A7,A8,A9,A10,
        B1,B2,B3,B4,B5,B6,B7,B8,B9,B10,
        SUM)          FIXED BIN(15) AUTO,
       (U(10),V(10)) FIXED BIN(15) STATIC EXT;

    IF MODE
      THEN DO;
        A1=U(1); A2=U(2); A3=U(3); A4=U(4); A5=U(5);
        A6=U(6); A7=U(7); A8=U(8); A9=U(9); A10=U(10);
      END;
      ELSE DO;
        B1=V(1); B2=V(2); B3=V(3); B4=V(4); B5=V(5);
        B6=V(6); B7=V(7); B8=V(8); B9=V(9); B10=V(10);
      END;

    LABEL: ;

    IF MODE
      THEN SUM = A1+A2+A3+A4+A5+A6+A7+A8+A9+A10;
      ELSE SUM = B1+B2+B3+B4+B5+B6+B7+B8+B9+B10;

    RETURN (SUM);

  END P;
```

At the point in the program P marked *LABEL* the ten A_i and the ten B_i are simultaneously live, and so is *MODE*. Thus with the first method of building the interference graph there is a 21-clique and the chromatic number of the graph is 21. [Recall that an n-clique is an n-node graph with all possible $n(n-1)/2$ edges.] With the second method, however, none of the ten A variables interferes with any of the ten B variables, and the chromatic number of the interference graph is only 11. (A technical point: we have ignored the fact that all of our interference graphs contain the 17-clique of machine registers as a subgraph. Thus the chromatic number is actually 17 instead of 11.)

4. Manipulating the Interferences

There are 3 stages in processing the interference graph of a procedure. The first stage is building the graph in the manner described above. This is done by the routine C_ITF. The second stage is coalescing nodes in this graph in order to force them to get the same color and be assigned to the same machine register. This is done by the routine C_LR. The third and final stage is attempting to construct a 17-coloring of the resulting graph. This is done by a fast routine called C_CLR, or by a slower routine C_NP which uses backtracking and is guaranteed to find a 17-coloring if there is one.

Of course, backtracking is dangerous; in some unusual circumstances C_NP uses exponential amounts of time.

We now make a few general remarks about the preprocessing of the interference graph which is done for the purpose of assuring that separate nodes in the graph must get the same color. This is done by coalescing nodes, i.e. taking two nodes which do not interfere and combining them in a single node which interferes with any node which either of them interfered with before. Note that coalescing nodes in the graph before coloring it is also a way of doing some pre-coloring, for any node which is coalesced with one of the 17 machine registers has in fact been assigned to that register. Of course, such pre-colorings are a strong constraint on the final coloring, and should be avoided if possible, preferably replaced by coalesces not involving real machine registers. It should be pointed out that preprocessing the graph in this manner gives much better results than warping the coloring algorithms to try to give certain nodes the same color.

Here is an example of a typical situation in which one might wish to coalesce nodes. If there is a *LR T,S* (load register *T* from *S*) in the object program, it is desirable to give the names *S* and *T* the same color so that it isn't actually necessary to copy the contents of register *S* into register *T* and thus the Final Assembly Phase needn't emit any code for this intermediate language instruction. (This optimization is traditionally referred to as subsumption.) C_LR achieves this by checking the source *S* and target *T* of each *LR* instruction in the object program to see whether or not they interfere. If they don't, then C_LR alters the graph by combining or coalescing the nodes for *S* and *T*. Thus any coloring of the graph will necessarily give them the same color.

However, in order to make this work well, the definition of interference presented above must be altered yet again! The refinement is that the target of an *LR* doesn't necessarily have to be allocated to a different register than its source. Thus a *LR T,S* at a point at which *S* and the k names N_i are live only yields the k interferences of the form (T, N_i), but not the interference (T, S). (See Appendix 1 for a consistent philosophy of the "ultimate" notion of interference and approximations to it.)

Subsumption is a very useful optimization, because intermediate language typically contains many *LR*'s. Some of these are produced for assignments of one scalar to another. But even more are generated for subroutine linkages and are introduced by value numbering and by reduction in strength. Besides eliminating *LR*'s by coalescing sources and targets, C_LR also attempts to coalesce computations with the condition code, and to coalesce the first operand and the result of instructions like subtract which are actually two-address (to avoid the need for the Final Assembly Phase to emit code to copy the operand). C_LR also attempts to coalesce the operands of certain instructions with real registers in order to assign them to register pairs.

How is the interference graph actually colored? This is done by using the following idea, which is surprisingly powerful. If one wishes to obtain a 17-coloring of a graph G, and if a node N has less then 17 neighbors, then no matter how they are colored there will have to be a color left over for N. Thus node N can be thrown out of the graph G. The problem of obtaining a 17-coloring of G has therefore been recursively reduced to that of obtaining a 17-coloring of a graph G' with one node (and usually several edges) less than G. Proceeding in this manner, it is often the case that the entire graph is thrown away, i.e. the problem of 17-coloring the original graph is reduced to that of 17-coloring the empty graph. In fact, C_CLR gives up if the original graph cannot be reduced to the empty graph, and so spill code has to be introduced.

On the other hand, C_NP won't give up until it proves that the graph is not 17-colorable; it uses an urgency criterion to select nodes for which to guess colors, and backtracks if guesses fail. The urgency of a node is defined to be (the current number of uncolored neighbors that it has) divided by (the number of possible colors that are currently left for it). C_CLR runs in time linear in the size of the graph, while C_NP in the worst case is exponential, although this doesn't seem to happen often. The usual situation is that C_NP quickly confirms that graphs for which C_CLR gave up indeed have no 17-coloring. In fact, up to now in our experiments running actual PL/I source programs through the experimental compiler, in the handful of cases in which C_NP found a 17-coloring and C_CLR didn't, C_NP has achieved this by guessing without having to backtrack. In view of this situation, we have disabled the dangerous backtracking feature of C_NP. Furthermore, C_NP is only invoked when C_CLR fails and the user of the compiler has requested a very high level of optimization.

5. Representation of the Interference Graph

One of the most important problems in doing register allocation via graph coloring is to find a representation for the interference graph, i.e. a data structure, for which doing the 3 different kinds of operations which are performed on it – namely building the graph, coalescing nodes, and coloring it – can be done with a reasonable investment of CPU time and storage. In order to do these three different kinds of manipulations efficiently, it is necessary to be able to access the interference graph both at random and sequentially. In other words, it is necessary to be able to quickly determine whether or not two given names interfere, and to also be able to quickly run through the list of all names that interfere with a given name.

While building the graph one accesses it at random in order to determine whether an edge is already in the graph or must be added to it. While coloring the graph one accesses it sequentially, in order, for example, to count the number of neighbors that a node has (so that if this number is less than 17 the node can be deleted). And while coalescing nodes one accesses the graph both in a random and in a sequential fashion. For each LR T,S in the object code one must first check whether or not T and S interfere, which is a random access. If T and S don't interfere, one must then make all interferences of the form (S, X) into ones of the form (T, X). To do this requires sequential access to all names that interfere with S, and random access to see which interferences (T, X) are new and necessitate adding an edge to the graph.

Our solution to the problem of satisfying both of these requirements – fast random and sequential access – is to simultaneously represent the interference graph in two different data structures, one of which is efficient for random access, and the other for sequential access.

For random access operations we use an area $ITFS$ in which the interference graph is represented in the form of a bit matrix. We take advantage of the fact that the adjacency matrix of the interference graph is symmetrical to halve the storage needed. The precise addressing rule is as follows. Consider two nodes numbered i and j, where without loss of generality we assume that i is less than or equal to j. Then these are adjacent nodes in the interference graph if the $i + j^2/2$ th bit of the area $ITFS$ is a 1, and if this bit is a 0 they are not adjacent. (Here the result of the division is truncated to an integer.)

Since the adjacency matrix is usually quite sparse, and the number of bytes in the $ITFS$ area grows roughly as a quadratic function $f(n) = n^2/16$ of the number n of nodes in the interference graph, for large programs it would be better if hashing were used instead of direct addressing into a bit matrix (somewhat more CPU time would be traded for much less main memory). Since the coefficient $1/16$ of n^2 is small, if the program is not too large our bit matrix approach is ideal since it uses a small amount of storage and provides immediate access to the desired information.

For sequential access operations we keep in an area $LSTS$ lists of all the nodes which are adjacent to a given one, in the form of linked 32-byte segments. Each segment begins with a 4-byte forward pointer which is either 0 or is the offset in $LSTS$ of the first byte after the next segment of the list. This forward pointer is followed in the segment by fourteen 2-byte fields for the adjacent nodes. For any given node J, and Jth element of the vector NXT is either 0, or gives the offset in $LSTS$ of the first empty adjacent-node field in the latest segment of the list of nodes which are adjacent to J, or, if the latest segment is full, it gives the offset of the first byte after the latest segment. All segments in a list are full (give all 14 adjacent nodes), except possibly the latest one.

6. Deleting Interferences and Propagating Coalesces

Consider a LR T,S at a point in the object program where besides S the names $L_1, L_2, \ldots$ are also live. Furthermore, suppose S was subsumed with L_i. We carefully avoided making T and S interfere, but it turns out that we erroneously made T and L_i interfere. This may have blocked our subsuming T and L_i, which in turn may have blocked other subsumptions. Our solution to this problem is as follows: After C_LR does all possible desirable coalesces, the entire interference graph is rebuilt from scratch, and typically there will be fewer interferences than before. We then run C_LR again to see if any of the coalesces which were impossible before have now become possible. This entire process is repeated either a fixed number of times (usually twice will do), or until no further coalesces are obtained. It turns out that in practice this is as fast and uses much less storage than the expensive data structure (described below) which directly supports deleting interferences and propagating coalesces.

Here is a more arcane example of a situation which requires interferences to be removed: If the source and target of a *LR* instruction are coalesced, then the *LR* no longer makes its source and target interfere with the condition code, nor does it make its target interfere with all names live at that point.

As it is of some theoretical interest, we now describe the alternate representation of the interference graph mentioned above. The graph has a count associated with each edge. This is called the interference count, and it is the number of program points at which the two computations interfere. As interferences are deleted, these counts are decremented, and if they reach zero then the two computations no longer interfere with each other.

Let us be more precise. In the framework necessary to directly propagate coalesces, the interference graph is best thought of as consisting of three sparse symmetric matrices. The first one gives the interference count of any two given names. The second one gives a pointer to the list of interferences that must be deleted if these two names are coalesced, and the third sparse matrix is boolean and indicates whether it is desired to coalesce the pair of names if their interference count hits zero. In practice these three sparse matrices can be combined into a single one. Hash tables are needed to provide random access to elements of the matrix, as well as pointers in both directions to chain rows and columns together for sequential access and to permit fast deletion.

The problem with this scheme for directly deleting interferences and propagating coalesces is the large amount of memory needed to represent the interference graph.

7. Representation of the Program During Coloring

Here are some details about the way we represent the program in terms of names. In order to avoid rewriting the intermediate language text, it is actually left in terms of symbolic registers. But it is supplemented by a vector NM_MAP giving the name of the result produced by each intermediate language instruction, and also by a "ragged" array giving for each basic block in the intermediate language text a list of ordered pairs (symbolic register live at entry to the basic block, corresponding name). And the name of a computation is represented as the index into the intermediate language text of an arbitrarily chosen canonical definition point for it. It is then possible to interpret one's way down a basic block maintaining at each moment a map from the symbolic registers into the corresponding names. C_ITF does this, keeping track of which names are live at each point, in order to build the interference graph. We also take advantage of this scheme to avoid rewriting the intermediate language text to reflect coalesces – only the ragged array and the NM_MAP vector are changed.

8. Handling of Machine Idiosyncrasies

It was mentioned above that one of the important advantages of the coloring approach to register allocation is that special case considerations can be taken care of by additional interferences in the graph. For example, the fact that the base register in a load instruction cannot be assigned to the register $R0$, is handled by making all names that are used as base registers interfere with $R0$. The fact that a call to a PL/I subprogram or a library routine has the side-effect of destroying the contents of certain machine registers is handled by making all names live across the call interfere with all registers whose contents are destroyed. Thus if j computations are live across the call and k registers are destroyed by it, a total of jk interferences are added to the graph to reflect this fact.

Although subtract is a destructive 2-address instruction, in the intermediate language subtract is 3-address and non-destructive. This is done to make possible a systematic uniform optimization process. Consider the intermediate language instruction $SR\ N1,N2,N3$ ($N1: = N2 - N3$). If $N1$ and $N2$ are assigned to the same register, then code emission in the Final Assembly Phase will emit a single instruction, subtract, for this intermediate language instruction. If not, it will emit $LR\ N1,N2$

followed by *SR* N1,N3. However, if N1 and N3 are assigned to the same register, then the Final Assembly Phase is in trouble, because copying N2 into N2 destroys N3. In order to avoid this code-emission problem, we make N1 and N3 interfere when building the interference graph.

A large set of special-purpose interferences has to do with intermediate language instructions involving the condition code (*CC*). The intermediate language ignores the fact that there is actually only one *CC*. The way to get around this is exemplified by contrasting the compare intermediate language instruction with the actual compare instruction. The intermediate language compare is three-address: two registers are compared, and bits 2 and 3 of the result register express the result of the compare. However compare always sets the bits of the *CC*, not those of an arbitrary register. Code emission in the Final Assembly Phase emits machine code for the compare intermediate language instruction in the following manner. If the result of the compare intermediate language instruction is assigned to the *CC*, then it merely generates a compare. If the result of the compare intermediate language instruction is assigned to one of the 16 general-purpose registers, then code emission generates a compare followed by a *BALR* which copies the contents of the *CC* into the indicated general-purpose register.

(A very special issue is how to deal with the fact that some instructions set the *CC* to reflect the sign of their result. For instance, subtract does this. In the Final Assembly Phase no code is emitted for a compare with zero of the result of a subtraction if it comes later in the same basic block as the subtract and none of the intervening instructions destroys the *CC*.)

9. Techniques for Inserting Spill Code

Our techniques for inserting spill code are quite heuristic and *ad hoc*. The following notion is the basis for our heuristic. At any point in the program, the *pressure on the registers* is defined to be equal to the number of live names (it might be interesting to change this to the number of live colors) plus the number of machine registers which are unavailable at that point because their contents are destroyed as a side-effect of the current instruction. Under the level two optimization compiler option, we insert spill code to immediately lower the maximum pressure on the registers in the program to 14. Under the level three optimization compiler option, successive tries are made. Spill code is inserted to bring the maximum pressure down to 20, then down to 19, etc., until a colorable program is obtained.

After inserting spill code it is necessary to recompute the def-use chains and the right number of names; there are generally more names than before. We also rerun dead code elimination, which has the side-effect of setting the operand-last-use flag bits in the intermediate language text – these flags are needed by C_ITF to keep track of which names are live at each point in the program. Note that since intermediate language text containing spill code is reanalyzed by optimization routines, and these routines only understand intermediate language written in terms of symbolic registers, the intermediate language text containing spill code must be correct in terms of symbolic registers as well as names.

How is spill code inserted to lower the register pressure? We attempt to respect the loop structure of the program and to put spill code in regions of the program which are not executed frequently. This is done in the following manner. First the decomposition of the program into flow-graphs is used bottom-up to compute the maximum register pressure in each basic block and each interval of all orders. As we do this we also obtain a bit vector of mentioned names for each basic block and interval. A *pass-through* is defined to be a computation which is live at entry to an interval but which is not mentioned (i.e. neither used nor redefined) within it. Clearly pass-throughs of high-order intervals are ideal computations to spill, i.e. to keep in storage rather than in a register throughout the interval for which they are a pass-through. We use the decomposition of the program into flow-graphs top-down in order to fix all those intervals in which the maximum pressure is too high by spilling pass-throughs.

We have explained how spill decisions are made for pass-throughs, but we have not explained how the spill code is actually inserted. This is done by using two rules. First of all, if a name is spilled anywhere, then we insert a store instruction at each of its definition points. And pass-throughs are reloaded according to the following rule: load at entry to each basic block *B* every name live at entry to *B* that is not spilled within *B*, but that is spilled in some basic block which is an immediate predecessor of B. These rules for inserting spill code are easy to carry out, but the other side of the coin is that they sometimes insert unnecessary code. However this unnecessary spill code is eliminated by a pass of dead code elimination which immediately follows.

Further remarks: Another idea used here is that some computations have the property that they can be redone in a single instruction whose operands are always available. We call such computations *never-killed*. An example of a never-killed computation is a load address off of the register which gives addressability to the DSA. Such computations are recalculated instead of being spilled and reloaded. Furthermore, if spilling pass-through computations doesn't lower the register pressure enough, as a last resort we traverse each basic block inserting spill code whenever the pressure gets too high.

Another approach to using recomputation instead as an alternative to spilling and reloading, is what we have called the *rematerialization* of uncoalesced LR instructions. Here the idea is to replace a LR which can't be coalesced away by a recomputation that directly leaves the result of the computation in the desired register. (Of course, this should only be done if repeating the computation at this point still gives the same result.) Rematerialization usually decreases the pressure on the registers. Furthermore, assuming that all intermediate language instructions seen at this stage of the compilation are single-cost, replacing an uncoalesced LR by a recomputation cannot increase object program path lengths, and it sometimes actually shortens them. Thus there is a sense in which rematerialization is an optimization as opposed to a spill technique.

Rematerialization is most helpful when there are LR's into real registers. Typically this occurs when parameters are passed in standard registers. The standard parameter registers are destroyed over calls so the computation to be passed cannot be kept in the standard register over the call. The adverse consequence of this is most severe in loops where many loop constant parameters may be kept in registers and are loaded into standard parameter registers before each procedure invocation. Rematerialization tends to reduce the requirement for registers to hold loop constant parameters.

An entirely different approach to spilling might be based on the following observation. It is possible to have C_CLR make the spill decisions as it colors the interference graph. Each time C_CLR is blocked because it cannot delete any more nodes (all of them have more than 16 neighbors), it simply deletes a node by deciding to always keep that computation in storage rather than in a register. By increasing the granularity in the names, one could perhaps develop this into a more global and systematic approach to spilling than the one sketched above.

10. Conclusions

We have shown that in spite of the fact that graph coloring is NP-complete, it can be developed into a practical approach to register allocation for actual programs. It is also a pleasant surprise that coalescing nodes of the graph turns out to be an important optimization technique, and that machine idiosyncrasies can be handled in a uniform manner. We believe that our approach is able to pack computations into registers globally across large programs more cleverly than a hand-coder can or should. However, when not all computations can be kept in registers across the entire program, then the spill code that we insert sometimes leaves much to be desired.

Acknowledgements

The authors wish to state that the experimental compiler described herein could not have been completed without the efforts of the remaining members of their team: Richard Goldberg, Peter H. Oden, Philip J. Owens, and Henry S. Warren Jr. Although they were not directly involved with the compiler's register allocation scheme, this enterprise was very much a team effort to which all involved made essential contributions. We also wish to thank Erich J. Neuhold for reading an earlier version of this paper and suggesting improvements in the exposition.

References

1. J. Cocke and P. W. Markstein, Measurement of program improvement algorithms. In *Information Processing 80* (Edited by S. H. Lavington), pp. 221-228. North-Holland, Amsterdam (1980).

2. F. E. Allen and J. Cocke, A program data flow analysis procedure. *Commun. ACM* **19**, 137-147 (1976).

3. A. P. Yershov, *The Alpha Automatic Programming System.* Academic Press, London (1971).

4. J. T. Schwartz, *On Programming: An Interim Report on the SETL Project.* Courant Institute of Math. Sciences, New York University (1973).

5. A. V. Aho, J. E. Hopcroft and J. D. Ullman, *The Design and Analysis of Computer Algorithms.* Addison-Wesley, Reading, MA (1974).

Appendix 1. The "Ultimate" Notion of Interference

The intuitive definition of the concept of interference is that two symbolic registers (i.e. results of computations) interfere if they cannot reside in the same machine register. Similarly, a symbolic register and a machine register interfere if the symbolic register cannot be assigned to that real register. Thus two registers interfere if there exists a point in the program, and a specific possible execution of the program for which:

1. Both registers are defined (i.e. they have been assigned by previous computations in the current execution);

2. Both registers will be used (note that we are considering a specific execution. Thus we mean use, *not* potential use);

3. The values of the registers are different.

It is clear that if these conditions are met, then assigning both symbolic registers to the same real register would be incorrect for that execution. It should also be clear that if any of the three conditions is not met, then such an assignment is correct at that point in the program, for that execution.

Of course, the criteria stated above are in general undecidable properties of the program. Thus a compiler must use more restrictive conditions of interference, potentially increasing the number of registers or amount of spill code required.

One particularly simple and sufficient condition is that two symbolic interfere if they are ever simultaneously live (in the data flow sense). Consideration or experiment will show that this criterion is both expensive to compute and overly conservative. The difficulty is that application of this standard involves adding interferences for all pairs of live values at every point in the program. One could attempt to reduce this cost by observing how the liveness set changes during a linear reading of the program, so that only potentially new interferences are added. Only growth of the liveness set need be taken into account, that is to say, the fact that (a) symbolic registers become alive on assignment, and (b) the set grows by union at a control flow join. The cost of computing the simultaneously alive criterion could be reduced by applying these observations.

However, one can safely take into account (a) all by itself, and ignore (b), the effect of control flow joins. This approach, which may be called point of definition interference, is not only inexpensive to compute, but omits certain apparent interferences for which both symbolic registers can never be defined simultaneously in any symbolic registers can never be defined simultaneously in any particular execution of the program. Thus we approximate interference by reading the program, using precomputed data flow information so that the set of live values is known at every computation. At each computation, the newly defined symbolic register is made to interfere with all currently live symbolic registers which cannot be seen to have the same value as the newly defined register.

Appendix 2. Proof That All Graphs Can Arise in Register Allocation

Consider the following program. It has declarations of the variables $NODE_i$, and there are just as many of these variables as there are nodes in the desired graph. For each edge ($NODE_i$, $NODE_j$) in the desired graph, the corresponding variables are summed in order to make them interfere.

```
P: PROC(EDGE,MODE) RETURNS(FIXED BIN);
   DCL (MODE,EDGE,X) FIXED BIN;
   DCL LABEL(number-of-edges) LABEL;
   ...
   DCL NODEi FIXED BIN STATIC EXT;
   ...
   GO TO LABEL(EDGE);
   ...
   /*************************************/
   /* THE CALL PREVENTS OPTIMIZATION    */
   /* FROM MOVING THE LOADS OF NODEi,j. */
   /* THE ASSIGNMENT STATEMENT          */
   /* MAKES NODEi AND NODEj INTERFERE.  */
   /* JOINi,j CODE FRAGMENTS MAKE       */
   /* NAMES COME OUT CORRECTLY.         */
   /*************************************/
   LABEL(edge-number):
   CALL EXTERNAL_ROUTINEedge-number;
   X = NODEi + NODEj;
   IF MODE THEN GO TO JOINi;
            ELSE GO TO JOINj;
   ...
   JOINi:
   RETURN (X*NODEi);
   ...
END P;
```

"Register Allocation by Priority-Based Coloring" by F. Chow and J. Hennessy from *Proceedings of the ACM SIGPLAN '84 Symposium on Compiler Construction SIGPLAN Notices,* Volume 19, Number 6, June 1984, pages 222-232. Copyright 1984, Association for Computing Machinery, Inc., reprinted by permission.

Register Allocation by Priority-based Coloring

Frederick Chow[†] and John Hennessy

Computer Systems Laboratory
Stanford University
Stanford, CA 94305

Abstract

The classic problem of global register allocation is treated in a heuristic and practical manner by adopting the notion of priorities in node-coloring. The assignment of priorities is based on estimates of the benefits that can be derived from allocating individual quantities in registers. Using the priorities, the exponential coloring process can be made to run in linear time. Since the costs involved in register allocation are taken into account, the algorithm does not over-allocate. The algorithm can be parameterized to cater to different fetch characteristics and register configurations among machines. Measurements indicate that the register allocation scheme is effective on a number of target machines. The results confirm that, using priority-based coloring, global register allocation can be performed practically and efficiently.

1. Introduction

The view of global register allocation as a graph coloring algorithm has long been established [7]. A coloring of a graph is an assignment of a color to each node of the graph in such a manner that each two nodes connected by an edge do not have the same color. In register allocation, each node in the graph, called the interference graph, represents a program quantity that is a candidate for residing in a register.

Two nodes in the graph are connected if the quantities interfere with each other in such a way that they must reside in different registers. In coloring the interference graph, the number of colors used for coloring, r, is the number of registers available for use in register allocation. The goal is to find the best way to assign the program variables to registers so that the execution time is minimized. In global register allocation, we take into account entire procedures in deciding on the variables to be colored.

The standard coloring algorithm to determine whether a graph is r-colorable is NP-complete. It involves selecting nodes for which to guess colors, and backtracking if the guesses fail [1]. The algorithm takes only linear time when the first trial succeeds. But if the graph is not r-colorable, or is near the borderline cases, an exponential amount of computation is needed to prove that it is indeed so, since it is necessary to backtrack and attempt all possible coloring combinations before reaching the final conclusion. Thus, the standard coloring algorithm works well only when the target machines have a large number of registers. A heuristic procedure with linear running time might be best in practice, and the exponential algorithm may be made only the last resort in critical situations.

Global allocation of registers by coloring usually does not take into account the cost and saving involved in allocating variables to registers. By cost, we refer to the presence of register-memory transfer operations that put variables in registers or update their home locations to make the registers available for other uses. By saving, we refer to the gain in execution speed due to individual variables being accessed in registers. Variables occur with different frequencies and with varying degrees of clustering, so that the relative benefits of assigning registers to variables differ.

---

† Present address: Daisy Systems Corp., 139 Kifer Court, Sunnyvale, CA 94086.

Permission to copy without fee all or part of this material is granted provided that the copies are not made or distributed for direct commercial advantage, the ACM copyright notice and the title of the publication and its date appear, and notice is given that copying is by permission of the Association for Computing Machinery. To copy otherwise, or to republish, requires a fee and/or specific permission.

©1984 ACM 0-89791-139-3/84/0600/0222$00.75

The standard coloring algorithm always tries to allocate as many items in registers as possible. It does not recognize that it is sometimes non-beneficial to assign certain variables to registers over some regions in the program, possibly due to the need to save registers before procedure calls or for letting other variables use the same registers. When it is found that an r-coloring is impossible, the decision regarding which variables to be excluded in the coloring (i.e. to be spilled) is difficult to make. The spilling decisions are separate from the coloring decisions, and it is hard to predict the effect of spilling a certain variable on the outcomes of the subsequent coloring attempts. The standard coloring algorithm also does not take into account the loop structure of the program. In practice, variables occurring in frequently executed regions should be given greater preference for residing in registers.

In this paper, we present a global coloring algorithm that overcomes the above problems. The algorithm finds reasonable, though not necessarily optimal, solutions quickly, and it works for most configurations of general-purpose registers in target machines up to and including the grouping into nonintersecting register classes. It involves assigning priorities to all register-residing candidates and ordering register assignments according to this priority. The algorithm does not backtrack, and the running time is proportional to the number of registers and the number of possible live ranges to be allocated to registers.

2. Background

The algorithm we present in this paper is the register allocation algorithm used in the production optimizer UOPT [2]. UOPT is a self-contained, portable and machine-independent global optimizer on a machine-independent intermediate language called U-Code [5]. This intermediate code is output from a Pascal front-end and a Fortran front-end. The optimized versions of U-Code are translated into different target machine code by different back-end code generators.

The global optimizer UOPT performs a comprehensive set of global and local optimizations. Global register allocation is done in UOPT as the last phase of optimization, when the final structure of the code to be emitted has been determined by earlier optimization phases and all potential register uses have been exposed. A fixed number of registers is reserved for use by the code generators. The rest are to be freely allocated by the optimizer. Since the input program is assumed executable without using the global optimizer, all program variables in the input are assumed to have been allocated in main memory. Temporaries generated by the previous phases of the optimizer are also assumed to have been allocated in home memory locations, and they are treated uniformly as variables. Due to these assumptions, it is not necessary to generate spill code for variables not allocated to registers. Instead, all objects have home memory locations and the optimizer attempts to remap memory accesses to register accesses. This contrasts with the approach used in the PL.8 compiler [1] in which the register allocation phase attempts to map the unlimited number of symbolic registers assumed during earlier compilation and optimization phases into hardware registers; if this is unsuccessful, code is added to spill computations from registers to storage and later re-load them.

The register allocation algorithm used is a combination of a local method based on usage counts and the global method based on coloring. The local phase allocates one block to a register each time. The global phase allocates one live range to a register each time. The local register allocation phase is inexpensive and near-optimal for straight-line code, but does little to contribute to the globally optimal solution. The global allocation phase is more computation-intensive. In our approach, the local allocation process is made to do as much allocation as possible so long as the allocation would not have any effect on the outcome of the global allocation phase.

3. Cost and Saving Estimates

In performing register allocation, we divide the program code into code segments, each not longer than a basic block, which represent the smallest extents of program code over which variables are allocated to registers. Assigning a variable to a register involves the loading of the variable from main memory to the assigned register prior to referencing the variable in a register in the subsequent code. If the value of the variable is changed in the intervening code where it resides in register, the home memory location of the variable has to be updated with the register content at the end of the code segment unless it is dead on exit. These extra move operations between registers and memory represent the execution time cost of the register assignment. The execution time saving of the register assignment refers to how much the code segment is rendered faster due to the variable's residing in a register. Thus, we define the following three parameters, which vary among target machines:

MOVCOST — The cost of a memory-to-register or register-to-memory move, which in practice is the execution time of the U-Code instructions RLOD (load to register) or RSTR (store from register) respectively in the target machine.

LODSAVE — The amount of execution time saved for each reference of a variable residing in register compared with the corresponding memory reference that is replaced.

STRSAVE — The amount of execution time saved for each definition of a variable residing in register compared with the corresponding store to memory being replaced.

4. Local Register Allocation

Local register allocation refers to allocation in a straight-line piece of program code, and it precedes the global allocation phase. The method of allocating registers locally using reference counts is well-established and inexpensive [3]. Locally optimal solutions to the register allocation problem do not necessarily add up to the globally optimal solution. However, it is possible to determine a portion of register allocation locally that also belongs to the global solution, so that the work load of the subsequent, more expensive global allocation phase can be made smaller.

For each variable in the local code segment being considered, the local saving that can be achieved by assigning the variable to register can be estimated by:

$$\text{NETSAVE} = \text{LODSAVE} \times u + \text{STRSAVE} \times d - \text{MOVCOST} \times n \quad (1)$$

where u is the number of uses of the variable,
d is the number of definitions and
n is either 0, 1 or 2.

n depends on whether a load of the variable to a register (RLOD) at the beginning of the code segment and a store from the register back to the variable's home location (RSTR) at the end of the code segment are to be inserted. If they are both needed, n is 2. If the first occurrence of the variable is a store, then the initial RLOD is not needed. If the variable is not altered, or if the variable is not live at the end of the code segment, then the RSTR is not necessary.

If the local code segment is considered together with its preceding and subsequent code, the term involving MOVCOST represents the uncertainty in cost with regard to NETSAVE that may or may not contribute to the final global solution. This is because if the variable is also allocated to the same register in the surrounding code, then the RLOD and RSTR at the beginning and end of the current code segment are unnecessary, and the actual value of NETSAVE is increased. Thus, for each variable in the local code, we consider two separate quantities:

$$\text{MAXSAVE} = \text{LODSAVE} \times u + \text{STRSAVE} \times d \quad (2)$$

$$\text{MINSAVE} = \text{LODSAVE} \times u + \text{STRSAVE} \times d - \text{MOVCOST} \times n \quad (3)$$

The quantity MINSAVE represents the minimum saving in the local code segment gained by allocating the variable to register. The quantity MAXSAVE is the maximum possible saving. The actual saving after all register allocation is performed will range between MINSAVE and MAXSAVE. The parameters MAXSAVE and MINSAVE also apply to variables which do not occur in the code segment, when they are both 0; in such cases, the two parameters are used only in the later global allocation process.

When the surrounding blocks are considered together with the current block, the local allocation may displace some other variable which has been assigned to the same register in the adjacent blocks and which, if allowed to occupy the same register in the current block, would enable the elimination of the RSTR's at the ends of the preceding blocks and the RLOD's at the starts of the succeeding blocks. Thus, the absolute criterion for determining the local allocation of a variable in register can be given as:

$$\text{MINSAVE} > \text{MOVCOST} \times (p + s) \quad (4)$$

where p is the number of predecessors,
   s is the number of successors of the block.

When this condition is satisfied, the variable can be locally allocated in register with certainty regardless of the rest of the program. In computing the above condition, the loop nesting depths of the blocks are used as weights.

The determination of exactly which register to assign is not done in the local allocation pass. It is delayed until the global allocation phase, when the optimizer will look for opportunities to assign the same register to a variable over contiguous code segments to minimize the number of RLOD's and RSTR's.

5. Computing the Live Ranges

A live range of a variable is an isolated and contiguous group of nodes in the control flow graph in which the variable is defined and referenced. No other definition of the variable reaches a reference point inside the live range. Also, the definitions of the variable inside the live range do not reach any other reference point outside the live range. Global register allocation assigns complete live ranges to registers, and if this is not possible, parts of live ranges are assigned. Throughout a procedure, each register is occupied by live ranges or parts of live ranges that do not overlap. Computations for the separate live ranges of the program variables require processing and representation overhead. We circumvent these computations by assuming one live range for each variable in a procedure at the beginning of the global register allocation phase, even though it may have non-adjacent parts. In the course of coloring, the live ranges are broken up into smaller segments when necessary.

By virtue of the contiguity of the blocks in a live range, when the live range is assigned to a register, RLOD's are needed only at entry points to the live range and RSTR's are required only at its exit points (Fig. 1). UOPT supports both the caller-save and callee-save convention regarding registers in procedure calls. In the caller-save context, all registers need to be freed at a procedure call so that they can be used in the called procedure. Thus, live ranges are never allowed to extend over a procedure call. The register allocator is responsible for indicating which

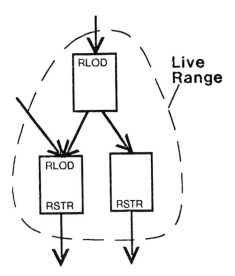

Fig. 1 A live range with associated RLOD's and RSTR's

variable home locations are to be updated from registers before a procedure call, and which variables are to be re-loaded to registers after the call. UOPT has a procedure integration pre-pass that replaces procedure calls by copying their code in-line, thus increasing non-call ranges. In the case of the callee-save convention, live ranges are allowed to extend over procedure calls, and registers are allocated across the calls.

6. The Global Coloring Algorithm

The cost and saving estimates we defined earlier, weighted by the loop-nesting depths of program points at which the variable accesses occur, play an important role in our global coloring algorithm. The coloring process is driven according to the cost and saving estimates. Each iteration assigns one live range to a register by picking the most promising live range according to the cost and saving estimates computed over each live range. By assigning the live ranges with high priorities first, it is hoped that the results of the allocation will be close to optimal. The algorithm terminates when either all live ranges or parts of live ranges have been allocated, or all registers have been used up over all code segments. Thus, the computation time does not deteriorate when r-coloring cannot be achieved. The algorithm allocates register to a live range only when the saving is higher than the cost. Thus, the over-allocation problem does not exist in our algorithm.

We assume that all variables have been assigned home locations before register allocation begins. This allows us not only to avoid the problem of having to introduce spill code. By taking into account the cost of register-memory transfer operations, we can factor the effects of not allocating in registers into the coloring decisions. Because the cost and saving estimates are weighted by loop-nesting depths, our algorithm also takes the loop structure of the program into account. Thus, variables in frequently executed regions have higher priority for residing in registers.

We assume a single live range for each variable in a procedure at the beginning of global register allocation. Apart from saving the cost of computing and representing separate live ranges prior to coloring, the interference graph is also made much simpler. The processing cost associated with accessing, manipulating and updating the interference graph during coloring is greatly reduced.

The standard coloring algorithm handles the situation of insufficient registers by spilling variables into main memory. We handle this situation by live range splitting. In the course of performing coloring, when a variable cannot be assigned the same color throughout the procedure, its live range is split into smaller live ranges. The new live ranges are treated the same way as variables as far as the coloring algorithm is concerned, and the interference graph is updated accordingly. As splitting proceeds further along, the split-out parts may not be true live ranges since the original def-use relationships may not be restricted to points inside the subranges. Splitting is repeated until all the split live ranges can be colored or until all the split live ranges consist of single code segments. If a split-out live range is left uncolored at the termination of coloring, the effect is equivalent to not allocating the variable over the region covered. Live range splitting is performed with the emphasis on not creating small live range fragments unless warranted by the situation.

As an illustration, Fig. 2(a) shows a region of code in which variables A, B and C are to be allocated in registers. Although the live range for variable A consists of two separate parts, they are initially taken as a single live range. Assume that a single register is left available to contain the three variables. Fig. 2(b)

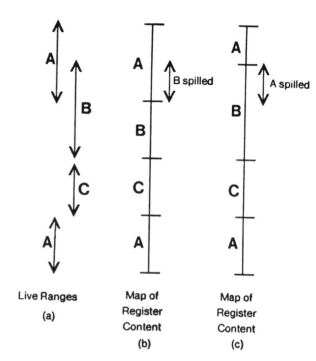

Live Ranges	Map of Register Content	Map of Register Content
(a)	(b)	(c)

Fig. 2 Possible allocation configurations

and (c) show two possible allocation results, depending on the occurrence frequencies of the variables in the live ranges covered. To arrive at the result of Fig. 2(b), variables A and C are allocated first. The live range of variable B is then split so that one part of it is allocated and the other part spilled. In Fig. 2(c), variables B and C are allocated first. The algorithm splits the live range of A into the two naturally separate parts, and the lower live range of A is then allocated. The top live range of A is then further split so that one part is allocated and the other part that interferes with B is spilled.

In the node coloring algorithm, variables which have a number of neighbors in the interference graph less than the original number of colors available are left uncolored until the very end, since it is certain that an unused color can be found for them. These are called *unconstrained* variables or live ranges. The rest of the live ranges are assigned colors by successive iterations of Step 2 of the algorithm. Each iteration selects a live range and assigns a color to it. New live ranges are formed out of splitting during the iterations, and if any of these are unconstrained, they are added to the unconstrained pool of variables.

Algorithm *Priority-based Node Coloring.*

1. Find the live ranges whose number of neighbors in the interference graph is less than the number of colors available, and set them aside in the pool of unconstrained live ranges.

2. Repeat Steps a to c, each time assigning one color to a live range until all constrained live ranges have been assigned a color, or there is no register left that can be assigned to any live range in any code segment (taking into account registers allocated in the preceding local allocation phase).

   a. Perform Step (i) or (ii) for each live range lr until TOTALSAVE for all original or newly formed live ranges are computed:

      (i). If lr has a number of colored neighbors less than the total number of colors available, assume a color is assigned to it covering all its live blocks. Then compute and record TOTALSAVE for the variable lr as follows:

         1. In each block i of the live range lr, determine whether register load and store is necessary based on whether the adjacent blocks in the flow graph belong to the same live range. Let the number of register loads and stores be n, which ranges from 0 to 2.

         2. Compute NETSAVE$_i$ as

         $$NETSAVE_i = LODSAVE \times u + STRSAVE \times d \\ - MOVCOST \times n$$

         where u is the number of uses, and

            d is the number of definitions of the live range variable in block i.

         3. Let w_i denotes the loop-nesting depth of block i in the flow graph. Compute TOTALSAVE for the live range lr as:

         $$TOTALSAVE = \sum_{i \in lr} (NETSAVE_i \times w_i).$$

      (ii). If the number of colored neighbors of lr is already equal to the number of colors

available, then the live range lr has to be split. A new live range lr_1 is split out from lr as follows:

A new node in the interference graph is created for lr_1. A definition block from lr, preferably one at an entry point to lr, is first added to lr_1. Blocks adjacent to lr_1 that also belong to lr are successively added to lr_1, updating the neighbors in the interference graph until the number of colored neighbors of lr_1 in the interference graph is one less than the number of available colors. The motivation of this is to produce the largest possible live range that can still be colored. This is continued until no more blocks can be added to the new live range lr_1.

If the newly formed live range lr_1 has a number of neighbors in the interference graph less than the number of colors available, set it aside in the pool of unconstrained variables. Otherwise, add it to the pool of candidates for estimation of TOTALSAVE.

As a result of the new node in the interference graph, some previously unconstrained live ranges may now become constrained. These have to be transferred from the unconstrained pool to the constrained pool.

   b. For each live range lr, compute ADJSAVE as

   $$ADJSAVE = \frac{TOTALSAVE}{\langle number\ of\ nodes\ in\ lr \rangle}.$$

   (The quantities TOTALSAVE and ADJSAVE do not have to be recomputed if the live range has not changed since the previous iteration.)

   c. Looking at the values of ADJSAVE computed for all the uncolored but constrained live ranges in Steps a and b, choose the live range with the highest value of ADJSAVE and assign a color to it.

3. Assign colors to the unconstrained live ranges, each time using a color that has not been assigned to one of their neighbors in the interference graph.

Thus, the algorithm orders the assigning of colors according to which variable currently has the highest value of ADJSAVE (Step 2c). ADJSAVE can be visualized as the total number of occurrences of the variable in the live range, weighted by loop-nesting depths and normalized by the length of the live range. The adjustment by the live range length (the number of nodes in the live range) is needed because a live range occupying a larger region of code takes up more register resource if allocated in register. In the local allocation phase, we have already taken pure occurrence frequencies into account. Thus, when entering the global allocation phase, all the variables that remain unallocated in each code segment have occurrence frequencies that do not differ widely, so the important consideration is whether the allocation enables the same register to be assigned across contiguous code segments so that register loads and stores can be minimized. The value of ADJSAVE comprises a measure of this connectedness. The more connected the code segments in the live ranges of a variable are, the more worthy is the variable to be allocated in register, and the more difficult it will be to find the same register for it throughout; so, it is important to assign a color to it before other variables. The use of the ADJSAVE criterion is justified only if the local allocation phase precedes global allocation.

The determination of n in Step 2a(i) can make use of more information than previously possible in the local allocation phase of Section 4. If the first occurrence of the variable at an entry block is a store, then the RLOD is not needed. If all the predecessors of a block also belong to the live range, then the RLOD is also not necessary, unless any of the predecessor contains a procedure call. By the same token, RSTR's at points internal to live ranges are not always necessary. An RSTR is necessary at the exit blocks of a live range only if the live range contains at least one assignment to the live range variable and the variable is not dead on exit. At blocks internal to live ranges, RSTR's are also generated if any successor node has an RLOD, or contains a procedure call.

The computation time complexity of the above algorithm can be estimated. We are mainly concerned with Step 2 of the algorithm, since this step takes a lot more time compared with Step 3 for the unconstrained live ranges. Let r be the number of registers. Let l be the number of live ranges, and assume that this stays fixed during the course of the algorithm. Also assume that each register is assigned to one and only one live range in the procedure, though in reality this is not always the case. Then there is r iterations for Step 2 of the algorithm. For the first iteration, a live range is to be chosen out of l live ranges. For the second iteration, the choice is to be made out of the $l - 1$ live ranges remaining. Summing all the iterations, we get

$$l + (l - 1) + \ldots + (l - r + 1) = \frac{r(2l - r + 1)}{2}.$$

Thus, the algorithm is $O(r(l - r))$. The time of the algorithm proportional to both the number of registers available and the number of candidates to reside in registers.

The algorithm can easily extend to the case of multiple classes of registers. The interference graph will only give interferences between variables of the same class. The algorithm is repeated once for each class of register. In each case, the number of colors corresponds to the number of registers in the class being considered.

The relative importance between the local and global phases can be varied by changing the maximum length of code segments allowed. By setting an option, a limit on the maximum number of variable appearances allowed in a basic block is imposed. If this limit is exceeded, the remaining code is made to belong to a new block. A default value for this option serves to guard against the presence of large blocks which can degrade the output of the register allocator. When blocks are small, the local phase will not be able to allocate as many items to registers based on its allocation criteria, and more work is left to the more expensive global phase. As the limit on block lengths becomes smaller and smaller, the overall allocation also approaches the optimal solution since registers can now be allocated across shorter segments to cater to any irregular clustering of accesses. The processing cost also increases correspondingly because of the larger number of blocks involved and the greater amount of work being performed by the global phase. Thus, the register allocation algorithm has a large amount of built-in flexibility with respect to processing cost and quality of results. In practice, basic

Program	Perm	Tower	Queen	Intmm	Mm	Puzzle	Quick
% of var. references in registers	.65	.40	.76	.95	.95	.94	.67
% of var. assignments in registers	.70	.23	.72	.96	.96	.77	.77

Program	Bubble	Tree	Fft	Sieve	Quick2	Inverse	Average
% of var. references in registers	.91	.78	.87	.87	.62	.71	.77
% of var. assignments in registers	.92	.74	.80	.89	.62	.75	.76

Table 1(a). Static register allocation statistics in the DEC 10

Program	Perm	Tower	Queen	Intmm	Mm	Puzzle	Quick
% of var. references in registers	.94	.69	.87	.96	.96	.95	.80
% of var. assignments in registers	.95	.54	.88	.95	.95	.78	.80

Program	Bubble	Tree	Fft	Sieve	Quick2	Inverse	Average
% of var. references in registers	.90	.77	.86	.86	.79	.80	.86
% of var. assignments in registers	.91	.76	.81	.83	.75	.91	.84

Table 1(b). Static register allocation statistics in the 68000

blocks are usually short, and most of the work is done by the global phase.

7. Measurements

The priority-based register allocation algorithm has been implemented in the production optimizer UOPT and tested on a number of target machines. The results have shown that it is effective on a wide range of machines. We now present measurements that give us some ideas about the performance and effectiveness of our register allocation algorithm. The measurements are based on running and optimizing a set of benchmarks consisting of 13 Pascal and Fortran programs. These benchmark programs are standard, compute-bound application programs, with minimal calls to un-optimizable external routines and run-times.

7.1. Statistical counts

Table 1(a) and Table 1(b) display the register allocation statistics for the benchmark programs in the DEC 10 and 68000 respectively. It shows the percentages of variable references and the percentages of variable assignments that are in the global registers. The table does not include register usage by the code generators for code generating purposes. The data are obtained by static counts in the optimized programs. The dynamic counts are expected to be much better, since the register allocator in UOPT takes loop-nesting depths into account.

The percentages of allocation displayed in the two tables are not 100% because both of the two machines are not load/store machines, and infrequently accessed variables will not be allocated. The two machines also have a good set of memory addressing modes, so that a variable will not be allocated unless a payoff is obtained.

The DEC 10 uses the caller-save linkage convention, and the DEC 10 code generator allows UOPT to allocate up to 9 registers out of the 14 available. Programs that have many procedure calls (e.g. Tower)

Program	Perm	Tower	Queen	Intmm	Mm	Puzzle	Quick
0. No optimization	9.62 (1.0)	1.68 (1.0)	3.95 (1.0)	1.29 (1.0)	1.42 (1.0)	5.22 (1.0)	1.60 (1.0)
1. Only local optimizations	10.92 (1.14)	1.68 (1.0)	4.22 (1.07)	1.10 (.85)	1.23 (.87)	5.24 (1.0)	1.42 (.89)
2. Only local optimizations and reg. alloc.	8.46 (.88)	1.39 (.83)	3.99 (1.01)	1.05 (.81)	1.19 (.84)	4.85 (.93)	1.25 (.78)
3. All except register alloc.	8.87 (.92)	1.36 (.81)	3.76 (.95)	.65 (.50)	.78 (.55)	3.74 (.72)	1.60 (1.0)
4. Full global optimization	7.44 (.77)	1.27 (.75)	2.67 (.68)	.42 (.33)	.55 (.38)	2.47 (.47)	1.30 (.70)

Program	Bubble	Tree	Fft	Sieve	Quick2	Inverse	Average
0. No optimization	3.69 (1.0)	1.01 (1.0)	2.85 (1.0)	5.09 (1.0)	.719 (1.0)	4.71 (1.0)	(1.0)
1. Only local optimizations	3.79 (1.03)	1.05 (1.04)	1.82 (.64)	5.22 (1.03)	.703 (.98)	3.89 (.83)	(.95)
2. Only local optimizations and reg. alloc.	2.04 (.55)	.91 (.90)	1.68 (.59)	3.30 (.65)	.487 (.68)	3.67 (.78)	(.79)
3. All except register alloc.	4.60 (1.25)	1.08 (1.07)	1.40 (.59)	5.86 (1.15)	.807 (1.12)	3.17 (.67)	(.87)
4. Full global optimization	2.33 (.63)	.93 (.93)	1.07 (.37)	3.52 (.69)	.572 (.80)	2.36 (.50)	(.61)

Running times in Seconds
(Ratio to un-optimized running times in parentheses)

Table 2. Running times to show effects of register allocation on the DEC 10

Program	Perm	Tower	Queen	Intmm	Mm	Puzzle	Quick
0 registers	8.87 (1.0)	1.36 (1.0)	3.76 (1.0)	.65 (1.0)	.78 (1.0)	3.74 (1.0)	1.60 (1.0)
2 registers	8.25 (.93)	1.28 (.94)	3.62 (.96)	.64 (.98)	.78 (.99)	2.56 (.68)	1.48 (.93)
4 registers	7.44 (.84)	1.28 (.94)	3.29 (.88)	.58 (.89)	.71 (.91)	2.54 (.68)	1.42 (.89)
6 registers	7.44 (.84)	1.27 (.93)	2.68 (.71)	.43 (.66)	.56 (.72)	2.54 (.68)	1.42 (.89)
All 9 registers	7.44 (.84)	1.26 (.92)	2.68 (.71)	.42 (.65)	.55 (.71)	2.47 (.68)	1.30 (.81)

Program	Bubble	Tree	Fft	Sieve	Quick2	Inverse	Average
0 registers	4.60 (1.0)	1.08 (1.0)	1.40 (1.0)	5.86 (1.0)	.807 (1.0)	3.17 (1.0)	(1.0)
2 registers	3.71 (.81)	.96 (.89)	1.24 (.89)	4.02 (.69)	.724 (.90)	2.89 (.91)	(.88)
4 registers	3.84 (.83)	.93 (.86)	1.14 (.81)	3.99 (.68)	.669 (.83)	2.75 (.87)	(.84)
6 registers	2.33 (.51)	.93 (.86)	1.09 (.78)	3.53 (.60)	.621 (.77)	2.40 (.76)	(.75)
All 9 registers	2.33 (.51)	.93 (.86)	1.05 (.75)	3.25 (.55)	.572 (.71)	2.35 (.74)	(.73)

Running times in Seconds
(Normalized running times in parentheses)

Table 3. Effects of the number of registers available for register allocation (DEC 10)

tend to diminish the percentage allocated because the numerous instances of register saves and re-loads around procedure calls tend to increase the cost of the allocations.

The 68000 code generator allows UOPT to use up to 6 data registers and 4 address registers, out of the 8 data registers and 8 address registers available. The register allocation statistics for the 68000 is markedly different from that for the DEC 10, which is due to the use of the callee-save linkage convention in the 68000. The percentages of variable accesses allocated in registers in the 68000 are always greater than those in the DEC 10, since register saves and re-loads do not occur around procedure calls unless there are side effects. Tables 1(a) and (b) show that the linkage convention concerning the handling of registers does affect register allocation.

7.2. Selective application

Another method to study the effectiveness of our register allocation is by comparing the running times of the benchmarks with and without register allocation. Table 2 displays the running times of the benchmarks on the DEC 10 for different extents of optimization. Rows 1 and 2 show between them the effects of adding the register allocation phase if the optimizer performs only the minimal local optimizations. Rows 3 and 4 show between them the effects of leaving out the register allocation phase when the optimizer performs its full set of optimization. The data show that the register allocation is very effective, especially when the optimizer performs other global optimizations. Without register allocation, the benefits of the other global optimizations cannot be fully exposed, because the cost of saving intermediate quantities in main memory is high enough in some cases to cancel out the benefits that can be derived from the optimizations.

7.3. Varying the number of registers

In Table 3, we investigate the effects of allowing different numbers of registers to be allocated by UOPT out of the 14 available in the DEC 10. The results displayed in Table 3 show that the optimized running times always improve when a larger number of registers are available to UOPT. The 5 registers normally used by the code generator is enough

for most practical purposes, and increasing the number used by the code generator (i.e. decreasing the number used by UOPT) does not cause appreciable improvement in execution speed.

As expected, different programs require different numbers of registers for optimal register allocation. In the programs Perm, Tower and Tree, 4 registers seem to be all that are needed; for others, increasing the number further yields better execution speeds. In the programs Puzzle and Sieve, just 2 registers can dramatically improve the program running time. Different programs have different cut-off points regarding the number of registers they need for optimal register allocation. The cut-off number of registers required is related to the *chromatic numbers* of the interference graphs — the numbers of colors needed to color the graphs.

8. Concluding Remarks

In this paper, we have shown that, by using a priority-based coloring algorithm, the traditional register allocation problem can be approached practically and efficiently. Moreover, it can be performed in the machine-independent context using a few machine parameters. Among the parameters we use are characterizations of the benefits of register accesses over memory accesses. The performance and efficiency of the algorithm are not affected by the number of registers available in the target machines.

There are possibilities for further enhancement to the register allocation scheme we have presented. In the global coloring phase, register allocation priorities are computed by assuming that the register-memory move instructions are at fixed positions. The results can be improved if the priority ordering takes into account the possibility of moving the register-memory transfer instructions to positions that can minimize execution time cost.

The problem of allocating overlapping registers of different sizes have not been considered in this paper. It would be interesting to see to what extent the priority-based coloring scheme can be adapted to such situations.

Acknowledgement

This work represents part of the research performed for the S–1 project, under Contract 2213801 from the Lawrence Livermore National Laboratory. The development of the S–1 computer is funded by the Office of Naval Research of the U. S. Navy and the Department of Energy.

References

[1] G.J. Chaitin, "Register Allocation and Spilling via Graph Coloring," *ACM SIGPLAN Notices, 17,* 6 (June 1982), *(Proceedings of the SIGPLAN 82 Symposium on Compiler Construction)*, pp. 201 – 207.

[2] F. Chow, "A Portable Machine-independent Global Optimizer — Design and Measurements," Ph.D. Thesis and Technical Report 83-254, Computer System Lab, Stanford University, Dec. 1983.

[3] R.A. Freiburghouse, "Register Allocation Via Usage Counts," *Comm. ACM 17,* 11, Nov. 74.

[4] B. W. Leverett, "Register Allocation in Optimizing Compilers," Ph.D. Thesis and Technical Report CMU CS-81-103, Carnegie-Mellon University, February 1981.

[5] D. Perkins and R. Sites, "Machine-independent Pascal Code Optimization," *ACM SIGPLAN Notices, 14,* 8 (August 1979), *(Proceedings of the SIGPLAN 79 Symposium on Compiler Construction)*, pp. 201–207.

[6] R.L. Sites and D.R. Perkins, "Machine-independent Register Allocation," *ACM SIGPLAN Notices, Vol. 14, Number 8 (August 1979), (Proceedings of the SIGPLAN 79 Symposium on Compiler Construction)*, pp. 221–225.

[7] J.T. Schwartz, "On Programming: An Interim Report on the SETL Project," Courant Institute of Math. Sciences, New York University, 1973.

Strategies for Managing the Register File in RISC

YUVAL TAMIR, STUDENT MEMBER, IEEE, AND CARLO H. SÉQUIN, FELLOW, IEEE

Abstract—The RISC (reduced instruction set computer) architecture attempts to achieve high performance without resorting to complex instructions and irregular pipelining schemes. One of the novel features of this architecture is a large register file which is used to minimize the overhead involved in procedure calls and returns. This paper investigates several strategies for managing this register file. The costs of practical strategies are compared with a lower bound on this management overhead, obtained from a theoretical *optimal strategy*, for several register file sizes.

While the results concern specifically the RISC processor recently built at U.C. Berkeley, they are generally applicable to other processors with multiple register banks.

Index Terms—Cache fetch strategies, computer architecture, procedure calls, register file management, RISC, VLSI processor.

I. INTRODUCTION

INVESTIGATIONS of the use of high-level languages show that procedure call/return is the most time-consuming operation in typical high-level language programs [8], [9] due to the related overhead of passing parameters and saving and restoring of registers. The RISC architecture [8], [9] includes a novel scheme that results in highly efficient execution of this operation.

In conventional, register-oriented computers, the procedure call/return mechanism is based on a LIFO stack of variable size *invocation frames* (activation records). When a procedure is called, an area on top of the stack is used for storing the input arguments, saving the return address and register values, allocating local variables and temporaries, and, if the procedure calls another procedure, storing output arguments. A procedure's invocation frame denotes this area on the stack. At any point in time, the number of invocation frames in the stack is the current *nesting depth*. The invocation frame of the calling procedure overlaps that of the called procedure so that the memory locations containing the parameters passed from the calling procedure to the called procedure are part of both frames.

In most computers, register/register operations can be performed faster than the corresponding memory/memory operations. Therefore, the most heavily used local variables and temporaries are placed in registers. When a procedure is called, it must save the value of all the registers it will use and restore these values before returning control to the calling

Manuscript received July 14, 1982; revised January 3, 1983. This work was supported by the Defense Advanced Research Projects Agency under ARPA Order 3803, and monitored by Naval Electronic System Command under Contract N00039-81-K-0251.

The authors are with the Computer Science Division, Department of Electrical Engineering and Computer Sciences, University of California, Berkeley, CA 94720.

procedure. Analysis of the dynamic behavior of Pascal and C programs, executing on a VAX 11/780, has shown [8], [9] that saving and restoring register values and writing and reading of parameters from the common area of the caller and the callee are responsible for more than 40 percent of the data memory references.

In RISC, the call/return mechanism is based on *two* LIFO stacks. One of the stacks (henceforth "STACK1") contains *fixed size* frames which hold scalar quantities of the invocation frame (i.e., scalar input arguments, the return address, scalar output parameters, and scalar local variables and temporaries). The second stack (henceforth "STACK2") contains variable size frames, some of which may be empty (i.e., their size is zero). This stack is used for all nonscalar variables which are normally placed on the single stack in conventional computers. It is also used for scalars in case there is not enough space in the fixed size frame on STACK1.

The size of the STACK1 frame in RISC was determined based on a study by Halbert and Kessler [5]. The dynamic behavior of nine noninteractive UNIX™ C programs was analyzed. These programs included the main part of the C compiler *ccom*, the Pascal interpreter *pi*, the UNIX copy command *cp*, the *troff* text formatter, and the UNIX *sort* program. This study showed that a fixed frame size of 22 "words" (22 registers), with an overlap of six "words" between adjacent frames, is sufficient for all the scalar variables and arguments in over 95 percent of the procedure calls.

The implementation of STACK2 in RISC is identical to the implementation of the single LIFO stack in conventional computers: the stack itself resides in memory, there is a processor register that serves as a stack pointer, and there is another register that serves as the frame pointer [4]. There is no special hardware support for operations on STACK2 but, due to STACK1, such operations are far less frequent than operations on the LIFO stack of conventional computers. Since the implementation and operation of STACK2 is identical to those of the stack in conventional computers, STACK2 will not be discussed any further in this paper.

In conventional computers, registers are used for storing part of the invocation frame of the currently executing procedure (i.e., the top frame on the stack). In RISC, there is a large register file that is divided into several fixed size "register banks," each of which can hold one STACK1 frame. Since each STACK1 frame partially overlaps the previous STACK1 frame and the next STACK1 frame, each register bank shares

™ UNIX is a trademark of Bell Laboratories.

Reprinted from *IEEE Transactions on Computers*, Volume C-32, Number 11, November 1983, pages 977-989. Copyright 1983 by The Institute of Electrical and Electronics Engineers, Inc.

some of its registers with the two neighboring register banks.

The STACK1 frame used by the currently executing procedure, is always in one of the register banks. At each point in time, the contents of one of the register banks are addressable as registers, thus providing a "window" into the register file. This register bank is always the one containing the STACK1 frame of the currently executing procedure. A procedure call modifies a hardware pointer and "moves" the window to the next register bank in the register file, where the STACK1 frame of the called procedure resides. Thus, for example, register 15 (R15) in the calling procedure is in a different physical position in the register file from R15 in the called procedure, although the operand specifier for R15 is identical in the two procedures.

A return instruction restores the previous value of the above mentioned hardware pointer so the previous values of all the registers are "restored" without any data movement. Furthermore, no memory references are required for passing arguments since they are passed in registers which are in the region of overlap between the register banks containing the STACK1 frames of the caller and the callee.

By using this scheme, a procedure call in RISC can be made as fast as a jump and with fewer accesses to data memory than are required in conventional computers.

Since the size of the register file is limited, there is a need for a mechanism which will handle the case when the procedure nesting depth exceeds the number of STACK1 frames which fit in the register file. When a procedure call is executed, a new "empty" register bank is needed. If all the register banks in the register file are in use, an "overflow" occurs. This overflow causes a trap which is handled by operating system software. The operating system must free one or more register banks to make room for the new frame. Since the STACK1 frames in the register banks which are "freed" must be preserved, the software copies the frames to a conventional LIFO stack which is kept in memory and contains only STACK1 frames.

When a return instruction is executed, the window must be moved to a register bank containing the previous frame (i.e., the frame of the calling procedure). If all the register banks are free (i.e., the calling frame is not resident), an "underflow" occurs. This underflow causes a trap, upon which the operating system software loads one or more frames from memory where they were stored when an overflow occurred.

The register file is simply a write-back cache of STACK1. The cache blocks are the STACK1 frames. The top few frames of STACK1 are in the register file while the rest are in memory. When an underflow occurs, one or more occupied STACK1 frames are *fetched* from memory. When an overflow occurs, one or more register banks are "freed." This can be interpreted as "fetching" empty STACK1 frames from memory. Since in both cases the "fetching" is done by software, there is great flexibility in defining the cache *fetch strategy* (algorithm) [10]. This strategy determines the number of frames to be moved to/from memory when an overflow/ underflow occurs.

In this paper, several fetch strategies are considered. A theoretical "optimal strategy" is developed and is used as a reference point for evaluating the performance of several practical strategies. In addition, the effect of register file size on the performance of different strategies is investigated.

II. THE OPTIMAL STRATEGY

In this section an *optimal strategy* for managing the register file will be discussed. This strategy requires unbounded lookahead (possibly to the end of the call/return trace) and is therefore only useful as a lower bound on the cost of practical strategies. A proof that the proposed strategy is, in fact, "optimal" is presented.

A. Definitions

In order to facilitate further discussion, some formal definitions are required.

When a program is executing, its nesting depth constantly changes: every procedure call increases the nesting depth by one and every return decreases the nesting depth by one. Hence, for every execution of a program, there is a corresponding sequence of nesting depths. This sequence will be called a *procedure nesting depth sequence* (PNDS).

Definition 1: A *procedure nesting depth sequence* (PNDS) is a sequence of integers $D = (d_1, d_2, \cdots, d_n)$ where $d_1 = 1$, $d_i > 0$ for $1 \leq i \leq n$ and $|d_i - d_{i-1}| = 1$ for $2 \leq i \leq n$.

The integer i is an index into the PNDS; d_1 is the nesting depth at the beginning of the program. For each $i, 2 \leq i \leq n$, d_i is the nesting depth after $i - 1$ calls and returns are executed (i.e., after $i - 1$ changes in the nesting depth). Henceforth, an index into the PNDS will be called a *location.* An example of a PNDS is shown in Fig. 1.

The frames of STACK1 are numbered from 1 to m (with m being the current nesting depth, i.e., the number of the frame of the currently executing procedure). The top (i.e., highest numbered) few frames of the stack are always in the register file while the rest are in memory.

Definition 2: The *register file position* (RFP) is the number of the lowest numbered frame which is in the register file.

When an overflow occurs, the lowest number frame(s) in the register file are copied to memory and the register banks they occupy in the register file are "freed." This increases the register file position. Similarly, when an underflow occurs the RFP is decreased. Thus, the number of times the RFP is changed during the execution of the program is equal to the sum of the number of overflows and the number of underflows which occur.

Definition 3: A *register file move* (RFM) denotes an increase or decrease in the register file position.

Definition 4: The *size* of the register file move is the absolute value of the difference between the RFP before the move and the RFP after the move.

If the current nesting depth is d, the STACK1 frame being used by the currently executing procedure, is the one labeled d. The register file position must be such that this frame is contained in the register file. Hence, if the register file can hold w frames and if the RFP is p, then $p \leq d < p + w$. Before execution begins, the RFP is some positive integer p_0. During the execution of a program with a PNDS $D = (d_1, d_2, \cdots, d_n)$, for each nesting depth d_i, the corresponding RFP p_i must be such that the above condition is satisfied, i.e., $p_i \leq d_i < p_i + w$.

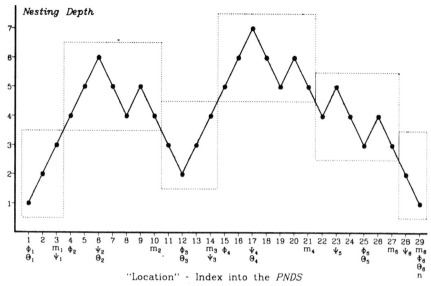

Fig. 1.   PNDS and optimal RFP's.

Definition 5: Given a PNDS $D = (d_1, d_2, \cdots, d_n)$ and a register file that can hold w frames, a valid *register file position sequence* (RFPS) is a sequence of RFP's: $P = (p_0, p_1, p_2, \cdots, p_n)$ such that the p_i's are positive integers and for all i, $1 \leq i \leq n$, $p_i \leq d_i < p_i + w$.

There is a one-to-one correspondence between nesting depths in the PNDS and RFP's in the RFPS. Successive RFP's, p_{j-1} and p_j, in the RFPS may be unequal or equal depending on whether the register file position is modified between the $j - 2$ and $j - 1$ change in the nesting depth.

Definition 6: If $P = (p_0, p_1, p_2, \cdots, p_n)$ is an RFPS, an RFM is said to occur in *location j* $(1 \leq j \leq n)$ of P, if and only if $p_j \neq p_{j-1}$.

The number of RFM's which occur during some interval in which the program is executing is of interest in this paper. The interval is defined as a subsequence of the RFPS (which corresponds to a subsequence of the PNDS).

Definition 7: If $P = (p_0, p_1, p_2, \cdots, p_n)$ is an RFPS, the number of RFM's occurring in location range $[i, j]$ of P, where $1 \leq i \leq j \leq n$, is the number of unique integers k, such that $i \leq k \leq j$ and $p_k \neq p_{k-1}$. This number will be denoted by $\text{RFM}_P[i, j]$.

Definition 8: If $P = (p_0, p_1, p_2, \cdots, pn)$, is an RFPS, the *memory traffic* occurring in location range $[i, j]$ of P, where $1 \leq i \leq j \leq n$, is the total number of STACK1 frames moved to/from memory as the RFP is set to $p_i, p_{i+1}, \cdots, p_j$ successively. This number is denoted by $\text{MT}_P[i, j]$:

$$\text{MT}_P[i, j] = \sum_{k=i}^{j} \left| p_k - p_{k-1} \right|.$$

B. What is an "Optimal Strategy"?

There is some overhead involved in handling overflow/underflow traps: saving the current state, determining the cause of the trap, activating the proper trap handling routine, restoring state, and returning to normal execution. Hence, it is desirable to minimize the number of register file overflows and underflows. In addition, there is the direct *cost* involved in actually moving the data to/from memory. For each register file move, this cost is proportional to the number of frames moved (i.e., to the size of the register file move). Hence, it is desirable to minimize the number of frames moved for each overflow/underflow, i.e., the memory traffic which is the result of overflows and underflows.

The problem of finding the "best" RFPS is similar to finding optimal strategies for handling page faults in virtual memory systems. In virtual memory systems it is also desirable to minimize both the number of page faults (since there is overhead involved in handling such faults) and the I/O involved in moving memory pages to/from disk or drum. For the virtual memory problem, Belady [1] developed an "optimal" page replacement algorithm which causes the fewest possible page faults for a program which executes in a fixed number of main memory page frames. Belady's algorithm is not realizable since it requires knowledge of the future portion of the page trace.

In the next sections it is shown that if the entire call return trace of the program (i.e., the PNDS) is known, there exists a RFPS which achieves *both* the minimum number of overflow/underflow traps and the minimum memory traffic resulting from register file moves. It is further shown that knowledge of the entire PNDS is *necessary* for achieving an optimum RFPS.

C. The Existence of an Optimal RFPS

In order to prove the existence of an optimal RFPS, an algorithm for deriving such an RFPS from a given PNDS, is presented. The optimality of the RFPS produced by the algorithm is shown by proving that no other valid RFPS can have fewer register file moves or result in less memory traffic.

An optimal RFPS can be obtained as follows. We start with the RFP at 1 and keep it there until the nesting depth exceeds the number (w) of register banks in the register file. Now the RFP must be changed, i.e., an RFM must occur. In order to determine the *optimal size* of the RFM, we must look ahead in the call/return trace (i.e., in the PNDS). Starting from the current location, we determine the longest subsequence of the PNDS for which a constant RFP is possible (i.e., in which the difference between the maximum nesting depth and the minimum nesting depth does not exceed $w - 1$). The new RFP is chosen so that it is valid for this entire subsequence. From the end of this subsequence we repeat the procedure until the entire PNDS is covered.

Special handling is required when determining the RFP for the last subsequence in the PNDS. In this case the difference between the maximum and minimum nesting depth within the subsequence may be less than $w - 1$. Hence, there is some freedom in setting the RFP. In order to minimize the memory traffic, the new RFP is chosen so that it is valid for the entire subsequence *and* the absolute value of the difference between the new RFP and the previous RFP is minimized. An example of a PNDS and the corresponding optimal RFPS is shown in Fig. 1.

More formally, the procedure can be stated as follows. Given an arbitrary PNDS $D = (d_1, d_2, \cdots, d_n)$, an optimal RFPS $P = (p_0, p_1, p_2, \cdots, p_n)$, for a register file that can hold w frames, can be obtained as follows:

[1]   **let** $i = 1, p_0 = 1$
[2]   **repeat**
[3]   **let** $E = (d_i, d_{i+1}, \cdots, d_m)$
        where m is the maximum integer such that
        $i \leq m \leq n$ and $\max(E) - \min(E) < w$
[4]   **if** $(m < n)$ **or** $(p_{i-1} > \min(E))$ **then**
[5]   **for** $j = i$ **to** m
            let $p_j = \min(E)$
[6]   **else**
[7]   **for** $j = i$ **to** m
            let $p_j = \max(E) - w + 1$
[8]   **let** $i = m + 1$
[9]   **until** $i > n$

First, it must be shown that the algorithm generates a valid RFPS for the given PNDS. Proof of the validity of the algorithm and of the generated RFPS requires proving the following lemmas.

Lemma 1: The **repeat** and **for** loops terminate after a finite number of iterations, i.e., the algorithm always terminates.

Proof: Since n is finite and i is incremented by at least 1 during each iteration of the **repeat** loop, n is an upper bound on the number of iterations through the **repeat** loop.

It is always true that $i \geq 1$ and $m \leq n$. Hence, n is an upper bound on the number of iteration through the **for** loop (either one) each time it is entered. ∎

Lemma 2: For all $i, 1 \leq i \leq n, p_i \leq d_i < p_i + w$, i.e., the RFP's generated by the algorithm are valid.

Proof: From the algorithm, if p_i is set in step 5, then $p_i \leq d_i$ [since $p_i = \min(E)$] and $d_i - p_i < w$ (since $\max(E) - \min(E) < w$). Hence, $p_i \leq d_i < p_i + w$.

If p_i is set in step 7, then $p_i \geq d_i - w + 1$ (since $p_i = \max(E) - w + 1$) and $p_i + w - 1 - d_i < w$ (since $\max(E) = p_i + w - 1$ and $\max(E) - \min(E) < w$). From the first inequality, $d_i \leq p_i + w - 1$ and from the second inequality $p_i < d_i + 1$. Hence, $p_i \leq d_i < p_i + w$. ∎

The proof of the optimality of the generated RFPS requires some additional notation. The subsequence E which is defined during the kth iteration of the **repeat** loop will be denoted E_k

(it corresponds to the kth setting of the RFP). The corresponding integer m will be denoted m_k. For convenience in notation, we define $m_0 = 0$. The number of iterations that the **repeat** loop executes before terminating will be denoted by K (it corresponds to the number of times that the RFP is adjusted). Note that $1 \leq m_1 < m_2 < \cdots < m_K = n$.

For each location range, $[m_{k-1} + 1, m_k]$, the RFP's in the RFPS generated by the algorithm are constant. Within this location range, Φ_k and Ψ_k are the locations of the first occurrence of the minimum and maximum nesting depths, respectively. More formally, see the following.

Definition 9: Φ_k and Ψ_k are the smallest integers, such that for each k ($1 \leq k \leq K$), both are in the location range $[m_{k-1} + 1, m_k]$, where $d_{\Phi_k} = \min(E_k)$ and $d_{\Psi_k} = \max(E_k)$.

In order to prove the optimality of the RFPS generated by the algorithm, it must be shown that this RFPS results in the lowest possible memory traffic. This will be done by using induction on the K boundaries of $K - 1$ location ranges. These boundaries are defined below and are denoted by Θ_k, for all k such that $1 \leq k \leq K$. The boundary point Θ_k is the location of the first minimum or maximum nesting depth within the location range $[m_{k-1} + 1, m_k]$. If the RFP in the RFPS generated by the algorithm for location range $[m_{k-1} + 1, m_k]$ is less than the RFP for location range $[m_{k-2} + 1, m_{k-1}]$, then $\Theta_k = \Phi_k$, otherwise $\Theta_k = \Psi_k$. More formally:

Definition 10: Θ_k is an integer such that for each $k, 2 \leq k \leq K, \Theta_k = \Phi_k$ if $d_{\Phi_k} < d_{\Phi_{k-1}}$, and $\Theta_k = \Psi_k$ otherwise. For convenience in notation, we define $\Theta_1 = 1$.

Fig. 1 shows the PNDS from the execution of Ackerman's function with arguments (2, 1). The dotted squares show the "optimal" RFP's for a register file that can hold three frames. In this example, five RFM's are necessary ($\text{RFM}_P[1, 29] = 5, K = 6$) and the memory traffic resulting from those RFM's is 12 frames ($\text{MT}_P[1, 29] = 12$).

Let $Q = (q_0, q_1, q_2, \cdots, q_n)$ be an arbitrary valid RFPS for D.

The rest of this section contains a formal proof that the number of RFM's in P and the memory traffic resulting from those RFM's are at most equal to the number of RFM's in Q and the memory traffic resulting from those RFM's, respectively.

Lemma 3: If $K > 1$, then for all $k, 1 \leq k < K, \text{RFM}_Q[1, m_k + 1] \geq k$.

Proof: See the Appendix.

From the algorithm, for all $k, 1 \leq k \leq K, d_{\Psi_k} - d_{\Phi_k} \leq w - 1$. It is now shown that for $1 \leq k \leq K - 1, d_{\Psi_k} - d_{\Phi_k} = w - 1$.

Lemma 4: If $K > 1$, then for all $k, 1 \leq k \leq K - 1, d_{\Psi_k} - d_{\Phi_k} = w - 1$.

Proof: See the Appendix.

It should be noted that Lemma 4 makes no claims about the value of $(d_{\Psi_K} - d_{\Phi_K})$, i.e., it makes no claims about the case $k = K$. From the algorithm it is clear that $d_{\Psi_K} - d_{\Phi_K} < w$. So it is quite possible that $d_{\Psi_K} - d_{\Phi_K} < w - 1$.

Lemma 5: If $K > 1$, for all $k, 1 \leq k \leq K - 1$, for all $i, m_{k-1} + 1 \leq i \leq m_k, p_i = d_{\Phi_k} = d_{\Psi_k} - w + 1$. For the last subsequence, i.e., $k = K$: if $\Theta_k = \Phi_k$, then $p_i = d_{\Phi_k}$, else $p_i = d_{\Psi_k} - w + 1$.

Proof: See the Appendix.

Lemma 6: If $K > 1$, then for all k, $1 \leq k \leq K$, $MT_Q[1, \Theta_k]$ $\geq MT_P[1, \Theta_k] + |q_{\Theta_k} - p_{\Theta_k}|$.

Proof: See the Appendix.

Using the above lemmas, we can formally prove the "optimality" of the RFPS generated by the algorithm.

Theorem 1: The RFPS P generated by the algorithm for the PNDS D is an *optimal* RFPS for D, i.e., if Q is an arbitrary valid RFPS for D, then

$$RFM_P[1, n] \leq RFM_Q[1, n]$$

and

$$MT_P[1, n] \leq MT_Q[1, n].$$

Proof: If $K = 1$, then there are no RFM's in P so $RFM_P[1, n] = 0$, $MT_P[1, n] = 0$, and the theorem holds.

Assume $K > 1$. In the algorithm, all the RFP's, corresponding to the same subsequence, are set to the same value (step 5 or step 7). Hence, the only way that $p_i \neq p_{i+1}$ can occur is if $i = m_k$ for some k, $1 \leq k \leq K - 1$. Thus, $RFM_P[1, n] \leq K - 1$.

From Lemma 3, $K - 1 \leq RFM_Q[1, m_{K-1} + 1]$. Since $m_{K-1} + 1 \leq n$, $RFM_Q[1, m_{K-1} + 1] \leq RFM_Q[1, n]$. Hence, $K - 1 \leq RFM_Q[1, n]$. Thus, $RFM_P[1, n] \leq RFM_Q[1, n]$.

From Lemma 6, $MT_Q[1, \Theta_K] \geq MT_P[1, \Theta_K] + |q_{\Theta_K} - p_{\Theta_K}|$. Since $|q_{\Theta_K} - p_{\Theta_K}| \geq 0$, $MT_Q[1, \Theta_K] \geq MT_P[1, \Theta_K]$. Since $\Theta_K \leq n$, $MT_Q[1, n] \geq MT_Q[1, \Theta_K]$. Since $d_{\Theta_K} \in E_K$ and $d_n \in E_K$, $p_{\Theta_K} = p_{\Theta_K+1} = \cdots = p_n$. Thus, $MT_P[\Theta_K + 1, n] = 0$, so $MT_P[1, \Theta_K] = MT_P[1, n]$. Hence, $MT_P[1, n] \leq MT_Q[1, n]$.

Q.E.D.

D. The Unrealizability of an Optimal Strategy

When a computer is executing a program, the entire call/return trace is not known ahead of time. In fact, it is unlikely that there is any look-ahead possible. In this section it is shown that knowledge of the entire PNDS is necessary for finding an optimal RFPS.

First, it should be noted that no simplifying assumptions about the properties of the call/return trace of "real" programs can be made. In other words, for every given sequence of integers which satisfies the definition of a PNDS (Definition 1), it is possible to construct a real program whose sequence of nesting depths is the given sequence. This is demonstrated by the program in Fig. 2 (which is written in the C language [7]). When this program is executed, its sequence of nesting depths is identical to the sequence of integers in the array *depthlist* (assuming that the sequence of integers in *depthlist* is a valid PNDS).

To show that unbounded look-ahead on the call/return trace is necessary for achieving an optimal RFPS, consider a system where there is a bounded (or nonexistent) look-ahead; more specifically, a system where at each point in time only the next t calls and returns are known in advance. (Note that in most systems $t = 0$.) Assume that the register file of the system can hold w frames and that there are two programs to be executed: PROG1 and PROG2. These programs have identical call/return traces for the first s calls and returns, where $w + t < s$. At some point, before $s - t$ calls/returns are executed, the nesting depth (in both programs) reaches $w + 1$. The nesting

```
int depthlist[] = {  /* This is the PNDS, 0 terminated */
  1, 2, 3, 2, 3, 4, 3, 2, 1, 0 } ;
int depthind = 1 ;
main()
{
  while (depthlist[depthind] > 1) {
    deeper(2) ;
    depthind = depthind + 1 ;
  }
}
deeper(curdep)
  int curdep ; /* The current nesting depth */
{
  depthind = depthind + 1 ;
  while (depthlist[depthind] > curdep) {
    deeper(curdep+1) ;
    depthind = depthind + 1 ;
  }
  if (depthlist[depthind] == 0)
    exit(0) ;
}
```

Fig. 2. A program whose "behavior" follows an arbitrary PNDS.

depth stays between 2 and $w + 1$ until a total of s calls/returns are executed. After that, in PROG1 the nesting depth decreases and the program terminates at nesting depth 1. In PROG2, on the other hand, the nesting depth increases to $w + 2$ and then decreases until the program terminates at nesting depth 1.

In both programs, when the nesting depth first reaches $w + 1$, the same information about the call/return trace is available, and therefore any strategy for managing the register file will result in the same action being taken for both programs. This action is clearly *not* optimal for at least one of the programs. For PROG1, the optimal action is to move one frame to memory. This action is not optimal for PROG2 since another overflow will occur when a nesting depth of $w + 2$ is reached. The optimal action for PROG2 is to move two frames to memory so that only one overflow will occur during the execution of the program. Moving two frames to memory is *not* the optimal action for PROG1 since it results in unnecessary memory traffic: moving two frames to and from memory instead of one.

The fact that an optimal strategy is not realizable does not imply that all practical strategies for managing the register file are equally bad. As seen in the next section, simple changes in the strategy for managing the register file may significantly affect the cost of handling calls and returns.

III. PRACTICAL STRATEGIES FOR MANAGING THE REGISTER FILE

In most real systems, no look-ahead at the call/return trace is possible. Thus, the decision as to how many frames should be moved to/from memory when an overflow/underflow occurs must be based on the previous behavior of the executing program or be completely independent of the PNDS of the executing program.

As indicated above, two factors contribute to the *cost* (execution time) of handling register file overflows and underflows: the handling of the interrupt/trap that is initiated by the overflow/underflow and the actual transfer of the STACK1 frames to/from memory. If the number of frames which are moved when an interrupt occurs is not fixed, some computation may be required in order to calculate this number. The cost of this calculation is included in the cost of handling the interrupt. In order to evaluate the effectiveness of different strategies for managing the register file, these strategies can be tried out on the call/return trace of benchmark programs. The number of overflows/underflows and transfers of STACK1 frames which result from each strategy can thus be determined. These numbers can then be related to the *cost* of the overflow/underflow handler using the following formula:

cost = α × (number overflows + number underflows)
$$+ \beta \times \text{(number frames moved)}$$

where α and β are constants: α is the cost of responding to the interrupt and calculating the number of frames to be moved, and β is the cost of moving one STACK1 frame to or from memory.

A. Measurement Technique

The method used for obtaining the call/return trace of the benchmark programs used in this paper relies on the fact that the call/return trace of a program executing on a RISC computer is identical to the call/return trace of the same program executing on any similar computer. In this case, the benchmark programs are all written in the C language [7], and their call/return trace is obtained from their execution on a VAX 11/780. The assembly code produced by the C compiler is processed by an editor script which inserts calls to special procedures before and after each procedure call instruction. When the program is executed, in addition to producing its normal output, it creates a file containing a string of bits. The *i*th bit in the string corresponds to the *i*th call/return executed by the program. This bit is 1 if a call was executed, 0 if a return was executed. The bit string is the call/return trace of the program. Routines which simulate different strategies for managing the register file use this string to obtain the number of overflows/underflows and the resulting memory traffic which will occur if the benchmark program is executed using the simulated strategy.

For this study, three benchmark programs were used:

rcc	The RISC C compiler [2] which is based on Johnson's portable C compiler [6]. The call/return trace used was generated by the compiler compiling the UNIX file concatenation utility *cat*. 88 606 calls and returns were executed and a nesting depth of 26 was reached.
puzzle	This is a bin-packing program which solves a three-dimensional puzzle. It was developed by Forest Baskett. During the execution of the program, 42 710 calls and returns were executed and a nesting depth of 20 was reached.
tower	This is a Tower of Hanoi program. The call/return trace used, was obtained for the program moving 18 disks. 1 048 574 calls and returns were executed and a nesting depth of 20 was reached.

In this paper, the cost of handling register file overflows and underflows is assumed to be directly proportional to the number of RISC instructions they require. If no calculation is needed in order to determine the number of frames to be moved, the cost of responding to the interrupt is approximately 30 instructions ($\alpha = 30$ in the above discussion). The cost of moving one STACK1 frame is 16 instructions ($\beta = 16$ in the above discussion).

B. The Cost of "Fixed" Strategies

The simplest strategy for managing the register file is to always move the same number of frames (say *i*) *to* memory, when an overflow occurs, and always move the same number of frames (say *j*) *from* memory, when an underflow occurs. For a register file that can hold *w* frames, such a strategy will be denoted *fixed*(*i*, *j*) where *i* and *j* are integers such that $1 \leq i \leq w$ and $1 \leq j \leq w$.

When a *fixed* strategy is used, no computation is required in order to determine the number of frames to be moved. Hence, the equation

cost = 30 × (number overflows + number underflows)
$$+ 16 \times \text{(number frames moved)}$$

is used to evaluate the cost of managing the register file. This equation is also used in evaluating the cost of the optimal strategy, which serves as a lower bound on the cost of other strategies.

1) Measurement Results: The actual "performance" of the optimal strategy and *fixed* strategies is presented in this section. All possible fixed strategies for register files containing 3, 5, 7, 9, 13, and 17 register banks have been tried with the three benchmark programs.

Tables I–III summarize the results for each one of the three benchmark programs with six different register file sizes and for seven different strategies. The results include the number of overflows, number of underflows, memory traffic, and cost. For the optimal strategy, the "raw" numbers are presented. For the other six strategies, the figures shown are normalized with respect to the corresponding entries for the optimal strategy with the same register file size. In the three tables *w* denotes the number of register banks in the register file.

The *fixed* strategies included in the tables are: the best of all *fixed* strategies (i.e., the strategy resulting in the least cost) for the particular program and register file size, the worst of all *fixed* strategies (i.e., the strategy resulting in the greatest cost) for the particular program and register file size, *fixed*(*w*, 1) which guarantees the minimum number of overflows, *fixed*(1, *w*) which guarantees the minimum number of underflows, *fixed*(1, 1) which guarantees the minimum memory traffic, and *fixed*($\lceil w/2 \rceil$, $\lceil w/2 \rceil$) which is "symmetrical."

2) Discussion of Measurement Results: Although the three benchmark programs used are quite different, the results show many common characteristics in their behavior, as far as the management of the register file is concerned. In addition, the results for the *fixed*(*w*, 1), *fixed*(1, *w*), and *fixed*(1, 1) strategies provide an experimental verification to the fact that the "optimal strategy," presented in Section II, does indeed minimize the number of overflows/underflows and memory traffic simultaneously.

The register file size and the way that the register file is managed can significantly affect the cost of procedure calls. Table IV shows the average number of instructions per procedure call required for managing the register file. For every

TABLE I
FIXED STRATEGIES WITH *rcc*

Reg File Size (w)		3	5	7	9	13	17
Best Fixed Strategy		(1,1)	(1,1)	(2,2)	(2,2)	(2,2)	(2,2)
Worst Fixed Strategy		(3,3)	(5,5)	(7,7)	(9,9)	(13,13)	(17,17)
Optimal Strategy (raw)	#Overflows	5828	1483	548	236	83	16
	#Underflows	6200	1232	474	171	71	14
	Mem. Traffic	19006	5554	2482	1378	458	74
	Cost	664936	170314	70372	34228	11948	2084
Best Fixed Strategy (normalized)	#Overflows	1.63	1.87	1.65	1.87	1.67	1.56
	#Underflows	1.53	2.25	1.91	2.58	1.96	1.79
	Mem. Traffic	1.00	1.00	1.46	1.28	1.21	1.35
	Cost	1.31	1.50	1.59	1.60	1.44	1.49
Worst Fixed Strategy (normalized)	#Overflows	2.30	7.06	9.49	10.64	43.40	79.31
	#Underflows	2.16	8.50	10.97	14.69	50.73	90.64
	Mem. Traffic	4.24	18.85	29.33	32.86	204.48	583.05
	Cost	3.15	13.53	20.99	25.54	143.50	367.79
fixed(w,1) (normalized)	#Overflows	1.00	1.00	1.00	1.00	1.00	1.00
	#Underflows	2.82	6.02	8.09	12.42	15.20	19.43
	Mem. Traffic	1.84	2.67	3.09	3.09	4.71	7.35
	Cost	1.89	2.96	3.61	4.05	5.81	8.32
fixed(1,w) (normalized)	#Overflows	3.19	3.88	5.44	5.66	4.83	3.94
	#Underflows	1.00	1.00	1.00	1.00	1.00	1.00
	Mem. Traffic	1.96	2.07	2.40	1.94	1.75	1.70
	Cost	2.01	2.31	2.83	2.57	2.26	2.08
fixed(1,1) (normalized)	#Overflows	1.63	1.87	2.26	2.92	2.76	2.31
	#Underflows	1.53	2.25	2.62	4.02	3.23	2.84
	Mem. Traffic	1.00	1.00	1.00	1.00	1.00	1.00
	Cost	1.31	1.50	1.62	1.85	1.76	1.63
fixed($\lfloor\frac{w}{2}\rfloor,\lfloor\frac{w}{2}\rfloor$) (normalized)	#Overflows	1.85	2.73	2.38	2.51	1.46	4.19
	#Underflows	1.55	3.29	2.76	3.46	1.70	4.79
	Mem. Traffic	2.02	4.38	4.21	4.30	3.70	16.30
	Cost	1.79	3.71	3.49	3.81	2.88	11.19

TABLE III
FIXED STRATEGIES WITH *tower*

Reg File Size (w)		3	5	7	9	13	17
Best Fixed Strategy		(1,1)	(3,3)	(1,1)	(1,1)	(1,1)	(3,3)
Worst Fixed Strategy		(3,3)	(4,5)	(6,6)	(9,9)	(13,13)	(17,17)
Optimal Strategy (raw)	#Overflows	74898	16912	4128	1026	64	4
	#Underflows	74898	16912	4128	1026	64	4
	Mem. Traffic	262142	65534	16382	4094	254	14
	Cost	8688152	2063264	509792	127064	7904	464
Best Fixed Strategy (normalized)	#Overflows	1.75	1.11	1.98	2.00	1.98	1.00
	#Underflows	1.75	1.11	1.98	2.00	1.98	1.00
	Mem. Traffic	1.00	1.71	1.00	1.00	1.00	1.71
	Cost	1.39	1.42	1.48	1.48	1.48	1.34
Worst Fixed Strategy (normalized)	#Overflows	2.00	4.84	32.26	128.00	64.00	16384.00
	#Underflows	2.00	3.88	32.26	128.00	64.00	16384.00
	Mem. Traffic	3.43	10.00	97.54	577.41	419.28	159158.86
	Cost	2.69	7.23	65.82	359.68	248.67	85309.80
fixed(w,1) (normalized)	#Overflows	1.00	1.00	1.00	1.00	1.00	1.00
	#Underflows	3.00	5.00	7.00	9.00	13.00	17.00
	Mem. Traffic	1.71	2.58	3.53	4.51	6.55	9.71
	Cost	1.86	2.79	3.76	4.75	6.77	9.34
fixed(1,w) (normalized)	#Overflows	3.00	5.00	6.99	8.99	7.00	3.00
	#Underflows	1.00	1.00	1.00	1.00	1.00	1.00
	Mem. Traffic	1.71	2.58	3.52	4.50	3.53	1.71
	Cost	1.86	2.79	3.75	4.74	3.78	1.86
fixed(1,1) (normalized)	#Overflows	1.75	1.94	1.98	2.00	1.98	1.75
	#Underflows	1.75	1.94	1.98	2.00	1.98	1.75
	Mem. Traffic	1.00	1.00	1.00	1.00	1.00	1.00
	Cost	1.39	1.48	1.48	1.48	1.48	1.39
fixed($\lfloor\frac{w}{2}\rfloor,\lfloor\frac{w}{2}\rfloor$) (normalized)	#Overflows	2.33	1.11	8.47	16.48	1.00	64.00
	#Underflows	2.33	1.11	8.47	16.48	1.00	64.00
	Mem. Traffic	2.67	1.71	17.07	41.31	3.53	329.14
	Cost	2.49	1.42	12.89	29.28	2.30	192.00

TABLE II
FIXED STRATEGIES WITH *puzzle*

Reg File Size (w)		3	5	7	9	13	17
Best Fixed Strategy		(1,1)	(1,1)	(1,1)	(2,2)	(7,7)	(3,3)
Worst Fixed Strategy		(3,3)	(5,5)	(7,7)	(9,9)	(13,13)	(17,17)
Optimal Strategy (raw)	#Overflows	736	159	26	8	1	1
	#Underflows	747	159	30	5	1	1
	Mem. Traffic	2056	514	94	30	14	6
	Cost	77386	17764	3184	810	284	156
Best Fixed Strategy (normalized)	#Overflows	1.40	1.62	1.81	1.87	1.00	1.00
	#Underflows	1.38	1.62	1.57	2.00	1.00	1.00
	Mem. Traffic	1.00	1.00	1.00	1.33	1.00	1.00
	Cost	1.22	1.33	1.36	1.53	1.00	1.00
Worst Fixed Strategy (normalized)	#Overflows	9.80	39.50	130.58	70.83	1462.00	2791.00
	#Underflows	9.65	39.50	113.17	85.00	1462.00	2791.00
	Mem. Traffic	21.05	122.20	505.84	255.00	2715.14	15815.87
	Cost	14.54	77.79	302.82	182.59	2450.39	10806.18
fixed(w,1) (normalized)	#Overflows	1.00	1.00	1.00	1.00	1.00	1.00
	#Underflows	2.96	5.00	6.07	10.80	13.00	17.00
	Mem. Traffic	2.15	3.09	3.87	3.60	1.86	5.67
	Cost	2.05	3.04	3.79	4.36	2.94	6.95
fixed(1,w) (normalized)	#Overflows	3.04	4.99	7.85	6.50	7.00	3.00
	#Underflows	1.00	1.00	1.00	1.00	1.00	1.00
	Mem. Traffic	2.18	3.09	4.34	2.60	1.00	1.00
	Cost	2.08	3.04	4.26	3.17	1.63	1.38
fixed(1,1) (normalized)	#Overflows	1.40	1.62	1.81	2.50	7.00	3.00
	#Underflows	1.38	1.62	1.57	3.00	7.00	3.00
	Mem. Traffic	1.00	1.00	1.00	1.00	1.00	1.00
	Cost	1.22	1.33	1.36	1.70	2.27	1.77
fixed($\lfloor\frac{w}{2}\rfloor,\lfloor\frac{w}{2}\rfloor$) (normalized)	#Overflows	1.30	2.38	2.38	1.17	1.00	2.00
	#Underflows	1.28	2.38	2.07	1.40	1.00	2.00
	Mem. Traffic	1.86	4.42	5.28	2.33	1.00	6.00
	Cost	1.53	3.33	3.66	1.90	1.00	4.46

TABLE IV
COST OF REGISTER FILE MANAGEMENT PER PROCEDURE CALL

Reg File Size (w)		3	5	7	9	13	17
Optimal Strategy	rcc	15.01	3.84	1.59	0.77	0.27	0.05
	puzzle	3.62	0.83	0.15	0.04	0.01	0.01
	tower	16.57	3.94	0.97	0.24	0.02	0.00*
Best Fixed Strategy	rcc	19.73	5.77	2.53	1.23	0.39	0.07
	puzzle	4.43	1.11	0.20	0.06	0.01	0.01
	tower	23.00	5.57	1.44	0.36	0.02	0.00*
Worst Fixed Strategy	rcc	47.24	52.00	33.33	19.73	38.70	17.30
	puzzle	52.66	64.71	45.15	6.93	32.59	78.94
	tower	44.57	28.44	84.00	87.17	3.72	75.50

cost of managing the register file may become prohibitive if the register file is too small (three register banks). In this case, for two out of the three programs (*rcc* and *tower*), it is likely that a conventional stack mechanism for handling procedure calls would have resulted in better performance. If a larger register file is used, the cost of managing the register file drops sharply. The results indicate that, for a register file of five or more register banks, this scheme compares favorably with the conventional stack mechanism.

Invoking a high-level language procedure and returning from it requires several RISC instructions in addition to those used for managing the register file. Specifically, arguments have to be copied to the area of overlap between the current STACK1 frame and the next STACK1 frame; if the procedure returns a value, it may have to be copied from this overlap area; the stack pointer and frame pointer for STACK2 may need to be updated; the actual RISC *call* and *ret* instructions must be executed. C procedures typically have less than four arguments [5]. Hence, in addition to the RISC instructions that manage the register file, between three and seven instructions will be executed for each procedure call/return pair.

call there is a corresponding *return*. Hence, in this context, "procedure call" includes returning from the procedure as well as invoking it.

The data indicate that, even with the optimal strategy, the

If an efficient strategy (such as the "best fixed strategy") is used, the cost of managing the register file decreases as the number of register banks in the register file increases. Once this cost reaches approximately one RISC instruction per procedure call/return pair (e.g., using the "best fixed strategy" with a register file containing nine register banks), it no longer dominates the total number of instructions required for each procedure call/return. In a single chip VLSI microprocessor, chip area is a precious resource. Rather than adding more register banks (e.g., beyond nine), the limited chip area can be used more effectively for other purposes, such as an on-chip cache or hardware support for multiply, that are likely to make a greater contribution to overall processor performance. Even for the benchmarks used here, which reach a relatively high nesting depth [5], a register file with between five and nine register banks seems optimal.

Choosing a "good" strategy is critical to the success of the register file scheme. Tables II and III show that choosing the "wrong" strategy can result in more than four orders of magnitude increase in the cost of managing the register file. Furthermore, if an inefficient strategy is used, an increase in the register file size can result in an *increase* in the cost of managing the register file (since there is an opportunity to generate more useless memory traffic). In most cases, the best fixed strategy is to minimize the memory traffic (i.e., use the *fixed*(1, 1) strategy). This can be explained by the fact that the cost of moving one frame to memory and then from memory back to the register file is about the same as the cost of handling the trap when an overflow or underflow occurs. Hence, the immediate cost of unnecessarily moving a frame (which results in one frame's worth of traffic to memory and later back to the register file) is about equal to the cost of not moving a frame when it should have been moved (an extra overflow or underflow trap). In addition, if an unnecessary move is made, the cost may include the cost of an extra overflow or underflow which will occur later. Hence, the "penalty" for moving one more frame than necessary, when an overflow or underflow occurs, is greater than the "penalty" for moving one fewer frame than necessary. Thus, if the call/return sequence is random, the best fixed strategies are likely to be those that require the movement of only one or two frames when an overflow or underflow occurs. The use of such strategies is further supported by the fact that with the optimal strategy, in cases where there are more than ten overflows/underflows throughout the execution of the program, the average number of frames moved when an overflow or underflow occurs is between 1.4 and 3 and in most cases is approximately 2.

C. Taking the Past into Account

The *fixed* strategies do not attempt to take into account the previous behavior of the executing program. It is conceivable that a strategy that does take past behavior into account would result in a lower cost, closer to that of the optimal strategy.

One way of "taking the past into account" involves keeping track of which register banks have been used since the last overflow or underflow. If two or more STACK1 frames are moved whenever an overflow or underflow occurs, it is clear that, in some cases, it will turn out that too many frames will be moved, resulting in unnecessary memory traffic. When an overflow occurs, register banks are "freed" by copying their contents to memory. If some of the freed register banks remain unused until the next underflow, their contents remain intact and need not be copied from memory to the register file. Similarly, if too many register banks are loaded when an underflow occurs, the contents of those that are unused until the next overflow need not be copied to memory since their contents are already in the appropriate memory locations.

Many practical strategies result in unnecessary memory traffic, i.e., more memory traffic than is required by the optimal strategy. The above technique reduces the memory traffic resulting from any such strategy. Our measurements indicate that with the useless "worst fixed strategy," which produces an exorbitant number of unnecessary moves of STACK1 frames, keeping track of which register banks are used can reduce this memory traffic by up to an order of magnitude. However, with "reasonable" strategies, the gains are less impressive. If the "best fixed strategy" is *fixed*(1, 1) then clearly no gain is possible. With the *fixed*(2, 2) strategy, the decrease in memory traffic is less than ten percent. The above technique requires some extra hardware and a few more instructions in the trap handling routine. When the overhead of these extra instructions is taken into account, the total cost of managing the register file for the *fixed*(2, 2) strategy is about the same as without this extra mechanism. For the *fixed*(1, 1) strategy, the extra instructions will simply add to the cost of managing the register file without any saving in memory traffic.

We have investigated two other methods for "taking the past into account." They both involve determining the number of frames to be moved when an overflow or underflow occurs based on the previous behavior of the program. The first method (henceforth denoted C/R) is to use the call/return trace immediately preceding the overflow or underflow. The second method (henceforth denoted O/U) is to use the trace of overflows and underflows which preceded the trap being handled.

The C/R method can be implemented by adding a special shift register to the processor. Every call instruction shifts a 1 into the register and every return shifts a 0. The routine which handles the overflow/underflow trap examines the contents of this register and determines the immediately preceding call/return trace of the program. This pattern is used to access a table containing the "optimal" number of frames that should be moved, given a particular call/return pattern. This scheme adds very few instructions to the cost of handling the overflow/underflow trap.

The O/U method does not require any additional hardware. The "overflow/underflow trace" is kept in a fixed memory location and is updated each time an overflow or underflow occurs by the routine that handles these traps. The pattern in this memory location is used in the same way as the contents of the shift register for the C/R method.

Both the C/R method and O/U method require finding a mapping between "call/return patterns" or "overflow/underflow patterns" and "number of frames to be moved" so that the total cost is reduced. In order to find such a mapping (for either one of the methods) we tabulated the optimal number of frames to be moved (which can be found given unbounded look-ahead) following various call/return or overflow/underflow patterns for the three benchmark programs. We attempted to use these tables to determine which patterns indicate that a single frame should be moved and in which cases moving more than one frame would be preferable. However, we could not find a single mapping which worked better than the *fixed*(1, 1) strategy for all three programs!

For the three benchmark programs used in this work, it appears that the optimal number of frames to be moved is, for all practical purposes, independent of the immediately preceding call/return pattern of length ten or less. The O/U method shows more promise but the results are inconclusive. Following a suggestion by Denning [3], we tested an O/U method which involved moving two frames after two consecutive overflows or underflows and moving one frame otherwise. For register file sizes of interest (between five and nine frames), the cost of managing the register file using this method was compared to the cost using the *fixed*(1, 1) strategy. Reductions of up to 28 percent in the number of overflows and underflows and increases of up to 59 percent in the memory traffic were measured. When the extra instructions in the trap handling routines are taken into account, the overall cost was either equal to or greater than the cost of the *fixed*(1, 1) strategy in all but one case.

IV. CONCLUSIONS

The success of the RISC architecture is due, in part, to the reduction in the number of memory accesses which is possible through the use of the register file [11]. We have shown that the effectiveness of the register file is dependent on choosing the "right" size for the register file and an efficient strategy for deciding how many frames should be moved to/from memory when an overflow/underflow occurs.

Our measurements indicate that with the simple *fixed* strategy, *fixed*(1, 1), the cost of managing the register file is within a factor of two of the cost of the optimal strategy (which requires unbounded look-ahead). For a register file containing more than eight register banks, the *fixed*(2, 2) strategy yields slightly better performance.

If a "reasonable" strategy is used, the cost of managing the register file is inversely proportional to its size. If the register file is too small, the number of overflows and underflows becomes prohibitively large. Since the STACK1 frames have a fixed size, the large number of overflows and underflows results in a lot of memory traffic even when the number of registers actually used (for arguments and local variables) is small. Hence, if the register file is too small, the overall cost of procedure calls may be greater than if a conventional stack mechanism is used. Our measurements indicate that if the register file contains five or more frames, the use of the register file scheme rather than a conventional stack mechanism is worthwhile.

We have attempted to use past behavior of the program in order to predict the future behavior and reduce the cost of managing the register file. So far, our attempts have not succeeded.

The first method (keeping track of which register banks have been used since the last overflow or underflow), reduces the cost of managing the register file only for inefficient strategies.

For efficient strategies, such as *fixed*(1, 1) or *fixed*(2, 2), the extra overhead in the trap handling routine was greater than the savings from the reduced memory traffic.

The two other methods attempt to determine the "optimal" number of frames to be moved from the immediately preceding pattern of calls/returns or overflows/underflows. These methods appear ineffective since we could not find a single mapping between either type of patterns and number frames to be moved, which reduces the cost for all three programs. These results, while preliminary, raise serious doubts that a mapping which reduces the cost of managing the register file for a majority of programs could be found. Even in this context, the simplest solution appears to also be the best.

APPENDIX

PROOF OF LEMMAS 3-6

Lemma 3: If $K > 1$, then for all k, $1 \le k < K$,

$$\text{RFM}_Q[1, m_k + 1] \ge k.$$

Proof: By induction on k.

Basis: $k = 1$. It is shown that $\text{RFM}_Q[1, m_1 + 1] \ge 1$. From the algorithm,

$$\max(E_1) - \min(E_1) < w$$

while

$$\max(E_1 \cup \{d_{m_1+1}\}) - \min(E_1 \cup \{d_{m_1+1}\}) \ge w.$$

Hence, either

$$d_{m_1+1} < \min(E_1)$$

or

$$d_{m_1+1} > \max(E_1).$$

By Definition 1, $d_1 = 1$ and $d_i \ge 1$ for all i, $1 \le i \le n$. Hence,

$$d_1 = \min(E_1 \cup \{d_{m_1+1}\}) = \min(E_1)$$

and

$$d_{m_1+1} = \max(E_1 \cup \{d_{m_1+1}\}).$$

Thus,

$$d_{m_1+1} - d_1 \ge w.$$

Since Q is a valid RFPS for D, $q_1 \le d_1 < q_1 + w$ and $q_{m_1+1} \le d_{m_1+1} < q_{m_1+1} + w$. $d_{m_1+1} \ge d_1 + w$ and $d_1 \ge q_1$ imply that $d_{m_1+1} \ge q_1 + w$. But $q_{m_1+1} + w > d_{m_1+1}$. Hence,

$$q_{m_1+1} + w \ge q_1 + w,$$

i.e., $q_{m_1+1} > q_1$. The fact that $q_{m_1+1} \ne q_1$ implies that at least one RFM occurs in the location range $[2, m_1 + 1]$, so $\text{RFM}_Q[1, m_1 + 1] \ge 1$.

Induction Step: Assuming that this lemma holds for $k = \alpha - 1$, where $2 \le \alpha < K$, it is now proven that it holds for $k = \alpha$. In other words, assuming $\text{RFM}_Q[1, m_{\alpha-1} + 1] \ge \alpha - 1$, it is proven that $\text{RFM}_Q[1, m_\alpha + 1] \ge \alpha$:

If $\text{RFM}_Q[1, m_{\alpha-1} + 1] \ge \alpha - 1$, then either

$$\text{RFM}_Q[1, m_{\alpha-1} + 1] \ge \alpha$$

or

$$\text{RFM}_Q[1, m_{\alpha-1} + 1] = \alpha - 1.$$

The former case implies that $\text{RFM}_Q[1, m_\alpha + 1] \geq \alpha$ (since $m_\alpha + 1 \geq m_{\alpha-1} + 1$) and the lemma is proved. Hence, we can assume $\text{RFM}_Q[1, m_{\alpha-1} + 1] = \alpha - 1$.

The rest of the proof is similar to the proof of the *basis*:

From the algorithm,

$$\max(E_\alpha) - \min(E_\alpha) < w$$

while

$$\max(E_\alpha \cup \{d_{m_\alpha+1}\}) - \min(E_\alpha \cup \{d_{m_\alpha+1}\}) \geq w.$$

Hence, either $d_{m_\alpha+1} < \min(E_\alpha)$ or $d_{m_\alpha+1} > \max(E_\alpha)$.

Assume $d_{m_\alpha+1} < \min(E_\alpha)$:

From the algorithm and the definition of Ψ, $d_{\Psi_\alpha} - d_{m_\alpha+1} \geq w$. Since Q is a valid RFPS for D,

$$q_{\Psi_\alpha} \leq d_{\Psi_\alpha} < q_{\Psi_\alpha} + w$$

and

$$q_{m_\alpha+1} \leq d_{m_\alpha+1} < q_{m_\alpha+1} + w.$$

Hence,

$$q_{\Psi_\alpha} + w > d_{\Psi_\alpha} \geq d_{m_\alpha+1} + w \geq q_{m_\alpha+1} + w,$$

i.e., $q_{\Psi_\alpha} > q_{m_\alpha+1}$.

Assume $d_{m_\alpha+1} > \max(E_\alpha)$:

From the algorithm and the definition of Φ,

$$d_{m_\alpha+1} - d_{\Phi_\alpha} \geq w.$$

Since Q is a valid RFPS for D,

$$q_{\Phi_\alpha} \leq d_{\Phi_\alpha} < q_{\Phi_\alpha} + w$$

and

$$q_{m_\alpha+1} \leq d_{m_\alpha+1} < q_{m_\alpha+1} + w.$$

Hence,

$$q_{m_\alpha+1} + w > d_{m_\alpha+1} \geq d_{\Phi_\alpha} + w \geq q_{\Phi_\alpha} + w,$$

i.e., $q_{m_\alpha+1} > q_{\Phi_\alpha}$.

The fact that $q_{\Psi_\alpha} \neq q_{m_\alpha+1}$ ($q_{\Phi_\alpha} \neq q_{m_\alpha+1}$) implies that there is at least one RFM in the location range $[\Psi_\alpha + 1, m_\alpha + 1]$ ($[\Phi_\alpha + 1, m_\alpha + 1]$). But $\Psi_\alpha \geq m_{\alpha-1} + 1$ ($\Phi_\alpha \geq m_{\alpha-1} + 1$). Hence, there is at least one RFM in the location range $[m_{\alpha-1} + 2, m_\alpha + 1]$, i.e., $\text{RFM}_Q[m_{\alpha-1} + 2, m_\alpha + 1] \geq 1$. But by assumption $\text{RFM}_Q[1, m_{\alpha-1} + 1] = \alpha - 1$. Hence, $\text{RFM}_Q[1, m_\alpha + 1] \geq \alpha$. ∎

Lemma 4: If $K > 1$, then for all k, $1 \leq k \leq K - 1$,

$$d_{\Psi_k} - d_{\Phi_k} = w - 1.$$

Proof: From the algorithm,

$$\max(E_k) - \min(E_k) < w$$

while

$$\max(E_k \cup \{d_{m_k+1}\}) - \min(E_k \cup \{d_{m_k+1}\}) \geq w.$$

Hence, either $d_{m_k+1} < \min(E_k)$ or $d_{m_k+1} > \max(E_k)$.

By Definition 1, $|d_{m_k+1} - d_{m_k}| = 1$. Since $d_{m_k} \in E_k$, either $d_{m_k+1} = \min(E_k) - 1$ or $d_{m_l+1} = \max(E_k) + 1$. Hence,

$$\max(E_k \cup \{d_{m_k+1}\}) - \min(E_k \cup \{d_{m_k+1}\})$$
$$= \max(E_k) - \min(E_k) + 1.$$

Thus, $\max(E_k) - \min(E_k) \geq w - 1$. But from the algorithm, $\max(E_k) - \min(E_k) \leq w - 1$. Hence,

$$\max(E_k) - \min(E_k) = w - 1,$$

i.e., $d_{\Psi_k} - d_{\Phi_k} = w - 1$. ∎

Lemma 5: If $K > 1$, for all k, $1 \leq k \leq K - 1$, for all i,

$$m_{k-1} + 1 \leq i \leq m_k, p_i = d_{\Phi_k} = d_{\Psi_k} - w + 1.$$

For the last subsequence, i.e., $k = K$: if $\Theta_k = \Phi_k$, then $p_i = d_{\Phi_k}$, else $p_i = d_{\Psi_k} - w + 1$.

Proof: For all i, $1 \leq i \leq n$, the value of p_i is set in step 5 or in step 7 of the algorithm.

If $1 \leq k \leq K - 1$, then by Lemma 4,

$$d_{\Psi_k} - d_{\Phi_k} = w - 1.$$

Hence,

$$d_{\Phi_k} = d_{\Psi_k} - w + 1$$

and the same value (d_{Φ_k}) will be assigned to p_i in step 5 or step 7 of the algorithm.

If $k = K$, then it may be the case that $d_{\Psi_k} - d_{\Phi_k} < w - 1$. Hence, it may make a difference whether the value of p_i is assigned in step 5 or in step 7. This is controlled by the value of Θ_k.

If $\Theta_k = \Phi_k$, then, by the definition of Θ,

$$d_{\Phi_k} < d_{\Phi_{k-1}}.$$

Since $k - 1 < K$,

$$p_{m_{k-1}} = p_{\Phi_{k-1}} = d_{\Phi_{k-1}}.$$

Hence,

$$\min(E_k) < p_{m_{k-1}},$$

and the second clause in step 4 of the algorithm is satisfied. Thus, p_i ($m_{k-1} + 1 \leq i \leq m_k$) is assigned a value in step 5 of the algorithm. So

$$p_i = d_{\Phi_k}.$$

If $\Theta_k = \Psi_k$, then, by the definition of Θ,

$$d_{\Phi_k} \geq d_{\Phi_{k-1}}.$$

Since $k - 1 < K$,

$$p_{m_{k-1}} = p_{\Phi_{k-1}} = d_{\Phi_{k-1}}.$$

Hence,

$$\min(E_k) \geq p_{m_{k-1}},$$

and the second clause in step 4 of the algorithm is *not* satisfied. Since $k = K$, $m_k = n$, and the first clause in step 4 of the algorithm is also *not* satisfied. Thus, p_i ($m_{k-1} + 1 \leq i \leq m_k$) is assigned a value of step 7 of the algorithm. So

$$p_i = d_{\Psi_k} - w + 1.$$

Lemma 6: If $K > 1$, then for all k, $1 \leq k \leq K$,

$$MT_Q[1, \Theta_k] \geq MT_P[1, \Theta_k] + |q_{\Theta_k} - p_{\Theta_k}|.$$

Proof: By induction on k.

Basis: $k = 1$. It is shown that $MT_Q[1, \Theta_1] \geq MT_P[1, \Theta_1] + |q_{\Theta_1} - p_{\Theta_1}|$.

By the definition of Θ, $\Theta_1 = 1$. Hence,

$$MT_Q[1, \Theta_1] = MT_Q[1, 1] = |q_1 - q_0|$$

and

$$MT_P[1, \Theta_1] + |q_{\Theta_1} - p_{\Theta_1}| = MT_P[1, 1] + |q_1 - p_1|$$
$$= |p_1 - p_0| + |q_1 - p_1|.$$

By Definitions 2 and 5, for all i, $1 \leq i \leq n$,

$$1 \leq q_i \leq d_i < q_i + w$$

and

$$1 \leq p_i \leq d_i < p_i + w.$$

By Definition 1, $d_1 = 1$. Hence, $q_1 = p_1 = 1$. From the algorithm, $p_0 = 1$. Hence,

$$MT_P[1, \Theta_1] + |q_{\Theta_1} - p_{\Theta_1}| = |p_1 - p_0| + |q_1 - p_1| = 0.$$

Since $|q_1 - q_0| \geq 0$,

$$MT_Q[1, \Theta_1] \geq 0.$$

Thus,

$$MT_Q[1, \Theta_1] \geq MT_P[1, \Theta_1] + |q_{\Theta_1} - p_{\Theta_1}|.$$

Induction Step: Assuming that this lemma holds for $k = \alpha - 1$, where $2 \leq \alpha \leq K$, it is now proven that it holds for $k = \alpha$. In other words, assuming

$$MT_Q[1, \Theta_{\alpha-1}] \geq MT_P[1, \Theta_{\alpha-1}] + |q_{\Theta_{\alpha-1}} - p_{\Theta_{\alpha-1}}|,$$

it is proven that

$$MT_Q[1, \Theta_\alpha] \geq MT_P[1, \Theta_\alpha] + |q_{\Theta_\alpha} - p_{\Theta_\alpha}|.$$

From Definition 8,

$$MT_Q[1, \Theta_\alpha] = MT_Q[1, \Theta_{\alpha-1}] + MT_Q[\Theta_{\alpha-1} + 1, \Theta_\alpha]$$

and

$$MT_P[1, \Theta_\alpha] = MT_P[1, \Theta_{\alpha-1}] + MT_P[\Theta_{\alpha-1} + 1, \Theta_\alpha].$$

Using the induction hypothesis,

$$MT_Q[1, \Theta_\alpha] \geq MT_P[1, \Theta_{\alpha-1}] + |q_{\Theta_{\alpha-1}} - p_{\Theta_{\alpha-1}}| + MT_Q[\Theta_{\alpha-1} + 1, \Theta_\alpha].$$

$MT_Q[\Theta_{\alpha-1} + 1, \Theta_\alpha]$ is the number of STACK1 frames transferred to/from memory in location range $[\Theta_{\alpha-1} + 1, \Theta_\alpha]$. A change by one in the RFP indicates that one STACK1 frame is transferred to or from memory. Hence, the memory traffic in location range $[\Theta_{\alpha-1} + 1, \Theta_\alpha]$ is at least the difference between the RFP at the beginning of the range and the RFP at the end of the range, i.e.,

$$MT_Q[\Theta_{\alpha-1} + 1, \Theta_\alpha] \geq |q_{\Theta_\alpha} - q_{\Theta_{\alpha-1}}|.$$

Hence,

$$MT_Q[1, \Theta_\alpha] \geq MT_P[1, \Theta_{\alpha-1}] + |q_{\Theta_{\alpha-1}} - p_{\Theta_{\alpha-1}}| + |q_{\Theta_\alpha} - q_{\Theta_{\alpha-1}}|.$$

From Definition 8 and the algorithm,

$$MT_P[\Theta_{\alpha-1} + 1, \Theta_\alpha] = \sum_{\beta=\Theta_{\alpha-1}+1}^{\Theta_\alpha} |p_\beta - p_{\beta-1}|$$

$$= \sum_{\beta=\Theta_{\alpha-1}+1}^{m_{\alpha-1}} |p_\beta - p_{\beta-1}| + |p_{m_{\alpha-1}+1} - p_{m_{\alpha-1}}|$$

$$+ \sum_{\beta=m_{\alpha-1}+2}^{\Theta_\alpha} |p_\beta - p_{\beta-1}| = |p_{m_{\alpha-1}+1} - p_{m_{\alpha-1}}|.$$

Since $\alpha - 1 < K$, by Lemma 5, $p_{m_{\alpha-1}} = d_{\Phi_{\alpha-1}}$. From the algorithm, $p_{m_{\alpha-1}+1} = p_{m_\alpha}$. Hence,

$$MT_P[\Theta_{\alpha-1} + 1, \Theta_\alpha] = |p_{m_\alpha} - d_{\Phi_{\alpha-1}}|.$$

Thus,

$$MT_P[1, \Theta_\alpha] = MT_P[1, \Theta_{\alpha-1}] + |p_{m_\alpha} - d_{\Phi_{\alpha-1}}|.$$

In the rest of the proof, the following four cases will be handled separately:

Case A: $\Theta_\alpha = \Phi_\alpha$ and $\Theta_{\alpha-1} = \Phi_{\alpha-1}$
Case B: $\Theta_\alpha = \Phi_\alpha$ and $\Theta_{\alpha-1} = \Psi_{\alpha-1}$
Case C: $\Theta_\alpha = \Psi_\alpha$ and $\Theta_{\alpha-1} = \Phi_{\alpha-1}$
Case D: $\Theta_\alpha = \Psi_\alpha$ and $\Theta_{\alpha-1} = \Psi_{\alpha-1}$.

Case A: $\Theta_\alpha = \Phi_\alpha$ and $\Theta_{\alpha-1} = \Phi_{\alpha-1}$:

$$|q_{\Theta_{\alpha-1}} - p_{\Theta_{\alpha-1}}| + |q_{\Theta_\alpha} - q_{\Theta_{\alpha-1}}|$$
$$= |q_{\Phi_{\alpha-1}} - p_{\Phi_{\alpha-1}}| + |q_{\Phi_\alpha} - q_{\Phi_{\alpha-1}}|$$
$$= |p_{\Phi_{\alpha-1}} - q_{\Phi_{\alpha-1}}| + |q_{\Phi_{\alpha-1}} - q_{\Phi_\alpha}| \geq p_{\Phi_{\alpha-1}} - q_{\Phi_{\alpha-1}}$$
$$+ q_{\Phi_{\alpha-1}} - q_{\Phi_\alpha} = p_{\Phi_{\alpha-1}} - q_{\Phi_\alpha}$$
$$= (p_{\Phi_{\alpha-1}} - p_{\Phi_\alpha}) + (p_{\Phi_\alpha} - q_{\Phi_\alpha}).$$

By Lemma 5, since $\Theta_\alpha = \Phi_\alpha$ and $\alpha - 1 < K$, $p_{\Phi_\alpha} = d_{\Phi_\alpha}$ and $p_{\Phi_{\alpha-1}} = d_{\Phi_{\alpha-1}}$. Hence,

$$|q_{\Theta_{\alpha-1}} - p_{\Theta_{\alpha-1}}| + |q_{\Theta_\alpha} - q_{\Theta_{\alpha-1}}|$$
$$\geq (d_{\Phi_{\alpha-1}} - d_{\Phi_\alpha}) + (d_{\Phi_\alpha} - q_{\Phi_\alpha}).$$

Since Q is a valid RFPS for D,

$$q_{\Phi_\alpha} \leq d_{\Phi_\alpha} < q_{\Phi_\alpha} + w.$$

Hence, $(d_{\Phi_\alpha} - q_{\Phi_\alpha}) \geq 0$. Thus,

$$|q_{\Theta_{\alpha-1}} - p_{\Theta_{\alpha-1}}| + |q_{\Theta_\alpha} - q_{\Theta_{\alpha-1}}| \geq d_{\Phi_{\alpha-1}} - d_{\Phi_\alpha}.$$

From the definition of Θ, since $\Theta_\alpha = \Phi_\alpha$, $d_{\Phi_{\alpha-1}} > d_{\Phi_\alpha}$. Hence,

$$d_{\Phi_{\alpha-1}} - d_{\Phi_\alpha} = |d_{\Phi_{\alpha-1}} - d_{\Phi_\alpha}|.$$

Thus,

$$|q_{\Theta_{\alpha-1}} - p_{\Theta_{\alpha-1}}| + |q_{\Theta_\alpha} - q_{\Theta_{\alpha-1}}| \geq |d_{\Phi_{\alpha-1}} - d_{\Phi_\alpha}|.$$

Therefore,

$$MT_Q[1, \Theta_\alpha] \geq MT_P[1, \Theta_{\alpha-1}] + |d_{\Phi_{\alpha-1}} - d_{\Phi_\alpha}|.$$

By Lemma 5, since $\Theta_\alpha = \Phi_\alpha$, $p_{m_\alpha} = d_{\Phi_\alpha}$. Hence,

$$MT_P[1, \Theta_\alpha] = MT_P[1, \Theta_{\alpha-1}] + |d_{\Phi_\alpha} - d_{\Phi_{\alpha-1}}|.$$

Thus,

$$\mathrm{MT}_Q[1, \Theta_\alpha] \geq \mathrm{MT}_P[1, \Theta_\alpha].$$

Case B: $\Theta_\alpha = \Phi_\alpha$ and $\Theta_{\alpha-1} = \Psi_{\alpha-1}$:

$$\begin{aligned}
|q_{\Theta_{\alpha-1}} &- p_{\Theta_{\alpha-1}}| + |q_{\Theta_\alpha} - q_{\Theta_{\alpha-1}}| \\
&= |q_{\Psi_{\alpha-1}} - p_{\Psi_{\alpha-1}}| + |q_{\Phi_\alpha} - q_{\Psi_{\alpha-1}}| \\
&= |p_{\Psi_{\alpha-1}} - q_{\Psi_{\alpha-1}}| + |q_{\Psi_{\alpha-1}} - q_{\Phi_\alpha}| \geq p_{\Psi_{\alpha-1}} \\
&\quad - q_{\Psi_{\alpha-1}} + q_{\Psi_{\alpha-1}} - q_{\Phi_\alpha} = p_{\Psi_{\alpha-1}} - q_{\Phi_\alpha}.
\end{aligned}$$

From the algorithm, $p_{\Psi_{\alpha-1}} = p_{\Phi_{\alpha-1}}$. Hence,

$$|q_{\Theta_{\alpha-1}} - p_{\Theta_{\alpha-1}}| + |q_{\Theta_\alpha} - q_{\Theta_{\alpha-1}}| \geq p_{\Phi_{\alpha-1}} - q_{\Phi_\alpha}.$$

The rest of the proof for this case is identical to the proof of Case A.

Case C: $\Theta_\alpha = \Psi_\alpha$ and $\Theta_{\alpha-1} = \Phi_{\alpha-1}$:

$$\begin{aligned}
|q_{\Theta_{\alpha-1}} &- p_{\Theta_{\alpha-1}}| + |q_{\Theta_\alpha} - q_{\Theta_{\alpha-1}}| \\
&= |q_{\Phi_{\alpha-1}} - p_{\Phi_{\alpha-1}}| + |q_{\Psi_\alpha} - q_{\Phi_{\alpha-1}}| \\
&\geq q_{\Phi_{\alpha-1}} - p_{\Phi_{\alpha-1}} + q_{\Psi_\alpha} - q_{\Phi_{\alpha-1}} = q_{\Psi_\alpha} - p_{\Phi_{\alpha-1}} \\
&= (q_{\Psi_\alpha} - p_{\Psi_\alpha}) + (p_{\Phi_\alpha} - p_{\Phi_{\alpha-1}}).
\end{aligned}$$

By Lemma 5, since $\Theta_\alpha = \Psi_\alpha$ and $\alpha - 1 < K$, $p_{\Phi_\alpha} = d_{\Psi_\alpha} - w + 1$ and $p_{\Phi_{\alpha-1}} = d_{\Phi_{\alpha-1}}$. Hence,

$$\begin{aligned}
|q_{\Theta_{\alpha-1}} - p_{\Theta_{\alpha-1}}| + |q_{\Theta_\alpha} - q_{\Theta_{\alpha-1}}| &\geq (q_{\Psi_\alpha} - d_{\Psi_\alpha} + w - 1) \\
&\quad + (d_{\Psi_\alpha} - w + 1 - d_{\Phi_{\alpha-1}}).
\end{aligned}$$

Since Q is a valid RFPS for D,

$$q_{\Psi_\alpha} \leq d_{\Psi_\alpha} < q_{\Psi_\alpha} + w.$$

Hence, $q_{\Psi_\alpha} - d_{\Psi_\alpha} + w > 0$, so

$$q_{\Psi_\alpha} - d_{\Psi_\alpha} + w - 1 \geq 0.$$

Thus,

$$|q_{\Theta_{\alpha-1}} - p_{\Theta_{\alpha-1}}| + |q_{\Theta_\alpha} - q_{\Theta_{\alpha-1}}| \geq d_{\Psi_\alpha} - w + 1 - d_{\Phi_{\alpha-1}}.$$

From the definition of Θ, since $\Theta_\alpha = \Psi_\alpha$, $d_{\Phi_\alpha} > d_{\Phi_{\alpha-1}}$. From the algorithm,

$$\max (E_{\alpha-1}) - \min (E_{\alpha-1}) < w$$

while

$$\max (E_{\alpha-1} \cup \{d_{m_{\alpha-1}+1}\}) - \min (E_{\alpha-1} \cup \{d_{m_{\alpha-1}+1}\}) \geq w.$$

Hence, either $d_{m_{\alpha-1}+1} < d_{\Phi_{\alpha-1}}$ or $d_{m_{\alpha-1}+1} > d_{\Psi_{\alpha-1}}$. In this case, since $d_{\Phi_\alpha} > d_{\Phi_{\alpha-1}}$ and $d_{m_{\alpha-1}+1} \geq d_{\Phi_\alpha}$, it must be true that $d_{m_{\alpha-1}+1} > d_{\Psi_{\alpha-1}}$. By the definition of Ψ, $d_{\Psi_\alpha} \geq d_{m_{\alpha-1}+1}$. Hence,

$$d_{\Psi_\alpha} > d_{\Psi_{\alpha-1}}.$$

By Lemma 4, since $\alpha - 1 < K$, $d_{\Psi_{\alpha-1}} = d_{\Phi_{\alpha-1}} + w - 1$. Hence, $d_{\Psi_\alpha} > d_{\Phi_{\alpha-1}} + w - 1$, so

$$d_{\Psi_\alpha} - w + 1 - d_{\Phi_{\alpha-1}} > 0.$$

Thus,

$$d_{\Psi_\alpha} - w + 1 - d_{\Phi_{\alpha-1}} = |d_{\Psi_\alpha} - w + 1 - d_{\Phi_{\alpha-1}}|.$$

By Lemma 5, since $\Theta_\alpha = \Psi_\alpha$, $p_{m_\alpha} = d_{\Psi_\alpha} - w + 1$. Hence,

$$|q_{\Theta_{\alpha-1}} - p_{\Theta_{\alpha-1}}| + |q_{\Theta_\alpha} - q_{\Theta_{\alpha-1}}| \geq |p_{m_\alpha} - d_{\Phi_{\alpha-1}}|.$$

Therefore,

$$\mathrm{MT}_Q[1, \Theta_\alpha] \geq \mathrm{MT}_P[1, \Theta_{\alpha-1}] + |p_{m_\alpha} - d_{\Phi_{\alpha-1}}|.$$

It has been shown above that $\mathrm{MT}_P[1, \Theta_\alpha] = \mathrm{MT}_P[1, \Theta_{\alpha-1}] + |p_{m_\alpha} - d_{\Phi_{\alpha-1}}|$. Hence,

$$\mathrm{MT}_Q[1, \Theta_\alpha] \geq \mathrm{MT}_P[1, \Theta_\alpha].$$

Case D: $\Theta_\alpha = \Psi_\alpha$ and $\Theta_{\alpha-1} = \Psi_{\alpha-1}$:

$$\begin{aligned}
|q_{\Theta_{\alpha-1}} &- p_{\Theta_{\alpha-1}}| + |q_{\Theta_\alpha} - q_{\Theta_{\alpha-1}}| \\
&= |q_{\Psi_{\alpha-1}} - p_{\Psi_{\alpha-1}}| + |q_{\Psi_\alpha} - q_{\Psi_{\alpha-1}}| \\
&\geq q_{\Psi_{\alpha-1}} - p_{\Psi_{\alpha-1}} + q_{\Psi_\alpha} - q_{\Psi_{\alpha-1}} = q_{\Psi_\alpha} - p_{\Psi_{\alpha-1}}.
\end{aligned}$$

From the algorithm, $p_{\Psi_{\alpha-1}} = p_{\Phi_{\alpha-1}}$. Hence,

$$|q_{\Theta_{\alpha-1}} - p_{\Theta_{\alpha-1}}| + |q_{\Theta_\alpha} - q_{\Theta_{\alpha-1}}| \geq q_{\Psi_\alpha} - p_{\Phi_{\alpha-1}}.$$

The rest of the proof for this case is identical to the proof of Case C.

∎

ACKNOWLEDGMENT

We would like to thank P. Denning, D. Ferrari, M. Katevenis, J. Ousterhout, R. Sherburne, and A. Smith for their useful suggestions on improving this paper and D. Patterson for his help with the development of some of the initial RISC analysis tools.

REFERENCES

[1] L. A. Belady, "A study of replacement algorithms for a virtual storage computer," *IBM Syst. J.*, vol. 5, no. 2, pp. 78–101, 1966.
[2] R. Campbell, "A C compiler for RISC," M.S. rep., Univ. California, Berkeley, Dec. 1980.
[3] P. J. Denning, private communication, May 1982.
[4] *VAX11 Architecture Handbook*, Digital Equipment Corp., 1979.
[5] D. Halbert and P. Kessler, "Windows of overlapping register frames," in *CS292R Final Project Reports* (unpublished), Univ. California, Berkeley, June 1980, pp. 82–100.
[6] S. C. Johnson, "A portable compiler: Theory and practice," in *Proc. 5th ACM Symp. Principles of Programming Languages*, Jan. 1978, pp. 97–104.
[7] B. W. Kernighan and D. M. Ritchie, *The C Programming Language*. Englewood Cliffs, NJ: Prentice-Hall, 1978.
[8] D. A. Patterson and C. H. Séquin, "RISC I: A reduced instruction set VLSI computer," in *Proc. 8th Annu. Symp. Comput. Architecture*, Minneapolis, MN, May 1981, pp. 443–457.
[9] ——, "A VLSI RISC," *Computer*, vol. 15, pp. 8–21, Sept. 1982.
[10] A. J. Smith, "Cache memories," *Comput. Surveys*, vol. 14, pp. 473–530, Sept. 1982.
[11] Y. Tamir, "Simulation and performance evaluation of the RISC architecture," Electron. Res. Lab., Univ. California, Berkeley, Memo. UCB/ERL, M81/17, Mar. 1981.

Yuval Tamir (S'78) received the B.S.E.E. degree ("with highest distinction") from the University of Iowa, Iowa City, in 1979 and the M.S. degree in electrical engineering and computer science from the University of California, Berkeley, in 1981.

Since 1979 he has been a Research Assistant in the Electronics Research Laboratory at U.C. Berkeley where he is currently working on his Ph.D. dissertation. His research interests are fault-tolerant computing, computer architecture, and distributed systems.

Mr. Tamir is a student member of the IEEE Computer Society and the Association for Computing Machinery.

Carlo H. Séquin (M'71–SM'80–F'82) received the Ph.D. degree in experimental physics from the University of Basel, Basel, Switzerland, in 1969.

In 1969–1970 he performed postdoctoral work at the Institute of Applied Physics, University of Basel, which concerned interface physics of MOS transistors and problems of applied electronics in the field of cybernetic models. From 1970 to 1976 he worked at Bell Laboratories, Murray Hill, NJ, in the MOS Integrated Circuit Laboratory on the design and investigation of charge-coupled devices for imaging and signal processing applications. He spent 1976–1977 on leave of absence with the University of California, Berkeley, where he lectured on integrated circuits, logic design, and microprocessors. In 1977 he joined the faculty in the Department of Electrical Engineering and Computer Sciences, where he is Professor of Computer Science. Since 1980 he has headed the CS Division as Associate Chairman for Computer Sciences. His research interests lie in the field of computer architecture and design tools for very large scale integrated systems. In particular, his research concerns multimicroprocessor computer networks, the mutual influence of advanced computer architectures and modern VLSI technology, and the implementation of special functions in silicon. Since 1977 he has been teaching courses in structured MOS-LSI design. He is an author of the first book on charge-transfer devices, and has written many papers in that field.

Dr. Séquin is a member of the Association for Computing Machinery and the Swiss Physical Society.

Analyzing Multiple Register Sets

Charles Y. Hitchcock III and H. M. Brinkley Sprunt
Department of Electrical and Computer Engineering
Carnegie-Mellon University
Pittsburgh, PA 15213

Abstract

This paper summarizes results from recent experiments which quantify the performance effects of multiple register sets on computer architectures[1]. These experiments started with the simulation of procedure-intensive benchmarks on three different computer architectures which had various register set schemes added to them. The results from these simulations were dramatic, yet they were difficult to interpret since many interacting factors were involved. This led to a more focussed study to characterize the parameter passing and procedure context switching costs of various register set schemes. The basic hypothesis behind this work, that the performance gains from multiple register sets are independent of instruction set complexity, is supported by the results. Also of interest is the perspective this study gives on the interactions between parameter passing, procedure state saving, and machine architecture.

Introduction

As members of the Archons project [6] at CMU, we are interested in decentralized resource management and are considering computer architectures to "support" such a system. The RISC (Reduced Instruction Set Computer) advocates are prescribing minimalist architectures tied to single-cycle implementations to obtain the high performance that we desire. This stands in stark contrast to our CISC (Complex Instruction Set Computer) tendency to migrate complex functions, ones that might perform interprocess communication or resource allocation, into an architecture. Naturally, we examined the RISC literature to see what we might gain from such an approach.

The many papers about the RISC I[2] project at Berkeley have claimed impressive performance for this single-chip processor. In spite of these attractive results, we were unable to see the RISC I as constituting proof that RISC machines are superior. The results were inconclusive because the RISC I's performance is not solely determined by its instruction set, but is also aided by a powerful scheme of multiple register sets (MRSs).

Most computer architectures that employ general purpose registers have their single logical register set implemented as a single physical register set (SRS). Yet for many years designers have made computers that physically contain multiple register sets (MRSs). These MRSs were usually used to retain the state of multiple processes. For example, up to 32 processes' states could be maintained in the SDS Sigma 7 computer (circa 1966). Such an MRS scheme can, however, be used to cache the procedure state of a single process. Rather than having to save the local variables, temporary values, and parameters contained in the register set during a procedure call, a new, empty register set is provided. Procedure calls and returns become largely a matter of changing a pointer which determines the active physical register set. Furthermore, these register sets can overlap so that parameters can be passed between procedures without the cost of moving them to and from memory. Such overlapping was done on the BELLMAC-8, although its "registers" are mapped into main memory. A detailed description of an overlapping register set (ORS) scheme is found in [7], with a designer's overview in [4].

It was impossible to draw conclusions about the effects of the RISC I's "reduced" nature since its ORS performance was not factored out of its reported results. This lack of differentiation moved us to do our own experiments to calibrate the effects that ORS and MRS schemes can have on a computer architecture. It was believed that such effects would be completely orthogonal to an architecture's instruction set complexity. A previous paper [1] outlined the goals of this study, along with those of a complementary set of experiments. [2] The results from this MRS exploration [5] are summarized here.

---

[1] This research is sponsored in part by the Department of the Army under contract DAA B07-82-C-J164

[2] In this paper, the term *RISC* always refers to a computer design philosophy, while *RISC I* refers to a particular research project.

Reprinted from *The Proceedings of the 12th Annual International Symposium on Computer Architecture*, 1985, pages 55-63. Copyright ©1985 by The Institute of Electrical and Electronics Engineers, Inc.

EH0251-9/86/0000/0168$01.00 © 1985 IEEE

Ideally, the goal of this study would have been to answer the question "What are the effects and costs involved in incorporating multiple register sets in a computer architecture?" This question could be broken down into these five issues:

1. In what ways is an architecture's performance changed by incorporating multiple register sets?

2. What changes are necessary to a machine's instruction set and internal structures to support such register sets?

3. How do multiple register sets affect the task of writing a compiler for an architecture?

4. What is the impact of multiple register sets on a machine which needs quick context swaps?

5. How does the choice of high-level language or application affect the usefulness of multiple register sets?

While we hoped to explore these and other considerations, our focus was on gauging the effects that MRSs can have on an architecture's performance experimentally, the first issue listed above. In implementing our experiments, we were forced to think about and make decisions involving the other four issues.

Experimental Methodology

To establish the performance effects of MRSs, we decided to run a series of simulations. First, we would simulate benchmarks on an existing machine that has a single set of general purpose registers. We would then alter its architecture to include eight register sets and repeat the simulations. Any difference observed would be attributable to the MRSs. Similarly, we could alter the architecture to include an ORS scheme and again observe the effects.

The key metric used in this study is processor-memory traffic, a metric indicative of an architecture's performance and independent of any particular implementation. Processor-memory traffic is an especially good metric for studying MRSs. This is because the use of MRS is predicated on reducing the amount of data traffic produced by procedure calls, which is often the most costly high-level language operation in terms of memory

references. [7] It is also worth noting that processor-memory traffic does accurately characterize the performance of machines that saturate their memory busses, as does the RISC I.

Note that this study only claims to make valid intra-machine comparisons. These experiments were designed to vary only register structures within an architecture so as to expose the effects of MRSs. We believe that the performance differences produced by altered register structures can largely be characterized by our chosen metrics. The differences between architectures cannot be expressed so simply. As such, drawing conclusions by comparing results from different architectures is not valid. We added eight register sets to the CISC machines since the RISC I had eight register sets. This was done only to allow the *trends* between machines to be comparable, not to make cross-architecture comparisons valid.

Three variations of simulators were created for three different architectures. MRSs and ORSs were "added" to the DEC VAX/11 and the Motorola 68000, both originally SRS machines. The third architecture, RISC I, already had these features. Two additional RISC I's were created, one with multiple non-overlapping register sets and one with only a single register set. These three architectures were chosen because they all use general-purpose registers, both RISC and CISC were represented, and reasonable software support was available for each. Furthermore, the two CISCs are commercial successes and were the subjects of previous RISC studies.

Of course, programs were needed to exercise these simulators. The obvious source for such programs was Berkeley. They had gathered a number of C benchmarks for their RISC I studies and some of these were purposefully procedure-intensive so as to demonstrate the power of ORSs. Since ORS, MRS, and SRS variations of the same machine should perform identically when not executing procedure calls, we concentrated on highly-recursive benchmarks hoping that these would expose the effects of MRSs most dramatically. If so, then they would provide a good means of testing the hypothesis that MRS performance benefits are orthogonal to instruction set complexity. It should be emphasized, however, that the benchmarks we used are not necessarily representative of any "real" computing environment but are merely used to examine the effects of MRSs.

Most of the modifications necessary to conduct our experiments were hardware changes; however, it was also necessary in some cases to modify the software. The SRS and MRS variations of the architectures examined in this study can run the same code. The actual operations performed during the call and return instruction sequences of the MRS machines do change to make use of the MRSs, but the instruction sequence itself is unaltered. The code for the ORS machines, however, does need to be modified. This is because the parameters are passed by a different mechanism, via overlapped registers instead of a memory stack. While reworking a compiler could produce the desired result, it was much easier for us to change the assembly code by hand. Altering it in a rote fashion was simple since only the parameter-passing code had to be changed. Care was taken not to introduce any special optimizations in the process. If an aspect of the alteration was in doubt, the result was modelled as closely as possible to the RISC I code, which was compiled and optimized by software.

Results and Interpretation

The results from these experiments support the hypothesis that the performance effects of multiple register sets are orthogonal to the complexity of an architecture's instruction set. The MRS and ORS versions of the VAX and the 68000 both show decreases in processor-memory traffic when compared to the standard versions of these architectures, as seen in Figures 1 and 2. Similarly, the SRS version of RISC I requires many more memory reads and writes than does the standard RISC I with overlapped register sets (see Figure 3). The procedure intensive benchmarks Towers of Hanoi, Fibonnacci, and Ackermann probably do not represent any typical application environment, but they do show the effects of the multiple and overlapped register set mechanisms.

Though each of these architectures exhibits a decrease in processor-memory traffic from the SRS to ORS versions, the average decrease is greatest for RISC I (68% as compared to 53% for the 68000 and 45% for the VAX). The RISC I shows a large decrease partly because the same overflow/underflow scheme used by the standard ORS RISC I is also used for both the MRS and SRS versions. This scheme always saves/restores 16 registers (10 local and 6 overlap) on every overflow/underflow regardless of whether these registers are being used or not. The reason for using this scheme was to make the MRS and SRS versions as close to the original architecture as possible. The scheme's effect is most dramatic when only one register set is available since every call or return must save or restore 16 registers, as in the SRS version. A more reasonable save/restore scheme is used by both the 68000 and the VAX in which each procedure has a mask specifying the registers that the procedure will modify. Only the specified registers are saved and restored on procedure boundaries. Though the mask register scheme is not optimal, it is much more efficient for procedures which do not use many registers.

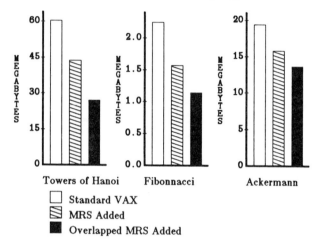

Figure 1: Total processor-memory traffic for benchmarks on the standard VAX and two modified VAXes, one with multiple register sets and one with overlapping multiple register sets.

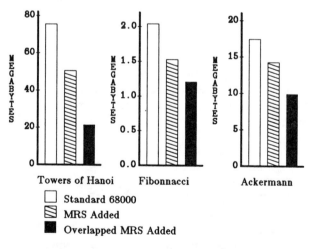

Figure 2: Total processor-memory traffic for benchmarks on the standard 68000 and two modified 68000's, one with multiple register sets and one with overlapping multiple register sets.

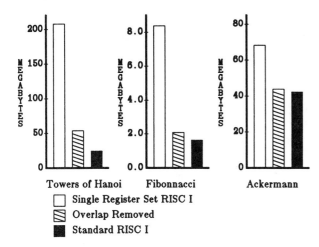

Figure 3: Total processor-memory traffic for benchmarks on the standard RISC I and two modified RISC I's, one with no overlap between register sets and one with only one register set.

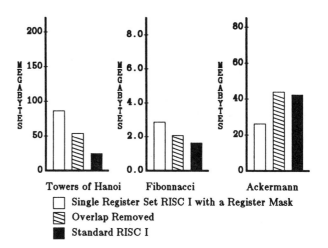

Figure 4: Total processor-memory traffic for benchmarks on the standard RISC I and two modified RISC I's, one with no overlap between register sets and one with a single register set which makes use of a register mask to indicate which registers should be saved and restored on procedure calls and returns.

To examine further the effect of the register saving/restoring scheme a register mask scheme similar to those of the VAX and 68000 was added to the SRS version of the RISC I. This addition does increase the complexity of the RISC I but it is a reasonable change since the required chip area would be made available by reducing the number of register sets from eight to one. The results from this new simulator are presented in Figure 4. As expected, the amount of processor-memory traffic for the register mask SRS versions dropped significantly. The most interesting result is that the register mask SRS RISC I performs better than the standard ORS RISC I on Ackerman's function. This behavior is counter-intuitive for three reasons:

1. SRS versions of an architecture typically do not perform better than ORS versions.

2. Ackermann's function performs better on the register mask SRS version of RISC I while Hanoi and Fibonnacci do not.

3. The VAX and the 68000 do not show similar behavior even though they use register mask schemes.

A better understanding of these benchmarks and the multiple register set mechanisms is needed to explain this seemingly anomalous behavior.

Each of these benchmarks are similar in that they perform a lot of procedure calls but they are very different in the number of procedure calls per overflow of the register file. For the standard ORS RISC I with eight overlapping register sets, the number of calls per overflow is 2 for Ackermann, 22 for Fibonnacci, and 65 for Hanoi. RISC I's register file overflows very often while executing Ackermann's function whereas overflows are rare for Fibonnacci and Hanoi. It is this difference in the number of calls per overflow that accounts for the apparent discrepancy in the performance of the register mask SRS RISC I on these benchmarks.

The register mask SRS RISC I performs better than the standard ORS RISC I on Ackermann's function because the register mask SRS version saves and restores less state than the standard ORS version does. The difference between the SRS versions of RISC I in Figures 3 and 4 is solely attributable to the processor-memory traffic overhead due state saving and restoring on register file overflows. Using the standard state saving/restoring scheme for the SRS RISC I is very wasteful since overflows occur on every procedure call. The register mask scheme for the SRS RISC I is not as wasteful; it decreases the processor memory traffic for each benchmark by better than 50%.

This explanation of the seemingly anomalous behavior reminds us that two performance issues are being tested here: parameter passing efficiency and state saving and restoring efficiency. To properly evaluate test these MRS mechanisms, these performance factors should not be mixed together as they are in these benchmarks. Doing so made interpreting our benchmark results difficult for several reasons:

- While the benchmarks were picked to display the effects of MRSs, it is difficult to attribute performance differences to actual mechanism differences. Determining when an observed difference is due to parameter passing changes or to a new overflow-handling strategy requires detailed examination of instruction count summaries and memory traffic counts. The amount of non-procedure call activity that these benchmarks perform further obfuscates the results.

- Performance predictions are difficult to generalize or adapt for a specific application. If a particular application generally uses many more parameters or exhibits a fairly unusual call/return profile, then it is not obvious how the performance of any of these schemes would change. The benchmark results are not helpful in this regard. While they might show performance trends, they can not be used to analyze performance for a real workload.

- Even small changes made to the parameter passing or call instruction mechanisms can dramatically affect the benchmark results. Trying a whole spectrum of mechanism variations would be appealing if it were not for the limited result interpretation due to the factors mentioned.

- The benchmarks do not represent any realistic computing environment. Ackermann's function was used only to show procedure call performance since this operation dominates this program's execution. Yet, its worth for showing the performance of an MRS architecture is dubious since its call per overflow rate is so low.

In considering these factors, a more narrow analysis of the mechanisms involved provides more easily interpreted results. Similarly, determining memory traffic as a function of the architecture and environment-related factors, such as the average number of parameters to be passed, yields more general results.

The original interest of this study was the performance of various parameter passing schemes and the efficiency of using MRSs. By coding the call/return sequences of hypothetical or real architectures, it is possible to generate equations that describe the performance of various parameter passing schemes in terms of instruction and data traffic. By properly parameterizing these equations, a general gauge of performance is obtained. The next section examines the creation and use of equations to compare parameter passing schemes, while the one following it evaluates different state saving strategies.

Call Sequence Costs

In order to analyze the costs involved in a call/return sequence, we first list the operations that are involved. The actions that characterize a call/return sequence are:

1. Prepare any parameters for passing: This code, if necessary, would move any parameters into position, onto a parameter passing stack for instance. Often these moves can be optimized away since some parameters are calculated into position before the call.

2. Call the procedure: This instruction places the processor in a new procedure context. We are not concerned with the method of creating a new (empty) procedure context here. (Explicit calculations that compare mechanisms that prepare a new procedure context are developed in the next section.) The saving of registers in use, and similar state preserving functions, are presumed to be free.

3. Prepare parameters for use by procedure: Sometimes parameters are moved into the CPU before they are used in a calculation. If this movement is done as part of a calculation which uses the parameter (i.e., is not done in a separate instruction), then this code is not explicitly present and, hence, does not add to the procedure call's overhead.

4. Prepare any result for return: This code is analogous to that for preparing a parameter to be passed.

5. Return from procedure: This instruction returns the processor to the caller's procedure context. As with the call instruction, the restoration of procedure state is assumed to be free.

6. Prepare the result for use: This code is analogous to that for preparing parameters for use.

We will examine an example of such code, and the equation that derives from it. The code that characterizes the RISC I's call/return sequence is:

a. add r0, rParam, rOverlap

b. call r15, destination

c. nop

** change to the called procedure context **

d. add r0, rOverlap, rUse

** body of called procedure is executed **

e. add r0, rResult, rOverlap

f. ret r31

g. nop

** change back to calling procedure context **

h. add rOverlap, r0, rUse

Each of the above operations is described below:

a. Move parameter to an overlap register, repeat as necessary for multiple parameters.

b. Branch to a new procedure, saving the old PC in register 15.

c. Insert a NOP if necessary (RISC I branching is delayed and often another instruction is placed here).

d. Move parameter into a register to be used, repeat for multiple parameters.

e. Move result to overlap register.

f. Return to calling the procedure, restoring the PC with register 31's value (the calling procedure's register 15).

g. Insert a NOP if necessary (RISC I branching is delayed and often another instruction is here).

h. Move result out of the overlap area.

Note that (a.) (d.) (e.) and (h.) can sometimes be optimized away.

By counting the instruction bytes for the above code, we calculate the call/return overhead for a highly unoptimized call with a single parameter which receives a single result. By generating equations which characterize number of parameters, whether there is a result, and the likelihood of optimizations, a far more general result is produced.

Total Memory Bytes Transferred:

$$= \text{Sum of instruction bytes from (a.) to (h.)}$$
$$= 4[N(PP + TP) + R(PR + TR) + CN + RN + 2]$$

where

N - number of parameters
PP - fraction of prepare parameter moves (a.)
CN - fraction of nop's following calls (c.)
TP - fraction of take parameter moves (d.)
R - fraction of returns that produce a result
PR - fraction of prepare result moves (e.)
RN - fraction of nop's following returns (g.)
TR - fraction of take result moves (h.)

To be of any specific use, actual values for these variables need to be found for the application code of interest. For this study, values were borrowed from existing analyses where possible (see [3] for a good summary). If unavailable, they were estimated based on samples of code. This was often the case since many code characteristics which are of interest when analyzing MRS machines, such as calls per overflow, have not commonly been measured. It should be stressed here that the values we used and the results from our equations are not meant to be definitive. They do, however, result from a process that can be adapted to known applications.

When analyzing the RISC I in this way, the considerations leading to its call/return overhead equation are few. This is largely due to its load/store ORS architecture and its 32 bit implementation. For a 68000 using a memory stack to pass parameters, many more complications arise:

- Traffic created by data reads and writes needs to be counted.

- Different addressing modes can be used which vary the instruction size.

- Parameters can vary in size (byte, halfword, word).

- The sources and destinations of the parameters are not always registers, as is almost always the case with the RISC I.

This can lead to an unmanageable proliferation of variables. Rather than attempt to deal with this wealth of information for the general case, we constrained our call/return example to the passing of 32-bit values which are found in registers.

Equations and values were generated for four styles of RISC I. The first was the standard ORS RISC I which passes its parameters in its overlapping registers. Since the MRS and SRS versions of the RISC I execute the same call/return sequence, passing parameters on a stack in memory, one equation characterizes both of them. Two other variations of parameter passing were tried. One added push and pop instructions to the RISC I architecture and used these for passing parameters on a memory stack. Where the SRS RISC I required two instructions to perform a push (a subtract followed by a store), this version was assumed to require only one. The last version passed parameters in the RISC I's global registers. These physical registers exist in the logical register address space of every procedure. A parameter can be placed into a global register, a call instruction executed, and the parameter will be found in the same global register unchanged. This eliminates the need to move a parameter on and off a stack in memory.

Equations and values were also generated for three 68000 versions (ORS, SRS using global registers, and SRS using a memory stack) as well as three VAX versions (ORS, SRS using global registers, and SRS using a memory stack). The cost of each of these call/return sequences, in terms of total memory bytes transferred, are plotted in Figures 5, 6, and 7. Since all three architectures use the same code for both SRS and non-overlapping MRS versions, the SRS results presented also apply to MRS machines.

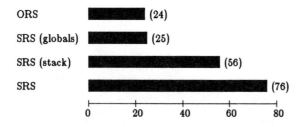

Figure 5: Total memory bytes transferred for a call/return sequence on four variations of RISC I.

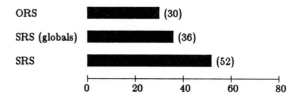

Figure 6: Total memory bytes transferred for a call/return sequence on three variations of 68000.

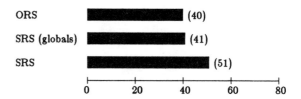

Figure 7: Total memory bytes transferred for a call/return sequence on three variations of VAX.

The bar graphs above show a much greater variation among the RISC I machines than among the VAX machines, with the 68000 variations somewhere in between. This is due to three factors.

1. The VAX has very compact push and pop register instructions which account for only 6 bytes of traffic apiece. This is not much more than the register-to-register moves that they replace (which create 3 bytes of traffic apiece) and is half the size of RISC I's synthesized push and pop.

2. The procedure calling convention used by our VAX C compiler returns results in register 0. This feature was retained, and as such register 0 acts as a global register for return values. This means that the ORS and SRS versions are identical for their return sequences.

3. The VAX architecture maintains an elaborate stack structure. In keeping with our goal of changing an architecture as little as possible for these experiments, this stack mechanism was kept. The processor-memory traffic overhead imposed as a result constitute roughly half of the totals in Figure 7.

The 68000, in fact, shares the first two factors with

the VAX, accounting in part for its intermediate role.

State Saving Costs

This section discusses the costs involved in saving and restoring procedure state when an overflow or underflow of a processor's register file occurs. As with analyzing the costs involved to pass parameters between procedures, a general analysis of the costs associated with procedure state saving could be quite complex. The actual operations involved are simple: save the previous procedure state on an overflow and restore state on an underflow. However, the methods used can be very elaborate.

The factors that affect the cost of procedure state saving and restoring are:

- Frequency of state saving: This varies with the number of register sets available and the call/return profile of the application program. More register sets reduce the frequency of state saving. A call/return profile which exhibits a high degree of call locality will overflow the register file less often than a profile with frequent large changes in call depth.

- Amount of state to be saved: This depends on the number of registers available in each register set, how the application program uses those registers, and how the state to be saved is specified (whether the entire state is always saved, or whether a mask feature is provided to save only the state that might be changed).

- Complexity of the instructions used to save and restore state: This ranges from having no special state saving mechanisms to very elaborate and complex mechanisms. Processors without special instructions to handle state saving (like RISC I) must perform this function using other primitive instructions. A microcoded mechanism, like the VAX's, is very complex but eliminates the need for multiple state saving instructions.

Though many things affect the efficiency of state saving and restoring, some distinct methods exist to reduce the amount of state that must be saved.

- Provide multiple register sets which reduce the frequency of register file overflows.

- Provide special instructions to save and restore state. This reduces the processor-memory traffic cost by eliminating the need for many primitive instructions to do the same jobs.

- Provide methods to specify which state should not be lost (using register masks, for example).

- Use smart register allocation strategies and other optimization strategies to avoid the necessity of saving some state.

We have already seen an example of the difference a smart state saving algorithm can make with the two versions of the SRS RISC I. The cost in terms of processor-memory traffic of an overflow on the original ORS RISC I is approximately 188 bytes (31 instructions, 16 of which are stores). This figure is independent of the number of registers that actually need to be saved. The RISC I saves 16 registers whenever it overflows. A more elaborate scheme which stores the subset of registers that are actually being used would involve iterative testing. Such testing, with the RISC I's primitive instruction set, would greatly increase the cost of an overflow.

The register mask RISC I machine, however, is assumed to be microcoded. As such it requires no instruction bytes and it has a processor-memory traffic cost of 4 bytes times the number of registers saved (a total of 24 bytes for Ackermann and Fibonnacci and 32 bytes for Hanoi). This much lower cost accounts for its superior performance on Ackermann which has a very high overflow rate.

Other Issues

We have discussed, in this paper, the performance gains due to MRSs, the machine changes required to support MRSs, and how MRSs affect compiled code. This discussion leaves points 4 and 5, as outlined earlier, unexplored. An examination of these remaining points, context swap performance and suitability to various high-level languages, can be found in [5] as well as further detail on all issues described in this paper.

Conclusion

The results presented in this paper support the hypothesis that performance gains due to multiple register sets are independent of instruction set complexity. The magnitude of such gains is determined by the register structure implemented, the mechanisms used to manage that structure, and the calls per overflow rate which is dependent on the usage environment of the machine. All three of these factors were explored and discussed in this paper. The results from this paper do not relieve a computer designer from running his own simulations, or creating his own equations, but they do provide insight into what may be expected from incorporating multiple register sets.

Acknowledgements

We would like to thank Prof. E. Douglas Jensen and Robert P. Colwell for sharing with us their insights on this topic. We would also like to that the RISC I creators at the University of California at Berkeley for sharing their RISC I software with us.

References

1. Robert P. Colwell, Charles Y. Hitchcock III, and E. Douglas Jensen. "Peering Through the RISC/CISC Fog: An Outline of Research". *Computer Architecture News 11*, 1 (March 1983), 44-50.

2. Robert P. Colwell. The Performance Effects of Functional Migration and Architectural Complexity in Object-Oriented Systems. PhD thesis, Carnegie-Mellon University. Expected completion in May, 1985.

3. Reinhold P. Weicker. "Dhrystone: A Synthetic Systems Programming Benchmark". *Communications of the ACM 27*, 10 (October 1984), 1013-1030.

4. Daniel C. Halbert and Peter B. Kessler. Windows of Overlapping Register Frames. CS292R Final Reports, University of California, Berkeley, June 9, 1980.

5. Charles Y. Hitchcock III and H. M. Brinkley Sprunt. An Evaluation of Multiple Register Sets. Carnegie-Mellon University, May, 1985. To be published.

6. E. Douglas Jensen. The Archons Project: An Overview. Proceedings of the International Symposium on Synchronization, Control, and Communication in Distributed Systems, 1983. Academic Press.

7. David A. Patterson and Carlo H. Sequin. "A VLSI RISC". *Computer 15*, 9 (September 1982), 8-21.

Section 4: RISC Compilers

4.1 Background

One of the major goals of the RISC approach is to achieve high performance. Success depends not only on the organization and architecture of the processor but on the effectiveness of the compiler. In most cases, programmers (even systems programmers) use high-level languages. Thus the performance of a program will depend critically on how well it has been compiled into the target machine language.

The importance of the compiler for performance is true on any machine, but is especially significant on RISC machines. Most of the RISC designers on the various projects report that (1) they expect that more effective compilers can be built for RISC as opposed to CISC machines and (2) the success of their design depends on the development of a good RISC compiler.

The reasoning behind the first point above is this: Because RISC instructions are primitive, a compiler can use them more efficiently to generate optimized code. In contrast, CISC instructions are difficult to use effectively because the compiler is limited to dealing with more aggregated, less primitive building blocks. This hinders the compiler in performing such tasks as efficient register allocation.

The evidence to date suggests that RISC compilers, on average, will expend more compile-time effort than CISC compilers in an attempt to optimize the target code. The expected payoff, of course, is enhanced run-time performance.

The articles in this section discuss the RISC compilers used on three commercially available machines. It can be seen that two concerns are of major importance in all of these efforts: optimized register usage and efficient exploitation of pipelining. The topic of register usage was examined in detail in Section 3. To provide some context for this section, the concept of instruction pipelining is discussed next.

4.2 Instruction Pipelining

As computer systems evolve, greater performance can be achieved by taking advantage of improvements in technology, such as faster circuitry. In addition, organizational enhancements to the CPU can improve performance. Two examples of this are the use of multiple registers rather than a single accumulator and the use of a cache memory. Another organizational approach, which is quite common, is instruction pipelining.

4.2.1 Pipelining Strategy

Instruction pipelining is similar to the use of an assembly line in a manufacturing plant. An assembly line takes advantage of the fact that a product goes through various stages of production. By laying the production process out in an assembly line, products at various stages can be worked on simultaneously. This process is also referred to as *pipelining*, because, as in a pipeline, new inputs are accepted at one end before previously accepted inputs appear as outputs at the other end.

To apply this concept to instruction execution, we must recognize that, in fact, an instruction has a number of stages. Figure 1-1, for example, breaks the instruction cycle up into eight tasks, which occur in sequence. Clearly, there should be some opportunity for pipelining.

As a simple approach, consider subdividing instruction processing into two stages: fetch instruction and execute instruction. There are times during the execution of an instruction when main memory is not being accessed. This time could be used to fetch the next instruction in parallel with the execution of the current one. Figure 4-1a depicts this approach. The pipeline has two independent stages. The first stage fetches an instruction and buffers it. When the second stage is free, the first stage passes the buffered instruction to the second stage. While the second stage is executing the instruction, the first stage takes advantage of any unused memory cycles to fetch and buffer the next instruction. This is called *instruction prefetch* or *fetch overlap*.

It should be clear that this process will speed up instruction execution. If the fetch and instruction stages were of equal duration, the instruction cycle time would be halved. However, if we look more closely at this pipeline (Figure 4-1b), we will see that this doubling of execution rate is unlikely for two reasons:

1. The execution time will generally be longer than the fetch time. Execution will involve reading and storing operands and the performance of some operation. Thus the fetch stage may have to wait for some time before it can empty its buffer.

2. A conditional branch instruction makes the address of the next instruction to be fetched unknown. Thus the fetch stage must wait until it receives the next instruction address from the execute stage. The execute stage may then have to wait while the next instruction is fetched.

EH0251-9/86/0000/0177$01.00 © 1986 IEEE

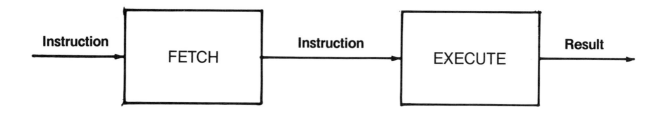

(a) Simplified View

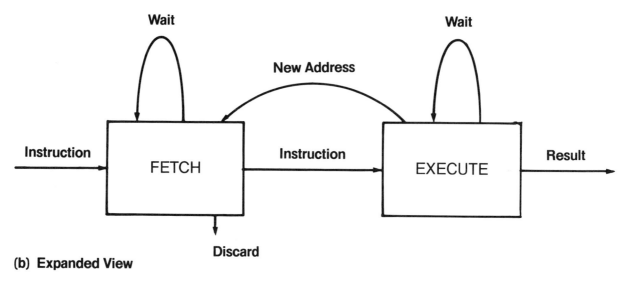

(b) Expanded View

Figure 4.1:   Two-Stage Instruction Pipeline

The time loss from the second reason can be reduced by guessing. A simple rule is the following: When a conditional branch instruction is passed on from the fetch to the execute stage, the fetch stage fetches the next instruction in memory after the branch instruction. Then, if the branch is not taken, no time is lost. If the branch is taken, the fetched instruction must be discarded and a new instruction fetched.

While these factors reduce the potential effectiveness of the two-stage pipeline, some speedup occurs. To gain further speedup, the pipeline must have more stages. Let us consider the following decomposition of the instruction processing.

- *Fetch Instruction (FI):* Read the next expected instruction into a buffer.

- *Decode Instruction (DI):* Determine the opcode and the operand specifiers.

- *Calculate Operands (CO):* Calculate the effective address of each source operand. This may involve displacement, register indirect, indirect, or other forms of address calculation.

- *Fetch Operands (FO):* Fetch each operand from memory. Operands in registers need not be fetched.

- *Execute Instruction (EI):* Perform the indicated operation and store the result, if any, in the specified destination operand location.

With this decomposition, the various stages will be of more nearly equal duration. For the sake of illustration, let us assume equal duration and assume that only one stage that accesses memory may be active at a time. Then, Figure 4-2 illustrates that a five-stage pipeline can reduce the execution time for four instructions from 20 time units to 13 time units. Note that the FI stage always involves a memory access. The FO and EI stages may or may not involve memory access, but the diagram is based on the assumption that they do.

Again, several factors serve to reduce the performance enhancement. If the five stages are not of equal length, there will be some waiting involved at various pipeline stages, as discussed before. A conditional branch instruction can invalidate several instruction fetches. A similar unpredictable event is an interrupt. Figure 4-3 indicates the logic needed for pipelining to account for branches and interrupts.

Other problems arise that did not appear in our simple two-stage organization. The CO stage may depend on the

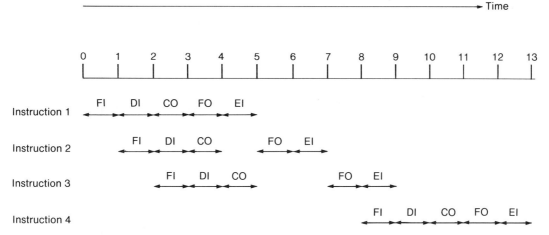

Figure 4.2:   Timing Diagram for Pipelined Operation

contents of a register that could be altered by a previous instruction still in the pipeline. Other such register and memory conflicts could occur. The system must contain logic to account for this type of conflict.

The system should also contain additional logic to improve pipeline efficiency. For example, if an EI stage is not going to access memory, then another memory-accessing stage in another instruction can be performed in parallel.

From the preceding discussion, it might appear that the greater the number of stages in the pipeline, the faster the execution rate. However, two factors work against this conclusion:

1. At each stage of the pipeline, there is some overhead involved in moving data from buffer to buffer and in performing various preparation and delivery functions. This overhead can appreciably lengthen the total execution time of a single instruction, which can produce significant delays when the ideal pipeline pattern is not followed either through branching or memory access dependencies.

2. The amount of control logic required to handle memory and register dependencies and to optimize the use of the pipeline increases enormously with the number of stages. This can lead to a situation where the control logic controlling the gating between stages is more complex than the stages being controlled.

Thus instruction pipelining is a powerful technique for enhancing performance but requires careful design to achieve optimum results with reasonable complexity.

4.2.2 Dealing with Branches

One of the major problems in designing an instruction pipeline is assuring a steady flow of instructions to the initial stages of the pipeline. The primary impediment, as we have seen, is the conditional branch instruction. Until the instruc-

tion is actually executed, it is impossible to determine whether the branch will be taken or not.

In what follows, we briefly summarize some of the more common approaches to be taken for dealing with branches.

- *Multiple Streams:* A simple pipeline suffers a penalty for a branch instruction because it must choose one of two instructions to fetch next and may choose erroneously. A brute-force approach is to allow the pipeline to fetch both instructions, making use of multiple streams. One problem with this approach is that additional branch instructions may enter the pipeline (either stream) before the original branch decision is resolved. These instructions need their own multiple streams beyond what is supported in the hardware.

- *Prefetch Branch Target:* When a conditional branch is recognized, the target of the branch is prefetched, in addition to the instruction following the branch. This target is then saved until the branch instruction is executed. If the branch is taken, we have already prefetched the target.

- *Branch Prediction:* Various techniques can be used to predict whether a branch will be taken. These can be based on historical analysis of past executions (e.g., by opcode) or on some dynamic measure of the recent frequency of branching.

- *Delayed Branch:* It is possible to improve pipeline performance by automatically rearranging instructions within a program so that branch instructions occur later than actually desired.

The first three approaches are built into the hardware and are exercised at run time. The last approach listed above is performed at compile time and is used in most of the RISC compilers. This technique was introduced in some of the articles in section 2 and is further explored by the articles in this section.

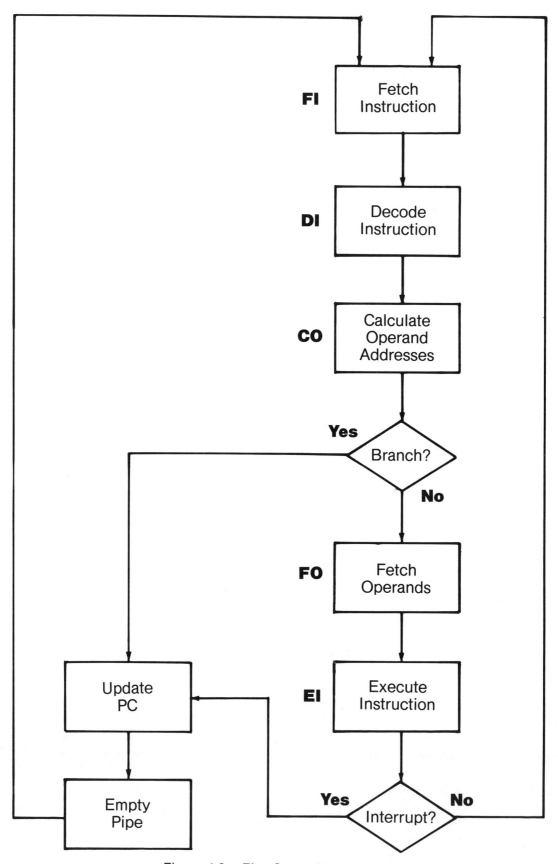

Figure 4.3: Five-Stage CPU Pipeline

4.3 Article Summary

The first article, by Coutant et al., presents the family of compilers developed for the new RISC-based Hewlett-Packard computers. The paper provides considerable detail on the optimization techniques employed. It also examines RISC-related design issues and explains how these have been addressed by the compiling system.

The article by Hopkins describes the compiler for the IBM PC RT. The most important optimizations performed by this compiler are moving code out of loops, elimination of redundant computations, and register allocation. Examples of each are given.

Finally, "Engineering a RISC Compiler System" examines the compiler suite for the product from MIPS Computer Systems, which is based on the Stanford MIPS project. Pipeline-optimization and register-allocation techniques are described.

COMPILERS FOR THE NEW GENERATION OF HEWLETT-PACKARD COMPUTERS

Deborah S. Coutant, Carol L. Hammond, and Jon W. Kelly
Hewlett-Packard
1501 Page Mill Road
Palo Alto, CA 94304

WITH THE ADVENT of any new architecture, compilers must be developed to provide high-level language interfaces to the new machine. Compilers are particularly important to the reduced-complexity, high-precision architecture currently being developed at Hewlett-Packard in the program that has been code-named Spectrum. The Spectrum program is implementing an architecture that is similar in philosophy to the class of architectures called RISCs (reduced instruction set computers).[1] The importance of compilers to the Spectrum program was recognized at its inception. From the early stages of the new architecture's development, software design engineers were involved in its specification.

The design process began with a set of objectives for the new architecture.[2] These included the following:

- It must support high-level language development of systems and applications software.
- It must be scalable across technologies and implementations.
- It must provide compatibility with previous systems.

These objectives were addressed with an architectural design that goes beyond RISC. The new architecture has the following features:

- There are many simple instructions, each of which executes in a single cycle.
- There are 32 high-speed general-purpose registers.
- There are separate data and instruction caches, which are exposed and can be managed explicitly by the operating system kernel.
- The pipeline has been made visible to allow the software to use cycles normally lost following branch and load instructions.
- Performance can be tuned to specific applications by adding specialized processors that interface with the central processor at the general-register, cache, or main memory levels.

The compiling system developed for this high-precision architecture* enables high-level language programs to use these features. This paper describes the compiling system design and shows how it addresses the specific requirements of the new architecture. First, the impact of high-level language issues on the early architectural design decisions is described. Next, the low-level structure of the compiling system is explained, with particular emphasis on areas that have received special attention for this architecture: program analysis, code generation, and optimization. The paper closes with a discussion of RISC-related issues and how they have been addressed in this compiling system.

Designing an Architecture for High-Level Languages

The design of the new architecture was undertaken by a team made up of design engineers specializing in hardware, computer architecture, operating systems, performance analysis, and compilers. It began with studies of computational behavior, leading to an initial design that provided efficient execution of frequently used instructions, and addressed the trade-offs involved in achieving additional functionality. The architectural design was scrutinized by software engineers as it was being developed, and their feedback helped to ensure that compilers and operating systems would be able to make effective use of the proposed features.

A primary objective in specifying the instruction set was to achieve a uniform execution time for all instructions. All instructions other than loads and branches were to be realizable in a single cycle. No instruction would be included that required a significantly longer cycle or significant additional hardware complexity. Restricting all instructions by these constraints simplifies the control of execution. In conventional microcoded architectures, many instructions pay an overhead because of the complexity of control required to execute the microcode. In reduced-complexity computers, no instruction pays a penalty for a more complicated operation. Functionality that is not available in a single-cycle instruction is achieved through multiple-instruction sequences or, optionally, with an additional processor.

As the hardware designers began their work on an early implementation of the new architecture, they were able to discover which instructions were costly to implement, required additional complexity not required by other instructions, or required long execution paths, which would increase the cycle time of the machine. These instructions were either removed, if the need for them was not great, or replaced with simpler instructions that provided the needed functionality. As the hardware engineers provided feedback about which instructions were too costly to include, the software engineers investigated alternate ways of achieving the same functionality.

For example, a proposed instruction that provided hardware support for a 2-bit Booth multiplication was not included because the additional performance it provided was not justified by its cost. Architecture and compiler engineers worked together to propose an alternative to this instruction. Similarly, several instructions that could be

---

*The term "high-precision architecture" is used because the instruction set for the new architecture was chosen on the basis of execution frequency as determined by extensive measurements across a variety of workloads.

Copyright 1986 Hewlett-Packard Company. © Reproduced with permission.

used directly to generate Boolean conditions were deleted when they were discovered to require a significantly longer cycle time. The same functionality was available with a more general two-instruction sequence, enabling all other operations to be executed faster.

The philosophy of reduced-complexity computers includes the notion that the frequent operations should be fast, possibly at the expense of less frequent operations. However, the cost of an infrequent operation should not be so great as to counterbalance the efficient execution of the simple operations. Each proposed change to the architectural specification was analyzed by the entire group to assess its impact on both software and hardware implementations. Hardware engineers analyzed the instruction set to ensure that no single instruction or set of instructions was causing performance and/or cost penalties for the entire architecture, and software engineers worked to ensure that all required functionality would be provided within performance goals. Compiler writers helped to define conditions for arithmetic, logical, and extract/deposit instructions, and to specify where carry/borrow bits would be used in arithmetic instructions.

As an example of such interaction, compiler writers helped to tune a conditional branch nullification scheme to provide for the most efficient execution of the most common branches. Branches are implemented such that an instruction immediately following the branch can be executed before the branch takes effect.[1] This allows the program to avoid losing a cycle if useful work is possible at that point. For conditional branches, the compiler may or may not be able to schedule an instruction in this slot that can be executed in both the taken-branch and non-taken-branch cases. For these branches, a nullification scheme was devised which allows an instruction to be executed only in the case of a taken branch for backward branches, and only in the case of a non-taken branch for forward branches. This scheme was chosen to enable all available cycles to be used in the most common cases. Backward conditional branches are most often used in a loop, and such branches will most often be taken, branching backwards a number of times before falling through at the end of the iteration. Thus, a nullification scheme that allows this extra cycle to be used in the taken-branch case causes this cycle to be used most often. Conversely, for forward branches, the nullification scheme was tuned to the non-taken-branch case. Fig. 1 shows the code generated for a simple code sequence, illustrating the conditional branch nullification scheme.

Very early in the development of the architectural specification, work was begun on a simulator for the new computer architecture and a prototype C compiler. Before the design was frozen, feedback was available about the ease with which high-level language constructs could be translated to the new instruction set. The early existence of a prototype compiler and simulator allowed operating system designers to begin their development early, and enabled them to provide better early feedback about their needs, from the architecture as well as the compiler.

At the same time, work was begun on optimization techniques for the new architecture. Segments of compiled code were hand-analyzed to uncover opportunities for optimization. These hand-optimized programs were used as a guideline for implementation and to provide a performance goal. Soon after the first prototype compiler was developed, a prototype register allocator and instruction scheduler were also implemented, providing valuable data for the optimizer and compiler designers.

Compiling to a Reduced Instruction Set

Compiling for a reduced-complexity computer is simplified in some aspects. With a limited set of instructions from which to choose, code generation can be straightforward. However, optimization is necessary to realize the full advantage of the architectural features. The new HP compiling system is designed to allow multiple languages to be implemented with language-specific compiler front ends. An optimization phase, common to all of the languages, provides efficient register use and pipeline scheduling, and eliminates unnecessary computations. With the elimination of complex instructions found in many architectures, the responsibility for generating the proper sequence of instructions for high-level language constructs falls to the compiler. Using the primitive instructions, the compiler can construct precisely the sequence required for the application.

For this class of computer, the software architecture plays a strong role in the performance of compiled code. There is no procedure call instruction, so the procedure calling sequence is tuned to handle simple cases, such as *leaf routines* (procedures that do not call any other procedures), without fixed expense, while still allowing the complexities of nested and recursive procedures. The saving of registers at procedure call and procedure entry is dependent on the register use of the individual procedure. A special calling convention has been adopted to allow some complex operations to be implemented in low-level routines known as *millicode*, which incur little overhead for saving registers and status.

Compiling to a reduced instruction set can be simplified because the compiler need not make complicated choices among a number of instructions that have similar effects. In the new architecture, all arithmetic, logical, or conditional instructions are register-based. All memory access is done through explicit loads and stores. Thus the compiler need not choose among instructions with a multitude of addressing modes. The compiler's task is further simplified by the fact that the instruction set has been constructed in

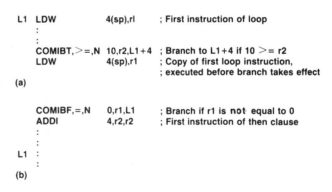

Fig. 1. *An illustration of the conditional branch nullification scheme. (a) The conditional branch at the end of a loop will often be followed by a copy of the first instruction of the loop. This instruction will only be executed if the branch is taken. (b) The forward conditional branch implementing an if statement will often be followed by the first instruction of the then clause, allowing use of this cycle without rearrangement of code. This instruction will only be executed if the branch is not taken.*

a very symmetrical manner. All instructions are the same length, and there are a limited number of instruction formats. In addition to simplifying the task of code generation, this makes the task of optimization easier as well. The optimizer need not handle transformations between instructions that have widely varying formats and addressing modes. The symmetry of the instruction set makes the tasks of replacing or deleting one or more instructions much easier.

Of course, the reduced instruction set computer, though simplifying some aspects of the compilation, requires more of the compilers in other areas. Having a large number of registers places the burden on the compilers to generate code that can use these registers efficiently. Other aspects of this new architecture also require the compilers to be more intelligent about code generation. For example, the instruction pipeline has become more exposed and, as mentioned earlier, the instruction following a branch may be executed before the branch takes effect. The compiler therefore needs to schedule such instructions effectively. In addition, loads from memory, which also require more than a single cycle, will interlock with the following instruction if the target register is used immediately. The compiler can increase execution speed by scheduling instructions to avoid these interlocks. The optimizer can also improve the effectiveness of a floating-point coprocessor by eliminating unnecessary coprocessor memory accesses and by reordering the floating-point instructions.

In addition to such optimizations, which are designed to exploit specific architectural features, conventional optimizations such as common subexpression elimination, loop invariant code motion, induction variable elaboration, and local constant propagation were also implemented.[3] These have a major impact on the performance of any computer. Such optimizations reduce the frequency of loads, stores, and multiplies, and allow the processor to be used with greater efficiency. However, the favorable cost/performance of the new HP architecture can be realized even without optimization.

The Compiler System

All of the compilers for the new architecture share a common overall design structure. This allows easy integration of common functional components including a symbolic debugger, a code generator, an optimizer, and a linker. This integration was achieved through detailed planning, which involved the participation of engineers across many language products. Of the new compilers, the Fortran/77, Pascal, and COBOL compilers will appear very familiar to some of our customers, since they were developed from existing products available on the HP 3000 family of computers. All of these compilers conform to HP standard specifications for their respective languages, and thus will provide smooth migration from the HP 1000, HP 3000, and HP 9000 product lines. The C compiler is a new product, and as mentioned earlier, was the compiler used to prototype the instruction set from its earliest design phase. The C compiler conforms to recognized industry standard language specifications. Other compilers under development will be integrated into this compiler system.

To achieve successful integration of compilers into a homogeneous compiling system it was necessary to define distinct processing phases and their exact interfaces in terms of data and control transfer. Each compiler begins execution through the *front end*. This includes the lexical,

syntactic, and semantic analysis prescribed by each language standard. The front ends generate intermediate codes from the source program, and pass these codes to the code generators. The intermediate codes are at a higher level than the machine code generated by a later phase, and allow a certain degree of machine abstraction within the front ends.

Two distinct code generators are used. They provide varying degrees of independence from the front ends. Each interfaces to the front ends through an intermediate code. One of these code generation techniques has already been used in two compiler products for the HP 3000. Fig. 2 shows the overall design of the compilers. Each phase of the compilation process is pictured as it relates to the other phases. The front ends are also responsible for generating data to be used later in the compilation process. For example, the front end generates data concerning source statements and the types, scopes and locations of procedure/function and variable names for later use by the symbolic debugger. In addition, the front end is responsible for the collection of data to be used by the optimizer.

These compilers can be supported by multiple operating systems. The object file format is compatible across operating systems.

Code Generation

The code generators emit machine code into a data structure called SLLIC (Spectrum low-level intermediate code). SLLIC also contains information regarding branches and their targets, and thus provides the foundation for the building of a control flow graph by the optimizer. The SLLIC data structure contains the machine instructions and the

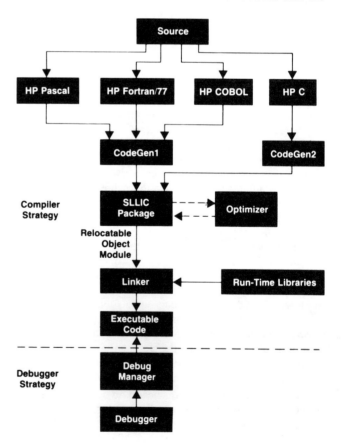

Fig. 2. *The compiler system for HP's new generation of high-precision-architecture computers.*

specifications for the run-time environment, including the program data space, the literal pool, and data initialization. SLLIC also holds the symbolic debug information generated by the front end, is the medium for later optimization, and is used to create the object file.

The reduced instruction set places some extra burden on the code generators when emitting code for high-level language constructs such as byte moves, decimal operations, and procedure calls. Since the instruction set contains no complex instructions to aid in the implementation of these constructs, the code generators are forced to use combinations of the simpler instructions to achieve the same functionality. However, even in complex instruction set architectures, complex case analysis is usually required to use the complex instructions correctly. Since there is little redundancy in the reduced instruction set, most often no choice of alternative instruction sequences exists. The optimizer is the best place for these code sequences to be streamlined, and because of this the overall compiler design is driven by optimization considerations. In particular, the optimizer places restrictions upon the code generators.

The first class of such restrictions involves the presentation of branch instructions. The optimizer requires that all branches initially be followed by a NOP (no operation) instruction. This restriction allows the optimizer to schedule instructions easily to minimize interlocks caused by data and register access. These NOPs are subsequently replaced with useful instructions, or eliminated.

The second class of restrictions concerns register use. Register allocation is performed within the optimizer. Rather than use the actual machine registers, the code generators use symbolic registers chosen from an infinite register set. These symbolic registers are mapped to the set of actual machine registers by the register allocator. Although register *allocation* is the traditional name for such an activity, register *assignment* is more accurate in this context. The code generators are also required to associate every syntactically equivalent expression in each procedure with a unique symbolic register number. The symbolic register number is used by the optimizer to associate each expression with a value number (each run-time *value* has a unique *number*). Value numbering the symbolic registers aids in the detection of common subexpressions within the optimizer. For example, every time the local variable i is loaded it is loaded into the same symbolic register, and every time the same two symbolic registers are added together the result is placed into a symbolic register dedicated to hold that value.

Although the optimizer performs transformations at the machine instruction level, there are occasions where it could benefit from the existence of slightly modified and/or additional instructions. *Pseudoinstructions* are instructions that map to one or more machine instructions and are only valid within the SLLIC data structure as a software convention recognized between the code generators and the optimizer. For example, the NOP instruction mentioned above is actually a pseudoinstruction. No such instruction exists on the machine, although there are many instruction/operand combinations whose net effect would be null. The NOP pseudoinstruction saves the optimizer from having to recognize all those sequences. Another group of pseudoinstructions has been defined to allow the optimizer to view all the actual machine instructions in the same canonical form, without being restricted by the register use prescribed by the instructions. For example, some instructions use the same register as both a source and a target. This makes optimization very difficult for that instruction. The solution involves the definition of a set of pseudoinstructions, each of which maps to a two-instruction sequence, first to copy the source register to a new symbolic register, and then to perform the operation on that new register. The copy instruction will usually be eliminated by a later phase of the optimizer.

Another class of perhaps more important pseudoinstructions involves the encapsulation of common operations that are traditionally supported directly by hardware, but in a reduced instruction set are only supported through the generation of code sequences. Examples include multiplication, division, and remainder. Rather than have each code generator contain the logic to emit some correct sequence of instructions to perform multiplication, a set of pseudoinstructions has been defined that makes it appear as if a high-level multiplication instruction exists in the architecture. Each of the pseudoinstructions is defined in terms of one register target and either two register operands or one register operand and one immediate. The use of these pseudoinstructions also aids the optimizer in the detection of common subexpressions, loop invariants, and induction variables by reducing the complexity of the code sequences the optimizer must recognize.

Control flow restrictions are also placed on generated code. A *basic block* is defined as a straight-line sequence of code that contains no transfer of control out of or into its midst. If the code generator wishes to set the carry/borrow bit in the status register, it must use that result within the same basic block. Otherwise, the optimizer cannot guarantee its validity. Also, all argument registers for a procedure/function call must be loaded in the same basic block that contains the procedure call. This restriction helps the register allocator by limiting the instances where hard-coded (actual) machine registers can be *live* (active) across basic block boundaries.

Optimization

After the SLLIC data structure has been generated by the code generator, a call is made to the optimizer so that it can begin its processing. The optimizer performs intraprocedural local and global optimizations, and can be turned on and off on a procedure-by-procedure basis by the programmer through the use of compiler options and directives specific to each compiler. Three levels of optimization are supported and can also be selected at the procedural level.

Optimization is implemented at the machine instruction level for two reasons. First, since the throughput of the processor is most affected by the requests made of the memory unit and cache, optimizations that reduce the number of requests made, and optimizations that rearrange these requests to suit the memory unit best, are of the most value. It is only at the machine level that all memory accesses become exposed, and are available candidates for such optimizations. Second, the machine level is the common denominator for all the compilers, and will continue to be for future compilers for the architecture. This allows the implementation of one optimizer for the entire family of compilers. In addition to very machine specific optimizations, a number of theoretically machine independent optimizations (for example, loop optimizations) are also included. These also benefit from their low-level implementation, since all potential candidates are exposed. For example, performing loop optimizations at the machine level allows the optimizer to move constants outside the loop, since the machine has many registers to hold them. In summary, no optimization has been adversely affected by this strategy; instead, there have been only benefits.

Level 0 optimization is intended to be used during program development. It is difficult to support symbolic debugging in the presence of all optimizations, since many optimizations reorder or delete instruction sequences. Nonsymbolic debugging is available for fully optimized programs, but users will still find it easier to debug nonoptimized code since the relationship between the source and object code is clearer. No code transformations are made at level 0 that would preclude the use of a symbolic debugger. In particular, level 0 optimizations include some copy and NOP elimination, and limited branch scheduling. In addition, the components that physically exist as part of the optimizer, but are required to produce an executable program, are invoked. These include register allocation and branch fixing (replacing short branches with long branches where necessary).

After program correctness has been demonstrated using only level 0 optimizations, the programmer can use the more extensive optimization levels. There are two additional levels of optimization, either of which results in code reordering. The level any particular optimization component falls into is dependent upon the type of information it requires to perform correct program transformations. The calculation of data flow information gives the optimizer information regarding all the resources in the program. These resources include general registers, dedicated and status registers, and memory locations (variables). The information gleaned includes where each resource is defined and used within the procedure, and is critical for some optimization algorithms. Level 1 optimizations require no data flow information, therefore adding only a few additional optimizations over level 0. Invoking the optimizer at level 2 will cause all optimizations to be performed. This requires data flow information to be calculated.

Level 1 optimization introduces three new optimizations: peephole and branch optimizations and full instruction scheduling. Peephole optimizations are performed by pattern matching short instruction sequences in the code to corresponding templates in the peephole optimizer. An example of a transformation is seen in the C source expression

if (flag & 0x8)

which tests to see that the fourth bit from the right is set in the integer flag. The unoptimized code is

```
LDO       8(0), 19      ; load immediate 8 into r19
AND       31,19,20      ; intersect r31 (flag) with r19 into r20
COMIBT, = 0,20,label    ; compare result against 0 and branch
```

Peephole optimization replaces these three instructions with the one instruction

```
BB,> =    31,28,label   ; branch on bit
```

which will branch if bit 28 (numbered left to right from 0) in r31 (the register containing flag) is equal to 0.

Level 1 optimization also includes a branch optimizer whose task is to eliminate unnecessary branches and some

unreachable code. Among other tasks, it replaces branch chains with a single branch, and changes conditional branches whose targets are unconditional branches to a single conditional branch.

The limited instruction scheduling algorithm of level 0 is replaced with a much more thorough component in level 1. Level 0 scheduling is restricted to replacing or removing the NOPs following branches where possible, since code sequence ordering must be preserved for the symbolic debugger. In addition to this, level 1 instructions are scheduled with the goal of minimizing memory interlocks. The following typify the types of transformations made:

- Separate a load from the instruction that uses the loaded register
- Separate store and load instruction sequences
- Separate floating-point instructions from each other to improve throughput of the floating-point unit.

Instruction scheduling is accomplished by first constructing a dependency graph that details data dependencies between instructions. Targeted instructions are separated by data independent instructions discovered in the graph.

The same register allocator is used in level 0 and level 1 optimization. It makes one backwards pass over each procedure to determine where the registers are defined and used and whether or not they are live across a call. It uses this information as a basis for replacing the symbolic registers with actual machine registers. Some copy elimination is also performed by this allocator.

Level 2 optimizations include all level 1 optimizations as well as local constant propagation, local peephole transformations, local redundant definition elimination, common subexpression and redundant load/store elimination, loop invariant code motion, induction variable elaboration and strength reduction, and another register allocator. The register allocator used in level 2 is partially based on graph coloring technology.[4] Fully optimized code contains many more live registers than partially optimized or nonoptimized code. This register allocator handles many live registers better than the register allocator of levels 0 and 1. It has access to the data flow information calculated for the symbolic registers and information regarding the frequency of execution for each basic block.

Control Flow and Data Flow Analysis

All of the optimizations introduced in level 2 require data flow information. In addition, a certain amount of control flow information is required to do loop-based optimizations. Data flow analysis provides information to the optimizer about the pattern of definition and use of each resource. For each basic block in the program, data flow information indicates what definitions may reach the block (reaching definitions) and what later uses may be affected by local definitions (exposed uses). Control flow information in the optimizer is contained in the basic block and interval structures. *Basic block analysis* identifies blocks of code that have no internal branching. *Interval analysis* identifies patterns of control flow such as if-then-else and loop constructs.[5] Intervals simplify data flow calculations, identify loops for the loop-based optimizations, and enable partial update of data flow information.

In the optimizer, control flow analysis and data flow analysis are performed in concert. First, basic blocks are identified. Second, local data flow information is calculated for each basic block. Third, interval analysis exposes the structure of the program. Finally, using the interval structure as a basis for its calculation rules, global data-flow analysis calculates the reaching definitions and exposed uses.

Basic block analysis of the SLLIC data structure results in a graph structure where each basic block identifies a sequence of instructions, along with the predecessor and successor basic blocks. The interval structure is built on top of this, with the smallest interval being a basic block. Intervals other than basic blocks contain subintervals which may themselves be any type of interval. Interval types include basic block, sequential block (the subintervals follow each other in sequential order), if-then, if-then-else, self loop, while loop, repeat loop, and switch (case statement). When no such interval is recognized, a set of subintervals may be contained in either a *proper interval* (if the control flow is well-behaved) or an *improper interval* (if it contains multiple-entry cycles or targets of unknown branches). An entire procedure will be represented by a single interval with multiple descendants. Fig. 3 shows the interval structure for a simple Pascal program.

Calculation of data flow information begins with an analysis of what resources are used and defined by each basic block. Each use or definition of a resource is identified by a unique *sequence number*. Associated with each sequence number is information regarding what resource is

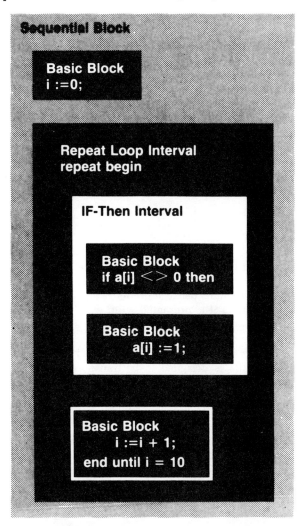

Fig. 3. *This figure illustrates the interval structure of a simple sequence of Pascal code. The nested boxes represent the interval hierarchy.*

being referenced, and whether it is a use or a definition. Each SLLIC instruction entry contains sequence numbers for all of the resources defined or used by that instruction. The local data flow analysis determines what local uses are exposed at the top of the basic block (i.e., there is a use of a resource with no preceding definition in that block) and what local definitions will reach the end of the block (i.e., they define a resource that is not redefined later in the block). The local data flow analysis makes a forward and backward pass through the instructions in a basic block to determine this information.

Local data flow information is propagated out from the basic blocks to the outermost interval. Then, information about reaching definitions and exposed uses is propagated inward to the basic block level. For known interval types, this involves a straightforward calculation for each subinterval. For proper intervals, this calculation must be performed twice for each subinterval, and for improper intervals, the number of passes is limited by the number of subintervals.

As each component of the optimizer makes transformations to the SLLIC graph, the data flow information becomes inaccurate. Two strategies are employed to bring this information up-to-date: *patching* of the existing data flow information and partial recalculation. For all optimizations except induction variable elimination, the data flow information can be patched by using information about the nature of the transformation to determine exactly how the data flow information must be changed. All transformations take place within the loop interval in induction variable elimination. The update of data flow information within the loop is performed by recalculating the local data flow information where a change has been made, and then by propagating that change out to the loop interval. The effect of induction variable elimination on intervals external to the loop is limited, and this update is performed by patching the data flow information for these intervals.

Aliasing

The concept of resources has already been presented in the earlier discussion of data flow analysis. The optimizer provides a component called the *resource manager* for use throughout the compiler phases. The resource manager is responsible for the maintenance of information regarding the numbers and types of resources within each procedure. For example, when the code generator needs a new symbolic register, it asks the resource manager for one. The front ends also allocate resources corresponding to memory locations for every variable in each procedure. The resources allocated by the resource manager are called *resource numbers*. The role of the resource manager is especially important in this family of compilers. It provides a way for the front end, which deals with memory resources in terms of programmer variable names, and the optimizer, which deals with memory resources in terms of actual memory locations, to communicate the relationship between the two.

The most basic use of the resource numbers obtained through the resource manager is the identification of unique programmer variables. The SLLIC instructions are decorated with information that associates resource numbers with each operand. This allows the optimizer to recognize uses of the same variable without having to compare addresses. The necessity for communication between the front ends and the optimizer is demonstrated by the following simplified example of C source code:

```
proc() {
 int i, j, k, *p;
 .
 .
 .
 i = j + k;
 *p = 1;
 i = j + k;
 .
 .
 .
}
```

At first glance it might seem that the second calculation of j + k is redundant, and in fact it is a common subexpression that need only be calculated once. However, if the pointer p has been set previously to point to either j or k, then the statement *p = 1 might change the value of either j or k. If p has been assigned to point to j, then we say that *p and j are *aliased* to each other. Every front end includes a component called a *gatherer*[6] whose responsibility it is to collect information concerning the ways in which memory resources in each procedure relate to each other. This information is cast in terms of resource numbers, and is collected in a similar manner by each front end. Each gatherer applies a set of language specific alias rules to the source. A later component of the optimizer called the aliaser reorganizes this information in terms more suitable for use by the local data flow component of the optimizer.

Each gatherer had to solve aliasing problems specific to its particular target language. For example, the Pascal gatherer was able to use Pascal's strong typing to aid in building sets of resources that a pointer of some particular type can point to. Since C does not have strong typing, the C gatherer could make no such assumptions. The COBOL compiler had to solve the aliasing problems that are introduced with the REDEFINE statement, which can make data items look like arrays. Fig. 4 shows the structure of the new compilers from an aliasing perspective. It details data

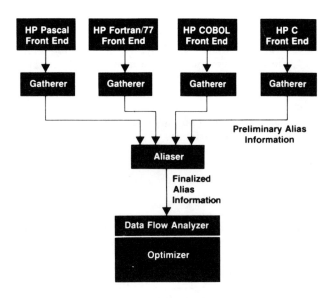

Fig. 4. *Scheme for the collection of alias information.*

and control dependencies. Once the aliasing data has been incorporated into the data flow information, every component in the optimizer has access to the information, and incorrect program transformations are prevented.

The aliaser also finishes the calculation of the aliasing relationships by calculating the transitive closure* on the aliasing information collected by the gatherers. The need for this calculation is seen in the following skeleton Pascal example:

```
procedure p;
 begin
 p : ^integer;
 q : ^integer;
 .
 .
 .
 p := q;
 .
 .
 .
 q := p;
 .
 .
 .
 end;
```

The aliasing information concerning q must be transferred to p, and vice versa, because of the effects of the two assignment statments shown. The aliaser is an optimizer component used by all the front ends, and requires no language specific data. Another type of memory aliasing occurs when two or more programmer variables can overlap with one another in memory. This happens within C unions and Fortran equivalence statements. Each gatherer must also deal with this issue, as well as collecting information concerning the side effects of procedure and function calls and the use of arrays.

The SLLIC Package

The SLLIC data structure is allocated, maintained, and manipulated by a collection of routines called the *SLLIC package*. Each code generator is required to use these routines. The SLLIC package produces an object file from the SLLIC graph it is presented with, which is either optimized or unoptimized. During implementation it was relatively easy to experiment with the design of the object file, since its creation is only implemented in one place. The object file is designed to be transportable between multiple operating systems running on the same architecture.

The SLLIC graph also contains the symbolic debug information produced by the front end. This information is placed into the object file by the SLLIC package. The last step in the compilation process is the link phase. The linker is designed to support multiple operating systems. As much as possible, our goal has been for the new compilers to remain unchanged across operating systems, an invaluable characteristic for application development.

*Transitive closure: For a given resource, the set of resources that can be shown to be aliased to the given resource by any sequence of aliasing relationships.

Addressing RISC Myths

The new compiling system provides a language development system that is consistent across languages. However, each language presents unique requirements to this system. Mapping high-level language constructs to a reduced-complexity computer requires the development of new implementation strategies. Procedure calls, multiplication, and other complex operations often implemented in microcode or supported in the hardware can be addressed with code sequences tuned to the specific need. The following discussion is presented in terms of several misconceptions, or myths, that have appeared in speculative discussions concerning code generation for reduced-complexity architectures. Each myth is followed by a description of the approach adopted for the new HP compilers.

Myth: An architected procedure call instruction is necessary for efficient procedure calls.

Modern programming technique encourages programmers to write small, well-structured procedures rather than large monolithic routines. This tends to increase the frequency of procedure calls, thus making procedure call efficiency crucial to overall system performance.

Many machines, like the HP 3000, provide instructions to perform most of the steps that make up a procedure call. The new HP high-precision architecture does not. The mechanism of a procedure call is not architected, but instead is accomplished by a software convention using the simple hardwired instructions. This provides more flexibility in procedure calls and ultimately a more efficient call mechanism.

Procedure calls are more than just a branch and return in the flow of control. The procedure call mechanism must also provide for the passing of parameters, the saving of the caller's environment, and the establishment of an environment for the called procedure. The procedure return mechanism must provide for the restoration of the calling procedure's environment and the saving of return values.

The new HP machines are register-based machines, but by convention a stack is provided for data storage. The most straightforward approach to procedure calls on these machines assumes that the calling procedure acquires the responsibility for preserving its state. This approach employs the following steps:

- Save all registers whose contents must be preserved across the procedure call. This prevents the called procedure, which will also use and modify registers, from affecting the calling procedure's state. On return, those register values are restored.
- Evaluate parameters in order and push them onto the stack. This makes them available to the called procedure which, by convention, knows how to access them.
- Push a *frame marker*. This is a fixed-size area containing several pieces of information. Among these is the *static link*, which provides information needed by the called procedure to address the local variables and parameters of the calling procedure. The return address of the calling procedure is also found in the stack marker.
- Branch to the entry point of the called procedure.

To return from the call, the called procedure extracts the return address from the stack marker and branches to it. The calling procedure then removes the parameters from the stack and restores all saved registers before program flow continues.

This simple model correctly implements the steps needed to execute a procedure call, but is relatively expensive. The model forces the caller to assume all responsibility for preserving its state. This is a safe approach, but causes too many register saves to occur. To optimize the program's execution, the compiler makes extensive use of registers to hold local variables and temporary values. These registers must be saved at a procedure call and restored at the return. The model also has a high overhead incurred by the loading and storing of parameters and linkage information. The ultimate goal of the procedure call convention is to reduce the cost of a call by reducing memory accesses.

The new compilers minimize this problem by introducing a procedure call convention that includes a register partition. The registers are partitioned into *caller-saves* (the calling procedure is responsible for saving and restoring them), *callee-saves* (the called procedure must save them at entry and restore them at exit), and *linkage* registers. Thirteen of the 32 registers are in the caller-saves partition and 16 are in the callee-saves partition. This spreads the responsibility for saving registers between the calling and called procedures and leaves some registers available for linkage.

The register allocator avoids unnecessary register saves by using caller-saves registers for values that need not be preserved. Values that must be saved are placed into registers from the callee-saves partition. At procedure entry, only those callee-saves registers used in the procedure are saved. This minimizes the number of loads and stores of registers during the course of a call. The partition of registers is not inflexible; if more registers are needed from a particular partition than are available, registers can be borrowed from the other partition. The penalty for using these additional registers is that they must be saved and restored, but this overhead is incurred only when many registers are needed, not for all calls.

In the simple model, all parameters are passed by being placed on the stack. This is expensive because memory references are made to push each parameter and as a consequence the stack size is constantly altered. The new compilers allocate a permanent parameter area large enough to hold the parameters for all calls performed by the procedure. They also minimize memory references when storing parameters by using a combination of registers and memory to pass parameters. Four registers from the callee-saves partition are used to pass user parameters; each holds a single 32-bit value or half of a 64-bit value. Since procedures frequently have few parameters, the four registers are usually enough to contain them all. This removes the necessity of storing parameter values in the parameter area before the call. If more than four 32-bit parameters are passed, the additional ones are stored in the preallocated parameter area. If a parameter is larger than 64 bits, its address is passed and the called procedure copies it to a temporary area.

Additional savings on stores and loads occur when the called procedure is a leaf routine. As mentioned previously, the optimizer attempts to maximize the use of registers to hold variable values. When a procedure is a leaf, the register allocator uses the caller-saves registers for this purpose, thus eliminating register saves for both the calling and called procedures. It is never necessary to store the return address or parameter registers of a leaf routine since they will not be modified by subsequent calls.

Leaf routines do not need to build a stack frame, since they make no procedure calls. Also, if the allocator succeeds in representing all local variables as registers, it is not necessary to build the local variable area at entry to the leaf procedure.

The convention prescribes other uses of registers to eliminate other loads and stores at procedure calls. The return address is always stored in a particular register, as is the static link if it is needed.

To summarize, the procedure call convention used in the new HP computers streamlines the overhead of procedure calls by minimizing the number of memory references. Maximal use of registers is made to limit the number of memory accesses needed to handle parameters and linkage. Similarly, the convention minimizes the need to store values contained in registers and does not interfere with attempts at optimization.

Myth: The simple instructions available in RISC result in significant code expansion.

Many applications, especially commercial applications, assume the existence of complex high-level instructions typically implemented by the system architecture in microcode or hardware. Detractors of RISC argue that significant code expansion is unavoidable since the architecture lacks these instructions. Early results do not substantiate this argument.[7,8] The new HP architecture does not provide complex instructions because of their impact on overall system performance and cost, but their functionality is available through other means.

As described in an earlier article,[2] the new HP machines do not have a microcoded architecture and all of the instructions are implemented in hardware. The instructions on microcoded machines are implemented in two ways. At the basic level, instructions are realized in hardware. More complex instructions are then produced by writing subroutines of these hardware instructions. Collectively, these constitute the microcode of the machine. Which instructions are in hardware and which are in microcode are determined by the performance and cost goals for the system. Since HP's reduced instruction set is implemented solely at the hardware level, subroutines of instructions are equivalent to the microcode in conventional architectures.

To provide the functionality of the complex instructions usually found in the architecture of conventional machines, the design team developed the alternative concept of *millicode instructions* or routines. Millicode is HP's implementation of complex instructions using the simple hardware instructions packaged into subroutines. Millicode serves the same purpose as traditional microcode, but is common across all machines of the family rather than specific to each.

The advantages of implementing functionality as millicode are many. Microcoded machines may contain hidden performance penalties on all instructions to support multiple levels of instruction implementation. This is not the case for millicode. From an architectural viewpoint, millicode is just a collection of subroutines indistinguishable from other subroutines. A millicode instruction is executed by calling the appropriate millicode subroutine. Thus, the expense of executing a millicode instruction is only present when the instruction is used. The addition of millicode instructions has no hardware cost and hence no direct influence on system cost. It is relatively easy and inexpensive to upgrade or modify millicode in the field, and it can continue to be improved, extended, and tuned over time.

Unlike most microcode, millicode can be written in the same high-level languages as other applications, reducing development costs yet still allowing for optimization of the resultant code. Severely performance-critical millicode can still be assembly level coded in instances where the performance gain over compiled code is justified. The size of millicode instructions and the number of such instructions are not constrained by considerations of the size of available control store. Millicode resides in the system as subroutines in normally managed memory, either in virtual memory where it can be paged into and out of the system as needed, or in resident memory as performance considerations dictate. A consequence of not being bound by restrictive space considerations is that compiler writers are free to create many more specialized instructions in millicode than would be possible in a microcoded architecture, and thus are able to create more optimal solutions for specific situations.

Most fixed instruction sets contain complex instructions that are overly general. This is necessary since it is costly to architect many variations of an instruction. Examples of this are the MVB (move bytes) and MVW (move words) instructions on the HP 3000. They are capable of moving any number of items from any arbitrary source location to any target location. Yet, the compiler's code generators frequently have more information available about the operands of these instructions that could be used to advantage if other instructions were available. The code generators frequently know whether the operands overlap, whether the operands are aligned favorably, and the number of items to be moved. On microcoded machines, this information is lost after code generation and must be recreated by the microcode during each execution of the instruction. On the new HP computers, the code generators can apply such information to select a specialized millicode instruction that will produce a faster run-time execution of the operation than would be possible for a generalized routine.

Access to millicode instructions is through a mechanism similar to a procedure call. However, additional restrictions placed on the implementation of millicode routines prevent the introduction of any barriers to optimization. Millicode routines must be leaf routines and must have no effect on any registers or memory locations other than the operands and a few scratch registers. Since millicode calls are represented in SLLIC as pseudoinstructions, the optimizer can readily distinguish millicode calls from procedure calls. Millicode calls also use different linkage registers from procedure calls, so there is no necessity of preserving the procedure's linkage registers before invoking millicode instructions.

The only disadvantage of the millicode approach over microcode is that the initiation of a millicode instruction involves an overhead of at least two instructions. Even so, it is important to realize that for most applications, millicode instructions are infrequently needed, and their overhead is incurred only when they are used. The high-precision architecture provides the frequently needed instructions directly in hardware.

Myth: RISC machines must implement integer multiplication as successive additions.

Integer multiplication is frequently an architected instruction. The new architecture has no such instruction but provides others that support an effective implementation of multiplication. It also provides for inclusion of a high-speed hardware multiplier in a special function unit.[2]

Our measurements reveal that most multiplication operations generated by user programs involve multiplications by small constants. Many of these occurrences are explicitly in the source code, but many more are introduced by the compiler for address and array reference evaluation. The new compilers have available a trio of instructions that perform shift and add functions in a single cycle. These instructions, SH1ADD (shift left once and add), SH2ADD (shift left twice and add) and SH3ADD (shift left three times and add) can be combined in sequences to perform multiplication by constants in very few instructions. Multiplications by most constants with absolute values less than 1040 can be accomplished in fewer than five cycles. Negatively signed constants require an additional instruction to apply the sign to the result. Multiplication by all constants that are exact powers of 2 can be performed with a single shift instruction unless overflow conditions are to be detected. Additionally, multiplications by 4 or 2 for indexed addressing can be avoided entirely. The LDWX (load word indexed) and LDHX (load half-word indexed) instructions optionally perform unit indexing, which combines multiplication of the index value with the address computation in the hardware.

The following examples illustrate multiplication by various small constants.

```
Source code:
    4*k
Assembly code:
    SH2ADD    8,0,9         ;  shift r8 (k) left 2 places,
                               add to r0 (zero) into r9
Source code:
    -163*k
Assembly code:
    SH3ADD    8,8,1         ;  shift r8 (k) left 3 places, add
                               to itself into r1
    SH3ADD    1,1,1         ;  shift r1 left 3 places, add to
                               itself into r1
    SH1ADD    1,8,1         ;  shift r1 left 1 place, add to
                               k into r1
    SUB       0,1,1         ;  subtract result from 0 to
                               negate; back into r1
Source code:
    A(k)
Assembly code:
    LDO       -404(30),9    ;  load array base address
                               into r9
    LDW       -56(0,30),7   ;  load unit index value into r7
    LDWX,S    7(0,9),5      ;  multiply index by 4 and
                               load element into r5
```

When neither operand is constant or if the constant is such that the in-line code sequence would be too large, integer multiplication is accomplished with a millicode instruction. The multiply millicode instruction operates under the premise that even when the operands are un-

known at compile time, one of them is still likely to be a small value. Application of this to the multiplication algorithm yields an average multiplication time of 20 cycles, which is comparable to an iterative hardware implementation.

Myth: RISC machines cannot support commercial applications languages.

A popular myth about RISC architectures is that they cannot effectively support languages like COBOL. This belief is based on the premise that RISC architectures cannot provide hardware support for the constructs and data types of COBOL-like languages while maintaining the one-instruction-one-cycle advantages of RISC. As a consequence, some feel that the code expansion resulting from performing COBOL operations using only the simple architected instructions would be prohibitive. The significance of this is often overstated. Instruction traces of COBOL programs measured on the HP 3000 indicate that the frequency of decimal arithmetic instructions is very low. This is because much of the COBOL program's execution time is spent in the operating system and other subsystems.

COBOL does place demands on machine architects and compiler designers that are different from those of languages like C, Fortran, and Pascal. The data items provided in the latter languages are represented in binary and hence are native to the host machine. COBOL data types also include packed and unpacked decimal, which are not commonly native and must be supported in ways other than directly in hardware.

The usual solution on conventional machines is to provide a commercial instruction set in microcode. These additional instructions include those that perform COBOL field (variable) moves, arithmetic for packed decimal values, alignment, and conversions between the various arithmetic types.

In the new HP machines, millicode instructions are used to provide the functionality of a microcoded commercial instruction set. This allows the encapsulation of COBOL operations while removing the possibility of runaway code expansion. Many COBOL millicode instructions are available to do each class of operation. The compiler expends considerable effort to select the optimal millicode operation based on compile-time information about the operation and its operands. For example, to generate code to perform a COBOL field move, the compiler may consider the operand's relative and absolute field sizes and whether blank or zero padding is needed before selecting the appropriate millicode instruction.

Hardware instructions that assist in the performance of some COBOL operations are architected. These instructions execute in one cycle but perform operations that would otherwise require several instructions. They are emitted by the compiler in in-line code where appropriate and are also used to implement some of the millicode instructions. For example, the DCOR (decimal correct) and UADDCM (unit add complement) instructions allow packed decimal addition to be performed using the binary ADD instruction. UADDCM prepares an operand for addition and the DCOR restores the result to packed decimal form after the addition. For example:

```
r1 and r2 contain packed decimal operands
r3 contains the constant X'99999999'

UADDCM 1,3,31    ; pre-bias operand into r31
ADD    2,31,31   ; perform binary add
DCOR   31,31     ; correct result
```

Millicode instructions support arithmetic for both packed and unpacked decimal data. This is a departure from the HP 3000, since on that machine unpacked arithmetic is performed by first converting the operand to packed format, performing the arithmetic operation on the packed data, and then converting the result back to unpacked representation. Operations occur frequently enough on unpacked data to justify the implementation of unpacked arithmetic routines. The additional cost to implement them is minimal and avoids the overhead of converting operands between the two types. An example of the code to perform an unpacked decimal add is:

```
r1 and r2 contain unpacked decimal operands
r3 contains the constant X'96969696'
r4 contains the constant X'0f0f0f0f'
r5 contains the constant X'30303030'

ADD    3,1,31    ; pre-bias operand into r31
ADD    31,2,31   ; binary add into r31
DCOR   31,31     ; correct result
AND    4,31,31   ; mask result
OR     5,31,31   ; restore sum to unpacked decimal
```

In summary, COBOL is supported with a blend of hardware assist instructions and millicode instructions. The compiled code is compact and meets the run-time execution performance goals.

Conclusions

The Spectrum program began as a joint effort of hardware and software engineers. This early communication allowed high-level language issues to be addressed in the architectural design.

The new HP compiling system was designed with a reduced-complexity machine in mind. Register allocation, instruction scheduling, and traditional optimizations allow compiled programs to make efficient use of registers and low-level instructions.

Early measurements have shown that this compiler technology has been successful in exploiting the capabilities of the new architecture. The run-time performance of compiled code consistently meets performance objectives. Compiled code sizes for high-level languages implemented in this low-level instruction set are comparable to those for more conventional architectures. Use of millicode instructions helped achieve this result. Complex high-level language operations such as procedure calls, multiplication, and COBOL constructs have been implemented efficiently with the low-level instructions provided by the high-precision architecture. A later paper will present performance measurements.

Acknowledgments

The ideas and results presented in this paper are the culmination of the work of many talented engineers involved with the Spectrum compiler program. We would like to acknowledge the individuals who made significant technical contributions to the work presented in this paper in the following areas: early compiler development and optimizer investigation at HP Laboratories, optimizer development, aliasing design and implementation in the compiler front ends, code generator design and implementation, procedure call convention design, and object module specification.

Megan Adams	Tom Lee
Robert Ballance	Steve Lilker
Bruce Blinn	Daniel Magenheimer
William Buzbee	Tom McNeal
Don Cameron	Sue Meloy
Peter Canning	Terrence Miller
Paul Chan	Angela Morgan
Cary Coutant	Steve Muchnick
Erik Eidt	Karl Pettis
Phil Gibbons	David Rickel
Adiel Gorel	Michelle Ruscetta
Richard Holman	Steven Saunders
Mike Huey	Carolyn Sims
Audrey Ishizaki	Ron Smith
Suneel Jain	Kevin Wallace
Mark Scott Johnson	Alexand Wu
Steven Kusmer	

We feel privileged to have the opportunity to present their work. We would like to extend special thanks to Bill Buzbee for his help in providing code examples, and to Suneel Jain for providing the description of the optimization components.

References

1. D.A. Patterson, "Reduced Instruction Set Computers," *Communications of the ACM*, Vol. 28, no. 1, January 1985, pp. 8-21.
2. J.S. Birnbaum and W.S. Worley, Jr., "Beyond RISC: High-Precision Architecture," *Hewlett-Packard Journal*, Vol. 36, no. 8, August 1985, pp. 4-10.
3. A.V. Aho and J.D. Ullman, *Principles of Compiler Design*, Addison-Wesley, 1977.
4. G.J. Chaitin, "Register Allocation and Spilling via Graph Coloring," *Proceedings of the SIGPLAN Symposium on Compiler Construction*, June 1982, pp. 98-105.
5. M. Sharir, "Structural Analysis: A New Approach To Flow Analysis in Optimizing Compilers," *Computer Languages*, Vol. 5, Pergamon Press Ltd., 1980.
6. D.S. Coutant, "Retargetable High-Level Alias Analysis," *Conference Record of the 13th ACM Symposium on Principles of Programming Languages*, January 1986.
7. J.A. Otto, "Predicting Potential COBOL Performance on Low-Level Machine Architectures," *SIGPLAN Notices*, Vol. 20, no. 10, October 1985, pp. 72-78.
8. G. Radin, "The 801 Computer," *Symposium on Architectural Support for Programming Languages and Operating Systems*, March 1982, pp. 39-47.

Components of the Optimizer

The optimizer is composed of two types of components, those that perform data flow and control flow analysis, and those that perform optimizations. The information provided by the analysis components is shared by the optimization components, and is used to determine when instructions can be deleted, moved, rearranged, or modified.

For each procedure, the control flow analysis identifies basic blocks (sequences of code that have no internal branching). These are combined into intervals, which form a hierarchy of control structures. Basic blocks are at the bottom of this hierarchy, and entire procedures are at the top. Loops and if-then constructs are examples of the intermediate structures.

Data flow information is collected for each interval. It is expressed in terms of resource numbers and sequence numbers. Each register, memory location, and intermediate expression has a unique resource number, and each use or definition of a resource has a unique sequence number. Three types of data flow information are calculated:

- Reaching definitions: for each resource, the set of definitions that could reach the top of the interval by some path.
- Exposed uses: for each resource, the set of uses that could be reached by a definition at the bottom of the interval.
- UNDEF set: the set of resources that are not available at the top of the interval. A resource is available if it is defined along all paths reaching the interval, and none of its operands are later redefined along that path.

From this information, a fourth data structure is built:

- Web: a set of sequence numbers having the property that for each use in the set, all definitions that might reach it are also in the set. Likewise, for each definition in the set, all uses it might reach are also in the set. For each resource there may be one or many webs.

Loop Optimizations

Frequently the majority of execution time in a program is spent executing instructions contained in loops. Consequently, loop-based optimizations can potentially improve execution time significantly. The following discussion describes components that perform loop optimizations.

Loop Invariant Code Motion. Computations within a loop that yield the same result for every iteration are called loop invariant computations. These computations can potentially be moved outside the loop, where they are executed less frequently.

An instruction inside the loop is invariant if it meets either of two conditions: either the reaching definitions for all its operands are outside the loop, or its operands are defined by instructions that have already themselves been identified as loop invariant. In addition, there must not be a conflicting definition of the instruction's target inside the loop. If the instruction is executed conditionally inside the loop, it can be moved out only if there are no exposed uses of the target at the loop exit.

An example is a computation involving variables that are not modified in the loop. Another is the computation of an array's base address.

Strength Reduction and Induction Variables. Strength reduction replaces multiplication operations inside a loop with iterative addition operations. Since there is no hardware instruction for integer multiplication in the architecture, converting sequences of shifts and adds to a single instruction is a performance improvement. Induction variables are variables that are defined inside the loop in terms of a simple function of the loop counter.

Once the induction variables have been determined, those that are appropriate for this optimization are selected. Any multiplications involved in the computation of these induction variables are replaced with a COPY from a temporary. This temporary holds the initial value of the function, and is initialized preceding the loop. It is updated at the point of all the reaching definitions of the induction variable with an appropriate addition instruction. Finally, the induction variable itself is eliminated if possible.

This optimization is frequently applied to the computation of array indices inside a loop, when the index is a function of the loop counter.

Common Subexpression Elimination

Common subexpression elimination is the removal of redundant computations and the reuse of the one result. A redundant computation can be deleted when its target is not in the UNDEF set for the basic block it is contained in, and all the reaching definitions of the target are the same instruction. Since the optimizer runs at the machine level, redundant loads of the same variable in addition to redundant arithmetic computations can be removed.

Store-Copy Optimization

It is possible to promote certain memory resources to registers for the scope of their definitions and uses. Only resources that satisfy aliasing restrictions can be transformed this way. If the transformation can be performed, stores are converted to copies and the loads are eliminated. This optimization is very useful for a machine that has a large number of registers, since it maximizes the use of registers and minimizes the use of memory.

For each memory resource there may be multiple webs. Each memory web is an independent candidate for promotion to a register.

Unused Definition Elimination

Definitions of memory and register resources that are never used are removed. These definitions are identified during the building of webs.

Local Constant Propagation

Constant propagation involves the folding and substitution of constant computations throughout a basic block. If the result of a computation is a constant, the instruction is deleted, and the resultant constant is used as an immediate operand in subsequent instructions that reference the original result. Also, if the operands of a conditional branch are constant, the branch can be changed to an unconditional branch or deleted.

Coloring Register Allocation

Many components introduce additional uses of registers or prolong the use of existing registers over larger portions of the procedure. Near-optimal use of the available registers becomes crucial after these optimizations have been made.

Global register allocation based on a method of graph coloring is performed. The register resources are partitioned into groups of disjoint definitions and uses called register webs. Then, using the exposed uses information, interferences between webs are computed. An interference occurs when two webs must be assigned different machine registers. Registers that are copies of each other are assigned to the same register and the copies are eliminated. The webs are sorted based on the number of interferences each contains. Then register assignment is done using this ordering. When the register allocator runs out of registers, it frees a register by saving another one to memory temporarily. A heuristic algorithm is used to choose which register to save. For example, registers used heavily within a loop will not be saved to free a register.

Peephole Optimizations

The peephole optimizer uses a dictionary of equivalent instruction patterns to simplify instruction sequences. Some of the patterns identify simplifications to addressing mode changes, bit manipulations, and data type conversions.

Branch Optimizations

The branch optimizer component traverses the instructions, transforming branch instruction sequences into more efficient instruction sequences. It converts branches over single instructions to instructions with conditional nullification. A branch whose target is the next instruction is deleted. Branch chains involving both unconditional and conditional branches are combined into shorter sequences wherever possible. For example, a conditional branch to an unconditional branch is changed to a single conditional branch.

Dead Code Elimination

Dead code is code that cannot be reached at program execution, since no branch to it or fall-through exists. This code is deleted.

Scheduler

The instruction scheduler reorders the instructions within a basic block, minimizing load/store and floating-point interlocks. It also schedules the instructions following branches.

Suneel Jain
Development Engineer
Information Technology Group

An Optimization Example

This example illustrates the code generated for the following C program for both the unoptimized and the optimized case.

```
test ( )
{
int i, j;
int a1[25], a2[25], r[25][25];

    for (i = 0; i < 25; i + +) {
        for (j = 0; j < 25; j + +) {
            r [i] [j] = a1 [i] * a2 [j];
        }
    }
}
```

In the example code that follows, the following mnemonics are used:

rp	return pointer, containing the address to which control should be returned upon completion of the procedure
arg0	first parameter register
arg1	second parameter register
sp	stack pointer, pointing to the top of the current frame
mret0	millicode return register
mrp	millicode return pointer.

The value of register zero (r0) is always zero.

The following is a brief description of the instructions used:

LDO	immed(r1),r2	$r2 \leftarrow r1 + immed.$
LDW	immed(r1),r2	$r2 \leftarrow *(r1 + immed)$
LDWX,S	r1(r2),r3	$r3 \leftarrow *(4*r1 + r2)$
STW	r1,immed(r2)	$*(r2 + immed) \leftarrow r1$
STWS	r1,immed(r2)	$*(r2 + immed) \leftarrow r1$
STWM	r1,immed(r2)	$*(r2 + immed) \leftarrow r1$ AND $r2 \leftarrow r2 + immed$
COMB,< =	r1,r2,label	if $r1 <= r2$, branch to label
BL	label,r1	branch to label, and put return address into r1 (for procedure call)
BV	0(r1)	branch to address in r1 (for procedure return)

ADD	r1,r2,r3	$r3 \leftarrow r1 + r2$
SH1ADD	r1,r2,r3	$r3 \leftarrow 2*r1 + r2$
SH2ADD	r1,r2,r3	$r3 \leftarrow 4*r1 + r2$
SH3ADD	r1,r2,r3	$r3 \leftarrow 8*r1 + r2$
COPY	r1,r2	$r2 \leftarrow r1$
NOP		no effect

In the following step-by-step discussion, the unoptimized code on the left is printed in black, and the optimized code on the right is printed in color. The code appears in its entirety, and can be read from the top down in each column.

Save callee-saves registers and increment stack pointer. Unoptimized case uses no register that needs to be live across a call.

LDO	2760(sp),sp	STW	2, − 20(0,sp)
		STWM	3,2768(0,sp)
		STW	4, − 2764(0,sp}

Assign zero to i. In the optimized case, i resides in register 19.

STW	0, − 52(0,sp)	COPY	0,19

Compare i to 25. This test is eliminated in the optimized case since the value of i is known.

LDW	− 52(0,sp),1
LDO	25(0),31
COMB,< = ,N	31,1,L2

In the optimized version, a number of expressions have been moved out of the loop:

{maximum value of j}	LDO	25(0),20
{address of a1}	LDO	− 156(sp),22
{address of a2}	LDO	− 256(sp),24
{address of r}	LDO	− 2756(sp),28
{initial value of 100*i}	LDO	0(0),4
{maximum value of 100*i}	LDO	2500(0),2

Initialize j to zero, and compare j to 25. This test has also been eliminated in the optimized version, since the value of j is known. Note that j now resides in register 21.

L3			
STW	0, − 56(0,sp)	COPY	0,21
LDW	− 56(0,sp),19		
LDO	25(0),20		
COMB,< = ,N	20,19,L1		

In the optimized version, the load of a1[i] is moved out of the inner loop, since the value of i is constant in the inner loop.

LDWX,S	19(0,22),23

Register 28 contains the address of r, and register 4 contains the value 100*i, which is the offset of the ith row of array r. This is constant over the inner loop, and has been moved out.

ADD	28,4,3
L6	

The loop begins with the load of a1[i] into the first parameter register. This value has already been loaded in the optimized version, and need only be copied.

LDO	− 156(sp),21		
LDW	− 52(0,sp),22		
LDWX,S	22(0,21),arg0	COPY	23,arg0

The value of a2[j] is loaded into the second parameter register, and the multiply millicode instruction is called. In the optimized case, the address of a2[0] and the value of j are both already in registers.

```
LDO      -256(sp),1
LDW      -56(0,sp),19
BL       mull,mrp          BL        mull,mrp
LDWX,S   19(0,1),arg1      LDWX,S    21(0,24),arg1
```

Store the result into r[i][j]. The three SHxADD instructions calculate 100*i. Note that most of the following is loop invariant, and has been moved out of the loop in the optimized case.

```
LDO     -2756(sp),19  {address of r}
LDW     -52(0,sp),20  {value of i}
SH1ADD  20,20,21      {r21 ← 3*i}
SH3ADD  21,20,22      {r22 ← 25*i}
SH2ADD  22,0,1        {r1 ← 100*i}
ADD     19,1,31       {address of r + 100*i}
LDW     -56(0,sp),19  {value of j}
SH2ADD  19,31,20      {add j*4 to address}  SH2ADD  21,3,31
STWS    mret0,0(0,20) {store}               STWS    mret0,0(0,31)
```

Increment j.

```
LDW     -56(0,sp),21           LDO     1(21),21
LDO     1(21),22
STW     22,-56(0,sp)
```

Compare j to the value 25 (already in register 20 in the optimized version). The position after the conditional branch contains no useful instruction in the unoptimized case. In the op-

timized version, the first instruction of the loop has been copied to this position, and the target adjusted to the following instruction. Because the branch has the nullification flag set (,N), the following instruction will not be executed when the branch is not taken.

```
LDW       -56(0,sp),1
LDO       25(0),31
COMBF,<=  31,1,L6    COMBF,<=,N  20,21,L6+4
NOP                  LDWX,S      21(0,24),25
L1
```

Increment i, and test for the end of the loop. In the optimized version, induction variable elaboration has removed the 100*i multiplication, and added a new induction variable to contain that value. This value, in register 4, is now tested against a maximum value of 2500, contained in register 2. This branch has been scheduled like the previous branch.

```
LDW      -52(0,sp),19
LDO      1(19),20        LDO    1(19),19
STW      20,-52(0,sp)    LDO    100(4),4
LDW      -52(0,sp),21
LDO      25(0),22
COMBF,<= 22,21,L3        COMBF,<=,N 2,4,L3+4
NOP                      COPY    0,21
L2
```

Finally, the registers are restored, and control is returned to the calling procedure.

```
                          LDW    -2788(0,sp),2
                          LDW    -2764(0,sp),4
BV    0(rp)               BV     0(rp)
LDO   -2760(sp),sp        LDWM   -2768(0,sp),3
```

Compiling·for the RT PC ROMP

M.E. Hopkins

Introduction

The IBM RT PC ROMP architecture is relatively low level and simple. A natural consequence is that the primitive instructions should execute rapidly on most implementations. Does the choice of such a low level interface make sense given that almost all programming today is, or should be, done in a high level language? Could compiler writers do a better job if the CPU was somewhat more elaborate, with additional functions tailored to the constructs commonly found in high-level languages? Of course it is clear that code can be generated for any execution model. Examples of execution models are register transfer, stack, and·storage-to-storage. Unlike human coders, compilers will tirelessly and accurately generate long sequences of code to map one model of a language onto a machine with another model. The hard task is to obtain efficient code for a particular machine.

Which style of machine is best? Our preference for a machine like the ROMP is based partly on fundamental engineering constraints and partly on our ability to use well understood compilation techniques to obtain high quality code. An example of a fundamental engineering constraint is that operations that are internal to the CPU, such as register-to-register add, run faster than instructions that reference storage, even on machines with caches. (The fact that some machines slow down basic arithmetic to memory reference speed should not concern us.) Examples of compilation techniques will be given later. We also have a certain bias to simple hardware solutions. Part of this is aesthetic, but we also have a suspicion grounded on experience that the next language just may not match the complex operation which is built into an elaborate architecture.

The discussions that follow are based on the PL.8 compiler, which accepts source programs written in C, Pascal and PL.8, a systems dialect of PL/I. A description of the compiler is given in Auslander and Hopkins[1]. PL.8 produces optimized object code for System/370 and MC68000 as well as ROMP and the 801 minicomputer [2]. The compiler largely relies on global optimization and register allocation to produce good object code. The VRM and various ROMP tools were developed using PL.8. Originally, the compiler was an experimental vehicle used to build software for the 801 minicomputer, but in recent years it has been used in a number of internal IBM projects. It is not presently available to customers.

Hardware/Software Cooperation

Both hardware and software affect system performance. The compiler writer must accept his share of the responsibility. The ROMP architecture divides the task in ways that lead to better performance without excessive burden on either hardware or software. A few examples will indicate how responsibility is shared.

One of the more expensive operations on many computers is branching. As long as instruction execution proceeds sequentially it is possible to prefetch and decode instructions ahead of their actual execution. This overlapping is usually termed pipelining. When a branch is encountered a new instruction stream must be found. Conditionality and computed branch targets complicate the decisions that must be made in hardware. Very-high-performance machines do prefetch on multiple paths and retain branch history tables to avoid "flushing the pipe." Most one-chip processors simply accept expensive branches as a fact of life. The ROMP solution is to define a family of

Reprinted by permission from *IBM RT Personal Computer Technology*, IBM Publication Number SA23-1057, © 1986 by International Business Machines Corporation.

execute branches that perform the next ("subject") instruction in parallel with the branch. Implementing this facility only complicates the hardware a little. It thus becomes the responsibility of the compiler to produce execute branches. Through most of compilation, the compiler only deals with branches in the familiar non-execute format. At one point a scheduling process is run which rearranges code between labels and branches. (This unit is termed a basic block.) One of the goals of scheduling is to place an instruction that could become the subject of an execute branch just in front of the branch. (The main constraint is that the branch cannot depend on the result of the subject instruction.) Other optimizations are unaware of the compilation of execute branches. Final assembly then looks at the instruction that precedes every branch and flips the pair if it is valid to convert a normal to an execute branch. Branches tend to constitute over 20% of all instructions executed. Even if only half of all branches can be transformed to the execute form, a modest increase in hardware and compiler complexity has resulted in the effect of a 10% reduction in the path length or number of instructions executed.

A similar situation exists with loads. Loads tend to take substantially more time than register-to-register (RR) ops, but it is possible for the hardware (in Real mode) to overlap the load with execution of the following instruction if the next instruction does not require the result of the load. The scheduling process also rearranges code to facilitate such overlap. If loads constitute 15% or 20% of all executions, it is easy to see that another 10% or greater reduction in effective path length may be achieved here. Notice that a machine that bundles the fetch of an operand from memory with a computation cannot easily overlap fetching with some other function.

Of course the object code that comes from such a compiler looks strange. In some sense, you are seeing the equivalent of the internal state of a very costly high-performance pipelined processor. Writing optimal assembly language code requires some care on the ROMP. It is rather like microcoding. However, on the ROMP the process is systematic, if tedious, making it

fortunate that most programming is done in a high-level language.

Compilation Strategies
The most important optimizations performed by the PL.8 compiler are probably moving code out of loops, the elimination of redundant computations (commoning), and register allocation. The ROMP makes these operations easier and more profitable.

Let us examine these optimizations in the light of machine models and how they evaluate expressions:

- Stack computation

- Memory-to-memory

- Memory-to-register

- Register-to-register

Consider the source code fragment:

    x = a + b;
    (a few statements, which destroy x, leaving
    a and b)
    y = a + b;

If the recomputation of a + b is to be avoided on the stack machine, an explicit copy in storage must be made and then the value must be refetched from storage when assigning to y. The trouble with this strategy is that "remembering" is very costly. On the ROMP an RR Add costs one cycle, while Loads and Stores take between three and five cycles depending on whether the machine is in real or virtual mode and whether or not it is possible to overlap another instruction with the load. Unless an operation is very expensive, it is often as efficient to recompute as to "remember" on a stack machine. On a memory-to-memory machine one must often pay for an explicit copy as in the following code for a hypothetical memory-to-memory machine:

    temp = a + b
    x = temp
       :   .
    y = temp

The added storage references may well make commoning counterproductive. We shall say no more about the stack or memory model. Whatever their virtues for simplifying compilation, they seem to guarantee more storage references and thus worse performance than the other two models.

The storage-to-memory model is shared by 370 and MC68000. At first glance a 370-type approach seems attractive.

```
x = a + b;  L R1, a
            A R1,b
            ST R1, x

y = a + b;  ST R1, y
```

On the ROMP we get:

```
x = a + b;  L R1, a
            L R2, b
            CAS R3, R1, R2 Add
            ST R3, x

y = a + b;  ST R3,y
```

The ROMP takes one more instruction. (It does have some opportunities to obtain overlap on the Loads by inserting unrelated instructions, but let us ignore that benefit). If the example is changed slightly to:

```
x = a + b;
y = a − b;
```

We then get on 370:

```
x = a + b;  L R1, a
            A R1, b
            ST R1, b

y = a − b;  L R1, a
            S R1, b
            ST R1, y
```

After the first statement, neither a nor b are available and they are the operands of the next statement. On the ROMP, both are available and so there is no need for an expensive refetch. Of course we can turn the 370 into a ROMP-style, register-to-register machine. The problem is that the 370 Add instruction destroys one of its operands, while CAS, an Add that doesn't set the condition code on the ROMP, is three-address. The PL.8 compiler goes to considerable effort to give 370 code the benefits of both the

storage-to-register and register-to-register approaches. It is not clear that the effort is worth it. On some 370 models, two Loads and an Add Register may be as fast as Load, Add from Storage. In any case there are relatively few storage-to-register computational operations in a typical snapshot of 370 execution. One typical mix shows the following most frequently-executed storage-to-register ops.

Instruction	% of execution
C: compare	1.74
N:and	1.26
AL:add logical	1.07
CL:compare logical	.44
A:add	.39
S:subtract	.37
O:or	.36
CH:compare half	.33
AH:add half	.24
SH:subtract half	.10
MH:multiply half	.07

If all such ops are included, the percentage of executions is less than 6.5%. Modest as this figure is, it overstates the advantage to be gained from memory-to-register ops, as many of these instructions are addressing literals. On the ROMP they would be immediate ops. In light of frequency of usage, potential performance improvement, hardware requirements and compiler complexity it is hard to believe that storage-to-register ops are cost effective.

The reader may not be impressed with optimizing a + b, and would be correct if the only benefit of optimization was a rewrite of the user's program at the source level. The most potent effects of an optimizing compiler are derived from reducing the administrative code used to implement high-level constructs. Consider what it takes to implement the following code fragment in PL.8.

```
1 a               static ext,
2 b               integer,
2 c (0:10),
    3 d           integer,
    3 e           integer,
    3 f           char (16);
  x = e(i);
```

The reference to e(i) includes the following factors:

- The address of the structure a

- The displacement of e within a

- i times the stride of c.

In PL.8 and Pascal, subscript range testing is normally done even on production code. Thus there is also a trap to ensure that the value of i is between zero and ten. The fetch of e(i) may be commoned or moved out of a loop, but there are many other opportunities for optimization. The load of the address constant to locate the structure need not be repeated when a reference is made to b. Storing into d(i) requires no additional instructions. Programs are filled with opportunities to reuse portions of this administrative type code. The higher the level of the machine, the less chance there will be for reuse, as one factor may change.

An example of this phenomenon is in subscript computations. As the ROMP does not have a built-in multiply instruction, the compiler generates a series of shifts, adds and subtracts when the stride is a constant. Thus a multiply by 24 is implemented as:

shiftl(i, 4) + shiftl(i, 3)

If somewhere else in the program there is a multiply of i by 8 or 16, one of the shifts already used to compute i*24 will suffice. By systematically exploiting the many small opportunities for optimization that occur in real programs, the PL.8 compiler can produce programs that execute very rapidly on the ROMP.

It is now necessary to discuss register allocation. So far we have tacitly assumed that there would be enough registers to hold all the intermediate results which optimization creates. A large number of registers require, not only more hardware, but more bits in the instruction to name the particular register. Compiler studies showed that, while 32 registers were beneficial, 16 were a reasonable compromise. A PL.8-type compiler approach would probably not be very effective with substantially fewer than 16 registers. The code would tend to look like the memory-to-memory model of computation. The PL.8 compiler uses a graph coloring algorithm [3] to assign the infinite number of symbolic registers used during optimization to the 16 available on the ROMP, but other methods can be used.

It is particularly important that a machine not restrict the register allocation by typing registers or otherwise constraining their use. Implicit usage is also undesirable. Even the ROMP has some minor problems here, but they are easily overcome. Register 0 cannot be used as a base because the CPU assumes this means the value zero. The register allocation phase of the compiler overcomes this problem by introducing an interference in the coloring graph. Each symbolic register used as a base interferes with real register zero; thus, the compiler will not assign such a symbolic register to R0. Branch and Link implicitly uses R15. This was chosen by the compiler writers to match the proposed linkage conventions. The most bothersome constraint is paired shifts. Normal shifts on the ROMP are of the form:

Shift   RA, shift amount

The value to be shifted is in RA and is returned to the same register. If only this form of instruction were available, implementing a multiply by an arbitrary constant using shifts and adds would often require intermediate copies. Rather than introduce a 4-byte nondestructive shift instruction, the paired shift was introduced. Every register has a twin whose name is obtained by complementing the low bit of the name (e.g., the twin of R2 is R3 and vice versa). The PL.8 register allocator handles this in the following manner. The internal form of the program used by optimization has shifts with separate target, source and shift count fields. Prior to register coloring an attempt is made to coalesce the source and target. If this fails, an attempt is made to coalesce the source and target onto a particular pair of real registers. Other cases, which seem to be rare, result in an extra load register.

On machines like the 370 there are a plethora of problems associated with registers:

- The 370 really has fewer than 16 registers because at least one must be reserved for program addressability.

- The fact that integer multiply destroys a

pair of registers introduces complications.

- The PL.8 compiler has never really exploited 370 instructions that use register pairs such as the loop closing BXLE op and double length shifts. (We are not alone in not using BXLE. It has a frequency of less than .01% on most execution samples.)

- The fact that some arithmetic and logical instructions work on less than a full word is a constant problem. It takes a lot of special analysis to decide when a short op can be used.

While the ROMP does have some minor irregularities in its register scheme, it is a substantial improvement on our past architectures, resulting in few problems for an optimizing compiler whose goal is to retain many available quantities in registers.

Checking and Linkage

In recent years programming languages have attempted to guard against programming errors and raise the level of the source language. The ROMP instruction set supports both.

The trap instructions provide an economic method to test for unusual or erroneous conditions during execution. Pascal and PL.8 both customarily run in production with checking enabled. However, it is possible to eliminate these checks. By having separate checking ops and then optimizing code, the compiler writer can ensure that the correctness criteria of a wide variety of languages are efficiently enforced.

The efficient implementation of a language like C, in which primitives are coded as basic functions, clearly depends on linkage. However, higher level languages which implement data abstractions also depend on the subroutine mechanisms. In implementing procedure call, the ROMP convention is to load the first four parameters into registers. The invoked procedure may then use them in place or copy them into other registers. The important point is that they seldom need to be copied into storage, an expensive operation. Longer parameter lists must be put in storage, but these are relatively infrequent. This strategy is much more efficient than the traditional 370 or UNIX type linkage, which passes parameters in storage. When invoking

a procedure, it is not normally necessary to load its address. System routines such as multiply or the primitive storage allocator are kept in low memory and the 24-bit absolute branch can be used to access them. Relative branching within a bound module, which is as large as a megabyte, is also possible with a single instruction. On entry to a procedure it is merely necessary to do a Store Multiple to save any registers that will be used and bump the stack pointer. Stack overflow is normally caught by an attempt to reference a protected page. (For procedures with large stack frames an explicit check is made.) Exit from a procedure consists of loading the return value in a register, restoring the saved registers and executing a branch register.

In practice, there are many variations on this theme, depending on the language, system conventions, and the user's program. For example, in Figure 1 we see the object code for a function that performs the typical C storage-to-storage move. Because it is able to work entirely out of registers that are, by convention, not saved over a call, it has no prologue and an epilogue that consists of a branch register. As source programs and languages become more complex, procedure call overhead will increase, but the compiler writer can always choose the minimum code sequence for the task at hand. One interesting consequence of the MMU relocate is that, given inverted page tables, many systems will want to allocate a very large contiguous stack when a process is created. There is no reason to maintain the stack in disjoint sections, as the mere existence of address space does not degrade performance as is the case with conventional page tables.

High-Level Functions

High-level functions on the ROMP are implemented with subroutines rather than microcode. The most obvious examples are

```
/* move to a byte of zeros. */
move (t, s)
char *t, *s;

while (*t + + = *s + +);
return;
```

multiply, divide and storage-to-storage move. On 370 instruction traces, move constitutes about 2% of all executions, making it, by far, the most important complex instruction. It

Object Code for ROMP

```
2: 000000                      PDEF   move
5: 000000              %6:
5: 000000 LCS   4003          LCS    r0,$MEMORY+*s(r3)
5: 000002 INC   9131          INC    r3,r3,1
5: 000004 INC   9121          INC    r2,r2,1
5: 000006 CIS   9400          CIS    cr,r0,0
5: 000008 BNBX  89AF FFFC     BFX    cr,b26/eq,%6
5: 00000C STC   DE02 FFFF     STC    r0,$MEMORY+*t-1(r2)
7: 000010 BNBR  E88F          BFR    24,r15
```

Figure 1   Example

tends to consume close to 10% of the execution time. On large 370 machines 2 bytes are moved per cycle. (A cycle is taken to mean the time for a minimum op such as a register add.) For aligned moves, the ROMP can achieve close to this rate by means of an "unrolled" loop. For unaligned moves, a carefully handcrafted subroutine has been written. It uses ops which are of otherwise marginal utility, such as MCxx. There are even some compensations for not having the 370 MVC op. The ROMP move subroutine has been tailored to make moves of overlapped data nondestructive, thus satisfying the PL.8 rule. Once again we note that high-level instructions never quite do what they are supposed to do, but low-level ops can be specialized to the specific requirements.

The various versions of multiply on 370 constitute about .1% of all instructions executed. High-performance 370 machines tend to have a very expensive multiplier. Low-end machines implement the multiply instruction with a microcode operator that is the functional equivalent of the ROMP Multiply Step instruction. It is hard to see how the ROMP solution results in significantly worse performance. Sometimes there may be better performance. Constant multiplies can be done with adds and shifts. Some applications may not require a full 32-bit multiply. If the multiplier is only 12 bits long, then it is possible to get a product with six rather than 16 multiply step instructions. Once again the basic instruction set permits the user or compiler writer to do exactly what he wants with great efficiency rather than depending on the foresight of some computer architects. (Those of us who participated in the development of the ROMP architecture are constantly grateful that we did not enshrine our more exotic requirements in silicon.)

One of the sadder sequences of code is to see a divide by two in a binary search or heap sort implemented with a divide rather than a shift instruction. Even on high-performance machines, divide can take almost ten times a shift. That is a big loss of performance in a loop that is likely to be very important. This doesn't occur because compiler writers are unaware that a right shift can sometimes replace a divide by a power of two. The problem is negative numbers as dividends. $(-1)/2$ is 0 on 370. -1 shifted right one bit is still -1. The substitution of a shift for a divide only works for positive dividends. For the PL.8 language we decided to implement a true twos complement divide subroutine using the Euclidean algorithm that rounds down rather than toward 0. Thus replacing divides with shifts gives the same result. In this case a low-level instruction set gave us a new view of source language semantics. We simply implemented the divide subroutine that we wanted rather than accepting built-in semantics.

The ROMP does have Load and Store Multiple ops. It would be possible to get along without them. However, this is one case where a high-level instruction improves performance. This is because they permit the CPU to send one address to the memory subsystem and then do a series of Loads or Stores without the interference of fetching a series of instructions and sending effective addresses to the memory subsystem.

The ROMP approach to implementing high-level function frees the compiler writer and user from the tyranny of instruction sets without giving up any significant performance. Furthermore, the engineer can concentrate on making Load, Store and Branch run well. Here is the frequency of execution of the top ten instructions in a typical snapshot of 370 execution.

Instruction	% of Executions
BC:Branch Condition	20.2
L:Load	15.5
TM:Test Under Mask	6.1
ST:Store	5.9
LR:Load Register	4.7
LA:Load Address	4.0
LTR:Test Register	3.8
BCR:Branch Register	2.9
MVC:Move Characters	2.1
LH:Load Half Word	1.8

Together these constitute 67% of all instructions executed. Clearly the vast majority of the over two hundred 370 instructions occur a good deal less than 1% of the time. Most of the above have direct counterparts in the ROMP instruction set. Other than move, it is hard to think of any 370 instruction which might have improved ROMP performance if it had been implemented.

Code Size and Path Length
The 801 minicomputer was designed to have the shortest possible path length, and code size was sacrificed to achieve this. This is highly appropriate on a machine with a cache. In a machine with a storage hierarchy, most of the faults come from referencing data. Doubling the size of the code only marginally increases the number of faults. However, the ROMP does not have a cache. In order to multiplex the 32-bit memory channel with instructions and data, it helps to have short instructions.

For this reason the ROMP has short forms of many commonly occurring full-function instructions. In addition, a compromise was made such that, of the register-to-register operations, only CAS, the form of add that does not set the condition register, is fully three-address. Shifts have the paired form while subtract and the logical ops destroy one operand. This is a compromise. Add occurs so frequently that a 16-bit, three-address format has a big benefit. There are not enough code points to have all the other RR instructions in 16-bit, nondestructive format. Because the register allocator was able to coalesce operands most of the time, a 16-bit, two-operand format was chosen for the other RR ops. Similar reasoning led us to have short-form increment and decrement instructions.

All in all, the ROMP is surprisingly space efficient without undue performance loss. The average length of a ROMP instruction varies from application to application, but is usually well under 3 bytes. In some cases, the ROMP does require an added instruction but it is relatively infrequent and an easy decision for the compiler.

Details
A number of small details contribute to

making the ROMP a good target for compilers.

- Condition codes tend to be an awkward match for many systematic methods of compilation. In the ROMP, those instructions that set the relational bits of the condition register set them in the same way as a compare with zero. This permits the compiler to eliminate all compares with zero that are preceded by an instruction that sets the same register as the register comparand. It is also important to not set the condition register on Load, Store, or the basic Adds that compute addresses. This permits code to be inserted, or rearranged without worrying about the condition register. The condition register test bit provides an efficient means to move and compare arbitrary bits even when their position in a word must be computed at run time. This makes it very efficient to implement packed arrays of bits and Pascal-type sets.

- Load instructions that fetch bytes and half-words from storage either set the remainder of the register to zero or fill it with sign bits. This makes it easier to treat partial words as algebraic or logical quantities. On 370 one of the most common idioms is a subtract of a register from itself followed by an insert character. LC does the entire job on the ROMP.

- The Load and Store Multiple instructions can be used to do block moves or zero large areas in an efficient manner.

- Sometimes constant data will not fit into the ROMP 16-bit immediate field. Instructions are provided that treat the immediate field as a left-justified quantity. It is thus possible to follow either of two strategies. Use two ops if either the upper or lower form is insufficient. The alternative is to manufacture the constant in a register, which requires two instructions, but then the constant may be reused many times by short, fast RR ops.

Other Methodologies
Not all source languages will be implemented with optimizing compilers like PL.8.

Where high-quality object code is not crucial it may pay to have a very fast compiler that

202

produces mediocre object code. A number of features make this a reasonably easy task. Even code from a very naive compiler is quite compact. The large number of general-purpose registers means it is easy to reuse values over short stretches. The large displacement means one can reserve large areas for intermediate results without fearing overflow. High-level function can be invoked via subroutines with a reasonable in-line overhead. Finally, code can be addressed and constants can always be manufactured on-the-fly without establishing or maintaining addressability to code segments and a literal pool as is required on 370.

Another method of implementation is interpretation. The ROMP is a very good interpreter. This should not surprise us as it is really a general-purpose micro engine.

Conclusion

The ROMP architecture provides the high-level language compiler writer with the right set of implementation primitives. Its strength is the ability to combine the basic operations in new ways suited to the task at hand. In Figure 1 we have an example of how a common idiom in C is efficiently implemented. It is hard to see how the most specialized instruction could improve very much on this. After all, there will have to be a fetch and store, as well as a test and bumps for each character moved. A high-level instruction would be further complicated by considerations of crossing page boundaries, running too long, etc. If we build in this instruction we are tailoring the machine to C; other languages such as Pascal, ADA, FORTRAN and COBOL that do not share the

C convention that character strings are terminated with a zero, will find the op useless. However, even C may not find this the best strategy for character movement all the time. Large buffers should not be moved 1 byte at a time. Then there are other idioms in C, for searching tables, scanning input forward and backward, looking for other characters and an infinite number of other tasks. Is each of these to be a special op? Will the compiler have to look for complicated patterns trying to match a complex function to a complex instruction? The ROMP permits the compiler writer to combine primitives to efficiently solve the particular problem at hand for a wide variety of source languages.

As the programming community moves toward languages that are more powerful than C it becomes even more urgent to rely on basic constructs. Only the simplest languages can be based on complex, high-level messages. Thousands of hieroglyphics are much less powerful than an alphabet of twenty-odd characters. Fast, primitive operations will be required to efficiently implement the high level languages of the future.

References

1. M. Auslander and M.E. Hopkins, "An Overview of the PL.8 compiler," *Proc. of the Sigplan '82 Symposium on Compiler Writing,* Boston, MA, June 23-25, 1982.

2. George Radin, "The 801 Minicomputer," *Proc. of Symposium on Architectural Support for Programming Languages and Operating Systems,* Palo Alto, California, March 1-3, 1982.

3. Gregory J. Chaitin, Marc A. Auslander, Ashok K. Chandra, John Cocke, Martin E. Hopkins, and Peter W. Markstein, "Register Allocation via Coloring," *Computer Languages,* Vol 6, No 1, 1981, 47-57.

ENGINEERING A RISC COMPILER SYSTEM

F. Chow, M. Himelstein, E. Killian, L. Weber

MIPS Computer Systems
930 Arques Ave
Sunnyvale, CA 94086

Abstract

RISC machine compilers play a more important role in enhancing system performance than conventional compilers. In a RISC system, traditional boundaries between hardware, compiler, and operating system are modified to optimize overall system performance. Responsibility for a given function shifts to the compiler system when the compiler can do a better job, often using special techniques to accomplish its new tasks. With careful engineering, such a system can be both run-time and compile-time efficient.

Introduction

The MIPS machine, like other RISC machines, provides an interesting challenge for compiler writers. A RISC machine provides primitive hardware functions rather than bundling functionality into complex instructions, allowing the compiler to optimize below the level of other architectures. The compiler can generate optimal code for a simple machine more easily since the architecture provides fewer alternatives in performing a given function. This allows the compiler to focus its attention on other aspects of optimization, including global optimization and an efficient run-time environment.

The MIPS machine was designed according to RISC principles: maximizing performance through trade-offs between hardware and software. As such, the architectural design[1] was developed in parallel with the operating system[2] and compiler effort. Many architectural decisions were made based on special support provided by the compilers.

The MIPS compiler system was designed to satisfy a number of objectives:
- It must support a reduced instruction set by providing for functions not present in the hardware.
- It must produce code and data that achieve maximum run-time efficiency.
- It must be compile-time efficient.
- It must be tested and bootstrapped before having hardware.

This paper presents the MIPS compiler system by addressing these issues and relating them to the relevant components in the system.

Overview of the MIPS Compiler Suite

The MIPS compiler suite contains compilers for C, Pascal and FORTRAN 77. FORTRAN and Pascal adhere to the existing ANSI Standards, and C conforms to the defacto standard.[3] MIPS Pascal and FORTRAN contain common extensions. As figure 1 shows, each language has its own front-end, while common back-end phases generate and optimize code. MIPS' run-time libraries provide language-dependent functions for each language.

The front-ends translate the semantics of the different languages into an intermediate

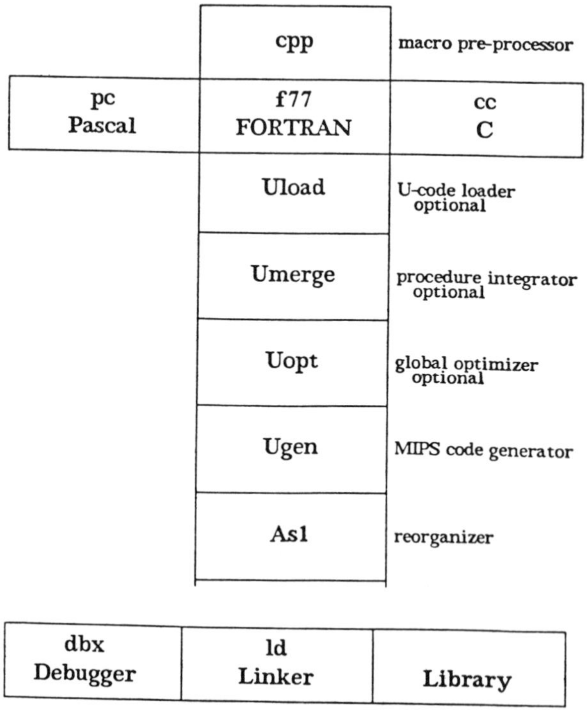

	cpp	macro pre-processor
pc Pascal	f77 FORTRAN	cc C
	Uload	U-code loader optional
	Umerge	procedure integrator optional
	Uopt	global optimizer optional
	Ugen	MIPS code generator
	Asl	reorganizer

dbx Debugger	ld Linker	Library

Figure 1 - MIPS Compiler Structure

EH0251-9/86/0000/0204$01.00 © 1986 IEEE

Reprinted from *The Proceedings of COMPCON Spring 86*, 1986, pages 132-137. Copyright © 1986 by The Institute of Electrical and Electronics Engineers, Inc.

representation, called U-Code, used by several of the common phases. U-Code is a stack-oriented pseudo-machine language originating from the version in use at Stanford University.[4] With U-Code as the intermediate representation, the system provides uniform compilation and optimization support to C, Pascal and FORTRAN.

Each front-end produces a symbol table file that contains loader and debugger information. Each compiler phase may add to or modify the symbol table to provide information for the loader or extend debugger information. The loader uses the symbol table information for relocation and merges it into the final object module. The source-level debugger uses the symbol table to provide a robust debugging environment even in the face of optimizations.

Every compiler phase performs optimizations. An optional phase, called Uopt, performs global optimization and register allocation. The code generator, called Ugen, does local optimizations and produces MIPS assembly language output. The final assembly phase, called As1, does peep-hole optimizations and architecture-dependent pipeline scheduling and produces a MIPS machine language object module.

Supporting a Reduced Instruction Set

The MIPS machine has a simple and uniform instruction set. All instructions are 32 bits in length and execute in one cycle. The compiler synthesizes operations that require greater instruction length or cycles from sequences of instructions.[5] Close interaction between compiler design and architecture design[6] results in synthesized operations that are as efficient as their counterparts in conventional machines, and sometimes more efficient.

Accessing Data

The MIPS architecture provides only one addressing mode: the sum of a register and a 16-bit signed offset. Addressing static memory requires a 32-bit absolute address, so the assembler uses two instructions to synthesize an absolute address reference: the first loads a register with the high 16 bits of the address and the second performs the reference using the low 16 address bits as the offset from that register. This 8-byte sequence is comparable in length to an absolute address reference in other architectures (for example, it is 7 bytes on a

VAX*), and is just as fast. Other optimizations further reduce the cost of this synthesis. For example, pipeline reorganization may schedule these instructions separately to occupy idle cycles in other sequences, or peephole optimization may recognize the high 16 bits of the address as common to two references.

To reduce the cost of static memory references even further, the system dedicates one register, called the global pointer, to address 64K of static data. The code generator, assembler, and linker all participate in grouping small pieces of static data so they can be addressed by this one register in a one cycle, 4-byte reference, which is a substantial improvement in density and speed. Control over all components of the system was key in using this simple technique.

The global optimizer also plays a role in reducing the cost of accessing 32-bit constants and addresses. Since it is expensive to load such constants into registers, the optimizer analyzes their appearances and assigns them to registers in the regions where they occur. It also eliminates load redundancies by moving the loading of these constants out of loops.

Calling Procedures

Procedure call, entry, and return is another area where the compiler must synthesize the proper functionality. A good design allows effective subsetting of the complete procedure call mechanism. In our design, a procedure call, entry, and return can be as fast and simple as two instructions in two cycles. The protocol specifies only how to pass parameters and what registers to preserve across the procedure call. This allows the called procedure to organize its stack frame (if any) as appropriate.

For each procedure, the code generator allocates space for the largest parameter list used in the body. The code allocates this space once on entry to the procedure. Each point of call requires no further stack manipulation. The first four words of parameters are placed in specific registers (often the parameter computation is done directly into the appropriate register), and other parameters are placed in the stack. 95% of the calls require no memory references because they pass fewer than four words of parameters. An instruction stores the return address in a register and transfers control to the called procedure. The contract between caller and callee specifies that the callee may freely use the *unsaved* registers, but must preserve the

---

* VAX is a Trademark of Digital Equipment Corporation.

saved registers. Variables live at the point of call will be allocated to saved registers by Uopt and Ugen. The result of a function is returned in a register.

On entry to a procedure, the first four parameters and the return address appear in registers and the other parameters are on the the stack. The called procedure then allocates a stack frame by subtracting the frame size from the stack pointer, saving registers with explicit store instructions, and moves register parameters and the return address to home locations. On return, the sequence is reversed.

A procedure that does not call any other procedure is called a *leaf procedure*. Leaf procedures do not need parameter and return address registers for further calls, and the parameters and return address are assigned to their input registers. No data movement is necessary. A leaf can allocate register variables to unsaved registers, eliminating the need to save and restore registers. With no registers to save and no calls to make, a leaf often needs no stack frame because everything resides in registers. At this point the subtract and add from

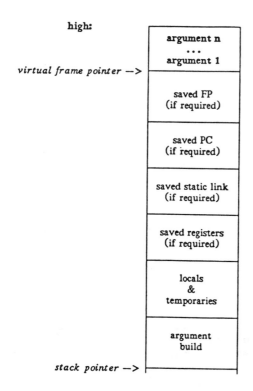

Figure 2 - MIPS Stack Frame

the stack pointer are eliminated, leaving only the call and return jumps as overhead.

A frame pointer is used in most linkage conventions to support the allocation of data on the activation stack. The frame pointer mechanism is not used in the MIPS compiler system. This is possible because the the frame pointer is usually known to the compiler to be at a fixed offset from the stack pointer, which is computed to be the maximum size of the stack frame. A compile-time fixed offset from the stack pointer is called the *virtual frame pointer*. When a procedure uses dynamic allocation, which is rare, the code generator allocates the fixed-size portion of the stack frame and then uses another register to remember this point in the stack before allocating the variable-sized data. Figure 2 illustrates the activation stack frame at the point of a call.

To support stack traces and general debugging, the compiler adds symbol table entries to specify the register and size that together represent a virtual frame pointer. The symbol table specifies the location of the return address (either in its input register or in the stack frame). We have shifted the task of maintaining a simple activation stack for debugging from procedure entry to compile and debug time.

Scheduling Instructions in Software

In the MIPS machine's pipeline, "load" and "branch" instructions cause memory delays. Rather than providing expensive scheduling and interlocking in hardware, we rely on the final assembly phase of the compiler, As1, to ensure consistency between instructions.[7] An optimization called pipeline reorganization improves performance by 20% on average, by ordering instructions to remove memory delays and to overlap floating point instruction with other instructions.

A load delay occurs when one instruction loads a value into a register and the next instruction uses that register. As1 changes the instruction order so that the instruction following the load does not depend on the load. This permits one instruction to access memory in parallel while executing another instruction.

Branches in the MIPS architecture take effect after the instruction following the branch instruction; this is called a *delayed branch*. The hardware can execute the instruction already in the pipeline while accessing the instruction determined by the branch. As1 places an instruction that logically precedes the branch instruction in the delay slot of the branch.

If As1 cannot find a suitable instruction from above the branch, it replicates the instruction at the target of the branch provided no side-effects occur if the branch falls through.

The independent floating point unit can execute its instructions in parallel with ordinary instructions and memory operations. As1 orders instructions so that the machine does useful work while the floating point unit executes its slightly slower instructions.

Reorganization presents an interesting challenge to the debugger. Source-level debuggers provide facilities to stop and examine program state on any source line. A reorganized program may have already executed instructions from lines following the desired source line and may not have executed all the instructions preceding the line.

To permit the debugging of production programs, the MIPS compiler system stores procedure-relative line number information for each instruction. The debugger uses the line number information to simulate a source-code consistent view of program execution.

Handling Complex Operations

The MIPS instruction set lacks bit field operations. The front-ends of the compiler assume responsibility for translating bit field inserts and extracts into machine primitive instructions such as shifts, bit-wise AND and bit-wise OR. The global optimizer can recognize these simpler operations and apply its optimization techniques on all or part of them. For example, optimization improves assignments to multiple bit fields in the same word.

Another example of a complex operation is multiplication. The final assembly phase of the compiler translates multiplication into optimal instruction sequences. Even though the MIPS machine has a hardware multiplication unit, it is often better to synthesize a multiplication from simpler instructions when multiplying by simple constants. For example, multiplication by 14 executes in three cycles (two shifts and a subtract), which is faster than a hardware multiply.

The MIPS machine only provides the fastest executing forms of branch instructions, which comprise the majority of branches based on dynamic frequency. More complex branch conditions are synthesized by the final assembly phase. The assembler can use the extra instruction to fill a delay slot of another instruction.

Achieving Run-time Efficiency

The MIPS machine provides an ideal target for many optimizations. Work at Stanford[8] shows that machine-independent optimizations are particularly effective on RISC machines. The global optimizer, which operates on U-code, is derived from that work. MIPS has refined the U-Code intermediate language to make it expose most MIPS machine primitives to the optimizer. In addition, most of the optimizations were specifically tailored to the MIPS environment. The global optimizations performed include: copy propagation, common subexpressions, invariant code motion, removal of redundant assignments, strength reduction, and linear function test replacements.

Uopt also provides register allocation among its optimizations. The load/store nature of RISC machines makes register allocation especially effective. By globally analyzing usage patterns, the register allocator decides which variables best reside in registers. Uopt uses a priority-based global graph-coloring algorithm,[9] which often achieves optimal results with reasonable compile-time cost. Register allocation helps realize the full benefits of the other global optimizations, since intermediate computational results are best saved in registers. The 31 general-purpose registers provided by the MIPS machine also increases the versatility of the register allocator.

The MIPS global optimizer operates on one procedure at a time. Because large procedures generally offer more opportunities for optimization, MIPS provides a procedure integrator, called Umerge, which selectively copies procedures in-line at their point of call, eliminating call overhead while increasing the global optimizer's impact.

Both Uopt and Umerge operate on a single compilation unit at a time. The MIPS compiler also provide the framework for supporting global optimizations across an entire load module. The U-Code loader, called Uload, merges separate compilation units into a single file at the U-Code level. This enables multi-module programs to achieve the same degree of optimization as single-module programs.

The code generator was designed specifically for the MIPS architecture and generates very good local code. Although attention to detail is critical, we found code selection straight-forward for the MIPS machine. To improve local code quality, Ugen recognizes and optimizes local common subexpressions, performs simplification and folding in expressions, deletes dead code, and does branch and label optimization. Ugen also allocates expression temporaries to registers in a manner which maximizes reorganization opportunities.

Assuring Compile-time Efficiency

To reduce compilation time, the MIPS compiler system uses binary forms for all interfaces, including U-Code, symbol table files and assembler code. The compilers are self compiling, and therefore self optimizing.

The MIPS compiler system employs a sophisticated symbol table. The symbol table supplies a large amount of source file information to the symbolic debugger and external symbol information to the loader. The design goals for the symbol table included minimizing disk space usage and reducing the cost to compiler passes. The symbol table also contains enough information to help debug optimized code. Due to the symbol table design, full debugging symbol tables are typically a third to a half smaller than 4.2BSD or System V COFF symbol tables, even though they contain more information.

The loader is another example of compiler efficiency. In a multi-module program, changing one module requires recompiling only that module, but requires relinking all the modules and libraries. Therefore, we have stressed efficiency in the loader design. For example, we have optimized library scanning by including a hash table in the library for externals. To process a library, the loader hashes the remaining undefined symbols into the library's hash table. This scan is efficient because a program typically contains fewer undefined symbols during a load than defined externals in the library.

Sophisticated optimizations such as those found in our compiler system can significantly lengthen compilation time. We are using execution time statistics to provide the compiler with accurate information on what areas of a program require optimization. This feedback mechanism allows the global optimizer and procedure integrator to optimize only those areas which promise the greatest gains.

Testing Strategies

The RISC approach is most effective when the hardware, compiler, and operating system are developed simultaneously. In development of the compiler, the goal has been to have a fully-tested production-quality system available at the same time as the hardware. To support operating system work with a similar goal, a well-debugged compiler was actually needed substantially earlier. No compiler system can achieve production-quality status without extensive testing, particularly on many large programs.

Simulation is the answer, but conventional simulation is far too slow to permit extensive testing of large programs. A novel simulator, called Moxie, was developed that translates a MIPS object file to a VAX object file. Moxie translates object file formats as well as converting MIPS instructions to VAX instructions. The resulting VAX program is then run, and in effect simulates the MIPS code. Moxie also translates MIPS UNIX* system calls to VAX UNIX system calls, thus allowing the simulation of programs that do arbitrary I/O and system interaction.

This technique allows MIPS code to "run" at the rate of 600K instructions per second on a VAX 780, sufficiently fast to run numerous UNIX programs (such as yacc, grep, diff, and cpp), to bootstrap the MIPS compiler itself, and to test the compilers with C, FORTRAN, and Pascal validation suites.

Moxie also has extensive tracing facilities that provide precise instruction counting statistics and a cache simulator that models the effects of program interaction with main memory. With these tools, accurate benchmark (e.g. whetstone, linpack) results were obtained before hardware was available.

A symbolic debugger layered on top of Moxie uses both the original and translated binaries along with a Moxie-generated table mapping MIPS instruction addresses to their VAX counterparts. This environment provides both machine-level access to MIPS registers and instructions (use for compiler development) and source-level debugging (useful for applications written in C, FORTRAN, and Pascal).

Conclusion

The compiler is an integral part of a RISC-based computer system. The MIPS compiler system is responsible for providing functionality not present in the hardware. Supporting absolute address references, multiplication, and procedure call mechanism using more primitive hardware functions are a few examples of operations that the MIPS compiler system does better than an equivalent hardware-only implementation. The techniques are simple, but quite effective. The

---

* UNIX is a Trademark of AT&T.

compiler also performs important traditional optimizations. The net effect is a system that is both compile-time and run-time efficient. We believe this approach, based on careful engineering of the compiler system with respect to the underlying hardware, results in a superior compiler compared to current multi-targeted compilers.

Acknowledgement

We would like to thank the members of the compiler development group for their fine job in implementing the compiler system. We would also like to thank the MIPS architecture group for providing a very clean machine architecture. And, we especially thank all those users who found that last bug in the compiler.

1. John Moussouris, Les Crudele, Dan Freitas, Craig Hansen, Ed Hudson, Steve Przybylski, Tom Riordan, and Chris Rowen, "A CMOS RISC Processor with Integrated System Functions," *Proceedings COMPCON*, IEEE, (March 4-6, 1986).

2. Mike DeMoney, Jim Moore, and John Mashey, "Operating System Support on a RISC," *Proceedings COMPCON*, IEEE, (March 4-6, 1986).

3. Brian W. Kernighan and Dennis M. Ritchie, *The C Programming Language*, Prentice-Hall (1978).

4. Peter Nye and Fred Chow, "A Transporter's Guide to the Stanford U-Code Compiler System," *Technical Report*, Computer Systems Laboratory, Stanford University, (June 1983).

5. M. E. Hopkins, "Compiling High-Level Functions on Low-Level Machines," *Proceedings ICCD*, IEEE , (October 1983).

6. John L. Hennessy, "VLSI Processor Architecture," *IEEE Trans. on Computers* C-33(12) pp. 1221-1246 (Dec 1984).

7. Thomas Gross, "Code Optimization of Pipeline Constraints," *Technical Report No. 83-255*, Computer Systems Laboratory, Stanford University, (December 1983).

8. Fred Chow, "A Portable Machine-Independent Global Optimizer — Design and Measurements," *Ph.D. Thesis and Technical Report 83-254*, Computer Systems Laboratory, Stanford University, (Dec 1983).

9. Fred Chow and John Hennessy, "Register Allocation by Priority-based Coloring," *Proceedings SIGPLAN*, ACM, (June 17-22, 1984).

Section 5: Example Systems

5.1 Background

The pioneering work on RISC has produced three experimental or prototype systems: the RISC I from Berkeley, the 801 from IBM, and MIPS from Stanford. Quite recently, commercially-available systems based on RISC principles have begun to appear. This section provides a survey of both categories of systems.

5.2 Article Summary

"The 801 Minicomputer" reports on the seminal work and resulting prototype from IBM. This work inspired later efforts and marks the true beginning of the RISC movement. "A VLSI RISC" reports on the RISC I machine developed at Berkeley. This was perhaps the first use of the term RISC. The RISC I is the best-documented and most-studied of all the RISC machines. In both of these articles, the developers provide a detailed rationale for the design decisions taken.

The article by Mokhoff provides a brief survey of existing commercially available machines. He points out that these, inevitably, are not pure RISC machines but contain both RISC and CISC features. The article focuses on what are undoubtedly the two most significant of current offerings: those of IBM and Hewlett-Packard.

The next two articles discuss the IBM PC RT. This machine is an outgrowth of the experimental IBM 801 system. "ROMP/MMU Technology Introduction" defines the product objectives and describes RT/801 differences. "The IBM RT PC ROMP and Memory Management Unit Architecture" is a more detailed look at the processor and MMU chips.

The RISC-based product family from Hewlett-Packard is introduced in "Beyond RISC: High Precision Architecture." Design objectives and the resulting design principles are discussed.

"A CMOS RISC Processor with Integrated System Functions" describes the product from MIPS Computer Systems, which is an outgrowth of the Stanford MIPS project.

To provide the reader a point of comparison, the final article, "The Intel 80386—Architecture and Implementation," looks at one of the contemporary 32-bit microprocessors. This article illustrates the direction that the mainstream of computer architecture has been taking.

George Radin

The 801 Minicomputer

This paper provides an overview of an experimental system developed at the IBM Thomas J. Watson Research Center. It consists of a running hardware prototype, a control program, and an optimizing compiler. The basic concepts underlying the system are discussed, as are the performance characteristics of the prototype. In particular, three principles are examined: (1) system orientation towards the pervasive use of high-level language programming and a sophisticated compiler, (2) a primitive instruction set which can be completely hard-wired, and (3) storage hierarchy and I/O organization to enable the CPU to execute an instruction at almost every cycle.

Introduction

In October 1975, a group of about twenty researchers at the IBM Thomas J. Watson Research Center began the design of a minicomputer, a compiler, and a control program whose goal was to achieve significantly better cost/performance for high-level language programs than that attainable by existing systems. The name 801 was chosen because it was the IBM number of the building in which the project resided. (The twenty creative researchers were singularly uninspired namers.) This paper describes the basic design principles and the resulting system components (hardware and software).

Basic concepts

• *Single-cycle implementation*
Probably the major distinguishing characteristic of the 801 architecture is that its instructions are constrained to execute in a single, straightforward, rather primitive machine cycle. A similar general approach has been pursued by a group at the University of California [1].

Complex, high-function instructions, which require several cycles to execute, are conventionally realized by some combination of random logic and microcode. It is often true that implementing a complex function in random logic will result in its execution being significantly faster than if the function were programmed as a sequence of primitive instructions. Examples are floating-point arithmetic and fixed-point multiply. We have no objection to this strategy, provided the frequency of use justifies the cost and, more importantly, provided these complex instructions in no way slow down the primitive instructions.

But it is just this pernicious effect on the primitive instructions that has made us suspicious. Most instruction frequency studies show a sharp skew in favor of high usage of primitive instructions (such as LOAD, STORE, BRANCH, COMPARE, ADD). If the presence of a more complex set adds just one logic level to a ten-level basic machine cycle (e.g., to fetch a microinstruction from ROS), the CPU has been slowed down by 10%. The frequency and performance improvement of the complex functions must first overcome this 10% degradation and then justify the additional cost. If the presence of complex functions results in the CPU exceeding a packaging constraint on some level (e.g., a chip, a board), the performance degradation can be even more substantial.

Often, however, a minicomputer that boasts of a rich set of complex instructions has not spent additional hardware at all, but has simply microprogrammed the functions. These microinstructions are designed to execute in a single cycle and, in that cycle, to set controls most useful for the functions desired. This, however, is exactly the design goal of the 801 primitive instruction set. We question, therefore, the need for a separate set of instructions.

In fact, for "vertical microcode," the benefits claimed are generally not due to the power of the instructions as much as to their residence in a high-speed control store. This amounts to a hardware architect attempting to guess which subroutines, or macros, are most frequently used and assigning high-speed memory to them. It has resulted, for instance, in functions like EXTENDED-PRECISION FLOATING-

©Copyright 1982, Association for Computing Machinery, Inc., reprinted by permission. This paper originally appeared in the *Proceedings of the Symposium for Programming Languages and Operating Systems*, published in the *ACM SIGARCH Computer Architecture News*, Vol. 10, No. 2, March 1982; it is republished here, with only slight revisions.

Reprinted with permission from *IBM Journal of Research and Development*, Volume 27, Number 3, May 1983, pages 237-246. The article was slightly revised from one that appeared in *ACM SIGARCH Computer Architecture*, Volume 10, Number 2, March 1982. Copyright © 1983 by International Business Machines, Inc.

POINT DIVIDE and TRANSLATE AND TEST on System/370 computers residing in high-speed storage, while procedure prologues and the first-level-interrupt handler are in main storage. The 801 CPU gets its instructions from an "instruction cache" which is managed by least-recently-used (LRU) information. Thus, all frequently used functions are very likely to be found in this high-speed storage, exhibiting the performance characteristics of vertical microcode.

Programming complex functions as software procedures or macros rather than in microcode has three advantages:

First, the CPU is interruptible at "microcode" boundaries, hence more responsive. Architectures with complex instructions either restrict interrupts to instruction boundaries, or (as in, for instance, the MOVE CHARACTERS LONG instruction on the System/370) define specific interruptible points. If the instruction must be atomic, the implementation must ensure that it can successfully complete before any observable state is saved. Thus, in the System/370 MOVE CHARACTERS instruction, before the move is started all pages are pretouched (and locked, in an MP system) to guard against a page-fault interrupt occurring after the move has begun. If interruptible points are architected, the state must be such that the instruction is restartable.

The second advantage of programming these functions is that an optimizing compiler can often separate their components, moving some parts out of a loop, commoning others, etc.

Third, it is often possible for parts of a complex instruction to be computed at compile time. Consider, for instance, the System/370 MOVE CHARACTERS instruction once again. Each execution of this instruction must determine the optimal move strategy by examining the lengths of the source and target strings, whether (and in what direction) they overlap, and what their alignment characteristics are. But, for most programming languages, these may all be known at compile time. Consider also a multiply instruction. If one of the operands is a constant, known at compile time, the compiler can often produce more efficient "shift/add" sequences than the general multiply microcode subroutine.

The major disadvantage to using procedures instead of microcode to implement complex functions occurs when the microinstruction set is defined to permit its operands to be indirectly named by the register name fields in the instruction which is being interpreted. Since, in the 801 and in most conventional architectures, the register numbers are bound into the instructions, a compiler must adopt some specific register-usage convention for the procedure operands and must move the operands to these registers when necessary.

A computer whose instructions all execute very efficiently, however, is attractive only if the number of such instructions required to perform a task is not commensurately larger than that required of a more complex instruction set. The 801 project was concerned only with the execution of programs compiled by our optimizing compiler. Therefore, within the constraints of a primitive data flow, we left the actual definition of the instructions to the compiler writers. The results, discussed later, generally show path lengths (that is, number of instructions executed) about equivalent to those on a System/370 for systems code, and up to 50% longer for commercial and scientific applications (given no hardware floating point).

• *Overlapped storage access*
Instruction mixes for the 801 show that about 30% of instructions go to storage to send or receive data, and between 10% and 20% of instructions are taken branches. Moreover, for many applications, a significant portion of the memory bandwidth is used by I/O. If the CPU is forced to wait many cycles for storage access its internal performance will be wasted.

The second major design goal of the 801 project, therefore, was to organize the storage hierarchy and develop a system architecture to minimize CPU idle time due to storage access. First, it was clear that a cache was required whose access time was consistent with the machine cycle of the CPU. Second, we chose a "store-in-cache" strategy (instead of "storing through" to the backing store) so that the 10% of expected store instructions would not degrade the performance severely. (For instance, if the time to store a word through to the backing store is ten cycles, and 10% of instructions are stores, this will add up to one cycle to each instruction on average depending on the amount of execution overlap.)

But a CPU organization that needs a new instruction at every cycle as well as accessing data every third cycle will still be degraded by a single conventional cache that delivers a word every cycle. Thus, we decided to split the cache into a part containing data and a part containing instructions. In this way we effectively doubled the bandwidth to the cache and allowed asynchronous fetching of instructions and data at the backing store.

Most conventional architectures make this decision difficult because every store of data can be a modification of an instruction, perhaps even the one following the store. Thus, the hardware must ensure that the two caches are properly synchronized, a job that is either expensive or degrading, or both. Even instruction prefetch mechanisms are complex, since the effective address of a store must be compared to the Instruction Address Register.

Historically, as soon as index registers were introduced into computers the frequency of instruction modification fell dramatically until, today, instructions are almost never modified. Therefore, the 801 architecture does not require this hazard detection. Instead it exposes the existence of the split cache to software and provides instructions by which software can synchronize the caches when required. In this system, the only program that modifies instructions is the one that loads programs into memory.

Similarly, in conventional systems in which the existence of a cache is unobservable to the software, I/O must (logically) go through the cache. This is often accomplished in less expensive systems by sending the I/O physically through the cache. The result is that the CPU is idle while the I/O proceeds, and that after an I/O burst the contents of the cache no longer reflect the working set of the process being executed, forcing it back into transient mode. Even in more expensive systems a broadcasting or directory-duplication strategy may result in some performance degradation.

We observed that responsibility for the initiation of I/O in current systems was evolving towards paging supervisors, system I/O managers using fixed-block transfers, and, for low-speed devices, a buffer strategy which moves data between subsystem buffers and user areas. This results in the I/O manager knowing the location and extent of the storage being accessed, and knowing when an I/O transfer is in process. Thus, this software can properly synchronize the caches, and the I/O hardware can transmit directly to and from the backing store. The result of this system approach in our prototype is that, even when half of the memory bandwidth is being used for I/O, the CPU is virtually undegraded.

Notice that in the preceding discussions (and in the earlier discussion of complex instructions) an underlying strategy is being pervasively applied. Namely, wherever there is a system function that is expensive or slow in all its generality, but where software can recognize a frequently occurring degenerate case (or can move the entire function from run time to compile time), that function is moved from hardware to software, resulting in lower cost *and* improved performance.

An interesting example of the application of this strategy concerns managing the cache itself. In the 801 the cache line is 32 bytes and the largest unit of a store is four bytes. In such a cache, whose line size is larger than the unit of a store and in which a "store-in-cache" approach is taken, a store directed at a word which is not in the cache must initiate a fetch of the entire line from the backing store into the cache. This is because, as far as the cache can tell, a load of another word from this line might be requested subsequently. Fre-quently, however, the store is simply the first store into what to the program is newly acquired space. It could be a new activation on a process stack just pushed on procedure call (e.g., PL/I Automatic); it could be an area obtained by a request to the operating system; or it could be a register save area used by the first-level-interrupt handler. In all of these cases the hardware does not know that no old values from that line will be needed, while to the compiler and supervisor this situation is quite clear. We have defined explicit instructions in the 801 for cache management so that software can reduce these unnecessary loads and stores of cache lines.

One other 801 system strategy leads to more effective use of the cache. Conventional software assumes that its memory is randomly addressable. Because of this assumption, each service program in the supervisor and subsystems has its own local temporary storage. Thus, an application program requesting these services will cause references to many different addresses. In a high-level-language-based system like the 801, control program services are CALLed just like a user's subroutines. The result is that all these service programs get their temporary areas from the same stack, resulting in much reuse of cache lines and, therefore, higher cache hit ratios.

So far we have discussed 801 features that result in overlapped access to the cache between instructions and data, overlapped backing store access among the caches and I/O, less hardware synchronizing among the caches and I/O, and techniques to improve the cache hit ratios. One other aspect of the 801 CPU design and architecture should be described to complete the picture.

Even if almost all instruction and data references are found in the cache, and the cache and backing store are always available to the CPU, a conventional CPU will still often be idle while waiting for a load to complete or for the target of a branch to be fetched. Sophisticated CPUs often keep branch-taken histories or fetch ahead on both paths in order to overcome this idle time. In the 801 project we observed that, with a small number of hardware primitives, software (i.e., the compiler) could reorder programs so that the semantics remained unchanged but the hardware could easily overlap this idle time with useful work.

On load instructions the register that is to be the target of the load is locked by the CPU. The CPU then continues execution of the instruction stream until it reaches an instruction that requires this register, at which time it idles until the load is completed. Thus, if the compiler can find a useful instruction to put after the load that does not require the result of the load, the CPU will not be idle at all while the data cache fetches the requested word. (And if the compiler can find several such instructions to put after the load, execution of these will even overlap cache miss.)

Similarly for branches, the 801 architecture defines, for every type of branch instruction, an alternate form called BRANCH WITH EXECUTE. (This is similar to the delayed branch in the RISC computer [1].) These instructions have exactly the same semantics as their corresponding branch instructions, except that while the instruction cache is fetching the branch target the CPU executes the instruction that has been placed immediately after the BRANCH WITH EXECUTE instruction. For instance, in the sequence

LOAD R1,A

BNZ L

the CPU would be idle while the instruction cache was fetching L, if the branch was taken. Changing the BRANCH NON-ZERO to a BRANCH NON-ZERO WITH EXECUTE and moving the LOAD instruction results in

BNZX L

LOAD R1,A

which has exactly the same semantics but allows the CPU to execute the LOAD while the instruction cache is fetching the instruction at L. The 801 compiler is able, generally, to convert about 60% of the branches in a program into the execute form.

- *A compiler-based system*
So far we have discussed two major ideas which pervade the 801 system. First, build a CPU that can execute its instructions quickly (i.e., in one relatively short machine cycle), and define these instructions to be a good target for compilation so that resulting path lengths are generally commensurate with those for the same functions on more complex instruction sets (e.g., System/370). Second, define the storage hierarchy architecture, the CPU instructions, the I/O architecture and the software so that the CPU will generally not have to wait for storage access. The third major idea centers about the 801 compiler. A fundamental decision of the 801 project was to base the entire system on its pervasive use. This has resulted in the following system characteristics.

Instruction sets for conventional CPUs have been defined with an implicit assumption that many programmers will use assembly language. This assumption has motivated the definition of complex instructions (such as EDIT AND MARK, TRANSLATE AND TEST) almost as much as has the notion of a fast control store. But, increasingly, programmers do not use assembly language except where optimal performance is essential or machine functions are required that are not reflected in the source language.

The compiler for the 801 has demonstrated that it can produce object code that is close enough to best hand code generally so that assembly language programming is almost never needed for performance. The operating system has isolated those machine-dependent functions not reflected in the language (such as DISABLE, START I/O, DISPATCH) and developed efficient procedures which provide these functions with minimal linkage overhead.

The result is a system in which less than a thousand lines of supervisor code (and some of the "microcode" subroutine implementations of the complex functions) are written in assembly language. This has relieved the 801 architecture of the burden of being easy to program directly. Virtually the only programmers who are concerned with the nature of the architecture are the compiler writers and the "core" supervisor writers. All others see the system only through a high-level language. Because of this, the 801 architects were able to base their decisions solely on the needs of these few programmers and on cost/performance considerations.

Thus, the 801 architecture was defined as that set of run-time operations which

- could not be moved to compile time,
- could not be more efficiently executed by object code produced by a compiler which understood the high-level intent of the program, or
- was to be implemented in random logic more effectively than the equivalent sequence of software instructions.

It might at first seem surprising that compiler writers would not want powerful high-level instructions. But in fact these instructions are often hard to use since the compiler must find those cases which exactly fit the architected construct. Code selection becomes not just finding the fewest instructions, but the right instructions. And when these instructions name operands in storage instead of in registers, code selection depends upon the results of register allocation.

The 801 approach to protection is strongly based upon this compiler intermediary between users and the hardware. Conventional systems expect application programmers, and certainly subsystem programmers, to use assembly language or other languages in which it is possible to subvert the system (either deliberately or accidentally). Thus, hardware facilities are required to properly isolate these users. The most popular examples of these facilities are storage protect keys, multiple virtual address spaces, and supervisor state. These facilities are often costly and sometimes degrade performance. But what is more important is that they are often inadequate. Since even 16 different keys are insufficient for unique assignment, for instance, different users are sometimes given the same key or the system limits the number of active users. Also, because the key disciplines are only two-level, many subsystems are forced to run with full addressing capability.

If, however, users are constrained to a properly defined source language, and their programs are processed by an intelligent compiler and run on an operating system that understands the addressing strategies of the compiler, it is possible to provide better protection at less cost. The 801 system, therefore, is based upon the assumption that certain critical components of the compiler are correct, and that all programs executing on the system (except for a small supervisor core) have been compiled by this compiler. The system will guarantee

- that all references to data (scalars, arrays, structures, areas) really do point to that data, and that the extents of the references are included in the extents of the data,
- that a reference to dynamically allocated-and-freed data is made only between an allocation and a free,
- that all branches are to labels, and all calls are to proper entry points in procedures,
- that the extents of all arguments to a procedure match the extents of their corresponding parameters, so that the protection persists across calls, and
- that all declarations of global (external) variables in separately compiled procedures have consistent extents.

This checking is often done at compile time, link-edit time, or program-fetch time, but, when necessary, trap instructions are introduced into the object code to check at run time. The resulting increase in path length due to this run-time checking is generally less than 10% because this code is optimized along with the rest of the program [2].

Notice that this is not a "strongly typed" approach to checking. Overlays of one data type on another are permitted, provided the domains are not exceeded. But our experience in running code conventionally on the System/370 and then on the 801 with this checking has shown that many program bugs are discovered and that, more importantly, they tend to be the kinds of bugs that elude normal component test procedures.

It was noted earlier that, because the operating system was also written in the 801's high-level language and compiled by the 801 compiler, its service programs were simply CALLed like any external procedure, resulting in better cache behavior. An even more important consequence of this design, however, is that the checking of matches between arguments and parameters is performed at the time a program is loaded into memory and linked to the supervisor. This results in efficient calls to supervisor services, especially when compared to conventional overhead. It means also that the compiler-generated "traceback" mechanism continues into the operating system, so that when an error occurs the entire symbolic call chain can be displayed.

The linkage between procedures on the 801 is another example of a consistent machine design based on a system used solely via a high-level language. We wanted applications on the 801 to be programmed using good programming style. This implies a large number of procedures and many calls. In particular, it implies that very short procedures can be freely written and invoked. Thus, for these short procedures, the linkage must be minimal.

The 801 procedure linkage attempts to keep arguments in registers where possible. It also expects some register values to be destroyed across a CALL. The result is that a procedure call can be as cheap as a BRANCH AND LINK instruction when the called procedure can execute entirely out of available registers. As more complex functions are required they increase the overhead for linkage incrementally.

Finally, the pervasive use of a high-level language and compiler has given the project great freedom to change. The architecture has undergone several drastic changes and countless minor ones. The linkage conventions, storage mapping strategies, and run-time library have similarly been changed as experience provided new insights. In almost every case the cost of the change was limited to recompilations.

This ability to preserve source code, thus limiting the impact of change, can have significant long-range impact on systems. New technologies (and packaging) often offer great performance and cost benefits if they can be exploited with architecture changes.

System components

- *The programming language*

The source language for the 801 system is called PL.8. It was defined to be an appropriate language for writing systems programs and to produce optimized code with the checking described previously.

PL.8 began as an almost-compatible subset of PL/I, so that the PL.8 compiler was initially compiled by the PL/I Optimizer. It contains, for instance, the PL/I storage classes, functions, floating-point variables, varying character strings, arrays with adjustable extents, the structured control primitives of PL/I, the string-handling built-in functions, etc. It differs from PL/I in its interpretation of bit strings as binary numbers, in its binary arithmetic (which simply reflects the arithmetic of the 801 hardware) and in some language additions borrowed from Pascal. It does not contain full PL/I ON conditions, multiple entry points, or the ability to develop absolute pointers to Automatic or Static storage. Relative pointers, called Offsets, can be developed only to Areas. This discipline has several advantages:

- All program and data areas can be moved freely by the system, since absolute addresses are never stored in user-addressable data structures.
- Any arithmetic data type can be used as an offset (relative pointer) and all arithmetic operations can be freely performed, since the extent checks are made on every use.
- A store, using a computed offset, can only affect other data in that particular area. Thus, the locations whose values could have been changed by this store are significantly limited. This enhances the power of the optimization algorithms.
- It leads to better structured, more easily readable programs.

- *The optimizing compiler*
There have been about seven programmers in the compiler group since the project began. A running compiler was completed after about two years. Since then the group has been involved with language extensions, new optimization techniques, debugging, and usability aids. It should be noted, however, that for about twenty years the Computer Sciences department at Yorktown Heights has been working on compiler algorithms, many of which were simply incorporated into this compiler.

The PL.8 compiler adopts two strategies which lead to its excellent object code. The first is a strategy which translates, in the most straightforward, inefficient (but correct) manner, from PL.8 source language to an intermediate language (IL). This translation has as its only objective the production of semantically correct object code. It seeks almost no special cases, so that it is relatively easy to debug. Moreover, the intermediate language which is its target is at a very low level, almost at that of the real 801 machine.

The next phase of the compiler develops flow graphs of the program as described in [3], and, using these graphs, performs a series of conventional optimization algorithms, such as

- common sub-expression elimination,
- moving code out of loops,
- eliminating dead code, and
- strength reduction.

Each of these algorithms transforms an IL program into a semantically equivalent, but more efficient, IL program. Thus, these procedures can be (and are) called repetitively and in any order. While these procedures are quite sophisticated, since each of them acts on the entire program and on all programs, a bug in one of them is very easily observed.

The power of this approach is not only in the optimizing power of the algorithms but in the fact that they are applied to such a low-level IL. Conventional global optimizing compilers perform their transformations at a much higher level of text, primarily because they were designed to run in relatively small-size memory. Thus, they can often not do much more than convert one program to another which could have been written by a more careful programmer. The PL.8 compiler, on the other hand, applies its optimization algorithms to addressing code, domain checking code, procedure linkage code, etc.

The second compiler strategy which is different from conventional compilers is our approach to register allocation [4, 5]. The IL, like that of most compilers, assumes an arbitrarily large number of registers. In fact, the result of each different computation in the program is assigned a different (symbolic) register. The job for register allocation is simply to assign real registers to these symbolic registers. Conventional approaches use some subset of the real registers for special purposes (e.g., pointers to the stack, to the code, to the parameter list). The remaining set is assigned locally within a statement, or at best a basic block (e.g., a loop). Between these assignments, results which are to be preserved are temporarily stored and variables are redundantly loaded.

The 801 approach observes that the register-assignment problem is equivalent to the graph-coloring problem, where each symbolic register is a node and the real registers are different colors. If two symbolic registers have the property that there is at least one point in the program where both their values must be retained, we model that property on the graph as a vertex between the two nodes. Thus, the register-allocation problem is equivalent to the problem of coloring the graph so that no two nodes connected by a vertex are colored with the same crayon.

This global approach has proven very effective. Surprisingly many procedures "color" so that no store/load sequences are necessary to keep results in storage temporarily. (At present the compiler "colors" only computations. There is, however, no technical reason why local variables could not also be "colored," and we intend to do this eventually.) When it does fail, other algorithms which use this graph information are employed to decide what to store. Because of this ability of the compiler to effectively utilize a large number of registers, we decided to implement 32 general-purpose registers in the hardware.

The compiler also accepts Pascal programs, producing compatible object code so that PL.8 and Pascal procedures can freely call one another. It also produces efficient object code for the System/370, thus providing source code portability.

Instructions and operands

Instruction formats and data representations are areas which saw significant change as the project evolved. This section describes the current version of the architecture. The kind of instruction and operand set requested by the compiler developers turned out, fortunately, to be precisely one which made hardware implementation easier. The overriding theme was regularity. For instance,

- All operands must be aligned on boundaries consistent with their size (i.e., halfwords on halfword boundaries, words on word boundaries). All instructions are fullwords on fullword boundaries. (This results in an increase in program size over two- and four-byte formats, but the larger format allows us to define more powerful instructions resulting in shorter path lengths.) Since the 801 was designed for a cache/main store/hard disk hierarchy and virtual-memory addressing, the consequence of larger programs is limited to more disk space and larger working sets (i.e., penalties in cache-hit-ratio and page-fault frequencies).

  With this alignment constraint, the hardware is greatly simplified. Each data or instruction access can cause at most one cache miss or one page fault. The caches must access at most one aligned word. Instruction prefetch mechanisms can easily find op codes if they are searching for branches. Instruction alignment and data alignment are unnecessary. Instruction Length Count fields (as in the System/370 PSW) are unnecessary and software can always backtrack instructions. Moreover, for data, traces show that misaligned operands rarely appear, and when they do are often the result of poor programming style.

- Given four-byte instructions, other benefits accrue. Register fields in instructions are made five bits long so that the 801 can name 32 registers. (This aspect of 801 architecture makes it feasible to use the 801 to emulate other architectures which have 16 general-purpose registers, since 16 additional 801 registers are still available for emulator use.)

  Four-byte instructions also allow the target register of every instruction to be named explicitly so that the input operands need not be destroyed. This facility is applied pervasively, as in "Shift Reg A Left by contents of Reg B and Store Result in Reg C." This feature of the architecture simplifies register allocation and eliminates many MOVE REGISTER instructions.

- The 801 is a true 32-bit architecture, not a 16-bit architecture with extended registers. Addresses are 32 bits long; arithmetic is 32-bit two's complement; logical and shift instructions deal with 32-bit words (and can shift distances

up to 32). A useful way to reduce path length (and cache misses) is to define a rich set of immediate fields, but of course it is impossible to encode a general 32-bit constant to fit into an immediate field in a four-byte instruction. The 801 defines the following subsets of such constants which meet most requirements:

- A 16-bit immediate field for arithmetic and address calculation (D field) which is interpreted as a two's-complement signed integer. (Thus, the constants $\pm 2^{15}$ can be represented immediately.)
- A 16-bit logical constant. Each logical operation has two immediate forms—upper and lower, so that in at most two instructions (cycles) logical operations can be performed using a 32-bit logical constant.
- An 11-bit encoding of a Mask (i.e., a substring of ones surrounded by zeros or zeros surrounded by ones). Thus, for shift, insert, and isolate operations the substring can be defined immediately.
- A 16-bit immediate field for branch-target calculation (D field) which is interpreted as a signed two's-complement offset from the address of the current instruction. (Thus, a relative branch to and from anywhere within a 32K-byte procedure can be specified immediately.)
- A 26-bit immediate field specifying an offset from the address of the current instruction or an absolute address, so that branches between procedures, to supervisor services, or to "microcode subroutines" can be specified without having to establish addressability.

- LOAD and STORE instructions are available in every combination of the following options:

- LOAD or STORE.
- Character, halfword, sign-extended halfword, or fullword.
- Base + Index, or Base + Displacement effective address calculation. (Usage statistics for System/370 show low use for the full B + X + D form. Thus, a three-input adder did not seem warranted.)
- Store the effective address back into the base register (i.e., "autoincrement") or not.

- Branches are available with the following branch-target specifications:

- Absolute 26-bit address,
- Instruction Address Register + Displacement (signed 16- or 26-bit word offset), or
- Register + Register,

BRANCH AND LINK forms are defined normally. But conditional branches are defined not only based upon the state of the Condition Register but on the presence or absence of a one in any bit position in any register. [This allows the TEST UNDER MASK – BRANCH CONDI-

TION sequence in System/370 to be executed in one machine cycle (and no storage references) if the bit is already in a register. Again, the power of global register allocation makes this more probable.]

- There are COMPARE AND TRAP instructions defined which allow the System/370 COMPARE – BRANCH CONDITION sequence to be executed in one machine cycle for those cases where the test is for an infrequently encountered exception condition. These instructions are used to implement the run-time extent checking discussed earlier.

- Arithmetic is 32-bit two's complement. There are special instructions defined to allow MAX, MIN, and decimal add and subtract to be coded efficiently. There are also two instructions defined (MULTIPLY STEP and DIVIDE STEP) to allow two 32-bit words to be multiplied in 16 cycles (yielding a 64-bit product) and a 64-bit dividend to be divided by a 32-bit divisor in 32 cycles (yielding a 32-bit quotient and a 32-bit remainder).

- The 801 has a rich set of shift and insert instructions. These were developed to make device-controller "microcode," emulator "microcode," and systems code very efficient. The functions, all available in one machine cycle, are as follows:

  - Ring-shift a register up to 31 positions (specified in another register or in an immediate field).
  - Using a mask (in another register or in an immediate field), merge this shifted word with all zeros (i.e., isolate the field) or with any other register (i.e., merge), or with the result of the previous shift (i.e., long shift),
  - Store this back into any other register or into storage (i.e., move character string).

(This last facility allows misaligned source and target character string moves to execute as fast as two characters per cycle.)

Interrupts and I/O

I/O in the 801 prototype is controlled by a set of adapters which attach to the CPU and memory by two buses. The External Bus attaches the adapters to the CPU. It is used by software to send commands and receive status, by means of synchronous READ and WRITE instructions. Data are transmitted between the adapters and the 801 backing store through the MIO (Memory-I/O) bus. (As described previously, it is the responsibility of the software to synchronize the caches.)

Rather than support integrated and complex (multi-level) interrupt hardware, the 801 again moves to software functions that can be performed more efficiently by program-

ming. Software on systems that provide, say, eight interrupt levels often find this number inadequate as a distinguisher of interrupt handlers. Thus, a software first-level-interrupt handler is programmed on top of the hardware, increasing the real time to respond. Moreover, the requirement to support eight sets of registers results in these being stored in some fast memory rather than in logic on-chip. This results in a slower machine cycle. If the real-time responsiveness of a system is measured realistically, it must include not only the time to get to an interrupt handler but the time to process the interrupt, which clearly depends on the length of the machine cycle. Thus, in a practical sense the 801 is a good real-time system.

Interrupt determination and priority handling is packaged outboard of the CPU chips in a special unit called the external interrupt controller (along with the system clocks, timers, and adapter locks). (This packaging decision allows other versions of 801 systems to choose different interrupt strategies without impacting the CPU design.) In this controller, there are (logically) two bit vectors. The first, the Interrupt Request Vector (IRV) contains a bit for each device which may wish to interrupt the CPU (plus one each for the clocks, timers, and the CPU itself for simulating external interrupts). These bits are tied by lines to the devices.

The second vector, called the Interrupt Mask Vector (IMV) contains a bit corresponding to each bit in the IRV. The IMV is loaded by software in the CPU. It dynamically establishes the priority levels of the interrupt requesters. If there is a one in a position in the IRV corresponding to a one in the corresponding position of the IMV, and the 801 CPU is enabled for interrupt, the CPU is interrupted.

On interrupt, the CPU becomes disabled and unrelocated and begins executing the first-level-interrupt handler (FLIH) in lower memory. The FLIH stores the interrupted state, reads the IRV, and determines the requester. Using this position number, it sends a new IMV (reflecting the priority of the requester) and branches to the interrupt handler for that requester, which executes enabled and relocated. Path lengths for the FLIH are less than 100 instructions (and can be reduced for a subclass of fast-response interrupts), and less than 150 instructions for the dispatcher (when the interrupt handler completes).

Internal bus

We have, so far, described a CPU that must have the following (logical) buses to storage:

- a command bus to describe the function requested,
- an address bus,
- a source data bus for stores, and
- a target data bus for loads.

Table 1 Performance comparison: System/370-168 and 801, for a Heap Sort programmed in PL.8.

CPU	In inner loop				
	Code size (bytes)	No. of instruc- tions	Data refs.	Cycles	Cycles/ inst.
System/370-168	236	33	8	56	1.7
801	240	28	6	31	1.1

Table 2 Performance comparison: randomly selected modules on PL.8 compiler. (Note: Relative numbers are the ratios of 801 parameters to System/370 parameters.)

Module (In order of increasing size)	Relative code size	Dynamic comparisons	
		Relative instructions executed	Relative data storage references
FIND	1.02	0.91	0.60
SEARCHV	0.93	0.83	0.38
LOAD S	0.83	0.91	0.43
P2_EXTS	1.00	1.00	0.57
SORT_S1	0.86	0.78	0.59
PM_ADD1	0.86	0.96	0.63
ELMISS	0.87	0.86	0.69
PM_GKV	0.92	0.76	0.46
P5DBG	0.98	0.81	0.52
DESCRPT	0.86	0.75	0.42
ENTADD	0.79	0.76	0.42
Total	0.90	0.80	0.50

We observed that other functions might be implemented outboard of the CPU and could attach to the CPU via these same buses (e.g., floating point). Therefore, we exposed these buses in an 801 instruction, called INTERNAL BUS OPERATION (IBO). This instruction has operands to name the following:

- the bus unit being requested,
- the command,
- the two operands (B,D or B,X) which will be added to produce the output on the address bus,
- the source register, and
- the target register, if needed,

and three flags:

- privileged command or not,
- target register required or not, and
- address bus sent back to Base register or not.

Having defined this generic instruction, we gave bus-unit names to the instruction and data caches, the external-interrupt controller, the timer, and the relocate controller, and assigned the IBO op code to all instructions directed to these units.

Prototype hardware

A hardware prototype has been built for an early version of the 801 architecture, out of MECL 10K DIPs (Motorola Emitter Current Logic dual in-line packages). It runs at 1.1 cycles per instruction. (This number must be taken as an out-of-cache performance figure because the applications which currently run show hit ratios at close to 100% after the initial cache load.) We do not yet have multiple-user measurements.

The register file is capable of reading out any three and writing back any two registers within a single cycle. Thus, the CPU is pipelined as follows.

The first level of the pipeline decodes the instruction, reads two registers into the ALU, executes the ALU, and either latches the result or, for LOAD or STORE instructions, sends the computed address to the cache. On a STORE instruction, the data word is also fetched from the register file and sent to the cache.

The second level of the pipeline sends the latched result through the shifter, sets the condition register bits, and stores the result back into a register. During this cycle also, if a word has been received from the cache as the result of a load instruction, it is loaded into the register.

(The hardware monitors register names to bypass the load when the result is being immediately used.)

The cache is designed so that, on a miss, the requested word is sent directly to the CPU, thus reducing lockout while the cache line is being filled.

Performance comparisons

Tables 1 and 2 show some early performance comparisons. Since the compiler produces object code for the System/370 as well as the 801, these comparisons are possible for the same source programs and the same compiler. We use the number of cycles in the inner loops and the number of storage references in the inner loops to approximate dynamic performance.

Table 1 shows results for an in-memory sort procedure. Table 2 shows the results for randomly selected modules from the compiler itself. Note that as the modules get larger the power of global register allocation results in fewer storage references. Note also that, in spite of the fact that the

801 contains no complex instructions, the 801 modules contain fewer instructions and fewer instruction executions. This is because the complex instructions are generally very infrequent, whereas the 801 has a more powerful set of primitive instructions.

Conclusions

While we do not have nearly enough measurements to draw hard conclusions, the 801 group has developed a set of intuitive principles which seem to hold consistently.

At least in low-to-mid-range processor complexity, a general-purpose, register-oriented instruction set can be at least as good as any special vertical microcode set. Thus, there should be only one hard-wired instruction set, and it should be directly available to the compiler.

A good global register allocator can effectively use a large number of general-purpose registers. Therefore, all the registers which the CPU can afford to build in hardware should be directly and simultaneously addressable. Stack machines, machines that hide some of the registers to improve CALL performance, and multiple-interrupt-level machines all seem to make poorer use of the available registers.

Protection is far more effectively provided at a level where the source language program is understood.

It is easy to design and build a fast, cheap CPU, and it will become more so as VLSI evolves. The harder problem is to develop software, architecture, and hardware which do not keep the CPU idling due to storage access.

Acknowledgments

The seminal idea for the 801 and many subsequent concepts are due to John Cocke. The list of contributors has grown too large to list here. The following people were with the project from the beginning and were responsible for most of the design and implementation: Hardware: Frank Carrubba, manager; Paul Stuckert, Norman Kreitzer, Richard Freitas, and Kenneth Case. Software: Marc Auslander, manager; Compiler: Martin Hopkins, manager; Richard Goldberg, Peter Oden, Philip Owens, Peter Markstein, and Gregory Chaitin; Control Program: Richard Oehler, manager; Albert Chang. Joel Birnbaum was the first manager of the project and later a constant supporter. Bill Worley also contributed significantly through the years.

References

1. D. A. Patterson and C. H. Séquin, "RISC-I: A Reduced Instruction Set VLSI Computer" *Proceedings of the Eighth Annual Symposium on Computer Architecture*, May, 1981.
2. V. Markstein, J. Cocke, and P. Markstein, "Optimization of Range Checking," *Research Report RC-8456*, IBM Thomas J. Watson Research Center, Yorktown Heights, NY, 1980.
3. J. Cocke and P. W. Markstein, "Measurement of Program Improvement Algorithms," *IFIP 80 Proceedings, Information Processing*, S. H. Lavington, Ed., North-Holland Publishing Co., Amsterdam, 1980, pp. 221–228.
4. G. J. Chaitin, M. A. Auslander, A. K. Chandra, J. Cocke, M. E. Hopkins, and P. W. Markstein, "Register Allocation via Coloring," *Computer Languages* (British) **6**, 47–57 (1981).
5. G. J. Chaitin, "Register Allocation and Spilling via Coloring," *Research Report RC-9124*, IBM Thomas J. Watson Research Center, Yorktown Heights, NY, 1981.

Received May 6, 1982; revised November 11, 1982

George Radin *IBM System Products Division, 44 South Broadway, White Plains, New York 10601.* Mr. Radin is an IBM Fellow and director of architecture responsible for the definition of advanced architectures for System Products Division processors. He joined IBM in 1963 at the New York Programming Center. Since then he has worked on PL/I language definition in New York, as senior manager at the Thomas J. Watson Research Center, Yorktown Heights, New York, as manager of advanced system architecture and design in Poughkeepsie, New York, and as a member of the Corporate Technical Committee, Armonk, New York. Before joining IBM, he was manager of the computer center at the New York University College of Engineering. Mr. Radin received his B.A. in 1951 from Brooklyn College, New York, in English literature, his M.A. in 1954 from Columbia University, New York, in English literature, and his M.S. in 1958 from New York University in mathematics.

*The reduced instruction set computer is an alternative to the
general trend toward increasingly complex instruction sets.
It executes most instructions in a single, short cycle.*

A VLSI RISC

David A. Patterson and Carlo H. Séquin

University of California, Berkeley

$\mathbf{A}$ general trend in computers today is to increase the complexity of architectures commensurate with the increasing potential of implementation technologies, as exemplified by the complex successors of simpler machines. Compare, for example, the DEC VAX-11[1] to the PDP-11, the IBM System/38[2] to the System/3, and the Intel iAPX-432[3,4] to the 8086. The complexity of this class of computers, which we call CISCs for complex instruction set computers, has some negative consequences: increased design time, increased design errors, and inconsistent implementations.[5]

Investigations of VLSI architectures indicate that the delay-power penalty of data transfers across chip boundaries and the still-limited resources (devices) available on a single chip are major design limitations. Even a million-transistor chip is insufficient if a whole computer has to be built from it.[6] This raises the question of whether the extra hardware needed to implement a CISC is the best use of "scarce" resources.

The above findings led to the Reduced Instruction Set Computer Project. The purpose of the RISC Project is to explore alternatives to the general trend toward architectural complexity. The hypothesis is that by reducing the instruction set one can design a suitable VLSI architecture that uses scarce resources more effectively than a CISC. We also expect this approach to reduce design time, design errors, and the execution time of individual instructions.

Our initial version of such a computer is called RISC I. To meet our goals of simplicity and effective single-chip implementation, we somewhat artificially placed the following design constraints on the architecture:

(1) *Execute one instruction per cycle.* RISC I instructions should be about as fast and no more complicated than microinstructions in current machines such as the PDP-11 or VAX.

(2) *Make all instructions the same size.* This again simplifies implementation. We intentionally postponed attempts to reduce program size.

(3) *Access memory only with load and store instructions; the rest operate between registers.* This restriction simplifies the design. The lack of complex addressing modes also makes it easier to restart instructions.

(4) *Support high-level languages.* The degree of support is explained below. Our intent is to optimize the performance of RISC I for use with high-level languages.

RISC I supports 32-bit addresses, 8-, 16-, and 32-bit data, and several 32-bit registers. We intend to examine support for operating systems and floating-point calculations in the future.

It would appear that these constraints, based on our desire for simplicity and regularity, would result in a machine with substantially poorer code density, poorer performance, or both; but in spite of these constraints, the resulting architecture competes favorably with other

An earlier version of this article, entitled "RISC I: A Reduced Instruction Set VLSI Computer," appeared in the *Proc. Eighth Int'l Symp. Computer Architecture*, May 1981, pp. 443-457.

Reprinted from *Computer,* September 1982, pages 8-22. Copyright © 1982 by The Institute of Electrical and Electronics Engineers, Inc.

EH0251-9/86/0000/0222$01.00 © 1982 IEEE

Recent developments

Since this article was submitted, we have received our first good silicon, and it looks like beginner's luck applies to VLSI. These chips correctly ran all diagnostic programs used to verify our original design. We (foolishly) created new diagnostics and uncovered a design error associated with the optional setting of condition codes on the load and shift instructions. Defying historical precedent for solving the problem by announcing a new architectural "feature," we decided to cover this minor error by modifying the RISC I assembler. (This was possible because ALU operations properly set all condition codes, whereas load and shift instructions do not set the negative condition bit. The patch consists of inserting an arithmetic test instruction when a conditional jump needs the *N* condition from a load or shift operation.)

The fastest of these chips runs all diagnostics at 1.5 MHz, or 2 μsec per RISC I instruction. Several factors explain the difference between expected and measured performance. The chief one is inexperience; this was the first chip that any of us had built. A second is raw speed of transistors from this fabrication. Test structures ran about half the speed of other runs. The last stage of design involved connecting cells, and we concentrated our re-sources on logical correctness rather than circuit speed. We recently reexamined the design and found four long clocked control lines that an analog circuit simulator predicts will limit the maximum clock speed to 4 MHz. Furthermore, many of our diagnostics can be run with a 3-MHz clock, suggesting that only a few RISC instructions are limiting performance. Finally, as we have still tested only 20 percent of the chips, we may well find faster RISC I's.

Even at 1.5 MHz and the assembler correction of the error, RISC I still runs programs faster than commercial microprocessors. RISC I was put onto a board with memory, I/O, and memory management on June 11, 1982, and ran its first program.

The bottom line of the RISC I effort is that students, as part of the graduate curriculum, designed and evaluated an architecture, learned Mead-Conway design, built new CAD tools, and tested their design. The end product, a 44,500-transistor integrated circuit, has one minor design error; it worked on the first good silicon and runs programs faster than commercial microprocessors.

More details can be found in an article in the September/October 1982 issue of *VLSI Design* entitled "Running RISCs."

microprocessors and minicomputers. This is due largely to a scheme of register organization we call overlapped register windows.

Support for high-level languages

Clearly, new architectures should be designed with the needs of high-level language programming in mind. It should not matter, however, whether a high-level language system is implemented mostly by hardware or mostly by software, provided the system hides any lower levels from the programmer.[7] Given this framework, the role of the architect is to build a cost-effective system by deciding what pieces of the system should be in hardware and what pieces in software.

The selection of languages for consideration in RISC I was influenced by our environment; we chose "C" because of its large user community and, hence, considerable local expertise. Given the limited number of transistors that can be integrated into a single-chip computer, most of the pieces of a RISC high-level language system are in software, with hardware support for only the most time-consuming events.

To determine what constructs are used most frequently and, if possible, what constructs use the most time in average programs, we first looked at the frequency of classes of variables in high-level language programs. Data collected for Pascal and C are shown in Table 1.

The most important observation was that integer constants appeared almost as frequently as arrays or structures. What is not shown is that more than 80 percent of the scalars were local variables and more than 90 percent of the arrays or structures were global variables.

We also looked at the relative dynamic frequencies of high-level language statements for the same eight programs; average occurrences over one percent are shown in Table 2. This information does not tell what statements use the most time in the execution of typical programs. To answer that question, we have to look at the code produced by typical versions of each of these statements. A "typical" version of each statement was supplied by Wulf as part of his study into judging the quality of compilers.[8] We used C compilers for the VAX, PDP-11, and 68000 to determine the average number of instructions and mem-

Table 1.
Dynamic percentage of operands in Pascal and C.

	P1	P2	P3	P4	C1	C2	C3	C4	AVERAGE
INTEGER CONSTANT	14	18	11	20	25	11	29	28	20 ± 7
SCALAR	63	68	46	54	37	45	66	62	55 ± 11
ARRAY/STRUCTURE	23	14	43	25	36	43	5	10	25 ± 14

PROGRAM   EXPLANATION

P1   COMP - a Pascal P-code style compiler
P2   MACRO - the macro expansion phase of the SCALD I design system
P3   PRINT - a prettyprinter for Pascal
P4   DIFF - a program that finds the differences between two files
C1   PCC - the portable C compiler for the VAX
C2   CIFPLOT - a program that plots VLSI mask layouts on a dot plotter
C3   NROFF - a text formatting program
C4   SORT - the Unix sorting program

Table 2.
Relative frequency of Pascal and C statements.

STATEMENTS*	P1	P2	P3	P4	AVERAGE	C1	C2	C3	C4	AVERAGE
ASSIGN	39	52	35	53	45 ± 8	22	50	25	56	38 ± 15
IF	35	30	36	16	29 ± 8	59	31	61	22	43 ± 17
CALL	15	14	16	15	15 ± 1	6	17	9	16	12 ± 5
WITH	2	0	5	13	5 ± 5	2	2	3	5	3 ± 1
LOOP	5	5	5	4	5 ± 0	9	0	1	1	3 ± 4
CASE	4	0	1	0	1 ± 1	2	-	-	0	< 1 ± 1

*Because statements can be nested, we count each occurrence of a statement. Loop statements are counted once per execution rather than once per loop iteration. For example, if two IF statements and three assignment statements appear in a loop that iterates 5 times, we would count 26 statements with 15 assignments, 10 IF statements, and one loop. The WITH statement qualifies a record name.

ory references per statement. By multiplying the frequency of occurrence of each statement with the corresponding number of machine instructions and memory references, we obtain Table 3, which is ordered by memory references.

The data in Table 3 suggest that the procedure call/return is the most time-consuming operation in typical high-level language programs. These results corroborate studies by Lunde[9] and Wichmann.[10] The statistics on operands found in Table 1 emphasize the importance of local variables and constants. RISC I supports HLLs by enhancing performance of the most time-consuming features of typical HLL programs, as opposed to making the architecture "close" to a particular HLL; thus, RISC I attempts to handle local variables, constants, and procedure calls efficiently while leaving less frequent operations to instruction sequences or subroutines.

Basic architecture of RISC I

The RISC I architecture has 31 instructions, most of which do simple ALU and shift operations on registers. As shown in Table 4, they have been grouped into four

Table 3.
Weighted relative frequency of HLL statements (ordered by memory references).

STATEMENTS* HLL	HLL (OCCURRENCE) P	C	WEIGHTED (MACHINE INSTR.) P	C	WEIGHTED (MEM. REF.) P	C
CALL/RETURN	15 ± 1	12 ± 5	31 ± 3	33 ± 14	44 ± 4	45 ± 19
LOOPS	5 ± 0	3 ± 1	42 ± 3	32 ± 6	33 ± 2	26 ± 5
ASSIGN	45 ± 5	38 ± 15	13 ± 2	13 ± 5	14 ± 2	15 ± 6
IF	29 ± 8	43 ± 17	11 ± 3	21 ± 8	7 ± 2	13 ± 5
WITH	5 ± 5	—	1 ± 0	—	1 ± 0	—
CASE	1 ± 1	< 1 ± 1	1 ± 1	1 ± 1	1 ± 1	1 ± 1
GOTO	—	3 ± 1	—	0 ± 0	—	0 ± 0

*For the CALL statement we counted passing parameters, saving/restoring general registers, and saving/restoring the program counter. The IF and CASE statements include instructions to evaluate expressions and to jump. For LOOP statements we count all the machine instructions executed during each iteration.

categories: arithmetic-logical, memory access, branch, and miscellaneous. Instructions, data, addresses, and registers are 32 bits. The execution time of a RISC I cycle is given by the time it takes to read and add two registers, and then store the result back into a register. Register 0, which always contains zero, allows us to synthesize a variety of operations and addressing modes.

Load and store instructions move data between registers and memory. Rather than lengthen the general cycle to permit a complete memory access, these instructions use two CPU cycles. There are eight variations of memory access instructions to accommodate sign-extended or zero-extended 8-bit, 16-bit, and 32-bit data. Although there appears to be only the index-plus-displacement addressing mode in data transfer instructions, absolute and register-indirect addressing can be synthesized using register 0 (see Table 5).

Branch instructions include call, return, conditional, and unconditional jump. The conditional instructions are the standard set used originally in the PDP-11 and found in most 16-bit microprocessors today. Most of the innovative features of RISC I are found in call, return, and jump; they will be discussed later.

Figure 1 shows the 32-bit format used by register-to-register instructions and memory access instructions. For register-to-register instructions, DEST selects one of the 32 registers as the destination of the result of the operation performed on the registers specified by SOURCE1 and SOURCE2. If IMM = 0, the low-order five bits of SOURCE2 specify another register; if IMM = 1, SOURCE2 expresses a sign-extended 13-bit constant. As mentioned above, the frequency of integer constants in HLL programs suggests architectural support, so immediate operands are available in every instruction. SCC determines whether or not the condition codes are set. Memory access instructions use SOURCE1 to specify the index register and SOURCE2 to specify the offset. One other format combines the last three fields to form a 19-bit PC-relative address and is used primarily by the branch instructions.

The examples in Table 6 show that many of the important VAX instructions can be synthesized from simple RISC I addressing modes and opcodes. Comparative measurements of benchmarks will demonstrate the effectiveness of the chosen instruction set.

Table 4.
Assembly language definition for RISC I.

INSTRUCTION	OPERANDS	COMMENTS	
ADD	Rs,S2,Rd	Rd ← Rs + S2	integer add
ADDC	Rs,S2,Rd	Rd ← Rs + S2 + carry	add with carry
SUB	Rs,S2,Rd	Rd ← Rs − S2	integer subtract
SUBC	Rs,S2,Rd	Rd ← Rs − S2 − carry	subtract with carry
SUBR	Rs,S2,Rd	Rd ← S2 − Rs	integer subtract
SUBCR	Rs,S2,Rd	Rd ← S2 − Rs − carry	subtract with carry
AND	Rs,S2,Rd	Rd ← Rs & S2	logical AND
OR	Rs,S2,Rd	Rd ← Rs | S2	logical OR
XOR	Rs,S2,Rd	Rd ← Rs xor S2	logical EXCLUSIVE OR
SLL	Rs,S2,Rd	Rd ← Rs shifted by S2	shift left
SRL	Rs,S2,Rd	Rd ← Rs shifted by S2	shift right logical
SRA	Rs,S2,Rd	Rd ← Rs shifted by S2	shift right arithmetic
LDL	(Rx)S2,Rd	Rd ← M[Rx + S2]	load long
LDSU	(Rx)S2,Rd	Rd ← M[Rx + S2]	load short unsigned
LDSS	(Rx)S2,Rd	Rd ← M[Rx + S2]	load short signed
LDBU	(Rx)S2,Rd	Rd ← M[Rx + S2]	load byte unsigned
LDBS	(Rx)S2,Rd	Rd ← M[Rx + S2]	load byte signed
STL	Rm,(Rx)S2	M[Rx + S2] ← Rm	store long
STS	Rm,(Rx)S2	M[Rx + S2] ← Rm	store short
STB	Rm,(Rx)S2	M[Rx + S2] ← Rm	store byte
JMP	COND,S2(Rx)	pc ← Rx + S2	conditional jump
JMPR	COND,Y	pc ← pc + Y	conditional relative
CALL	Rd,S2(Rx)	Rd ← pc, next pc ← Rx + S2, CWP ← CWP − 1	call and change window
CALLR	Rd,Y	Rd ← pc, next pc ← pc + Y, CWP ← CWP − 1	call relative and change window
RET	Rm,S2	pc ← Rm + S2, CWP ← CWP + 1	return and change window
CALLINT	Rd	Rd ← last pc; next CWP ← CWP − 1	disable interrupts
RETINT	Rm,S2	pc ← Rm + S2; next CWP ← CWP + 1	enable interrupts
LDHI	Rd,Y	Rd<31:13> ← Y; Rd<12:0> ← 0	load immediate high
GTLPC	Rd	Rd ← last pc	to restart delayed jump
GETPSW	Rd	Rd ← PSW	load status word
PUTPSW	Rm	PSW ← Rm	set status word

Register windows. Investigations into the use of high-level languages suggest that the procedure call is the most time-consuming operation in high-level language programs. Potentially, RISC programs may have even more calls, because the complex instructions found in CISCs are subroutines in RISCs. Thus, the procedure call must be as fast as possible, perhaps no longer than a few jumps. Because of its register window scheme, RISC I approaches this goal and reduces data memory traffic.

Using procedures involves two groups of time-consuming operations: saving or restoring registers on each call or return, and passing parameters and results to and from the procedure. The frequency of local scalar variables justifies the architectural support of placing locals in registers, and Baskett[11] and Sites[12] have proposed that

Table 5.
Synthesizing VAX addressing modes.

ADDRESSING	VAX	RISC EQUIVALENT
REGISTER	Rx	Rx
IMMEDIATE	#LITERAL	S2 (13-BIT LITERAL)
INDEXED	Rx + DISPL	Rx + S2 (13-BIT DISPLACEMENT)
ABSOLUTE	@#ADDRESS	r0 + S2 (r0 ≡ 0)
REG INDIRECT	(Rx)	Rx + 0

OP CODE <7>	SCC <1>	DEST<5>	SOURCE1<5>	IMM<1>	SOURCE2<13>

Figure 1. RISC I basic instruction format.

Table 6.
Synthesizing VAX instructions.

OPERATION	VAX		RISC I EQUIVALENT	
REG-REG MOVE	MOVL	Rm,Rn	ADD	R0,Rm,Rn (r0 ≡ 0)
COMPARE	CMPL	Rm,Rn	SUB	Rm,Rn,r0,{c}
COMPARE TO 0	TSTL	Rn	SUB	Rn,r0,r0,{c}
	TSTL	A	LDL	(r0)A,r0,{c}
CLEAR	CLRL	Rn	ADD	r0,r0,Rn
	CLRL	A	STL	r0,(r0)A
TWOS COMPLEMENT	MNEGL	Rm,Rn	SUB	r0,Rm,Rn
ONES COMPLEMENT	MCOML	Rm,Rn	XOR	Rm,#−1,Rn
LOAD CONST	MOVL	$N,Rm($\mid N \mid < 2^{12}$)	ADD	r0,#N,Rm
	MOVL	$N,Rm($\mid N \mid \geq 2^{12}$)	LDHI	#N<31:13>,Rm
			ADD	r0,#N<12:0>,Rm
INCREMENT	INCL	Rn	ADD	Rn,#1,Rn
DECREMENT	DECL	Rn	SUB	Rn,#1,Rn
CHECK INDEX BOUNDS,	INDEX	Rm,#0,#U,	SUB	Rm,#U,r0{c};
(A[0:U])		#1,A,Rn;	JMP	lequ,OK;*
TRAP IF ERROR,	MOVB	(Rn),Rp	CALL	error;
AND READ A[Rm]			OK: LDBU	(Rm)A,Rp

*This approach is better than the normal algorithm. We can think of an index as an unsigned integer since 0 ≤ index ≤ U. A two's complement negative number (1X...X) is then a large unsigned number, so we only need make one unsigned test instead of two signed tests. Nonzero lower bounds are handled by subtracting the lower bound from the index, and multiple indices are handled by repeating the sequence and including a multiply and an add. This idea resulted from a discussion between Bill Joy, Peter Kessler, and George Taylor. Taylor coded the examples and found that on the VAX-11/780, the sequence of simple instructions was always faster than the index instruction. This optimization is found in the Unix C optimizer.

microprocessors keep multiple banks of registers on the chip to avoid register saving and restoring. A similar scheme was adopted by RISC I. Each procedure call allocates a new "window" of registers from the large register file for use by that procedure, and the return resets a pointer, restoring the old set. But some of the registers are not saved or restored on each procedure call; these registers (r0 through r9) are called global registers.

Furthermore, the sets of registers used by different procedures overlap, allowing parameters to be passed in registers. In other machines, parameters are usually passed on the stack, and the calling procedure uses a register (frame pointer) that points to the beginning of the parameters (and also the end of the locals). Thus, all references to parameters are indexed references to mem-

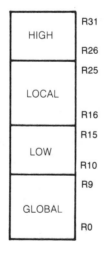

Figure 2. Naming within one virtual RISC I register window.

ory. Our approach partitions the set of window registers (10-31) into the three parts defined by their respective overlap. Every procedure sees the set of registers shown in Figure 2.

High registers 26 through 31 contain parameters passed from "above" the current procedure—that is, from the calling procedure. Local registers 16 through 25 are used for local scalar storage. Low registers 10 through 15 are used for temporaries and parameters passed to the procedure "below" the current procedure (the called procedure). On each procedure call a new set of registers, numbered 10-31, is allocated. The low registers of the "caller" become the high registers of the "callee" because of the hardware overlap between subsequent register windows. Thus, without moving information, parameters in registers 10-15 appear in registers 25-31 of the called window. Figure 3 illustrates this approach for the case where procedure A calls procedure B, which calls procedure C.

If the nesting depth is sufficiently large, all register windows will be used. RISC I handles a call overflow with a separate stack in memory. Overflow and underflow are handled with a trap to a software routine that adjusts that stack. Because this routine can save or restore several sets of registers, the overflow/underflow frequency is based on local variations in the depth of the stack rather than absolute depth. The effectiveness of this scheme depends on the relative frequency of overflows and underflows. Studies by Halbert and Kessler[13] show that with eight register banks overflow will occur in less than one percent of the calls. This suggests that programs exhibit locality in the dynamic nesting of procedures, just as they exhibit locality in memory references.

Another problem with variables in registers occurs in referencing them with pointers, since this requires variable addresses. Because registers normally do not have memory addresses, we could let the compiler determine which variables have pointers and put these variables in memory, but this precludes separate compilation and slows access to these variables. RISC I solves that problem by giving addresses to the window registers. By reserving a portion of the address space, we can determine, with one comparison, whether a register address points to a CPU register or to one that has overflowed into memory. Because the only instructions accessing memory—load and store—already take an extra cycle, we can add this feature without reducing their performance. This permits the use of straightforward compiler technology and still leaves most of the variables in registers.

This addressing technique also solves the "up-level addressing" problem. Pascal and other languages allow nested procedure declarations, thereby creating a class of variables that are neither global variables nor local to a single procedure. Compilers keep track of each procedure environment using static and dynamic links or displays. Such a compiler for RISC I would also associate the memory address for the window of local variables. These variables would then be accessed by using the display or dynamic chains to find the corresponding memory addresses.

Delayed jump. The normal RISC I instruction cycle is just long enough to execute the following sequence of operations: read a register, do an ALU operation, and store the result back into a register. We increase performance by prefetching the next instruction during the execution of the current instruction. This introduces difficulties with branch instructions. Several high-end machines have elaborate techniques to prefetch the appropriate instruction after the branch,[14] but these techniques are too complicated for a single-chip RISC. Our solution was to redefine jumps so that they do not take effect until after the *following* instructions; we refer to this as the delayed jump.

The delayed jump allows RISC I to always prefetch the next instruction during the execution of the current instruction. The machine language code is suitably arranged so that the desired results are obtained. Because RISC I is always intended to be programmed in high-level languages, we will not burden the programmer with this complexity; the "burden" will be carried by the programmers of the compiler, the optimizer, and the debugger.

Table 7 illustrates the delayed branch. Machines with normal jumps would execute the sequence in Table 7a in the order 100, 101, 102, 105, ... To get that same effect in RISC I, we would have to insert a no operation instruction (Table 7b). The sequence of instructions for RISC I is now 100, 101, 102, **103**, 106, ... In the worst case, every jump could take two instructions. The RISC I compiler, however, includes an optimizer that tries to rearrange the sequence of instructions to do the equivalent operations while making use of the instruction slot where the NOP appears. As shown in Table 7c, the optimized RISC I sequence is 100, 101, **102**, 105, ... Because the instruction following a jump is always executed and the jump at 101 is not dependent on the add at 102, this sequence is equivalent to the original program segment in Table 7a.

Architectural heritage. Since architects of new machines build on the work of others, we believe it is important to trace the genealogy of RISC I. Its earliest ancestor is the 1951 Ferranti-Manchester MADM—the first machine with index registers—which also used a register to supply zero.[15] Seymour Cray revived the idea in 1964 with the CDC-6400 and continued to use it in the CDC-7600 and the Cray 1. The delayed jump was first used in the Maniac I, which was completed just a year after the MADM, but we adopted the idea from microprogrammed control units, where delayed jumps are the norm.

The leading proponent of reduced instruction set computers for floating-point data is Cray. For the last 15 years, he has combined simple instruction sets with so-

**Table 7.
Normal and delayed jumps.**

ADDRESS	(a) NORMAL JUMP		(b) DELAYED JUMP		(c) OPTIMIZED DELAYED JUMP	
100	LOAD	X,A	LOAD	X,A	LOAD	X,A
101	ADD	1,A	ADD	1,A	**JUMP**	**105**
102	**JUMP**	**105**	**JUMP**	**106**	**ADD**	**1,A**
103	ADD	A,B	**NOP**		ADD	A,B
104	SUB	C,B	ADD	A,B	SUB	C,B
105	**STORE**	**A,Z**	SUB	C,B	**STORE**	**A,Z**
106			**STORE**	**A,Z**		

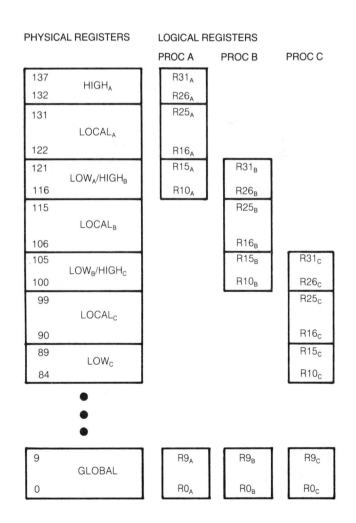

Figure 3. Use of three overlapped register windows.

phisticated pipelined implementations to create the most powerful floating-point engines in the world. While Cray concentrates. on impressive floating-point rates at impressive costs, RISC I concentrates on improved performance at lower cost for integer programs written in HLLs.

A machine with similar goals that predates RISC I is the IBM 801. This project, led by John Cocke and George Radin, began in 1975 by reexamining the relationship between instruction sets, compilers, and operating systems. They pushed the state of the art of compiler technology and created an extremely fast, reduced-instruction-set ECL minicomputer. Alas, the architecture community was left to speculate on the truth of widely varying rumors about the technical details[16] as well as the success or failure of the project.[17] Fortunately, accurate information is beginning to emerge.[18] It will be interesting to see the similarities between RISC I and the 801; one difference is that RISC I uses traditional compiler technology and the 801 uses a traditional register set.

In searching the annals of computer architecture we cannot find a clear reference to overlapped register windows. To our best knowledge, no machine uses the scheme for fast, multiport registers in the CPU. Most modern machines support procedure call by having instructions that manage a portion of main memory as a stack to pass parameters and allocate locals. Theoretically, a cache should then make such a scheme as fast as the overlapped register windows. Registers are faster than caches because of the difference in speed between a small memory and a large memory, the difference in speed between a deterministic access and a probabilistic access, and the difference in speed between a nontranslated register access and a translated virtual memory access. Theoretically, hardware can overcome almost any obstacle, but it occasionally stumbles in implementation. The advantages of registers become apparent when we look at concrete realizations; as we shall see, procedure call/return on the VAX-11/780, using a software stack enhanced by a hardware cache, is about an order of magnitude slower than the overlapped register windows of RISC I.

There are a few machines that share features of RISC I's overlapped register window scheme. The BBN C/70, a recent machine, allocates a new set of registers on every procedure call, but it does not overlap register sets.

Figure 4. Photomicrograph of RISC I.

228

Table 8.
VLSI design metrics for Z8000, MC68000, iAPX-432, and RISC I.

| | ZILOG Z8000 | MOTOROLA 68000 | INTEL iAPX-432 | | | RISC I |
			43201	43202	43203	
TOTAL DEVICES	17.5K	68K	110K	49K	60K	44K
TOTAL MINUS ROM	17.5K	37K	44K	49K	44K	44K
DRAWN DEVICES	3.5K	3.0K	5.6K	9.5K	5.7K	1.8K
REGULARIZATION FACTOR	5.0	12.1	7.9	5.2	7.7	25
SIZE OF CHIP (MILS)	238×251	246×281	318×323	366×313	358×326	406×305
(AREA IN MIL^2)	60K	69K	103K	115K	117K	124K
SIZE OF CONTROL (MIL^2)	37K	35K	67K	45K	47K	7K
PERCENT CONTROL	53%	50%	65%	39%	40%	6%
TIME TO FIRST SILICON (MONTHS)	30	30	33	33	21	19
DESIGN EFFORT (MAN MONTHS)	60	100	170	170	130	15
LAYOUT EFFORT (MAN MONTHS)	70	70	90	100	50	12

A popular architecture that comes close to RISC I is the Texas Instruments 990-9900 family. These machines allocate their general "registers" in memory, so adding the contents of one register to another results in three memory accesses. A single register points to the register work space; most of the machines allow the pointer to overlap work spaces. The latest generation of this family, the TI 99000, includes on-chip main memory, but the first models appear to still have slow register access.[19] The machine that comes closest to the overlapped register windows is the Bell Labs MAC-8. The state of NMOS technology in 1975 precluded having a rich instruction set *and* a register file on the chip; the architects chose the rich instruction set. The main difference between the MAC-8 and TI 990 is that the Bell architects realized that overlapping the registers could improve the performance of the procedure call and provided instructions to specifically overlap the register windows in memory. It is our understanding that some C compilers used this feature. This machine was never implemented with on-chip registers, and the logical successor to this machine, the BellMAC-32, has abandoned this approach.

VLSI implementation

The transition from theoretical architecture to concrete circuits began on January 6, 1981. Mask descriptions were completed June 22, and we received first silicon on October 23. Figure 4 is a photomicrograph of RISC I. We followed the Mead-Conway design philosophy for NMOS with lambda at two microns and no buried contacts. This first version, RISC I "Gold" as it is known internally, implements the complete instruction set and six windows with a total of 78 registers. The only piece of the architecture not implemented is the mapping of registers into the memory address space.

We collected statistics on the design and layout of RISC I.[20] Table 8 compares these results to VLSI implementations of more complex architectures. The most visible impact of the reduced instruction set is the reduced control

area: control is only six percent of RISC I compared to 50 percent in others. RISC I is also more regular. Lattin defines the regularity factor as the total number of transistors (less those in ROM) divided by the number of individually drawn transistors.[21] By this measure RISC I is two to five times more regular than the Z8000, 68000, or 432. The time from the first discussion of the RISC I architecture to the masks was 14 months—less than the development periods of other machines. This was due in part to the reduced instruction set and in part to the Berkeley CAD software, a good match for this style of VLSI design. The primary interface was Caesar, an excellent color graphics layout editor developed by Ousterhout.[22]

Evaluation

Register windows. Two benchmarks—"puzzle" and "quicksort"—showed the effectiveness of window registers in reducing procedure cost. The two recursive programs behave quite differently. Quicksort has a large percentage of procedure calls. Puzzle has such a low density of calls that it is almost atypical for modern structured programs, but it does have a large nesting depth. In both cases, the window scheme proved to be beneficial. Table 9 shows the maximum depth of recursion, the number of register window overflows and underflows, and the total

Table 9.
Memory traffic due to call/return.

| | CALLS PLUS RETURNS, % INSTRS | MAXIMUM NESTED DEPTH | RISC I OVERFLOWS + UNDERFLOWS | DATA MEMORY TRAFFIC | |
				RISC I, WORDS	VAX, WORDS
PUZZLE	43K 0.7%	20	124	8K 0.8%	444K 28.0%
QUICKSORT	111K 8.0%	10	64	4K 1.0%	696K 50.0%

number of words transferred between memory and the RISC CPU as a result of the overflows and underflows. It also shows the memory traffic due to saving and restoring registers in the VAX. For this simulation we assumed that half of the registers were saved on an overflow and half were restored on an underflow. We found that for RISC I, an average of 0.37 words are transferred to memory per procedure invocation for the puzzle program and 0.07 for quicksort. Note that half of the data memory references in quicksort are the result of the call/return overhead of the VAX.

Table 10 compares the average "cost" of the RISC procedure mechanism—measured in execution time, number of instructions executed, and data memory accesses—to that of three traditional machines. The data was collected by looking at the code generated by C compilers for these machines for procedure call and return statements, assuming that two parameters are passed and requiring that three registers be saved.

The window scheme also reduces off-chip memory accesses. In traditional machines, 30 to 50 percent of the instructions generally access data memory, but no more than 20 percent of the instructions are register-to-register.[23,24] Because RISC I arithmetic and logical instructions cannot access memory, one might expect a higher percent of data transfer instructions. This is not the case. The static frequencies of RISC I instructions for nine typical C programs show that less than 20 percent of the instructions are loads and stores, but more than 50 percent are register-to-register. RISC I has successfully changed the allocation of variables from memory into registers, thus minimizing the slower off-chip memory accesses. This demonstrates that complex addressing modes are not necessary to obtain an effective machine.

Delayed jump. The effectiveness of rearranging the code around jump instructions can be evaluated by counting the NOP instructions in a program. Static figures before optimization show that in typical C programs about 18 percent of the instructions are NOPs inserted after jump instructions. A simple peephole optimizer reduces this to about eight percent. The optimizer does well on unconditional branches (removing about 90 percent of the NOPs) but not so well with conditional branches (removing only about 20 percent of the NOPs). Note that these are the static numbers; the dynamic numbers can be worse.

This optimizer was improved to replace the NOP by the instruction at the target of a jump. This technique can be applied to conditional branches if the optimizer determines that the target instruction modifies temporary resources—for example, an instruction that only modifies the condition codes. In quicksort, this removes all NOPs except those that follow return instructions, dropping NOPs from 12 percent statically to three percent. The dynamic effectiveness of the delayed branch must now include the NOPs plus the instructions after conditional branches that need not be executed for a particular jump condition. The total percentages of either type of instruction are again program dependent, ranging from 4 to 22 percent.

Overall performance. Prototype versions of a RISC 1 compiler for C, optimizer, linker, assembler, and simulator were developed early in the project to predict the code size and performance of RISC I. The minicomputers and microprocessors chosen for this comparison are described in Table 11. We didn't have working hardware for either the 68000 or RISC I, so we used simulators to predict performance. The cycle time for the first RISC I prototype is expected to be 400 nsec to read and add two 32-bit registers, store the result in a register, and prefetch the next instruction. This estimate is both optimistic and pessimistic: optimistic in that it is unlikely that students can successfully build something that fast on their first

**Table 10.
Procedure call/return overhead
(including parameter passing).**

	EXECUTION TIME (μSECS)	INSTRUCTIONS EXECUTED	DATA MEMORY ACCESSES
VAX-11	26	5	19
PDP-11	22	19	15
68000	19	9	12
RISC I	2	6	0.2

**Table 11.
Characteristics of six machines.**

	MICROPROCESSORS—NMOS VLSI			MINICOMPUTERS—SHOTTKY TTL MSI		
	RISC I	68000	Z8002	VAX-11/780	PDP-11/70	C/70
YEAR OF INTRODUCTION	1981	1980	1979	1978	1975	1980
BASIC INSTRUCTIONS	31	61	110	248	65	40
GENERAL REGISTERS	32	15	14	13	6	8
ADDRESSING MODES	2	14	12	18	12	17
ADDRESS SIZE (BITS)	32	24	16	32	16	20
BASIC CLOCK FREQUENCY	7.5MHz	10MHz	6MHz	5MHz	7.5MHz	6.7MHz
REG. TO REG. ADD (μsec)	0.4	0.4	0.7	0.4	0.5	?
MODIFY INDEX, BRANCH IF ZERO (BRANCH TAKEN)	1.2	1.0	2.2	1.4	0.8	?

try, and pessimistic because an experienced IC design team could build a much faster machine.

We chose 11 C programs for the performance comparison. The first five programs are HLL versions of the *EDN* benchmarks.[25] The other C programs range from toy programs (e.g., towers of Hanoi) to programs from the Unix environment that are used every day (e.g., SED, a batch-oriented text editor).

The compilers used are quite similar: the VAX, C/70, Z8002, 68000, and RISC I C compilers are based on a Unix portable C compiler,[26] and the one for the PDP-11 is based on the Ritchie C compiler.[27] Experiments comparing the Ritchie and portable C compilers for the PDP-11 have shown that the average difference in the size of generated code is within one percent.[28]

Tables 12 and 13 compare the relative performance and code size of these minicomputers and microprocessors on the 11 C programs. A surprising result is that, even though size optimization was virtually ignored, RISC I programs are—at worst—a factor of two larger than programs for the other machines. To us, the most important figure of merit for a new architecture is execution time. Table 13 shows that RISC I executes C programs faster than currently available microprocessors—faster even than most minicomputers.

Discussion

The presentation of the RISC concept has led to many stimulating discussions. Listed below are frequently heard comments followed by a short discussion of that comment.

CISCs provide better support of HLLs since they include HLL primitives (CASE, CALL).

CISC architectures support HLLs by narrowing the gap between the semantics of the assembly language and

Table 12.
C benchmarks: RISC I program size (in bytes) and RISC I size ratio.

| BENCHMARK | RISC I | PROGRAM SIZE RELATIVE TO RISC I | | | | |
		68000	Z8002	VAX-11/780	11/70	C/70
E—STRING SEARCH	144	.8	.9	.7	.8	.7
F—BIT TEST	120	1.2	1.5	1.2	1.4	1.0
H—LINKED LIST	176	.7	.8	1.2	1.7	.8
K—BIT MATRIX	288	1.1	1.3	1.0	1.3	1.1
I— QUICKSORT	992	.7	1.1	.9	1.1	.9
ACKERMAN(3,6)	144	—	2.1	.5	.6	.5
PUZZLE(SUBSCRIPT)	2736	—	.5	.5	.6	.6
PUZZLE(POINTER)	2796	.9	.5	.5	.5	.6
RECURSIVE QSORT	752	—	.8	.6	.8	.6
SED(BATCH EDITOR)	17720	—	1.0	.6	.5	.5
TOWERS HANOI(18)	96	—	2.5	.8	1.0	.7
AVERAGE		.9± .2	1.2± .6	.8± .3	.9± .4	.7± .2

Table 13.
C benchmarks: RISC I execution time (in milliseconds) and RISC I performance ratio.

| BENCHMARK | RISC I | NUMBER OF TIMES SLOWER THAN RISC I | | | | |
		68000	Z8002	VAX-11/780	11/70	C/70
E—STRING SEARCH	.46	2.8	1.6	1.3	0.9	2.2
F—BIT TEST	.06	4.8	7.2	4.8	6.2	9.2
H—LINKED LIST	.10	1.6	2.4	1.2	1.9	2.5
K—BIT MATRIX	.43	4.0	5.2	3.0	4.0	9.3
I— QUICKSORT	50.4	4.1	5.2	3.0	3.6	5.8
ACKERMAN(3,6)	3200	—	2.8	1.6	1.6	—
RECURSIVE QSORT	800	—	5.9	2.3	3.2	1.3
PUZZLE(SUBSCRIPT)	4700	—	4.2	2.0	1.6	3.4
PUZZLE(POINTER)	3200	4.2	2.3	1.3	2.0	2.1
SED(BATCH EDITOR)	5100	—	4.4	1.1	1.1	2.6
TOWERS HANOI(18)	6800	—	4.2	1.8	2.3	1.6
AVERAGE		3.5± 1.8	4.1± 1.6	2.1± 1.1	2.6± 1.5	4.0± 2.8

the semantics of an HLL. Support can also, however, be measured as the inverse of the "costs" of using typical HLL constructs on a particular machine. If the architect provides a feature that "looks" like the HLL construct but runs slowly, the compiler writer will omit the feature or, worse, the HLL programmer concerned with performance will avoid the construct. A recent study shows that CISCs penalize the use of HLLs far more than RISCs.[29]

It is more difficult to write a compiler for a RISC than a CISC.

A recent paper by Wulf[30] helps explain why this is not true. He says that compiling is essentially a large "case analysis." The more ways there are to do something (more instructions and addressing modes), the more cases must be considered. The compiler writer must balance the speed of the compiler with his desire to get good code. In CISCs there may not be enough time to analyze the potential usage of all available instructions. Thus, Wulf recommends, "There should be precisely one way to do something, or all ways should be possible." In RISC we have taken the former approach. There are few choices; for example, if an operand is in memory, it must first be loaded into a register. Simple case analysis implies a simple compiler, even if more instructions must be generated in each case.

RISC I is tailored to C and will not work well with other HLLs.

Studies of other HLLs[23,31] indicate that the most frequently executed operations are the same simple HLL constructs found in C, for which RISC I has been optimized. Unless an HLL significantly changes the way people program, we expect to see similar results. For languages that have unusual data types, such as Cobol, we need to find the simple operations that are used repeatedly in that environment and incorporate them into a RISC. Even if the RISC I architecture does not map Cobol efficiently, we believe this philosophy can lead to a RISC that does.

Comparisons of RISC I with the VAX are unfair in that the VAX provides a virtual address space; RISC I would be much slower if it had virtual memory.

To answer the question "How much slower?" we looked at solutions used by other microprocessors. National Semiconductor has announed the 16082, a memory management chip with an address cache that normally translates virtual address into physical addresses in 100 nsec.[32] If we were to put this chip in a system with a RISC CPU, it would add another 100 nsec to every memory access. Memory is referenced every 400 nsec in RISC I, so such a combination would reduce RISC performance by 20 percent. Because 80 to 90 percent of memory references in RISC I are to instructions,[1] more sophisticated approaches, such as translating addresses only when crossing a page boundary, might limit performance reduction to only five percent. A final observation is that even if the addition of virtual memory doubled the cycle

time of NMOS RISC I, it would still be faster than most present-day microprocessors.

The good performance is due to the overlapped register windows; the reduced instruction set has nothing to do with it.

Certainly, a significant portion of the speed is due to the overlapped register windows of RISC I. A key point is that there would have been no room for register windows if control had not dropped from 50 to 6 percent. Furthermore, control is so simple in RISC that microprogramming is unnecessary; this eliminates the control loop as the limiting factor of the machine cycle, as is frequently the case in microprogrammed machines.

There is no difference between overlapped register windows and a data cache.

A cache is ineffective if it is too small. An effective data cache would require a much larger area than our register file, especially if it must provide the same number of ports as the register file. The more complicated virtual address translation and decoding would likely stretch the basic CPU cycle time. Finally, the more complicated cache control would have extended the design phase of RISC I.

RISC I represents a new style of computers that take less time to build yet provide higher performance. While traditional machines "support" HLLs with instructions that look like HLL constructs, this machine supports the use of HLLs with instructions that HLL compilers can use efficiently. The loss of complexity has not reduced RISC's functionality; the chosen subset, especially when combined with the register window scheme, emulates more complex machines. It also appears we can build such a single-chip computer much sooner and with less effort than traditional architectures.

As we go to press, we are just testing the RISC I chips. Unfortunately, the polysilicon layer was processed improperly, and we believe this accounts for the fact that the chips are only partially operational. We have not yet found any circuit design errors.

This research area is by no means closed. For example, an investigation of a RISC with two ALU operations per cycle and dual-port main memory has begun at Stanford,[33] and we are working on a new implementation with a denser register file and a more sophisticated timing scheme.[34] Some of the other topics to be investigated include the applicability of RISCs to other HLLs (e.g., Lisp, Cobol, Ada), the effectiveness of an operating system on RISC (e.g., Unix), the architecture of coprocessors for RISC (e.g., graphics, floating point), migration of software to RISC (e.g., a 370 emulator written in RISC machine language), and the implementation of RISC in other technologies (CMOS, TTL, ECL). This list is too big for one project; we hope to cooperate with industry and academia in exploring RISCy architectures. ∎

Acknowledgments

The RISC Project has been sustained by a large group of volunteers. We would like to thank all those in the Berkeley community who have helped push RISC from a concept to a chip. We would also like to give special thanks to a few.

John Ousterhout created, maintained, and revised Caesar, our principal design aid, and consistently provided useful technical and editorial advice. Lloyd Dickman was actively involved with the design of RISC during his sabbatical at Berkeley, supplying technical and managerial expertise. We also want to thank Richard Newton for dedicating his VLSI class to the RISC project.

The RISC research was investigated over a four-quarter sequence of graduate courses at Berkeley. Many have participated but a few contributed significantly. Manolis Katevenis did the initial block structure and the initial timing description and provided many important simplifications and ideas about the implementation and the architecture. Ralph Campbell wrote the initial C compiler, the optimizer, assembler, and linker. Yuval Tamir wrote a simulator, ran the benchmarks,[35] and provided many suggestions in the initial design of RISC I. Gary Corcoran wrote the initial ISPS description of RISC I. Jim Peek, Korbin Van Dyke, John Foderaro, Dan Fitzpatrick, and Zvi Peshkess were the principal VLSI designers of the first RISC I chip. Michael Arnold, Dan Fitzpatrick, John Foderaro, and Howard Landman all wrote CAD tools that were crucial to the VLSI implementation of RISC I. Peter Kessler helped derive the overlapped register windows and helped with the CAD software. Jim Beck and Bob Cmelik created the VLSI testing hardware and software. Bob Sherburne is currently working with Katevenis on a more efficient VLSI implementation of RISC. Earl Cohen and Neil Soiffer collected statistics on C programs, and Shafi Goldwasser collected similar statistics for Pascal.

We would also like to thank Korbin Van Dyke for his useful suggestions on improving this paper.

This research was funded in part by the Defense Advance Research Projects Agency, ARPA Order No. 3803, and monitored by the Naval Electronic System Command under Contract No. N00039-78-G-0013-0004. We would like to thank Duane Adams, Paul Losleben, and DARPA for providing the resources that allow universities to attempt projects involving high risk.

References

1. W. D. Strecker, "VAX-11/780: A Virtual Address Extension to the DEC PDP-11 Family," *AFIPS Conf. Proc.,* Vol. 47, 1978 NCC, pp. 967-980.

2. B. G. Utley et al., *IBM System/38 Technical Developments,* IBM GS80-0237, 1978.

3. P. Tyner, *iAPX-432 General Data Processor Architecture Reference Manual,* Order No. 171860-001, Intel, Santa Clara, Calif., 1981.

4. E. Organick, *A Programmer's View of the Intel 432 System,* McGraw-Hill, Hightstown, N.J., 1982.

5. D. A. Patterson and D. R. Ditzel, "The Case for the Reduced Instruction Set Computer," *Computer Architecture News,* Vol. 8, No. 6, Oct. 15, 1980, pp. 25-33.

6. D. A. Patterson and C. H. Séquin, "Design Considerations for Single-Chip Computers of the Future," *IEEE Trans. Computers,* Joint Special Issue on Microprocessors and Microcomputers, Vol. C-29, No. 2, pp. 108-116.

7. D. R. Ditzel and D. A. Patterson, "Retrospective on High-Level Language Computer Architecture," *Proc. Seventh Annual Int'l Symp. Computer Architecture,* May 6-8, 1980, pp. 97-104.

8. W. Wulf, private communication, Nov. 1980.

9. A. Lunde, "Empirical Evaluation of Some Features of Instruction Set Processor Architecture," *Comm. ACM,* Mar. 1977, Vol. 20, No. 3, pp. 143-153.

10. B. A. Wichmann, "Ackermann's Function: A Study in the Efficiency of Calling Procedures," *BIT,* Vol. 16, No. 1, Jan. 1976, pp. 103-110.

11. F. Baskett, "A VLSI Pascal Machine," public lecture, University of California, Berkeley, Fall 1978.

12. R. L. Sites, "How to Use 1000 Registers," *Caltech Conf. VLSI,* Jan. 1979.

13. D. Halbert and P. Kessler, *Windows of Overlapping Registers,* CS292R Final Reports, June 9, 1980.

14. D. Morris and R. N. Ibbett, *The MU-5 Computer System,* Springer-Verlag, New York, 1979.

15. F. C. Williams and T. Kilburn, "The University of Machester Computing Machine," *Inaugural Conf. Machester University Computer,* July 1951, pp. 5-11.

16. "Altering Computer Architecture is Way to Raise Throughput, Suggests IBM Researchers," *Electronics,* Vol. 49, No. 25, Dec. 23, 1976, pp. 30-31.

17. "IBM Mini a Radical Departure," *Datamation,* Vol. 25, No. 11, Oct. 79, pp. 53-55.

18. G. Radin, "The 801 Minicomputer," *Proc. Symp. Architectural Support for Programming Languages and Operating Systems,* Mar. 1-3, 1982.

19. R. V. Orlando and T. L. Anderson, "An Overview of the 9900 Microprocessor Family," *IEEE Micro,* Vol. 1, No. 3, Aug. 1981, pp. 38-42.

20. D. T. Fitzpatrick et al., "A RISCy Approach to VLSI," *VLSI Design,* Vol. 2, No. 4, Oct. 81, pp. 14-20.

21. W. W. Lattin et al., "A Methodology for VLSI Chip Design," *Lambda—The Magazine of VLSI Design,* Second Quarter 1981, pp. 34-44.

22. J. Ousterhout, "Caesar: An Interactive Editor for VLSI Circuits," *VLSI Design,* Vol. 2, No. 4, Nov. 1981, pp. 34-38.

23. W. C. Alexander and D. B. Wortman, "Static and Dynamic Characteristics of XPL Programs," *Computer,* Vol. 8, No. 11, Nov. 1975, pp. 41-46.

24. L. Shustek, "Analysis and Performance of Computer Instruction Sets," PhD Thesis, Stanford University, Jan. 1978.

25. R. G. Grappel and J. E. Hemmengway, "A Tale of Four Microprocessors: Benchmarks Quantify Performance," *Electronic Design News,* Vol. 26, No. 7, Apr. 1, 1981, pp. 179-265.

26. S. C. Johnson, "A Portable Compiler: Theory and Practice," *Proc. Fifth Annual ACM Symp. Programming Languages,* Jan. 1978, pp. 97-104.

27. B. W. Kernighan and D. M. Ritchie, *The C Programming Language,* Prentice-Hall, Englewood Cliffs, N.J., 1978.

28. S. C. Johnson, private communication, Jan. 1981.

29. D. A. Patterson and R. S. Piepho, "RISC Assessment: A High-Level Language Experiment," *Proc. Ninth Int'l Symp. Computer Architecture,* Apr. 26-29, 1982, pp. 3-8. (Scheduled to appear in an upcoming issue of IEEE Micro.)

30. W. A. Wulf, "Compilers and Computer Architecture," *Computer,* Vol. 14, No. 7, July 1981, pp. 41-48.

31. D. R. Ditzel, "Program Measurements on a High-Level Language Computer," *Computer,* Vol. 13, No. 8, Aug. 1980, pp. 62-72.

32. Y. Lavi et al., "16-bit Microprocessor Enters Virtual Memory Domain," *Electronics,* Vol. 53, No. 9, Apr. 24, 1980, pp. 123-129.

33. J. Hennessy et al., "The MIPS Machine," *Digest of Papers Compcon Spring 82*, Feb. 1982, pp. 2-7.

34. R. W. Sherburne et al., "Datapath Design for RISC," *Proc. Conf. Advanced Research in VLSI,* Jan. 25-27, 1982, pp. 53-62.

35. Y. Tamir, "Simulation and Performance Evaluation of the RISC Architecture," Electronics Research Laboratory Memorandom No. UCB/ERL M81/17, University of California, Berkeley, Mar. 1981.

David A. Patterson has been a member of the faculty in the Computer Science Division, Department of Electrical Engineering and Computer Sciences, University of California, Berkeley, since 1977. He was named associate professor in 1981 and currently teaches computer architecture at the graduate and undergraduate levels. His research combines popular software, experimental architecture, and VLSI to create more effective computer systems.

Patterson spent the fall of 1979 on leave of absence at Digital Equipment Corporation developing microprogram design tools and reviewing computer designs. In the next academic year he developed courses that led to the design and implementation of RISC I, a 45,000-transistor microprocessor. In 1982 he received the Distinguished Teaching Award from the Berkeley division of the Academic Senate of the University of California. Patterson received a BA in mathematics and an MS and PhD in computer science from UCLA.

Carlo H. Séquin is a professor of computer science at the University of California, Berkeley. Since 1980, he has headed the Computer Science Division as associate chairman for computer sciences in the Department of Electrical Engineering and Computer Science. He joined the faculty in 1977. His research interests lie in the field of computer architecture and design tools for very large scale integrated systems. In particular, his research concerns multi-microprocessor computer networks, the mutual influence of advanced computer architecture and modern VLSI technology, and the implementation of special functions in silicon.

From 1970 to 1976, Séquin worked on the design and investigation of charge-coupled devices for imaging and signal processing applications at Bell Telephone Laboratories, Murray Hill, New Jersey. He has written many papers in that field and is an author of the first book on charge-transfer devices. Séquin received his PhD in experimental physics from the University of Basel, Switzerland, in 1969. He is a member of the ACM and the Swiss Physical Society, and a fellow of the IEEE.

New RISC machines appear as hybrids with both RISC and CISC features

With both IBM and Hewlett-Packard hopping onto the RISC bandwagon earlier this year, a new era in computer design and architecture has been launched. But neither IBM's engineering workstations nor HP's minicomputers are true RISC machines; they're hybrids that combine the best of both complex-instruction-set computer and reduced-instruction-set computer architectures.

IBM has been doing research in RISC architectures since the mid-70s under the project name of the 801 minicomputer, and its new RT PC is a direct outgrowth of this effort. But neither the earlier, commercially available RISC-based machines from companies such as Ridge Computers (Santa Clara, CA) and Pyramid Technology (Mountain View, CA), nor the new contenders from IBM (Rye Brook, NY) and Hewlett-Packard (Palo Alto, CA) can claim to be true RISC machines. Computer designers are actually hard put to identify a true RISC machine because it's unclear how far an instruction set can be reduced or simplified and still efficiently perform all of the functions necessary for a practical machine.

Whatever IBM's novel architecture is specifically called, IBM can at least make the "invented here" claim. Coupling that with its well-established reputation for product support, IBM's move should serve as an added impetus for other computer vendors to follow suit with RISC-based designs.

On the way to RISC

The road to the development of a RISC machine is a bumpy one. RISC architecture is a radical departure from the way computer designers have thought of computer architectures for the past two to three decades. During this time, instruction

Nicolas Mokhoff
Senior Editor

sets grew larger, more complex and harder to implement without degrading a machine's performance. In 1975, IBM started looking for alternative architectures implementing smaller instruction sets that would simplify the programmer's chore and provide performance improvements at the same time.

> *"Although specification of instructions, their format and their number are the primary focus of most of the RISC literature, the best generalization of RISC philosophy goes well beyond this narrow activity."*
> *—E. Douglas Jensen*
> *Carnegie-Mellon University*

The search for a simpler solution was picked up by university-based groups as well, giving birth to projects such as RISC I and II and the MIPS microprocessor. RISC I and II microprocessors were the results of graduate projects at the University of California at Berkeley and the MIPS microprocessor was its counterpart at Stanford University. These have remained laboratory curiosities although they come the closest to the ideal RISC machine defined by most computer scientists.

Although IBM has applied the RISC concepts developed on the 801 minicomputer to a family of stand-alone engineering workstations, the original aim of the 801 project was simply to restrict the instruction set to include a minimum of highly repe-

titive instructions for a specific application. When IBM decided to enter the CAD/CAM workstation market, it seized the opportunity to introduce a family of workstations using such a reduced instruction set to execute the repetitive functions inherent in the mathematically intensive problems handled on workstations.

IBM's RISC architecture was designed to speed up computer operation by using its relatively simple 118 instructions—such as add, subtract, shift and compare—most of which can be executed within a single 170-ns machine cycle. This feature, coupled with innovative virtual memory techniques, gives IBM's $12,000 to $20,000 workstations the ability to perform CAE/CAD/CAM tasks usually reserved for larger computers (see "IBM RISC workstation features 40-bit virtual addressing," *Computer Design,* Feb 15, 1986, p 28).

While the RT PC's 118 instructions are less than half the number of instructions used in a complex-instruction-set computer, such as the VAX 11/780, the number of instructions isn't the only criterion used to define a RISC machine. As proposed by E. Douglas Jensen, professor of computer science at Carnegie-Mellon University (Pittsburgh, PA), there are six synergistic elements that seem essential to the RISC philosophy: single-cycle operation, load/store design, hard-wire control, relatively few instructions and addressing modes, fixed instruction format and more compile-time effort than for a CISC machine.

"Although specification of instructions, their format and their number are the primary focus of most of the RISC literature," says Jensen, "the best generalization of RISC philosophy goes well beyond this narrow activity. More properly, it connotes a willingness to consciously make design trade-offs between architecture and implementation, hardware and software, and compile time and run

Copyright by *Computer Design* © April 1, 1986. All rights reserved. Reprinted by permission.

time in order to maximize performance as measured in some specific context.''

RISC proponents have to make these design trade-offs when designing their machines. As a result, all current commercial designs are hybrid CISCs/RISCs of some type. But the fact that designers are trying out the RISC concepts in the first place signals the beginning of a new generation of computers and not just a migration to the next advanced processors. In IBM's case, it was a clearcut move into the CAD/CAM workstation area with a separate line of new machines that don't fit into IBM's other computer lines. This isn't the case with HP's Spectrum family of RISC-based minicomputers, however.

Compatible with existing machines

HP, being a technology-driven engineering-oriented company, made a conscious effort several years ago to base its next-generation line of computers on RISC concepts. But the company also decided to maintain compatibility with its installed base of HP 3000 family members. This, in part, accounted for the seemingly endless delays in introducing the new Spectrum family.

Software developers were busy making the new Series 930 and 950 RISC computers operationally compatible with the other HP 3000 systems, and also making compatible object codes, source codes, data bases and networks. As HP's president, John A. Young, explains, ''Protecting customers' hardware and software investments has been a major objective with this new generation of computers. We feel customers' migration to the new systems will be easier than the industry has come to expect for a major system rollover.''

According to HP, many current applications can be moved to the new Series 930 and 950 over a weekend

Hewlett-Packard's RISC-based HP 3000 Series 930 provides higher performance than its earlier Series 68, while protecting existing hardware and software investments. The 140 instructions maximize throughput while retaining compatibility over a wide range of price and performance.

because the new systems can run the existing HP 3000 object code without the need for modification, recompilation or data conversion. The same compatibility will be ensured with the new HP 9000 Series 500 engineering workstation when it's made available mid-year. Since both current and new models are Unix-based, the fact that the new model will be a RISC-type machine will make little difference to the end user. The only perceptible difference is that the new RISC-based model will be twice as fast as the current HP 9000 Series 500.

HP's RISC-like architecture, labeled Precision Architecture, is the result of engineering decisions based on extensive experimental data. ''We believe that the analysis and measurement techniques used to evaluate and balance this architecture demonstrate conclusively that no one need settle any longer for the ad hoc techniques so widely used to make engineering trade-offs,'' says Joel Birnbaum, vice president of research and development at HP's Palo Alto laboratories. Birnbaum says that HP plans to publish the measurement results so that anyone can see that engineering decisions made to extend the RISC

architecture into the Precision Architecture were correct. ''We've made computer design a little more like astrophysics than astrology,'' asserts Birnbaum.

RISC performs better than CISC

The increase in performance of RISC-based machines over CISC-based ones is largely the result of two factors: instructions that are simple and can be implemented directly in hardware and an innovative hierarchical memory design. In a RISC machine, frequently used instructions and data are stored in a large number of CPU registers, which operate up to eight times faster than main memory.

''Much of the efficiency of RISC architectures comes from using registers for most operations,'' emphasizes William F. Zachmann, vice president of the office of technology assessment at International Data Corp (Framingham, MA). ''Instead of directly operating on data in main memory, a RISC system will typically perform arithmetic and logical operations only on data previously loaded into registers. Load and store operations to main storage are much slower than register operations and if these occur in the critical path of program execution, they can completely obliterate whatever advantage in CPU speed a RISC architecture may have to offer.''

Zachmann notes that the numerous main storage references required for context switching in a typical multiuser, multitasking environment pose a significant problem for pure RISC architectures. In addition, key applications require instruction mixes which involve a large number of complex operations, frequent storage references or both, and these work against efficiency in a true RISC architecture. As an example, Zachmann cites both floating-point arithmetic and decimal arithmetic—essential for scientific and commercial data applications—as complex operations that wouldn't be included in a true RISC design.

Commercially available RISC machines aren't true RISCs, claims Zachmann, because they include complex floating-point and decimal instructions in their instruction sets. These systems represent a compromise between the goal of achieving a reduced instruction set and the reality of sufficiently complex instructions to make a system practical. "No pure RISC architecture is ever likely to be a viable practical system,'' concludes Zachmann.

Howard Sachs, general manager of Fairchild's advanced processor division (Mountain View, CA), agrees. "The architecture of a supercomputer, which has always been RISC-oriented, coupled with the operating system support of CISCs and the capabilities of the VLSI memory to provide caching, make it feasible to come up with a new high-performance, low-cost computer architecture.'' Sachs adds that achieving this performance requires balancing all aspects of the system.

To support his position, Sachs points to Fairchild's Clipper module, a 32-bit three-chip set that uses the basic elements of RISC architecture coupled with a macroinstruction unit that provides high-level instructions and functions. Instead of microcoded instructions, the Clipper uses 101 hard-wired instructions to achieve peak performance levels of 33 Mips. This translates to a 5-Mips execution rate in a system configuration.

Two identical cache/memory-management chips complement the CPU chip and provide fast access for both data and instructions. To accommodate the scientific applications that Fairchild has targeted, the floating-point unit has been incorporated on the CPU chip. This eliminates the need for transfers of op codes over the bus and synchronization.

Transputer instead of RISC

Another IC vendor dabbling with simpler instruction sets is Inmos (Colorado Springs, CO). As in RISC designs, the transputer instruction set implements complex operations as a sequence of simple, very tightly encoded high-speed instructions. Unlike typical RISCs that have a large amount of general-purpose registers, the transputer has a large amount of registers incorporated on the same chip as the processor.

Rather than keep variables in the general-purpose registers, the transputer keeps them in memory, copying their values to and from registers attached to the ALU when they're needed in a computation. This is beneficial for context switching since the variables don't have to be constantly saved and restored. And there's no arbitrary limit set on the number of local variables, as there would be if a fixed number of registers were used to hold the variables. The transputer is different from both RISCs and CISCs in its choice of physically short, simple instructions, a syntax that's close to that of a high-level language (because of its dependence on Occam) and the use of microcode for greater efficiency in frequently used complex operations.

RISC versus CISC trade-offs have led Celerity Computing (San Diego, CA) to develop a family of supermini-computers based on a RISC architecture. Each of Celerity's systems, designed for compute-intensive research and design projects, uses a CPU and a floating-point processor in a RISC-like architecture with more than 150 instructions. "Celerity used that many instructions to maintain the enhanced execution speeds of a reduced instruction set without limiting the processor to too few commands and thus sacrificing function,'' says Andrew McCrocklin, vice president of software engineering.

A three-stage pipeline architecture with delayed jumps provides a basic cycle time as low as 100 ns. Single-cycle execution of most instructions is possible even though the instruction set is not reduced in the sense of RISCs. Instead, a rich set of instructions includes operations based on half-words, bytes and digits as well as words. The instruction set is reduced only in format and register orientation, not functionality. The architecture extends the RISC stacked-register concept by adding a set of dedicated 64-bit floating-point registers that's also managed as a stack. Celerity believes that this is the only approach to complex, floating-point calculations.

With at least six vendors offering RISC-type machines and chips, and the research that's being conducted by some large computer makers, such as Digital Equipment Corp, there are bound to be more RISCs springing up within the next year or so. The debate has just begun on what constitutes a RISC machine and whether it makes sense for the entire industry to switch from CISC to RISC for the next generation of machines. One thing is sure: when instruction sets become so complex that they become unmanageable and slow machine performance, designers will start finding ways to design simpler instruction sets, keeping any features inherent in complex instruction sets that help tackle an application. **CD**

Alain J. Hanover
President
Viewlogic Systems

The RT PC: An evaluation

IBM's introduction of the RT PC is both good news and bad news for the CAE workstation industry. It's good news for vendors who have committed themselves to building personal workstations based on the IBM PC and compatible platforms, but it's bad news for vendors of multiuser workstations based on non-IBM platforms.

The RT retains the open architecture and compatibility that have made the IBM PC the most popular platform for CAE workstations. Yet it offers a significant increase in performance plus a state-of-the-art operating system that will allow development of more sophisticated applications on a personal workstation.

The price of the RT, though greater than that of previous personal computers, is still within the upper range of what most CAE workstation users are willing to pay for a personal system, especially considering the greatly improved performance it offers. Moreover, the inevitable emergence of RT-compatible computers will drive down prices, making it even more attractive.

Because of its superior performance, the RT is destined to fill the high end of the PC line and complement the PC AT as the standard platform for personal CAE workstations, with the PC AT maintaining the low end of the PC line. But the use of the RT as a CAE workstation platform won't happen overnight. The proprietary RISC architecture will present software-transport problems for those PC-based workstation vendors whose software is written in machine language. But those with software based on high-level languages should have a relatively easy time porting software, especially since the initial RT offering includes a full complement of language translators and DOS compatibility.

The initial RT offering includes a few disappointments, however. One is the lack of support for sophisticated network applications, which will make it difficult initially to support resource sharing and information exchange among workstations. Another disappointment is the lack of a low-cost, high-resolution graphics subsystem, but communications support and low-cost, high-resolution graphics subsystems should emerge shortly from IBM and third parties. Moreover, the next two years should see the transport of horizontal applications packages, such as Lotus 1-2-3 and Ashton-Tate's Framework, to the RT, allowing it to be used as a multifunction personal workstation in the tradition of previous members of the IBM PC family.

The RT spells trouble for vendors of traditional multiuser CAE workstations, who have already seen their markets eroded by PC-based personal workstations and thus have begun to move into personal workstations themselves. But the introduction of the RT is perhaps most ominous for non-IBM platform vendors. With the CAE market shifting to personal workstations based on AT and RT architectures, such vendors will find themselves competing for a steadily dwindling market segment. To survive, they may be forced to adopt the IBM standard.

Although the RT will pose problems for some vendors, the ultimate beneficiary of its introduction will be the CAE workstation user. Its addition to the PC line means that users will soon have a full spectrum of personal workstations to match their budgets and design requirements. By continuing the IBM PC tradition of an open architecture, it will encourage competition that will drive down the cost of CAE workstations, while increasing their power and ease of use.

ROMP/MMU Technology Introduction

D.E. Waldecker and P.Y. Woon

The ROMP/PL.8 project was initiated by the IBM Office Products Division (OPD) in mid-1977 in Austin. OPD architects were motivated to develop a high-performance microprocessor which could be efficiently programmed using a high-level language. The "801 Project" at IBM Research in Yorktown Heights, New York had many of the same goals. (This project is described by George Radin in [1] and [2].) It was decided to take the 801 architecture and modify it as appropriate for OPD objectives. This cooperative effort became known as the Research – OPD – MicroProcessor and was given the acronym ROMP.

ROMP/801 Objectives

Objectives of both the 801 and ROMP projects were to provide high performance, Reduced Instruction Set Computer (RISC) architectures which were especially well-suited as the target for an advanced, optimizing compiler (the PL.8 compiler). The RISC architectures are characterized by use of general-purpose registers, use of only Load and Store instructions for referencing memory, and execution of most instructions in a single processor cycle. The PL.8 compiler was under development at IBM Research in Yorktown Heights in conjunction with the 801 project. The goal of the PL.8 compiler was to produce code which is almost as efficient as code developed in assembly language. Attention was given to ensure that both the 801 and ROMP machines were good compiler targets. Instruction set definition was driven by compiler requirements as opposed to performance on bench marks or optimization for a particular software kernel.

The ROMP definition was influenced by many factors. Maintaining a strong relationship with the 801 activities in Research was important in order to take advantage of compiler advances which continued throughout the development phase. Cost was a key consideration and influenced both architecture and technology selection. Storage economy was a main factor that led to differences between the ROMP and the 801 instruction sets. A technology goal was to fit the processor (ROMP) and the Memory Management Unit (MMU) on a single chip each. Another goal was to fully exercise the Burlington Silicon Gate Process (SGP) technology while maintaining chip sizes that would produce reasonable manufacturing yields.

An initial TTL model of the ROMP was operational in Austin at the end of 1978. Differences between this first ROMP and the current chip were driven by technology and, to a greater extent, by changes in the Research 801 definition. The original machines performed 24-bit arithmetic and had both 16- and 32-bit instructions. The 801 evolved to 32-bit arithmetic and addressing and the ROMP followed this lead, primarily because the need for a 32-bit address was recognized and maintaining the desired PL.8 compiler compatibility required that this change be made to both machines.

ROMP/801 Differences

Although the 801 and ROMP have a common heritage, some important differences exist between the two. The 801 assumed the use of two cache memories, one for instructions and one for data. A requirement for caches was not incorporated into the ROMP design for cost and complexity reasons. Since the ROMP can execute an instruction almost every processor cycle, an efficient memory interface capable of high bandwidth was a requirement. Two key features of the ROMP design which greatly reduce memory bandwidth limitations are: the Instruction

Reprinted by permission from *IBM RT Personal Computer Technology*, IBM Publication Number SA23-1057, © 1986 by International Business Machines Corporation.

Prefetch Buffer and the use of 16-bit, in addition to 32-bit, instructions. The ROMP contains a 16-byte instruction prefetch buffer which practically guarantees that all sequentially accessed instructions are available for execution when they are needed.

The 801 migrated to all 32-bit instructions while the ROMP maintained both 16- and 32-bit instructions. The judicious use of 16-bit instructions decreases memory code space and allows more code per real-page frame in a virtual memory system, resulting in fewer page faults and improved system performance. More importantly, the shorter average instruction length of the ROMP decreases the memory bandwidth required for instruction fetches. For example, an instruction mix containing 30% Load and Store instructions (which require 32 bits of memory reference each for data) would require 41.6 bits of memory bandwidth per instruction if all instructions are 32 bits long. The same instruction mix executed in the ROMP, where the average instruction length (weighted average of 16- and 32-bit instructions) is about 20 bits (2.5 bytes), only requires an average of 29.6 bits for each instruction. This is a reduction in memory bandwidth requirement of almost 30% per instruction for the ROMP over a design which contains only 32-bit instructions. Since memory bandwidth is usually the performance-limiting factor, a 30% reduction in the bandwidth requirement will certainly improve performance in a non-cache system.

It must be recognized that a machine with all 32-bit instructions should do more "work" for each instruction executed than a machine with some instructions that can only be executed in a 16-bit format. That is, an equivalent MIP (Million Instructions Processed per second) rate for a machine with only 32-bit instructions should represent more processing capability than the same MIP rate for a machine with both 16- and 32-bit instructions. One of the limitations of 16-bit instructions is the limited number of bits available to specify operation codes, registers, displacements, etc. This limitation is one of the reasons that the 801 uses 32-bit instructions exclusively. Use of only 32-bit instructions permits the register specification fields to contain the 5 bits required to select one of 32 general-purpose registers (GPRs).

The limit of 16 registers for the ROMP results in only a modest increase in Load and Store frequency, since the PL.8 compiler perform an efficient register optimization. A primary motivation for having 32 registers is efficient emulation of other architectures which have 16 general-purpose registers (i.e., System/370). The ROMP does an excellent job of emulating other machines which have a more limited register set. The 801 is significantly better at 370 emulation. Aside from emulation, the use of all 32-bit instructions is estimated to make the 801 MIP rate about 15% to 20% more powerful than the ROMP MIP rate. That is, software path lengths for 801 programs are about 15% to 20% shorter than they are for equivalent ROMP programs.

The use of both 16- and 32-bit instructions adds some design complexity. Instruction handling and decoding must account for instruction location on both 16- and 32-bit boundaries. The 16-byte Instruction Buffer and its management also adds complexity. However, studies have shown that the 16-byte Instruction Buffer provides about the same performance advantage as a 256-byte instruction cache, with a significant savings in the silicon required for implementation.

The design point chosen for the ROMP is well suited for a microprocessor VLSI design. Good performance is achieved with readily available memories and the silicon area requirements are a good fit for our SGP technology. The ROMP's dual 16- and 32-bit instruction format provides about a 10% net performance advantage over an equivalent 801 microprocessor in non-cache systems.

Compiler Development for ROMP & 801
The PL.8 compiler was initially developed for the 801 project in Research as part of the exploration of the interaction of computer architecture, system design, programming language, and compiler techniques. The adaptation of this compiler to the ROMP architecture was done in Austin. A single compiler was maintained with the addition of another "backend" for the ROMP. This involved a complex working relationship between Research and Austin. This excellent relationship has continued over the years with enhancements and modifications being made by both groups. The compiler is currently owned by Austin with enhancements being

made by both groups.

The PL.8 compiler currently supports three source languages, Pascal, C, and PL.8, a PL/I variant designed to be suitable for generation of efficient object code for systems programming. Object code is produced for the 801, ROMP, System/370, and MC68000.

The ROMP PL.8 compiler development influenced the design of the ROMP instructions in a number of significant ways. The goal of program storage (byte) efficiency caused the following modifications to be made:

1. Short (16 bits) forms of several instructions were introduced to provide for the special case of an immediate operand with value less than 16. For example, Add Immediate, Subtract Immediate, Compare Immediate, and Load Immediate were provided.

2. A short-form relative jump instruction was added with maximum displacement of plus or minus 256 bytes.

3. The long (32-bit) Branch instructions were defined to be relative rather than absolute in order to reduce the storage necessary for relocation information from modules.

4. A Load Character instruction was added in order to handle character data with fewer bytes.

    In addition, Load Multiple and Store Multiple instructions were provided to improve the speed of subroutine linkage.

The resultant ROMP architecture proved to require about 30% fewer bytes than 801 for a selected set of bench marks.

In addition, the ROMP instruction set design includes only instructions which can be used effectively by the compiler. The ROMP does not contain complex instructions and addressing modes which a compiler finds difficult to generate. The ROMP does not have complex loop closing instructions which require several free registers in order to operate. It does not contain instructions like repeat, rotate, and edit—instructions which are not primitives for PL.8 constructs.

Register allocation is simplified by the requirement that variables be loaded into registers before being operated upon.

The PL.8 compiler employs state-of-the-art compiler technology [3] utilizing several independent advances in the theory of compiler design. John Cocke and Fran Allen [4] published a procedure of data flow analysis—a technique for analyzing the interval of execution over which a variable is used, and using that information for optimization and assignment of variables to registers. The technique allows efficient use of registers and enhances the reliability of generated code.

The compiler's scheduling algorithms make use of the data flow analysis results to produce a program which takes advantage of the pipelined implementation of the ROMP. Since only Load and Store operations reference memory, the compiler can very effectively intersperse memory references and register-to-register (RR) operations in the instruction stream so that processing of the RR operation can overlap the memory reference. The compiler also makes effective use of the Branch with Execute instruction. This instruction allows execution of an instruction following the Branch while the branch target instruction is being fetched. This overlap of instruction execution with the fetching of the new instruction stream results in better CPU utilization.

In addition the PL.8 compiler uses LALR parser generator [5] techniques. Syntax-directed translation enables the compiler to associate the intermediate code generation directly with the syntactic structure of the source language. Furthermore, it uses a map-coloring algorithm from topology for register allocation [6]. Most programs of reasonable size color in 16 GPR without spilling. 32 GPR would reduce spilling on larger programs but would require 5 bits for register specification which would require 32-bit instructions. The trade-off was made in favor of the use of 16-bit instructions (with the 25% to 30% performance advantage) at the performance detriment of large programs.

The compiler incorporates the primary theoretical advances in compiler design achieved over the past decade. The proof of the theory lies in its effectiveness. The approach of developing the language and the instruction set as a joint effort has paid off in language efficiency and in ease of code generation. Benchmarks have shown that the compiler generates code that approaches the performance and storage requirements of assembly code produced by a good hand coder. These results are a testimony to the success of the design approach and the compiler technology used.

Silicon Technology

As stated earlier, the initial ROMP TTL Prototype was operational in Austin at the end of '78. The success of this Prototype in demonstrating the 801 concepts applied to the ROMP, motivated us to proceed with a ROMP VLSI design. In early '79, the IBM General Technology Division in Burlington, Vermont was interested in applying their SGP (Silicon Gate Process) technology to a logic part (as opposed to a memory part). One of their objectives for such a project was that the logic part selected should be complex enough to stress the technology ground rules. The ROMP appeared to fit the requirements for a "technology-proving" development. It contains a custom register file, ROM, custom logic in data registers, multiplexers, and the ALU, Off-Chip Drivers and Receivers, plus random logic designed with a master image approach.

The division of design tasks between Austin and Burlington was a rather complex arrangement. Austin was responsible for the Functional Specification and logic design. Burlington was responsible for the final chip layout but many macros and large portions of the chip were designed in Austin. Austin performed the logic simulation and also built a nodal model of the ROMP chip to verify functionality. Burlington designed the memory for this model and also wrote many of the Architectural Verifications Programs (AVPs) used to test the model, drive the logic simulation, and ultimately test the chip functionally. Manufacturing test patterns were generated in Austin but special test patterns to resolve unique problems early in the program were generated in Burlington.

Early ROMP parts did indeed stress the technology. We were required to change the

design several times as technology ground rules evolved. Changes were made to improve yields and chip reliability well after we had achieved functional parts. As we progressed, the chip was also made smaller. The initial pass was 8.35 mm square and the final version is 7.65 mm square.

Projected performance of the ROMP chip was significantly improved over time. Initial projections were for a cycle in the 250 - 300-nanosecond range. As we gained more data and modified the design to eliminate critical paths, the projections were reduced to the 200 - 250-nanosecond range. We also projected that 50% of the functional parts could be selected to execute at a 170-nanosecond cycle. The design which is in manufacture has virtually no fall-out of functional parts due to selection for 170-nanosecond operation. The typical ROMP will run at about a 135-nanosecond cycle. System considerations of memory and I/O interfacing, system clock skews, voltage variations, and tester tolerances limit our CPU cycle from being faster than 170 nanoseconds.

MMU Memory Management

The MMU is a 9 mm square SGP chip which performs the RT PC system memory management function.

The MMU chip used the same technology and design approach as ROMP. Since the ROMP had served as the vehicle to solidify the technology and design methods, the MMU design was more straightforward in many respects. However, the MMU functional requirements resulted in a larger chip than the ROMP. The MMU definition was initiated in late '81. The basis for the functional definition was System/38 and work done at Research on memory management approaches consistent with the 801 architecture. Some of the more prominent features are use of inverted page tables to minimize memory page table space, special segments to provide protection with 128-byte resolution, and ability to accomodate variable speed memories.

Favorable experience with ROMP logic simulation convinced us that there was no need to build a TTL nodal model of the MMU chip. However, in order to support early

RT PC prototypes, a three-card TTL equivalent of the MMU function was developed. The early prototypes were completed in early '83. When MMU chips were received in late '83, the three-card TTL version was replaced by less than one-half card containing the VLSI MMU.

Summary

The ROMP project is an excellent example of several IBM divisions at different sites working together to produce a successful program. The project ultimately resulted in the RT PC product design by the Engineering Systems Products group in Austin. It embodied the 801 RISC / PL.8 compiler concepts developed in IBM Research and served as an important vehicle to mature the Silicon Gate Process (SGP) technology of the IBM General Technology Division.

The close relationship of the PL.8 compiler development and the hardware design is a rare occurrence and, we believe, was one of the key elements in achieving an excellent and balanced design.

References

1. George Radin, "The 801 Minicomputer," in ACM, 0-89791-066-4 82/03/0039

2. George Radin, "The 801 Minicomputer," *IBM Journal of Research & Development,* 27, pp. 237-246, May 1983.

3. Marc Auslander and Martin Hopkins, "An Overview of the PL.8 Compiler," in ACM, 0-89791-074-5/82/006/0022.

4. F.E. Allen and J.A. Cocke, "A Program Data Flow Analysis Procedure," in *CACM,* 19, 3 (March 1976).

5. W.R. La Londe, "An Efficient LALR Parser Generator," University of Toronto, Technical Report CSRG-2 (April 1971).

6. Gregory J. Chaitin, Marc A. Auslander, Ashok K. Chandra, John Cocke, Martin E. Hopkins, and Peter W. Markstein, "Register Allocation via Coloring," *Computer Languages,* 6, No. 1, pp. 47-57, 1981.

The IBM RT PC ROMP and Memory Management Unit Architecture

P.D. Hester, Richard O. Simpson, Albert Chang

Introduction

This paper describes the ROMP microprocessor and companion Memory Management Unit (MMU) used in the IBM RT PC. The ROMP and MMU grew out of IBM's requirements in the late 1970s for a modern microprocessor for use in office equipment and small computers. Several major goals were identified at the start of the project.

- **High-Level Language Programming.** With software costs rising, it was decided that almost all programming for the new processor should be done in a high-level language because of its greater efficiency of programming. This meant that a good compiler was needed in conjunction with the processor. In fact, an excellent compiler was needed—one that would produce the tightest possible object code, to reduce the size of ROM and RAM storage required for office machines.

- **Addressability.** Sixteen-bit computers are limited to addressing 64K bytes or words unless some additional hardware, such as segment registers, is introduced in the addressing path. The difficulty of handling objects larger than 64K even with segment registers led to the decision to make the ROMP an all 32-bit machine, with 32-bit registers, 32-bit addresses, and 32-bit data quantities.

The ROMP and MMU have segment registers, but they are used for different purposes than in typical 16-bit computers. Each segment can span 256 megabytes; the segment registers are used to provide addressability to a number of different objects rather than to extend addressability beyond the first 64K bytes of an object.

- **Two Chips.** For cost reasons the number of VLSI chips in a small system must be minimized. Existing technology did not allow functions as complex as the ROMP and MMU to be combined into a single chip, so one chip was used for the processor and one for the Memory Management Unit. The split is about even; the two chips are of comparable complexity (the MMU is somewhat larger than the ROMP).

- **High Performance with Inexpensive Memory.** The 801 minicomputer [1], a Reduced Instruction Set Computer (RISC) then under development at the IBM Thomas J. Watson Research Center in Yorktown Heights, New York, had exceptionally high performance. However, much of its performance depends on its two caches, which can deliver an instruction word and a data word on each CPU cycle. Since such caches were prohibitively costly for small systems, pipelining techniques normally found in larger machines were adapted to the ROMP so that useful work could be done during the (comparatively) long time needed for memory operations. The techniques include asynchronous prefetching and partial decoding of instructions, a packet-switched channel between the ROMP and the MMU, execution of instructions beyond a "load" until the loaded data is actually needed, and delayed branches which overlap the execution of another instruction with the fetching of the branch target.

- **Virtual Memory.** This requirement was identified later than the others, after it was realized that the ROMP had the potential of being used in much more elaborate systems than just office machines. The virtual addressing mechanism provides 2^{40}

Reprinted by permission from *IBM RT Personal Computer Technology*, IBM Publication Number SA23-1057, © 1986 by International Business Machines Corporation.

bytes of virtual addressability and supports real memory sizes of up to 16 megabytes. It uses concepts from the System/38 [2], and additionally provides a means of controlling access to sections of virtual memory smaller than a page for assistance in database locking schemes.

The PL.8 compiler [3], which was developed at IBM Research in conjunction with the 801 architecture, offered the potential of generating extremely efficient code for a machine which matched its paradigm of a computer. Thus, the ROMP programming model and instruction set are derived from the 801 processor for which the PL.8 compiler was originally designed, but the ROMP is designed for greater byte efficiency (the programs are smaller) than the 801. That the ROMP instruction set is a good target for a compiler is demonstrated by the fact that the PL.8 compiler generates code that is within about 10% of the size of good hand code.

Together, the ROMP and MMU implement a system with the following major characteristics:

- A large uniformly-addressed virtual memory (2^{40} bytes)

- A large number of general-purpose registers (16)

- A simple, uniform instruction set with most instructions executing in a single cycle.

As with other RISC designs [4, 5], the ROMP instruction set performs all operations on data within general registers; the only memory operations provided are Load and Store. The compiler "pipelines" the Load operations by separating them from the use of the loaded data as far as possible.

Although most ROMP instructions execute in only one cycle, additional cycles are taken when it is necessary to wait for data to be returned from memory for Loads and Branches. As a result, the ROMP takes about three cycles on the average for each instruction. At the cycle time of 170 nanoseconds used in the RT PC, the ROMP runs at about 2 MIPs.

Details of the ROMP and MMU architecture are described in the following sections.

ROMP Processor
The RT PC ROMP processor was designed to:

- Provide an architected address and data width of 32 bits

- Provide an efficient target for an optimizing compiler

- Support virtual memory

- Provide system integrity through separate user and supervisor states

- Provide improved error detection and reporting facilities

- Provide high performance with low-cost memory.

The first requirement dictated an architecture providing both 32-bit address and data quantities. As a result, it was decided that all registers and computations would support 32-bit quantities. However, the architecture provides for specific support of 8-bit and 16-bit quantities in addition to 32-bit quantities.

The ROMP processor architecture was defined with the assumption that most software would be developed in a high-level language. At this same time, an optimizing compiler was being developed at IBM Research which supported a variant of the PL/I programming language. A joint study was conducted to evaluate this compiler and the architectural requirements to take advantage of the compiler optimization techniques. This study indicated the need for a large number (16 or 32) of 32-bit general-purpose registers, and an instruction set closely matched to the compiler intermediate language. Specifics of the resulting instruction set are provided later in this paper.

During the architecture definition, it became clear that systems using processors of this class must provide virtual memory. In order to support virtual memory, precise interrupts were defined for the ROMP so that the cause of a page fault can be identified easily. All instructions are restartable; an instruction causing a page fault can simply be re-executed after the fault is resolved. This sort of virtual memory support is common on mainframes and some minicomputers, but had not appeared in a microprocessor prior to the design of the ROMP.

The need to provide protection of user programs and isolation of control program functions resulted in the definition of separate user and supervisor states. Only instructions which cannot be used to affect system integrity are valid in user state. Instructions associated with control program functions are valid in supervisor state only.

In order to guarantee data integrity, certain requirements and facilities are provided for error detection and reporting, including:

- Parity checking on all external buses

- Bus timeout detection

- Non-maskable hardware error detection interrupts.

Good system performance with low-cost memory was an early requirement. Although cache memories were considered, they were quickly discarded due to their cost and complexity. A compromise was made between cost and performance that resulted in the decoupling of memory operations from CPU operations, and in the definition of an innovative high bandwidth packet switching storage channel that supports multiple outstanding operations. The MMU was designed to allow overlap of the address translation process with memory access. The MMU also supports two-way interleaved memory which provides a throughput of one memory operation every CPU cycle.

Programming Model
The ROMP provides 16 32-bit General Purpose Registers (GPRs) that can be used for either address or data quantities. There are no restrictions on which registers can be used for addresses or data. Figure 1 shows the 16 GPRs.

Note that the 16 GPRs are also grouped in eight pairs. These pairs (0-1, 2-3, etc.) are used with the paired shift instructions to

provide nondestructive shift capability. Details of the paired shifts are provided in the instruction set section of this paper.

A 32-bit register quantity can be treated as either a full 32-bit quantity, two 16-bit quantities, or four 8-bit quantities. Instructions are provided to manipulate data in any of these forms.

In addition to the 16 32-bit GPRs, a separate set of System Control Registers (SCRs) is provided. The SCRs include the following:

- Three registers associated with a 32-bit system timer facility

- The Multiplier Quotient (MQ) register used with the multiply and divide step instructions

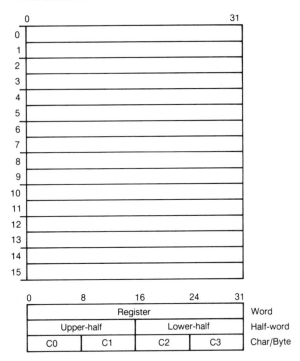

Figure 1   General-Purpose Registers

- The Machine Check Status (MCS) and Program Check Status (PCS) which are used to report hardware errors and software errors and exceptions respectively

- The Interrupt Request Buffer (IRB) used for posting interrupts

- The 32-bit Instruction Address Register (IAR)

- The Interrupt Control Status (ICS) register used for controlling interrupts and interrupt levels, address translation, memory protect, and other miscellaneous control functions

- The Condition Status (CS) which contains the condition code bits.

Instruction Set

The ROMP is generally a two-address architecture, with both 2- and 4-byte instructions of seven formats as shown in Figure 2. The various formats provide an opcode field, register fields (RA, RB, and RC) and an immediate field (I, JI, BI, and BA). RA, RB, and RC are each 4-bit fields which specify one of the 16 GPRs.

Although most ROMP instructions are two-address, the X format provides three register addresses. In all other formats, the RB and RC fields specify the source registers, with RB also specifying the destination register. A single instruction called Compute Address Short (CAS) is implemented in the X format, where the contents of registers RB and RC are added together and the sum placed in

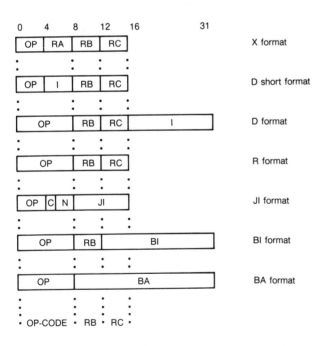

Figure 2   Instruction Formats

register RA. Extensive studies indicated the need for a three-address add instruction for address computations so that both source register quantities could be preserved.

The various instruction formats were defined so that the opcode and two register fields (RB and RC) are always in the same bit positions within each instruction format. This allows these fields to be used as defaults to unconditionally control fetching of instruction microcode and register operands without instruction pre-decoding. This is necessary to support a goal of single-cycle execution of each instruction. Note that in certain formats (JI, BI, BA for example) one or both register fields are not used. However, these fields are still used to fetch register operands. During the execute phase of instruction processing, a decision is made to use the immediate information rather than the register quantities. Since this decision is not made until the execute phase, the register information can be fetched by default and later discarded with no undesirable results. This approach is required to achieve the goal of single-cycle instruction execution, without creating implementation constraints.

During the definition of the ROMP instruction set, several studies were conducted to determine the frequency of use of each proposed instruction. These studies indicated that certain instructions (Increment, Immediate Shift, Short Branch, Loads and Stores with small displacements, etc.) were very heavily used. Some of these were defined as 2-byte instructions in order to achieve the desired byte efficiency and to reduce the memory bandwidth requirements of the processor to less than one word per cycle. Four-byte versions of certain of the 2-byte instructions were also defined for completeness that allowed a 16-bit immediate field instead of the 4-bit immediate field provided by the 2-byte format. Several evaluations were made trading off the byte efficiency of the 2-byte instructions versus their limited displacement capability. The final instruction set definition included 79 2-byte instructions and 39 4-byte instructions. Ongoing analysis of compiler-generated code indicates an average instruction length of 2.4 to 2.7 bytes, indicating good use of the 2-byte formats.

In certain formats (X, D Short, and JI) a 4-bit opcode is used. Opcodes were chosen so that these particular formats could be easily determined with a minimum of pre-decoding.

The ROMP provides a total of 118 instructions in the following ten classes:

Instruction Class	Number of Instructions
1. Memory Access	17
2. Address Computation	8
3. Branch and Jump	16
4. Traps	3
5. Moves and Inserts	13
6. Arithmetic	21
7. Logical	16
8. Shift	15
9. System Control	7
10. Input and Output	2
Total	118

The Memory Access instructions permit loading and storing data between the 16 GPRs and main memory. These instructions support four types of data:

- 8-bit (character) quantities
- 16-bit (halfword) quantities
- 16-bit algebraic (sign extended halfword) quantities
- 32-bit (fullword) quantities.

Load and Store Multiple instructions are also included in this class that permit loading or storing of from one to 16 of the GPRs to memory. A test and set instruction is also provided for multiprocessor synchronization.

All Memory Access instructions compute the effective memory address as the sum of a GPR contents plus an immediate field specified in the instruction (base + displacement addressing). Two-byte memory access instructions provide a 4-bit immediate field, with 4-byte instructions providing a 16-bit immediate field.

The Memory Access instructions operate only between memory and one or more GPRs. No memory-to-memory operations are provided. The architecture allows instruction execution to continue beyond a load instruction if subsequent instructions do not use the load data. This increases system performance by overlapping memory access with subsequent instruction execution.

Address Computation instructions are provided which compute memory addresses without changing the condition codes. These instructions include a three-address add instruction (Compute Address Short), Increment, Decrement, and 2- and 4-byte instructions which permit loading a GPR with a 4-bit or 16-bit immediate value respectively. Separate Compute Address Lower and Compute Address Upper instructions are provided to load a 16-bit immediate value into either the lower half or upper half of a GPR. Two Address Computation instructions are provided specifically to aid in the emulation of 16-bit architectures. They allow computing a 16-bit quantity that replaces the low-order 16 bits of a GPR without altering the upper 16 bits.

Standard Branch and Jump instructions are provided for decision making. Two-byte Jump instructions are provided that provide a relative range of plus or minus 254 bytes. Four-byte Branch instructions provide a range of up to plus or minus 1 megabyte. A group of Branch and Link (BAL) instructions is also provided for subroutine linkage.

A delayed branch (called "Branch with Execute") is provided to allow overlap of the branch target fetch with execution of one instruction following the branch (called the subject instruction). Execution of the subject occurs in parallel with fetching of the target instruction, thereby eliminating dead cycles that would normally occur during fetching of the target instruction.

Three Trap instructions are provided for run-time address checking. These instructions compare a register quantity against a limit, and cause a program check interrupt if the limit is exceeded.

The Move and Insert class of instructions support testing the value of any bit in a GPR, and the movement of any of the four 1-byte fields in a GPR. A Move instruction is provided that allows moving any one of the 32 bits in a GPR to a test bit in the condition status register, with a corresponding instruction that moves the test bit value to any of the 32 bits in a GPR. A series of Move Character instructions are included that move any of the four 1-byte fields in a GPR to another 1-byte field in a GPR.

The Arithmetic class supports standard Add and Subtract operations in both single and extended precision modes. Other instructions in this class include Absolute Value, Ones and Twos Complement, Compare, and Sign

Extend. Also, Multiply Step and Divide Step instructions are provided. The Multiply Step instruction produces a 2-bit result per step, and can be used to construct variable length multiply operations. The Divide Step instruction produces a single bit result per step, and can be used to construct variable length divide operations.

The Logical class provides AND, OR, XOR, and negation operations using two register quantities or one register and an immediate value. A group of Set and Clear Bit instructions is also included in this class that allows any bit in any GPR to be set to one or zero.

The Shift class provides Algebraic Shift Right, Shift Right, Shift Left, and left and right paired shifts. Shift amounts from 0 to 31 bits can be specified as either an immediate quantity in the instruction, or as an indirect amount using the value in a GPR. The concept of paired shifts was introduced to provide non-destructive shifts that shift a specified GPR a given amount, and place the result in a different register (the "twin" of the source register) without altering the source register. The twin of a given register is determined by complementing the low-order bit of the register number (i.e., the twin of register 4 is 5, the twin of 11 is 10, etc.).

Instructions in the System Control class are generally privileged instructions that are valid only in supervisor state. Included in this class are instructions that move GPRs to and from SCRs, set and clear SCR bits, Load Program Status, and Wait for interrupt. Also included is a nonprivileged Supervisor Call instruction.

Two instructions that load and store GPRs to I/O devices are included in the Input and Output class. These instructions are normally used to access control registers in the MMU or other system elements.

Interrupt Facility
The ROMP implements a priority-based interrupt scheme supporting seven external interrupt levels. In addition, two error reporting interrupt levels are also provided. The program check level is used for reporting software errors and exceptions such as page fault, protection violations, and attempted execution of a reserved opcode. The machine check level is used to report hardware failures such as bus parity errors, uncorrectable memory ECC errors, and bus timeouts.

The interrupt facility includes old and new program status words (PSWs) similar to those of System/370. Each PSW pair contains the IAR, condition status, and interrupt control information. Hardware automatically performs a PSW swap when an interrupt occurs. GPRs are not automatically saved by hardware, with system software using a Store Multiple instruction to save required GPRs. A Load Program Status (LPS) instruction is provided that automatically restores the machine state from the old PSW once interrupt servicing is complete.

Memory Management Unit
The MMU combines the functions of virtual addressing support and memory control. From the system point of view, it translates virtual addresses to real addresses, implements the memory protection model, performs "lock-bit" processing (explained below), and provides interrupts to the ROMP for exceptional conditions such as page faults.

As a memory controller, the MMU is responsible for the hardware-level control of up to 16M bytes of RAM and ROM. Separate controls are provided for RAM and ROM that support different speed memories and allow interleaving of RAM for improved memory bandwidth. Internal logic is provided to support Error Correcting Code (ECC) for RAM and parity for ROM. The MMU also provides control signals for the external Reference-and-Change Array (R/C).

The support for ECC on the RAM is new in the microprocessor field and is a reflection of the large memory sizes expected to be used with the ROMP. The lockbit mechanism provides a sub-page-level protection and locking mechanism and is new with the MMU.

Virtual Address Translation
Figure 3 shows the memory model which the MMU implements. When the ROMP is operating in Real mode (Translate bit in Interrupt Control Status off), the MMU functions simply as a hardware memory controller. In this mode, up to 16M bytes of

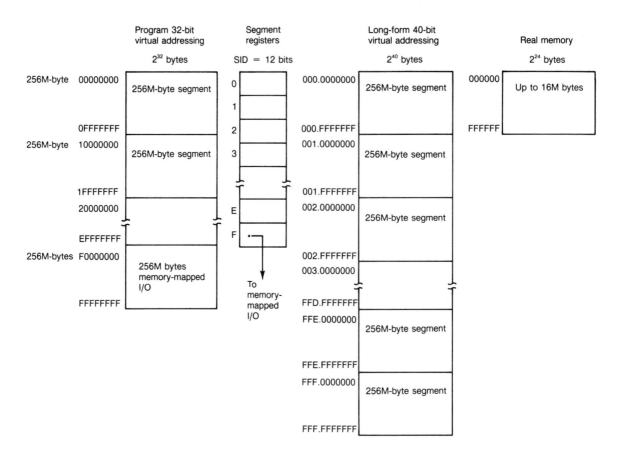

Figure 3 Storage Model

real memory can be addressed. When the ROMP is in Translate mode (Translate bit in ICS on), the MMU translates each address from the ROMP from virtual to real and then uses the real address to access the memory arrays. Memory access from adapters on the I/O Channel is also supported by the MMU, with a control bit for each access indicating whether the access is real or translated.

Program virtual addresses generated by the ROMP are 32 bits. These are expanded in the MMU to 40 bits by using the high-order 4 bits of the program virtual address to select one of 16 Segment Registers (SRs), and then concatenating the 12-bit Segment Identifier (SID) contained within the SR to the remaining 28 bits of the incoming address. To the executing program, memory appears to be 4 gigabytes of virtual memory broken into 16 segments of 256M bytes each.

The largest addressable entity is normally the 256M-byte segment, but system software can construct larger objects by (for example) assigning consecutively-numbered SIDs to

adjacent SRs, creating an object whose maximum size is any multiple of 256M bytes up to 4 gigabytes. Objects larger than 4 gigabytes will require special techniques.

The Segment Registers reside in the MMU, and can be read and written from the ROMP by supervisor-state programs, using I/O instructions. Each SR contains the following:

- Segment Present bit
- ROMP Access Protect bit
- I/O Access Protect bit
- 12-bit Segment ID
- Special Segment bit
- Key bit.

Because the virtual addresses generated by programs are only 32 bits long, while translation is performed on 40-bit virtual addresses, each program is restricted to addressing only those segments supplied to it (i.e., SIDs loaded into SRs) by the operating system. Segments can be shared between processes by placing the same SID value into an SR for each process (not necessarily the same SR).

250

The 40-bit virtual addresses are translated to real by looking them up in an Inverted Page-Table (IPT) as shown in Figure 4. The table is "inverted" because it contains one entry for each real memory page rather than one per virtual page. Thus a fixed proportion of real memory is required for the IPT regardless of the number of processes or virtual segments supported. To translate an address, a hashing function is applied to the virtual page number (high-order part of the 40-bit virtual address, less the byte offset) to obtain an index to the Hash Anchor Table (HAT). Each HAT entry points to a chain of IPT entries with the same hash value. A linear search of the hash chain yields the IPT entry (and thus the real page number) which corresponds to the original 40-bit virtual address. If no such entry is found, then the virtual page is not mapped and a page fault interrupt is taken.

The hashing technique results in chains which are typically short—between one and two entries. Even so, translating a virtual address using only the HAT and IPT would require several memory accesses for each translation. In order to eliminate most of the IPT searches, the MMU maintains a cache of recently-translated addresses in a Translate Look-aside Buffer (TLB). The TLB is two-way set-associative, with 32 entries. If the required entry is in the TLB, then the MMU can complete its translation in one cycle. If a TLB

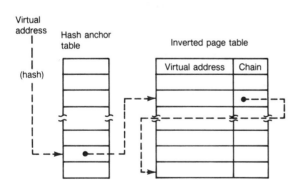

Figure 4 Hash Anchor Table and Inverted Page Table (Conceptual)

"miss" occurs, then the MMU automatically searches the IPT and reloads the least recently used entry for the appropriate congruence class. This typically adds 8 to 11 cycles to the translation time. An IPT "miss" is a page fault.

The MMU provides functions for use by supervisor-state software which cause selected entries in the TLB to be purged and thus reloaded from the IPT the next time they are needed. Such purging is required at certain times to keep the TLB contents synchronized with changes to the IPT. Purging can be done for an individual page, for an entire segment, or for the entire TLB. A task switch by itself does not require that any of the TLB be purged; only the segment registers need be loaded. A "load real address" function is also provided for supervisor-state software to allow determining the real address corresponding to a given virtual address.

Memory Protection
Several functions performed by the MMU combine to provide memory protection for programs running with address translation on.

In order for the MMU to respond to a virtual address at all, the Segment Present bit in the appropriate SR must be set. This feature is used not only for protection, but to provide memory-mapped I/O by arranging for the address range covered by one or more SRs to be ignored by the MMU but responded to by the I/O Channel Controller.

For SRs which have the Segment Present bit set, access through the MMU is controlled by the settings of the ROMP Access Protect and I/O Access Protect bits. A segment register can thus be assigned to the ROMP processor, to I/O devices via the I/O channel controller, to both, or to neither.

For virtual accesses which are allowed by the control bits described above, one of two types of memory protection is applied. Which one to use is determined by the Special Segment bit in the SR. If this bit is 0, then a key matching scheme adapted from System/370 is used. Processes are given key 0 or key 1 access to segments via the Key bit in each SR. Individual pages have 2-bit keys in their IPT (and thus TLB) entries. The types of access allowed are defined by the following table:

Page Key	Type of page	SR Key	Load	Store
00	Key 0 fetch-protected	0	Yes	Yes
		1	No	No
01	Key 0 read/write	0	Yes	Yes
		1	Yes	No
10	Public read/write	0	Yes	Yes
		1	Yes	Yes
11	Public read-only	0	Yes	No
		1	Yes	No

Current TID compared to TID in IPT	Write Bit in IPT	Lockbit value for selected line	Access permitted Load	Access permitted Store
Equal	1	1	Yes	Yes
		0	Yes	No
Equal	0	1	Yes	No
		0	No	No
Not Equal	—	—	No	No

If the Special Segment bit in the SR is 1, then a finer granularity of protection is applied. Each page is considered to be made up of 16 "lines" of 128 bytes each (with 2K-byte pages) or 256 bytes each (with 4K-byte pages). Access to a particular line within a page is controlled by the value of a "lockbit" associated with each line. Each IPT (and TLB) entry contains 16 lockbits for each page, a "write" bit that determines how the lockbits are interpreted, and an 8-bit Transaction Identifier (TID). In addition, the MMU contains a Current TID register which is loaded by the operating system when a process is dispatched. Access to the lines within pages of "special segments" is determined by the following table:

Use of the Special Segment facilities allows interprocess locking of items smaller than pages. Interrupts caused by disallowed accesses can be used to grant locks, to cause processes to wait, or to indicate actual protection violations.

Conclusions
Together, the ROMP and MMU provide many of the characteristics of a mainframe computer—large virtual memory, 32-bit addressing and data flow, high performance—while requiring only a few chips to implement. The Reduced Instruction Set Computer concept allows the hardware architecture to be relatively simple, while the combination of ROMP and MMU hardware and modern system software can produce a very powerful computer system which is small enough to reside on a desk top.

The realm of personal computers need not be restricted to those applications which can fit on 8- or 16-bit machines with limited addressability and CPU speed. Programs typically considered mainframe applications can take advantage of the addressability, virtual memory, and speed of the ROMP.

References
1. George Radin, "The 801 Minicomputer," *Proc. of Symposium on Architectural Support for Programming Languages and Operating Systems,* Palo Alto, CA, March 1-3, 1982. Published in *ACM SIGARCH Computer Architecture News* Vol. 10, No. 2, March 1982. Also published in *IBM Journal of Research and Development* Vol. 27, pp. 237-246 (1983).
2. G.G. Henry, "Introduction to IBM System/38 Architecture," *IBM System/38 Technical Developments,* IBM Corporation, Atlanta, GA, 1978.
3. M. Auslander and M.E. Hopkins, "An Overview of the PL.8 compiler," *Proc. of the SigPlan '82 Symposium on Compiler Writing,* Boston, MA, June 23-25, 1982.
4. J. Hennessy, N. Jouppi, S, Przybylski, C. Rowen, T. Gross, F. Baskett, and J. Gill, "MIPS: A Microprocessor Architecture", *Proc. of the SigMicro 15th Annual Microprogramming Workshop,* 1982.
5. D.A. Patterson, "Reduced Instruction Set Computers", *CACM 28,* 1 (January 1985).

BEYOND RISC:HIGH-PRECISION ARCHITECTURE

Joel S. Birnbaum and William S. Worley, Jr.
Hewlett-Packard
1501 Page Mill Road
Palo Alto, CA 94304

Introduction

Computer architecture and implementation are quite analogous to building architecture and construction. An architect designs a building to achieve a certain balance of aesthetics and function; it is up to the construction engineers to realize this concept subject to the structural integrity of materials and the laws of physics. Similarly, computer architects must make design decisions to achieve the goal of performing useful work within a set of constraints imposed by product size, range, cost, and usability. Hardware and software engineers must then translate this architecture into viable implementations, but unfortunately no comprehensive theory of computation guides their trade-offs. Modern computers are often the result of ad hoc decisions by these engineers, and tradition has frequently played too large a role.

In 1981, a group of architects and engineers at Hewlett-Packard Laboratories, with help from representatives of HP's computer divisions, began a series of precision measurements about computational behavior under a wide range of execution scenarios so that design trade-offs could be made more knowledgeably. The results of those studies led, through a process of iterative optimization, to the specification of a neoclassical, register intensive, hardwired logic computer architecture which defines a unified family of scalable computers offering significant cost/performance advantages over contemporary, microcode-based designs. Refinements by engineers in HP's product divisions followed, and ensuing implementations of this architecture have verified its potential over a broad range of size and function. This paper will discuss the design objectives and some of the basic principles of the architecture, emphasizing departures from orthodoxy. It will serve as an introduction to later papers which will present detailed treatments of the architecture, engineering level discussions of some implementations, and the results of performance analyses.

Design Objectives and Basic Principles

The program at HP to develop implementations of the new architecture is code-named Spectrum. From the outset, the objective for the Spectrum program was to develop a microcomputer and minicomputer family with scalable cost and performance across the full range of product sizes and application areas then addressed by all existing Hewlett-packard computer products. This task was further tempered by a very important overriding constraint: the new architecture must provide a smooth application migration path from all of these exiting products. It is this albatross of compatibility that has usually prevented computer manufacturers from unifying their disparate product lines, for the cost of recording applications is usually too great to be borne, and designs that compromise the specific requirements of technical, commercial, and real-time applications for the benefit of uniformity usually suffer degraded performance when compared with specifically optimized machines.

As a design objective, however, such a scalable unified architecture offers many incentives. If subsystem and peripheral interfaces can be consistent across family members and application domains, then the development effort for the family will be greatly reduced, as will the cost of maintenance and modification of both the hardware and the software. There are concomitant customer advantages in terms of cost of ownership, flexibility of configuration, and modularity, particularly in networks, where the same code can now run on workstations, network servers, and timeshared distributed mainframes. The challenge is to create a common, simple core, which can be incrementally enhanced by the addition of functionally specific structures for particular application execution environments. At the outset, we established and have adhered to three design doctrines:

Copyright 1986 Hewlett-Packard Company. © Reproduced with permission.

o The architecture must support essentially all systems and applications programming being done in high-level languages.

o The architecture must scale in a technology-independent and implementation-independent way.

o It must be able to support the efficient emulation of or migration from previous architectures including their I/O subsystems.

In many ways, the new HP architecture is an architecture determined from the point of view of the software it must run. It was designed by a team of hardware and software engineers who sat side by side during all phases of its design. It falls roughly into the class of what have come to be known as reduced instruction set computers, or RISC machines. In many ways, as we shall see, the term RISC is unfortunate, since a reduced instruction set is not the goal, and is, in fact, only one part of the story. It does no good, for example, to build an engine capable of rapid execution if it cannot efficiently support a large virtual address space, or if it is idle much of the time waiting for information to arrive from the storage subsystem, or if execution is blocked by contention with the input/output mechanisms. It is crucially important to consider the storage hierachy and the input/output subsystems as integral to any systes as integral to any system design, for it is the taste with which these elements are combined that determines performance at the system throughut level and that further determines the effectiveness with which specific instantiations of the architecture can be optimized.

In many ways, RISC machines in general and HP's new architecture in particular appear to fly in the face of conventional wisdom about computer design. Many of the conventional axioms were formulated in the pre-VLSI era, and at a time when software technology, particularly that of control programs and compilers, was far less sophisticated than it is today. Rethinking of fundamental assumptions has often been curtailed by the need for compatibility with an installed product base. HP's new architecture is the result of a reexamination of these assumptions, aided by extensive and precise measurements, in the light of the capabilities of modern integrated circuits and systems software. To highlight differences, the major design principles will be presented as a series of paradoxical assertions.

Paradoxical Assertions

An architecture based on a primitive hardwired instruction set, constrained to permit implementations that can execute most instructions in a single cycle, can lead to better cost/performance than a more complex microcode-based architecture.

For many years, the principal limitation to the growth of computing has been the extremely poor productivity of software application development. In fact, at least two thirds of the world's programmers are still involved in the maintenance and modification of old code. Therefore, it is not surprising that computer architects for many years have sought to raise the level of abstraction for the creation of both systems and applications programs, since programming in high-level languages has been shown to improve productivity in both the creation and maintenance phases.

The principal architectural trend of the 1970s was to take advantage of the rapidly decreasing costs of hardware, brought about by increased chip densities, by implementing in hardware as high-level an interface for the instruction set as possible. The most common way of achiving this was through microcode interpretation of the architected instructions into the fundamental machine level. The justifucation for the microcode was often given in terms of greater performance, but in fact, this performance depended mostly on the microcode's being resident in high-performance control store. The effectiveness of this scheme is then dependent upon the ability of the system architects to guess in advance which instructions can most benefit from being rsident in the control store. In fact, a second advantage of microcode was probably more responsible for its pervasive use: system development modifications and tuning could now be done through microprogramming rather than hardware redesign, purportedly improving development costs and schedules because of the enhanced flexibility. For many machines in the intermediate (supermini) class, the microcode became large and complex because the architects relegated many complicated decisions relating to the specific execution environments to this interpreter.

Architecture Genealogy

The first von Neumann computers (Fig. 1a) were simple, hardwired machines built from vacuum tubes. Their unreliability imposed strict physical limits on their complexity, and as a result they had very few registers in their data paths. Logic speed and memory speed were in approximate balance. When vacuum tubes gave way to solid-state designs, volume and power dropped by two orders of magnitude and logic speed increased by an order of magnitude. This led to a serious imbalance between logic and memory speeds. The response of designers was the microcoded machine (Fig. 1b). Such a machine exploits the speed imbalance between logic and main memory to reduce the real logic in the machine by substituting a microcoded interpreter, running out of a small, fast control store, for the missing hardware. More significantly, however, this design removes the physical constraint on architectural complexity, since the architecture is now a function of software (firmware) in the control store.

Since the microcoded machine did not address the central problem, which was slow memory access, the situation was ripe for the invention of an effective memory buffering mechanism known as a cache (Fig. 1c), which provides (almost) the access speed of a small memory with the capacity of a large, slower primary memory.

The success of cache designs and the insights provided by studying the instruction traces collected to aid in their design led to the proposed design shown in Fig. 1d, which provides all the data memory bandwidth of a cache design without the overhead of instruction interpretation.

The new HP architecture that is now the basis of the Spectrum program is an optimized case of Fig. 1d in which the data path complexity has been minimized to reduce cycle time and instruction coding has been tuned to prevent significant code size expansion.

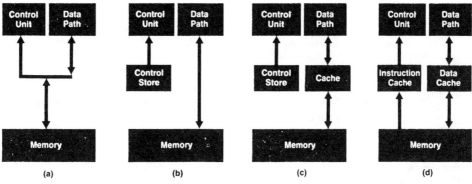

Computer architecture types: (a) von Neumann (b) microcoded (c) cache (d) proposed.

During the mid-70s, far less intrusive and more precise performance measurements than had been possible before began to be made in a variety of university and industrial laboratories. Through the mechanism of instruction tracing across a wide variety of workloads, these measurements brought a new level of understanding of what was actually going on inside the computer execution units. It was discovered that the simple instructions, such as branch, load, store, and add, dominated the instruction execution frequencies and that the complex instructions were seldom used. The justification for executing such simple instructions interpretively in microcode is difficult, since a several-cycle performance penalty is usually exacted.

These observations led to a new breed of machine which had a reduced number of primitive hardwired instructions- the ones that were executed most frequently- which could be constrained to execute in a single cycle (with the exception, of course, of instructions that must access storage, such as loads and branches).

The Spectrum program design team at HP Laboratories analyzed billions of instruction executions and used the results to create an instruction set in which the most frequently used instructions are implemented directly in hardware. While the early literature on so-called reduced instructions set computers tended to emphasize the distinction between microcoded and hardwired instructions, an equally important characteristic of the new HP architecture is that its designers have invested in high-speed general-purpose registers instead of microcode. A computer whose highest (fastest) level of the storage hierarchy is general-purpose registers has several advantages. The obvious one is that register-to-register instructions are intrinsically faster than those requiring storage access. Another is that modern compilers can analyze data and control flows and can thus allocate registers efficiently. The reuse of information held in registers is enhanced dramatically, in most instances producing shorter total path lengths and far fewer storage accesses. Yet another advantage of simple register-based instruction sets is that computations can often be broken into independent portions, which frequently permits greater overlap between the processing units and the storage hierarchy.

Modern computers typically have an execution pipeline which permits new instructions to be begun before prior ones are completed. HP's new architecture acknowledges this reality by making characteristics of the pipeline achitecturally visible; delayed branches and loads are two consequences that will be discussed later. The effect is that an instruction can be executed almost every cycle. The pipeline can be relatively simple, because advances in compiler technology enable the clever scheduling of instructions to take advantage of cycles that would otherwise be idle.

Some complex microcode-based machines have writable control store to permit different complex instruction execution environments to be created to match the task at hand. This has proven, in general, a very complicated task, and very few end users have availed themselves of this capability. In one sense, the new HP architecture can be thought of as having no microcode, but it is equally valid to consider it as having only microcode. The distinction is that the HP microstore is the normal dynamically managed storage hierarchy instead of a special control store. It is thus dynamically alterable and operates at a far higher level. This type of microcode can be written using high-level languages and standard development environments and can be paged in and out of the system in a straightforward fashion. In this way, further performance enhancements often result from the specialized construction of complicated instructions from· the primitive hardwired ones, since these subroutines are frequently a better match for the specific run-time situation than generalized microcoded instruction sets.

The critical question about reduced complexity architecture is whether or not the performance gains that result from direct execution will be lost through increased path length resulting from having to formulate complex instructions in terms of the simple ones. This valid question does not have a single simple answer. In many cases, an optimizing compiler will be able to produce path lengths no longer than conventional solutions. In other cases, it is judicious to add hardware to implement complex facilities; examples might be floating-point instructions, decimal arithmetic instructions, high-performance multiplications, and array operations. In general, the applications workload is the determining factor. More will be said later about the capabilities of the new architecture to permit flexible trade-offs beween the hardware and soft-

ware. The design philosophy used throughout is to preserve the performance of the primitive instructions and not to invest in hardware assists until both frequency of occurrence and functional need justify it.

A primitive instruction set is a better match to high-level languages than a complex one.

Although the dramatic advances in shrinking the size of computing devices with concomitant benefits in power, speed and cost have garnered most of the attention over the last three decades, there has been steady and important progress in software technology as well. In particular, compilers have grown far more capable of analyzing and optimizing programs. A modern globally optimizing compiler can produce code that rivals handcode in all but low-level routines requiring direct control of machine resources. The new HP instruction set has been chosen to be the target for such a compiler. As a result, it is very regular; all instructions are 32 bits in length, opcodes and register fields always occur in the same locations, and there is great symmetry in the functions provided. The result is that with the exception of a few performance-critical routines such as the first-level interrupt handler, virtually all programming is done in high-level language. Furthermore, short, precise instructions serve as an excellent base for interpretation, so languages like LISP can be executed quite effectively, even without hardware assists.

Some insight into why a simple instruction set is a better match for a high-level language compiler can be gained by recognizing that human beings are quite good at formulating complex strategies and data structures to use powerful instructions. Compilers, however, are most effective at simple repetitive execution with a minimum of special cases. Compiler accuracy and code performance both suffer dramatically as the complexity increases. The compilers for the new HP architecture are designed to maximize register reuse and reschedule instruction sequences to maintain pipeline efficiency. By elimination of unused code and precalculation of many quantities at compile time, further performance gains are achieved.

A cache should not be hidden.

The efficiency of the storage hierarchy is crucial to any high performance machine, since storage is intrinsically always slower than logic. The high-speed register set is the highest level of this hierarchy and has been discussed above; the next level is the cache or high-speed buffer memory, which helps to lessen the speed mismatch between the logic units and main memory. Its purpose is to achieve almost the bandwidth of the cache but with the capacity of the main store. The cache, as its name implies, is usually hidden from the perspective of the software, because it is generally not part of the architecture but an implementation afterthought. In the new HP architecture, the cache is exposed and the storage hierarchy is explicitly managed. This is made possible by the careful design of the operating system kernels, and by disallowing run-time instruction modification unless responsibility for it is taken in the software. The architecture allows implementations to buffer information in the high-speed storage to reduce the time required to translate virtual addresses, fetch instructions, and fetch and store data. The architecture supports up to 2^{32} virtual address spaces, each 2^{32} bytes long (Fig. 1). Virtual address translation is done by translation look-aside buffers, or TLBs. Separate TLBs can be used for instructions and data, or one can be used for both. The high-speed caches can also be separate for instructions and data, thus increasing the bandwidth from memory substantially, or one can be used for both. Splitting the cache effectively doubles its bandwidth since it allows

us to fetch data and instructions simultaneously. This departure from the von Neumann concept of indistinguishability of instructions and data is achieved through the provision of instructions to permit the synchronization and management of the caches when modifications of instructions by stores are involved.

Several other strategies are employed to minimize the idle time of the processor while the storage hierarchy is being exercised. One example is the ability to execute delayed branch instructions, which differ from conventional branches in that the processor executes the instruction after the branch while the branch target is being fetched from storage, often using what would otherwise be an idle cycle (Fig. 2a). HP's new architecture also contains novel facilities for performing program logic functions without requiring branch instructions. Similarly, code rearrangements can often overlap the execution of other instructions with instructions that access storage (Fig. 2b). The register intensive computation model reduces the number of storage accesses, since only load and store instructions access main memory, all other computation being performed among registers or between a register and an immediate field contained in an instruction. The generous number of registers ensures that the register allocation scheme of the compiler can assign the most frequently used variables to them so as to incur a fraction of the memory references required by traditional architectures.

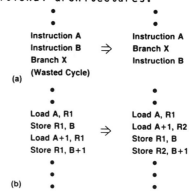

Fig. 2. *Branch and load scheduling. (a) One-cycle delayed branches can almost always be used to eliminate a cycle of cache delay by permuting instructions to occupy the branch's "delay slot" usefully. (b) Two ways of moving two words from A, A + 1 to B, B + 1. The straightforward code on the left incurs "load interlocks" between each load instruction and its adjacent store instruction, since the cache can be expected to require a full cycle to respond. The rescheduled code on the right uses an additional register to overlap the data fetch delays, resulting in a two-cycle saving.*

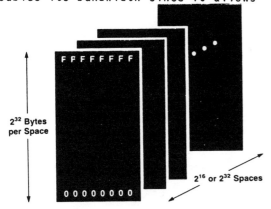

Fig. 1. *The new HP architecture provides for up to 2^{32} distinct virtual address spaces, each up to 2^{32} bytes long. Implementations may limit the number of virtual spaces to zero (real addressing only), 2^{16}, or the full 2^{32}.*

HP high-precision architecture provides a better base for a scalable range of specific product implementations than more customized microcoded architecture.

The new HP architecture is technology independent in the sense that implementers can choose a technology based only on considerations of size, cost, and performance trade-offs with the assurance that code written on any member of the family will execute unchanged on any other member. This means, for example, that a development system on a large mainframe can be used to develop code that will run on a single-chip microprocessor in a personal computer or workstation, or that code normally executed in the workstation environment can run on a network server or timeshared mainframe when that is convenient or desirable. Within a given technology, performance will depend strongly on the trade-offs between hardware and software that have been made and on the size and number of caches that have been provided, since efficiency for a given application is quite sensitive to the number and locality of storage accesses.

High-performance hardware in the form of assist processors can be added to any basic high-pecision achitecture system to enhance its performance or functionality (Fig.3). Three categories of assist processors are differentiated by the level at which they interface to the memory hierarchy. Special function units interface to the memory hierarchy at the general register level and can be thought of as alternative processing units or as an alternative path through the execution unit of the existing processor. Examples include fixed-point binary multiply and divide units, emulation assists, and encryption or decryption hardware.

Coprocessors attach to the memory hierarchy at the level of the caches. They generally have their own internal registers and hardware evaluation mechanism. Examples of coprocessors are high-performance graphics or floating-point arithmetic engines. Note that the cache-to-coprocessor bandwidth can be different from the cache-to-main-processor bandwidth.

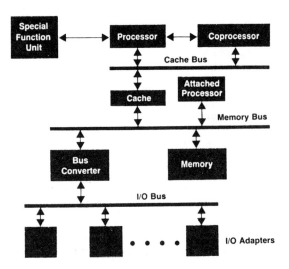

Fig. 3. *High-precision architecture system processing unit block diagram, showing high-performance assist processors added to enhance the performance or functionality of the basic system. Special function units connect directly to the processor, and can be thought of as alternative data paths associated with the processor's general registers. Coprocessors, on the other hand, have a control interface with the processor, but they have a private register set and a direct data interface with the cache. They are appropriate when special data types are supported that have little overlap with main processor data types, such as floating-point data. Attached processors are a third level of specialized assist. They have private registers, private data paths, and local storage. Attached processors execute separate instruction streams and are best suited for specialized operations on complex data types—for example, vector processing.*

The third type of assist processor attaches to the main memory bus. High-precision architecture supports various types of multiprocessing with special instructions and control features. Multiprocessing can be homogeneous and tightly coupled, or the attached processor can be specialized (e.g., an array processor or an I/O controller). In all cases, such attached processors typically have their own registers and local storage.

High-precision architecture permits great flexibility in choosing cost/performance points based primarily on the choice of technology and secondarily on the configuration of the memory hierarchy and special VSLI hardware assists. In this way, implementations can be tuned for specific application domains and the same fundamental architecture can serve commercial, scientific, and real-time applications.

The I/O architecture of the computers being developed by the Spectrum program has been designed to permit complete control of I/O devices by privileged or nonprivileged code written in high-level language. It is based on a memory-mapped addressing structure (that is, all communication with external devices is done through registers that are addressed using normal load and store instructions). This conforms with the objective of making it possible to do all programming in high-level language, since the uniformity of addressing makes it possible to treat device drivers in a nonspecialized way. Since the I/O devices are addressed exactly as if they were memory locations, the same protection structure can be used for both, which greatly simplifies the overall system. We believe that this will protect the I/O better than many other more expensive schemes and can even be extended to protect individual I/O devices. The architecture is flexible enough to accommodate adapters that convert the new HP I/O protocol to other protocols and vice versa, so that foreign devices can be connected to new HP systems when appropriate. Just as in the storage hierarchy, the I/O architecture supports several types of interfaces ranging from sparse, direct control of simple devices to very rich functional controllers. The direct memory access of I/O is organized so as to present minimum interference in the storage hierarchy, which enables the processor to run at reasonable speed even when the full I/O bandwidth is being used.

Since some members of the new HP computer family will be used as instrument and real-time process controllers, we have attempted to optimize the ability of the new architecture to respond to a wide range of external and internal interrupt conditions. Here again, the speed and uniformity of the instruction set and the simplicity and regularity of the control interfaces yield significant prformance and functional advantages over more conventional hardware-independent implementations. This structure has also enabled us to build an unusually rich set of hardware instrumentation into some of the early implementations. This has proven valuable during development, and we think it will help customers a great deal in tuning the performance of their configurations for particular workloads.

A reduced-complexity, high-precision architecture enables more graceful migration from other architectures than conventional approaches.

This is, of course, the overriding constraint for any new architecture proposed by a manufacturer with a large installed base of application programs. We believe that migration from existing HP products to the new computers will be among the least difficult that the industry has yet seen. There are many reasons for this, but perhaps the principal one is that the simplicity of the instruction set and control paths and inclusion of versatile field-isolation facilities make the new machines extremely good interpreters, and so guarantee that software emulation of previous machines will be unusually effective where time dependencies are not critical, particularly since the system spends much of its time in the control program and software subsystems, which run in native mode. The emulated code can be freely combined with recoded native versions of the most critical routines, thus providing a continual incremental upgrade path. For many applications, simply recompiling the source code will yield significant improvements in performance. When source code is unavailable, an optimizing object-code compiler, which treats the object code of an earlier machine as input, has been found to produce important performance gains with acceptable code size expansions in a large percentage of cases. For those few cases where direct emulation or recompilation is not effective, migration tools have been developed.

Although the new HP high-precision architecture is very efficient at software-based emulation, hardware assists in the form of special function units, coprocessors, or attached processors can be provided where indicated. The I/O subsystem is designed to permit native and foreign mode device attachments, including adapters from seleced previous HP I/O architectures. Future versions of the system will incorporate features for fault tolerance and high availability. Since the software is able to identify each module in a particular system, self-configuration without operator intervention will also be possible.

Conclusion

The high-precision architecture being developed by the Spectrum program provides the base for the next-generation family of HP computers. We think it will provide a cost/performance leadership position for commercial, scientific, and real-time applications and will scale across a wide range of function and performance. It will enable all HP computer systems to converge to a single architecture, with almost all programming done in a consistent way in a variety of high-level languages and operating system environments. Systems based on the new architecture will be able to provide compatible execution of application programs written for most earlier-generation HP systems. When required, attachment of older I/O devices will be possible.

The Spectrum program does not result from a single new idea, but rather is the result of the tasteful synthesis of the enormous progress in semiconductor technology with an increased understanding of the role of compilers and operating system design.

We have tried to learn from nature that simplicity is a relative term and have added complexity only where usage justifies it.

Later articles in other conferences and technical journals will present greater architectural detail and will chronicle the specific implementations and their performance.

Acknowledgments

The Spectrum program is the result of the ideas and accomplishments of many people from many different areas within HP. Space does not permit inclusion of a list of the names of all those whose contributions should be acknowledged. Future papers and articles on the Spectrum program will provide the opportunity of these individuals to describe their work and to be recognized for their accomplishments. The authors wish to thank Michael J. Mahon for materials that have been included in this article.

A CMOS RISC PROCESSOR WITH INTEGRATED SYSTEM FUNCTIONS

J. Moussouris, L. Crudele, D. Freitas, C. Hansen, E. Hudson
R. March, S. Przybylski, T. Riordan, C. Rowen, D. Van't Hof

MIPS Computer Systems
930 Arques Ave.
Sunnyvale, CA 94086

Abstract

By omitting complex features and streamlining the most frequent operations, reduced instruction set computers (RISC) can achieve high peak performance at relatively low hardware cost, particularly when implemented in VLSI.[1,2] But to sustain this performance across a broad range of environments, integration of critical system functions is as essential as reduction of the instruction set. We describe a single-chip CMOS processor that consists of a very lean RISC CPU that achieves 16 mips peak, along with a system coprocessor that integrates the functions needed to keep the CPU from idling for storage access.

Introduction

MIPS Computer Systems of Sunnyvale, Ca. has developed a full-custom CMOS VLSI processor consisting of two tightly-coupled 16 MHz units on a single chip. The first unit is a RISC CPU that has powerful data handling facilities, but is simpler at the machine code / compiler interface than most other RISC processors.

The second unit is a system coprocessor that is designed to fit the needs of a multi-tasking operating system for virtual memory, exception handling, and error recovery. This coprocessor incorporates a memory/cache interface with on-chip tag comparators, parity generators and checkers. It generates the clock and control signals needed to achieve peak bus bandwidths of more than 128 Mbyte/sec with external caches of up to 128 Kbytes of standard 25-35 nsec CMOS static RAMS. Finally, it supports a synchronous coprocessor interface that supplies this bandwidth to external coexecution units for floating point and other special compute-intensive functions.

The MIPS processor was developed jointly with an optimizing compiler suite and UNIX* OS port. The

---

* UNIX is a Trademark of AT&T.
VAX is a Trademark of Digital Equipment Corp.

compiler was bootstrapped and tested, and the critical paths through the OS were running on a cross-assembler, well before hardware design was complete. Hence design decisions could be made in the presence of quantitative measurements of impact on overall system performance. Many tradeoffs were explored. Some innovations not only enhanced performance, but also simplified life for the VLSI and system designers, and for the OS and compiler developers as well! The final result is a 16 MHz TTL-compatible CMOS chip which dissipates less than 2 W in a 144-pin ceramic PGA package, and provides sustained performance about 8 times a VAX* 11/780 across a broad range of application and system programming environments.

This paper describes the hardware: what was left out and what was put into the VLSI implementation. Two companion papers discuss some of the tradeoffs and innovations in compiler[3] and OS.[4]

What we left out

The MIPS instruction set is designed to execute effectively in a single cycle, in a deep synchronous pipeline, interruptible on cycle boundaries. There is no microcode. As in other RISC machines, all computation is register-to-register, and all data accesses are simple loads and stores.[5]

The MIPS architecture is, however, even simpler and leaner than most other RISC machines. The hard-wired machine code is free of factors that could degrade cycle time, pipeline efficiency, or responsiveness and precision of the exception mechanism. After extensive performance analysis, a number of features that are common even in RISC machines were left out, including the following:

Hidden registers. Figure 1 illustrates the MIPS CPU registers: 32 general-purpose 32-bit registers, a double-word (64-bit) special register for multiply and divide results, and a 32-bit program counter. The general-purpose registers are all directly and simultaneously addressable from every instruction. There are no mechanisms for hiding a portion of the

Reprinted from *The Proceedings of COMPCON Spring 86*, 1986, pages 126-137. Copyright © 1986 by The Institute of Electrical and Electronics Engineers, Inc.

EH0251-9/86/0000/0261$01.00 © 1986 IEEE

General Purpose Registers:

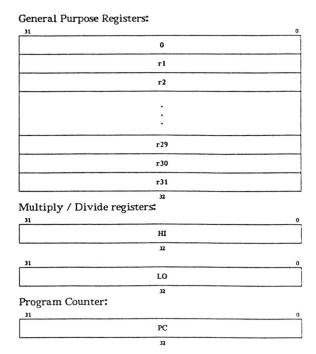

Figure 1 - CPU Registers

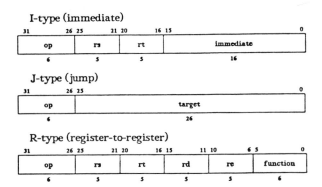

Figure 2 - Instruction Formats

register file, such as the following schemes implemented in other RISC machines: register windows,[6] stack caches,[7] separate user/kernel registers,[8] or process register sets.[9] Instead, the register file is symmetric, and the compiler and OS implement various software strategies (some of which are described in the two companion papers), for dramatically reducing the overhead of saving and restoring registers. The cache and memory controller also assist by buffering successive storage operations.

Condition codes. In the MIPS architecture, conditions generated by SET instructions are loaded directly into the general-purpose registers (except for overflow, which is trapped). There is no condition code register. Hence the pipeline design is freed from any special mechanisms to bypass condition codes, interlock on them, or abort writing them on exceptions -- beyond those implemented for the register file itself. Moreover, conditions mapped onto the register file are subject to the same compile-time optimizations in allocation and reuse as other register variables.[10]

Variable-length instructions.[11] Figure 2 illustrates the three CPU instruction formats, all of which are are fixed 32-bit words. Simple instruction decoding guarantees 100% utilization of the instruction cache bandwidth, without prefetch buffers and

complications in the exception model caused by having instructions straddle page boundaries. The effect of long instructions can be synthesized at compile time. For example, 32-bit immediate addresses are synthesized by concatenating two I-type instructions (see Figure 2) containing the upper and lower 16-bits of the immediate respectively.

Multiple address modes. All MIPS loads and stores are I-type instructions, implementing a single (base + 16-bit offset) address mode. Similarly, all branches are I-type with a single (PC + 16-bit offset) address mode, and all jumps are either J-type with a 26-bit absolute word address or R-type with a 32-bit register target. In each case, the mode implemented is the one most frequently needed by compilers. Complex modes, such as (base + index + offset), are synthesized at compile time, subject to optimizations that eliminate redundancy.[12]

Implementing only the frequent mode in hardware minimizes register ports, datapath busses, and pipeline latencies for loads and branches.

What we put in

Omission of complicated features from the MIPS machine code makes available silicon area and power for data handling, concurrency, and system functions that substantially enhance the performance and versatility of the processor. As before, we emphasize how the MIPS design differs in these areas from other RISC machines.

Data Handling

Since loads and stores have only one address mode, a lot of opcode space is available for multiple data types. MIPS supports signed and unsigned loads and stores of bytes, halfword, and full words. In addition, there are some special data handling features:

Unaligned reference support. MIPS defines instructions for accessing unaligned words and halfwords. For example, LWR (LWL) extracts the right (left) fragment of an unaligned word from a given aligned word in memory, and right (left) justifies it into a designated general purpose register. Two of these instructions can be concatenated to perform a general unaligned word reference in the minimal two cycles (the load aligner is bypassed internally to merge the fragments).

Dual byte sex. The MIPS processor has two byte sex configurations: little-endian (VAX, x86, 32x) and big-endian (370, 68k). Hence it is compatible with existing databases generated by machines that access bytes in either order.

Concurrency

The MIPS machine achieves single-cycle execution of its simplified instructions, including loads and branches, thanks to the concurrency achieved in an efficient pipeline and multiple functional units.

Single cycle loads and branches. MIPS loads and branches execute in precisely one cycle, with a single additional cycle of latency. There are no restrictions on concatenating storage instructions back-to-back, and no hardware interlocks.[13] Instead, loads and branches always take effect just after the instruction that follows them (the "delay slot"). The MIPS assembler reorders instructions to fill delay slots with useful code 70-90% of the time.

Efficient pipeline. Figure 3 illustrates four successive instructions in the MIPS pipeline. The 16.6 MHz clock cycle is divided into two 30 nsec phases. Note that the external instruction and data caches each have 60 nsec to cycle. The major internal operations (OP, DA, IA) each occur in 60 nsec as well. Instruction decode is simple enough, however, to occur in a single 30 nsec phase, overlapped with register fetch. Calculation of a branch target (IA) also overlaps IDEC, so that a branch at instruction 0 can address the ICACHE access of instruction 2 (see dotted line A in figure 3). Similarly, a load at instruction 0 gets its data bypassed into the OP of instruction 2 (dotted line C), but an ALU/shift result gets bypassed directly into instruction 1 with zero latency (dotted line B).

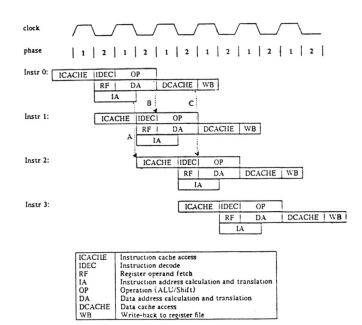

ICACHE	Instruction cache access
IDEC	Instruction decode
RF	Register operand fetch
IA	Instruction address calculation and translation
OP	Operation (ALU/Shift)
DA	Data address calculation and translation
DCACHE	Data cache access
WB	Write-back to register file

Figure 3 - Pipeline

Note that the IA-ICACHE and DA-DCACHE cycles are displaced by one phase, so that the corresponding TLB and cache accesses can be interleaved on a single set of busses.

Multiple functional units. Figure 4 is a block diagram of the MIPS processor. On the right side is the CPU datapath that implements the pipeline of Figure 3. There is a stack of functional units, including ALU, 32-bit shifter, and an autonomous 32-bit multiply/divide unit. An address adder and incrementer/mux for the PC generate data and instruction virtual addresses alternately at 30 nsec intervals. After a 60 nsec latency, operands or instructions are transferred (again, on alternate phases) across the external DATA bus. Instructions are latched into a central local decode core, and also into a master pipeline/bus controller that coordinates internal and external pipeline events in the presence of stalls and exceptions.

The datapath is organized so that all units can initiate their functions under local control. When instruction decode is complete, the master control unit can then late-select the desired results at the destination point, and abort any unused functions.

Referring again to Figure 3, we see that during a typical phase 1, instruction 3 might be bringing back an instruction onto the DATA bus from ICACHE, 2 might calculate a data address, 1 might initiate a DCACHE access, and 0 might be writing back the result of a previous load to the register

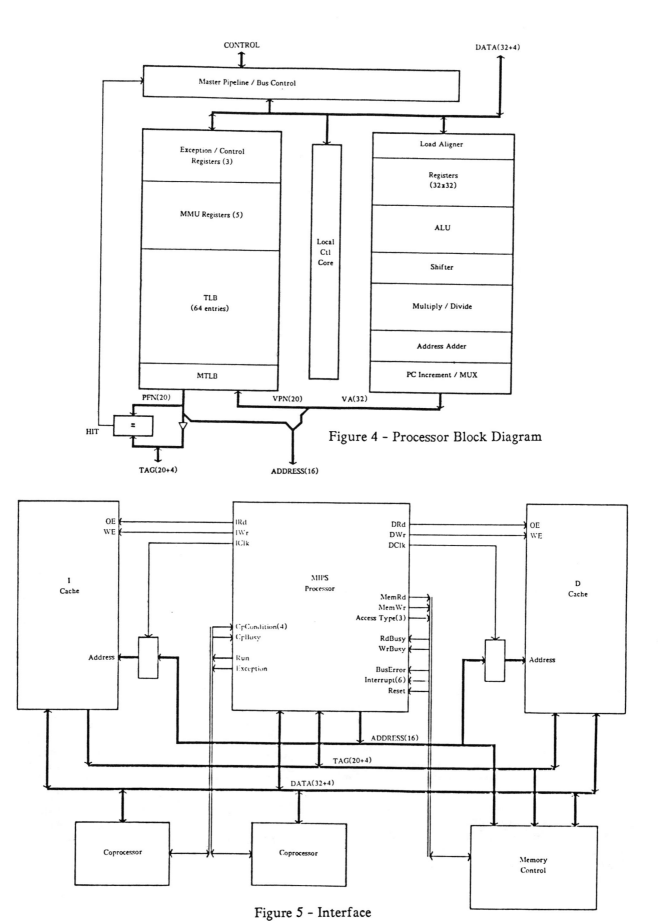

Figure 4 - Processor Block Diagram

Figure 5 - Interface

file. Meanwhile, a multiply or divide operation that was initiated during a still earlier cycle might be preparing a 64-bit result to load into the HI/LO registers.

Integrated system coprocessor

On the left side of the Figure 4 block diagram is the datapath of the system coprocessor, which implements yet another level of concurrent functions as follows:

Virtual memory. The major element in the system coprocessor data path is a 64-entry fully associative translation lookaside buffer (TLB), which translates a 20-bit virtual page number into a 20-bit physical page frame number in a 30 nsec phase. Instruction addresses translate in a faster 2-entry micro-TLB (MTLB), to compensate for branch target calculation exceeding 30 nsec. When the MTLB misses, it is filled from the main TLB in a single cycle — a small penalty, since accesses stay within the two most recent pages 95-99% of the time. When the TLB itself misses, 5 special-purpose MMU registers and 3 exception/control registers in the coprocessor assist the operating system in refilling from an external page table, using a TLB miss handler with fewer than 10 instructions for the most frequent case. The format and function of the TLB and system coprocessor registers are detailed in the OS paper in this series.[4]

Exception handling and error recovery. The MIPS machine supports a rich set of exception types, including address and translation exceptions, and illegal operation, overflow, and program traps. External asynchronous exceptions include six maskable external interrupts, bus error, and reset.

All exceptions can occur at cycle boundaries. The exception model is precise. That is, each exception is handled in a state that reflects serial completion of all instructions prior to the exception and none of the instructions subsequent to it. The simple CPU register set (Figure 1), reduced instruction set (Figure 2), and synchronous contention-free pipelining (Figure 3) play a key role in flushing and restarting the pipe gracefully to maintain precise exceptions with only 60 nsec latency.

The system Status register contains fields which assist in error diagnosis and recovery. Further details of the exception-handling and error-recovery mechanisms are given in the OS paper in this series.

External cache interface. As shown in Figure 4, the physical address coming out of the TLB is split across two external busses: ADDRESS low (16 bits) and TAG (20 bits, plus valid and 3 parity bits). The system coprocessor includes on-chip parity checkers and generators, as well as a tag comparator that detects cache HIT.

Figure 5 illustrates the external interface of the MIPS processor. Two external arrays of standard CMOS SRAMs are organized as direct-mapped split instruction and data caches. The processor interleaves accesses to the two caches on the ADDRESS, TAG, and DATA busses. Instruction fetch begins with ADDRESS clocked through a latching buffer by ICLK during phase 2, and continues until DATA and TAG are latched on the chip at the end of the next phase 1. Similarly, data fetch begins with ADDRESS clocked by DCLK during phase 1, and completes with DATA and TAG latched on the chip at the end of phase 2. During data stores, all three busses are outputs from the chip to the memory controller: the full 32-bit real address is transmitted on ADDRESS and TAG during phase 1, and the 32-bit DATA during phase 2.

This cache interface integrates all circuitry that normally intervenes between processor and raw cache RAMs. Even the control lines for cache write and tristate output enables and for the address buffer clocks are all generated on chip, for precision in control of clock skews. Without this level of integration it would not be feasible to sustain bus bandwidth in excess of 128 Mbyte/sec with standard 25-35 nsec CMOS SRAMs. The OS also plays a role in managing the caches to maintain consistency with DMA I/O activity without hardware bus watching overhead.

Memory interface. The memory control interface on the right side of Figure 5 includes several signals that synchronize storage events. MemRd and MemWr are asserted on cache miss and store respectively, while AccessType distinguishes null, byte, halfword, tribyte, and word transfers. RdBusy and WrBusy control termination and initiation of the stalls that occur when the cache misses or the write buffer is full. Bus Error warns of hard storage errors, such as non-recoverable ECC conditions or bus timeout. Other asynchronous events are signalled on six external interrupt lines. The memory interface can also support configurations with one or both caches missing.

External coprocessor interface. Figure 5 also illustrates the external coprocessor interface, which is designed to support a floating point unit, extensions to the system coprocessor, and up to two additional coexecution units. Coprocessors are connected to the DATA bus only.

Each coprocessor has up to 32 internal registers. There are 4 opcodes, one for each type of coprocessor, dedicated to register-to-register operations that execute without intervention of the main CPU. Another 4 opcodes each are dedicated to loads and stores between cache and coprocessor registers. These instructions are recognized both by the main CPU (which computes and translates the address, and manages the cache interface) and by the coprocessor (which grabs the DATA bus to transfer the operand exactly 5 run phases after the corresponding instruction appeared on the bus).

A CpCondition signal, one for each coprocessor type, allows the main processor to branch on a coprocessor condition set up by a prior operation. Any coprocessor can assert CpBusy to stall the main CPU when a coprocessor instruction is issued while the coprocessor still has the required functional unit busy with an earlier operation. Finally, the main processor asserts Run and Exception to advance or abort operations in the coprocessors, so that the respective pipelines can remain synchronized across stalls and exceptions.

Chip Statistics

The MIPS processor is implemented in a 2 micron double-metal single-poly CMOS technology with 400 angstrom gate oxide. The die size is 8.5x10 mm, with a transistor count of about 100,000. Power dissipation is less than 2W in a 144-pin ceramic PGA package with 109 TTL-compatible signal I/Os. There are 35 power and ground pins to reduce switching noise transients. A simple two-phase clocking methodology is maintained. Pipeline stalls and all external TTL events occur on 16 MHz boundaries. The chip layout uses a twin-tub methodology with conservative latchup protection, for robustness in transporting or shrinking the design to faster technologies.

Acknowledgements

M. Wageman, D. Reebel, L. Reebel, and B. Leone assisted in mask design; J. Kinsel assisted in the design and verification of the execution unit; J. McHugo and M. Mills helped with logic simulation; R. Patrie generated the testing strategy; K. DeVaughn and R. Abramowitz assisted with diagnostics; J. Hennessy performed benchmark performance analysis and architecture verification; L. Weber and the MIPS Compiler Group fine-tuned the architecture as target for compilers; J. Mashey and the MIPS Operating System Group played a central role in the definition of the System Coprocessor.

1. John L. Hennessy, "VLSI Processor Architecture," *IEEE Trans. on Computers* C-33(12) pp. 1221-1246 (Dec 1984).

2. David A. Patterson, "Reduced Instruction Set Computers," *Comm. ACM* 28(1) pp. 8-21 (Jan 1985).

3. Fred Chow, Mark Himelstein, Earl Killian, and Larry Weber, "Engineering a RISC Compiler," *Proceedings 1986 COMPCON*, IEEE, (March 4-6, 1986).

4. M. DeMoney, J. Moore, and J. Mashey, "Operating System Support on a RISC," *Proceedings 1986 COMPCON*, IEEE, (March 4-6, 1986).

5. George Radin, "The 801 Minicomputer," *IBM J. Res Develop* 27(3) pp. 237-246 (May 1983).

6. David A. Patterson and Carlo H. Sequin, "A VLSI RISC," *IEEE Computer* 15(9) pp. 8-18 (Sept 1982).

7. D. Ditzel and R. McLellan, "Register Allocation for Free: The C Machine Stack Cache," *SIGPLAN Notices* 17(4) pp. 48-56 ACM, (April 1982).

8. H. Sachs and W. Hollingsworth, "A High Performance 846,000 Transistor UNIX Engine: The Fairchild CLIPPER," *Proceedings ICCD*, IEEE , (October 1985).

9. R. Ragen-Kelley and R. Clark, "Applying RISC Theory to a Large Computer," *Computer Design*, (November 1983).

10. Fred Chow and John Hennessy, "Register Allocation by Priority-Based Coloring," *SIGPLAN Notices* 19(6) pp. 222-232 (June 1984).

11. E. Basart, "Computer Architecture - Designing for Speed," *IEEE Computer*, pp. 25-30 (1983).

12. Martin E. Hopkins, "A Definition of RISC," *International Workshop on High-Level Computer Architecture*, University of Maryland, (May 1984).

13. John Hennessy, Norman Jouppi, Forest Basket, and John Gill, "MIPS: A VLSI Processor Architecture," CSL Tech. Report 223, Stanford U., Stanford, CA (June 1983).

The Intel 80386—Architecture and Implementation

Khaled A. El-Ayat and Rakesh K. Agarwal

Intel Corporation

The Intel 80386—Architecture and Implementation

Khaled A. El-Ayat and Rakesh K. Agarwal

Intel Corporation

The Intel 80386 represents the state of the art in high-performance, 32-bit microprocessors. It features absolute object code compatibility with previous members of the iAPX 86 family of microprocessors, including the 80286, 80186, 80188, 8086, and 8088. This protects major investments in application and operating systems software developed for the iAPX 86 family, while offering a significant enhancement in performance. The 80386's architecture and performance should allow it to be used in a wide range of demanding applications—e.g., in engineering workstations, office systems, robotic and control systems, and expert systems.

The 80386 implements a full 32-bit architecture with a 32-bit-wide internal data path including registers, ALU, and internal buses; it provides 32-bit instructions, addressing capability, and data types, and a 32-bit external bus interface. It extends the iAPX 86 family architecture with additional instructions, addressing modes, and data types. It incorporates a complete memory management unit. The 80386 extends the 80286 segmentation model to support four-gigabyte segments and to provide a standard two-level paging mechanism for physical memory management. System designers can use segmentation or paging or both, without performance penalties, to meet their memory management requirements.

The 80386 architecture is complemented by a bus interface that uses only two clocks per bus cycle; this allows efficient interfacing to high-speed as well as low-speed memory systems. At 16 MHz, the bus can sustain a 32-megabyte-per-second transfer rate. Other bus features include dynamic bus sizing to support mixed 16/32-bit port interfacing and a dynamically selectable pipelined mode to facilitate high-speed memory interleaving and allow longer access times.

The 80386 is implemented in Intel's CHMOS-III 1.5-micrometer process. Typical instruction mixes indicate an average processing rate of 4.4 clocks per instruction and an overall execution rate of three to four MIPS. To facilitate system debugging, the chip incorporates hardware debug features and self-testing.

80386 base architecture

Different microprocessor applications require different types of architectural support. Some applications—such as those running under Berkeley UNIX—may prefer a linear address space. Others that manage a multitude of dynamic data structures may require hardware-enforced rules to protect the visibility of the dynamically created objects. The 80386 architecture supports these diverse require-

EH0251-9/86/0000/0268$01.00 © 1985 IEEE

Reprinted from *IEEE Micro*, December 1985, pages 4-22. Copyright 1985 by The Institute of Electrical and Electronics Engineers, Inc.

ments by providing the user with several memory management and addressing models. Further, its repertoire of addressing modes, data types, instructions, and special constructs make it well suited to modern high-level languages.

The base architecture of the 80386 encompasses the register model, data types, addressing modes, and instruction set. It forms the basis for high-level-language compiler code generation and for assembly-language-level application programming. Other features of the machine useful for implementing operating systems are discussed in the section on OS architecture.

Registers. The 80386 possesses several on-chip register sets to support various machine features. Figure 1 shows the eight general-purpose registers available for calculations and memory addressing, the flags register, and the instruction pointer. Other registers include control registers, six segment registers used to structure the four-gigabyte address space and to facilitate system debug, and six debug registers used to control the setting of up to four code or data breakpoints.

The 32-bit general registers are named EAX, EBX, ECX, EDX, ESP, EBP, ESI, and EDI. To allow 16-bit operations and to provide compatibility with the 16-bit members of the iAPX 86 family, eight 16-bit registers are superimposed onto the low-order parts of the 32-bit registers. Similarly, there are eight 8-bit registers that are aliases for the lower and upper halves of each of the 16-bit registers. Operations on 8-bit or 16-bit registers affect only the corresponding superimposed registers. For example, the carry out of bit 7 during an 8-bit add is not propagated into bit 9 of the destination; instead, the carry flag (CF) of the flags register is set appropriately. This is true for all condition code settings in the flags.

Operand addressing. 80386 operands may reside on the chip (in registers), in main memory, or in the I/O address space. Furthermore, an operand may be implied in the instruction or specified explicitly as a part of the instruction.

Storing operands in registers generally provides the fastest method of processing data. The contents of any 80386 general register can be operated on by any arithmetic or logical operator. Alternatively, 8-, 16-, or 32-bit constants (immediates) can be embedded directly in an instruction. Sixteen- and 32-bit operations may specify 8-bit sign-extended or zero-extended immediates. Table 1 includes sample instructions employing registers and immediates as

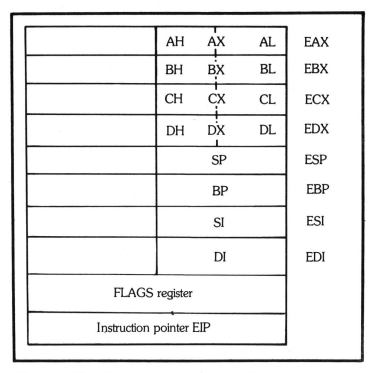

Figure 1. The 80386 general register set, FLAGS, and instruction pointer.

operands. In general, register-to-register operations execute in two clocks on the 80386. At a clock rate of 16 MHz, this translates to 125 nanoseconds per operation.

Most operands are stored in main memory. The 80386 has a full complement of address generation mechanisms for specifying the effective address of such operands. These mechanisms were developed in response to the storage paradigms present in high-level languages.

In its simplest form, the effective address of a memory operand can be encoded directly in an instruction. Usually, however, a particular memory address is not known until the program is actually executing. In this case, the effective address can be obtained by summing the contents of one or two general-purpose registers and an optional immediate value or *displacement*. This register-based effective address scheme can be summarized as

[base register] + [index register] * (scale) + [displacement].

Here the base register is any general-purpose register and the index register is any general-purpose register

Table 1.
Examples of operand addressing in the 80386.

Instruction	Clocks	Semantics
INC EAX	2	Increment contents of EAX by 1.
IMUL EBX, -3	9	Multiply the integer in EBX by -3.
CMP CX, 0	2	Compare contents of CX with 0 and set condition codes.
MOVSX EAX, SI	3	Sign extend the contents of the 16-bit register SI and move into EAX.
MOV DWORD PTR [56], -12445654	2	Assign -12445654 to the 32-bit integer at address 56.
JMP jumpTable[EBX*4]	10	Jump to the address stored at entry EBX of jump table.
SUB DX, WORD PTR [EBP + EDI*2-10]	7	Subtract from DX the 16-bit quantity at address [EBP + EDI*2-10].

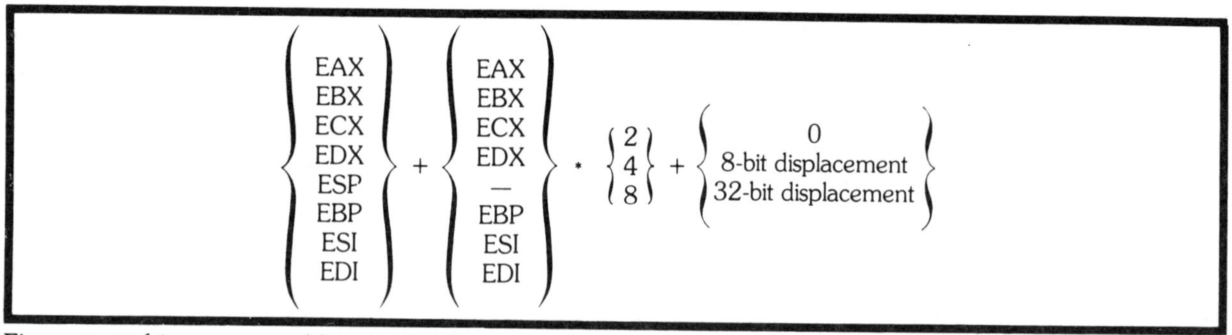

$$\begin{Bmatrix} EAX \\ EBX \\ ECX \\ EDX \\ ESP \\ EBP \\ ESI \\ EDI \end{Bmatrix} + \begin{Bmatrix} EAX \\ EBX \\ ECX \\ EDX \\ - \\ EBP \\ ESI \\ EDI \end{Bmatrix} * \begin{Bmatrix} 2 \\ 4 \\ 8 \end{Bmatrix} + \begin{Bmatrix} 0 \\ \text{8-bit displacement} \\ \text{32-bit displacement} \end{Bmatrix}$$

Figure 2. 32-bit memory addressing modes.

Table 2.
80386 support of high-level-language memory addressing.

Storage class	Type specifier	Addressing mode
Static	Scalar	[disp]
	Structure	[disp]
	Array of scalars	[disp + index]
	Array of structures	[disp + index] ·
Automatic	Scalar	[base + disp]
	Structure	[base + disp]
	Array of scalars	[base + disp + index]
	Array of structures	[base + disp + index]
Heap	Scalar	[base]
	Structure	[base + disp]
	Array of scalars	[base + index]
	Array of structures	[base + disp + scale]

other than ESP. The scale specification is a constant value, either 2, 4, or 8. If specified, it scales the index register by the required amount, thus simplifying indexing into arrays of multibyte elements. The displacement field is also a constant, its value ranging from -2^{31} to $+2^{31} - 1$. Figure 2 shows all of the 80386's 32-bit memory addressing modes, and Table 2 correlates high-level-language addressing forms with those modes. (Example of memory addressing appear in Table 1.)

Data types. As shown in Figure 3, the 80386 directly supports the fundamental data types found in most high-level languages. The basic operations provided by the 80386 for each of these data types are shown in Table 3. Most of these operations execute in two clocks when register or immediate operands are used. Furthermore, because of pipelining and the two-clock memory bus, stores to memory also execute in two clocks.

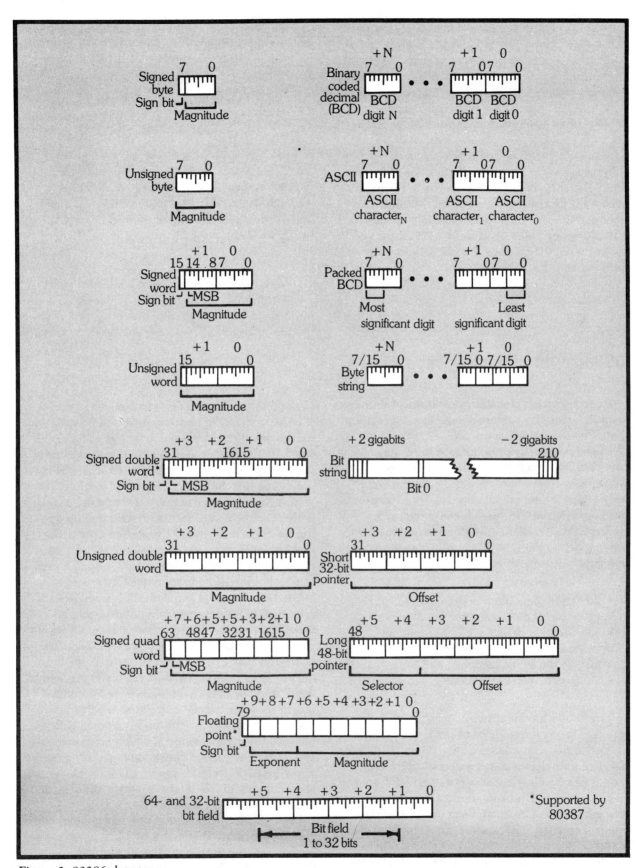

Figure 3. 80386 data types.

The basic unit of storage is a *byte*; a 16-bit quantity is a *word*, and a 32-bit quantity is a *double word*, or *d-word*. Words are defined as having a length of 16 bits so that notational compatibility with the other members of the iAPX 86 processor family will be retained. In the 80386, most data types are represented in the form of bytes, words, or d-words, or combinations thereof.

Words comprise two consecutive bytes in memory, with the low-order byte at the lower-numbered address. D-words comprise four consecutive bytes in memory, with the low-order byte at the lowest address and the high-order byte at the highest address. The address of a word or d-word is the address of the low-order byte. Hence, the 80386 utilizes the little-endian storage scheme.

Ordinal. An ordinal is an unsigned number. If it is in the range 0 through 4,294,967,295, it corresponds to a d-word value. If it has a magnitude of less than zero, it corresponds to a word or byte value. An example of an ordinal operation is the instruction sequence

```
MUL    EBX,vec[EDX*4]  ; EBX := EBX * vec[EDX]
INTO                   ; Generate an exception if
                       ; overflow
```

Here, the content of EBX is multiplied by the EDXth element of the d-word-sized ordinal array vec, and the product is stored in EBX. An overflow exception is generated if the product exceeds 4,294,967,295.

Integer. An integer is a signed number in the range $-2,147,483,648$ through $+2,147,483,647$. As with ordinals, d-word, word, and byte integers are supported. Integers are represented in two's-complement

80386 system debug capabilities

A large portion of system development time is usually devoted to system debugging and verification. The magnitude of the problem is strongly influenced by system complexity at both the software and the hardware levels. In highly complex systems, external hardware and software debug aids alone cannot provide the level of support needed; internal CPU assistance is required.

To facilitate system development and real-time system debugging, the 80386 provides the following capabilities:

- detection of instruction breakpoints,
- detection of data reference breakpoints,
- specification of four separate breakpoint addresses,
- instruction single-stepping, and
- a one-byte trap instruction.

The 80386 has six system debug registers (see figure). The first four, DR0 to DR3, store the required breakpoint addresses. Registers DR6 and DR7 contain debug status and control information, respectively. Registers DR4 and DR5 are reserved by Intel. Breakpoint addresses must be linear addresses of instructions or data items. The control register, DR7, specifies the conditions under which a breakpoint is recognized and includes enable/disable masking fields, the breakpoint type, and the breakpoint length fields.

The enable/disable masking fields determine whether a detected breakpoint condition will be recognized by the CPU and whether an exception will be generated or simply stored in the debug status register for future examination. The breakpoint type field indicates the type of memory reference—e.g., an instruction execution, a data write reference, or a data read/write reference—that is intended to cause the system break. The breakpoint length field is used primarily for data references and selects byte, word, or double-word ranges for data item breakpoints. This field is needed because of a problem that arises in data referencing. Simply specifying the starting address of a data item is too restrictive and is insufficient for matching a breakpoint condition. The problem exists because there are three different data item lengths (8, 16, and 32); under erroneous conditions the generated address and data type length may not exactly match the specified breakpoint condition. The length field adds flexibility by selecting a range in which breakpoints can occur. Instruction breakpoints always specify a one-byte length field, since system breakpoints should uniquely specify the byte-granular starting address of intended instructions.

Let us illustrate the use of the debug capability with an example. To cause a break at a particular instruction, the user loads the starting address of that instruction into one of the breakpoint address registers, DR0 to DR3. The

Table 3.

Table 3.
Data types supported by the 80386 instruction set.
(Floating point is available when numeric coprocessor is added.)

Operation	Ordinal	Integer	BCD	Floating point	String	Bit string
Move to/from memory, convert precision	X	X	X	X	X	X
Arithmetics add, subtract, multiply, divide, negate	X	X	X	X		
Logicals AND, OR, XOR, shift	X	X				
Compare	X	X	X	X	X	X
Transcendentals				X		

corresponding enable bit for the selected register must be set, and the type and length field must be set to instruction break (length = one byte). When the CPU is certain it is about to execute that instruction, it completes the execution of the current instruction, and a debug exception is generated. Note that if a successful branch or transfer of control precedes the intended breakpoint instruction, the break does not occur. An instruction break occurs before the instruction causing it is executed, whereas a data reference break occurs after the instruction causing it is executed.

The single-stepping-by-instruction feature forces an exception after each instruction execution. It can be used for system monitoring on an instruction-by-instruction basis. The one-byte trap instruction causes a software trap when executed and is useful for debugging exception-handling code.

80386 system debug registers.

31					0	
Breakpoint 0 linear address						DR0
Breakpoint 1 linear address						DR1
Breakpoint 2 linear address						DR2
Breakpoint 3 linear address						DR3
					Break Point Status	DR6
Break pt. length type	Break pt. length type	Break pt. length type	Break pt. length type		Break pt. enable/ disable	DR7

notation. This allows a common set of instructions for addition and subtraction. For example,

```
SUB    ESP, 5
```

subtracts five from ESP whether ESP stores an integer or an ordinal. The settings of the overflow, sign, zero, and carry flags allow a program to determine whether a signed or an unsigned overflow has occurred. However, special instructions are provided for determining overflow in multiply and divide operations involving integers, since an integer multiply has its own rules for overflow and an integer divide produces its own unique bit patterns.

Pointers. A pointer is a memory address. There are two types of pointers in the 80386: near pointers and far pointers. A near pointer is another term for an effective address. A far pointer has two components: a word-sized selector and a d-word-sized effective address. The selector names the logical address space in which the effective address resides. This ability to define logical address spaces gives a user greater flexibility in structuring memory. (This is discussed in greater detail below.) To retain compatibility with 16-bit members of the iAPX 86 processor family, the 80386 also supports pointers having word-sized selectors and word-sized effective addresses.

Bit fields. The 80386 can do fetches from, or perform stores into, contiguous bit sequences of up to 31 bits each, where such bit fields themselves reside in a bit string of up to four gigabits. Single-bit values can also be tested and modified. Furthermore, bit fields can be scanned for the first set bit in either a forward or a reverse direction. This feature can be used to implement the *set* type of Pascal. For example, if *col* is an object of the type *set of color*, then the Pascal fragment

while c **in** col **do**

can be translated into

```
BSF    EAX, col   ; Find first set element. Store in EAX
JZ     loopExit   ; Exit if none left
```

Floating-point operations. By adding the 80287 floating-point coprocessor, or the higher-performance 80387, the user can extend the 80386 instruction set to support 32-bit, 64-bit, and 80-bit IEEE-standard floating-point arithmetic directly. These coprocessors provide the accuracy and performance demanded by numerically intensive applications such as robotics and graphics.

Multiprecision operations. The 80386 provides limited support for 64-bit operands. Integer and ordinal multiply and divide operations may have 64-bit products and dividends; the multiplier, multiplicand, divisor, quotient, and remainder are limited to d-word quantities. Multiprecision add and subtract operations can be easily synthesized with the add-with-carry (ADC) and subtract-with-borrow (SBB) operations.

Besides multiprecision arithmetic operations, the 80386 provides double-width shift instructions that accept a 64-bit input and generate a 32-bit output. These instructions can be viewed as generalizations of the normal logical shifts, except that the value shifted in is not zeroes but is specified by the contents of another 32-bit operand. Double-width shifts are especially useful for buffering intermediate data when performing operations on unaligned bit strings. A barrel shifter within the 80386 makes the execution times of these instructions independent of the size of the shift—any register-based, double-shift operation can be done in three clock periods.

Logical addresses. Thus far we have discussed memory addresses only in the context of effective addresses. We shall now investigate the logical address spaces provided by the 80386 to allow convenient memory partitioning. Each logical address space is named by means of a word-sized selector. All memory addresses have two components: the selector that names the logical address space (or segment) and an effective address (or offset) that indexes into the named logical address space. The full selector:offset form of address is the far pointer mentioned previously. The selector is not usually directly specified in an instruction's operand field; it is instead stored in a segment register.

There are six segment registers named CS, DS, ES, FS, GS, and SS, as shown in Figure 4. Segment registers are not usually encoded in instructions; the segment register to be used is instead implied in the operand type. For example, code is fetched from the logical address space named by the selector in CS, at the offset specified by the instruction pointer EIP. Similarly, the stack is located in the logical address space named by the selector in SS, with the top-of-stack at offset ESP.

For memory operands not residing in the stack, the implied segment is usually DS. If a memory operand's default segment register is not desired, it

The 80386 physical implementation

The 80386 measures 390 mils on a side and is implemented in CMOS with Intel's CHMOS-III process, which provides 1.5-micrometer geometries and two layers of metallization. This allows 16-MHz operation with low power consumption. The chip contains over 275,000 transistors and is housed in a 132-pin pin grid array to simplify external interfacing and improve reliability.

To meet the high performance objectives of the 80386 architecture, the chip's designers organized the CPU into eight pipelined logical units and provided for a high degree of execution overlap among them. The units, which are shown in the die photo are the bus interface unit, the instruction (code) prefetch unit, the instruction decode unit, the segmentation unit, the paging unit, the protection test unit, the control unit, and the data unit. The last three comprise the execution section of the CPU, which consists of a microengine, a register file, an ALU, a barrel shifter, and miscellaneous control logic. On-chip memory management is implemented by the protection test, segmentation, and paging units.

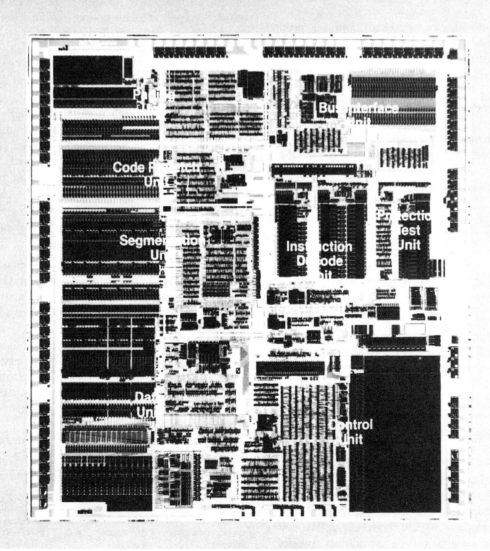

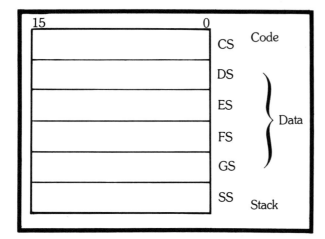

Figure 4. Segment registers.

can be overridden by placing one of six unique prefix bytes just before the instruction at which the override is to take effect. This allows rapid switching between different address spaces without requiring that a segment register be loaded with the correct selector value every time. It should be noted that segment descriptors are cached on the chip from their respective descriptor tables to allow rapid address translation and protection checking. Along with allowing the creation of address spaces, selectors form the basis for the 80386 memory management and protection scheme.

OS architecture—the memory management and protection model

Many computational environments require memory to be protected from unauthorized access. Furthermore, the allocation and deallocation of memory according to a process's needs must be managed. The 80386 provides a comprehensive set of mechanisms for supporting these requirements. The overall memory address generation structure is shown in Figure 5.

The logical address's selector and offset components specified by the instruction are mapped into a *linear address* via segment tables. Figure 6 shows how the selector specifies a segment descriptor. A segment descriptor is an eight-byte record. The main information it contains is the linear address and size

of the base of the segment, and the type of reference that is allowed to be made into the segment. (Segment access rights are discussed below.) The linear address is constructed from a logical address by adding the offset to the linear base address. If this address exceeds the bounds of the segment (as specified by its size), a segmentation exception is signaled. An instruction encountering such an exception is fully restartable. Note that there are two segment tables of 8192 entries each (see Figure 6 again). This permits a total of 16,383 logical address spaces,* or roughly 14 bits of addressability. Since the offset furnishes 32 bits of addressability, the total logical address space of the 80386 provides 2^{46} bits of addressability.

The linear address is passed through a two-level page map table to generate a physical address. The physical address is the address delivered to the microprocessor's external bus for a memory access.

If a particular environment requires only one logical address space, the selector mechanism can be easily bypassed. This is done by defining one large logical address space spanning the entire linear address space and loading the corresponding selector into all segment registers. The difference between a logical address and a linear address then disappears, since the effective address component of the logical address matches the linear address. Similarly, if a linear address to a physical address mechanism is not required, paging can be disabled by resetting a bit in a control register. When paging is disabled, the linear address bypasses the page table look-up and appears directly as the physical address.

Since both translation steps are optional, the 80386 can allow the user to choose from one of four distinct views of memory:

• Unsegmented unpaged memory. Here both translation steps are bypassed, thereby making the effective address the same as the physical address. This is useful, for example, in a low-complexity, high-performance controller application, which requires a simple view of memory.

• Unsegmented paged memory. Here memory is viewed as a paged linear address space. Protection and management of memory is done via paging. This view is favored by some operating systems—e.g., Berkeley UNIX.

• Segmented unpaged memory. Here memory is viewed as a collection of logical address spaces. The advantage of this view over a paged approach is that

---

*Entry zero of the global descriptor table is special-cased to indicate a *null selector*. Hence, only a total of 16,383 descriptors is supported.

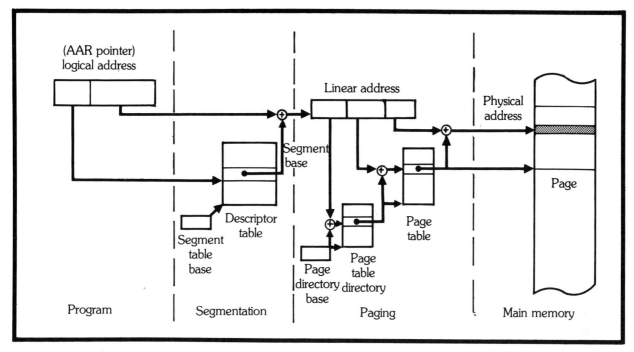

Figure 5. Memory address translation mechanism.

it affords protection down to the level of a single byte. Furthermore, unlike paging, it guarantees that when a linear address is generated the translation information is on-chip. Hence, segmented unpaged memory results in predictable access times.

• Segmented paged memory. This is the most comprehensive view of memory supported by the 80386. It uses segmentation to define logical memory partitions and paging to manage the allocation of memory within the partitions. Operating systems such as UNIX System V favor this view.

Segmentation mechanism. Memory protection is enforced in the 80386 through a concept called a *privilege level*. At any instant the processor is in one of four privilege levels. The current privilege level, or CPL, is stored as a number in the range 0 through 3, with level 0 being the most privileged level and level 3 the least. Furthermore, every logical address space (segment) has a privilege-level attribute associated with it called the descriptor privilege level, or DPL. The DPL is encoded in a field in the descriptor for a segment. Data access to a logical address space by a process operating at a given CPL is disallowed if the CPL is less privileged than the DPL of the logical address space. The CPL itself can change whenever CS is loaded with a new segment. Thus, the CPL is usually the DPL of the current code segment.

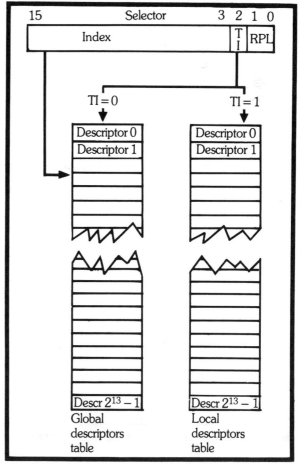

Figure 6. How a selector names a descriptor.

In addition to the DPL, a logical address space possesses an access attribute. This attribute is also stored in the descriptor for a segment. For address spaces containing data, it specifies whether read/write or read-only accesses are permitted. For address spaces containing code, it specifies whether read/execute or execute-only accesses are permitted. An access to a logical address space is allowed only if the access request passes a privilege level check and an access type check. The access attribute, privilege level, base address, and segment limit are contained in a segment descriptor. Each descriptor is an entry in either the global descriptor table (GDT) or the local descriptor table (LDT). The GDT specifies logical address spaces shared by all tasks, whereas the LDT specifies logical address spaces specific to a single task.

To support memory management, all descriptors have a *present bit* and an *accessed bit*. An access to a logical address space whose present bit is clear causes a fault, which is signaled via an interrupt. The fault handler can bring the logical address space's contents into the linear address space, set the linear address space's base and limit in the descriptor, and set the present bit. The faulting instruction can then be restarted. This implements a demand-swapping scheme for logical address spaces. The accessed bit is provided to help with the replacement policy implementation. This bit is set whenever a selector defining a logical address space is loaded into a segment register, thereby indicating which logical address spaces have been used recently.

Paging mechanism. To complement logical-to-linear address translation, the linear address is translated via paging into a physical address, as shown in Figure 5. The paging scheme involves a standard, two-level, table look-up process. The linear address to be translated is divided into three fields: a direc-tory table index, a page table index, and a byte index. The directory table index is a 10-bit field that selects one of 1024 page tables. This page table is in turn indexed by the 10-bit page table index, which selects one out of 1024 pages. This page is a 4096-byte block which is indexed by the 12-bit byte index. The byte thus addressed specifies the low-order byte of the operand addressed. The entries in the directory and page tables are d-word quantities that store the physical base addresses of page tables (for directory tables) or of pages (for page tables). These entries also provide the traditional dirty, ac-cessed, and present bits to allow for the implementa-tion of replacement policies in demand-paged sys-tems. The layout of each entry is shown in Figure 7.

The paging mechanism also provides protection at the page level. This is done via the user/supervisor and read/write bits in the directory and page table entries. A process is considered to be executing in user mode if CPL is set to 3; it is considered to be executing in supervisor mode if CPL is 2, 1, or 0. Therefore a user process is allowed to read a page only if both the directory entry and page table entry for it have the user/supervisor bit set. Similarly, a user write is allowed only if both entries have both the user/supervisor bit and the read/write bit set. A supervisor process is allowed to read or write all pages without restraint. Any violation of the page protection rules causes a paging exception. An in-struction encountering such an exception is fully restartable. This permits the construction of demand-paged systems and, it should be noted, allows the use of the copy-on-write trick in implementing UNIX's *fork* primitive.

Task switching support. In addition to the memory management and protection facilities described above, the 80386 assists the operating system by pro-viding hardware to implement task switching. This

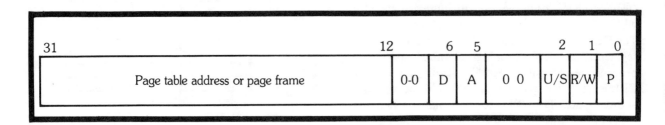

Figure 7. Directory table and page table entries.

hardware allows fast and efficient task switching in multitasking applications.

In task switching, the state of a task is stored in a data structure called a task state segment, or TSS. The fields of the TSS store images of the general registers, flags, instruction pointer, and segment registers, and an image of a pointer to the page directory table base and the local descriptor table. The TSS is itself described by a specially tagged descriptor residing in the global descriptor table. For a task switch to be performed, a call or jump is made via a selector that names such a descriptor. The processor recognizes the TSS and does a task switch by saving the current machine state in the currently active TSS and loading the state in the target TSS.

Compatibility with the 80286. Full compatibility with the 80286—to protect investments in operating systems and applications software—was clearly one of the key objectives of the 80386 architecture. Such compatibility was achieved by making the 80386 instruction set object code compatible with the 80286 instruction set; all architectural extensions to the 80286 instruction set, data types, and addressing modes adhere to strict compatibility rules. Furthermore, as the discussion earlier in this article showed, the basic 80286 memory management model was maintained and extended by the 80386.

Compatibility with the 8086. The 80386 is compatible with the 8086 in the same way that the 80286 is compatible with the 8086. The 80386 is similar to the 80286 in that it too powers up in 8086-compatible mode (also called real mode). Real mode is useful for initialization and for configuration of the processor data structures needed to run in native 80386 protected mode. The recommended method for running 8086 code is called virtual 86 mode.

To allow 8086 code to run harmoniously with its native code, the 80386 employs the notion of a virtual 8086, or VM86, task. Except for I/O and interrupt-related instructions, a VM86 task executes code using 8086 semantics. Memory addresses generated are treated as linear addresses and are subject to translation via paging. Mapping each VM86 task's linear address space to a different physical address virtualizes 8086 memory. However, operations that use global resources, such as I/O and interrupt operations, also need to be virtualized. This is done by trapping the instructions for such operations and allowing the virtual machine monitor (executing as a native 80386 program) to emulate them. VM86 mode is a key feature of the 80386—it allows the large

body of 8086 software to run concurrently with native code in high-performance environments, and thereby allows 86, 286, and 386 tasks to run simultaneously.

80386 implementation

To meet the 80386's performance objectives, the chip's designers gave careful consideration to the internal implementation of the architecture—i.e., the microarchitecture. Performance enhancements in advanced microprocessor CPU designs can be obtained through

- advances in technology and circuit design,
- higher clock rates,
- wider data paths,
- advances in system and bus architecture, and
- advances in microarchitecture.

The first four of these were discussed earlier along with their effects on performance. The following sections describe the 80386 microarchitecture, focusing on performance-enhancing features such as pipelining and parallelism.

The 80386 is organized as eight logical units, with each unit assigned a task or step in the fetching and execution of each instruction. This arrangement allows as much parallel execution of the instruction stream as possible. The units are pipelined and, for the most part, operate autonomously. The units and their interconnections are shown in Figure 8 in the functional block diagram of the 80386.

The eight units are the bus interface unit, the prefetch unit, the instruction decode unit, the control unit, the data unit, the protection test unit, the segmentation unit, and the paging unit. The control, data, and protection test units comprise the execution section of the CPU.

The bus interface unit interfaces the CPU to the external system bus and controls all address, data, and control signals to and from the CPU. The prefetch unit is responsible for fetching instructions from memory. It uses an advance-instruction-fetch pointer to prefetch code from memory and store it in a temporary code queue. This queue also acts as a buffer between the prefetch unit and the instruction decode unit. Since addresses generated by the prefetch unit are linear, they must be translated to physical addresses by the paging unit before the prefetch bus cycle request can be sent to the bus interface unit.

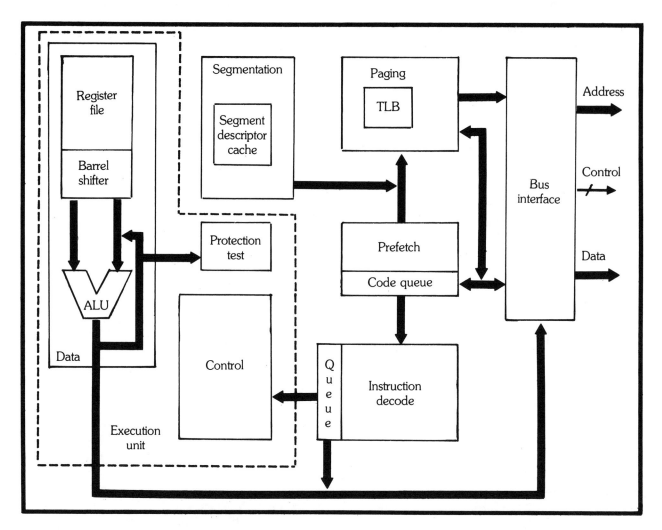

Figure 8. Block diagram of 80386.

The instruction decode unit prepares and decodes instructions for immediate execution by the execution unit. It does this by fetching bytes of code from the prefetcher's code queue, transforming them into a fully decoded instruction, and then storing that instruction in a three-level decoded instruction queue. The execution unit then operates on the decoded instruction, performing the steps needed to execute it.

Instructions requiring memory references send their requests to the segmentation unit for logical address computation and translation and segment protection violation checking. The segmentation unit produces a translated linear address which the paging unit then translates into a physical address. The paging unit also checks for paging violations before it sends a bus request and the address to the bus interface unit and external bus.

Pipelining and parallelism. Advanced microprocessors are normally pipelined by overlapping the fetching, decoding, and execution of instructions. In the 80386 microarchitecture, however, the operations of all eight of the logical units are overlapped. This allows the parallel and autonomous operation of the units. They can simultaneously operate on different instructions, thereby significantly boosting the overall instruction processing rate of the CPU. For example, while the bus interface unit is completing a data write cycle for one instruction, the instruction unit can be decoding another, and the execution unit processing a third.

The sections below describe each of the logical units of the 80386 and discuss how each was designed to maximize the benefits of pipelining.

Bus interface unit. The bus interface unit provides a high-speed interface between the CPU and the system. Its function is to efficiently meet the CPU's requirements for external bus transfers during code fetches, data fetches, paging unit requests, and segmentation unit requests. To accomplish this, it has been designed to accept and prioritize multiple internal bus requests so that it can make maximum use of the available bus bandwidth in servicing those requests. This activity is overlapped with any current bus transaction. As mentioned earlier, the 80386 bus uses only two clocks per cycle; if the pipelined mode is used, the 80386 bus is capable of starting the next address of a new bus cycle before the completion of a current bus transaction.

Prefetch unit. This unit is responsible for prefetching instructions from memory. It stores the aligned code in its code queue for efficient decoding by the instruction unit. It maintains a linear address pointer and a segment prefetch limit that are initially obtained from the segmentation unit to be used as a prefetch instruction pointer and for checking segment limit violations, respectively. The prefetcher attempts to keep its code queue filled with valid bytes of code by sending prefetch bus cycle requests to the bus interface unit through the paging unit. Prefetch bus cycle requests are made whenever the prefetch code queue is partially empty or after the occurrence of a control transfer. The prefetcher's bus cycle requests are assigned a lower priority than execution-related, operand fetch/store bus cycle requests and page-miss processing and segmentation-specific bus cycle requests. At zero wait states, there is no interference between prefetch and data bus cycles. Idle cycles are used to prefetch code from memory and keep the code queue filled.

Instruction decode unit. This unit decodes and prepares instructions for processing by the execution unit. Whenever the instruction unit's own queue or pipe is partially empty, it fetches bytes of code from the prefetcher code queue, decodes and prepares them, and stores the result in its own three-word-deep queue. The decoded instruction queue words are very wide; they contain all the instruction fields the execution unit needs to immediately execute the instruction without further decoding. The combined prefetch unit/instruction unit pipe operates on a two-clock cycle. The instruction unit, however, can decode at only one clock per opcode byte.

Execution unit. The next logical unit in the pipe is the execution unit. As mentioned previously, it is composed of the control, data processing, and protection test units. Its responsibility is to execute the instruction given to it. It does so by using its own resources as well as by communicating control and sequencing information to other logical units needed to complete the execution of the instruction. The fully decoded instruction is popped out of the instruction queue, and the execution unit uses its various fields, such as microcode starting addresses, operand references, data types, and ALU operators, to execute it.

The control section consists of a microcode-driven engine that has special-purpose hardware for decoding, assisting, and speeding up microcycle execution. The data processing section—or data path—contains all data registers, an ALU, a barrel shifter, multiply/divide hardware, and special control logic; it performs the data operations selected by the control section. The protection test section performs all static segmentation-related violation checks under microcode control.

The microengine has a two-clock execution latency, but by overlapping microinstruction fetching and execution and by using the delayed microjump technique, it provides an execution rate of only one clock per microcycle (62.5 ns at 16 MHz). To enhance the effective instruction processing rate of the execution unit further, parallel or overlapped execution of instructions is employed. Since memory reference instructions, including stack push and pop instructions (heavily utilized in procedure calls), constitute a large portion of the instruction mix in a typical program, a special technique is used to reduce the number of clocks needed to execute such instructions. The method used partially overlaps the execution of every memory reference instruction, including stack push and pop instructions, with the execution of the preceding instruction. This parallel execution of two instructions enhances the instruction processing rate of the CPU—with a typical mix of instructions, it yields a nine-percent improvement in performance.

The implementation of the execution unit required the addition of a 32-bit internal bus and special control logic to ensure the correct completion of the current instruction, prevent the use of stale register values, and provide the control needed to handle the simultaneous execution of two instructions.

Segmentation unit. This unit performs effective address computation upon request of the execution unit. It does this logical-to-linear address translation at the same time it does bus cycle segmentation violation checks. (Static violation checks—e.g., of segment descriptors—are performed by the protection test unit and are not part of the bus cycle activity.) The translated linear address is then sent to the paging unit along with bus cycle transaction information. The paging unit then becomes responsible for requesting bus service from the bus interface unit.

Paging unit. Linear addresses generated by the segmentation or code prefetch units are passed on to the paging unit, where they are translated into physical addresses. As explained in the section on architecture above, paging translation is implemented through a two-level page relocation mechanism. To improve performance, the paging unit uses a 32-entry translation look-aside buffer (TLB) to perform the translation. Page table and page frame entries are cached into the TLB. This results in a translation time of one half of a clock period—much faster than if

memory-based page tables were referenced instead of the TLB. The combined logical-to-physical address translation pipe, which includes effective address formation, segmentation, and paging relocation, requires only two clocks of processing. No additional clocks are needed for paging since TLB look-up and translation are performed in the same clock (second phase) as the linear address calculation.

Integrated segmentation and paging. The 80386 implements a segmentation-plus-demand-paging memory management function for virtual memory translation and protection violation checking. To enhance system performance, memory management functions are integrated into the chip. All virtual-to-physical address translation, segmentation, and paging violation checking are performed by the on-chip memory management unit (MMU), which is imple-

80386 bus operation

The 80386 external interface (Figure B) connects the chip to memory and peripherals over a high-performance bus. This interface provides separate address and data pins to support efficient high-speed bus transfers and bus cycle pipelining. It uses its other pins to maintain simple and efficient interfaces—pins are dedicated to cy-

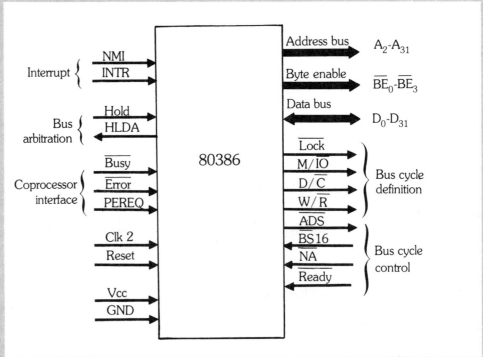

Figure B. iAPX 80386 external interface.

mented by the segmentation, protection test, and paging units. All memory management protection and translation descriptors are cached into the on-chip MMU. Segment descriptors are cached into segment descriptor caches in the segmentation unit, while page descriptors are cached into the TLB. Virtually all protection and translation activities utilize the on-chip descriptors.

There are several advantages to integrating memory management and the CPU on the same chip:

• The implementation can take advantage of pipelining and parallel execution by overlapping the steps from effective address formation to linear address and physical address generation. Under such an arrangement the next memory address will already be known while the current transaction is still on the bus. The logical-to-physical address translation in many cases will overlap other bus cycles and will be completed by the time the current bus cycle is finished. Pipelining to an off-chip MMU would clearly be more difficult.

• No additional clocks need to be added to the bus cycle to implement the MMU translation, since the memory management functions are internal and not part of the external bus cycle.

• System complexity and cost are reduced, and board design is simplified, since no off-chip memory management components are needed.

Special-purpose hardware. To enhance performance, the 80386 implements several important pro-

cle definition, cycle control, interrupts, bus arbitration, and coprocessor support.

Some typical 80386 bus cycles are shown in Figure C. With zero wait states, each bus cycle consists of only two clocks; at 16-MHz operation, the 32-bit bus can sustain a 32-megabyte-per-second transfer rate. When the bus operates in pipelined mode, the address of the next bus cycle is sent on pins A31-A2 before the current cycle is completed. This mode, which is dynamically selectable from the interface, can be used to implement a fast interleaved memory subsystem with inexpensive dynamic RAMs. In such a system, the current bus transaction uses one bank of memory while the new address is used to access another. The pipelined mode can also be used to overlap the current bus cycle with address decode delays of the next cycle, making available longer system access times. Slower memory or I/O systems use the $\overline{\text{READY}}$ pin to extend the current bus cycle as needed. Dynamic bus sizing allows software-transparent interfaces to 16-and 32-bit ports.

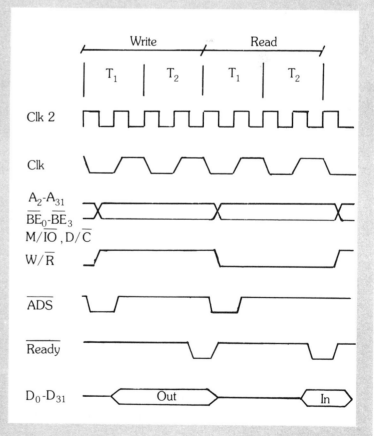

Figure C. 80386 bus operation.

cessing functions with special-purpose hardware. These special blocks include the TLB for paging translation, a 64-bit barrel shifter, multiply/divide hardware, multiple ALUs and adders, and miscellaneous random-logic control function implementations that take the place of PLA or microcode approaches that are too slow.

Translation look-aside buffer. As explained above, the time required to perform the two-step table lookup paging translation function is significantly reduced by the use of a TLB. With 32 entries in its cache, the TLB enjoys a relatively high hit ratio of 98 percent. A TLB miss occurs when an entry is not in the cache and references to memory-based page

Design for testability

To guarantee high quality in a complex VLSI microprocessor, the chip development team must

- use good, conservative design techniques,
- employ rigorous design verification at all levels,
- carefully choose the criteria against which manufacturing, testing, and quality assurance will be measured, and
- ensure the testability of the device.

Intel's goal is to manufacture the highest-quality silicon as inexpensively as possible. Adequate device testing helps achieve that goal. However, the testing of complex VLSI circuits is difficult. Here we explore the features that have been designed into the 80386 to make testing easier and ensure its adequacy.

A VLSI microprocessor is difficult to test for two reasons:

- It contains a large number of transistors but has a small number of external pins. The external pin count is too small to allow for a convenient and thorough interface to all the internal blocks of the microprocessor.
- It exhibits a fairly large number of states. It is virtually impossible to force the microprocessor to sequence through all possible states under all possible conditions.

These limitations make it very difficult to control and observe a VLSI microprocessor that is being tested.

To alleviate these problems, the 80386's designers incorporated test circuits into the device to ensure its testability. They designed these circuits to support proven test techniques. The test capability thus added facilitates component testing in the lab and in production environments and simplifies board and system testing in end user applications. Test capabilities built into the 80386 include

- self-test of all large PLAs,
- self-test of the control ROM and microengine, and
- signature analysis.

Special microcode and instructions are also provided to facilitate testing, and there is special test circuitry for the translation look-aside buffer (TLB).

PLA testing. In the 80386, self-test of large PLAs is needed because of the large number of possible input combinations. A maximal polynomial counter is used as a pseudorandom vector generator to drive the inputs to the PLA and to ensure sequencing through all possible combinations of the inputs. This is illustrated in the accompanying figure. As the inputs change in a pseudorandom fashion, the outputs from the PLA are fed into a linear feedback shift register with appropriate polynomial coefficients to accumulate a unique *signature* of the block. This signature is then read and analyzed by special software to determine correctness. This technique is referred to as *signature analysis*.

Signature analysis has been used for many years—primarily at the board and system level—to facilitate testing and fault diagnosing. It has the advantage of being able to reduce a large amount of data, uniquely encode it, and store it in a register (the linear feedback shift, or signature, register). It should be noted that the polynomials used to configure this register must be carefully chosen to provide maximum test coverage and error detection.

Control ROM testing. Self-test of the microcode ROM consists of sequencing through all addresses and word locations and, as in PLA testing, accumulating the result in a signature register. The accumulated microcode signature is then read by software. The microcode address counter logic is used to do the sequencing in the

tables are needed to complete the address translation. Even with a high hit ratio, the memory-referencing table look-up function is clearly time-consuming and should be designed to minimize the degradation of system performance. The 80386 paging unit incorporates special-purpose hardware to implement the table look-up functions instead of using the more economical but slower microcode approach. TLB miss processing by this special hardware consumes only nine clocks, whereas a microcode-driven look-up would consume three times as many clocks.

Barrel shifter. A 64-bit barrel shifter is provided to implement shift, rotate, and bit manipulation in-

ROM test sequence, to share hardware, and to provide address sequencing logic for the microengine self-test.

TLB test circuitry. Testing the TLB RAM and CAM (content-addressable memory) for all entries and with all data sensitivity patterns would be very cumbersome and time-consuming without special assistance.

To simplify such testing and improve its coverage, the 80386's designers added special-purpose hardware—two registers, plus special instructions to control them—to allow for the direct writing of any data pattern into the RAM or CAM blocks of the TLB. This hardware can also force the comparison of any data pattern against existing entries in the TLB to test the TLB's matching capability.

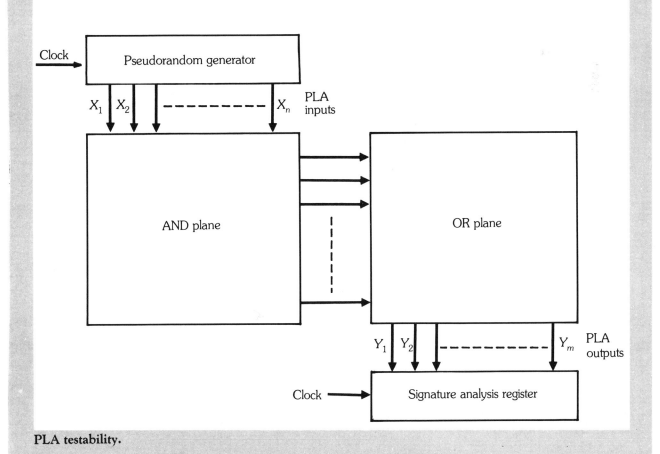

PLA testability.

structions efficiently as well as to assist in multiply and other miscellaneous operations. It can shift any data type by any shift count in a single clock, and it is significantly faster than an ALU/microcode implementation.

Multiply/divide hardware. A one-bit-per-clock multiply/divide mechanism permits a 32-bit multiply or divide in 40 clocks, maximum. To speed multiply execution, additional special hardware is included to detect early completion of a multiply and correctly terminate the operation. Early completion of a multiply is detected when all significant multiplier bits have been exhausted and the final product can be obtained by an appropriate shift operation. Since many multiply operations do not require the full 32-bit multiply, the average number of clocks needed for a multiply is 20.

The 80386 represents the state of the art in 32-bit microprocessor architecture and performance. It maintains object code compatibility with existing members of the 86 family of microprocessors, thus protecting end users' investments in software. Its implementation exploits pipelining and parallel execution to provide high performance. These characteristics make it an excellent candidate for application in engineering workstations, office systems, and robotic and control systems.

Khaled A. El-Ayat is a project manager in the Intel High-Performance Microprocessor Operation. With Intel eight years, he has contributed to the definition, design, and development of the company's microprocessors. He designed the control structures of the 80386. His technical interests include microprocessor architectures and all aspects of VLSI design.

A member of the IEEE, El-Ayat holds a BSc from Cairo University, an MSc in electrical engineering and computer science from the University of Toronto, and a PhD in electrical engineering and computer science from the University of California, Santa Barbara. He is a part-time lecturer in microprocessors at the University of Santa Clara.

Rakesh K. Agarwal is a senior design engineer in the Intel High-Performance Microprocessor Operation. He contributed to the architectural specification, microcoding, and logic design of the 80386. His primary technical interest is in the definition of the interface needed between hardware and software to make the most optimal use of computer system resources. He is also interested in the design of CAD tools that can be used to assist the architecture-to-logic transformation.

Agarwal received the BSc in computer science from the University of British Columbia and the MSc in computer science from the University of Toronto.

Questions about this article can be directed to El-Ayat at Intel Corporation, Mail Stop SC4-59, 2625 Walsh Avenue, Santa Clara, CA 95051.

Acknowledgments

The authors wish to acknowledge the superb efforts of the entire 80386 team, including the project managers, the chip architects group, the design engineers, and the mask designers.

Section 6: An Assessment of RISC

6.1 Background

For many years the general trend in computer architecture has been toward increasing CPU complexity: more instructions, more addressing modes, more specialized registers, and so on. The RISC movement represents a fundamental break with the philosophy behind that trend. Naturally, the appearance of RISC systems, and the publication of papers by its proponents extolling RISC virtues, has led to a reaction from what might be called the mainstream of computer architecture.

The work that has been done on assessing the merits of the RISC approach can be grouped into two categories

- *Quantitative:* attempts to compare program size and execution speed of programs on RISC and CISC machines that use comparable technology.
- *Qualitative:* examination of issues such as high-level language support and optimum use of VLSI real estate.

The success of the RISC approach in the marketplace is far from assured. As research, development, and product introduction continues, the assessment goes on. The articles in this section should give the reader an appreciation of the current status of that assessment.

6.2 Article Summary

The first article, "MIPS, Dhrystones, and Other Tales," serves to introduce the topic of quantitative assessment. The author points out the pitfalls of quantitative comparison and discusses several alternative techniques. Results are presented that compare some RISC and CISC machines.

The next three articles compare the Berkeley RISC machines to other contemporary computers. The Berkeley RISC machines are the best-documented and most-studied RISC systems. "Assessing RISCs in High-Level Language Support" compares the RISC I to five other processors, focusing on execution speed. "Re-evaluation of RISC I" attempts to decouple the effects of a large register file from a reduced instruction set and analyze the program size and execution time effects of the latter. "RISC Watch" assesses the performance of the second Berkeley machine, the RISC II.

The next two articles, "More Hardware Means Less Software" and "Toward Simpler, Faster Computers," provides a qualitative comparison of RISCs and CISCs.

The final article (with two responses) reports on a large and ongoing effort at Carnegie-Mellon University to assess RISCs versus CISCs. This is the most thorough, objective analysis yet published and serves as a fitting conclusion to our study of reduced instruction set computers.

EH0251-9/86/0000/0287$01.00 © 1986 IEEE   287

MIPS, DHRYSTONES AND OTHER TALES
Omri Serlin

Summary: Simple performance indices are desirable, but can never capture the complex factors involved. Lack of standards and independent certification further detract from the usefulness of such popular measures as MIPS, Dhrystones, Whetstones, and Linpack MFLOPS. End users should rely on applications-related workloads to compare competing systems.

(This is a revised version of an article from the April, 1986 issue of the *Supermicro* newsletter; a condensed version of this article also appeared in the June 1st, 1986 issue of *Datamation*.)

+++

The recent "RISC MIPS" vs. "real MIPS" debate has refocused the industry's attention on computer performance measurement. But the quest for simple measures of computer performance dates back to the very early days of the modern digital computer[1]. Over the years, many different performance indexes have been developed, including MIPS, Whetstones, Dhrystones, LINPACK MFLOPS, and transactions/second (tps), to name a few.

There are several reasons for the continuing, intense interest in this subject. End-users would like to have simple performance indicators so that they could make straight-forward comparisons of several competing alternatives. Another end-user concern is capacity planning: the ability to predict when a particular system would have to be augmented or replaced in order to service the expected future load.

Manufacturers are concerned with performance measurements that help designers optimize future hardware architectures, operating systems, and language compilers for their intended applications.

Journalists and Wall Street analysts love to construct neat comparison tables, replete with dollars-per-MIPS factors, which are always popular with readers in the industry and the investment community.

Technical economists use performance indices to chart the chronological progress of technology, such as the decline in the cost-per-computation over the years. Technology trend charts have also played an important role in, for example, the debate about Grosch's Law and the merits of distributed vs. centralized computing[2].

What's wrong with simple indicators?
There are two key problems with such indicators. First, there is a fundamental difficulty in reducing a set of complex considerations and conditions into one simple number. It is not reasonable to expect that a single number could meaningfully characterize a computer system, just as it is unlikely that a single number could capture the essence of the various factors that affect the "goodness" of an automobile, a much simpler system.

Moreover, different users may value each aspect of the system's performance quite differently. A user with a transaction processing

Reprinted with revisions from *The SUPERMICRO Newsletter*, Issue Number 54, April 1986. Copyright © 1986 ITOM International Co., POB 1450, Los Altos, CA 94023, USA, Telephone (415) 948-4516.

application is interested in the efficiency of the I/O system, database software, and communication protocols. Such a user is likely to be concerned with the magnitude and the consistency of the system's response time, but may care little for the CPU's ability to process floating point operations, or the compilation speed of the various compilers. In a technical, scientific, real-time or university environment, the set of priorities may be quite different.

The second problem is that, contrary to common misconception, there are no accepted industry standards for computing the value of MIPS or tps. Thus there is no assurance whatever that MIPS ratings reported for various system from various manufacturers are comparable in any sense. The recent arrival of RISC machines on the scene aggravates the problem.

Problems with "Standard" Benchmarks

Even when a sort of a standard does exist (e.g., Whetstones, Dhrystones, and LINPACK MFLOPS), there is no independent authority to certify performance claims. For example, Jack Dongarra of the Argonne National Laboratory, who publishes the very-widely-used results of the LINPACK benchmark, gives no guarantees regarding the authenticity of the performance data, which is supplied by a variety of sources. (He did tell this author, though, that he has "a 90% confidence in the numbers... I know the performance of the machines, and it matches the numbers").

Another complicating factor with the "standard" benchmarks is that multiple versions exist, which are not always identical. For example, version 1.0 of the Dhrystone benchmark, distributed by AT&T's Rick Richardson, whose results are posted on USENET and are widely quoted, yields about 15% better results relative to the version distributed by Reinhold Weicker, the benchmark's author. Richardson's "Version 1.1" is, supposedly, much closer to Weicker's intent.

A third difficulty is that the standard benchmarks can be run under a variety of conditions. For example, the Dhrystone benchmark can be run with and without registers. The Whetstone benchmark exists in single and double precision versions. Linpack can be run with standard, rolled, or assembly-coded BLAS (a key subroutine); in long or short precision; with 100 or 1000 equations; and with or without compiler directives to help in multiprocessor situations. Reported results often neglect to state these important conditions.

Operational problems can also lead to complications. For example, in 1985, grossly understated results were published in the press for one of AT&T's new 3B machines under the AIM Unix benchmarks. The problem was that, in interpreting the benchmark results, the machine's clock period was assumed to be much longer than it actually was. Most standard benchmarks are self-timing and rely on the system's hardware clocking facilities; any errors in interpreting these facilities, or in adapting the benchmark to use the internal clock, could seriously affect the results. It is generally better to repeat the test in a loop enough times so it can be timed with a stop watch.

Finally, reported results often neglect to mention important environmental factors that could have a significant impact. Among these: the operating system version; the machine's memory speed, when several options are available; the compiler version, and level of optimization invoked; the disk transfer rate and capacity (in I/O benchmarks); whether or not a floating point accelerator or coprocessor was employed; and so on. No serious comparison should ever be attempted unless the environment for each run is completely specified, and its implications understood.

Major Vendors' Approach

Major computer manufacturers rarely publish MIPS ratings for their systems; although DEC did advertise 6 MIPS for its 8650 system, and HP publicly claims 4.5 MIPS for the Spectrum processor in the models 3000/930 and 9000/840. Vendors are worried, on the one hand, that they may penalize themselves unnecessarily by quoting a conservative figure; and on the other, that some user might consider their claims excessive enough to justify legal action. Similar considerations apply with other performance measures for which there is no standard derivation procedure.

Instead, IBM and other major manufacturers typically characterize their new machines in relation to previous models. Performance data for that determination is usually derived from running a "job mix" of several representative programs on the new and old machines. With a few exceptions, manufacturers are very reluctant to publicly describe the exact procedure and programs used in deriving their relative performance figures; possibly because they do not wish competitors or users to be able to reproduce these.

Large vendors often have no company-wide standards for establishing relative performance. In 1982, for example, one Hewlett Packard division was characterizing the engineering-oriented Series 9000 (based on a proprietary, 32-bit microprocessor) as a 1 MIPS machine. At the same time, another HP division was claiming 3 MIPS for a much-lower cost, 16-bit A900 measurement and control computer. The two divisions were (and still are) using entirely different procedures to derive their performance claims. HP did introduce performance measurement standards for Spectrum-based models, which are currently being offered by two independent divisions.

Among major vendors, IBM is probably the most meticulous in measuring relative performance. To compare the low-end of 4300 series (4331 and 4341 models), introduced in 1979, to the older, System/370 models, IBM used a new suite of benchmarks, called the "Standard

Intermediate Systems Workload". The programs, developed jointly by SPD and several of the marketing divisions, included 7 typical commercial batch jobs, used to determine internal (CPU) performance; a transaction-oriented, CICS-based benchmark; and an interactive benchmark consisting of a collection of scripts simulating users doing various types of work under the VM operating system.

Great care was taken to assure identical conditions (peripherals, operating system parameters, etc.); when this was impossible, the differences were clearly enumerated. (Such differences are often due to differing characteristics of successive generation of equipment. Sometimes, however, even major vendors may have difficulty assembling substantial, identical configurations of several machines for "non productive" benchmark work). All told, more than 100 runs were required to complete the load under a variety of specified operating systems and other conditions. The internal IBM report on the results included more than 60 pages of small print and dozens of tables and charts.

Yet because IBM is highly compartmentalized into multiple, autonomous divisions, even today there is no single work load that can be used to compare the complete line of compatible mainframes (4300, 308X, 309X), even when using the same operating system. Incompatible operating systems (DOS/VSE, MVS, VM) further complicate the problem. The non-compatibles systems (S/1, S/36, S/38) present an even tougher problem, since their operating systems, support software, and language compilers are so drastically different than those for the mainline offerings.

Still, some progress has been made. Three key IBM performance centers (at Poughkeepsie and Endicott, NY; and Washington, DC) are today using a common workload to measure performance under the MVS operating system. The workload appears to be an extension of the SPD SISW mentioned above; it includes commercial batch, engineering/scientific batch, TSO interactive, IMS on-line, and CICS on-line work. Most of the measurements under this workload were performed on 308X and 4381 models; some portions were also run on the 4361 Mod 5 (in Germany).

Two internal IBM documents describe the results in exhaustive detail, one for MVS/370 and one for MVS/XA (the latter is the MVS version for the newer systems with 31-bit addressing; the original 360/370 used 24 bit addressing). These documents, while not generally available, are distributed to IBM sales people and are often discussed with prospective buyers.

International Data Corp. (Framingham, MA) is one of several independent organizations that have over the years attempted to provide their own relative performance measures, not just for IBM, but also for other vendors' gear. However, IDC numbers were not based on actual testing. Instead, they were derived from a paper-and-pencil formula, which assigned a performance basis of 45 "cuples" to the IBM System/370 Model 158-3, and relied mostly on the published IBM relative performance claims thereafter.

IDC never described this formula publicly, nor did it ever reveal how it derived numbers for non-IBM machines. There is reason to believe that the process included a good deal of "guesstimating" and group consensus. IDC decided to stop publishing its relative performance numbers, apparently because it reached the conclusion that the process by which they were derived was no longer adequate.

IBM goes on the Offensive

IBM became so concerned about performance claims by competitors vis-a-vis the latest 4381 models that, in mid-March, 1986, it hosted a special consultants' seminar on the subject, and even gave a special briefing dealing with performance measurement to the *Wall Street Journal*. IBM was principally worried about performance claims that suggested that DEC's 8650 and 8800 and DG's MV/20000 were considerably better in absolute performance and in price/performance relative to the latest 4381 Models 11, 12, 13 uniprocessor, and the dyadic Model 14.

In the presentation (which used "Vendor A" and "Vendor B" as thin disguises for DEC and DG, respectively), IBM showed how under different benchmarks and conditions, different conclusions could be drawn regarding the 4381 in relation to the competing machines. The 4381 gave best account of itself in engineering & scientific tasks requiring long (64 bit) precision, which IBM claims is really needed by the majority of such applications.

Based on direct testing of the DEC 8600, plus published claims of DEC and of DG relative to DEC, and using such published results as LINPACK, IBM concluded that, in long precision Whetstones, the 4381-14 dyadic matches DG's MV/20000 and is about 86% as fast as the DEC 8800. However, in long-precision LINPACK, as well as in running NASTRAN in LP, the 4381-13 matches the MV/20000, and the 4381-14 beats the 8800 by a factor of more than 1.5. The obvious moral of the story: simple numbers can't tell all; a detailed look behind the scenes is required for full understanding.

The origin and meaning of MIPS

One of the earliest attempts to characterize computer performance, in more meaningful terms than just its Add and Multiply execution times, was done around 1960 by IBM staffer J.C. Gibson[3]. He performed several *dynamic instruction traces* on programs written for the IBM 650 and 704 machines, and came up with his Gibson Mix, which made it possible to compute the execution time of an "average" instruction. The inverse of this measure became known as KIPS (later, MIPS): the number of average instructions executed per second.

A dynamic instruction trace requires either software or hardware instrumentation to record the type of each instruction as it is being executed. By performing such traces on a large (and, presumably, representative) body of programs, it is possible to determine how often a particular type of instruction is likely to be used in typical programs. Given the frequency of, and execution time for each instruction class, it is then possible to develop the execution time for an average instruction. Figure 1 shows such a Gibson Mix computation for a fairly representative non-IBM computer system from the early 1970s.

Fig. 1
Deriving MIPS from a Gibson Mix
For a 1970-Vintage Supermini

Instruction Category	Gibson Mix %	cpi	Weighted cpi
Load/Store	31.2	1.9	0.593
Add/Subtract	6.1	1.8	0.110
Multiply	0.6	10	0.060
Divide	0.2	18	0.036
Floating Add/Subtract	6.9	4	0.276
Floating Multiply	3.8	10	0.380
Floating Divide	1.5	18	0.270
Search/Compare	3.8	2	0.076
Test/Branch	16.6	1	0.166
Shift	4.4	2.8	0.123
Logical	1.6	1.3	0.021
No Memory Reference	5.3	1	0.053
Indexing	18.0	0	0.000
Cycles per average instruction (cpai) =			2.164

$$\text{MIPS} = 1 / (\text{cpai} \times \text{cycle time in us})$$
$$= 1 / (2.164 \times 0.6)$$
$$= 0.77$$

Source: O. Serlin, except mix % data: J.C. Gibson (see note 3).

Representative of the many other notable attempts at deriving performance figures based on instruction tracing was the one done in 1963 by Kenneth E. Knight on the IBM 704 and 7090 "scientific" and 705 "commercial" computers (see *Datamation*, September 1966, pp. 40-54). Knight computed his measure for 225 systems introduced between 1944 and 1963; but he was principally interested in quantifying technological change, rather than in accurate characterization of the performance of individual machines relative to each other.

At least three important recent architectures have been characterized by instruction frequencies obtained by tracing. Figures 2, 3, and 4 give the results for the IBM System/370, DEC VAX 11/780, and the Motorola 68000 family.

Fig. 2

System/370 Ten Most Frequent Instructions

Instruction		% Executions
BC -	Branch on Condition	20.2
L -	Load	15.5
TM -	Test under Mask	6.1
ST -	Store	5.9
LR -	Load Register	4.7
LA -	Load Address	4.0
LTR-	Test Register	3.8
BCR-	Branch on Register	2.9
MVC-	Move Characters	2.1
LH -	Load Halfword	1.8

Source: *IBM RT PC Computer Technology*, IBM Form No. SA23-1057, 1986, p. 81.

The chief advantage of the mix-based MIPS calculation was its simplicity. MIPS could be readily calculated from published instruction execution times, if one assumed Gibson's frequency data was correct for the specific target machine. The key drawback of the method was that this was rarely a correct assumption.

MIPS figures are useful only for comparisons among members of the same architectural family; they cannot be relied upon to compare systems which are architecturally substantially different. The following examples illustrate this point.

Some of the subtleties and difficulties involved in mix-based MIPS calculation can be seen by examining Figs. 1-4. For example, Gibson had provided a significant category for *indexing instructions* (e.g., "add 1 to index register 3"), which were popular on some computers in the late 1950s. Such instructions are not needed by most modern architectures, which permit any register to be used in indexing operations. Note in Figure 1 that the indexing category is weighted at zero, because the particular supermini involved (an SEL 86) had no indexing instructions, and entailed no indexing time penalty.

Fig. 3
DEC VAX 11/780 Instruction Frequencies

Group Name	Types	Frequency %
SIMPLE		83.60
	Move instructions, simple arithmetic operations, boolean operations, simple & loop branches, subroutine call & return.	
FIELD		6.92
	Bit field operations	
FLOAT		3.62
	Floating point operations, integer multiply & divide	
CALL/RETURN		3.22
	Procedure call & return; multiple register push & pop	
SYSTEM		2.11
	Privileged operations, context switch, system services, request & return, queue manipulation, protection probe instructions	
CHARACTER		0.43
	Character & string instructions	
DECIMAL		0.03
	Decimal instructions	

Source: Emer, J.S. & Clark, D.W.: *A Characterization of Processor Performance in the VAX 11/780*, 11th Int'l Symposium on Computer Architecture, June 1984, p. 304.

Will the real MIPS please stand?

An excellent illustration of the value of this caveat is the great "RISC vs. CISC" debate. While there is no accepted definition of the term, the general aim of RISC architectures is to obtain enhanced performance by simplifying the underlying hardware, so that it handles only a small set of (hopefully) the most-frequently-used instructions. More complex (and hopefully rare) instructions are delegated to the software; for example, the in-line "millicode" in the HP Spectrum architecture.

Fig. 4: Performance of the Motorola 68000 family

	68000	68010	68020 0% hit	68020 64% hit	68020 100% hit
Cycles/Av. Instruction	12.567	12.107	7.682	7.159	6.373
MIPS @ 8 MHz	0.64	0.66	-	-	-
MIPS @ 10 MHz	0.80	0.83	-	-	-
MIPS @ 12.5 MHz	-	1.03	1.63	1.74	1.96
MIPS @ 16.6 MHz	-	-	2.17	2.33	2.62

Hit rate is for the on-chip instruction cache.

Cycles/average instruction derived from actual instruction tracing.

Source: MacGregor, D. & Rubinstein, J.: *A Performance Analysis of MC68020-based Systems*; IEEE Micro, December 1985, pp. 55, 56.

How well a RISC machine achieves this aim can be measured by the number of clock cycles per average instruction (cpai). The ultimate goal of a RISC machine is to come as close to 1 cpai as possible; i.e., the great majority of executed instructions should take 1 clock. HP claims its Spectrum is at the 1.6-1.7 cpai level. The IBM RT PC, according to IBM published literature, averages 3 cycles per instruction. Once the cpi figure is established, MIPS can be directly calculated as 1/(cpai x us) where us = microseconds/cycle.

When comparing such RISC MIPS to those from conventional architectures, the key question is whether a given function or task at the user level translates into the same number of instructions on the two systems. The formal measure of this property is the *dynamic path length*. The information released to date is somewhat sketchy; but it seems to indicate that at least some RISC machines tend to be substantially more verbose than conventional CISC implementations. For example, there is some evidence that C programs compiled on the IBM RT PC produce 20%-40% more code than the same programs using the same compiler on the DEC VAX 11/780.

In translating *object code* from current HP3000 programs to Spectrum, an expansion factor of about 6:1 has been observed; i.e., each HP3000 instruction translates on the average into *six* Spectrum instruction. However, recompilation with native Spectrum compilers reduces the expansion factor to about 20%.

(It is also possible to run unmodified HP3000 binary code on a *simulator* running on the Spectrum. The simulator executes about 16-20 instructions for each simulated instruction. However, the simulator is said to run very nearly at 1 cpai on the 8 MHz Spectrum, achieving nearly 8 MIPS).

In making its MIPS claims for the Spectrum, HP carefully eliminated some of the verbosity sources, in order to make such claims more comparable with previous HP models and competitors' systems. Actual instruction counts were obtained by a passive (non-obtrusive) analyzer co-processor. Then these counts were reduced by accounting for Nullifies and TLB misses.

Nullifies are instances when the compiler can't find a useful instruction to stuff in the slot following a delayed branch; in such cases, a No-Op must be executed. Approximately 3-4% of all instructions fall in this category. Spectrum TLB misses are handled by software; a count of actual TLB misses is taken, and the estimated number of instructions involved in handling the miss is subtracted. Clearly, it would not be meaningful to compare MIPS from code sequences containing a great deal of No-Ops and TLB handling to code that performs the same function, but is not burdened by such excess baggage.

A third example is the Inmos Transputer, used most notably in Floating Point Systems' T-Series hypercube. Inmos claims 10 MIPS for its fastest version, while FPS claims a more modest 7.5 MIPS for a the slower version it is using. Both claims are several times higher than such leading 32-bit microprocessors as the Motorola 68020 or Intel's 386.

However, the Transputer's architecture is extremely rudimentary: it has no addressable registers at all, just a 3-level stack; and its basic instruction set features only sixteen 8-bit instructions. More complex instructions must be constructed *at run-time* using the basic set. This suggests that the Transputer's dynamic path lengths should be much greater than conventional machines', although Inmos claims this is not the case.

Furthermore, the Transputer's performance claims are based on finding all instructions and data in the 2KB on-chip memory, which is too small for realistic programs. Since the Transputer is so far programmable only in Occam, a unique language, none of the benchmarks couched in C, Pascal, Fortran, or other current languages can be run on it; so its true performance relative to conventional processors remains untested.

Synthetic Benchmarks
Well before RISC or the Transputer became hot issues, it was realized that instruction-level performance figures, such as MIPS, would always be unreliable in comparing systems whose underlying architectures are dissimilar. Furthermore, as more end-user activity became directed to high-level languages, the ability of the compiler to produce good (optimized) code became an increasingly important performance measure.

Synthetic benchmarks were developed in response to one or both of these needs. The goal is to create a simple, relatively small program that approximates the way typical applications, coded in high-level languages, behave. In particular, the synthetic benchmark is supposed to mimic the relative frequencies of the various types of high-level language statements and constructs, and the types of data structures real programs deal with, but in the framework of a manageably-small program.

Collecting dynamic execution statistics for high-level language programs is much more difficult than obtaining instruction traces, because it is generally impossible to determine language constructs from the resulting machine-level instruction sequences generated by the compiler. Hence designers of synthetic benchmarks are forced to rely on a mixture of static and dynamic data from a wide variety of sources[4]. Such benchmarks are therefore not accurate in reflecting the nature of typical programs. However, since they are cast in terms of specific programs, which are usually self-timing, they are far less subject to interpretation or "personal creativity" than are MIPS ratings.

Two of the best-known synthetic benchmarks are the Whetstone and Dhrystone programs. The Whetstone benchmark was developed in the early 1970s by Curnow and Wichman[5] at the U.K.'s National Physical Laboratory. It is based on statistics originally collected by Wichman from 949 programs compiled with the interpretive "Whetstone" Algol-60 compiler. However, its most popular implementation today is in Fortran. The program is constructed so as to represent the execution of one million "Whetstone instructions". The inverse of the measured run-time (in seconds) yields millions of Whetstone instructions per second, or simply (mega) Whetstones. A double-precision version of this benchmark merely changes the definitions of the relevant variables from single- to double-precision. The Whetstone benchmark is heavily biased towards numerical computing and floating point operations; in a general sense, it is representative of scientific and engineering applications. Some representative Whetstone ratings are shown in Figure 5.

Fig.5
KWhetstone Results, Single Precision

HP3000/930	2841.
IBM 4381-11	~2000.
DEC 11/780	1152.
HP1000/A900	1042.
MicroVAX II	877.
Sun 3/50	860.
Counterpoint	833.
Apollo 3000	780.
IBM RT PC	200.

Source: DEC: *Digital Review*, Jan. 1986, p.77; all others: company claims.

Dhrystone is a more recent benchmark, developed by Reinhold P. Weicker of Siemens, and first reported in 1984[4] as an Ada program. Dhrystone's emphasis is on the type of data and operations encountered in system, rather than numerical, programming. It contains 100 statements, of which 53 are assignment type, 32 are control statements, and 15 are procedure and function calls. C and Pascal versions also exist. Results are stated as thousands or millions of Dhrystones per second, or simply Dhrystones. Figure 6 shows a few Dhrystone results from the version distributed by AT&T's Rick Richardson, and reported by him regularly on USENET.

Fig. 6
Some Dhrystone Benchmark Results
(Best values, with registers)

IBM 3090/200	31,250*
Amdahl 5860	28,846*
HP3000/930	10,000
Alliant FX/8	7,655
DEC VAX 8600	7,142
Intel 386/16MHz	6,133
Gould PN9080	4,922*
Intel 386/12½MHz	4,794
NCR Tower 32	4,545
Sun 3/180	3,846
Celerity C1200	3,468
Pyramid 90x	3,333
HP9000/500	1,724#
IBM RT PC	1,698
DEC 11/780	1,640*
DEC MicroVAX II	1,399*
IBM PC/AT	1,388

* Version 1.1; all others Version 1.0.
\# Without registers.

Source: Rick Richardson, report of March 31, 1986; except IBM RT PC: & HP 3000/930; company claim.

A number of synthetic Cobol benchmarks have been proposed over the years. Perhaps the best known is the so-called "U.S. Steel Benchmarks"[6,] which consist of eleven "tests". They have been run on numerous systems since 1965. Results are presented as a productivity index relative to the IBM 1460; namely, the time for running the tests on the 1460 divided by the time on the tested machine. Under these tests, the IBM 3081 Model K yielded an index of 5505, while a DEC VAX 11/780 did 500.

The LINPACK benchmark

For the past several years, Jack J. Dongarra of the Argonne National Laboratory has been publishing the results of the so-called "LINPACK benchmark". LINPACK is a collection of Fortran subroutines for solving systems of linear equations. The benchmark consists of solving, in double-precision, a set of 100 such equations. Another version, which solves a set of 1,000 equations, has been recently introduced. Often used to compare the performance of supercomputers and vector processors, the benchmark has now been run on engineering workstations and even some personal computers. Results are given in terms of both LINPACK MFLOPS (millions of floating-point operations per second), and in relative terms, with the performance of the Cray 1S set at 1.0, and with faster machines registering under 1.0. Some selected LINPACK results are shown in Figure 7.

Fig. 7
Some LINPACK Results
(Best values, long precision, Fortran)

Machine	Ratio	MFLOPS
Cray XMP2 (1 proc.)*	0.50	24.
IBM 3090/200 w/VF*	1.0	12.
Cray 1S*	1.0	12.
Flt.Pt.Systs. FPS264*	2.2	5.6
Amdahl 5860 w/HSFPF	3.1	3.9
Alliant FX/8, 8 CEs*	4.9	2.5
IBM 3081K	5.7	2.1
IBM 4381 Mod 13	10.	1.2
DEC VAX 8800	12.	0.99
DEC VAX 8650	17.	0.70
HP3000/930	21.	0.57
Sun 3/160M w/FPA	30.	0.40
Celerity C1200	58.	0.21
DEC VAX 8200	80.	0.15
DEC MicroVAX II	97.	0.13
DEC 11/780 w/FPA	101.	0.13
IBM PC/AT w/80287	1054.	0.012

* Rolled BLAS.

Source: Dongarra, J.J.: *Performance of Various Computers Using Standard Linear Equations Software in a Fortran Environment;* Argonne National Laboratory Technical Memorandum No. 23, April 16, 1986. *HP 3000/930: Company claim.*

Transaction Processing

On line transaction processing (OLTP) is increasingly important in commercial applications (see Datamation, August 1, 1985, pp. 60-68). A transaction processing system maintains a typically-large database, to which multiple users at local and remote terminals have access, for both inquiries and updates. The transaction processing programs are generally small and not very demanding in terms of CPU utilization. Rather, the performance of the system is chiefly affected by the efficiency of its system and database software, I/O facilities, and communications protocols.

Performance measurements of such systems are best characterized in terms of transactions/second (tps), or tps/processor when more than one processor is available. A synthetic benchmark has been proposed[7]. This benchmark, dubbed the DebitCredit or DtCt benchmark, stipulates equivalent of 10,000 bank tellers doing an account update transaction once every 100 seconds, thus presenting the system with a load of 100 transactions/sec. The benchmark further specifies that 95% of all transactions must have a 1 second or less response time. The vendor is free to configure the lowest-cost system that will do the job, but is expected to report a cost-per-tps according to a specified formula. For less-demanding applications, the benchmark can be scaled down by reducing the number of tellers and the size of the relevant files.

Although this benchmark is hardly typical, it is the only one applicable to OLTP that has been given wide publicity to date. Several manufacturers, including IBM, DEC, NCR, Tandem, Stratus, and several others have performed this benchmark, although not all have reported results.

Unfortunately, since the benchmark is couched in functional terms only, it is open to some interpretation; reporting of the results often does not include key parameters, such as scaling. A compact description of the benchmark, along with critical analysis of its weaknesses, and a proposed standard reporting checklist, is contained in reference 8[8].

In measuring the on-line transaction performance of its IMS system, IBM has been using a standard workload developed in the late 1970s, based on GUIDE and SHARE user group surveys of IMS customer workloads. It represents an order entry and inventory control application. A subset of this workload has also been used to measure the transaction throughput of the relational database system, DB2. Performance measurements for both IMS and DB2 take place at the Santa Teresa Lab in San Jose, CA. Some DB2 measurements have been reported in reference 9[9].

Caveat Emptor
Measuring computer power is objectively difficult, and, due to competitive market pressures, politically explosive. It is, perhaps, futile to expect vendors to reveal how they derive their performance claims. Users should, whenever possible, test performance under loads that represent their typical applications; and employ wall-clock (stop-watch),

rather than internal timing. Users should insist that any benchmark results supplied by vendors or third parties should include complete environmental specifications, and complete specifications of the benchmark's version (an actual listing of the program would not be amiss).

Computer suppliers, like car manufacturers, should qualify all performance claims with a caveat of some sort. IBM already leads the way; some of its performance publications now carry the disclaimer, "Performance data determined by IBM in a controlled environment. Results obtained in other environments may vary significantly".

Footnotes and References

1. John von Neumann and his collaborator Herman Goldstine wrote about instruction frequency counts in technical reports they published in 1947-1948.

2. Industry gadfly Dr. Herbert R.J. Grosch informally stated his "law" in the 1950s as "proof" that large-scale systems were more cost effective than smaller, distributed systems. The law stated that a computer's performance is proportional to the square of its price; i.e., for double the price, a user should be able to get a system with four times the power. The debate about Grosch's Law raged on in the 1960s, until advancing VLSI technology made distributed processing (and later, personal computing) widely accepted. Even now the debate refuses to die; see *Grosch's Law Revisited* by Philip Ein-Dor (CACM, February 1985, pp. 142-151).

3. While the Gibson Mix was never published in the trade or professional press, I remember from first-hand knowledge that Gibson Mix data was already industry lore around 1964. Years later, Gibson did publish a 4-page, internal IBM Technical Report (TR-00.2043, June 18, 1970), which documented the mix data and gave a very terse description of the traces done on the IBM 704 and 650 machines in 1959, from which the mix was derived.

4. Weicker, Reinhold P.: *Dhrystone: A Synthetic Systems Programming Benchmark*, CACM, October, 1984, pp 1013-1090.

5. Curnow, H.J., & Wichman, B.A.: *A Synthetic Benchmark*, Computer Journal, February 1976, pp. 43-49. Whetstone (Leicester, U.K.) was the site of the English Electric Co.'s Atomic Power Division, where the interpretive Algol-60 compiler for the English Electric KDF9 computer was developed in the early 1960s. Interpreters for the Whetstone compiler were developed for three other British computers as well. Such interpreters made it possible for Wichman to collect run-time statistics on the frequencies of the various Algol constructs from 949 programs; that data was used as the model for the Whetstone benchmark.

6. Now called the Cobol Analysis System, and available through G.E. McKinzie, 1509 Muriel St., Pittsburgh, PA 15203.

7. See Anon et. al., *A Measure of Transaction Processing Power*, Datamation, April 1, 1985, pp. 112-118.

8. See *FT Systems* Newsletter, No. 47, July 1986, pp. 2-8. The publication is available from ITOM International Co., POB 1450, Los Altos, CA 94023.

9. See *InfoDB*, Summer, 1986 (Vol. 1, No. 2). The publication is available from Colin J. White Consulting, POB 20651, San Jose, CA 95160.

A reduced instruction set computer, RISC I, was compared to five traditional machines.

It provided the highest performance with the smallest penalty for using high-level language.

Assessing RISCs in High-Level Language Support

David A. Patterson and Richard S. Piepho*

University of California, Berkeley

Computer designers today generally increase the complexity of architectures commensurate with the increasing capabilities of implementation technologies. Negative consequences of such complexity are increased design time, more design errors, inconsistent implementations, and the delay in implementation typical of single-chip designs.[1] The class of computers characterized by this architectural complexity we call CISCs—complex instruction set computers. In this article, we will contrast CISCs to another class of computers we call RISCs—reduced instruction set computers. Examples of RISCs are the 801[2] at IBM, RISC I[3] at the University of California, Berkeley, and the MIPS machine[4] at Stanford; examples of CISCs are the DEC VAX-11[5] and the Intel iAPX-432.[6] Discussions arguing the merits of each style of design are found elsewhere.[1,7,8] Fairclough, apparently unaware of other work in the area, recently published evidence to support RISCs.[9]

Preliminary results from the RISC project at Berkeley are very encouraging. The design of RISC I began in spring 1980 and was completed in spring 1981. After we specified the architecture, we developed a C compiler, an optimizer, an assembler, a linker, and a simulator, and we designed a NMOS single-chip VLSI microprocessor.

The reduced instruction set had its most visible impact on the amount of control logic: It dropped by a factor of

*Richard S. Piepho is now with Bell Laboratories, Naperville, Illinois.

An earlier version of this article, entitled ''RISC Assessment: A High-Level Language Experiment,'' was presented at the *Ninth Annual Symposium on Computer Architecture*, April 1982, in Austin, Texas.

10.[10,11] The chip area saved by the simplicity of the control circuitry was devoted to a large set of 32-bit registers. The register file was partitioned in a way that allows a new set of registers to be allocated for each procedure call, thus avoiding the overhead of saving registers in memory. By giving memory addresses to these registers, and by overlapping sequential sets of registers, compilers can easily allocate local variables and parameters in registers.

Support for HLL

Computer architects agree on the need to support HLLs—high-level languages. Indeed, nearly every new architecture in the last five years has claimed that it was designed with HLLs in mind.[5,6,12,13,14] There is widespread disagreement, however, on the best way to provide HLL support.

Traditional architecture support for HLLs ranges from a simple stack pointer to direct execution of the source HLL program. Rather than define a HLL computer in terms of implementation, we define it in terms of its characteristics. An *HLL computer system*[15] (1) discovers and reports errors in terms of the HLL source program, and (2) does not have any outward appearance of transformations from the user programming language into internal languages. Its only important property is that the programmer is always interacting with the computer in terms of a high-level language. Thus it makes no difference to the user of a high-level language computer system whether that system is implemented with a CISC that maps one-to-one with the tokens of the language, or

Reprinted from *IEEE Micro*, November 1982, pages 9-18. Copyright © 1982 by The Institute of Electrical and Electronics Engineers, Inc.

if HLL support is provided largely by software on a very fast but simple machine.

A measure of the "quality" of an HLL computer system is the ratio of the execution time of programs written in the lowest-level language (usually assembly language) to the execution time of the same programs written in the HLL. This ratio is called the HLLESF—the HLL execution support factor.[15] A computer system with an HLLESF close to zero penalizes the use of an HLL, whereas a computer system with an HLLESF close to one does not reward the use of assembly language.

This article presents an informal experiment we conducted to determine whether RISCs or CISCs are better architectures for an HLL. Our hypothesis was that RISCs could provide as good an HLL environment as CISCs. We used two metrics to compare benchmark programs on a RISC with those on various CISCs. The first metric was simply performance—the speed at which the machines ran a set of HLL benchmarks. The second metric examined the penalty for using an HLL on a given machine—it is the HLLESF discussed above. We chose 11 benchmark programs and six computers for the experiment.

The HLL benchmark programs were compiled using the same compiler technology. Table 1 shows the absolute performance of the eleven HLL benchmarks on three minicomputers and three microprocessors. For the MC68000 and RISC I, we derived *predicted* performances through simulation, since at the time of the experiment we did not have working hardware for these two microprocessors. The 7.5-MHz RISC I microprocessor not only ran an average of two to four times faster than the other microprocessors and minicomputers, but of the 55 combinations of 11 programs with five machines, only one combination was faster than or equal to a 7.5-MHz RISC I.

We obtained the HLLESF by recoding the HLL benchmarks into assembly language and then comparing the performance of the HLL programs to that of the assembly programs. Machines penalizing an HLL the most will execute assembly language programs in much less time

than the HLL versions of those same programs; hence, the machines in Table 2 with HLLESFs closest to zero have the highest HLL penalties. This table suggests that there is significantly more reason to discard HLLs in the five traditional computers than in RISC I.

The results shown in Tables 1 and 2 indicate that a 7.5-MHz RISC I has the best absolute HLL performance and does the most to encourage the use of HLLs. These results, especially when combined with reduced design time, are a powerful argument that new architectures intended to be programmed in HLLs should follow the path of RISCs.

Conditions of the experiment

Since compiler technology affects the HLLESF, and since both compiler technology and hardware implementation technology affect absolute performance, the ideal experiment would vary only the architecture. As a result, we wanted to run a common set of benchmarks using a single compiler and programming language, to produce code for a variety of computer architectures in a given implementation technology. There were five variables in our experiment:

(1) benchmark programs,
(2) programming language,
(3) compiler technology,
(4) computer architecture, and
(5) implementation technology.

The sections below give our rationale for the decisions made in the experiment.

Benchmarks. We needed benchmarks coded in both an HLL and an assembly language for a variety of architectures. One common set of benchmarks is the Computer Family Architecture (CFA) Benchmarks.[16] In 1975, the

Table 1.
C benchmarks—7.5-MHz RISC I execution times and performance ratios.

BENCHMARK	RISC I 7.5 MHz msecs	68000 10 MHz	Z8002 6 MHz	VAX-11/780 5 MHz	11/70 7.5 MHz	C/70 7.4 MHz
		NUMBER OF TIMES SLOWER THAN 7.5-MHz RISC I				
E—STRING SEARCH	0.46	2.8	1.6	1.3	0.9	2.2
F—BIT TEST	0.06	4.8	7.2	4.8	6.2	9.2
H—LINKED LIST	0.10	1.6	2.4	1.2	1.9	2.5
K—BIT MATRIX	0.43	4.0	5.2	3.0	4.0	9.3
I—QUICKSORT	50.4	4.1	5.2	3.0	3.6	5.8
ACKERMANN (3,6)	3200	—	2.8	1.6	1.6	—
RECURSIVE QSORT	800	—	5.9	2.3	3.2	1.3
PUZZLE (SUBSCRIPT)	4700	—	4.2	2.0	1.6	3.4
PUZZLE (POINTER)	3200	4.2	2.3	1.3	2.0	2.1
SED (BATCH EDITOR)	5100	—	4.4	1.1	1.1	2.6
TOWERS HANOI (18)	6800	—	4.2	1.8	2.3	1.6
AVG. ±STD. DEV.		3.5±1.8	4.1±1.8	2.1±1.1	2.6±1.5	4.0±2.8

Army/Navy Computer Family Architecture Committee established a set of criteria to measure computer architectures.[17] They hoped to determine the criteria under which a commercial computer architecture could be evaluated for possible selection as a standard military computer.

The committee selected 12 programs as representative of frequent, "real-world" routines. These programs manipulate character, integer, and floating-point data, and also test interrupt handling and addressing modes.

A recent performance study, reported in the April 1, 1981 issue of *Electronic Design News* (*EDN*),[18] utilized the CFA benchmarks. The authors' goal was to have a fair set of criteria for selecting the best of the 16-bit microprocessors on the market. They presented the results of running a subset of the original benchmarks on the leading 16-bit machines.

Seven benchmarks (labeled A, B, E, F, H, K, and I in the CFA committee report) were coded by the individual manufacturers and run. An independent arbitrator, Hemmenway and Associates, confirmed the correctness of the routines and timing information. Five of the 12 original CFA benchmarks were omitted from the *EDN* study due to the lack of virtual memory (C and L) and floating-point arithmetic (D, G, and J). We further reduce the number of the benchmarks in our experiment by leaving out benchmarks A (I/O interrupt kernel) and B (I/O interrupt with FIFO processing), because of the difficulty of writing them in an HLL. Therefore, benchmark E (string search), benchmark F (bit test, set, and reset), benchmark H (linked-list insertion), benchmark I (quicksort), and benchmark K (bit matrix transposition) define our benchmark set. The sections below briefly describe each benchmark.[16,18]

String Search (E) examines a long character string for the first occurrence of a substring. If the search is successful, the procedure returns the substring's starting position. Otherwise the procedure returns a "not found" indicator. The starting addresses and the lengths of the string and substring are passed as parameters to the benchmark. This benchmark exercises an architecture's ability to move through character strings sequentially.

Bit test, set, and reset (F) tests, sets, or resets a bit within a tightly packed bit string beginning at a word boundary. A function code passed to the routine selects the operation performed. The base address of the bit string and the bit number are also passed as parameters to the benchmark. This benchmark tests, sets, and then resets three bits. It checks an architecture's bit-manipulation capabilities.

Linked-list insertion (H) inserts five new entries into a doubly linked list. The field length of each entry is 32 bits; the size of the forward and backward pointers depends on the architecture's addressing range. The address of a block of control information, and the address of the entry to be inserted, are passed as parameters. This benchmark tests pointer manipulation.

Quicksort (I) performs a nonrecursive quicksort algorithm on a large vector of fixed-length records. Unlike the original algorithm developed by C. A. R. Hoare, this one contains no procedure calls. The point at which the quicksort algorithm degrades into a simple insertion sort is passed as a parameter to the benchmark. The number of records and the starting address of the array are also passed to the benchmark. It thoroughly tests an architecture's addressing modes and character and stack manipulation capabilities.

Bit matrix transposition (K) takes a tightly packed, square bit matrix and transposes it. The matrix is of variable size and starts on a word boundary. However, the starting bit of the matrix within the first byte of the word is variable and is passed as a parameter to the benchmark. The size and starting byte address of the matrix are also passed as parameters to the benchmark. This benchmark exercises an architecture's bit manipulation and looping capabilities.

EDN published the assembly language version of each benchmark for each manufacturer. Since the results of this study could have influenced the sales of products, we were confident that each manufacturer had provided a highly tuned assembly language routine. To calculate the HLLESF,[19] we coded these benchmarks in an HLL—the C language—and recorded the execution speeds of the two versions.

The CFA benchmarks, however, lack tests for procedure call mechanisms. Recent studies on several architectures show that one out of every 20 executed instructions is a procedure call or return,[20,21,22] accounting for as much as 40 percent of execution time.[23,24,25] Hence, we also selected a set of programs more typical of the way HLLs are used in standard programming practice. This set of benchmarks includes Puzzle, Ackermann's Function, SED (a stream editor), Qsort (a sorting program), and Towers of Hanoi. All but the first program were written originally on the PDP-11/70. Ackermann's Function and Towers of Hanoi are well-known simple programs, but the others deserve further discussion.

Forest Baskett developed Puzzle, a recursive bin-packing program that solves a three-dimensional puzzle. He believes that the execution profile of this program typifies most HLL programs.[26] It has been written in several languages and has been run on several computers. Qsort is a *recursive* quicksort program frequently used in Unix. This version sorts 2600 fixed-length character strings. SED is a stream-oriented text editor that is one of the Unix software tools. It copies input files to the standard output after they have been edited according to a script of commands.

**Table 2.
HLLESF—ratio of assembly execution time to HLL execution time.**

BENCHMARK	RISC I	68000	Z8002	VAX-11/780	11/70
E—STRING SEARCH	0.62	0.17	0.32	0.23	0.53
F—BIT TEST	1.00	0.23	0.27	0.34	0.50
H—LINKED LIST	1.00	0.92	0.96	0.88	0.83
K—BIT MATRIX	0.94	0.21	0.29	0.34	0.24
I—QUICKSORT	0.92	0.16	0.44	0.47	—
AVERAGE ± STD. DEV.	0.9±0.1	0.3±0.3	0.5±0.3	0.4±0.2	0.5±0.2

A reduced instruction set

David A. Patterson

The philosophy of the reduced instruction set is to provide a very small set of very fast instructions and to rely on the compiler to produce optimized instruction sequences. Such instruction sets bring to mind early computers and vertical microprogrammed machines.

The RISC I architecture has 31 instructions, most of which do simple ALU and shift operations on registers. Instructions, data, addresses, and registers are 32 bits wide. The execution time of a RISC I cycle is given by the time it takes to read and add two registers and then store the result back into a register. The global register 0, which always contains zero, allows us to synthesize a variety of operations and addressing modes.

Table 1.
Synthesizing addressing modes.

ADDRESSING	RISC I	VAX EQUIVALENT
REGISTER	Rs	Rs
IMMEDIATE	S2 (13-bit literal)	#literal
INDEXED	Rx + S2 (13-bit displacement)	Rx + displ
ABSOLUTE	r0 + S2 (r0≡0)	@#address
REG INDIRECT	Rx + 0	(Rx)

Table 2.
Synthesizing VAX instructions.

OPERATION	VAX		RISC I EQUIVALENT	
REG-REG MOVE	movl	Rm,Rn	add	r0,Rm,Rn (r0≡0)
COMPARE	cmpl	Rm,Rn	sub	Rm,Rn,r0{c}
CLEAR	clrl	Rn	add	r0,r0,Rn
INCREMENT	incl	Rn	add	Rn,#1,Rn

Load and store instructions move data between registers and memory. Rather than lengthen the general cycle to permit a complete memory access, these instructions use two CPU cycles. There are eight variations of memory access instructions to accommodate sign-extended or zero-extended eight-bit, 16-bit, and 32-bit data. Although only the *index plus displacement* addressing mode appears to be included in data transfer instructions, *absolute* and *register indirect* addressing can be synthesized using register 0. (The last two entries in Table 1 show how this is done; the rest of the table shows how other addressing modes are synthesized.) Branch instructions include call, return, and conditional and unconditional jump. Most of the innovative features of RISC I are found in call and return; they will be discussed later. Figure 1 shows the 32-bit format used by register-to-register and memory access instructions.

For register-to-register instructions, DEST selects one of the 32 registers as the destination of the result of the operation performed on the registers specified by SOURCE1 and SOURCE2. If IMM (immediate) = 0, the low-order five bits of SOURCE2 specify another register; if IMM = 1, SOURCE2 expresses a sign-extended 13-bit constant. The frequency of integer constants in HLL programs suggests architectural support, so immediate operands are available in every instruction. SCC determines whether the condition codes are set. Memory access instructions use SOURCE1 to specify the index register and SOURCE2 to specify the offset. One other format combines the last three fields to form a 19-bit PC-relative address, and is used primarily by the branch instructions.

The examples in Table 2 show that many important VAX instructions can be synthesized from simple RISC I addressing modes and opcodes.

Procedure calls are time-consuming in typical high-level language programs. Potentially, RISC programs

Table 3.
Assembly programs for the VAX and the RISC I.

LINE NO.	VAX-11 (VARIABLES IN VAX MEMORY)		VAX-11 (VARIABLES IN VAX REGISTERS)		RISC I (r0≡0)	
1		moval _String, −4(fp)		moval _String,r9		add r0,#String,r28
2		clrl −8(fp)		clrl r8		add r0,r0,r27
3	L49:	movl −4(fp),r0			L49:	ldbs 0(r28),r6
4*		incl −4(fp)				add* r28,#1,r28
5		cmpb 8(ap),(r0)	L49:	cmpb r10,(r9)+		sub r29,r6,r0,{c}
6		jneq L50		jneq L50		jmpr* ne,L50
7		incl −8(fp)		incl r8		add r27,#1,r27
8	L50:	sobgeq 4(ap),L49	L50:	sobgeq r11,L49	L50:	sub r30,#1,r30,{c}
9						jmpr ge,L49

*The *delayed jump* of RISC I actually requires moving the add on line 4 below the jump on line 6. For more information, see Patterson and Séquin,[3] p. 13.

may have even more calls, because the complex instructions found in CISCs are subroutines in RISCs. Thus, the procedure call must be as fast as possible, perhaps no longer than a few jumps. Because of its *register window* scheme, RISC I comes close to this goal.

Using procedures involves two groups of time-consuming operations: saving or restoring registers on each call or return, and passing parameters and results to and from the procedure. In RISC I each procedure call results in the allocation of a new "window" of registers from the large register file, for use by the new procedure. The return just resets a pointer, restoring the old set. In addition, some of the registers are not saved or restored on each procedure call. These registers (r0 through r9) are called *global* registers.

Furthermore, the sets of registers used by different procedures are overlapped to allow parameters to be passed in registers. In other machines, parameters are usually passed on the stack, with the calling procedure using a register (frame pointer) to point to the beginning of the parameters (and also to the end of the locals). Thus, all references to parameters are indexed references to memory. The RISC approach is to partition the set of window registers (10-31) into the three parts defined by their respective overlap. Figure 2 shows this overlapped register window scheme.

Registers 26 through 31 (HIGH) contain parameters passed from "above" the current procedure, that is, from the calling procedure. Registers 16 through 25 (LOCAL) are used for local scalar storage. Registers 10 through 15 (LOW) are used for temporaries and parameters passed to the procedure "below" the current procedure (the called procedure). On each procedure call a new set of registers, numbered 10-31, is allocated. The LOW registers of the "caller" become the HIGH registers of the "callee" because of the hardware overlap between subsequent register windows. Thus, without the moving of any information, parameters in registers 10-15 appear in registers 25-31 of the called window. Figure 2 illustrates this approach for the case in which procedure A calls procedure B, which in turn calls procedure C.

If the nesting depth is sufficiently large, all register windows will be used. RISC I handles such overflow (as well as underflow) with a separate stack in memory, by trapping to a software routine that adjusts that stack. Because this routine can save or restore several sets of registers, the overflow/underflow frequency is based on the local variations in the depth of the stack rather than on the absolute depth. The effectiveness of this scheme depends on the relative frequency of overflows and underflows. Studies show that with eight register banks, overflow will occur in less than one percent of the calls. This suggests that programs exhibit locality in the dynamic nesting of procedures just as they exhibit locality in memory references.

Table 3 compares a VAX-11 assembly language program to its RISC I equivalent. The program counts the number of occurrences of a character in a string. There are two versions of the VAX-11 program; one is used with local variables allocated in memory, the other with them allocated in registers. The window register architecture of RISC I makes registers the natural depository of variables. The VAX depends on the programmer and compiler writer to be ingenious enough to use registers.

For more information on RISC I, see "A VLSI RISC" in the September 1982 issue of *Computer,* pages 8-21.

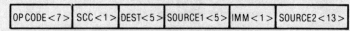

Figure 1. RISC I basic instruction format.

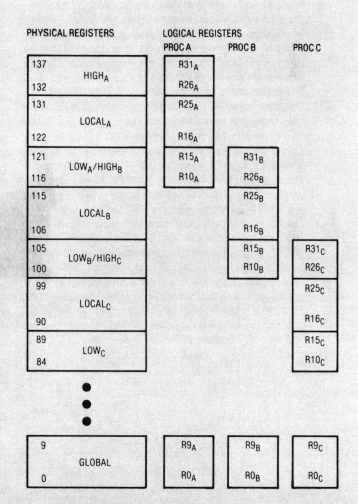

Figure 2. Use of three overlapped register windows.

The frequency of procedure calls plus returns in these programs varies from one in five instructions in Qsort to one in 235 in Puzzle. We used these five programs plus the subset of the CFA benchmarks discussed previously to estimate the performance of HLL programs executing on the machines in our experiment.

Programming language/compiler technology. To our knowledge, no compiler has been targeted to as many computer architectures as PCC—Johnson's Portable C Compiler.[27] A two-pass compiler with table-driven syntax analysis and code generation, it has been targeted to mainframes (IBM 370, Honeywell 6000, Univac 1110), minicomputers (VAX-11, PDP-11, BBN C/70), and microcomputers (Ii8085, Z8000, MC68000, Bellmac-32, RISC I). The first pass, identical in each version of this compiler, parses the C code and builds the symbol table. The second pass generates code according to table-driven algorithms, so only the tables are changed in each version. In each case, a simple peephole optimizer improves the code sequences and removes jump-to-jumps. Thus, saying that our experiment used the same compiler technology means that every version of the compiler used the same algorithms and that most of the code in each version was identical. One intangible was that different people built the compiler tables for each machine. We believed that their skills were roughly equal and that in any case the results were not biased in favor of RISC I.

An interesting question is how much performance is penalized to achieve portability. If the penalty is large, then perhaps PCC does not provide a fair evaluation of an architecture. DEC has recently announced a highly optimizing VMS C compiler written especially for the VAX family.[28] Robert Henry took the optimized assembly language output of the VMS C compiler, converted it to Unix assembler format, and timed the routines on the VAX-11/780 under Unix.[29] Table 3 presents the results for several programs that were compiled and executed using both the Unix PCC and the VMS C compilers. The VMS C compiler does an excellent job for loops with fixed bounds and allocates registers on the basis of common subexpression analysis. For large procedures, this combination produces excellent code, such as the subscripted version of the Puzzle program. PCC relies on register declaration to allocate registers, which can lead to slightly better performance, as in the pointer version of the Puzzle program. The exception is Towers of Hanoi, where the VMS C compiler uses more registers than PCC. Unfortunately, saving and restoring registers on the VAX-11/780 is fairly slow. Thus, the savings gained from more efficient execution between procedure calls is swamped by the extra overhead of saving registers. From Table 3 we conclude that PCC is a satisfactory C compiler for the VAX.

Although the popularity of C is on the rise, some critics maintain that it is a low-level programming language. If you don't share our opinion that C is a reasonable HLL, then you must believe that the HLLESF of C serves as an upper bound, since the HLLESF of a "real" HLL would be lower.

Architecture/implementation technology. We wanted to compare RISC I with a set of popular minicomputers and microprocessors. Unfortunately, implementations of these computers in the same technology do not exist. Thus, we do not distinguish architecture from implementation; one must consider the advantages arising from implementation technology when comparing performance.

The minicomputers we tested were the VAX-11/780, a 32-bit Schottky-TTL machine with a 200-nanosecond microcycle time; the PDP-11/70, a 16-bit Schottky-TTL machine with a 135-nanosecond cycle time; and the Bolt Beranek and Newman C/70, a 20-bit Schottky-TTL machine with a 150-nanosecond microcycle time. Both the VAX and PDP-11 have a cache. The VAX-11/780 and PDP-11/70 dominate today's minicomputer market. Digital Equipment Corporation specifies the VAX as being one or two times more powerful than the 11/70. The C/70 is a newly announced microcoded machine optimized for the execution of C. BBN claims the same performance for the C/70 as that of the PDP-11/70.

We also tested three microprocessors: the Zilog Z8002 and, via simulators, the Motorola MC68000 and RISC I. RISC I, a 32-bit machine with 32-bit addresses, uses NMOS technology almost at the same state of the art as that used by the Z8002 and MC68000. The transistor count is 17,500 for the Z8002, 45,000 for RISC I, and 68,000 for the MC68000. The Z8002 uses the smallest silicon area and RISC I the largest. The Z8002 is a 16-bit computer with 16-bit addresses, whereas the MC68000 works effectively as either a 16-bit or 32-bit machine with 24-bit addresses. Both the MC68000 and Z8002 come with a variety of clock rates. A 10-MHz MC68000 and a six-MHz Z8002 were used in the *EDN* study. We designed RISC I to run at 400 nanoseconds per instruction, implying a memory of the same speed at the 10-MHz MC68000, which can access memory in four clock ticks.

As mentioned above, C is a language of demonstrated portability. When moving it to a new architecture, the compiler writer must decide how many characters to fit into an integer variable. There are four characters per integer in the VAX, RISC I, and MC68000 versions of C, and two characters per integer in the C/70 and Z8002 versions. C also uses the default integer size to hold addresses. The small size of the C benchmark programs does not tax the limits of a 16-bit address space, and thus

**Table 3.
C benchmarks on the VAX-11/780—
VMS C compiler vs. Unix PCC.**

BENCHMARK	VMS C	UNIX PCC	VMS/UNIX (NUMBER OF TIMES SLOWER THAN UNIX)
ACKERMANN (3,6)	5750	5750	1.00
RECURSIVE QSORT	1750	2000	0.86
PUZZLE (SUBSCRIPT)	5650	10900	0.52
PUZZLE (POINTER)	4700	4750	1.01
SED (BATCH EDITOR)	6300	5850	1.08
TOWERS HANOI (18)	16050	12250	1.31
AVG. ± STD. DEV.	—	—	1.0 ± 0.2

smaller-word machines should enjoy a slight performance advantage, since with narrower data paths signals need not propagate as far. This advantage is strongest in VLSI implementations.

Running the experiment

To derive the two metrics, we ran the experiment several times, making adjustments as we went to give the various machines the "benefit of the doubt." Hence, each performance figure in Tables 1 and 2 are the best of several we obtained. Some of the results of the earlier runs, and the adjustments we made in response to them, are discussed below.

VAX. The C version of benchmark F on the VAX at first took 40 percent longer than the time indicated in Table 1. On examining the code, we found a patch to the compiler that was not allocating characters in registers. This patch was made because the allocation of characters in registers frequently leads to poorer performance on the VAX-11/780. We "corrected" the code for F and K, but the correction made no difference in the execution time of K.

MC68000. The architecture of the MC68000 spans the 32-bit *and* the 16-bit worlds. Our C compiler treats it as a 32-bit computer, while the assembly language programmer uses 32-bit data only when it improves performance. Thus, the HLLESF for the MC68000 may have been higher if our C compiler had used it strictly as a 16-bit computer. The simulated runs of the benchmarks on the MC68000 yielded execution times that were at first 15 percent slower than the times shown in the tables. The compiler for the MC68000 was the only one lacking an optimizer, so we estimated the performance improvement an optimizer would have provided by measuring the performance of the other five machines with and without optimization. The average improvement was 11 percent, but we picked 15 percent to give the "MC68000 optimizer" the benefit of the doubt.

Z8002. We measured the benchmarks on a four-MHz version of the Z8002 and got execution times 50 percent higher than what now shows in Table 1. Because we wanted a performance figure for a six-MHz Z8002 (as was used in the *EDN* study) instead of a four-MHz one, we reduced the measured execution time by 33 percent.

C/70. Although the C/70 does have a C compiler with a traditional assembly-language level, we excluded it from the HLLESF calculations simply because the manufacturer did not supply documentation of this level. The 10-bit bytes of the C/70 introduced problems with the C coding of benchmarks F (bit test, set, and reset) and K (bit matrix transposition). The shifts used to divide by eight in these benchmarks had to be replaced with actual divides by 10. Dividing is obviously much slower than shifting. If we assume that the C/70 can execute these two programs as fast as the 11/70, the average ratio of its performance to that of a 7.5-MHz RISC I drops from the 4.0 indicated in Table 1 to 3.2.

Questions raised by the RISC concept

The presentation of the RISC concept has led to many stimulating discussions with our coworkers and colleagues. Here, we present a brief review of the most popular topics.

Compilers. A comparison of the assembly language manual for the MC6800 to that for the MC68000, and of the manual for the PDP-11 to that for the VAX-11, shows an obvious increase in the "level" of the architecture. Concepts in HLLs become instructions in the new machines, e.g., CASE and CALL.

One would expect a CISC to have better HLL performance than a RISC, and thus it should be easier to write compilers for a CISC than for a RISC. A recent paper by Wulf[30] helps explain why neither statement is true. He considers compiling essentially a large "case analysis." The more *ways* to do something (the more instructions and addressing modes), the more cases we must consider. Since the compiler writer must balance the speed of the compiler with his desire to get good code, he may not have the time to perform the case analysis needed to generate all of the CISC instructions. Wulf further says that this trend towards "higher-level" assembly language, while commendable, may not be useful because a clash between the semantics of a HLL and the semantics of an instruction may render the instruction unusable. He argues that architectures should provide primitives rather than "solutions."

During the development of the RISC I compiler, we often observed that the task was not difficult, even though the instruction set was at a "lower level." This illustrates Wulf's recommendation that architectures provide either one way or every way to perform an operation. In RISC I we took the former approach. There are few choices in RISC I; for example, if an operand is in memory it must be loaded into a register. Simple case analysis implies a simple compiler, even if more instructions must be generated in each case.

Applicability to other HLLs. Studies of other algorithmic HLLs[31,32,] disclose the most frequently executed operations as the same simple HLL constructs found in C, for which RISC I has been optimized. Unless an HLL significantly changes the way people program, we expect to see similar results with any HLL. In the case of languages with unusual data types, such as Cobol, we need to find the simple operations used repeatedly in that environment and incorporate them into a RISC. Even if Cobol does not map efficiently onto the RISC I architecture, we believe the reduced instruction set philosophy can lead to an effective Cobol RISC.

Registers vs. a reduced instruction set. One reason for the good performance of RISC I is its overlapped register sets. Perhaps the instruction set is not even a first-order consideration!

We certainly agree that a significant portion of RISC I's speed is due to its overlapped register windows. RISC I's small amount of control logic (only six percent of the total circuitry on the chip, compared to the 50 percent typical of CISCs) created room for register windows—a key point in this discussion. Furthermore, the simplicity of control in RISC I rendered microprogramming unnecessary; this in turn eliminated the control loop—frequently the most critical timing path in microprogrammed machines—as the determining factor of the machine cycle. Moreover, any argument suggesting that instruction sets are not a primary performance factor is an argument for designing architectures that allow easy and efficient implementation—i.e., RISCs.

Virtual memory/protection. Our comparison of the six computers was somewhat unfair in that only the VAX provides a virtual address space that is larger than the physical address space. Given that RISC I doesn't provide the same function, perhaps RISC I should be considered in another class. Furthermore, RISC I provides no protection.

What about adding virtual memory capability to RISC I? In a virtual memory system, we first must have restartable instructions. Restarting a machine with simple instructions and addressing modes is quite easy, and RISC I is restartable. By how much would a virtual memory capability slow RISC I down? To find an accurate answer to this question, we looked at solutions used by other microprocessors. National Semiconductor has announced the 16082, a memory management chip that has an address cache and that normally translates virtual addresses into physical addresses in 100 nanoseconds.[33] If we put this chip in a system with a RISC I, it would add another 100 nanoseconds to every memory access. Memory is referenced every 400 nanoseconds in a 7.5-MHz RISC I, so such a combination would reduce RISC performance by 25 percent. Because 80 percent to 90 percent of memory references in RISC I are to instructions,[23] more sophisticated approaches, such as translating addresses only when crossing a page boundary (as is done in the VAX-11/780) or providing a virtual address cache (as is done in the Dorado[14]), would be needed to keep performance close to our goals.

Memory management subsumes protection. The most widely used computers rely on the separation of system and user states and associate protection with pages. If you believe this provides adequate security, then RISC I will suffice.

First silicon

The first RISC I was fabricated over the summer of 1981. The 44,500-transistor chip was designed in less time, with less manpower and fewer errors, than comparable CISC machines. Its original masks, for example, had only one design error. Programs first ran on a RISC I chip in the spring of 1982. Our first chips ran instructions at a clock rate of 1.5 MHz, considerably less than our projected 7.5 MHz. Even at that slow rate, however, RISC I ran programs faster than commercial microprocessors.[34] Discussions with IC professionals confirmed that a 7.5-MHz rate could be achieved with the NMOS fabrication technology we used. Hence, we have begun designing a new chip, with the goal of reaching 7.5 MHz.

Since our first implementation of RISC I was slower than planned, we feel we should wait for full-speed chips before altogether dismissing traditional architectures. Attaining expected performance on full-speed chips would certainly have been a more convincing argument for RISCs than falling short of expected performance on less than full-speed chips. However, we believe that the results from our experiment nonetheless make a strong case for the premise that the RISC I architecture can provide higher performance to HLL programs.

We attribute the lack of design errors and increased layout regularity to the simple RISC I architecture. As this was the first chip that any of us had designed, we think that inexperience (in addition to nonoptimal processing and missing CAD tools) were probably to blame for the poorer-than-expected performance.[34] As one of us stated in an earlier paper,[23]

This (7.5-MHz) estimate is both optimistic and pessimistic: optimistic in that it is unlikely that students can successfully build something that fast on their first try, and pessimistic because an experienced IC design team could build a much faster machine.

We believe the next chip will be much closer to our goals.

RISCs represent a new architectural style, one that enables designers not only to build working silicon faster than they can for CISCs, but also to obtain higher performance than CISCs. Whereas traditional machines "support" HLLs with instructions resembling HLL constructs, RISCs support HLLs with instructions that HLL compilers can use efficiently. We have performed a simple experiment to determine whether reduced or complex instruction set computers provide a better architectural base for high-level languages. We examined the support for HLLs by measuring both the absolute performance of eleven HLL programs and the performance benefits of recoding these programs by hand into assembly language. We compared the performance of six different architectures, using the same benchmarks, programming language, and compiler technology, and concluded that RISC I was the best.

Work on RISCs is by no means limited to one group of researchers. For example, John Hennessy of Stanford is investigating a pipelined RISC with software control of pipeline interlocks.[4] Many other topics remain to be investigated, such as the applicability of RISCs to HLLs like Lisp, Cobol, and Ada, the effectiveness of an operating system on RISCs (e.g., Unix), the architecture of coprocessors for RISCs (e.g., graphics, floating point), migration of software to RISCs (e.g., a 370 emulator written in a RISC machine language), and the implementation of RISCs in technologies such as CMOS, TTL, and ECL. This list surpasses the scope of one project; we hope to help industry and academia in exploring RISCy architectures. ■

Acknowledgments

The RISC project was aided by several people at Berkeley and other places. We would like to thank them all, and give special thanks to a few. Yuval Tamir created the RISC I simulator and helped with the assembly language benchmarks for RISC I and the VAX.[35] Michael Carey provided the support on the C compiler and suggestions on the measurements. More detailed information on this experiment can be found elsewhere.[19]

We would like to thank D. Clark, P. Hansen, R. Mayo, J. Ousterhout, M. Katevenis, R. Probst, C. Séquin, R. Sherburne, K. Van Dyke, and R. Wayman for their suggestions in improving this article.

The research reported in this article was supported in part by Bell Laboratories, and in part by the Department of Defense Advanced Research Projects Agency under ARPA Order No. 3803. The work was monitored by the Naval Electronic System Command under Contract No. N00039-81-K-0251.

We would also like to thank Duane Adams, Paul Losleben, and DARPA for providing the resources that allow universities to attempt projects involving high risk.

References

1. D. A. Patterson and D. R. Ditzel, "The Case for the Reduced Instruction Set Computer," *Computer Architecture News* (ACM Sigarch), Vol. 8, No. 6, Oct. 15, 1980, pp. 25-33.

2. G. Radin, "The 801 Minicomputer," *Proc. Symp. Architectural Support for Programming Languages and Operating Systems,* Mar. 1982, pp. 39-47.

3. D. A. Patterson and C. H. Séquin, "A VLSI RISC," *Computer,* Vol. 15, No. 9, Sept. 1982, pp. 8-21.

4. J. Hennessy et al., "The MIPS Machine," *Digest of Papers—Compcon Spring 82,* Feb. 1982, pp. 2-7.

5. W. D. Strecker, "VAX-11/780: A Virtual Address Extension to the DEC PDP-11 Family," *AFIPS Conf. Proc.,* Vol. 47, 1978 NCC, pp. 967-980.

6. W. W. Lattin et al., "A 32-bit VLSI Micromainframe Computer System," *Proc. IEEE Int'l Solid-State Circuits Conf.,* Feb. 1981, pp. 110-111.

7. D. W. Clark and W. D. Strecker, "Comments on 'The Case for the Reduced Instruction Set Computer'," *Computer Architecture News* (ACM Sigarch), Vol. 8, No. 6, Oct. 15, 1980, pp. 34-38.

8. R. Bernhard, "More Hardware Means Less Software," *IEEE Spectrum,* Vol. 18, No. 12, Dec. 1981, pp. 30-37.

9. D. A. Fairclough, "A Unique Microprocessor Instruction Set," *IEEE Micro,* Vol. 2, No. 2, May 1982, pp. 8-18.

10. D. T. Fitzpatrick et al., "VLSI Implementations of a Reduced Instruction Set Computer," *Proc. CMU Conf. VLSI Systems and Computations,* Oct. 1981, pp. 327-336.

11. D. T. Fitzpatrick et al., "A RISCy Approach to VLSI," *VLSI Design,* Vol. 2, No. 4, Fourth Qtr. 1981, pp. 14-20.

12. E. Stritter and T. Gunter, "A Microprocessor for a Changing World: The Motorola 68000," *Computer,* Vol. 12, No. 2, Feb. 1979, pp. 43-52.

13. B. L. Peuto, "Architecture of a New Microprocessor," *Computer,* Vol. 12, No. 2, Feb. 1979, pp. 10-21.

14. D. W. Clark, B. W. Lampson, and K. A. Pier, "The Memory System of a High-Performance Personal Comuter," *IEEE Trans. Computers,* Vol. C-30, No. 10, Oct. 1981, pp. 715-733.

15. D. R. Ditzel and D. A. Patterson, "Retrospective on High-Level Language Computer Architecture," *Proc. 7th Ann. Symp. Computer Architecture,* May 1980, pp. 97-104.

16. S. H. Fuller and W. E. Burr, "Measurement and Evaluation of Alternative Computer Architectures," *Computer,* Vol. 10, No. 10, Oct. 1977, pp. 24-35.

17. W. E. Burr, A. H. Coleman, and W. R. Smith, "Overview of the Military Computer Family Architecture Selection," *AFIPS Conf. Proc.,* Vol. 46, 1977 NCC, pp. 131-137.

18. R. G. Grappel and J. E. Hemmenway, "A Tale of Four Microprocessors: Benchmarks Quantify Performance," *Electronic Design News,* Apr. 1, 1981, pp. 179-265.

19. R. S. Piepho, "Comparative Evaluation of the RISC I Architecture via the Computer Family Architecture Benchmarks," MS degree project report, University of California, Berkeley, Aug. 1981.

20. D. Clark and H. Levy, "Measurement and Analysis of Instruction Use in the VAX-11/780," *Proc. 9th Ann. Symp. Computer Architecture,* Apr. 1982, pp. 9-17.

21. D. Ditzel and R. McLellan, "Register Allocation for Free: The C Machine Stack Cache," *Proc. Symp. Architectural Support for Programming Languages and Operating Systems,* Mar. 1982, pp. 48-56.

22. G. McDaniel, "An Analysis of a Mesa Instruction Set Using Dynamic Instruction Frequencies," *Proc. Symp. Architectural Support for Programming Languages and Operating Systems,* Mar. 1982, pp. 167-176.

23. D. A. Patterson and C. H. Séquin, "RISC I: A Reduced Instruction Set VLSI Computer," *Proc. 8th Ann. Symp. Computer Architecture,* May 1981, pp. 443-457.

24. A. Lunde, "Empirical Evaluation of Some Features of Instruction Set Processor Architecture," *Comm. ACM,* Vol. 20, No. 3, Mar. 1977, pp. 143-153.

25. B. A. Wichmann, "Ackermann's Function: A Study in the Efficiency of Calling Procedures," *BIT,* Vol. 16, No. 1, 1976, pp. 103-110.

26. F. Baskett, private communication, Nov. 1981.

27. S. C. Johnson, "A Portable Compiler: Theory and Practice," *Proc. Fifth Ann. ACM Symp. Programming Languages,* Jan. 1978, pp. 97-104.

28. P. Anklam et al., *Engineering a Compiler: VAX-11 Code Generation and Optimization,* Digital Press, Billerica, MA, 1982.

29. R. R. Henry, "Yet Another Benchmark: The VMS and UNIX C Compilers for Eight Favorite Programs on Two Different VAXes," internal working paper, University of California, Berkeley, Aug. 1982.

30. W. A. Wulf, "Compilers and Computer Architecture," *Computer,* Vol. 14, No. 7, July 1981, pp. 41-48.

31. W. C. Alexander and D. B. Wortman, "Static and Dynamic Characteristics of XPL Programs," *Computer,* Vol. 8, No. 11, Nov. 1975, pp. 41-46.

32. D. R. Ditzel, "Program Measurements on a High-Level Language Computer," *Computer,* Vol. 13, No. 8, Aug. 1980, pp. 62-72.

33. Y. Lavi et al., "16-bit Microprocessor Enters Virtual Memory Domain," *Electronics,* Apr. 24, 1980, pp. 123-129.

34. J. K. Foderaro, K. S. Van Dyke, and D. A. Patterson, "Running RISCs," *VLSI Design,* Vol. 3, No. 5, Sept./Oct. 1982, pp. 27-32.

35. Y. Tamir, "Simulation and Performance Evaluation of the RISC Architecture," Electronics Research Laboratory memorandum UCB/ERL M81/17, University of California, Berkeley, Mar. 1981.

David A. Patterson has been a member of the faculty in the Computer Science Division, Department of Electrical Engineering and Computer Sciences, University of California, Berkeley, since 1977. He was named associate professor in 1981 and currently teaches computer architecture at the graduate and undergraduate levels. His research combines popular software, experimental architecture, and VLSI to create more effective computer systems.

Patterson spent the fall of 1979 on leave of absence at Digital Equipment Corporation developing microprogram design tools and reviewing computer designs. In the next academic year he developed courses that led to the design and implementation of RISC I, a 45,000-transistor microprocessor. In 1982 he received the Distinguished Teaching Award from the Berkeley division of the Academic Senate of the University of California. Patterson received a BA in mathematics and an MS and PhD in computer science from UCLA.

Patterson's address is the Computer Science Division, Department of Electrical Engineering and Computer Sciences, University of California, Berkeley, CA 94720.

Richard S. Piepho is a member of the technical staff at Bell Telephone Laboratories in Naperville, Illinois. A member of the IEEE, Tau Beta Pi, and Eta Kappa Nu, he received a BSEE from Purdue University in 1980 and an MS in computer science and electrical engineering from the University of California, Berkeley, in 1981.

Contributions...

Re-evaluation of the RISC I

J. L. Heath,
North Dakota State University
Fargo, ND   58105

1.   INTRODUCTION

Recently reported research <3> indicates that the RISC I, a reduced instruction set computer, is able to outperform conventional processors. The validity of these results has, however, been questioned <7> since factors not directly related to the size and speed of the instruction set may have been utilized to the RISC I's advantage. By removing these extraneous factors, and re-evaluating the RISC I, this paper hopes to more completely evaluate the reduced instruction set computer.

2.   BACKGROUND

The Reduced Instruction Set Computer is a relatively new concept in computer architecture. The most publicized example of the reduced instruction set design philosophy is the RISC I, a 32 bit microprocessor which has been developed at the University of California, Berkeley. The results reported for the RISC I, when compared to conventional microprocessors, indicate that the RISC I offers improved performance when executing compiled C programs. The tests used in this evaluation compared the performance of the RISC I to the MC68000, the Z8000, and several other processors. The performance of these processors was measured via benchmark programs which were written in C and translated into machine language using a compiler.

There are, however, two factors other than the reduced instruction set which may have affected the performance of the RISC I. These are the register window (together with the large number of registers) and the type of compiler used for the C programs.

The register scheme, 138 registers allocated in overlapping groups of 32, provide a means of context switching which may have significantly increased the performance of the RISC I.

The programs written for the RISC I were compiled with the use of a peephole optimizer. The same programs when written for the conventional processors were compiled with a portable compiler. This discrepancy between the compilers used for the different machines being compared may have served to disproportionately benefit the RISC I.

Reprinted with permission from *Computer Architecture News*, March 1984,
pages 3-10. Copyright © 1984 by J.L. Heath.

3. ALTERNATIVES

There are two alternative methods of comparing the processors in question (within the context of using benchmark programs to measure performance). The first method is to use an optimized compiler for the conventional machines. The second method involves eliminating the effects of the register window and the optimizing compiler from the results of the RISC I, and comparing these results to similar studies performed for the other machines.

Both methods are useful for comparing the performance of different types of machines. The first method allows the highest performance levels of each processor to be measured, with the optimal use of all machine resources. The second method serves to isolate the benefits incurred by the reduced instruction set.

4. PREVIOUS STUDIES

The only major performance evaluation of the RISC I was done at Berkeley <3,4>. This evaluation involved writing a set of benchmark programs in C and compiling them for the RISC I and for several conventional processors. As stated earlier, the RISC I programs were compiled with a peephole optimizer whereas portable compilers were used on the other machines. The programs used in this evaluation included a subset of five programs from the Carnegie-Mellon test package. Processors used in this study were the RISC I, the Motorola MC68000, the Intel 8086, the DEC LSI-11/32, the Z8000, the VAX 11/780, the PDP 11/70, and the BBN C/70.

In 1981, Electronic Design News used a subset of seven programs from the Carnegie-Mellon test package to evaluate four processors <2>. Five of these programs were also used by Berkeley to evaluate the RISC I. The EDN study tested the Motorola MC68000, the Zilog Z8000, the DEC LSI-11/23, and the Intel 8086.

The programs used in each of these studies are indicated in Table 1.

By comparing the results of the EDN study to the Berkeley study for the MC68000 and the Z8000, it is apparent that the compiler used at Berkeley was relatively inefficient. One blatant example in support of this statement is the MC68000 programs which, when coded by hand, averaged over six times faster than the programs generated by the Berkeley C compiler (the hand coded programs were also smaller than the compiled C code).

The results of both the Berkeley and EDN studies are shown in Tables 2 and 3.

The results shown in Tables 2 and 3 indicate that the RISC I performance is comparable to that of the MC68000 and the Z8000. Although this would seem to justify the reduced instruction set computer philosophy, the results may be excessively biased in favor of the RISC I by the presence of, and use of, the large set of registers and the register window. This bias may be justified by the rationale that the implementation of both features was facilitated by the

```
+-------------------------------------------------------------------------+
!                              TABLE 1                                    !
!                                                                         !
!                     Carnegie-Mellon Benchmarks                          !
!                                                                         !
!                                                                         !
!       EDN    UCB      benchmark          description                    !
!                                                                         !
!        *                 A           I/O interrupt kernel               !
!        *                 B           I/O kernel with FIFO               !
!        *      *          E           Character-string search            !
!        *      *          F           Bit set, reset, test               !
!        *      *          H           Linked-list insertion              !
!        *      *          I           Quicksort                          !
!        *      *          K           Bit-matrix transposition           !
!                                                                         !
+-------------------------------------------------------------------------+
```

implementation of the small instruction set, i.e. the chip area necessary for the registers was available only because of the small amount of chip area used in the implementation of the instruction set.

5.   RE-EVALUATING THE RISC I

In order to eliminate the effects of the RISC I's register window, it was necessary to hand code each of the five Carnegie-Mellon benchmark algorithms directly in RISC I assembly code. Each program was run on a RISC I simulator to ensure correct program execution and to measure the execution times. These programs minimized the effects of the register window by only using 32 of the available registers. One residual benefit of the register windows does, however, remain; that is the contents of the registers used by the programs were not restored to the original register contents. Although this practice may violate some of the criteria set forth in the EDN study, the effects should be no more significant than those resulting from some of the 'questionable' practices used in the code written for the MC68000 and the Z8000 <4>.

The results of this study are also shown in Table 2 and 3.

TABLE 2

Benchmark Results, Program Size

Assembled C Code

Benchmark	RISC I	MC68000		Z8000	
E	144	115	(0.8)*	129	(0.9)*
F	120	144	(1.2)	180	(1.5)
H	176	123	(0.7)	140	(0.8)
I	992	694	(0.7)	1091	(1.1)
K	288	316	(1.1)	374	(1.3)
average			(0.9)		(1.12)

Machine Language Programs

Benchmark	RISC I	MC68000		Z8000	
E	112	44	(0.39)*	66	(0.59)*
F	84	36	(0.43)	44	(0.52)
H	164	106	(0.65)	96	(0.59)
I	692	266	(0.38)	386	(0.56)
K	232	74	(0.32)	110	(0.47)
average			(0.43)		(0.55)

* numbers in parenthesis indicate the number of times larger than the RISC I program.

TABLE 3

Benchmark Results, Program Execution Time

Assembled C Code

Benchmark	RISC I	processor	
		MC68000	Z8000
E	460	1228 (2.8)*	421 (0.9)*
F	60	288 (4.8)	242 (4.0)
H	100	160 (1.6)	137 (1.4)
I	50400	206640 (4.1)	149760 (3.0)
K	430	1720 (4.0)	1278 (3.0)
average		(3.5)	(2.5)

Machine Language Programs

Benchmark	RISC I	processor	
		MC68000	Z8000
E	417	244 (0.59)*	134 (0.32)*
F	83	70 (0.84)	70 (0.85)
H	66	153 (2.32)	135 (2.05)
I	39449	33527 (0.85)	66000 (1.67)
K	772	368 (0.48)	369 (0.45)
average		(1.01)	(1.07)

* numbers in parenthesis indicate the number of times slower than the RISC I program.

6. RISC I SIMULATOR

The simulator used for the RISC I programs was written in FORTRAN and run on an IBM computer system. The simulator implements each RISC I assembly language instruction as a FORTRAN subroutine. To run on the simulator, the RISC I program must therefore be transformed into a sequence of FORTRAN subroutine calls. This method of implementation, although somewhat slow, allows a large degree of flexibility, together with the ability to easily monitor the execution of the assembly language program.

One benefit of this type of simulator is that extensive and detailed knowledge of the hardware is not required. That is, since the instructions do not need to be represented as bit strings, the op codes for the particular instructions are not needed.

There are, however, some disadvantages to this type of simulator. Perhaps the major drawback is that the simulator does not represent a von Neumann machine, i.e. the instructions and data are not indistinguishable.

Before comparing the results, it should be noted that while the programs for the EDN study were coded by the processor manufacturers, Motorola and Zilog, the hand coded RISC I programs represent a first attempt at writing RISC I machine code. Therefore, the results may be slightly biased against the RISC I.

7. DYNAMIC PROGRAMMING STATISTICS

One additional feature of this simulator allows the dynamic programming statistics (i.e. the frequency of execution of individual instructions) to be gathered. The dynamic statistics for the five benchmark programs are given in Table 4.

TABLE 4

Dynamic Programming Statistics

	average frequency of execution	
instruction	machine language programs	assembled C programs
ADD	25 %	27 %
SUB	24	20
JMPR	25	15
other	26 *	38

* no single instruction in the 'other' category
accounted for more than 8 % of the total.

8. CONCLUSIONS

Several general observations may be made from comparing the results of the various studies. These are:

A) The discrepancy (both in program size and speed of execution) between the compiled C code and the hand written code (for both the Z8000 and the MC68000) indicate that the compiler used for these processors was not able to generate efficient code for those machines.

B) The hand coded RISC I programs were comparable, in terms of program size and speed of execution, to the results from the MC68000, the Z8000, and the compiled C code of the RISC I. Remember that the hand coded programs did not make use of the RISC I's register window or the large number of registers.

C) Comparing the results of individual programs indicates that for specific tasks the RISC I offers significantly better performance than either of the other processors. For instance, when executing benchmark H (Linked-list insertion), the RISC I performed much better than the other two processors.

D)   The dynamic programming statistics reveal that the RISC I makes extensive use of a very small subset of its already small instruction set. This indicates that a disproportionate increase in processor performance may be obtained by increasing the speed at which this subset of instructions executes.   This conclusion is not limited to reduced instruction set computers; it is, however, predicated on the assumption that the processor's software is written to effectively use these instructions.

1.   Jan L. Heath, "A Study of Reduced Instruction Set Computers", M.S. Thesis, EEE Dept., North Dakota State University, 1983

2.   R. Grappel, and J. Hemenway, "A tale of four uPs: Benchmarks quantify performance," Electronic Design News, Vol. 26, No. 7, April 1, 1981, pp. 179-265.

3.   D. Patterson, and C. Sequin, "A VLSI RISC," IEEE Computer, Vol. 15, No. 9, September, 1982, pp. 8-18.

4.   R. Piepho, "Comparative Evaluation of the RISC I Architecture Via the Computer Family Architecture Benchmarks," Research Project, University of California, Berkeley, August 17, 1981.

5.   D. Patterson, and D. Ditzel, "The Case for the Reduced Instruction Set Computer," Computer Architecture News, Vol. 8, No. 6, October, 1980, pp. 25-33.

6.   D. Fitzpatrick, D. Patterson, C. Sequin, et al.,¬"A RISCy Approach to VLSI," Computer Architecture News, Vol. 10, No. 1, March 1982, pp. 28-32.

7.   R. Colwell, C. Hitchcock III, E. Jensen, "Peering Through the RISC/CISC Fog: An Outline of Research," Computer Architecture News, Vol. 11, No. 1, March 1983, pp. 44-50.

RISC WATCH

David A. Patterson

Computer Science Division
Department of Electrical Engineering and Computer Sciences
University of California
Berkeley, California 94720

There have been several new computers and new studies relating to Reduced Instruction Set Computers (RISC) since our last article in *Computer Architecture News*. The first report is on RISC II, a much more aggressive implementation of the Berkeley RISC architecture. The studies of RISCs in new areas include floating point, big benchmarks, Lisp, and ECL. After reviewing the last stages of the Berkeley RISC project, I list the commercial RISCs, and conclude with a short description of our next project.

RISC II

We have just finished testing RISC II, a 32-bit NMOS microprocessor at Berkeley by Manolis Katevenis and Robert Sherburne. This 41,000 transistor chip is 25% smaller than RISC I even though it has 60 more 32-bit registers. Both designs were fabricated at λ of 2 microns (4 micron drawn gate length).

Like RISC I, RISC II worked on first silicon. This time, however, the performance was close to what we predicted—because of careful design and extensive Spice simulation of critical data-path delays and because of Crystal,[1] a MOS timing verifier developed by Prof. John Ousterhout. The predicted RISC II cycle time (i.e. execution of a register-to-register instruction) was 480 ns. In the lab, RISC II chips run at 500 ns per instruction (8MHz clock, VDD=5V, VBB=VSS=0V, room temperature, 1.25 Watts power dissipation).

Our architectural studies assumed 400 ns per instruction (10MHz clock) to predict performance of Berkeley RISCs. Benchmark simulations show that even at 500 ns, RISC II runs integer C programs faster than a 8-MHz iAPX-286, 10-MHz NS 16032, 12-MHz 68000, or 18-MHz HP 9000 CPU.

We resubmitted RISC II at smaller geometries ($\lambda = 1.5$). The resulting chip is, of course, about half the size—about 25% smaller than the 68000—yet runs at 330 ns per instruction (12MHz clock, VDD=5V, VBB=VSS=0V, room temperature, 1.8 Watts dissipation). Details on RISC II will be presented at the International Solid State Circuits Conference in San Francisco in February, 1984.[2]

FLOATING RISCS

Floating point arithmetic was ignored in our original studies because we rarely use floating point and because of the difficulty of implementation. Tim

Reprinted with permission from *Computer Architecture News*, March 1984, pages 11-19. Copyright © 1984 by D.A. Patterson.

Sippel studied floating point arithmetic and found that floating point routines written in C run only slightly faster on RISC than assembly language routines on the 68000, but neither is a match for a VAX. [3]

I have revised and summarized his study in the table below. The revisions include

- Using the measured cycle times of RISC II instead of the estimated time;

- Using the 10 MHz, 0 wait state 68010 in a SUN 2 workstation instead of the slower 8 MHz, 2 wait state 68000 of the Dual 8312 workstation;

- Using a faster floating point co-processor. Sippel originally estimated the performance of RISC with hardware support based on an 8-MHz 8087 co-processor. Here, I estimate the performance of based on the Weitek floating point chips.[4] This 2-chip set executes single precision floating add, subtract, and multiply in less than 1 microsecond. (Weitek also provide chips that are nearly twice as fast.) I have assumed that a double precision version of the Weitek chips would execute add, subtract, and multiply in 2 microseconds (not including the time to pass operands.) I also assume that divide takes 5 times as long as multiply.

The next question is selecting a floating point benchmark. The most widely quoted floating point benchmark is the Whetstone[5, 6], usually written in Fortran. We have no Fortran compiler for RISC II, but as the original Whetstone was written in Algol-60, we translated it into C.

Let me describe the circumstances of this experiment, to avoid misunderstandings. The motivation is comparability: showing relative CPU performance for the same software, and not giving the best possible performance for each architecture. This table shows single user CPU time using the UNIX[†] C compiler and the transcendental function library routines written in C. You can get better numbers for RISC II and the VAX if you write the transcendental routines in assembly language, if you use a more highly optimizing C compiler, if you use the Fortran version of this program with the VMS compiler, or if you calculate only single precision numbers.[‡] The point, however, is to reduce the number of variables in this study so that we can can more accurately compare CPU time. It is increasingly important to use the UNIX C compiler to compare CPU performance as Digital Equipment Corporation is now selling Berkeley UNIX, and Datamation estimates that more than 20% of the minicomputers sold in 1984 will be running some version of UNIX.[7]

The two variables in this table are the machines and the type of floating point support. RISC II, with the hypothetical double precision Weitek chip, is about half the speed of a 780 with the optional floating point accelerator, and faster than the standard 780 with microcoded floating point. The RISC II speed

---

[†] UNIX is a Trademark of Bell Laboratories.

[‡] For example, RISC II can run the Whetstones in single precision (using floating point arithmetic written in C) five times faster than double precision, and using the VMS Fortran compiler and VMS assembly language transcendental routines improves double precision performance by a third on the VAX.

Whetstone Benchmark in C		
(Double Precision using UNIX C compiler)		
(Transcendentals written in C)		
(Measuring single-user CPU time)		
Machine	Floating Point implementation	Time (sec.)
VAX 11/780	hardware	2.2
VAX 11/750	hardware	3.4
RISC II (12MHz)	hardware	4.5
VAX 11/780	microcode	5.5
RISC II (8MHz)	hardware	6.4
VAX 11/750	microcode	8.4
68010 (10MHz)	assembly	41.5
RISC II (12MHz)	C	67.1
RISC II (8MHz)	C	101.7

will be difficult to improve, for most of the floating point time is spent sending the operands between RISC II and the coprocessor. The software floating point routines written in C for RISC II are more than an order of magnitude slower than the coprocessor version.

Our interpretation of these results is that RISCs alone are not an effective vehicle for floating point applications, and that the CPU-coprocessor interface is an area we want to improve in future RISCs.

BENCHMARKS: BIGGER AND BETTER

The performance predictions for RISCs were based on small programs. This small size was dictated by the reliability of the simulator and compiler, the available simulation time, and the inability of the first simulators to handle UNIX system calls. I am sure that RISC advocates would like to know whether the performance predicted by the small programs holds for the larger ones.

The first step was finding a large benchmark. The large program that had the widest interest was the compiler. The compiler is usually a popular program on most systems and, as a large program, it likely strains the system.

Jim Miros ran his RISC C compiler and the VAX C compiler on both RISC II (simulated) and the VAX-11/780 (actual), and found that RISC II can compile faster the VAX-11/780.[8] (Since the RISC simulator cannot handle system calls, Miros made a version of each compiler with stubs in place of the system calls to make the comparison fair.) A 10 MHz RISC varied from 60% to 80% faster, just as the small programs predicted. I have revised his numbers for the 8 and 12 MHz RISC II and included them in the table below.

Compiled Program		VAX C Compiler					RISC C Compiler				
		on VAX	on RISC		$\frac{VAX}{RISC}$		on VAX	on RISC		$\frac{VAX}{RISC}$	
name	size (lines)	(secs)	8mhz	12mhz	8	12	(secs)	8mhz	12mhz	8	12
ld.c	1587	27.9	21.0	13.9	1.3	2.0	35.2	22.4	14.8	1.6	2.4
sort.c	873	17.4	13.2	8.7	1.3	2.0	20.0	13.2	8.7	1.5	2.3
puzzle.c	118	5.2	3.6	2.4	1.4	2.2	7.3	4.8	3.2	1.5	2.3
TOTAL	2578	50.5	37.8	25.0	1.3	2.0	62.5	40.4	26.7	1.5	2.3

UNIX C Compile Time Benchmarks
(Measuring single-user CPU time)
(VAX-11/780 vs. 8 & 12 MHz RISC II)

The 12 MHz RISC II runs either compiler more than twice as fast as the VAX-11/780. It is interesting to note that the VAX compiler runs faster than the RISC compiler on the same computer (50.5 vs. 62.5 or 25.0 vs. 26.7) even though the code generator was simpler for RISC (simpler instructions mean fewer decisions). It turns out that the heart of the UNIX C compiler is a pattern matching routine that matches the partially compiled object code to templates, so more instructions per program means more calls to this routine, thus slower compilation. However, even if we compare the RISC C Compiler running on RISC II to the VAX C Compiler running on the VAX-11/780, the 12MHz RISC II can still compile twice as fast.

PAPER STUDIES: Lisp and ECL

Carl Ponder studied how well RISCs could run Lisp.[9] His report was not based on implementing a Lisp system on RISC II, but was estimated by translating the output of VAX Lisp compilers to RISC II machine code. The Franz Lisp and PSL compilers generated VAX assembly code, which Ponder translated to RISC II. The next question was again what to use to compare performance. The mixture of competing programming environment philosophies, competing language factions, and competing companies has made Lisp benchmarking difficult. Dick Gabriel of Stanford, for example, has been working on the problem for two years and has yet to publish his results. Disregarding the warnings of the dangers of Lisp benchmarking, the table below lists compiled programs only and summarizes the results of running one highly recursive Lisp program on several machines.

Given that special case optimizations can result in a difference in performance of a factor of 8 on the same machine running the same language, it is dangerous to draw strong conclusions from this table. Ponder concludes that we can, at worst, expect better performance from RISC II than the VAX 11/750 for comparable Lisp systems.

Compiled TAK Lisp benchmark in Franz Lisp			
Machine	Lisp Dialect	Time (secs)	*Optimizations*
68010 (10MHz)	Franz Lisp	13.7	*(none)*
VAX 11/780	Franz Lisp	8.3	*(none)*
RISC II (8MHz)	Franz (est)	4.4	*direct call; tail recursion*
VAX 11/750	Franz Lisp	3.6	*fixed arithmetic*
RISC II (12MHz)	Franz (est)	2.9	*direct call; tail recursion*
68010 (10MHz)	Franz Lisp	2.5	*direct call; fixed arithmetic*
VAX 11/780	Franz Lisp	1.1	*direct call; fixed arithmetic*

Compiled TAK Lisp benchmark in PSL			
Machine	Lisp Dialect	Time (secs)	*Optimizations*
VAX 11/750	PSL	7.1	*(none)*
RISC II (8MHz)	PSL (est)	2.6	*direct call; tail recursion*
RISC II (12MHz)	PSL (est)	1.7	*direct call; tail recursion*
VAX 11/750	PSL	1.4	*direct call; fixed arithmetic*

Richard Blomseth investigated whether the RISC philosophy applies to computers built with technologies other than custom MOS.[10] He used a SCALDstation to design "Big RISC," a RISC II CPU built from ECL 100K chips. The timing verifier supplied a time estimate of the logic delays on the worst case path. Depending on your belief about wire delays and cache hit ratios, "Big RISC" is 4 to 8 times faster than RISC II, and the CPU fits on one large board.

Our conclusion is that the RISC philosophy works well for ECL 100K machines.

DOCUMENTED RISCS

In addition to the work mentioned above, several reports were written on the Berkeley RISC experiments. Jim Peek, the lead designer on RISC I, finished a report on the VLSI circuitry of RISC I.[11] Manolis Katevenis, the student who was principally responsible for the micro-architecture of RISC I and RISC II, has finished a dissertation that describes the rationale for RISCs, explains the micro-architecture of RISC II, and suggests directions for the next generation of machines.[12] Robert Sherburne, the lead circuit designer of RISC II and the last remaining RISC student, is completing his dissertation; in it, he analyzes the trade-offs in the circuit design of microprocessors and describes the ideas behind the circuits of RISC II.[13]

WILL OTHERS TAKE RISCS?

We stopped working on the RISC project a while ago, and it was interesting to see if others would pick up the ideas, and if so, when.

John Hennessy of Stanford started the MIPS project[14] shortly after we started the RISC project. They have recently fabricated a chip that works at the speed that meets or exceeds the performance predicted in his papers. MIPS can run Pascal programs about as fast as the DEC 20/60, or more than five times faster than a 8 MHz 68000. Like the IBM 801 project, MIPS relies on highly optimizing compilers in addition to streamlined computers to get high performance at low cost.15 Our studies report you can build a RISC faster than traditional computers even if both use the same simple compiler technology,[16] and Stanford has shown that the performance gap between RISCs and traditional machines is even greater when both use the same highly optimizing compiler technology.[17]

Three companies are selling RISC machines—at least according to their marketing departments. The Ridge Thirty-Two is a TTL minicomputer with a simple pipelined load/store architecture.[18] Pyramid has adopted the register window scheme of RISC I and also followed the load/store style of instruction set in building a TTL minicomputer.[19] INMOS has recently announced a single-chip VLSI computer with on-board memory and a simple instruction set.[20] All three companies claim performance exceeding the VAX-11/780, with INMOS claiming the largest advantage.

These three companies may not be the only ones to take risks, for according to one article[21] says

"A number of computer and chip makers including IBM, TRW, Fairchild Semiconductor, Hewlett-Packard, and Digital Equipment are reportedly investigating RISC architectures."

Although I doubt DEC is calling them RISCs, I certainly found it interesting that DEC's single chip VAXs do not implement the whole VAX instruction set.[22] A MicroVAX traps when it tries to execute some infrequent but complicated operations, and invokes transparent software routines that simulate those complicated instructions.

APPLES AND ORANGES

Fair comparisons of RISC architectures to traditional designs are difficult, and it certainly would be wonderful if "both architectures were designed from scratch in the same technology."[23] If we look at the technology used to build the CPU, most would conclude that the Mead/Conway 3 or 4 micron NMOS puts RISCs at a disadvantage. A RISC built either from the NMOS technology used to build the 68010 or the TTL gate arrays of the VAX-11/750 would certainly be faster, and we could build a much faster RISC using either the 1500 TTL chips in the VAX-11/780 CPU or using the 2 micron double level metal NMOS technology to build the 140,000 transistor MicroVAX 32.[24]

SUN 2 provides an answer to questions concerning the memory systems for RISCs. This machine has a 10 MHz 68010 that runs with no wait states with up to 4 megabytes of memory (built from 64K chips). This speed includes translating addresses from virtual to physical memory. The complete 2-level virtual memory tables—not just a translation buffer—are included on the same multibus board with the CPU. The 8MHz RISC II could run without wait states using this same scheme and same memory system. The 12MHz RISC II would require a new board design, either using the faster 256K memory chips or by building a cache like those found on the VAX-11/750 and the VAX-11/780.

RISCING BERKELEY'S FUTURE?

After working with C and UNIX, we decided to pick an architectural project that had far different problems and challenges. Experimental programming environments and objected-oriented computers seemed interesting, but traditional architectural support has meant:

- complex instruction sets; and

- poor performance.

In January 1983 we started our third architecture/VLSI course sequence, and our goal is to reverse that trend.

Our test vehicle is Smalltalk-80[†], an object-oriented programming language and programming environment created by the Software Concepts Group of Xerox PARC. This group has spent the last decade developing systems that improve programmer productivity, in part by using more computing power.

The only machine that has demonstrated adequate Smalltalk-80 performance is the Dorado,[25] an ECL minicomputer that costs over $100,000. Traditional computers have not been a good match for Smalltalk-80. The DEC Smalltalk-80 implementation for the VAX-11/780,[26] for example, is 15 to 30 times slower than the Dorado.[27]

Our next machine is called Smalltalk On A RISC, or SOAR[‡]. We hope SOAR will show that a Reduced Instruction Set Computer can be a low cost, high performance Smalltalk machine.

ACKNOWLEDGEMENTS

I thank the Berkeley students who had the courage to take our course sequences and to build "real stuff." Thanks also to Ricki Blau, Susan Eggers, Richard Fateman, Manolis Katevenis, Randy Katz, John Ousterhout, Allene Parker, Yale Patt, Carlo Séquin, and Nick Tredennick who gave valuable suggestions that improved the quality of this paper.

This research was sponsored by Defense Advance Research Projects Agency (DoD) ARPA Order No. 3803 Monitored by Naval Electronic System Command under Contract No. N00034-K-0251.

[†] Smalltalk-80 is a Trademark of Xerox Corporation.
[‡] SOAR is not a Trademark of Bell Laboratories nor of Xerox Corporation.

References

1. J.K. Ousterhout, "Crystal: A Timing Analyzer for nMOS VLSI Circuits," *Proc. Third Caltech Conference on Very Large Scale Integration*, pp. 57-70, 1983.

2. R.W. Sherburne, M.G.H. Katevenis, D.A. Patterson, and C.H. Séquin, "A 32b NMOS Microprocessor with a Large Register File," *31st International Solid States Circuit Conference*, San Francisco, February 23-25, 1984.

3. T. Sippel, "Floating RISCs," M.S. Project Report, U.C. Berkeley, September 1982. (Unpublished)

4. F. Ware, "Pipelined IEEE Floating Point Processor," *Compcon*, February 28-March 3, 1984.

5. H.J. Curnow and B.A. Wichmann, "A Synthetic Benchmark," *Computer Journal*, vol. 19, no. 1, 1975.

6. B.A. Wichmann and H.J. Curnow, "The Design of Synthetic Programs," in *Benchmarking: Computer Evaluation and Measurement,*, pp. 89-114, John Wiley & Sons, London, 1975.

7. J.W. Verity, "Minis Lose out to PCs," *Datamation*, vol. 29, no. 11, pp. 44-52, November 1983.

8. J. Miros, "A C Compiler for RISC I," M.S. Project Report, U.C. Berkeley, September 1982. (Unpublished)

9. C. Ponder, "... but will RISC run LISP? (a feasibility study)," Computer Science Technical Report No. UCB/CSD 83/122, U.C. Berkeley, August 1983. M.S. Project Report.

10. R. Blomseth, "A Big RISC," Computer Science Technical Report No. UCB/CSD 83/143, U.C. Berkeley, November 1983. M.S. Project Report.

11. J.B. Peek, "The VLSI Circuitry of RISC I," Computer Science Technical Report No. UCB/CSD 83/135, U.C. Berkeley, June 1983. M.S. Project Report.

12. M.G.H. Katevenis, "Reduced Instruction Set Computer Architectures for VLSI," Computer Science Technical Report No. UCB/CSD 83/141, U.C. Berkeley, October, 1983. PhD Dissertation.

13. R.W. Sherburne, *Processor Design Tradeoffs in VLSI,* U.C. Berkeley, May, 1984. PhD Dissertation (in preparation).

14. J. Hennessy, N. Jouppi, F. Baskett, A. Strong, T. Gross, C. Rowen, and J. Gill, "The MIPS Machine," *Proc. Compcon*, pp. 1-7, San Francisco, California, February 1982.

15. G. Radin, "The 801 Minicomputer," *Proc. Symposium on Architectural Support for Programming Languages and Operating Systems*, pp. 39-47, Palo Alto, California, March 1-3, 1982.

16. D.A. Patterson and R.S. Piepho, "RISC Assessment: A High-Level Language Experiment," *Proc. Ninth International Symposium on Computer Architecture*, Austin, Texas, April 26-29, 1982.

17. F.C. Chow, "A Portable Machine-Independent Global Optimizer—Design and Measurements," Computer Systems Laboratory Technical Note No. 83-254, Stanford University, December, 1983. PhD Dissertation

18. D. Folger and E. Basart, "Computer Architectures – Designing for Speed," *Compcon*, pp. 25-31, February 28-March 3, 1983.

19. R. Ragan-Kelley, "Performance of the Pyramid Computer," *Compcon*, February 28-March 1, 1983.

20. I. Barron, P. Cavill, D. May, and P. Wilson, "Transputer does 5 or more MIPS even when not used in parallel," *Electronics*, pp. 109-115., November 17, 1983.

21. C. Barney, "Fewer Instructions Speed Up VLSI," *Electronics*, vol. 55, no. 23, pp. 101-102, November 17, 1983.

22. B. Supnik and I. Evans, "MicroVAX 32 -- A VAX-Compatible Microprocessor," *Compcon*, February 28-March 3, 1984.

23. S.J. Metz, "Letter to the Editor," *Computer Architecture News*, vol. 11, no. 5, December 1983.

24. J. Beck, D. Dobberpuhl, M.J. Doherty, E. Dorenkamp, R. Grondalski, D. Grondalski, K. Henry, M. Miller, R. Supnik, S. Thierauf, and R. Witek, "A 32b Microprocessor with On-Chip Virtual Memory Management," *31st International Solid States Circuit Conference*, San Francisco, February 23-25, 1984.

25. D.W. Clark, B.W. Lampson, and K.A. Pier, "The Memory System of a High-Performance Personal Computer," *IEEE Transactions on Computers*, vol. C-30, no. 10, pp. 715-733, October 1981.

26. S. Ballard and S. Shirron, "The Design and Implementation of VAX/Smalltalk-80," in *Smalltalk-80: Bits of History, Words of Advice*, ed. Glenn Krasner, pp. 127-150, Addison Wesley, September, 1983.

27. K. McCall, "The Smalltalk-80 Benchmarks," in *Smalltalk 80: Bits of History, Words of Advice*, ed. Glenn Krasner, pp. 151-173, Addison-Wesley, Reading, MA, 1983.

References 9 – 12 are available from the Publications Office, Computer Science Division, 573 Evans Hall, University of California, Berkeley, California 94720. If you would like copies, please send the report name and number plus a check (made out to the Regents of the University of California) to cover the following publication costs: Ponder (#122): $2.50, Peek (#135): $2.50, Katevenis (#141): $6.00, and Blomseth (#143): $4.00.

Microprocessors

More hardware means less software

The trend is toward using ever-cheaper VLSI circuits in place of costly software—but some would reverse the trend

Recent trends in the semiconductor industry indicate that very large-scale integration (VLSI) will offer microprocessor designers two conflicting approaches to designing future systems: (1) They can continue the mainstream trend, where VLSI is used to build increasingly complex microprocessors—and where greater complexity is exhibited as more hardware to do functions previously done by software alone; or (2) They can, as proposed by a small number of designers, take the opposite tack and build simpler processors, where more functions are done by software.

Greater complexity lets designers use ever-cheaper VLSI circuits in place of increasingly expensive software. What's more, the takeover of many software functions by hardware is said to help programmers develop high-level language (HLL) programs that are shorter, more efficient, and easier to write, compile, and debug. More complex systems would, in theory, reduce the high cost of developing software and thus reduce the total life-cycle cost of a system.

But David A. Patterson, professor of computer science at the University of California, Berkeley, and David Ditzel, a computer scientist at Bell Laboratories in Murray Hill, N.J., disagree with this approach. The more complex machines, they say, do not offer worthwhile gains in performance or reductions in system cost. They propose a return to simpler—and therefore cheaper—processors, where they think compilers can be used more efficiently to optimize debugging and run-time performance.

A more cost-effective solution to the problem of soaring software costs, as they see it, would be the development of improved compilers that further simplify the programmer's job. Simpler systems are potentially faster, they add, since simpler chips have more area available for such speed-enhancing circuits as additional cache for pipelining instructions or data.

The fact is, however, that no generally accepted models exist for weighing the benefits of various architectures against the life-cycle costs of the final products.

Complex systems in the spotlight

The recent trend toward more complex microprocessors was highlighted by reports earlier this year that the Intel Corp. of Aloha, Ore., and Hewlett-Packard Inc. of Fort Collins, Colo., had developed micromainframes—32-bit processor chips with far more transistors and complex architecture than previous microprocessors, as well as processing rates that were competitive with some modern mainframes [Figs. 1 and 2].

Growing complexity had already been shown in the unusually powerful microprocessors—as powerful as minicomputers— introduced in 1980 by other companies: the 16-bit Z8000 from Zilog Corp. of Cupertino, Calif.; the MC68000 from Motorola

Inc. of Phoenix, Ariz.; and the 32-bit NSC16000 from National Semiconductor Corp. of Santa Clara, Calif.

These machines have instruction sets with varying amounts of complex instructions. A complex instruction is one that replaces a number of simpler ones and usually corresponds to a statement in such HLLs as Fortran, Pascal, and Ada. For example, a single such instruction may control the transfer of an entire data file between main storage and the central processing unit. In simpler machines, by contrast, software routines implement that transfer. The main point is that executing a complex instruction requires more hardware or microcode—code stored in read-only memory that controls the steps the machine must take to perform functions specified in the instruction set.

Recent examples of the simpler approach to design are the IBM 801 minicomputer, developed at the company's Watson Research Center in Yorktown Heights, N.Y., and an experi-

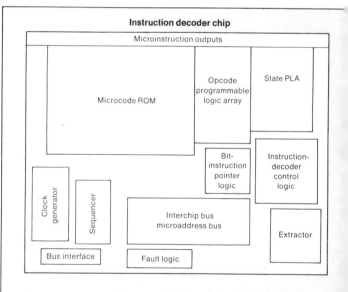

[1] Increasingly complex microprocessors—such as the Intel iAPX432 micromainframe shown above in a multiprocessor configuration—are the mainstream approach of the semiconductor industry to the cost-effective application of VLSI. Increasing complexity is defined as a trend toward using additional hardware to do functions previously done by software. The 432, for example, has a larger number of complex instructions that are done automatically by hardware (microcode). A complex instruction is one that replaces a number of simpler ones and usually corresponds to a statement in a high-level language.

Robert Bernhard   Associate Editor

Reprinted from *IEEE Spectrum*, December 1981, pages 30-37. Copyright © 1981 by The Institute of Electrical and Electronics Engineers, Inc.

EH0251-9/86/0000/0330$01.00 © 1981 IEEE

mental 32-bit microprocessor under development by Professor Patterson and a Berkeley colleague, Professor Carlo Sequin.

The IBM 801 is reported to be comparable in performance to the IBM 370/168 mainframe yet architecturally simpler, cheaper to build, and three times faster.

Simplified machines that are commercially available are represented by the TMS99000 family of microprocessors, introduced recently by Texas Instruments Inc. in Houston. The simpler memory-to-memory architecture of these systems is more cost-effective than the standard register-to-register architecture of other microprocessors, says Harvey Cragon, senior fellow at TI and adjunct professor of computer science at Southern Methodist University in Dallas. The TI systems are, indeed, in a class by themselves; they do not have general registers, accumulators, or stack pointers, and only by looking deeply into their architecture is it understood how they do any computing at all.

Throwbacks to earlier mainframes

The architectures of today's complex processors, at any rate, are similar in some ways to the revolutionary architectures of several past mainframes: the B5000, introduced in 1962 by the Burroughs Corp.; the Symbol computer, conceived in 1964 at Fairchild Camera and Instruments Corp. in Palo Alto, Calif., and introduced in 1971—but reclining now as a museum piece at Iowa State University in Ames; the IBM 360 and 370 series, introduced in the late 1960s and 1970s, respectively; and the recently introduced IBM System/38.

The Symbol computer was remarkable in that its designers believed future VLSI would require computers to be controlled solely by hardware. The resulting machine was the ultimate

complex-instruction-set computer (CISC), since hardware alone implemented such traditional software functions as compiling, text editing, memory management and timesharing, arithmetic, and variably sized data structures. The project was a commercial failure, its designers point out, because hardware and compiler technology were not advanced enough at that time to meet the system specifications.

The present-day microprocessor that comes closest to the ultimate CISC is the Intel iAPX432 micromainframe. The objections that some computer scientists have raised to CISCs may be better understood after a brief description of the controversial features of the 432 and other complex processor chips.

Intel innovates for programmers

Conventional proceedings have ample descriptions of how the iAPX432 achieves its mainframelike processing rates [see ''For further reading,'' p. 37]. However, some industry observers believe that the key innovation in the system is its unequaled emphasis on hardware or microcode implementation of an HLL—in this case Ada, the language adopted as a standard by the U.S. Department of Defense. Though other microprocessors have some similar features designed to speed the development of HLL programs, Intel is perhaps the first to unite all of these and more in a single architecture. The key architectural characteristics include the following:

• The instruction set is designed for efficient translation of Ada into machine-language programs. In many cases, therefore, an HLL instruction is translated into a single machine instruction, whereas conventional processors would need six or more instructions. There are send and receive instructions, for example, that

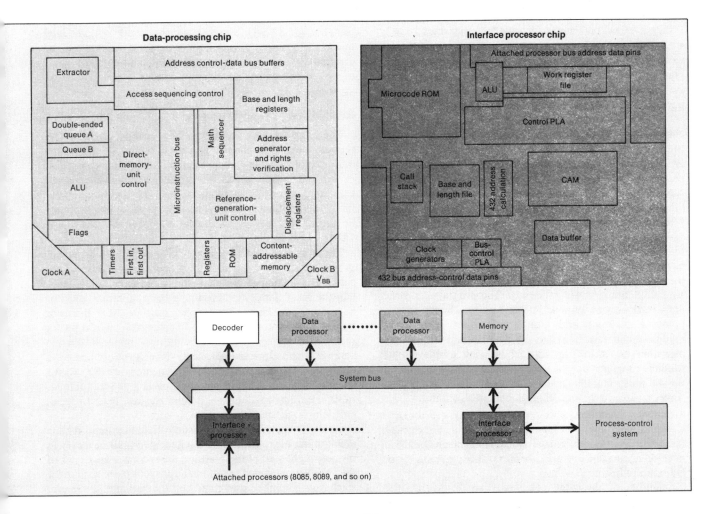

perform through hardware all the buffering and synchronizing operations needed to transmit such data structures as vectors, arrays, and files between programs.

• Microcode automatically performs various traditional operating system functions—for example, it distributes processing loads between different processors configured as a multiprocessing system. (In multiprocessing a single task is divided into subtasks that are processed concurrently by a system of coupled processors; this often yields far higher throughput at less cost than dividing the process load among many independent, single processors.) The distribution of loads is reported to reduce the time for programmers to develop custom operating systems for different applications. The programmer specifies only the parameters needed by a task scheduler, which is controlled by microcode. The parameters include task identification, user identification, and tasks to be performed.

• The most radical architectural characteristic is similar to the descriptor tables of the B5000 and the "object-oriented" architecture of the IBM System/38. Among nonspecialists the concepts of objects and descriptors may be widely misunderstood, though they have been publicized in the technical press.

Reliability and efficiency increased

The significance of object-oriented architecture is that it allows the hardware, the operating system, and the system programming language (Ada) to share in controlling automatically certain operations that help programmers develop reliable, efficient programs. These operations include such traditional compiler activities as type checking, range checking, and consistency checking. In previous microprocessors such functions were left to the programmer, to the compiler software alone, or to safeguards built into the HLL.

Object-oriented architecture has the following characteristics:

• The specification of data in programs (that is, what the data mean) is kept separate from how the data are referenced by program instructions or represented in memory. Programmers therefore can use data objects (or instructions as objects) without any knowledge of how the objects are implemented. The programmer uses them as if they were black boxes; the objects are abstractions in the sense that programmers have no direct access to the raw data but can access them indirectly through built-in hardware or software algorithms. Starting with simpler objects (integers, arrays, programs, lists, and so on), the programmer can build more complex objects, such as records, queues, lists of lists, lists of programs, and symbol tables.

• Hardware or software controls access to different types of data with passwords called descriptors. Through these a given object representation in memory (the actual physical data in a group of memory cells) may be accessed only by authorized programs. In theory programmers can thus use modular programming and structured design more efficiently. The programmer would design each program module (bubble in a typical bubble chart) to process a single task with a single data object. Access to the module would then be controlled automatically by hardware algorithms to ensure the required isolation of the module. Modular programs may be written for any microcomputer, but the 432 architecture is the only microcomputer system that enforces modular techniques through built-in algorithms.

• Hardware algorithms check whether each type of object is associated with operators that make sense for it. For example, the instruction "branch to data" would represent an illegal combination of data and operation (branch), since programs can only branch to instructions.

Examples of increased complexity are found in other microprocessors in the form of additional hardware or microcode. The HP chip, for example, has special machine instructions for debugging HLLs; they let programmers step through each instruction of a program to trace errors in either the source code or machine language. Special instructions help programmers develop operating systems.

Other complex processors

Designers of the Z8000 and MC68000 may have gone the furthest in appealing to programmers through additional complex instructions and addressing modes (different paths for information, such as between different types of working or index registers, or between registers and main memory). Operands may reside in general registers or main memory; this and the freedom of movement offered by various addressing modes reportedly lets compilers optimize programs more easily.

The MC68000 also has several unique instructions (LINK and UNLK) that are said to simplify implementation of HLLs because they maintain a linked list of data areas and parameters on the stack. (LINK is used at the start of a subprogram to keep track of program execution status, where frequent interrupts occur in nested subprograms; UNLK, used at the end of a subprogram, clears the stack prior to transferring program control to a higher-level subprogram.)

The NSC16000 supports HLLs with instructions and addressing modes that directly implement the manipulation of arrays, records, strings, and so on. The 16000 family is also the first to implement a true, demand-paged virtual memory system (through a separate memory-management unit), according to Subash Bal, product marketing director at National Semiconductor.

The iAPX432 has a unique method of paging that is also complex, but not as costly as a separate management unit. The Intel memory is segmented; each segment has a descriptor that indicates when a physical segment is present in memory and which of the current segments should be swapped (moved to fast, working memory) or overwritten by the new segment.

Alternative to complexity

The original reason for adding HLL instructions to microprocessors was that in years past memory was far slower and more costly than logic circuits in the central processor. HLL instructions executed much faster and needed less memory space than simpler instructions implemented with software subroutines. This imbalance between memory and the central processor no longer holds, in the view of Prof. Patterson, Dr. Ditzel, and TI's Mr. Cragon.

The memory-to-memory architecture of TI's 16-bit microprocessors is, in fact, based on the proposition that memory circuits are more compact and cheaper than processor logic circuits, and the speed gap is no longer significant. Whereas all other microprocessors locate their working registers (work spaces or stacks) on the processor chip, the TI processors have their work spaces in the system random-access memory. Because it is a less complex architecture to implement—fewer steps are needed to manipulate operands—memory-to-memory design allows speedier switching to and from work spaces in the face of interrupts, according to TI designers John Hughes, Peter Chappel, and John V. Schabowski.

To service interrupts (or switch contexts) in register-to-register architecture, the contents of 16 stack registers must be moved to memory at the start of the interrupt; this is done to keep track of the information needed to restore the previous context, since the stack registers will be used to process the interrupt. On return,

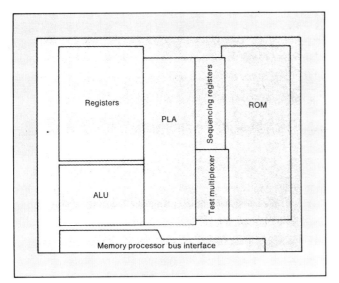

[2] A single-chip micromainframe built by Hewlett-Packard has 430 000 transistors on a chip area of 40 mm²; it has a stack-oriented instruction set that includes complex instructions to help programmers develop operating systems as well as do special stack manipulations that past processors did with software. The programmable logic array (PLA)—which holds the instruction decoder and controller—is a standard approach today in VLSI design. It provides the regular array of components that allows designers to use computer-aided design tools more cost-effectively. The interactions of PLA, test multiplexer, and sequencing registers implement conditional microcode skips, jumps, and subroutine calls.

the offloaded words must be reloaded in the stack. Besides the circuits and instructions needed to carry out these operations, the entire process entails one memory cycle to store and another to fetch each of many words.

The memory-to-memory architecture, its designers point out, requires just three programmable registers—a program counter, a work-space pointer, and a status register—along with a virtually unlimited supply of work space in virtual memory. Context switching is thus performed in two memory-read cycles and three memory-store cycles. The contents of the program counter are exchanged with those of the work-space pointer, the contents of the status register are saved, and data words stay in place. The overhead does increase as the number of different possible interrupts increases, but the TI designers contend that the overhead increases far more in register-based machines, since register capacity must be added in addition to control and housekeeping circuits.

Tagged, or descriptor, memories are not worth the cost, TI's Mr. Cragon believes, noting that the additional hardware complexity does not necessarily lead to more reliable, complex programs. Complexity itself, he says, is a significant source of errors. The run-time protection afforded by descriptor memories—although a benefit—tends, in his opinion, to suppress the innovativeness of programmers.

Benefit to compilers doubted

Complex instruction sets, Prof. Patterson and Dr. Ditzel say, appeal to designers who are unfamiliar with modern compiler technology.

Whereas HLL-oriented architecture serves largely that portion of the compiler that generates code from the HLL program, the size of the code-generating software is often dwarfed by the remaining portion of the compiler, which programmers generally find more important. The more important code includes the automatic lexical and syntax analyzers, parser generators, optimization routine, loaders, error detectors, and routines for error recovery and diagnostics.

The most complex architecture therefore would not significantly change the makeup or function of the compiler, Prof. Patterson and Dr. Ditzel maintain. Their long experience with compilers indicates that complex instructions are often impossible to generate from compilers; complex instructions are so specialized, moreover, that they are prone to implementing the wrong functions for languages other than those for which the machine was specifically designed.

The main point of their argument is that most of the presumed power that designers have put into CISC architecture is wasted; the machines would serve programmers better if the compilers were more intelligent and the architecture were simpler (and thus placed less burden on the compilers).

Another point about CISCs that critics challenge is the contention that they allow compilers to generate more compact code. The more compact code requires less memory and executes faster and so is cheaper, the argument goes. The critics raise these three points about code compaction:

1. Because the cost of memory is falling rapidly, more compact code offers insignificant savings in total system cost. The speed gap between memory and central processing unit has narrowed as well, and the recent use of pipelining (prefetching of instructions) has virtually closed the gap in fetching instructions from memory in microprocessors.

2. Experience indicates that more compact programs do not necessarily lead to significantly shorter execution times unless they result in at least a 20-to-30-percent savings. The limiting factor in execution speed is the rate at which data instructions are transferred from memory; but pipelining has greatly reduced the effect of this limitation.

3. Few systems are bought where the purchaser intends to run one particular fixed-size algorithm with one HLL; thus memory savings will differ for various HLLs. It is doubtful that under such conditions one instruction set could lead to significantly large savings.

Symbol of simplicity: the IBM 801

The designers of the IBM 801 conceived the machine about six years ago as a radically simpler alternative to the complex IBM 360 and 370 mainframes, according to Joel Birnbaum, formerly director of the computer science department at the Watson Research Center, but now at Hewlett-Packard. No performance details of this new minicomputer are available; however, the machine is currently used to monitor the hardware and software of the Model 3 370/168, where the 801 executes three or four instructions in a single memory cycle of the 168. Observers have extrapolated this to mean that the 801 can execute 10 MIPS (million instructions per second), compared with 2.4 MIPS for the 370/168 and 5 MIPS for the IBM 3033, one of the largest mainframes available.

The design of the 801 was based on the analysis of trace tapes carried out by IBM Fellow John Cocker and his colleagues at the Watson Research Center. Such analyses compare the patterns of instructions that are actually executed by the software of a given machine in daily use to the patterns that are possible in theory based on the machine architecture.

The analysis indicated, Dr. Birnbaum reports, that such relatively simple instructions as load, store, and branch are used far more often than the hundreds of other more complex instructions that CISCs may have in their instruction sets. The designers of the 801 therefore used hardwired logic to implement all such "primitives" (load, store, and so on) in one instruction cycle. As many higher-level instructions as possible were then implemented by software subroutines that use the primitives. The designers also made maximum use of the compiler to speed program execution through two techniques:

1. The compiler develops the best mix of hardware and software to minimize the number of machine cycles during run-time.

2. When the program is first compiled, the compiler and operating system execute those instructions that need to be performed only once, instead of on every execution of the program.

The execution of instructions in a single cycle is possible because the designers separated the caches for data from those for instructions. In a single cycle, therefore, the machine can simultaneously execute an instruction, fetch the next instruction from the cache, and either load or store data from the cache.

What is most significant about the 801 design, Dr. Birnbaum says, is that it lets programmers use the existing power of compilers and operating systems to analyze what a program is doing with stored information. This power is wasted in the typical CISC, he notes, since the basic idea is that complexity should be used to make such information transparent to users.

RISC-I: a bare-bones processor

The RISC-I, designed by Prof. Patterson and Prof. Sequin, is a 32-bit single-chip processor that has not yet been built; it has been simulated at the circuit level with benchmarking programs, however, and is reported to have the overall performance of the VAX 11/780 high-end minicomputer, manufactured by Digital Equipment Corp. of Tewksbury, Mass.

More power to computer-aided design

What some microprocessor makers have achieved in recent years seems amazing, considering the highly publicized reports that the industry is short of both engineers and computer-aided design (CAD) tools for designing very large-scale integrated systems. Either the existing manpower or CAD tools are more productive than the publicity indicates, or else the problems of VLSI design have been overstated.

The point is illustrated by the two micromainframes that are the current showpieces of VLSI: the three-chip iAPX432 from Intel Corp., with 200 000 transistors (110 000 on the data-processing chip alone), and a single-chip system from Hewlett-Packard Inc., with 430 000 transistors on a chip area 40 millimeters squared.

These are record IC densities for logic chips (64-kilobit random-access memories have about 100 000 transistors on a chip 25 mm² to 36 mm²). Yet Intel and HP designers achieved those densities through state-of-the-art circuits and optical lithography with line widths of from 1.5 to 5 micrometers [see figure]. In addition, gates were placed and interconnected on the chip, and the logic and circuit designs were checked by less powerful CAD systems than many experts predicted would be needed for such complex systems.

The HP designers used an in-house CAD system to place and interconnect an average of more than 180 devices per engineer-day. That was more than the minimum productivity that experts had said was needed for systems of the late 1980s with a life cycle of three years. (The design cycle must be less than the life cycle, of course, so manufacturers can make timely introductions of new products.) The Intel team, also using its own CAD systems, placed and interconnected about 25 devices per engineer-day. Yet the layout was completed in less than two years. This achievement defied some expert predictions that systems of this size could not be built in less than three years unless productivity was more than 250 devices per engineer-day.

"Considering the unprecedented complexity of the two systems, their circuits were designed and debugged with relatively little trouble," says Carver Mead, professor of computer science at the California Institute of Technology in Pasadena, who was a consultant on the Intel project. He attributed this to the so-called structured hierarchical design method that he pioneered several years ago with a colleague, Lynn Conway.

Designing 'regular' structures

The structured method emphasizes the design of "regular computer structures"—that is, the logic circuits are built up from more or less repeated patterns of identical devices and interconnections. For example, the control portion of microprocessor chips had traditionally been made with logic devices placed at random in the available space between other circuits; in the structured approach, however, programmable logic arrays implement the control units, resulting in more regular layouts that are easier to design, debug, and modify. A similar example, at a lower functional level, is a shift register cell (made with an inverter) that can be concatenated for as many bits as desired. The power, ground, and output lines of one cell align with the corresponding lines of the next. Each cell has a gating transistor that is driven by clock signals.

In designing a register, therefore, the designer can specify the entire register by drawing just one cell on the chip and then specifying such parameters as bit length and timing. Regular arrays increase design productivity, as measured by the "regularization factor," which was introduced some years ago by Intel's William W. Lattin, general manager of OEM microcomputer operations. The factor yields the effective number of devices that designers get for each one they draw. It is defined as the total number of devices on the chip (excluding memory arrays) divided by the number of devices that the designers had actually drawn.

In the hierarchical aspect of the Mead-Conway approach, the functional design is partitioned into successively smaller pieces to yield circuits of manageable complexity with as little as 20 to 50 transistors. For example, a frequency divider may be split into one counter plus one register, and the counter can be split further into individual bit positions. Most of the circuit design is then performed in bits and pieces that are later integrated.

Because of the reduced complexity and data in each piece, designers can use interactive graphics systems to generate the layouts for a given partition.

Separating the design into simpler pieces is not new. What is new in VLSI design is the need for computerized methods to integrate and speed the vast number of separate design activities.

No more 'paper dolls'

Prior to the development of modern CAD systems, designers used the "paper doll" approach, where they drew individual polygons by hand on Mylar sheets to represent IC mask patterns. With that method, it would have taken, by some estimates, at least 100 years to lay out either the HP or Intel chips.

Modern CAD systems, whether made by IC manufacturers themselves or commercial suppliers, have one or more stand-alone interactive graphics terminals linked to a computer system. Each terminal, or work station, allows a designer to build circuits from different combinations of progressively larger standard cells stored in a data base in the computer. The designer uses the interactive graphics as a sketch pad, where he can edit, add, or delete polygons or interconnections, as well as define standard cells and experiment with different layouts or IC densities.

In the structured design approach at HP, for example, the designer used a library of regular block structures. The blocks had a matching cell pitch and bus structure in the length dimension, but they varied in width. Similar cells with well-defined interfaces could be placed in regular patterns forming larger blocks. These structured cells differ from standard cells used in other CAD systems only in that they were designed to satisfy a given computer architecture and general interconnection pattern.

CAD systems therefore are basically data-base management systems that assist designers by placing and routing IC devices and verifying the correctness of a logic or circuit design through simulation. The systems are available from such suppliers as Applicon Inc. in Burlington, Mass.; Calma Inc. in Sunnyvale, Calif.; Avers Inc. in Scott's Valley, Calif.; AMI in Santa Clara, Calif.; Compeda Inc. in Palo Alto, Calif, and Computervision in Bedford, Mass.

The designers ascribe the excellent performance to their unique implementation of the call/return instruction, which their studies of programs showed was the most time-consuming instruction in most HLL programs run on the VAX, the PDP-11 (also manufactured by DEC), and the MC68000. The call/return instruction is used when the program jumps from one procedure (subroutine) to another, perhaps through a number of procedures nested one inside the other. It involves such time-consuming operations as saving or restoring register contents on each call or return and passing parameters and data to and from the procedures. (Procedures are programs in a program library that make code written by one person available to others; they are written so that subsequent users need not know their inner workings, but only the external details of what parameters and data they require.)

As envisioned by the Berkeley computer scientists, the RISC-I architecture would be based on four rules:

1. Instructions shall be executed in one cycle in as little time as are the microinstructions on such machines at the PDP-11 or VAX-11; yet instructions shall be so simple that no microcode is needed for their execution. A cycle is defined as the time to read a register, perform an arithmetic-and-logic-unit operation, and store the result back in a register.
2. Higher-level instructions, such as those found in CISCs, shall be implemented as software subroutines.
3. To simplify implementation, all instructions shall have the same word length.
4. The architecture shall support HLLs through implementation of the fastest method of executing such instructions as call/return, or of supporting the allocation of local (confined to

CAD tools for production IC artwork are of two general types:
1. Systems for custom layout performed with computer graphics, where the designer closely controls the IC density and may achieve maximum coverage of the chip area at the cost of relatively long development time.
2. Automated layout systems, where the designer submits logic diagrams and the system either automatically places and interconnects standard logic cells or routes the cells in a gate-array chip. This approach is far speedier than the first, but it results in relatively inefficient use of chip area.

The symbolic layout system

A recent development is the symbolic layout system, which represents an attempt to bridge the gap between the two general types. Symbolic systems have been developed by Applicon, AMI,

Calma, HP, National Semiconductor, and Intel, among other companies. They are divided roughly into static and dynamic types, depending on whether the symbols refer to cells that are in fixed positions or to cells that can be moved to optimize the layout or meet design rules.

In both types, for example, the designer can symbolize an enhancement-mode transistor on the interactive sketch pad as follows: he uses software commands to draw a horizontal line that crosses a vertical line on one mask level and a rectangle on a second, higher level. These lines define a polysilicon rectangle, which serves as a gate contact, and a vertical rectangle that serves as a diffusion line. The X and Y coordinates of the vertices of any geometric shape on the mask are declared through such software descriptions as LL, for lower left, or UR for upper right.

Static symbolic systems, however, use the symbols to represent

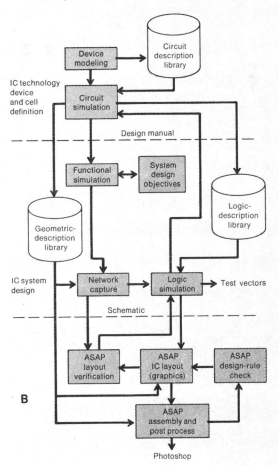

A

B

Advanced symbolic artwork preparation (ASAP) was used by Hewlett-Packard in Colorado Springs, Colo., to manage the design of its single-chip micromainframe, which has 430 000 transistors on a 40mm² chip. The IC designer writes a symbolic description of the desired circuits in the system language. The ASAP system generates a description of the IC mask by extending the software concept of mapping a program into a one-dimensional array of memory to that of mapping a symbolic hardware description into the two-dimensional physical planes of IC masks (A, above). Macrocells are groups of components with a given logic or circuit function. In the remainder of the design cycle (B), the ASAP assembly map, now stored in the geometric description library, involves device modeling, circuit simulation, and so on.

one procedure) as opposed to global variables (used in many different procedures). Studies of HLL programs had also shown that local scalar variables were the most frequent operands.

The so-called register windows in the RISC-I, the designers report, is a unique technique for maximizing the speed of execution of procedure calls [see Fig. 3]. The high speed, they say, stems from the reduction in off-chip memory accesses, compared with the way other processors perform the same operation.

In other processors the call instruction is implemented through a dedicated register (stack pointer) that saves a return address in the stack before the instruction causes the program to jump to the called procedure. Parameters are usually passed along to the stack through the help of another register (frame pointer) that points to the beginning of the parameters and the end of the local variables. The parameters are referenced by their memory ad-dresses, so that each time the procedure refers to the parameter, it refers to the address.

The RISC-I, by contrast, has multiple register banks (32 registers per bank), so that each call causes a new bank to be allocated to the called procedure. Thus the contents of registers are neither saved on jumping nor restored on return; on return a frame pointer simply indicates the bank that contains the current procedure.

The unique register windows are implemented as follows:
• Each bank of registers is divided into three parts: high, containing parameters passed from that portion of the program above the current (calling) procedure; local, where local scalars are stored; and low, for parameters passed to the procedure "below" the current procedure.
• On each procedure call, a register bank is allocated. The low

---

combinations of mask layers at a fixed position on the mask. Examples of such systems are AMI's SLIC (symbolic layout for integrated circuits), Applicon's CASL (computer-aided symbolic layout), and Calma's GDS II. Since the design rules may not be the same for all mask layers, the systems use variable grid spacings. For example, one grid spacing is used for metal lines and a different spacing for polysilicon, whereas different grids apply to horizontal and vertical lines.

National Semiconductor has extended the variable-grid concept with a program that varies the grid spacing continuously, subject to design rules, to maximize the amount of chip area covered by circuits.

A major drawback of the static type is reported to be that the designer must draw symbols exactly and place them carefully, to avoid violating design rules. Design rules must therefore be checked after the layout has been done—a time-consuming process.

Dynamic systems, on the other hand, adjust the final positions of the cells on the mask to obey design rules. Designers cannot violate the rules, and so no checking is required when the layout is finished.

Sticks: a dynamic design system

The most widely known dynamic system is Sticks. Developed at Hewlett-Packard several years ago by John Williams, now consultant in Palo Alto, Sticks is undergoing further commercial exploitation at Calma and HP. It is based on the principle that whereas human designers are inferior to computers in analyzing local details and observing design rules, they are superior in analyzing the overall characteristics of drawings and spotting areas of low circuit density.

The Sticks system, for example, allows designers to control the spacing of circuits by drawing windows in various parts of the mask and then specifying a direction; the result is that only the circuits inside the window are spaced according to design rules in the given direction. Repeated use of this procedure allows the designer to control the density of circuits over the entire mask. Designers may also use a "fencing" procedure to prevent excessive dispersion of circuits over given mask areas.

The symbolic drawings, referred to as sticks, can be rendered imperfectly by designers, since the system software can recognize valid drawings and indicate when the designer has made an error. The system can connect any stick structures that lie within certain distances of one another, since the drawings are not required to be fixed in any position. Designers can insert new structures between any number of existing stick structures by zooming in through interactive graphics, drawing in the structures, and connecting them. However useful these CAD tools may be, they do not help designers achieve the ultimate goal of design automation: to generate an entire mask set from a high-level description of chip architecture or function.

The ultimate CAD system

The ultimate automated system would implement the transition from a high-level description of architecture through the four re-maining levels of the design process: (1) high-level internal design, or the general floor plan of the microprocessor; (2) logic design; (3) circuit design; and (4) masks.

The ideal software package to accomplish that goal is generally called a silicon compiler, by analogy with traditional software compilers (which transform programs written in high-level languages into machine instructions). The silicon compiler is still in its infancy, largely at universities. Briefly the concept is this: the geometry of cells on the chip is described by various procedures in a programming language. Parameters are then passed to the procedures to generate cell structures representing either such logic blocks as adder/subtractors or shift registers, or such circuit elements as inverters.

For example, in the design of an inverter, the parameter would specify the circuit loading for the inverter amplifier. A procedure in the silicon compiler would use that parameter to compute the sizes of the transistors needed. That procedure would be linked to other procedures until the complete IC was described. In theory any architecture or circuit may be expressed in silicon compiler language.

The silicon compiler has been developed most extensively in the Bristle Blocks system written by David Johannsen, associate professor of computer science at the California Institute of Technology, based on the integrated-circuit language developed by Ronald Ayres of the Xerox Corp., in El Segundo, Calif. Given a high-level description of a microprocessor chip, Bristle Blocks produces a layout, a sticks diagram, and diagrams for transistors, logic, and functional blocks. The system is currently tailored to produce only chips of a few different architectures.

The basic unit is a cell that is analogous to a software subroutine. The subroutine manipulates lines, boxes, and polygons—each associated with a given mask layer—and it has a list of all the possible interconnections between cells. (The connection points are like bristles along the edge of the cells; hence the name.) For example, cells requiring inputs from pads have a connection point specifying the type of pad needed and where in the cell the pad should connect.

Whereas the cells in conventional CAD are data-base cells—akin to "frozen" frames of circuits stored as coordinates in data files—Bristle Blocks cells are little programs that can draw themselves, as well as stretch, compute their power requirements, and even simulate themselves.

The input to the silicon compiler has three parts:
1. The number of bits in each microcode word that is assigned to, for example, the register-select field, the arithmetic-and-logic-unit field, and so on.
2. The data-word width and the list of buses.
3. A list of the core elements, exclusive of pads, instruction decoders, the upper and lower buses, and the microcode.

The compiler is a three-pass type in which a core pass lays out the core elements, a control pass adds the instruction decoders, and a pad pass places the pads on the perimeter of the chip and routes wires to points in the core and decoders.

—R.B.

registers of the calling procedure then become the high registers of the called procedure; yet no information is moved, since the low registers of the calling frame overlap the high registers of the called frame.

• Associated circuitry intervenes when no free bank is available. Studies indicate that with four to eight banks, overflow occurs in only 1 percent of cases.

RISC's superiority questioned

The main criticisms of the RISC approach are stated most succinctly by Douglas W. Clark and William D. Strecker, architects of the VAX series of complex minicomputers, and Justin Rattner, architect of the iAPX432. The criticisms include the following:

1. RISC is still just a paper design. Before it can be realistically compared with modern processors, it must be completely designed and built, compilers and operating systems must be written, and performance measurements must be made in various applications.
2. A pillar of the RISC approach is that few operating codes account for most of a typical program's execution. However, the dominant codes differ for different HLLs, so that a RISC will always be less flexible than a machine with multiple instructions. (In the VAX 11/780, for example, the top 10 Fortran instructions account for 60 percent of all instruction executions, whereas the top 20 in Cobol account for a mere 8 percent of executions.) The execution time for an instruction is, in any case, more important than its frequency of execution. The RISC, in optimizing only the most frequently executed instruction, may degrade performance because rarely executed instructions can have very long execution times.
3. In the absence of any metric or model, there is no proof that a RISC—though implemented in less silicon than a complex machine—is more cost-effective.
4. A complex machine offers more opportunities to use specialized hardware to improve performance for specific applications. For example, a complex machine with a multiply instruction offers the potential of speeding the multiplication process through additional data paths and control; but a RISC that uses software for multiplication could speed the arithmetic only if the whole processor were speeded up.
5. Though the cost of memory is indeed decreasing over time, it will remain true that a small amount of cheap memory costs less than a large amount. What's more, the microcode cost for a machine is a one-time cost, whereas the memory for a given computer is added on for each system.

For further reading

Microcomputer Architecture and Programming, by John F. Wakely (John Wiley & Sons Inc., New York, 1981), is one of the rare textbooks with a detailed discussion of the trade-offs between microcomputer architecture, performance, and ease of programming.

In a debate over operating systems, published in *Interface,* Vol. 2, pp. 78–82, Harold Stone of the University of Massachusetts and Peter Denning of Purdue University discuss how computer architecture can close the "semantic gap"—the distance between the concepts in the computer instruction sets and the more powerful concepts in modern programming languages.

D.A. Patterson and C. Sequin generalize on the RISC concept in "Design considerations for single-chip computers of the future," *IEEE Journal of Solid-State Circuits,* SC-15 (1980), pp. 44–52.

The trade-offs in designing single-chip microcomputers—

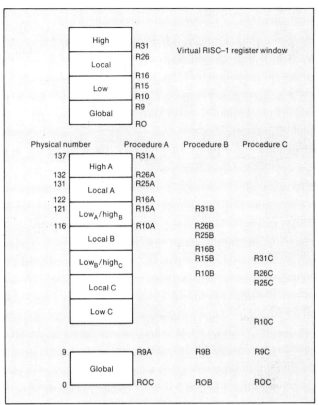

[3] The register windows in the RISC-I (Reduced Instruction Set Computer-I, proposed by Prof. David Patterson of Cal Tech) maximize the execution speed of procedure calls by reducing the number of accesses to off-chip memory. Multiple-register banks (32 per bank) are allocated by each call instruction to the called procedure, so that the contents of registers are neither saved on jumping nor restored on return. The "high" portion of each bank of registers contains parameters passed to the part of the program above the current calling procedure; the "local" portion contains local scalars; and the "low" portion contains parameters passed to the procedure from below the current procedure. On each call instruction the low registers become the high registers of the called procedure, yet no information is moved, since the low registers of the calling frame overlap the high registers of the called frame.

which differ from those well-proven in the design of computers, minicomputers, and microprocessor systems—are described by Harvey Cragon in "The elements of single-chip microcomputer architecture," *Computer,* October 1980, pp. 27–41. Unlike many articles of this type, the discussion is quite thorough and includes architecture trade-offs, memory-design factors, instruction and data word length, data-memory addressing, instruction-memory addressing, and so on. What's more, it weighs the classic alternatives in computer architecture: the von Neumann machine versus the Aiken machine. In the von Neumann machine, data words are not separate from instruction words; in Aiken machines, data and instructions are separate.

Richard J. Markowitz of Intel offers a well-balanced discussion of the relation between software and microcomputer architecture in "Software impact on microcomputer architecture," *Compcon 81* digest of papers pp. 40–48. Mr. Markowitz concludes that no quantitative method exists that "goes beyond these emotional arguments and can be applied dispassionately" to estimating the benefits of a new computer architecture. "Without metrics," he closes, "architecture remains a matter of taste." ◆

Toward simpler, faster computers

By omitting unnecessary functions, designers of reduced-instruction-set computers increase system speed and hold down equipment costs

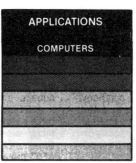

An overriding direction taken by computer design over the last 30 years—packing more and more functions into computing hardware to handle more complex problems—is being challenged as self-defeating.

Proponents of reduced-instruction-set computers (RISCs) contend that the way to make computers solve problems faster is to pare down the number of built-in functions they perform. Leaving instructions out of a central processing unit, much like leaving the automatic transmission out of a sports car, RISC supporters say, may improve its overall performance. By leaving out seldom-used instructions, computer designers may improve supermini and mainframe performance by a factor of 2 or 3 while reducing costs by an equal proportion.

Increasing density and complexity have been the rule in computer design for years. Integrated-circuit technology has let computer designers pack more power into smaller packages, and they have done so with abandon: a dozen or so chips can now contain as many gates as the entire CPU of a leading-edge mainframe of the early 1980s. The vast bulk of these newly available gates have been used for implementing additional instructions to support high-level languages or operating systems.

But should they? Examinations, some of them made as far back as the late 1960s, of which instructions computers actually execute and how much time they spend executing them appear to indicate that complex, specialized instructions are so infrequent that they cost more to implement than they are worth. A computer designed according to RISC precepts—which its proponents see as the fundamental direction for computer architectures for the next decade—would jettison such instructions, allowing designers to concentrate on making the core instruction set run faster. About half a dozen RISC computers have been built so far, some of them research machines and others commercial products, and all claim significantly better performance than equivalent conventional computers.

Some computer engineers, on the other hand, question the validity of the RISC approach. Among their objections are the following:
- RISCs require larger programs than complex-instruction-set computers to do equivalent problems.
- RISC instruction sets have been pared down to the point where certain operations that might take only a few instructions on a conventional computer require complex subroutines.
- RISC principles make no use of the increasing density available with advances in integrated-circuit technology.

The current RISC movement germinated in the early 1970s, when studies at IBM Corp. revealed that the vast bulk of a computer's time was spent loading data from memory into registers and storing them back into memory. Program branches—loop instructions or transfers to different parts of a program—also oc-

curred relatively frequently, as did arithmetic operations, but many other instructions were used infrequently. Nonetheless most modern large computers have enormous instruction sets: the DEC VAX-11, for example, has 304, each of which can be used with one or more or the computer's 18 addressing modes to operate on one or more of its 20 data types.

The rationale behind such a proliferation of instructions is to make the computer's low-level instruction set as much as possible like the high-level language instructions that it will presumably be executing, thereby reducing what has been called "the semantic gap." In an extreme example, Honeywell Inc. offered an instruction set for one of its mainframe computers in the early 1970s that reduced every Cobol verb to a single corresponding machine instruction [see "Microcode: hiding the real computer," p. 40]. This approach has the following problems, RISC proponents claim:
- Large instruction sets require complex and potentially time-consuming hardware steps to decode and execute them.
- Complex machine instructions may not match high-level language instructions exactly, in which case they may be of little use.
- Rich instruction sets present an overwhelming choice to language-compiling programs, which may not be capable of finding the correct specialized instruction to carry out a particular high-level function.
- Since complex machine instructions often have intricate execution sequences and side effects, programs using them can be difficult to optimize.

Defining terms

Compiler: a program that translates high-level language programs in a series of machine-code instructions for a computer to execute.

Opcode: the binary code for a particular machine instruction.

Operand: a code specifying the data that an instruction operates on, or the data themselves. Operands can be part of an opcode, or they can be extensions of the opcode.

Procedure call: a program branch in which control is transferred to an essentially independent subprogram that accepts parameters from the main program and returns values to it. Because procedures act as independent units, the contents of registers must be saved before calling and restored after returning from it.

RISC: reduced-instruction-set computer. A RISC eliminates complex instructions in the interest of speed and simplicity. "Reusable independent storage computer" has also been suggested as an expansion of the acronym to imply that the RISC's power comes from optimizing the use of CPU registers and main memory. Some controversy has arisen over the exact definition of a RISC, with contention focusing on whether computers with variable-length instructions, microcoded control, or floating-point arithmetic should properly be called RISCs.

Paul Wallich   Associate Editor

Reprinted from *IEEE Spectrum*, August 1985, pages 38-45. Copyright © 1985 by The Institute of Electrical and Electronics Engineers, Inc.

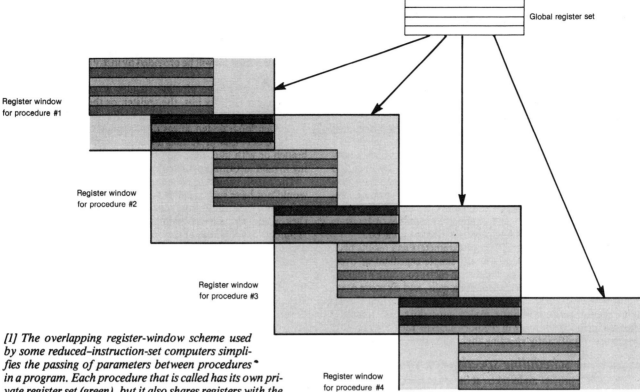

Global register set

Register window
for procedure #1

Register window
for procedure #2

Register window
for procedure #3

Register window
for procedure #4

[1] The overlapping register-window scheme used by some reduced–instruction-set computers simplifies the passing of parameters between procedures in a program. Each procedure that is called has its own private register set (green), but it also shares registers with the procedure that called it and with the procedure it calls (red). Parameters are passed to a called procedure by placing them in the lower set of shared registers, and results are passed back by placing them in the upper set of shared registers. A computer with overlapped register windows will generally also have a global register set (blue) accessible to all procedures.

• Instruction sets designed with specialized instructions for several high-level languages will carry excess baggage when executing any one language.

Computers based on RISC principles, on the other hand, make choices simpler for compilers, since there will usually be only one way to perform a particular function. Moreover, since their instructions break operations down to the simplest possible level, it is relatively easy for optimizing programs to combine operations and make software faster.

Two approaches to RISC

Three pioneering RISC efforts were the 801 project at IBM's Thomas J. Watson Research Laboratory in Yorktown, N.Y.; the Microprocessor without Interlocked Pipeline Stages (MIPS) project at Stanford University in Palo Alto, Calif.; and the Reduced Instruction Set Computer project at the University of California at Berkeley, which produced both the RISC I and RISC II processors. Two slightly different approaches have been taken to building RISC computers: the register-window approach, which relies on a large number of registers to store variables that would otherwise have to be fetched from the slower main memory, and the single–register-set approach, which pares hardware down to a minimum and relies on a smart compiler to allocate variables most efficiently to registers.

Both approaches share what is called a load/store architecture, meaning that only load and store instructions can access memory. All calculation is done explicitly in registers, thus eliminating multistage instructions in which the addresses of operands in main memory are calculated, the operands are fetched and run through the CPU, and the results are stored again in memory. Because of this simple architecture, all instructions can be executed in a single clock cycle.

The 801 project—started in 1975 and completed in 1979, though not publicly reported until 1981—grew out of research that had been done into computers with special instruction sets for special applications like number crunching and telephone switching. It was also an effort to find potential alternatives to the ever-increasing complexity of IBM's 370-series machines. "There was a group of people who were dissatisfied with the complexity of newer computers," recalled one IBM researcher, Martin Hopkins.

One aim of the 801 project, Hopkins asserted, was to point the way to computers with improved reliability and maintainability as well as higher speed. Such considerations can be traded off against one another fairly straightforwardly, he said, and "engineers should not spend all that capital up front" on complex instruction sets when attention might more profitably be devoted to overall system performance.

The 801 project succeeded in making a faster computer with a simpler instruction set and simpler data path compared with conventional machines using similar technology. Partly because of the concurrent development of a high-quality optimizing compiler, program path lengths—the total number of instructions executed to perform a particular algorithm—were also shorter. The compiler used relatively well-understood techniques, Hopkins said, such as moving code segments, eliminating common subexpressions, and precalculating constants, but it brought them all together for the first time. The compiler also did break new ground in allocating variables to registers.

An interesting result was that this same compiler could be used to generate code for a conventional IBM 370, using mostly the simplest 370 instructions. A 370 computer running program code generated by the 801 compiler executed twice as many instructions per second as it did when running programs compiled with a standard 370 compiler. This measurement is somewhat misleading, since the 801 used mainly the simplest and fastest-executing 370 instructions, but, Hopkins said, the programs also solved problems considerably faster.

The RISC project at Berkeley emerged from a similar backlash against commercial computer architecture. David Patterson, a professor of computer science at Berkeley, started the project after spending a sabbatical at Digital Equipment Corp. in Maynard, Mass., working on the prodigiously complex microcode of the VAX-11/780 superminicomputer. RISC I, the first product of the Berkeley research, had 31 instructions, compared with the VAX's 304, and only one addressing mode: all arithmetic and logical instructions operated on registers, and only load and store instructions accessed memory. The RISC II had 39 instructions and was also a load-store machine.

Into the silicon area where the complex instruction-decoding hardware and microinstruction sequencer would have gone, Patterson put an enormous register array. On a conventional computer, every procedure call and return requires saving the CPU registers in memory, loading the procedure's parameters, performing a computation, placing the result in a register or in memory, and then reloading the saved registers to return to the main program. But the RISC I and II allocate a new set of registers from its register set to each new procedure that is called.

Furthermore, the two RISCs pass parameters and results back and forth between procedures by the simple expedient of overlapping their register sets: six registers in each procedure's register set overlap with those of a procedure it calls, and six more overlap with the register set of the procedure that called it [see Fig. 1]. This register-window scheme makes procedure calls virtually free, reducing the number of memory accesses the RISC I and II make and significantly speeding their operation.

Execution scheduling speeds programs

The MIPS project undertaken at Stanford took a different approach to increasing speed in a RISC—it simplified pipelining. In a conventional computer, pipelining is used to decode and partly execute several instructions at the same time [see Fig. 2], but a conventional pipeline can break down for a number of reasons,

among them the following:

• The program takes a branch, thus requiring the pipeline to be cleared and new instructions to be fetched.

• Instructions in the pipeline require information that is not yet available because it will be provided by instructions further ahead in the pipeline.

• Instructions in the pipeline require access to the same resource—the memory bus, the register, or the ALU—simultaneously.

Conventional design solves these pipeline problems with special hardware that prefetches instructions at the destination of a branch or with interlocks that prevent instructions from accessing invalid information or from trying to use the same resource.

The MIPS project was intended to produce a computer that would not have such pipeline conflicts. It used special compiler software to rearrange programs and schedule instructions so that they would not interfere with one another, according to John Hennessy, who led the project as an assistant professor of computer science at Stanford and is currently on sabbatical as chief scientist of MIPS Computers Inc. in Mountain View, Calif. The processor also uses a delayed branch instruction—as do the Berkeley RISCs—to simplify the problem of refilling the pipeline after a change of control: the instruction following the branch is executed before control is transferred to the branch destination, giving the CPU time to fetch the proper instruction from the destination and start it through the pipeline.

But what happens to the instruction that gets executed before the branch takes effect? Does it perform useful work? Filling the slot after the branch is particularly tricky because most branches are conditional instructions: they transfer control to another portion of the program only at certain times. Even though a compiler can predict whether the branch will most often be taken or not, only instructions that should be executed in either case can

Microcode: hiding the 'real' computer

Most modern computers, including microprocessors, execute their instructions by what is called microcode, which is yet another level of coding below the individual bits of the instructions fetched from memory. These microinstructions give individual and detailed control over the registers, data paths, and arithmetic-and-logic units of the processor [see fig.].

Microcode serves to simplify both the programming and design of a central processing unit. For example, the machine-level instruction "Add the contents of register A to those of register B and deposit the result in register C" requires routing the contents of the two registers somehow to the inputs of the arithmetic-and-logic unit, setting the ALU to do addition, and then routing the output to the third register. Some of these operations can be done in parallel, while others must be done serially. Microcode simplifies the programming task, since the programmer (or the compiler program) is not required to consider which operations can or cannot proceed in parallel or exactly what bits to set on the ALU. Because they control the CPU at a much greater level of detail, microinstructions are typically much wider than macroinstructions; 40 bits is a typical width, and 60 bits is not uncommon.

Microcoding also simplifies the hardware design because designers can compose many high-level operations from a small number of microinstructions rather than adding entirely new hardware for each new instruction. They can implement a multiplication instruction, for example, as a series of addition and bit-shifting microinstructions rather than build a hardware multiplier.

Instructions that are put into microcode can often run faster than if they had to be spelled out in machine code—or macroinstructions—because microinstructions have access to internal registers and other machine resources that are not visible at the higher level. Furthermore, because microcode is built into the CPU, the microinstructions can be fetched from the control store much faster than macroinstructions can be retrieved from main memory.

Because microinstructions can be used to build specialized high-level functions from simpler low-level ones, they are also often used to hide the low-level architecture of a computer from a

programmer. IBM Corp. has followed this path with great success in the 370 series, all members of which look almost identical at the instruction-set level, even though their underlying architectures are quite different. Microcode routines for each instruction match the "virtual machine" to the underlying hardware resources.

Microinstructions also have their problems, of course. The difficulty of writing them is an obvious one; wide-word microcode is particularly hard to write and debug because it involves many actions occurring in parallel with hard-to-follow interactions between them. So-called vertical microcode, which allows much less parallelism, is easier to write but less efficient.

Another difficulty with microcode is that it adds a level of indirection to the execution of instructions; unless hardware is added to decode instructions and fetch their microcode quickly, a microcoded computer will run more slowly than one that executes instructions directly. With the advent of very fast memories, this may no longer be a problem, especially with wide-word microcoding, where most instructions require only a single line of microcode. In such cases, microcoding is simply an alternative method of getting the correct data to the processor's internal control lines and is equivalent to a programmed logic array or any other control structure.   —P.W.

A microcoded central processor decodes an instruction into an address in a control store memory, which in turn directs the execution of a sequence of low-level steps. Operands must be fetched from registers, cache, or main memory, arithmetic or logical operations performed, condition flags set, results written back to registers or memory, and the program counter adjusted to point to the next instruction. In the example above (not corresponding to any particular microcoded processor), two fields of an instruction are used to find an address in a first-level control store, which in turn directs a sequencer and selects a series of microinstructions—a microroutine—in a second-level control store. Several different instructions may use the same microroutine.

safely be put in the slot immediately following a branch. A typical example of a predictable branch is a program loop, which executes many times—branching back to the beginning each time—but eventually exits.

About 70 percent of the time, Hennessy explained, the position can be filled with an instruction that will be required whether the branch is taken or not. Perhaps 20 percent of the time it is filled by an instruction that does not advance the state of the computation—if the branch behaves according to the compiler's prediction, then the instruction performs useful work; but if it is taken, then no incorrect operations are performed. Finally, 10 percent of the slots are filled with no-operation instructions, which is what would be happening all the time for a conventional computer that had to refill its pipeline after every branch.

Hennessy said that since about 20 percent of the instructions executed were branches, the delayed branch yields a gain of about 15 percent in overall execution speed. The MIPS group at Stanford is currently working on MIPS-X, a virtual-address version of its machine, and the company Hennessy helped found is working on a CMOS implementation of the processor intended to execute about 3 to 5 million instructions per second. Hennessy will return to Stanford in the fall to head the university's computer science laboratory.

Among those making commercial forays into RISC work are Ridge Computers Inc., which manufactures a RISC that includes floating-point mathematics instructions; Pyramid Technology Corp., whose 90x is a many-user superminicomputer optimized for the UNIX operating system; and Harris Corp, whose HCX-7 is also optimized for UNIX. Hewlett-Packard Co. has announced that it will be using RISC architectures for its future minicomputer lines, although it has not yet announced a product, and DEC and IBM are also both rumored to be working on RISCs as CPUs for high-performance personal workstations.

The RISC philosophy seems sensible, research projects have achieved impressive performance, and commercial RISCs show remarkable throughput figures. But some computer scientists have criticized the move toward reduced instruction sets, however, and have voiced the following objections:
• RISC programs take up too much space, which degrades performance, since more instructions must be fetched from slower main memory to perform a given operation.
• RISC computers have not been tested in enough real-world situations to judge their performance.
• Overlapped-register-set RISCs, such as RISC I and II, suffer dramatic performance losses when executing programs where the register stack overflows and must be copied to main memory.
• Although RISC computers have simpler hardware, their program compilers must be proportionately more complex to wring performance out of the bare-bones CPU.
• The performance gains that RISC machines show are based on features such as overlapped register sets, which have nothing to do with reduced instruction sets and could as easily be implemented on complex machines.
• To compete in the real world, RISC machines must be loaded down with additional instructions and hardware—such as floating-point arithmetic and memory management—that make them just as complex as the complex-instruction-set computers they are supposed to replace. "It takes a lot of work to turn a RISC into a real computer," said one critic.

A group of researchers at Carnegie-Mellon University in Pittsburgh, Pa., pointed out that a rating method for computers used by the U.S. Department of Defense in its search for a new standard computer architecture put RISCs very low on the scale, whereas the VAX—an archetypal complex instruction set computer—was rated near the top. In studies of the number of times the RISC II had to access memory to fetch instructions, or to

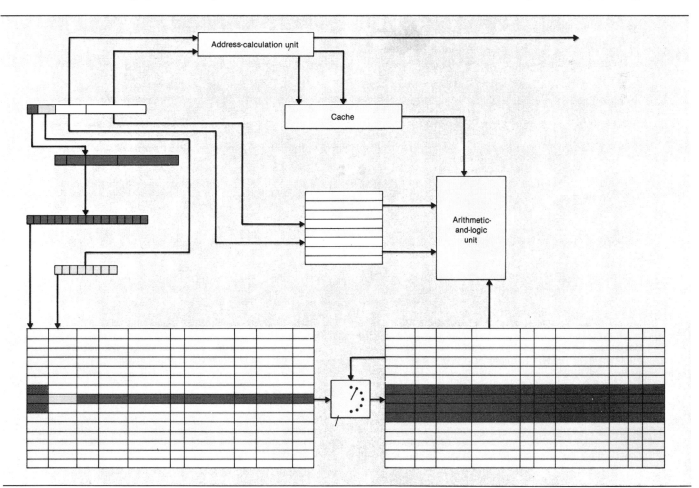

load and store data, it performed badly on programs that passed many parameters to their procedures, or that called huge numbers of procedures in succession. These cases were particularly difficult for the RISC II to handle because the overlapping register set could only handle a small number of procedure calls before overflowing to memory.

As soon as the RISC II had to make use of memory to save and restore its registers, the researchers found, its performance dropped precipitously, especially since it has no mechanism for saving or restoring only a few registers at a time—it must go through a software subroutine that saves or restores all 16 current registers, no matter how many are actually in use.

Two of the researchers, Charles Y. Hitchcock III and H.M. Brinkley Sprunt, also did studies in which they simulated the RISC, the MC68000, and the DEC VAX, adding or subtracting overlapping register sets to determine how much performance gain could be attributed to them when they did not overflow. They found that the RISC II's performance was largely dependent on its overlapping register set—without it, it ran about half as quickly on most problems. They also found that both the

MC68000 and the VAX could also benefit from having an overlapping register set added to their architectures, although the effect on them was less marked—only about a 30-percent difference.

RISC proponents counter that such an analysis is missing the point because overlapping register sets could not be added to the architecture of a 68000 or a VAX without reducing chip yield to unacceptable levels or increasing the number of boards in the CPU. "A VAX 780 has 27 boards in its CPU, and we have two," noted David Folger, president of Ridge Computers in Santa Clara, Calif. In applications such as integrated-circuit design, the Ridge outperforms a VAX 11/780 by a factor of 2 to 4.

On the other hand, one complex-microprocessor designer (whose company requested he not be named) said he believes that the RISC arguments "had their place at a certain point of technology," but that they have now been overtaken by the increasing density of semiconductor circuits. "Now we have eight times the density of RISC II," he noted. "So you put on a cache, and make addition and subtraction run faster, but what then?" He asserted that technological advances had made complex hard-

---

Compiler technology key to RISC success

Since what compilers do is break down high-level language programs into smaller actions, compiling for a reduced-instruction-set computer (RISC) simply requires a little more breaking down. A reduced instruction set provides fewer choices of instruction for the compiler, thus potentially leading to longer program code, but the reduced choice also simplifies the compiler, since it does not have to keep the complex accounting required to choose between several alternate ways of doing the same thing.

This simplification could have a salutary effect on compiler design. Martin Hopkins, a researcher at IBM Corp.'s Thomas J. Watson Research Center in Yorktown Heights, N.Y., for example, said he is a little disappointed with much recent university research on compilers because most of it has been aimed at "regularizing methods for making choices in special cases" rather than improving formal methods for global optimization and register allocation.

Simply generating machine code for a particular architecture is only the first stage in compilation. At least as significant for RISCs is the optimization stage, in which constants are precalculated, redundant subexpressions are eliminated, variables are shuffled among registers, and so forth.

And here the RISC shines: "It's almost undeniable that you can generate optimal code for a simple machine," said Robert Ragan-Kelley, vice president for computer architecture and planning at Pyramid Technology Corp. in Mountain View, Calif., "but it's difficult for a machine with lots of function." Complex-instruction-set computers present a difficult problem for optimization programs because there are too many choices for performing different operations, and even human experts may disagree on which is the best one.

In some RISCs, there is even a level below the compiler, called the assembler, which performs additional optimization and decoding of instructions. The assembler for the micro-Processor without Interlocking Pipeline Stage (MIPS) computer, built at Stanford University in Palo Alto, Calif., for example, translates such instructions as integer multiplication into the series of multiplication steps that the chip actually can do. In addition, the MIPS assembler contains a pipeline reorganizer that is responsible for scheduling the execution of instructions so that there will be no conflicts in the pipelined fetching of operands and no unused instruction slots due to branches that interrupt the pipeline.

The translation of a multiplication instruction into a series of smaller operations is exactly the same thing a microcoded complex-instruction-set computer does when it fetches the opcode for a multiplication, except, of course, that it is only

done once by the MIPS. John Hennessy, leader of the Stanford MIPS project and also chief scientist of MIPS Computers Inc. in Mountain View, said that this resemblance to traditional microcode is no mistake.

"Back in the 1960s and 1970s," he noted, "one of the big ideas was dynamic microcode"—an arrangement whereby the microcode that controlled the basic hardware of a computer would be changed on the fly to provide the most efficient execution sequence and machine instruction set at any given moment of program execution. Dynamic microcode ran into a host of problems, including the cost of reloading the high-speed memory of the control store and the difficulty of writing enormous amounts of microcode by hand.

Today, however, optimizing compilers can write the "microcode"—instructions for a RISC—and cheap CMOS memory chips can be built into large caches that are the equivalent of "a large writable control store," Hennessy said. Present compilers are up to the task of writing so-called vertical microcode, in which a relatively small number of operations take place in parallel, Hennessy asserted, but horizontal microcode, which controls an enormous number of simultaneous operations, is still some years in the future.

Because the compiler is an integral part of a RISC-based computer system, it is clear that most programming for RISCs will be done in high-level languages. But does this mean the end of assembly-language programming?

Certainly not, said IBM's Hopkins. For one thing, programming a RISC in assembly language is much simpler (although possibly more tedious) than programming a complex-instruction-set computer. And for another, there will always be a few applications where current compilers are not quite smart enough to recognize what tradeoffs they can make in the interests of speed. He cited such applications as interpreters for high-level languages as one area where human programmers have a edge in optimization.

"There are always going to be special-purpose routines for particular applications," said Hopkins, "and someone is going to have to code them in a high-level language or in assembly language." In fact, simple instruction sets may make it more feasible for programmers to write those routines in assembly language. Complex-instruction-set computers, Hopkins asserted, "take away power from individuals to solve their own performance problems and load the problems back onto some architectural group" of engineers who define the instruction set. RISC machines, on the other hand, give programmers direct access to the primitive operations required to do whatever they want.　　　　　　　　　　—P.W.

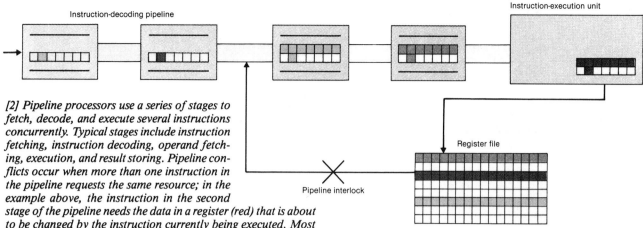

[2] Pipeline processors use a series of stages to fetch, decode, and execute several instructions concurrently. Typical stages include instruction fetching, instruction decoding, operand fetching, execution, and result storing. Pipeline conflicts occur when more than one instruction in the pipeline requests the same resource; in the example above, the instruction in the second stage of the pipeline needs the data in a register (red) that is about to be changed by the instruction currently being executed. Most computers use special hardware to stop the pipeline until the register has been changed; others omit interlocks and use special techniques either to ensure that there will be no conflicts or to accelerate the delivery of new data to the pipe stage that needs it.

Pipeline interlock

ware configurations much more feasible than they were even a few years ago.

Smaller instruction sets make bigger programs

The argument that RISC programs take up more space than the corresponding programs for a complex–instruction-set computer would seem to make sense: after all, if the compiler for a RISC breaks down high-level language instructions into very simple actions, it should take more instructions to accomplish a task than the conventional computer, where a single instruction often sets off a long chain of actions. The Intel 432 microprocessor, for example, had a single machine-level instruction—which triggered a substantial series of microinstructions—to send a message from one process to another, a job usually handled by an operating-system software routine.

In this view, the high instruction-execution rates of a RISC machine do not lead to correspondingly short execution times— "If you make each instruction brain-damaged enough, you can get a very high clock rate," noted Stephen Johnson of AT&T Bell Laboratories, in Summit, N.J., author of the portable C-language compiler used to compile benchmark programs for the RISC I and II.

But, on the other hand, Hennessy of Stanford asserted that "the RISC machines tend to execute about the same number of instructions" as their complex–instruction-set counterparts for a given problem.

This seeming paradox is explained, he said, by the amount of optimization that compilers can perform on RISC programs. By carefully allocating variables to registers, for example, a RISC machine can reduce the number of times it has to access main memory and the total number of instructions it has to do. Furthermore, all the registers of a RISC are directly accessible to the compiler, whereas complex–instruction-set computers often have hidden registers accessible only to particular instructions—for example, those that move data from one memory location to another, or add the contents of two memory locations. Such features make the optimizing of programs more difficult.

The question of program size is important, not merely because of potentially misleading execution speeds, but also because the effects of program size can snowball throughout an entire computer system. Larger programs require more memory to store them, thus affecting program-loading time. They are also more likely to cause page faults—portions of the program not in main memory—in virtual memory systems, thus reducing performance, and in computers with caches larger programs will reduce cache hit rates, thus diminishing performance further.

RISC machines are particularly dependent on caches—small,

high-speed memories—to feed them instructions at a rate fast enough that one instruction can be executed in each clock cycle. If a RISC has to wait for main memory to supply instructions and data, it can be slowed by a factor of 3 or more. Enhanced CPU performance can "get lost in the noise" in the face of such systemwide considerations, according to Robert Ragan-Kelley, vice president for architecture and planning at Pyramid. Overall evidence seems to indicate that program size is not a problem for RISCs so far, but it is certainly a pitfall to bear in mind when designing reduced instruction sets. "You can't just chop out instructions," he said. "The primitives must serve the application." If only a few crucial instructions are absent from its instruction set, a computer can take five or ten times as long to execute certain programs as it would if they were present.

Facing software questions

Because of their architectures, RISC machines may cross hardware thresholds and lose performance in a number of areas: not only in caches and main memory, but in registers as well. The two families of RISC machines face this problem differently. RISCs with a limited number of registers, such as the MIPS and the 801, may run out of registers because all calculations must be performed using them. Register-window RISCs, such as the RISC I and II and the Pyramid, may run out of registers for additional procedures, forcing an overflow to main memory.

The register-window RISCs face an additional problem when running multiple tasks at the same time, critics say: either they must allocate portions of the register set to each process, thus limiting how many tasks they can perform efficiently at the same time, or they must save and restore the entire register set when changing from one process to another, which represents a significant overhead penalty. (The RISC II has more than 100 registers, and the Pyramid has 528.)

Ragan-Kelley, on the other hand, contends that it is quite simple to implement a scheme whereby only a single register set is initially saved to make room for a new process and more are allocated as needed, thus reducing overhead substantially.

Much of the performance of RISC machines thus comes down to the technology of the compilers that convert high-level program code into the spare set of machine instructions the RISC will execute. If the compiler allocates variables to registers efficiently and eliminates redundant expressions, then all may be well, but if the compiler does not perform well, then code size can balloon and execution speed can plummet. Some critics assert that RISC designers have simply traded complexity in one place, hardware, for complexity in another, software.

But RISC proponents reply that writing compilers for a reduced-instruction set is at least as simple as writing a compiler for a complex–instruction-set computer—and potentially much easier, because the compiler usually has only one choice of instruction sequence for a particular operation. On a conventional computer, the same high-level language instruction could be executed in many different ways, each with its own specialized advantages and tradeoffs, but "on a RISC there's usually only one way to do things," said IBM's Hopkins.

Hennessy of Stanford contended that "the compiler issue has been exaggerated." For the most part, he pointed out, all a RISC compiler does is what typical complex–instruction–set computers do every time they execute an instruction: break an action down into smaller parts and execute these parts one by one. It stands to reason, he said, that efficiency is gained by paying the cost for that breakdown only once for each program and performing it as well as possible.

"Were not trying anything in our compilers that Fortran H doesn't do," said Ridge's Edwin Basart of his company's compiler technology. (Fortran H is a venerable optimizing compiler that has run on IBM mainframes for more than a decade.) Furthermore, he said, optimizing a program yields better and more predictable benefits on a RISC than on a complex–instruction–set computer, because eliminating an instruction always saves clock cycles, and the number of clock cycles saved by different alternatives is easy to calculate.

Compiler technology for RISCs has been attracting undue attention for two reasons, Basart contended. First, he said, "RISCs are new architectures, and so you have to build compilers for them; you can't just buy one off the shelf." Second, "Minicomputers haven't had good compilers—we're just doing what was done at Control Data 20 years ago."

Johnson, the compiler author at Bell Labs, agreed with this assessment of RISC compilers. After all, he points out, RISC instruction sets were designed after careful studies of exactly what instructions good compilers did generate.

IBM's Hopkins said, "Every trace tape ever run shows that nobody ever uses those fancy operations."

In a nutshell, according to Pyramid's Ragan-Kelley, "mature designers have always known that all computers do are loads and stores, procedure calls and returns, and so forth." Software complexity, he said, is not an issue.

Redefining a RISC

That major computer companies such as DEC, Hewlett–Packard, and IBM have either openly affirmed a commitment to RISC machines or sponsored extensive research and development efforts says something for the concept. But what of the three commercial RISCs already on the market? The Ridge, the Pyramid, and the Harris computers all stretch the definition of a RISC, and some critics question whether a computer like the Pyramid—with over 100 instructions, all implemented in microcode—should qualify as a RISC. Both the Ridge and the Pyramid are microcoded, and they also implement virtual memory, a technique usually reserved for complex computers.

Others, such as IBM's Hopkins, see elements of RISC philosophy being applied even in such complex machines as DEC's MicroVAX II, which achieves 80 percent of the performance of a VAX 11/780 even though it implements only about 60 percent of the VAX instruction set in hardware, relying on software for the rest.

The major reason to call the Ridge a RISC, said Folger, is the simplicity and regularity of its instruction set. The machine allows only load and store operations and operations that perform calculations on operands in registers. "The number of instructions isn't so important," he said. "For example, if you can do register-register addition, you get logical AND, OR, and exclusive-OR for free," because the same hardware is used for all those operations.

Because the Ridge instruction set is regular, the portion of the instruction specifying the operands can be sent to the register file to initiate the operand fetch, even while the instruction type is being decoded [Fig. 3]. Folger contrasted this with the VAX, where a series of extensions to the instruction opcode specify the kinds of operands, their locations, and their length. Because the oper-

ands can vary in length, the VAX cannot even determine the location of the second operand for an instruction until it has fully decoded the first, he pointed out.

Floating-point instructions, however, do appear to fall outside what is usually considered RISC architecture. "The IEEE floating-point standard has bells and whistles all over it," Johnson noted. Among these features are specifications for four different kinds of rounding, special extensions for very small numbers, and even a particular bit pattern to represent invalid numbers.

Both Ragan-Kelley and Folger pointed out, on the other hand, that floating-point calculations are an essential part of real computer applications, especially in science and engineering, so they must be included in a RISC manufactured for sale. Performance would be five to ten times worse without them, Ragan-Kelley asserted. In fact, since floating-point instructions do comprise such a large percentage of the instructions executed by scientific and engineering programs, including them in a commercial RISC is simply a reflection of the design principle that RISCs should include often-used instructions while leaving out those that are not used often or that can be efficiently emulated by subroutines.

RISCs that handle floating-point instructions are significantly more complex than RISCs that do not, but their complexity still does not approach that of conventional complex–instruction-set computers, Folger said. In fact, he asserted, one way of looking at the Ridge CPU would be as "a floating-point processor that also executes instructions on the side."

Another complex problem for RISCs is implementing virtual memory, a technique whereby programs can use far more space than is available in main memory by fetching "pages" from secondary storage as needed. Virtual memory requires a plethora of specialized hardware to translate between virtual and real addresses and to determine whether a page is in memory, as well as finely tuned software to decide which old page to swap out to make room for a new one. Nevertheless RISC machines have significant advantages in implementing virtual memory. Because RISCs perform all calculations in registers, only instruction fetches, loads, and stores can cause page faults that require swapping in a new page. And in any of these cases it is relatively easy to back up execution and restart the instruction after the required page has been brought in, because the instructions executed have no side-effect that must also be undone.

Since complex-instruction-set computers allow arithmetic and logical operations directly on memory, they run the risk of getting into states that are hard to untangle if a page fault occurs. For example, moving characters from one memory location to another on an IBM 370 could cause as many as eight page faults. Two page faults could occur fetching the portion of the instruction that sets the number of characters to be moved. Since instructions are allowed to straddle page boundaries, another two faults could occur fetching the move instruction itself, and four more page faults could occur in fetching the data from its source and storing it at its destination if each of those locations straddled a page boundary. The status of instruction execution and data movement would have to be saved when each page fault occurred and restored after the appropriate page was brought into memory. This problem would be significantly simplified by forcing instruction not to overlap page boundaries; some complex-instruction-set computers, on the other hand, do not even constrain instructions to begin and end at word boundaries.

RISCs change engineering tradeoffs

Complexities such as floating-point operations and virtual memory, however, are also fundamental to the problems that computers are being used to solve. "When you're doing a job that's inherently complicated, the complexity isn't going to go away," said Johnson. The point of designs like the RISCs is a willingness to trade off complexity across what were previously considered hard and fast system boundaries—making a little more work for the software so as to make a little less for the hardware. The present bias toward putting complexity in software

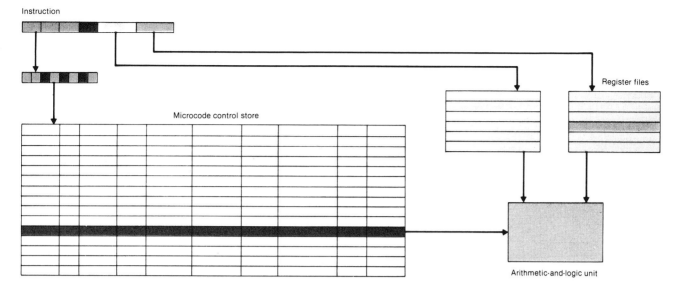

Instruction

Microcode control store

Register files

Arithmetic-and-logic unit

[3] A reduced-instruction-set computer uses a regular instruction format to speed execution. In this case, the first half of the instruction is decoded (red) whereas the second half is used to select operands from registers (green and blue). Complex-instruction-set computers often use several different instruction formats, so that the first part of the instruction must be fully decoded before the central processor can determine what to do with the rest of it. In extreme cases, each succeeding part of an instruction must be decoded for the processor to determine where the next part of the instruction begins.

arises because "bugs in the software are easier to fix," according to Johnson—certainly the turnaround time for compiling a piece of code is shorter than that for fabricating a piece of silicon.

"There's a wave of people now who are trained in the whole computer field from software to silicon," said Ridge's Basart, and these designers are better able to look at computers as systems consisting of many levels of hardware and software, rather than just at CPUs in isolation.

In addition, the rise of software standards has made it easier in the last half-decade to design new computer architectures. "UNIX is the unsung hero of all this," said Ragan-Kelley, "because without a retargetable operating system, there wouldn't have been a commercial environment for RISCs." With UNIX, a C language compiler, a few bright, dedicated programmers, and a great deal of hard work are about all that is needed to allow thousands of well-documented programs to be transported to a new computer.

If RISC concepts do point the way to a new design methodology for computers, what will be the result? Will conventional mainframes and minicomputers fade away? Probably not, since far too large an installed base of software would have to be converted. On the other hand, the increased speed of RISC architectures may place complex-instruction-set computers at an increasing disadvantage as time goes by.

"DEC has a terrible problem with the VAX, because you just can't build it to run fast," said one researcher who requested anonymity. "And, in the same way, IBM is stuck with the 370." One possibility for speeding such conventional machines is to apply some of the lessons learned from RISCs to their design. Although instruction sets and formats cannot be changed, their implementation can be, and it may be possible to emulate many instructions in software while maintaining performance. This kind of emulation, in fact, has been part of the designer's bag of trick for many years.

RISCs themselves will probably evolve as well. One possible direction is exemplified by the FRISC (fanatically reduced instruction set computer) in development at Schlumberger Palo Alto (Calif.) Research Center, which has no branch instructions in its CPU. Instead, in another example of tradeoffs across system boundaries, the processor relies on a special instruction-stream memory to feed it the correct next instruction to execute.

Another obvious direction for RISCs to take is toward added complexity. The Smalltalk on a RISC project at Berkeley, for example, adds hardware support for the Smalltalk language to the basic structure developed by Patterson. The MIPS-X project at Stanford is intended to provide a uniform virtual-memory structure for a RISC, eliminating address translation as far as possible. Folger and others speculate that Hewlett-Packard's RISC will include hardware support for packed-decimal arithmetic or memory-to-memory operations, two requirements of the Cobol language used in the mainstream data-processing environments inhabited by HP's current minicomputers.

"Once you've cleared the decks, you can now put more baggage on them," commented Basart of Ridge.

Ragan-Kelley, on the other hand, suggested that RISCs would be used as a basis for more complex system architectures. "The next generation of baroqueness," he said, "will be not at the CPU level, but rather with topologies and interconnections of multiple processor systems." Pyramid only recently announced a multiple-processor version of its RISC minicomputer.

As more computers based on RISC ideas are developed and used, their benefits and drawbacks will become clearer. What is already clear, though, is that computer architecture is changing. Formerly hard-and-fast divisions between software and hardware appear to be giving way to a systems approach.

To probe further

RISC proponents have published a number of papers expounding their views. One of the first was "A VLSI RISC," by David Patterson and Carlo Sequin of the University of California at Berkeley, in *IEEE Computer*, September 1982. "The 801 minicomputer," by George Radin of IBM, appeared in the *IBM Journal of Research and Development* in May 1983. A review of existing RISC efforts is "Reduced Instruction Set Computers," also by Patterson, in *Communications of the ACM*, January 1985.

The most thorough critical examination of reduced-instruction-set concepts is "Computers, Complexity, and Controversy," by Robert P. Colwell, Charles Y. Hitchcock III, E. Douglas Jensen, H.M. Brinkley Sprunt, and Charles P. Kollar of Carnegie-Mellon University in Pittsburgh, Pa., to be published in the September 1985 issue of *IEEE Computer*. A number of additional articles comparing RISCs and complex-instruction-set computers have appeared in *Computer Architecture News*. ◆

Instruction Sets and Beyond:

Computers, Complexity, and Controversy

**Robert P. Colwell, Charles Y. Hitchcock III,
E. Douglas Jensen, H. M. Brinkley Sprunt,
and Charles P. Kollar**

Carnegie-Mellon University

Computer design should focus on the assignment of system functionality to implementation levels within an architecture, and not be guided by whether it is a RISC or CISC design.

The avalanche of publicity received by the reduced instruction set computer has swept away objectivity in the technical communities and obscured many important issues. RISC design seriously challenges some implicit assumptions that have guided computer design for years. A study of its principles should yield a deeper understanding of hardware/software tradeoffs, computer performance, the influence of VLSI on processor design, and many other topics. Articles on RISC research, however, often fail to explore these topics properly and can be misleading. Further, the few papers that present comparisons with complex instruction set computer design often do not address the same issues. As a result, even careful study of the literature is likely to give a distorted view of this area of research. This article offers a useful perspective of RISC/Complex Instruction Set Computer research, one that is supported by recent work at Carnegie-Mellon University.

Much RISC literature is devoted to discussions of the size and complexity of computer instruction sets. These discussions are extremely misleading.

Instruction set design is important, but it should not be driven solely by adherence to convictions about design style, RISC or CISC. The focus of discussion should be on the more general question of the assignment of system functionality to implementation levels within an architecture. This point of view encompasses the instruction set—CISCs tend to install functionality at lower system levels than RISCs—but also takes into account other design features such as register sets, coprocessors, and caches.

While the implications of RISC research extend beyond the instruction set, even within the instruction set domain, there are limitations that have not been identified. Typical RISC papers give few clues about where the RISC approach might break down. Claims are made for faster machines that are cheaper and easier to design and that "map" particularly well onto VLSI technology. It has been said, however, that "Every complex problem has a simple solution...and it is wrong." RISC ideas are not "wrong," but a simple-minded view of them would be. RISC theory has many implications that are not obvious. Re-

Reprinted from *Computer*, September 1985, pages 8-19. Copyright © 1985 by The Institute of Electrical and Electronics Engineers, Inc.

EH0251-9/86/0000/0346$01.00 © 1985 IEEE

search in this area has helped focus attention on some important issues in computer architecture whose resolutions have too often been determined by defaults; yet RISC proponents often fail to discuss the application, architecture, and implementation contexts in which their assertions seem justified.

While RISC advocates have been vocal concerning their design methods and theories, CISC advocates have been disturbingly mute. This is not a healthy state of affairs. Without substantive, reported CISC research, many RISC arguments are left uncountered and, hence, out of perspective. The lack of such reports is due partially to the proprietary nature of most commercial CISC designs and partially to the fact that industry designers do not generally publish as much as academics. Also, the CISC design style has no coherent statement of design principles, and CISC designers do not appear to be actively working on one. This lack of a manifesto differentiates the CISC and RISC design styles and is the result of their different historical developments.

Towards defining a RISC

Since the earliest digital electronic computers, instruction sets have tended to grow larger and more complex. The 1948 MARK-1 had only seven instructions of minimal complexity, such as adds and simple jumps, but a contemporary machine like the VAX has hundreds of instructions. Furthermore, its instructions can be rather complicated, like atomically inserting an element into a doubly linked list or evaluating a floating point polynomial of arbitrary degree. Any high performance implementation of the VAX, as a result, has to rely on complex implementation techniques such as pipelining, prefetching, and multi-cycle instruction execution.

This progression from small and simple to large and complex instruction sets is striking in the development of single-chip processors within the past decade. Motorola's 68020, for example, carries 11 more addressing modes than the 6800, more than twice as many instructions, and support for an instruction cache and coprocessors. Again, not only has the number of addressing modes and instructions increased, but so has their complexity.

This general trend toward CISC machines was fueled by many things, including the following:

- New models are often required to be upward-compatible with existing models in the same computer family, resulting in the supersetting and proliferation of features.

- Many computer designers tried to reduce the "semantic gap" between programs and computer instruction sets. By adding instructions semantically closer to those used by programmers, these designers hoped to reduce software costs by creating a more easily programmed machine. Such instructions tend to be more complex because of their higher semantic level. (It is often the case, however, that instructions with high semantic content do not exactly match those required for the language at hand.)

- In striving to develop faster machines, designers constantly moved functions from software to microcode and from microcode to hardware, often without concern for the adverse effects that an added architectural feature can have on an implementation. For example, addition of an instruction requiring an extra level of decoding logic can slow a machine's entire instruction set. (This is called the "$n+1$" phenomenon.[1])

- Tools and methodologies aid designers in handling the inherent complexity of large architectures. Current CAD tools and microcoding support programs are examples.

Microcode is an interesting example of a technique that encourages complex designs in two ways. First, it provides a structured means of effectively creating and altering the algorithms that control execution of numerous operations and complex instructions in a computer. Second, the proliferation of CISC features is encouraged by the quantum nature of microcode memories; it is relatively easy to add another addressing mode or obscure instruction to a machine which has not yet used all of its microcode space.

Instruction traces from CISC machines consistently show that few of the available instructions are used in most computing environments. This situation led IBM's John Cocke, in the early 70's, to contemplate a departure from traditional computer styles. The result was a research project based on an ECL machine that used a very advanced compiler, creatively named "801" for the research group's building number. Little has been published about that project, but what has been released speaks for a principled and coherent research effort.

The 801's instruction set was based on three design principles. According to Radin,[2] the instruction set was to be that set of run-time operations that

- could not be moved to compile time,

- could not be more efficiently executed by object code produced by a compiler that understood the high-level intent of the program, and

- could be implemented in random logic more effectively than the equivalent sequence of software instructions.

The machine relied on a compiler that used many optimization strategies for much of its effectiveness, including a

powerful scheme of register allocation. The hardware implementation was guided by a desire for leanness and featured hardwired control and single-cycle instruction execution. The architecture was a 32-bit load/store machine (only load and store instructions accessed memory) with 32 registers and single-cycle instructions. It had separate instruction and data caches to allow simultaneous access to code and operands.

Some of the basic ideas from the 801 research reached the West Coast in the mid 70's. At the University of California at Berkeley, these ideas grew into a series of graduate courses that produced the RISC I* (followed later by the RISC II) and the numerous CAD tools that facilitated its design. These courses laid the foundation for related research efforts in performance evaluation, computer-aided design, and computer implementation.

The RISC I processor,[3] like the 801, is a load/store machine that executes most of its instructions in a single cycle. It has only 31 instructions, each of which fits in a single 32-bit word and uses practically the same encoding format. A special feature of the RISC I is its large number of registers, well over a hundred, which are used to form a series of overlapping register sets. This feature makes procedure calls on the RISC I less expensive in terms of processor-memory bus traffic.

Soon after the first RISC I project at Berkeley, a processor named MIPS (Microprocessor without Interlocked Pipe Stages) took shape at Stanford. MIPS[1] is a pipelined, single-chip processor that relies on innovative software to ensure that its pipeline resources are properly managed. (In machines such as the IBM System/360 Model 91, pipeline interstage interlocking is per-

formed at run-time by special hardware). By trading hardware for compile-time software, the Stanford researchers were able to expose and use the inherent internal parallelism of their fast computing engine.

These three machines, the 801, RISC I, and MIPS, form the core of RISC research machines, and share a set of common features. We propose the following elements as a working definition of a RISC:

(1) *Single-cycle operation* facilitates the rapid execution of simple functions that dominate a computer's instruction stream and promotes a low interpretive overhead.

(2) *Load/store design* follows from a desire for single-cycle operation.

(3) *Hardwired control* provides for the fastest possible single-cycle operation. Microcode leads to slower control paths and adds to interpretive overhead.

(4) *Relatively few instructions and addressing modes* facilitate a fast, simple interpretation by the control engine.

(5) *Fixed instruction format* with consistent use, eases the hardwired decoding of instructions, which again speeds control paths.

(6) *More compile-time effort* offers an opportunity to explicitly move static run-time complexity into the compiler. A good example of this is the software pipeline reorganizer used by MIPS.[1]

A consideration of the two companies that claim to have created the first commercial "RISC" computer, Ridge Computers and Pyramid Technology, illustrates why a definition is needed. Machines of each firm have restricted instruction formats, a feature they share with RISC machines.

Pyramid's machine is not a load/store computer, however, and both Ridge and Pyramid machines have variable length instructions and use multiple-cycle interpretation and microcoded control engines. Further, while their instruction counts might seem reduced when compared to a VAX, the Pyramid has almost 90 instructions and the Ridge has over 100. The use of microcoding in these machines is for price and performance reasons. The Pyramid machine also has a system of multiple register sets derived from the Berkeley RISC I, but this feature is orthogonal to RISC theory. These may be successful machines, from both technological and marketing standpoints, but they are not RISCs.

The six RISC features enumerated above can be used to weed out misleading claims and provide a springboard for points of debate. Although some aspects of this list may be arguable, it is useful as a working definition.

Points of attention and contention

There are two prevalent misconceptions about RISC and CISC. The first is due to the RISC and CISC acronyms, which seem to imply that the domain for discussion should be restricted to selecting candidates for a machine's instruction set. Although specification format and number of instructions are the primary issues in most RISC literature, the best generalization of RISC theory goes well beyond them. It connotes a willingness to make design tradeoffs freely and consciously across architecture/implementation, hardware/software, and compile-time/run-time boundaries in order to maximize performance as measured in some specific context.

The RISC and CISC acronyms also seem to imply that any machine can be classified as one or the other and that

---

* Please note that the term "RISC" is used throughout this article to refer to all research efforts concerning Reduced Instruction Set Computers, while the term "RISC I" refers specifically to the Berkeley research project.

the primary task confronting an architect is to choose the most appropriate design style for a particular application. But the classification is not a dichotomy. RISCs and CISCs are at different corners of a continous multidimensional design space. The need is not for an algorithm by which one can be chosen: rather, the goal should be the formulation of a set of techniques, drawn from CISC experiences and RISC tenets, which can be used by a designer in creating new systems.[4-6]

One consequence of the us-or-them attitude evinced by most RISC publications is that the reported performance of a particular machine (e.g., RISC I) can be hard to interpret if the contributions made by the various design decisions are not presented individually. A designer faced with a large array of choices needs guidance more specific than a monolithic, all-or-nothing performance measurement.

An example of how the issue of scope can be confused is found in a recent article.[7] By creating a machine with only one instruction, its authors claim to have delimited the RISC design space to their machine at one end of the space and the RISC I (with 31 instructions) at the other end. This model is far too simplistic to be useful; an absolute number of instructions cannot be the sole criterion for categorizing an architecture as to RISC or CISC. It ignores aspects of addressing modes and their associated complexity, fails to deal with compiler/architecture coupling, and provides no way to evaluate the implementation of other non-instruction set design decisions such as register files, caches, memory management, floating point operations, and co-processors.

Another fallacy is that the total system is composed of hardware, software, and application code. This leaves out the operating system, and the overhead and the needs of the operating system cannot be ignored in most systems. This area has received

far too little attention from RISC research efforts, in contrast to the CISC efforts focused on this area.[8,9]

An early argument in favor of RISC design was that simpler designs could be realized more quickly, giving them a performance advantage over complex machines. In addition to the economic advantages of getting to market first, the simple design was supposed to

---

The insinuation that the Micro-VAX-32 follows in a RISC tradition is unreasonable. It does not follow our definition of a RISC; it violates all six RISC criteria.

---

avoid the performance disadvantages of introducing a new machine based on relatively old implementation technology. In light of these arguments, DEC's MicroVAX-32[10] is especially interesting.

The VAX easily qualifies as a CISC. According to published reports, the MicroVAX-32, a VLSI implementation of the preponderance of the VAX instruction set, was designed, realized, and tested in a period of several months. One might speculate that this very short gestation period was made possible in large part by DEC's considerable expertise in implementing the VAX architecture (existing products included the 11/780, 11/750, 11/730, and VLSI-VAX). This shortened design time would not have been possible had DEC had not first created a standard instruction set. Standardization at this level, however, is precisely what RISC theory argues against. Such standards constrain the unconventional RISC hardware/software tradeoffs. From a commercial standpoint, it is significant that the MicroVAX-32 was born into a world where compatible assemblers, compilers, and operating systems abound, something that would certainly not be the case for a RISC design.

Such problems with RISC system designs may encourage commercial RISC designers to define a new level of standardization in order to achieve some of the advantages of multiple implementations supporting one standard interface. A possible choice for such an interface would be to define an intermediate language as the target for all compilation. The intermediate language would then be translated into optimal machine code for each implementation. This translation process would simply be performing resource scheduling at a very low level (e.g., pipeline management and register allocation).

It should be noted that the Micro-VAX-32 does not directly implement all VAX architecture. The suggestion has been made that this implementation somehow supports the RISC inclination toward emulating complex functions in software. In a recent publication, David Patterson observed:

Although I doubt DEC is calling them RISCs, I certainly found it interesting that DEC's single chip VAXs do not implement the whole VAX instruction set. A MicroVAX traps when it tries to execute some infrequent but complicated operations, and invokes transparent software routines that simulate those complicated instructions.[11]

The insinuation that the Micro-VAX-32 follows in a RISC tradition is unreasonable. It does not come close to fitting our definition of a RISC; it violates all six RISC criteria. To begin with, any VAX by definition has a variable-length instruction format and is not a load/store machine. Further, the MicroVAX-32 has multicycle instruction execution, relies on a microcoded control engine, and interprets the whole array of VAX addressing modes. Finally, the MicroVAX-32 executes 175 instructions on-chip, hardly a reduced number.

A better perspective in the Micro VAX-32 shows that there are indeed cost/performance ranges where microcoded implementation of certain functions is inappropriate and software emulation is better. The importance of carefully making this assignment of function to implementation level—software, microcode, or hardware—has been amply demonstrated in many RISC papers. Yet this basic concern is also evidenced in many CISC machines. In the case of the MicroVAX-32, floating point instructions are migrated either to a coprocessor chip or to software emulation routines. The numerous floating-point chips currently available attest to the market reception for this partitioning. Also migrated to emulation are the console, decimal, and string instructions. Since many of these instructions are infrequent, not time-critical, or are not generated by many compilers, it

would be difficult to fault this approach to the design of an inexpensive VAX. The MicroVAX-32 also shows that it is still possible for intelligent, competent computer designers who understand the notion of correct function-to-level mapping to find microcoding a valuable technique. Published RISC work, however, does not accommodate this possibility.

The application environment is also of crucial importance in system design. The RISC I instruction set was designed specifically to run the C language efficiently, and it appears reasonably successful. The RISC I researchers have also investigated the Smalltalk-80 computing environment.[12] Rather than evaluate RISC I as a Smalltalk engine, however, the RISC I researchers designed a new RISC and report encouraging performance results from simulations. Still, designing a processor to run a single

language well is different from creating a single machine such as the VAX that must exhibit at least acceptable performance for a wide range of languages. While RISC research offers valuable insights on a per-language basis, more emphasis on cross-language anomalies, commonalities, and tradeoffs is badly needed.

Especially misleading are RISC claims concerning the amount of design time saved by creating a simple machine instead of a complex one. Such claims sound reasonable. Nevertheless, there are substantial differences in the design environments for an academic one-of-a-kind project (such as MIPS or RISC I) and a machine with lifetime measured in years that will require substantial software and support investments. As was pointed out in a recent *Electronics Week* article, R. D. Lowry, market development manager for Denelcor,

Risc II and the MCF evaluation

In the mid 70's, a committee was created by the Department of Defense to "evaluate the efficiency of several computer architectures independently of their implementations."[1,2] This committee developed the Military Computer Family studies based on the premise that the "architectural efficiency" of a computer corresponds to its life-cycle cost, given some standard of implementation technology. The MCF committee developed a means of evaluating architectural efficiency that consisted of two parts: (1) an initial screening to determine the "reasonableness" of an architecture based on several qualitative and quantitative factors (described later) and (2) a methodical application of benchmarks for machines that successfully passed this screening.

The MCF evaluations have been considered by many to be an important milestone in the systematic evaluation of computer architectures. The published evaluations of RISC machines have indicated performance advantages large enough to merit attention and analysis. To learn about RISC architecture and the usefulness of the MCF evaluation procedure, we applied the complete MCF evaluation to the Berkeley RISC II since it posed the fewest obstacles.

The MCF program evaluates architectures standardized at the instruction set level, since, according to Burr, it "is the only [way to ensure] complete software transportability across a wide range of computer implementations.[1] This view is contrary to a fundamental RISC tenet that one should zealously pursue unconventional tradeoffs across the architecture/implementation boundary that can produce higher performance.

In addition, the architecture that was judged the best by the MCF evaluation criteria was the VAX, a particularly intriguing judgement considering the uniformly bad reviews given the VAX in RISC performance studies.

Furthermore many of these RISC performance studies used variations and carefully chosen subsets of the MCF benchmarks.[3] Evaluating the RISC II with a full MCF analysis sheds new light on this seeming discrepancy.

MCF evaluation criteria. The first part of the MCF evaluation is an initial screening to ensure that the candidate architecture contains features deemed essential to a successful military computer: virtual memory, protection, floating point, interrupts and traps, subsetability, multiprocessor support, I/O controllability, extensibility, and the ability to execute out of read-only memory. Current RISC II systems have not provided many of these features, but most of these requirements could be met with additional resources.

The initial screening also analyzes quantitative factors. Since this noted that "commercial-product development teams generally start off a project by weighing the profit and loss impacts of design decisions."[13] Lowry is quoted as saying, "A university doesn't have to worry about that, so there are often many built-in deadends in projects. This is not to say the value of their research is diminished. It does, however, make it very difficult for someone to reinvent the system to make it a commercial product." For a product to remain viable, a great deal of documentation, user training, coordination with fabrication or production facilities, and future upgrades must all be provided. It is not known how these factors might skew a design-time comparison, so all such comparisons should be viewed with suspicion.

Even performance claims, perhaps the most interesting of all RISC assertions, are ambiguous. Performance as measured by narrowly compute-bound, low-level benchmarks that have been used by RISC researchers (e.g., calculating a Fibonacci series recursively) is not the only metric in a computer system. In some, it is not even one of the most interesting. For many current computers, the only useful performance index is the number of transactions per second, which has no direct or simple correlation to the time it takes to calculate Ackermann's function. While millions of instructions per second might be a meaningful metric in some computing environments, reliability, availability, and response time are of much more concern in others, such as *space* and *aviation* computing. The extensive error checking incorporated into these machines at every level may slow the basic clock time and substantially diminish performance. Reduced performance is tolerable; but downtime may not be. In the extreme, naive application of the RISC rules for designing an instruction set might result in a missile guidance computer optimized for running its most common task—diagnostics. In terms of instruction frequencies, of course, flight control applications constitute a trivial special case and would not be given much attention. It is worth emphasizing that in efforts to quantify performance and apply those measurements to system design, one must pay attention not just to instruction execution frequencies, but also to cycles consumed per instruction execution. Levy and Clark make this point regarding the VAX instruction set,[14] but it has yet to appear in any papers on RISC.

When performance, such as throughput or transactions per second, is a first-order concern, one is faced with the task of quantifying it. The Berkeley RISC I efforts to establish the machine's throughput are laudable, but

screening includes such practicalities as the manufacturer's current customer base and the amount of existing software, the RISC II would compare unfavorably to the VAX in this part of the evaluation. While these factors were important in military computer standards, they are clearly irrelevant here.

After the initial screening, a series of test programs was executed on a simulator of the candidate architecture. To avoid compiler ambiguities, the benchmarks were programmed in the assembly language of the test system. The MCF committee was interested solely in compiled code performance, yet the members recognized that varying levels of compiler technology should not be allowed to affect the outcome of the study; compiler sophistication has nothing to do with inherent "architectural efficiency." At the time of the MCF evaluations, it was believed that even the best compilers would be unlikely to generate better code than expert programmers.

Sixteen benchmark programs were developed: they were representative of the tasks performed by military computers and were small enough for humans to write in a highly optimized form.

None of the sixteen benchmarks tests methods of subroutine linkage (although one of the benchmarks considered, but rejected, for the MCF study was the highly recursive Ackermann's function). Failure to test call efficiency was not an oversight by the MCF committee; two measures of subroutine efficiency are included in the quantitative factors section of the initial screening.

Rather than rely on combined architecture/implementation measurements such as execution throughput, the MCF measures of computer architecture efficiency were defined to be program size (S), memory bus traffic (M), and canonical processor cycles (R). The S measure includes the local data and stack space used by the benchmark, as well as its program space. (The benchmarks reflect a circa-1970 assumption that code and data each occupy about half of the available memory space.) The M measure for a benchmark is the number of bytes that the processor reads and writes to memory (no transparent caching scheme is used). To compute the R measure, the architecture being evaluated is emulated on a canonical processor. The R measure is the sum of the internal data register-to-register transfers required by the canonical processor. Thus, this measure is supposed to model the data traffic of the processor's internal activities during benchmark execution. To evaluate different architectures, these measures are used as dimensions of comparison.

RISC theory asserts that simple instructions can be made to execute very quickly if their implementations are unencumbered by the large con-

before sweeping conclusions are drawn one must carefully examine the benchmark programs used. As Patterson noted:

> The performance predictions for [RISC I and RISC II] were based on small programs. This small size was dictated by the reliability of the simulator and compiler, the available simulation time, and the inability of the first simulators to handle UNIX system calls. [11]

Some of these "small" programs actually execute millions of instructions, yet they are very narrow programs in terms of the scope of function. For example, the Towers of Hanoi program, when executing on the 68000, spends over 90 percent of its memory accesses in procedure calls and returns. The RISC I and II researchers recently reported results from a large benchmark, [11] but the importance of large,

heterogenous benchmarks in performance measurement is still lost on many commercial and academic computer evaluators who have succumbed to the misconception that "micro-benchmarks" represent a useful measurement in isolation.

Multiple register sets

Probably the most publicized RISC-style processor is the Berkeley RISC I. The best-known feature of this chip is its large register file, organized as a series of overlapping register sets. This is ironic, since the register file is a performance feature independent of any RISC (as defined earlier) aspect of the processor. Multiple register sets could be included in any general-purpose register machine.

It is easy to believe that MRSs can yield performance benefits, since procedure-based, high-level languages

typically use registers for information specific to a procedure. When a procedure call is performed, the information must be saved, usually on a memory stack, and restored on a procedure return. These operations are typically very time consuming due to the intrinsic data transfer requirements. RISC I uses its multiple register sets to reduce the frequency of this register saving and restoring. It also takes advantage of an overlap between register sets for parameter passing, reducing even further the memory reads and writes necessary. [15]

RISC I has a register file of 138 32-bit registers organized into eight overlapping "windows." In each window, six registers overlap the next window (for outgoing parameters and incoming results). During any procedure, only one of these windows is actually accessible. A procedure call changes the current window to the next

trol engine normally required for complex instructions. Consequently, since the MCF evaluation avoids measuring implementation features, any performance gains realized by such simplified control engines are ignored, while penalties, such as the increased processor-memory traffic of these load/store machines, are still taken into account. This effect has been noted before in applying the MCF evaluation to real machines.[4]

Results and interpretation. The RISC II architecture was evaluated by simulating assembly language versions of the 16 benchmarks. To gauge the results, its performance was compared to that of the VAX, rated "best" by the MCF measures. The VAX had a significantly lower S measure (memory space requirements) in 14 of the 16 benchmarks, requiring an average of three and a half times less memory than RISC II. This result seems inconsistent with published RISC reports which found that the RISC I took an

average of only 50 percent more memory. This difference is dramatic. Much of it may be due to the fact that previous studies used a compiler that produces reasonable code for the RISC II, but produces suboptimal code for the VAX (since it may not have been sophisticated enough to exploit the available complex instructions as a human would). If the latest compilers were used for both machines, the space difference between the machines would likely be reduced to that of handcoding in assembly language, which we used.

The RISC II had a much higher M (memory traffic measure) for 11 of the benchmarks, averaging over two and a half times more processor-memory traffic than the VAX. This MCF criterion shows the large penalty paid by RISC II because of its load/store architecture. It is accentuated by the generic RISC need to fetch more instructions per program, since RISC instructions have low semantic content.

The VAX also had a lower (better) R measure for 10 of the benchmarks, and it was substantially lower on five of them. Again, much of this difference was due to the increased number of instruction fetches required by RISCs. One of the ten benchmarks modelled the cost of a context swap, which is high on RISC II because of the amount of state information in the register file. On average, about half of the register file (approximately 64 registers) must be saved and restored in each process swap.

These benchmarks showed the RISC II to disadvantage on floating point,[5] integer multiplication, bit test and set operations, variable-sized block moves, and character string searches—operations for which RISC II has no primitive instructions. As a result, numerous instructions are required to emulate on a RISC

window by incrementing a pointer, and the six outgoing parameter registers become the incoming parameters of the called procedure. Similarly, a procedure return changes the current window to the previous window, and the outgoing result registers become the incoming result registers of the calling procedure. If we assume that six 32-bit registers are enough to contain the parameters, a procedure call involves no actual movement of information (only the window pointer is adjusted). The finite on-chip resources limit the actual savings due to register window overflows and underflows.[3]

It has been claimed that the small control area needed to implement the simple instruction set of a VLSI RISC leaves enough chip area for the large register file.[3] The relatively small amount of control logic used by a RISC does free resources for other uses, but a large register file is not the

only way to use them, nor even necessarily the best. For example, designers of the 801 and MIPS chose other ways to use their available hardware; these RISCs have only a single, conventionally sized register set. Caches, floating-point hardware, and interprocess communication support are a few of the many possible uses for those resources "freed" by a RISC's simple instruction set. Moreover, as chip technology improves, the tradeoffs between instruction set complexity and architecture/implementation features become less constrained. Computer designers will always have to decide how to best use available resources and, in doing so, should realize which relations are intrinsic and which are not.

The Berkeley papers describing the RISC I and RISC II processors claimed their resource decisions produced large performance improvements, two to four times over CISC machines like

the VAX and the 68000.[3,11] There are many problems with these results and the methods used to obtain them. Foremost, the performance effects of the reduced instruction set were not decoupled from those of the overlapped register windows. Consequently, these reports shed little light on the RISC-related performance of the machine, as shown below.

Some performance comparisons between different machines, especially early ones, were based on simulated benchmark execution times. While absolute speed is always interesting, other metrics less implementation-dependent can provide design information more useful to computer architects, such as data concerning the processor-memory traffic necessary to execute a series of benchmarks. It is difficult to draw firm conclusions from comparisons of vastly different machines unless some effort has been

what other machines provide in their instruction set; the MCF study provides a quantitative evaluation of this effect. The RISC II was comparable to the VAX on benchmarks that involved simple arithmetic and one-level array indexing.

Conclusions. Although the VAX achieves a better score on every aspect of the MCF evaluation than does the RISC II, it would be dangerous to conclude that the VAX is a "better" machine. The MCF study characterizes the life-cycle costs of various architectures based on a set of weighting factors culled from the military environment. The VAX can be said to be better only in the sense that the MCF life-cycle cost models clearly favor it.

Since RISC research explicitly gives up the possible benefits of the traditional architecture/implementation dichotomy to increase execution

throughput, the most basic MCF tenet does not hold for RISCs. The MCF life-cycle cost models did not include execution throughput, so the RISC II performance-related features were ignored, yet the price paid for these features is clear.

The MCF study's S,M, and R measures of architectural efficiency are open to question. For example, the R measure of internal processor overhead is of dubious utility when the architectures being compared are dissimilar. It is hard to see what canonical processor could be devised to serve as a common implementation of the RISC II and the Intel 432, for example.

The MCF study remains, however, the only large-scale evaluation of computer systems that includes as a primary figure of merit system life-cycle costs instead of easy throughput comparisons based on many arbitrary and implicit assumptions. The care taken by MCF in factoring out the myr-

iad interrelated elements of a computer system leaves it an excellent model for future evaluation efforts.

References

1. W.E. Burr, A.H. Coleman, and W.R. Smith, "Overview of the Military Computer Family Architecture Selection," *NCC Conference Proceedings* AFIPS, Montvale, N.J., 1977, pp. 131-137.

2. S.H. Fuller and W.E. Burr, "Measurement and Evaluation of Alternative Computer Architectures," *Computer*, Vol. 10, No. 10, Oct. 1977, pp. 24-35.

3. David A. Patterson, Richard S. Piepho, "RISC Assessment: A High-Level Language Experiment," *Proc. Ninth Ann. Symp. Computer Architecture*, 1982, pp. 3-8.

4. J.B. Mountain and P.H. Enslow Jr., "Application of the Military Computer Family Architecture Selection Criteria to the PRIME P400," *Computer Architecture News*, Vol. 6, No. 6, Feb. 1978.

5. D. Patterson, "RISC Watch," *Computer Architecture News*, Vol. 12, No. 1, Mar. 1984, pp. 11-19.

made to factor out implementation-dependent features not being compared (e.g., caches and floating point accelerators).

Experiments structured to accommodate these reservations were conducted at CMU to test the hypothesis that the effects of multiple register sets are orthogonal to instruction set complexity.[16] Specifically, the goal was to see if the performance effects of MRSs were comparable for RISCs and CISCs. Simulators were written for two CISCs (the VAX and the 68000) without MRSs, with non-overlapping MRSs and with overlapping MRSs. Simulators were also written for the RISC I, RISC I with non-overlapping register sets, and RISC I with only a single register set. In each of the simulators, care was taken not to change the initial architectures any more than absolutely necessary to add or remove MRSs. Instead of simulating execution time, the total amount of processor-memory traffic (bytes read and written) for each benchmark was recorded for comparison. To use this data fairly, only different register set versions of the same architecture were compared so the ambiguities that arise from comparing different architectures like the RISC I and the VAX were avoided. The benchmarks used were the same ones originally used to evaluate RISC I. A summary of the experiments and their results are presented by Hitchcock and Sprunt.[17]

As expected, the results show a substantial difference in processor-memory traffic for an architecture with and without MRSs. The MRS versions of both the VAX and 68000 show marked decreases in processor-memory traffic for procedure-intensive benchmarks, shown in Figures 1 and 2. Similarly, the single register set version of RISC I requires many more memory reads and writes than RISC I with overlapped register sets (Figure 3). This result is due in part to the method used for

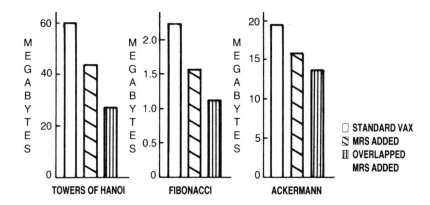

Figure 1. Total processor-memory traffic for benchmarks on the standard VAX and two modified VAX computers, one with multiple register sets and one with overlapped multiple register sets.

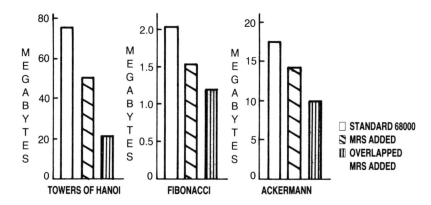

Figure 2. Total processor-memory traffic for benchmarks on the standard 68000 and two modified 68000s, one with multiple register sets and one with overlapped multiple register sets.

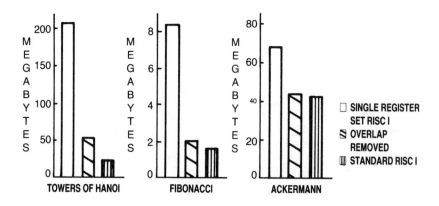

Figure 3. Total processor-memory traffic for benchmarks on the standard RISC I and two modified RISC I's, one with no overlap between register sets and one with only one register set.

handling register set overflow and underflow, which was kept the same for all three variations. With a more intelligent scheme, the single register set RISC I actually required fewer bytes of memory traffic on Ackermann's function than its multiple register set counterparts. For benchmarks with very few procedure calls (e.g., the sieve of Eratosthenes), the single register set version has the same amount of processor-memory traffic as the MRS version of the same architecture. [17]

Clearly, MRSs can affect the amount of processor-memory traffic necessary to execute a program. A significant amount of the performance of RISC I for procedure-intensive environments has been shown to be attributable to its scheme of overlapped register sets, a feature independent of instruction-set complexity. Thus, any performance claims for reduced instruction set computers that do not remove effects due to multiple register sets are inconclusive, at best.

These CMU experiments used benchmarks drawn from other RISC research efforts for the sake of continuity and consistency. Some of the benchmarks, such as Ackermann, Fibonacci, and Hanoi, actually spend most of their time performing procedure calls. The percentage of the total processor-memory traffic due to "C" procedure calls for these three benchmarks on the single register set version of the 68000 ranges from 66 to 92 percent. As was expected, RISC I, with its overlapped register structure that allows procedure calls to be almost free in terms of processor-memory bus traffic, did extremely well on these highly recursive benchmarks when compared to machines with only a single register set. It has not been established, however, that these benchmarks are representative of any computing environment.

The 432

The Intel 432 is a classic example of a CISC. It is an object-oriented VLSI microprocessor chip-set designed expressly to provide a productive Ada programming environment for large scale, multiple-process, multiple-processor systems. Its architecture supports object orientation such that every object is protected uniformly without regard to traditional distinctions such as "supervisor/user mode" or "system/user data structures." The 432 has a very complex instruction set. Its instructions are bit-encoded and range in length from six to 321 bits. The 432 incorporates a significant degree of functional migration from software to on-chip microcode. The interprocess communication SEND primitive is a 432 machine instruction, for instance.

Published studies of the performance of the Intel 432 on low-level benchmarks (e.g., towers of Hanoi[18]) show that it is very slow, taking 10 to 20 times as long as the VAX 11/780. Such a design, then, invites scrutiny in the RISC/CISC controversy.

One is tempted to blame the machine's object-oriented runtime environment for imposing too much overhead. Every memory reference is checked to ensure that it lies within the boundaries of the referenced object, and the read/write protocols of the executing context are verified. RISC proponents argue that the complexity of the 432 architecture, and the additional decoding required for a bit-encoded instruction stream contribute to its poor performance. To address these and other issues, a detailed study of the 432 was undertaken to evaluate the effectiveness of the architectural mechanisms provided in support of its intended runtime environment. The study concentrated on one of the central differences in the RISC and CISC design styles: RISC designs avoid hardware/microcode structures in-

tended to support the runtime environment, attempting instead to place equivalent functionality into the compiler or software. This is contrary to the mainstream of instruction set design, which reflects a steady migration of such functionality from higher levels (software) to lower ones (microcode or hardware) in the expectation of improved performance.

This investigation should include an analysis of the 432's efficiency in executing large-system code, since executing such code well was the primary design goal of the 432. Investigators used the Intel 432 microsimulator, which yields cycle-by-cycle traces of the machine's execution. While this microsimulator is well-suited to simulating small programs, it is quite unwieldy for large ones. As a result, the concentration here is on the low-level benchmarks that first pointed out the poor 432 performance.

Simulations of these benchmarks revealed several performance problems with the 432 and its compiler:

(1) The 432's Ada compiler performs almost no optimization. The machine is frequently forced to make unnecessary changes to its complex addressing environment, and it often recomputes costly, redundant subexpressions. This recomputation seriously skews many results from benchmark comparisons. Such benchmarks reflect the performance of the present version of the 432 but show very little about the efficacy of the architectural trade-offs made in that machine.

(2) The bandwidth of 432 memory is limited by several factors. The 432 has no on-chip data caching, no instruction stream literals, and no local data registers. Consequently, it makes far more memory references than it would otherwise have to. These reference requirements also make the code size much larger, since many more bits are required to reference data within an object than within a local register.

And because of pin limitations, the 432 must multiplex both data and address information over only 16 pins. Also, the standard Intel 432/600 development system, which supports shared-memory multiprocessing, uses a slow asynchronous bus that was designed more for reliability than throughput. These implementation factors combine to make wait states consume 25 to 40 percent of the processor's time on the benchmarks.

(3) On highly recursive benchmarks, the object-oriented overhead in the 432 does indeed appear in the form of a slow procedure call. Even here, though, the performance problems should not be attributed to object orientation or to the machine's intrinsic complexity. Designers of the 432 made a decision to provide a new, protected context for every procedure call; the user has no option in this respect. If an unprotected call mechanism were used where appropriate, the Dhrystone benchmark [19] would run 20 percent faster.

(4) Instructions are bit-aligned, so the 432 must almost of necessity decode the various fields of an instruction sequentially. Since such decoding often overlaps with instruction execution, the 432 stalls three percent of the time while waiting for the instruction decoder. This percentage will get worse, however, once other problems above are eliminated.

Colwell provides a detailed treatment of this experiment and its results. [20]

This 432 experiment is evidence that RISC's renewed emphasis on the importance of fast instruction decoding and fast local storage (such as caches or registers) is substantiated, at least for low-level compute-bound benchmarks. Still, the 432 does not provide compelling evidence that large-scale migration of function to microcode and hardware is ineffective. On the contrary, Cox et al. [21] demonstrated

that the 432 microcode implementation of interprocess communication is much faster than an equivalent software version. On these low-level benchmarks, the 432 could have much higher performance with only a better compiler and minor changes to its implementation. Thus, it is wrong to conclude that the 432 supports the general RISC point of view.

In spite of—and sometimes because of—the wide publicity given to current RISC and CISC research, it is not easy to gain a thorough appreciation of the important issues. Articles on RISC research are often oversimplified, overstated, and misleading, and papers on CISC design offer no coherent design principles for comparison. RISC/CISC issues are best considered in light of their function-to-implementation level assignment. Strictly limiting the focus to instruction counts or other oversimplifications can be misleading or meaningless.

Some of the more subtle issues have not been brought out in current literature. Many of these are design considerations that do not lend themselves to the benchmark level analysis used in RISC research. Nor are they always properly evaluated by CISC designers, guided so frequently by tradition and corporate economics.

RISC/CISC research has a great deal to offer computer designers. These contributions must not be lost due to an illusory and artificial dichotomy. Lessons learned studying RISC machines are not incompatible with or mutually exclusive of the rich tradition of computer design that preceded them. Treating RISC ideas as perspectives and techniques rather than dogma and understanding their domains of applicability can add important new tools to a computer designer's repertoire. □

Acknowledgements

We would like to thank the innumerable individuals, from industry and academia, who have shared their thoughts on this matter with us and stimulated many of our ideas. In particular, we are grateful to George Cox and Konrad Lai of Intel for their help with the 432 microsimulator.

This research was sponsored in part by the Department of the Army under contract DAA B07-82-C-J164.

References

1. J. Hennessy et al., "Hardware/Software Tradeoffs for Increased Performance," *Proc. Symp. Architectural Support for Programming Languages and Operating Systems*, 1982, pp. 2-11.

2. G. Radin, "The 801 Minicomputer," *Proc. Symp. Architectural Support for Programming Languages and Operating Systems*, 1982, pp. 39-47.

3. D. A. Patterson and C. H. Sequin, "A VLSI RISC," *Computer*, Vol. 15, No. 9, Sept. 1982, pp. 8-21.

4. R. P. Colwell, C. Y. Hitchcock III, and E. D. Jensen, " A Perspective on the Processor Complexity Controversy," *Proc. Int. Conf. Computer Design: VLSI in Computers*, 1983, pp. 613-616.

5. D. Hammerstrom, "Tutorial: The Migration of Function into Silicon," *10th Ann. Int'l Symp. Computer Architecture*, 1983.

6. J. C. Browne, "Understanding Execution Behavior of Software Systems," *Computer*, Vol. 17, No. 7, July 1984, pp. 83-87.

7. H. Azaria and D. Tabak, "The MODHEL Microcomputer for RISCs Study", *Microprocessing and Microprogramming*, Vol. 12, No. 3-4, Oct.-Nov. 1983, pp. 199-206.

8. G. C. Barton "Sentry: A Novel Hardware Implementation of Classic Operating System Mechanisms," *Proc. Ninth Ann. Int'l Symp. Computer Architecture*, 1982, pp. 140-147.

9. A. D. Berenbaum, M. W. Condry, and P. M. Lu, "The Operating System and Language Support Features of the BELLMAC-32 Microprocessor,"

Proc. Symp. Architectural Support for Programming Languages and Operating Systems, 1982, pp. 30-38.

10. J. Hennessy, "VLSI Processor Architecture," *IEEE Transactions on Computers,* Vol. C-33, No. 12, Dec. 1984, pp. 1221-1246.

11. D. Patterson, "RISC Watch," *Computer Architecture News,* Vol. 12, No. 1, Mar. 1984, pp. 11-19.

12. David Ungar et al., "Architecture of SOAR: Smalltalk on a RISC," *11th Ann. Int'l Symp. Computer Architecture,* 1984, pp. 188-197.

13. W. R. Iversen, "Money Starting to Flow As Parallel Processing Gets Hot," *Electronics Week,* Apr. 22, 1985, pp. 36-38.

14. H. M. Levy and D. W. Clark, "On the Use of Benchmarks for Measuring System Performance" *Computer Architecture News,* Vol. 10, No. 6, 1982, pp. 5-8.

15. D. C. Halbert and P. B. Kessler, "Windows of Overlapping Register Frames", CS292R Final Reports, University of California, Berkeley, June 9, 1980.

16. R. P. Colwell, C. Y. Hitchcock III, and E. D. Jensen, "Peering Through the RISC/CISC Fog: An Outline of Research," *Computer Architecture News,* Vol. 11, No. 1, Mar. 1983, pp. 44-50.

17. C. Y. Hitchcock III and H. M. B. Sprunt, "Analyzing Multiple Register Sets," *12th Ann. Int'l Symp. Computer Architecture,* 1985, in press.

18. P. M. Hansen et al., "A Performance Evaluation of the Intel iAPX 432," *Computer Architecture News,* Vol. 10, No. 4, June 1982, pp. 17-27.

19. R. P. Weicker, "Dhrystone: A Synthetic Systems Programming Benchmark," *Comm. ACM,* Vol. 27, No. 10, Oct. 1984, pp. 1013-1030.

20. R. P. Colwell, "The Performance Effects of Functional Migration and Architectural Complexity in Object—Oriented Systems," PhD. thesis, Carnegie-Mellon University, Pittsburgh, PA. Expected completion in June, 1985.

21. G. W. Cox et al., "Interprocess Communication and Processor Dispatching on the Intel 432," *ACM Trans. Computer Systems,* Vol. 1, No. 1, Feb. 1983, pp. 45-66.

Robert P. Colwell recently completed his doctoral dissertation on the performance effects of migrating functions into silicon, using the Intel 432 as a case study. His industrial experience includes design of a color graphics workstation for Perq Systems, and work on Bell Labs' microprocessors. He received the PhD and MSEE degrees from Carnegie-Mellon University in 1985 and 1978, and the BSEE degree from the University of Pittsburgh in 1977. He is a member of the IEEE and ACM.

Charles Y. Hitchcock III is a doctoral candidate in Carnegie-Mellon University's Department of Electrical and Computer Engineering. He is currently pursuing research in computer architecture and is a member of the IEEE and ACM. He graduated with honors in 1981 from Princeton University with a BSE in electrical engineering and computer science. His MSEE from CMU in 1983 followed research he did in design automation.

E. Douglas Jensen has been on the faculties of both the Computer Science and Electrical and Computer Engineering Departments of Carnegie-Mellon University for six years. For the previous 14 years he performed industrial R/D on computer systems, hardware, and software. He consults and lectures extensively throughout the world and has participated widely in professional society activities.

H. M. Brinkley Sprunt is a doctoral candidate in the Department of Electrical and Computer Engineering of Carnegie-Mellon University. He received a BSEE degree in electrical engineering from Rice University in 1983. His research interests include computer architecture evaluation and design. He is a member of the IEEE and ACM.

Charles P. Kollar is a senior research staff member in Carnegie-Mellon University's computer Science Department. He is currently pursuing research in decentralized asynchronous computing systems. He has been associated with the MCF and NEBULA project at Carnegie-Mellon University since 1978. Previous research has been in the area of computer architecture validation and computer architecture description languages. He holds a BS in computer science from the University of Pittsburgh.

Questions about this article can be directed to Colwell at the Computer Science Department, Carnegie-Mellon University, Pittsburgh, PA 15213.

"Any clod can have the facts,
but having opinions is an art."

Charles McCabe,
San Francisco Chronicle

THE OPEN CHANNEL

Response to "Computers, Complexity, and Controversy"

The causal reader of "Computers, Complexity, and Controversy" (September 1985, pp. 8-19) might erroneously conclude that the performance benefits of RISCs stem solely from multiple register sets, or MRSs, rather than from a wide range of benefits from the RISC approach. Furthermore, the authors suggest that architectural metrics—metrics we deny are of proven validity—show that RISCs are not good computers. They also declare that the 432 and MicroVAX 32 do not constitute evidence for the RISC approach, while the data suggest the opposite conclusion. While we welcome a scientific evaluation of the RISC approach, we feel most of the opinions in the article are not supported by evidence or by scientific reasoning.

The quantitative part of the article is the study on MRSs. A careful analysis of MRSs is worthwhile, but the relevance of the benchmarks used in such a study determine the relevance of its results. The authors mistakenly say that the "benchmarks used were the same ones originally used to evaluate RISC I." Table 1 shows the programs compiled, simulated, and published in papers about Berkeley RISCs. (We at Berkeley, by the way, supplied the authors with our compiler and simulator to run these programs.)

Table 1.
RISC programs ordered by size in lines of code.

SIZE (lines)	BENCHMARKS	SUBJECT	PUBLICATION (year)
29095	PCC	C compiler	1984
1608	SED	Text editor	1982
219	MCF #I	Iterative sort	1982
201	Whetstone	Floating point benchmark	1984
177	Puzzle	Bin-packing (pointer)	1982
136	Quicksort	Recursive sort	1981
133	Puzzle	Bin-packing (array)	1981
89	MCF #K	Bit matrix	1982
77	MCF #H	Linked list	1982
61	MCF #E	String search	1982
60	MCF #F	Bit test	1982
16	Towers	Recursive benchmark	1982
13	Ackerman	Recursive benchmark	1982

From this list, the authors chose the two smallest and most recursive programs, Ackerman and Towers of Hanoi, and added Fibonacci, a highly recursive two-line Lisp program. Since MRSs have major impact on procedure calls, their importance can be artificially inflated by programs with unusual procedure call patterns. Why did the authors choose the smallest programs with the largest number of recursive procedure calls to test their hypothesis that the effects of MRSs are orthogonal to instruction set complexity? We asked this question at the June '84 International Conference on Computer Architecture in Boston, where they reported their results. Their only explanation was that some of the other programs were not used because they did not have enough procedure calls to support their hypothesis.

In concluding their discussion here of MRSs, the authors acknowledge the pathological nature of the programs ("It has not been established, however, that these benchmarks are representative of any computing environment."), yet they claim that the performance of RISC I "has been shown to be attributable to (MRSs)" and that "performance claims for RISCs that do not remove effects due to MRSs are inconclusive at best." Furthermore, these remarks ignore the benefits of RISCs on average instruction execution time, obviously a key to performance. And even if the authors could

EH0251-9/86/0000/0358$01.00 © 1985 IEEE

Reprinted from *Computer*, November 1985, pages 142-143. Copyright © 1985 by The Institute of Electrical and Electronics Engineers, Inc.

apply their study to nonrecursive programs larger than 16 lines, they overlook that both the 801 and MIPS have the same significant benefits in cost and performance—and neither of these designs use MRSs. If, as the authors suggest, MRS is the "real secret" behind RISCs, we wonder why MRS wasn't included in their list of RISCs characteristics.

The authors report that architecture metrics show that the VAX outperforms RISCs. We believe the emphasis on architecture metrics over implementation issues is in part responsible for a generation of machines with good metrics but poor cost/performance and long development cycles. The measurement of those metrics by assembly language programs exacerbates the gap between abstract metrics and the real implementation, which will be measured by applications that use high-level languages and compilers. The RISC approach advocates a methodology that balances the needs of compilers with the implementation efficiency of the architecture.

The illusion created by measuring architectural metrics in isolation from the implementation is illustrated by the history of the VAX-like Nebula architecture, which has the best MCF metrics. Although the architecture was completed in 1980 and was reported in the February 1981 *Computer* (pp. 35-41), there are no commercial versions of this machine, and even though the Air Force funded this effort as a new standard computer, the government has yet to put out requests for bids to build Nebula machines. In sharp contrast, RISC architectures have been vigorously pursued by both startups and established computer manufacturers. Even though RISCs were not funded to be a standard, the government recently put out requests for bids to build both gallium arsenide and CMOS versions of the MIPS RISC architecture. If the validity of the MCF architecture metrics was widely endorsed, we would expect industry and government to have rushed to build Nebula and ignored RISCs, not vice versa.

The section of the article on the 432 inadvertently provides further support for RISC ideas. The authors start by citing papers that report the 432 is 10 to 20 times slower than the VAX-11/780. They then hypothesize the 432 would be faster if it were redesigned: if it had more pins, a wider bus, and a faster memory system, it would be 25 to 40 percent faster; if it had a less complicated and faster procedure call, it would be 20 percent faster; and if it didn't have variable bit length instructions, it would be three percent faster. According to their own numbers, the

new hypothetical 432 is still six to 12 times slower than the VAX, and likely three to six times slower than the 16-bit Motorola 68000 microprocessor. By concentrating on microcoding high-level functions, the 432 architects apparently sacrificed the performance of the more frequently occurring simple functions. Contrary to the authors' statement that "it is wrong to conclude that the 432 supports the general RISC point of view," we believe that the performance data and the authors' suggested simplifications—to increase the 432's performance—both provide evidence indeed for the value of the RISC approach.

Contrary to their conclusion, we think that the history of VLSI implementations of VAX supports the RISC approach.

Again contrary to their conclusion, we think that the history of VLSI implementations of the VAX, reported in the October 1984 *IEEE Journal of Solid-State Circuits* (pages 663-681), supports the RISC approach. The VLSI VAX is an eight-chip implementation of the full VAX architecture. During the course of the VLSI VAX project, DEC found that 20 percent of the instructions required 60 percent of the microcode, yet were only 0.2 percent of the executed instructions. Several years after the beginning of the project, DEC decided to modify the layout and microcode of the main CPU chip and then subset the architecture to fit the microcode memory and data path into a single chip, thus creating the MicroVAX-32. (The authors do not mention the VLSI VAX and mistakenly say that the MicroVAX-32 "was designed, realized, and tested in a period of several months." The paper by the MicroVAX designers reports that it took 20 months from the start of the project to produce the first pass of the descriptions of the circuit masks. Chip fabrication, testing, and redesign lengthens the design cycle.) Although this subset project started later, it finished first and is now a product. Furthermore, the performance degradation of the MicroVAX-32 for the omitted instructions is just 4 percent while the fivefold reduction in control store size cuts the active chip area almost in half. DEC's decision to subset its complex architecture to exploit VLSI—plus the reduced design effort of the simpler machine—is certainly some indirect support for the RISC approach.

The reader should note that this last year has been good for RISCs. John Cocke of IBM won the ACM-IEEE Eckert-Mauchly Award for Computer Architecture in part for his work on RISCs, and Manolis Katevenis' dissertation on VLSI RISCs won the ACM Doctoral Dissertation Award. Gordon Bell, another winner of the Eckert-Mauchly award and one of the designers of the PDP-11 and the VAX, cited the Berkeley and Stanford RISC research on VLSI computers last October in this magazine (pp. 14-30) and said that given "the current speed of logic relative to memory, it is time again to return to direct (versus microprogrammed) execution of the instruction set."

Without identifying a specific publication or quotation, the authors of "Computers, Complexity, and Controversy" claim that some RISC publications are "oversimplified, overstated, and misleading." Fortunately, disagreements in computer design are not resolved on the pages of a magazine; hardware is the final judge of architecture. Many computer scientists and commercial computer designers have been convinced by the research presented in the RISC papers and dissertations, so we encourage readers to investigate the issue carefully.

David Patterson
University of California, Berkeley
John Hennessy
Stanford University

Suggested reading

M. Hopkins, "A Perspective on Microcode," Proc. 21st Ann. Computer Conf., San Francisco, Calif., Feb. 1983, pp. 108-110.

M. Katevenis, "Reduced Instruction Set Computer Architecture for VLSI," ACM Doctoral Dissertation Award Series, MIT Press, Cambridge, Mass., 1985.

D. Patterson, "Reduced Instruction Set Computers," Comm. ACM, Vol. 28, No. 1, Jan. 1985, pp. 8-21.

S. Przybylski et al., "Organization and VLSI Implementation of MIPS," J. VLSI and Computer Systems, Vol. 1, No. 2, Fall 1984, pp. 170-208.

R. Sherburne et al., "A 32-bit NMOS Microprocessor with a Large Register File," IEEE J. Solid-State Circuits, Vol. 19, No. 5, Oct. 1984, pp. 682-689.

"Any clod can have the facts, but having opinions is an art."

Charles McCabe,
San Francisco Chronicle

THE OPEN CHANNEL

More controversy about "Computers, Complexity, and Controversy"

David Patterson and John Hennessy's response to our article, "Computers, Complexity, and Controversy," seems to indicate that they have misunderstood many important points that we tried to make. In this brief space we can only highlight their most serious misunderstandings. [1,2]

In our section on multiple register sets (MRS) we did not claim that RISC I's performance "has been shown to be attributable to (MRSs)."[1] Nor did we state that "MRS is the 'real secret' behind RISCs."[1] Our report was much different. To quote ourselves in context, we stated that "a significant amount of the performance of RISC I for procedure-intensive environments has been shown to be attributable to"[2] MRSs. Our experiments showed that the performance effects due to MRS are comparable for RISCs and CISCs. Consequently, we urge RISC researchers who incorporate this mechanism to factor out its performance effects when attempting to gauge performance due to the reduced nature of their machines. Similarly, one should do the same for any other mechanism which affects performance and is independent of instruction set complexity. In summary, it also seems necessary to restate that the goal of our MRS study was to evaluate the performance effects of MRS, *not* to re-evaluate the RISC I, the VAX-11 or the 68000. We simulated (using our own simulators) only procedure-intensive C benchmarks (all of which were supplied to us by Patterson) because MRS mechanisms are not exercised when procedure calls are not used. These benchmarks were appropriate for this study because they expose the performance effects of MRS, the focus of the study.

The tendency of many RISC supporters to emphasize throughput at the expense of architectural and other metrics is once again evident in the sentence, "The authors report that architectural metrics show that the VAX outperforms RISCs."[1] This is an incorrect paraphrase: we never said that "the VAX outperforms RISCs." In fact, we very clearly stated that throughput per se is *not* being measured by the MCF architecture evaluation scheme, and that this is arguably a shortcoming of the MCF model that unfairly penalizes machines which attempt to optimize throughput by making tradeoffs across the architecture/implementation boundary, as do RISCs: "The MCF life-cycle cost models did not include execution throughput, so the RISC II performance related features were ignored."[2] MCF was not designed to be a 100-yard dash for computer systems (as RISC performance studies usually are)—it was intended as a decathlon, reflecting our perception that actual systems in use need far more than large numbers of cycles-per-unit time in order to meet their goals.

In their response, Patterson and Hennessy have missed the most important point about performance comparisons with regard to the Intel 432. The 432's object orientation exacts an intrinsic performance cost, since it is manifested as a set of runtime checks and a large amount of additional information to be manipulated. Patterson and Hennessy state that an improved, "hypothetical 432 is still . . . three to six times slower than the 16-bit Motorola 68000."[1] This comparison, which we did not make, is meaningless because the two machines are not doing the same "work." To make a fair comparison, one would need either to migrate the object orientation of the 432 to the 68000 or to remove such support from the 432 (an enormous

task in either case). Perhaps Patterson and Hennessy's comparison addresses the throughput costs of supporting the 432's style of object orientation, but it does not "provide evidence . . . for the value of the RISC approach."[2]

As history shows, there is not necessarily any correspondence between technical merit and success in the senses of awards, salesmanship, and commercial products. Researchers should be willing to let their work stand or fall on the basis of its own scientific worth. While it may be that many computer scientists and commercial computer designers have been convinced by the research presented in the RISC papers and dissertations, it has been our experience that a significant number have not (and for very good reasons, as we have argued in our article).

Robert P. Colwell
Charles Y. Hitchcock III
E. Douglas Jensen
H.M. Brinkley Sprunt
Carnegie-Mellon University

References

1. David Patterson and John Hennessy, "Response to 'Computers, Complexity, and Controversy,'" in "Open Channel," *Computer*, Vol. 18, No. 11, November 1985, pp. 142-143.

2. Robert C. Colwell, Charles Y. Hitchcock III, H. M. Brinkley Sprunt, E. Douglas Jensen, and Charles P. Kollar, "Computers, Complexity, and Controversy," *Computer*, Vol. 18, No. 9, September 1985, pp. 8-19.

Reprinted from *Computer*, December 1985, page 93. Copyright © 1985 by The Institute of Electrical and Electronics Engineers, Inc.

Section 7: Glossary*

Some of the terms in this glossary are from the *American National Dictionary for Information Processing Systems*, developed by the American National Standards Committee X3, Information Processing Systems, or from the *Vocabulary for Data Processing, Telecommunications, and Office Systems*, IBM Report GC20-1699-5. These are indicated in the text by ANS and IBM, respectively.

ABSOLUTE ADDRESS (ANS) An address in a computer language that identifies a storage location or a device without the use of any intermediate reference.

ACCUMULATOR The name of the CPU register in a single-address instruction format. The accumulator, or AC, is implicitly one of the two operands for the instruction.

ADDRESS A number that uniquely identifies a memory location, register, or I/O port.

ADDRESS SPACE The range of addresses (memory, I/O) that can be referenced.

ADDRESSING MODE Technique used to determine the address of an operand based on the bits of the address field of the instruction.

ARITHMETIC AND LOGIC UNIT (ANS) A part of a computer that performs arithmetic operations, logic operations, and related operations.

ASSEMBLY LANGUAGE (ANS) A computer-oriented language whose instructions are usually in one-to-one correspondence with computer instructions and that may provide facilities such as the use of macroinstructions.

BASE ADDRESS (ANS) A numeric value that is used as a reference in the calculation of addresses in the execution of a computer program.

CACHE MEMORY A memory that is smaller and faster than main memory and that is interposed between the CPU and main memory. The cache acts as a buffer for recently used memory locations.

CENTRAL PROCESSING UNIT That portion of a computer that fetches and executes instructions. It consists of an arithmetic and logic unit (ALU), a control unit, and registers. Often simply referred to as a processor.

COMPUTER INSTRUCTION (ANS) An instruction that can be recognized by the processing unit of the computer for which it is designed. Synonymous with machine instruction.

COMPUTER INSTRUCTION SET (ANS) A complete set of the operators of the instructions of a computer together with a description of the types of meanings that can be attributed to their operands. Synonymous with machine instruction set.

CONDITION CODE A code that reflects the result of a previous operation (e.g., arithmetic). A CPU may include one or more condition codes, which may be stored separately within the CPU or as part of a larger control register. Also known as a flag.

CONDITIONAL JUMP (ANS) A jump that takes place only when the instruction that specifies it is executed and specified conditions are satisfied. Contrast with unconditional jump.

CONTROL REGISTERS CPU registers employed to control CPU operation. Most of these registers are not user visible.

CONTROL STORAGE (IBM) A portion of storage that contains microcode.

CONTROL UNIT That part of the CPU that controls CPU operations, including ALU operations, the movement of data within the CPU, and the exchange of data and control signals across external interfaces (e.g., the system bus).

DIRECT ADDRESS (ANS) An address that designates the storage location of an item of data to be treated as an operand. Synonymous with one-level address.

EMULATION (ANS) The imitation of all or part of one system by another, primarily by hardware, so that the imitating system accepts the same data, executes the same programs, and achieves the same results as the imitated system.

EXECUTE CYCLE That portion of the instruction cycle during which the CPU performs the operation specified by the instruction opcode.

FETCH CYCLE That portion of the instruction cycle during which the CPU fetches from memory the instruction to be executed.

FIRMWARE (ANS) The program instructions stored in a read-only storage.

GATE An electronic circuit that produces an output signal that is a simple Boolean operation on its input signals.

GENERAL-PURPOSE REGISTER (ANS) A register, usually explicitly addressable, within a set of registers, that can be used for different purposes, for example, as an accumulator, as an index register, or as a special handler of data.

---

*Based on Glossary in *Computer Organization and Architecture*, by William Stallings, Macmillan, 1987.

GLOBAL VARIABLE (IBM) A variable defined in one portion of a computer program and used in at least one other portion of that computer program.

IMMEDIATE ADDRESS (ANS) The contents of an address part that contains the value of an operand rather than an address. Synonymous with zero-level address.

INDEXED ADDRESS (ANS) An address modified by the content of an index register prior to or during the execution of a computer instruction.

INDEXING (IBM) A technique of address modification by means of index registers.

INDEX REGISTER (ANS) A register whose contents can be used to modify an operand address during the execution of computer instructions; it can also be used as a counter. An index register may be used to control the execution of a loop, to control the use of an array, as a switch, for table lookup, or as a pointer.

INDIRECT ADDRESS (ANS) An address that designates the storage location of an item of data to be treated as the address of the operand, but not necessarily as its direct address. Synonymous with multilevel address.

INDIRECT CYCLE That portion of the instruction cycle during which the CPU performs a memory access to convert an indirect address into a direct address.

INSTRUCTION ADDRESS REGISTER (ANS) A register from whose contents the address of the next instruction is derived.

INSTRUCTION CYCLE The processing performed by a CPU to execute a single instruction.

INSTRUCTION FORMAT The layout of a computer instruction as a sequence of bits. The format divides the instruction into fields, corresponding to the constituent elements of the instruction (e.g., opcode, operands).

INSTRUCTION REGISTER (ANS) A register that is used to hold an instruction for interpretation.

INTERRUPT (ANS) A suspension of a process, such as the execution of a computer program, caused by an event external to that process, and performed in such a way that the process can be resumed. Synonymous with interruption.

INTERRUPT CYCLE That portion of the instruction cycle during which the CPU checks for interrupts. If an enabled interrupt is pending, the CPU saves the current program state and resumes processing at an interrupt handler routine.

LOCAL VARIABLE (IBM) A variable defined and used only in one specified portion of a computer program.

MAIN MEMORY (ANS) Program-addressable storage from which instructions and other data can be loaded directly into registers for subsequent execution or processing.

MEMORY ADDRESS REGISTER (ANS) A register, in a processing unit, that contains the address of the storage location being accessed.

MEMORY BUFFER REGISTER A register that contains data read from memory or data to be written to memory.

MEMORY CYCLE TIME The inverse of the rate at which memory can be accessed. It is the minimum time between the response to one access request (read or write) and the response to the next access request.

MICROCOMPUTER (ANS) A computer system whose processing unit is a microprocessor. A basic microcomputer includes a microprocessor, storage, and input/output facility, which may or may not be on one chip.

MICROINSTRUCTION An instruction of a microprogram. Each instruction specifies one or more micro-operations. Execution of the instruction by the control unit causes the control unit to issue control signals to perform the required microoperations.

MICRO-OPERATION An elementary CPU operation, performed during one clock pulse.

MICROPROCESSOR A computer processor (CPU) all of whose components are on a single integrated-circuit chip.

MICROPROGRAM A program, consisting of microinstructions, that is executed by the control unit.

MICROPROGRAMMED CPU A CPU whose control unit is implemented using microprogramming.

MICROPROGRAMMING LANGUAGE An instruction set used to develop microprograms.

OPCODE Abbreviated form for operation code.

OPERAND (ANS) That which is operated upon. An operand is usually identified by an address part of an instruction.

OPERATION CODE (ANS) A code used to represent the operations of a computer. Usually abbreviated to opcode.

ORTHOGONALITY A principle by which two variables or dimensions are independent of one another. In the context of an instruction set, the term is generally used to indicate that other elements of an instruction (address mode, number of operands, length of operand) are independent of (not determined by) opcode.

PROCESSOR (ANS) In a computer, a functional unit that interprets and executes instructions.

PROCESSOR CYCLE TIME The time required for the shortest well-defined CPU micro-operation. It is the basic unit of time for measuring all CPU actions. Synonymous with machine cycle time.

PROGRAM COUNTER Instruction address register.

PROGRAM STATUS WORD (IBM) An area in storage used to indicate the order in which instructions are executed and to hold and indicate the status of the computer system. Synonymous with processor status word.

RANDOM-ACCESS MEMORY   Memory in which each addressable location has a unique addressing mechanism. The time to access a given location is independent of the sequence of prior accesses.

READ-ONLY MEMORY   Semiconductor memory whose contents cannot be altered, except by destroying the storage unit. Nonerasable memory.

REGISTERS   High-speed memory internal to the CPU. Some registers are user visible, that is, available to the programmer via the machine instruction set. Other registers are used only by the CPU for control purposes.

SCALAR (ANS)   A quantity characterized by a single value.

STACK (ANS)   A list that is constructed and maintained so that the next item to be retrieved is the most recently stored item n the list (i.e., last-in-first-out (LIFO)).

UNCONDITIONAL JUMP (ANS)   A jump that takes place whenever the instruction that specified it is executed.

USER-VISIBLE REGISTERS   CPU registers that may be referenced by the programmer. The instruction set format allows one or more registers to be specified as operands or addresses of operands.

Section 8: List of Acronyms

ALU   Arithmetic and Logic Unit
CISC   Complex Instruction Set Computer
CPU   Central Processing Unit
DMA   Direct Memory Access
HLL   High-Level Language
HP   Hewlett-Packard
IAR   Instruction Address Register
IBM   International Business Machines Corporation
IC   Integrated Circuit
I/O   Input/Output
IR   Instruction Register
LSI   Large-Scale Integration
MAR   Memory Address Register
MBR   Memory Buffer Register
MMU   Memory Management Unit
MSI   Medium-Scale Integration
PC   Program Counter
PROM   Programmable Read-Only Memory
PSW   Processor Status Word
RAM   Random-Access Memory
RISC   Reduced Instruction Set Computer
ROM   Read-Only Memory
ROMP   Research/Office-Products-Division Microprocessor
SSI   Small-Scale Integration
VLSI   Very-Large-Scale Integration

Section 9: Annotated Bibliography

The RISC field is relatively new and expanding rapidly. As yet, the available literature is rather sparse. An attempt has been made here to include most of the relevant recent material. The interested reader can pursue the topic in greater depth by consulting the references listed here.

AZAR83   Azaria, H. and Tabak, D.   "The MODHEL Microcomputer for RISCs Study." *Microprocessing and Microprogramming*, October-November 1983.

Examines the space of instruction sets containing from one to 32 instructions and concludes that instruction sets even smaller than that of the Berkeley RISC I may be superior.

BASA83   Basart, E. and Folger, D.   "Ridge 32 Architecture—A RISC Variation." *Proceedings, ICCD 83*, 1983.

Describes the RIDGE 32 RISC-based system. Includes performance comparison with some other machines.

BASA85   Basart, E.   "RISC Design Streamlines High-Power CPUs." *Computer Design*, July 1, 1985.

Describes the Ridge 32 RISC-based computer.

BELL86   Bell, C.   "RISC: Back to the Future?" *Datamation*, June 1, 1986.

Places RISC in the historical context of computer development since 1948. Bell shows that the roots of RISC can be traced to the CDC 6600. He also defends the position that RISC-based machines should provide superior performance.

BERN81   Bernhard, R.   "More Hardware Means Less Software." *IEEE Spectrum*, December 1981.

A qualitative comparison of the RISC approach to recent trends toward complex architectures.

BERN84   Bernhard, R. "RISCs—Reduced Instruction Set Computers—Make Leap." *Systems & Software*, December 1984.

A brief survey of current RISC projects and commercial offerings.

BIRN86   Birnbaum, J. and Worley, W.   "Beyond RISC: High-Precision Architecture." *Proceedings, COMPCON Spring 86*, March 1986.

Introduces Hewlett-Packard's new RISC-based architecture. Basic design principles are presented and defended.

BROW84   Browne, J.   "Understanding Execution Behavior of Software Systems." *Computer*, July 1984.

The author suggests aspects of execution behavior to be investigated to guide the design of computer architecture.

BRUN86   Bruno, C. and Brady, S.   "The RISC Factor." *Datamation*, June 1, 1986.

A survey of current RISC-based products and a discussion of their applicability in manufacturing environments.

CASE85   Case, B.   "Building Blocks Yield Fast 32-Bit RISC Machines." *Computer Design*, July 1, 1985.

Describes an approach to RISC implementation using bit-slice chips. The author discusses the advantages of this non-VLSI pproach.

CHAI82   Chaitin, G.   "Register Allocation and Spilling via Graph Coloring." *Proceedings of the SIGPLAN Symposium on Compiler Construction*, June 1982.

It is observed that the register-allocation problem is equivalent to the graph-coloring problem in topology. From this observation, a technique is developed that was used on the IBM 801 RISC machine.

CHOW86   Chow, F.; Himelstein, M.; Killian, E. and Weber, L.   "Engineering a RISC Compiler System." *Proceedings, COMPCON Spring 86*, March 1986.

Provides an introduction to the optimization techniques used for the compilers on the RISC-based processor from MIPS Computer Systems.

COLW85   Colwell, R.; Hitchcock, C. Jensen, E.; Brinkley-Sprunt, H. Kollar, C.   "Computers, Complexity, and Controversy." *Computer*, September 1985.

Reports on a large and ongoing effort at Carnegie-Mellon University to assess RISCs versus CISCs. Perhaps the most thorough, objective analysis yet published.

COUT86   Coutant, D. Hammond, C.; and Kelley, J.   "Compilers for the New Generation of Hewlett-Packard Computers." *Proceedings, COMPCON Spring 86*, March 1986.

Provides considerable detail on the optimization techniques used in HP's compilers for its RISC-based machines. The paper also examines RISC-related design issues and explains how these have been addressed by the compiling system.

DAVI86   Davidson, E.   "A Broader Range of Possible Answers to the Issues Raised by RISC." *Proceedings, COMPCON Spring 86*, March 1986.

A brief discussion of three RISC features (load/store architecture, few simple functional operations, and register stacks), in a variety of architectural contexts.

DEMO86 DeMoney, M.; Moore, J.; and Mashey, T. "Operating System Support on a RISC." *Proceedings, COMPCON Spring 86*, March 1986.

Discusses processor design features in the RISC-based system from MIPS Computer Systems that are intended to address operating system requirements. Using UNIX as an example, memory management and exception-handling are described.

FITZ81 Fitzpatrick, D. et al. "A RISCy Approach to VLSI." *VLSI Design*, 4th quarter, 1981. Reprinted in *Computer Architecture News*, March 1982.

Discusses design and implementation effort of RISCs versus CISCs.

FOTI84 Foti, L. et al "Reduced Instruction Set Multi-Microcomputer System." *Proceedings, National Computer Conference*, 1984.

Reports on a very simple processor with 16-bit words, 32-bit instructions, and less than 20 operations.

GANN85 Gannes, S. "Back-to-Basics Computers with Sports-Car Speed." *Fortune*, September 3, 1985.

The current status and commercial possibilities of RISC development are discussed.

GOOD85 Goodrich, P. "Simple Systems Approach Increases Throughput." *Mini-Micro Systems*, May 1985.

Describes the Whetstone XS-100 computer from Integrated Digital Products Inc. This RISC system was designed to be compatible with the Nova minicomputer.

GROS85 Gross, T. "Floating-Point Arithmetic on a Reduced Instruction-Set." *Proceedings, 7th Symposium on Computer Arithmetic*, 1985.

Current single-chip RISC processors do not support hardware floating-point operations. This paper describes a software approach implemented on the Standard MIPS. The strengths and limitations of this approach are analyzed.

HEAT84 Heath, J. "Re-evaluation of RISC I." *Computer Architecture News*, March 1984.

Attempts to decouple the effects of a large register file from a reduced instruction set and analyze the program size and execution time effects of the latter.

HENN82 Hennessy, J. et al. "Hardware/Software Tradeoffs for Increased Performance." *Proceedings, Symposium on Architectural Support for Programming Languages and Operating Systems*, March 1982.

Makes a case for simple rather than complex machine instructions to optimize compiler writing.

HENN83 Hennessy, J. and Gross, T. "Postpass Code Optimization of Pipeline Constraints." *ACM Transactions on Programming Languages and Systems*, July 1983.

A technique found in a number of RISC systems is the rearrangement of instructions at compile time to avoid pipeline interlocks. The basic problem is explored here with a detailed mathematical analysis.

HENN84 Hennessy, J. "VLSI Processor Architecture." *IEEE Transactions on Computers*. December 1984.

An exhaustive look at the relevant design issues for RISCs and CISCs, from the perspective of a RISC designer.

HIND86 Hinden, H. "IBM RISC Workstation Features 40-Bit Virtual Addressing." *Computer Design*, February 15, 1986.

A brief overview of the IBM PC RT, with an emphasis on the memory management unit.

HITC85 Hitchcock, C. and Brinkley, H. "Analyzing Multiple Register Sets." *The 12th Annual International Symposium on Computer Architecture*. June 17-19, 1985.

This study also attempts to separate the effects of a large register file from a reduced instruction set. It focuses on the effects of the former.

HOPK83 Hopkins, W. "HLLDA Defies RISC: Thoughts on RISCs, CISCs, and HLLDAs." *Proceedings, l6th Annual Microprogramming Workshop*, December 1983.

Recommends design principles for High Level Language Directed Architectures. The paper then compares CISC, RISC, and HLLDA approaches and concludes that the HLLDA avoids the usual CISC ineffiencies and compares favorably with the RISC.

KATE83 Katevenis, M. *Reduced Instruction Set Computer Architectures for VLSI*. PhD dissertation, Computer Science Department, University of California at Berkeley, October 1983. Reprinted by MIT Press, Cambridge, MA, 1985.

Contains a detailed description of the Berkeley RISC I and RISC II. Although this is a PhD thesis, it contains perhaps the best tutorial material on RISC technology.

KORT84 Korthaver, E. and Richter, L. "Are RISCs Subsets of CISCs? A Discussion of Reduced versus Complex Instruction Sets." *Microprocessing and Microprogramming*, August 1984.

Shows that the Berkeley RISC I instruction set can be synthesized by a subset of either the M68000 or the Z8000. The authors conclude that RISCs may offer benefits to compiler writers.

LUND77 Lunde, A. "Empirical Evaluation of Some Features of Instruction Set Processor Architectures." *Communications of the ACM*, March 1972.

This, along with TANE78, is one of the most influential papers on instruction execution characteristics. They have been referenced frequently in the RISC literature as providing evidence in favor of the use of a reduced instruction set.

MACD84 MacDougall, M. "Instruction-Level Program and Processor Modeling." *Computer*, July 1984.

Presents results of analysis of COBOL program execution on the IBM 370. The analysis is at the machine-instruction level.

MARK84 Markoff, J. "RISC Chips." Byte, November 1984.

An overview of RISC, concentrating on the Berkeley work.

MILL85 Miller, M. "Simplicity is Focus in Efforts to Increase Computer Power." *The Wall Street Journal*, August 23, 1985.

Reports on prospects for commercial RISC systems.

MOAD86 Moad, J. "Gambling on RISC." *Datamation*, June 1, 1986.

Speculation on the possible success of various RISC efforts. Analysis focuses on the Hewlett-Packard RISC-based product.

MOKH86 Mokhoff, N. "New RISC Machines Appear as Hybrids with Both RISC and CISC Features." *Computer Design*, April 1, 1986.

Discusses a number of RISC-based products, with emphasis on the IBM PC RT and HP 900/9000 series. CISC features in these products are discussed and justified.

MOUS86 Moussouris, J., et al. "A CMOS RISC Processor with Integrated System Functions." *Proceedings, COMPCON Spring 86*, March 1986.

Introduces the RISC processor from MIPS Computer Systems, based on the Stanford MIPS project. General design principles are discussed.

NEFF86a Neff, L. "Clipper™ Microprocessor Architecture Overview." *Proceedings, COMPCON Spring 86*, March 1986.

Introduces a microprocessor developed by Fairchild. The microprocessor exhibits RISC features. Both hardware and software design issues are briefly explored.

NEFF86b Neff, D. "C Compiler Implementation Issues on the Clipper™ Microprocessor." *Proceedings, COMPCON Spring 86*, March 1986.

Describes a compiler designed for use with a Fairchild processor that exhibits RISC features. The compiler takes advantage of the architecture to yield high performance, but with programming constraints.

OHR85 Ohr, S. "RISC Machines." *Electronic Design*, January 10, 1985.

A survey of commercial RISC ventures.

PATT82a Patterson, D. and Sequin, C. "A VLSI RISC." *Computer*, September 1982.

Describes the most influential of the RISC systems, the Berkeley RISC I. Provides a detailed rationale for design decisions taken.

PATT82b Patterson, D. and Piepho, R. "Assessing RISCs in High-Level Language Support." *IEEE Micro*, November 1982.

Compares the Berkeley RISC I to five other processors, focusing on execution speed.

PATT83 Patterson, D., et al. "Architecture of a VLSI Instruction Cache for a RISC." *Proceedings, Tenth International Conference on Computer Architecture*, 1983.

Reports on an instruction cache developed for the Berkeley RISC II. The authors introduce several novel design features, and evaluate their effectiveness.

PATT84 Patterson, D. "RISC Watch." *Computer Architecture News*, March 1984.

Assesses the performance of the Berkeley RISC II machine by comparing it with the VAX-11 and the M68010.

PATT85 Patterson, D. "Reduced Instruction Set Computers." *Communications of the ACM*, January 1985.

A survey article. The historical background and motivation that led to the research in RISC architecture is examined. The RISC approaches of Berkeley (RISC I and II), Stanford (MIPS), and IBM (801) are compared.

RADI83 Radin, G. "The 801 Minicomputer." *IBM Journal of Research and Development*, May 1983.

Describes the first RISC machine, the experimental IBM 801. Provides a detailed rationale for design decisions taken.

RAGA83 Ragan-Kelley, R. and Clark, R. "Applying RISC Theory to a Large Computer." *Computer Design*, November 1983.

A description of the Pyramid 90X RISC machine.

SEIT85 Seither, M. "Pyramid Challenges DEC with RISC Super-mini." *Mini-Micro Systems*, August 1985.

Describes the Pyramid 98X and compares it to the VAX 8600.

SERL86 Serlin, O. "MIPS, Dhrystones, and Other Tales." *Datamation*, June 1, 1986.

Argues that MIPS, the conventional benchmark for comparing performance of different machines, is useless. Several other techniques are discussed. Results are presented that compare some RISC machines with CISC machines.

TAMI83 Tamir, Y. and Sequin, C. "Strategies for Managing the Register File in RISC." *IEEE Transactions on Computers*, November 1983.

Explains the multiple-window approach used on the Berkeley RISC machines, and analyzes alternative techniques for optimizing register use.

TANE78 Tanenbaum, A. "Implications of Structured Programming for Machine Architecture." *Communications of the ACM*, March 1978.

This, along with LUND77, is one of the most influential papers on instruction execution characteristics. They have been referenced frequently in the RISC literature as providing evidence for the use of a reduced instruction set.

TREL82 Treleaven, P. "VLSI Processor Architectures." *Computer*, June 1982.

Examines a variety of new approaches to processor architecture based on VLSI implementation, including the RISC approach.

UNGA84   Ungar, D.; Blau, R.; Foley, P.; Samples, D.; and Patterson, D.   "Architecture of SOAR: Smalltalk on a RISC." *Proceedings, 11th International Conference on Computer Architecture*, 1984.

Smalltalk is a highly productive programming environment that poses tough challenges for the implementor: dynamic data typing, a high-level instruction set, frequent and expensive procedure calls, and object-oriented storage management. This paper describes a successful implementation on a RISC machine.

WALL85   Wallich, P.   "Toward Simpler, Faster Computers." *IEEE Spectrum*, August 1985.

Summarizes the motivations for the RISC approach and reports on the relative merits (compared to CISC) of the approach as seen by proponents and opponents.

WATE86   Waters, F., ed.   *IBM RT Personal Computer Technology*, IBM Publication SA23-1057, 1986.

A collection of papers by the developers of the RISC-based IBM RT PC. The papers cover major hardware components, microprocessor architecture, user interface, operating system design, and virtual resource management.

WILS84   Wilson, P.   "Thirty-Two Bit Micro Supports Multiprocessing." *Computer Design*, June 1, 1984.

Describes the Inmos Transputer which is a single-chip product combining processor, memory, and communication, and whose design reflects RISC principles.

AUTHOR BIOGRAPHY

William Stallings received a PhD from M.I.T. in computer science and a B.S. from Notre Dame in electrical engineering. He is an independent consultant and president of Comp/Comm Consulting of Great Falls, VA. He has been vice president of CSM Corp., a firm specializing in data processing and data communications for the health-care industry. He has also been director of systems analysis and design for CTEC, Inc., a firm specializing in command, control, and communications systems. He has also been senior communications consultant for Honeywell, where he was involved in the planning and design of communications and network products.

Dr. Stallings is the author of numerous technical papers and the following books:

- *LOCAL NETWORKS: AN INTRODUCTION, SECOND EDITION*, Macmillan 1987
- *COMPUTER ORGANIZATION AND ARCHITECTURE*, Macmillan, 1987
- *DATA AND COMPUTER COMMUNICATIONS*, Macmillan, 1985
- *REDUCED INSTRUCTION SET COMPUTERS*, IEEE Computer Society Press, 1987
- *COMPUTER COMMUNICATIONS: ARCHITECTURES, PROTOCOLS, AND STANDARDS*, IEEE Computer Society Press, 1985
- *INTEGRATED SERVICES DIGITAL NETWORKS (ISDN)*, IEEE Computer Society Press, 1985
- *LOCAL NETWORK TECHNOLOGY, SECOND EDITION*, IEEE Computer Society Press, 1985
- *A MANAGER'S GUIDE TO LOCAL NETWORKS*, Prentice-Hall, 1983